BLACKWELL COMPANIONS TO AMERICAN HISTORY

This series provides essential and authoritative overviews of the scholarship that has shaped our present understanding of the American past. Edited by eminent historians, each volume tackles one of the major periods or themes of American history, with individual topics authored by key scholars who have spent considerable time in research on the questions and controversies that have sparked debate in their field of interest. The volumes are accessible for the non-specialist, while also engaging scholars seeking a reference to the historiography or future concerns.

Published:
A Companion to the American Revolution
Edited by Jack P. Greene and J. R. Pole
A Companion to 19th-Century America
Edited by William L. Barney
A Companion to the American South
Edited by John B. Boles
A Companion to American Indian History
Edited by Philip J. Deloria and Neal Salisbury
A Companion to American Women's History
Edited by Nancy A. Hewitt
A Companion to Post-1945 America
Edited by Jean-Christophe Agnew and Roy Rosenzweig
A Companion to the Vietnam War
Edited by Marilyn B. Young and Robert Buzzanco
A Companion to Colonial America
Edited by Daniel Vickers

A Companion to 20th-Century America
Edited by Stephen J. Whitfield
A Companion to the American West
Edited by William Deverell
A Companion to American Foreign Relations
Edited by Robert D. Schulzinger
A Companion to the Civil War and Reconstruction
Edited by Lacy K. Ford
A Companion to American Technology
Edited by Carroll Pursell
A Companion to African-American History
Edited by Alton Hornsby
A Companion to American Immigration
Edited by Reed Ueda

In preparation:
A Companion to American Cultural History
Edited by Karen Haltunnen

BLACKWELL COMPANIONS TO HISTORY

Published
A Companion to Western Historical Thought
Edited by Lloyd Kramer and Sarah Maza

A Companion to Gender History
Edited by Teresa A. Meade and Merry E. Wiesner-Hanks

BLACKWELL COMPANIONS TO BRITISH HISTORY

Published
A Companion to Roman Britain
Edited by Malcolm Todd
A Companion to Britain in the Later Middle Ages
Edited by S. H. Rigby
A Companion to Tudor Britain
Edited by Robert Tittler and Norman Jones
A Companion to Stuart Britain
Edited by Barry Coward
A Companion to Eighteenth-Century Britain
Edited by H. T. Dickinson

A Companion to Nineteenth-Century Britain
Edited by Chris Williams
A Companion to Early Twentieth-Century Britain
Edited by Chris Wrigley
A Companion to Contemporary Britain
Edited by Paul Addison and Harriet Jones

In preparation
A Companion to the Early Middle Ages: Britain and Ireland
Edited by Pauline Stafford

BLACKWELL COMPANIONS TO EUROPEAN HISTORY

Published
A Companion to Europe 1900-1945
Edited by Gordon Martel
A Companion to Nineteenth-Century Europe
Edited by Stefan Berger
A Companion to the Worlds of the Renaissance
Edited by Guido Ruggiero

A Companion to the Reformation World
Edited by R. Po-chia Hsia

In preparation
A Companion to Europe Since 1945
Edited by Klaus Larres
A Companion to Eighteenth-Century Europe
Edited by Peter H. Wilson
A Companion to the Medieval World
Edited by Carol Lansing and Edward D. English

BLACKWELL COMPANIONS TO WORLD HISTORY

Published
A Companion to the History of the Middle East
Edited by Youssef M. Choueiri

In preparation
A Companion to Japanese History

Edited by William M. Tsutsui
A Companion to Latin American History
Thomas H. Holloway
A Companion to Russian History
Edited by Abbott Gleason

A COMPANION TO POST-1945 AMERICA

Edited by

Jean-Christophe Agnew and Roy Rosenzweig

Blackwell
Publishing

© 2002, 2006 by Blackwell Publishing Ltd

BLACKWELL PUBLISHING
350 Main Street, Malden, MA 02148-5020, USA
9600 Garsington Road, Oxford OX4 2DQ, UK
550 Swanston Street, Carlton, Victoria 3053, Australia

The right of Jean-Christophe Agnew and Roy Rosenzweig to be identified as the Authors of the Editorial Material in this Work has been asserted in accordance with the UK Copyright, Designs, and Patents Act 1988.

First published 2002 by Blackwell Publishing Ltd
First published in paperback 2006

1   2006

Library of Congress Cataloging-in-Publication Data has been applied for.

ISBN-13: 978-0-631-22325-2 (hardback)
ISBN-10: 0-631-22325-8 (hardback)
ISBN-13: 978-1-4051-4984-6 (paperback)
ISBN-10: 1-4051-4984-1 (paperback)

A catalogue record for this title is available from the British Library.

Set in 10 on 12 pt Galliard

The publisher's policy is to use permanent paper from mills that operate a sustainable forestry policy, and which has been manufactured from pulp processed using acid-free and elementary chlorine-free practices. Furthermore, the publisher ensures that the text paper and cover board used have met acceptable environmental accreditation standards.

For further information on
Blackwell Publishing, visit our website:
www.blackwellpublishing.com

Contents

Illustrations

About the Contributors

Jean-Christophe Agnew is Professor of American Studies and History at Yale University. He is the author of *Worlds Apart: The Market and the Theater in Anglo-American Thought, 1550–1750*, and of a number of articles on the history of market society and consumer culture.

Patrick N. Allitt was born and raised in Britain but studied for the Ph.D. in American History at the University of California, Berkeley. He has been Professor of American History at Emory University since 1988 and is the author of two books, and editor of a third, on religious and intellectual history.

Beth Bailey teaches in the American Studies department at Temple University, where she is also Regents Lecturer and director of the Feminist Research Institute. Her recent publications include *Sex in the Heartland* and *The Columbia Guide to America in the 1960s*.

Alan Brinkley is Allan Nevins Professor of History at Columbia University. He is the author of *Voices of Protest: Huey Long, Father Coughlin, and the Great Depression*; *The End of Reform: New Deal Liberalism in Recession and War*; and *Liberalism and its Discontents*. He is presently writing a biography of Henry R. Luce.

Thomas S. Blanton is Director of the National Security Archive at George Washington University. His books include *White House E-Mail: The Top Secret Computer Messages the Reagan–Bush White House Tried to Destroy* (1995), and as co-author, *The Chronology* (1987), *Litigation Under the Federal Open Government Laws* (1993), and *Atomic Audit: The Costs and Consequences of U.S. Nuclear Weapons Since 1940* (1998).

David L. Chappell teaches history at the University of Arkansas and is the author of *Inside Agitators: White Southerners in the Civil Rights Movement* (1994) and *A Stone of Hope: Prophetic Religion, Political Culture, and the Triumph of Civil Rights* (2002). His articles have appeared in the *Journal of American Studies*, *In These Times*, and *World Policy Studies*.

Susan G. Davis is Research Professor of Communications and Library and Information Science at the University of Illinois, Urbana-Champaign. She received her Ph.D. in Folklore and Folklife from the University of Pennsylvania, and has written and taught widely on folk performance and public space, popular culture and the commercial mass media, and tourism.

Erika Doss is Professor of Art History in the Department of Fine Arts, University of Colorado, and specializes in twentieth-century American art. She is the author of *Benton, Pollock, and the Politics of Modernism: From Regionalism to Abstract Expressionism* (1991); *Spirit Poles and Flying Pigs: Public Art and Cultural Democracy in American Communities* (1995); *Elvis Culture: Fans, Faith, and Image* (1999); *Looking at Life Magazine* (editor, 2001); and the forthcoming *Twentieth-Century American Art* (2002).

Susan J. Douglas is Catherine Neafie Kellogg Professor of Communication Studies at the University of Michigan. She is the author of *Inventing American Broadcasting, 1899–1922*; *Where the Girls Are: Growing Up Female with the Mass Media*; and *Listening In: Radio and the American Imagination*. She is completing a book on the changing representations of motherhood in the mass media since 1970.

Mary L. Dudziak teaches law and history at the University of Southern California Law School. She received her J. D. and Ph.D. in American Studies from Yale University. She is the author of *Cold War Civil Rights: Race and the Image of American Democracy* (2000).

Carolyn Eisenberg is Professor of US History and American Foreign Policy at Hofstra University. She is the author of *Drawing the Line: The American Decision to Divide Germany, 1944–49*. Her book received the Stuart L. Bernath Prize for the Historians of Foreign Relations and the 1996 Herbert Hoover Book Award.

James T. Fisher is a cultural historian of religion and ethnicity in the United States. He is the author of *The Catholic Counterculture in America, 1933–1962* (1989); *Dr. America: The Lives of Thomas A. Dooley, 1927–1961* (1997); and *Catholics in America* (2000).

Joshua B. Freeman is Professor of History at Queens College and the Graduate Center, City University of New York, and co-editor of *International Labor and Working-Class History*. His books include *In Transit: The Transport Workers Union in New York City, 1933–1966* and *Working-Class New York: Life and Labor Since World War II*.

Kevin Gaines teaches in the history department and the Center for Afro-American and African Studies at the University of Michigan. He is writing a book on African American and Caribbean expatriates in Ghana and the intersection between the US black freedom movement, the decolonization of Africa, and the Cold War.

Linda Gordon teaches history at New York University. Her most recent book is *The Great Arizona Orphan Abduction*. A completely revised and updated version of her history of birth control was due to be reissued in 2002.

Van Gosse received his Ph.D. from Rutgers, New Brunswick. He has taught at Wellesley and Trinity, and currently is at Franklin and Marshall. He has also worked as a Committee in Solidarity with the People of El Salvador (CISPES) organizer, director of the Center for Democracy in the Americas, and organizing director of Peace Action. He is writing a history of black politics and Black Power.

Greg Grandin worked with the Guatemalan Truth Commission and is an Assistant Professor of History at New York University. His book, *The Blood of Guatemala: A History of Race and Nation*, won the Latin American Studies Association's Bryce Wood Award. He is also the editor of *Denagado en su Totalidad*, a collection of United States declassified documents published in Guatemala.

David Hunt is a Professor of History at the University of Massachusetts at Boston, where he has been teaching and writing about the Vietnam War since 1969. His most recent publication is "Grunts and Historians: Recent Representations of Vietnam Veterans," *Bulletin of Concerned Asian Scholars*, 32/4 (2000): 61–70.

Matthew Frye Jacobson is Professor of American Studies, History, and African American Studies at Yale. He is the author of *Barbarian Virtues: The U.S. Encounters Foreign Peoples at Home and Abroad* (2000); *Whiteness of a Different Color: European Immigrants and the Alchemy of Race* (1998); and *Special Sorrows: The Diasporic Imagination of Irish, Polish, and Jewish Immigrants in the United States* (1995).

Richard H. King is Professor of American Intellectual History at the University of Nottingham, UK. He is the author most recently of *Civil Rights and the Idea of Freedom* (1992), and is completing an intellectual history of the ideas of race and culture between 1940 and 1975.

Stephen Lassonde teaches history at Yale University. He is associate editor of the *International Encyclopedia of the History of Childhood*, and author of *Learning to Forget: Schooling and Family Life in New Haven's Working Class, 1870–1940*. He is currently collaborating with Linda Mayes on a history of child development during the 1950s and 1960s.

Nelson Lichtenstein is the author of *State of the Union: A Century of American Labor*, *Walter Reuther: The Most Dangerous Man in Detroit*, and other books. He is writing a history of post-World War II politics and political economy in the United States. He teaches history at the University of California, Santa Barbara.

Melani McAlister is at the American Studies department at George Washington University in Washington, DC, where she teaches courses on globalization, cultural theory, and US cultural history. She is the author of *Epic Encounters: Culture, Media, and U.S. Interests in the Middle East, 1945–2000*.

Nancy MacLean is Associate Professor of History and African American Studies at Northwestern University. The author of *Behind the Mask of Chivalry: The Making of the Second Ku Klux Klan* (1994), she is now writing a history of affirmative action in employment, entitled *The Work of Inclusion: Contesting Racial and Gender Inequality on the Job in Modern America*.

James I. Matray is Professor of History at New Mexico State University. His research focuses on US foreign relations during and after World War II, with emphasis on Korea and Japan. Matray's publications include *The Reluctant Crusade: American Foreign Policy in Korea, 1941–1950*; *Korea and the Cold War: Division, Destruction, and Disarmament*; and *Japan's Emergence as a Global Power*.

Elaine Tyler May, Professor of American Studies and History at the University of Minnesota, is the author of *Great Expectations: Marriage and Divorce in Post-Victorian America* (1980); *Homeward Bound: American Families in the Cold War Era* (1988, 1999); *Pushing the Limits: American Women, 1940–1961* (1994); and *Barren in the Promised Land: Childless Americans and the Pursuit of Happiness* (1997).

David S. Painter, Department of History and Edmund A. Walsh School of Foreign Service, Georgetown University, is the author of *Oil and the American Century: The Political Economy of U.S. Foreign Oil Policy, 1941–1954* (1986), and *The Cold War: An International History* (1999), as well as co-editor (with Melvyn P. Leffler) of *Origins of the Cold War: An International History* (1994).

Roy Rosenzweig is College of Arts and Sciences Distinguished Professor of History and Director of the Center for History and New Media at George Mason University. He is the author, co-author, and co-editor of a number of books, including *The Presence of the Past: Popular Uses of History in American Life*.

Ellen Schrecker is Professor of History at Yeshiva University. She has written extensively about McCarthyism, including *No Ivory Tower: McCarthyism and the Universities* (1986) and *Many Are the Crimes: McCarthyism in America* (1998). She is currently revising *The Age of McCarthyism: A Brief History with Documents* and co-editing a collection of essays on the Cold War.

Robert O. Self is Assistant Professor of History and a fellow in the Michigan Society of Fellows at Brown University. His first book, to be published in 2003, deals with race, class and the geographies of urban political culture in California after 1945. His next project focuses on gender politics and cultures of masculinity in the postwar American city.

Thomas J. Sugrue is Bicentennial Class of 1940 Professor of History and Sociology at the University of Pennsylvania. His publications include *The Origins of the Urban Crisis*, which won the Bancroft Prize, and *W. E. B. DuBois, Race, and the City*. He is currently writing books on civil rights in the urban North and on the history of America in the twentieth century.

Allen Tullos is Associate Professor of American Studies at Emory University in Atlanta, Georgia. He is website coordinator of *americanroutes.com* and editor of the quarterly journal, *Southern Changes*.

Ian Tyrrell is a Professor in the School of History, University of New South Wales, in Sydney, Australia, and currently is Head of School. He is author, among other books, of *True Gardens of the Gods: Californian–Australian Environmental Reform, 1860–1930* (1999).

J. Samuel Walker is historian of the US Nuclear Regulatory Commission. He is the author or co-author of four books on the history of nuclear energy and has published articles on the subject in *Diplomatic History, Isis, JAMA: Journal of the American Medical Association, Pacific Historical Review, Technology and Culture*, and other journals.

Robert E. Weems, Jr. is a Professor of History at the University of Missouri-Columbia. His publications include *Black Business in the Black Metropolis: The Chicago Metropolitan Assurance Company, 1925–1985* (1996); *Desegregating the Dollar: African American Consumerism in the Twentieth Century* (1998); and *The African-American Experience: An Historiographical and Bibliographical Guide* (2001), co-edited with Arvarh E. Strickland.

Jon Wiener teaches American history at the University of California, Irvine, and is a contributing editor to the *Nation*. He has also written for the *New York Times Magazine*, the *Los Angeles Times*, and the *New Republic*, as well as the *American Historical Review* and *Past and Present*. His most recent book is *Gimme Some Truth: The John Lennon FBI Files*.

Robert Westbrook teaches American history at the University of Rochester. He is the author of *John Dewey and American Democracy* (1991), as well as a wide range of articles dissecting modern American political culture.

Julian E. Zelizer is Associate Professor of History and Public Policy at State University of New York, Albany. He is the author of *Taxing America: Wilbur D. Mills, Congress, and the State, 1945–1975*, winner of the 1998 D. B. Hardeman Prize and the 2000 Ellis Hawley Prize. He is completing a history of congressional reform between World War II and 2000. Additionally, he is editing the *Reader's Companion to the American Congress*.

Introduction

JEAN-CHRISTOPHE AGNEW AND ROY ROSENZWEIG

The title of this Blackwell Companion – *Post-1945 America* – says a good deal about the difficulties that beset anyone looking to encapsulate the past half-century of American history. The period is still unnamed and unplaced in the broad genealogy of the American past. At least, that is the impression one takes from the titles of many of the surveys that have thus far been published: *The Unfinished Journey, Moving On, Grand Expectations*, and, simplest of all, *More* (Chafe, 1998; Moss, 1994; Patterson, 1996; Collins, 2000). If the period is still "busy being born," perhaps that is because no one yet dares to write its epitaph. We know, or think we know, when the period began, which is to say on or around the dropping of the first atomic bomb on August 6, 1945. But we are not so certain when, or even whether, it has ended.

Some historians might point to the mid-1970s as an appropriate milestone or tombstone for the "postwar era"; Watergate, the oil crisis, and the defeat in Vietnam all marking the end of what Henry Luce had heralded in 1941 as the American Century. Others would no doubt choose 1989 or 1991 – the years of communism's collapse – to designate the end of the twentieth century, if not the end of history itself. Still others would identify September 11, 2001 as the point at which "everything changed." But even the most recent divisions leave the awkward remainder of our current moment. It is as if, having outlived our own historical obituary, we find ourselves belated and not much else: post-Cold War, yes, but postcolonial, postindustrial, and postmodern as well. Our title, then, is more than a convenient placeholder, for "*Post*-1945" captures the compound sense of our last half-century as a sequence of aftermaths: a series of almost compulsive reckonings with a world made *before* 1945. On the one hand, we are awash in books, films, and memorials on the Good War and the Greatest Generation; on the other, we behold a concerted effort to dismantle the so-called "safety nets" woven by that same generation – from Social Security to Anti-Ballistic Missile Treaties.

The ambivalence with which we look back upon the odyssey of the past fifty years is likewise visible in the titles of the historical surveys that have appeared in the interim: *A Troubled Journey, A Troubled Feast, Affluence and Anxiety, Present Tense*, to name just a few (Siegel, 1984; Leuchtenburg, 1973; Degler, 1968; Schaller et al., 1992). To be sure, these phrases bespeak something more than the mixed judgment of the historians who use them; they also evoke the conflicting emotions that Americans of the time experienced toward their new, global hegemony. A source of pride at one moment could in the blink of an eye feel like a hostage relationship. Vietnam, the oil embargo, and the Iranian embassy crisis were of course the most dramatic instances of that hostage-anxiety, while the strident Ramboism of foreign policy and popular culture in the Reagan–Bush years supplied the most conspicuous campaigns to redeem, if not erase, these humiliations. In one way or another, Americans were struggling to come to terms with what Tom Engelhardt (1995) has called the "end of victory culture."

Yet one could argue that Ramboism turned the knife in these wounds far more than it healed them. As a result, Americans in search of historical consolation in the 1990s found themselves looking past Vietnam, past Korea, to the unambiguously successful sacrifices of World War II. Steven Spielberg's *Saving Private Ryan* (1998) was the quintessential expression of this *fin-de-siècle* nostalgia, for its pitch-perfect reproduction of every formula of the classic combat film barely concealed the fact that its narrative energies were drawn almost entirely from the post-Vietnam missing-in-action story. Irony thus shadowed even this effort to push our nostalgia for victory culture to a politically "safer" place *before* 1945. How could one "save" Private Ryan, after all, without rescuing the same post-1945 triumphalist rationale that had so confidently and complacently dispatched eighteen-year-olds to Vietnam in the first place? How could one save Private Ryan, in other words, without also forgetting a good deal of postwar history – not just the Vietnam War, but also Korea and the red scare era of the 1940s and 1950s.

It is hardly a surprise, then, that scholars have stepped into the half-century gap between the beginning and end of victory culture in order to write history in place of nostalgia. Nostalgia-buffs steep the object of their desire in a warm, sepia bath of wistful, or camp, affection. (On pervasive nostalgia for the postwar period, see, for example, Lambrose, 1988.) Historians, in contrast, are more apt to wrestle with their subject, and never more so than in the narratives of post-1945 America, where many so often find their own autobiographies – their own memories – intersecting the chronicle of headlined events. For this very reason, traditionalists have dismissed "contemporary history" as mere journalism, the "first draft" for a more rigorously researched and sober-sided *history*. Yet given the enormous variety of documents available over the past fifty years – from opinion polls and television scripts to e-mail and Oval office tapes – and given the gradual declassification of many critical documents, it seems pointless to wait for yet more dust to settle when the true challenge is to make historical sense of the blooming, buzzing confusion of evidence. Road maps are in order, if only to be able to glimpse our destination.

So the "unfinished journey" is an especially appropriate description for a volume that, like this one, focuses on the *historiography* of the postwar even more than on its history. Even if we grant that the key events of the postwar era have already unfolded, we can hardly say the same thing for the key historical works that will ultimately characterize – and name – the period. Still, if there is anything we have discovered in the process of editing this volume, it is that the work historians have produced on the post-1945 period has been far more impressive than the traditionalists would have predicted. The "first draft," if that is what it is, looks pretty good.

And pretty comprehensive as well. In the 1970s, when the two of us were in graduate school, it would have been impossible to come up with a comprehensive exam reading list of books on the post-1945 period, at least one written by professional historians. Except perhaps for diplomatic history, where debates over the origins of the Cold War were already raging, there was simply no historiography to assign. A quarter-century later, the problem has been reversed: it is now virtually impossible for a single person to master the full historical literature on the era. A glance at the bibliographies to the essays in this volume will quickly confirm this claim. Surely no other period in US history has produced such an explosion of scholarship as this one has over the past two decades alone. Surely no other field has emerged so rapidly.

To take stock of this burgeoning historical literature, even as it continues to roll off the presses, is the daunting task that our authors have undertaken here. Necessarily, then, their essays and this volume must be offered as provisional and unfinished – a work in progress. While we might all wish for a more suitably meditative distance on the period, we have reason enough to take stock, in Lionel Trilling's phrase, in "the middle of the journey." At the very least, those who will be writing and reading the histories of the next two decades will need to assess in what ways and how well the terrain has already been charted. And though we do not claim this volume to be the definitive Michelin Guide to the historiography of the postwar era, we do see it as, well, a useful companion – a kind of "Lonely Planet" for the more adventurous traveler.

In keeping with that spirit of adventure, we have made this volume a wide-ranging exploration. We have included essays extending across economic, social, political, cultural, intellectual, and diplomatic history. Moreover, the essays themselves are panoramic. There are gaps, to be sure. Some reflect the uneven development of the historical literature; others simply could not fit into a volume even as long as this one. And in a few cases – political economy, science and technology, the United States and Africa, Native Americans, and the welfare state – the essays could not be completed in enough time to be included here. Historiography, like history, has its deadlines, and we did not want to delay publication of a volume that already offered both broad and timely coverage of the era.

Given the evolving state of the historical scholarship, it is not surprising that the maps offered in the thirty-four chapters that make up this guide differ greatly in cartographic strategy, not to mention the level of detail. The essays on political history – the Cold War, the Vietnam War, McCarthyism, the New Left, and civil rights, for example – address subfields rich in bibliography and steeped in controversy. In those cases, the essays resemble the more traditional historiographical review one is likely to find, say, on the Civil War or Reconstruction periods. In other essays – music and leisure and tourism, for example – the literature may be large without having coalesced around particular debates. Those authors provide something more like a bibliographic essay, surveying and cataloguing what has been written thus far. And in yet other essays – environmentalism and the visual arts, for instance – the authors are reporting on areas where the historical literature is only now emerging. The authors of such essays are more likely to devote their attention to the key events and themes of the period, effectively offering their own preliminary sketch of what the field or subfield is shaping up to be.

That is not to say that the new fields are the most "unfinished" ones. Take the Cold War essays, for example. Their topics may boast the oldest intellectual genealogies of the whole volume, but as the contributions of Ellen Schrecker, Greg Grandin, Carolyn Eisenberg, and David Painter and Thomas Blanton make clear, the ongoing and hotly debated process of document declassification – especially the US ones –

makes any definitive claim that "we now know" the history of the post-1945 era a dubious assumption at best. There are more than a few interpretive surprises in store for the reader of this companion.

Diverse as the topics and approaches may be, there are still some common themes that emerge from the essays as a whole. Not surprisingly, many authors still insist upon the key interpretive touchstones – especially the Cold War and the turbulent events summarized in the phrase "the Sixties." But if these landmarks survive, historians have found new ways to navigate around and through them, and of the first measures of distance to fall in the new historiography has been the decade-marker itself. If historians continue to write of the 1960s, for example, it is of a "decade" that begins in the mid-1950s and lingers into the mid-1970s. Here, perhaps, the intersection between history and autobiography is most visible, and more than one of our contributors reflects on the degree to which his or her field was itself generated, or regenerated, by the civil rights and liberation movements of the time. History "from the bottom up" has had its impact upon the last two decades of post-1945 historiography.

Yet pathbreaking as this work has been, we have nonetheless been struck by the persistence of older conventions and protocols of historical writing. The topics may be post-1945, but the approaches are rarely, if ever, poststructuralist, and you will find few contributors careening around the linguistic, or even culturalist, turn. Nor has there been much in the way of interdisciplinary exploration, as Julian Zelizer points out. True, this absence may be an artifact of our own editorial choices, but we suspect that it reflects as well the evidentiary burdens and methodological rigors felt by historians seeking to blaze new trails and, of course, to persuade skeptical colleagues. So, where we might have expected to announce the marriage of history and cultural studies in the post-1945 period, we can at this point report little more than the first, tentative engagement.

We have ourselves relied on relatively conventional organizational devices to place the thirty-four chapters in this volume into four roughly equal sections. Part I surveys "Society and Culture" in the postwar period; it includes chapters on family and demography, cities, religion, leisure and tourism, mass media, popular music, the visual arts, and social thought. Part II takes up social change and social movements in the post-World War II period, with chapters on political culture, immigrants and ethnicity, workers and unions, African Americans and civil rights, women and the women's movement, sexuality and movements for sexual liberation, the New Left, conservatism and environmentalism.

Part III surveys politics and foreign policy, including articles on political power, McCarthyism, and the Supreme Court, as well as key topics in American foreign relations – the origins of the Cold War in Europe, the United States and its relations with Latin America and Asia, the Vietnam War, the end of the Cold War, and the debates about nuclear weapons, nuclear fear, and nuclear power. The final section takes an entirely different approach. We wanted to devote some attention to particular works of importance – books that some scholars would regard as "essential reading." We asked eight scholars to offer reflections on a book that has shaped their thinking about the recent history of the United States. We thought that this would be an interesting way to focus attention on a set of books of lasting importance and an opportunity to comment on the significance (and limits) of a key book. We especially encouraged contributors to think about less obvious works and works by nonacademic historians. Significantly, six of the eight authors chose works that are more than fifteen years old (four of them more than twenty years old), a sign that while the field is mostly young and changing, a canon has already begun to form.

We are grateful to our thirty-six authors for their willingness to undertake this difficult and time-consuming assignment, for their responsiveness to our comments, for their adherence to a tight schedule, and, not least of all, for the very fine essays that they have written. We also greatly appreciate the help and support of Ken Provencher and Susan Rabinowitz at Blackwell. We are also indebted to Brigitte Lee for her careful and cheerful work on the copyediting and proofreading and to Jim O'Brien for his superb index. Our immediate families – Rita Rack, Winnie Agnew, and Deborah Kaplan – have cheerfully tolerated incessant interruptions caused by this project and have offered crucial advice and support, as have our many old friends in the Memorial Day picnic crowd. We also thank a number of scholars – especially Jennifer Brier, Philip Deloria, Gary Gerstle, Nancy Hewitt, Nelson Lichtenstein, James Sparrow, John Summers, Robert Westbrook, Shane White – who supplied helpful suggestions on potential authors and other matters. We have learned an enormous amount from our conversations with them and with our contributors, and we have learned even more from the essays that fill this volume. These essays have been our companions for some time now, and we are delighted to make them yours as well.

REFERENCES

Chafe, William H.: *The Unfinished Journey: America Since World War II* (New York: Oxford University Press, 1998).

Collins, Robert M.: *More: The Politics of Economic Growth in Postwar America* (New York: Oxford University Press, 2000).

Degler, Carl: *Affluence and Anxiety* (Glenview, Ill.: Scott, Foresman, and Company, 1968).

Engelhardt, Tom: *The End of Victory Culture: Cold War America and the Disillusioning of a Generation* (New York: Basic Books, 1995).

Lambrose, R. J.: "Rebel Without His Clothes," *Radical History Review*, 42 (1988): 195–6.

Leuchtenburg, William E.: *A Troubled Feast: American Society Since 1945* (Boston: Little, Brown, 1973).

Moss, George Donelson: *Moving On: The American People Since 1945* (Engelwood Cliffs: Prentice Hall, 1994).

Patterson, James T.: *Grand Expectations: The United States, 1945–1974* (New York: Oxford University Press, 1996).

Schaller, Michael, Scharff, Virginia, and Schulzinger, Robert D.: *Present Tense: The United States Since 1945* (Boston: Houghton Mifflin, 1992).

Siegel, Frederick F.: *Troubled Journey: From Pearl Harbor to Ronald Reagan* (New York: Hill and Wang, 1984).

PART I

Society and Culture

CHAPTER ONE

Family and Demography in Postwar America: A Hazard of New Fortunes?

STEPHEN LASSONDE

Since the mid-1960s the proportion of children living in two-parent households has declined for all groups in the United States, a trend that has elicited responses – popular and scholarly – ranging from consternation to mild satisfaction. While the ill-fated "Moynihan Report" (US Department of Labor, 1965) promoted single-parent headship as the chief cause of "family breakdown" among African Americans, the subsequent decline of two-parent households among whites has provoked more generalized concern about the health of family life in the United States. As long as single-parent headship was linked exclusively to the "disorganization" of a group as patently oppressed as African Americans and the cause of their immiseration could be hung on slavery and Jim Crow, single-parenthood could be regarded as a remote, if malformed, adaptation to the harsh conditions imposed by the evils and ignorance of generations past. At the close of the twentieth century, however, it became increasingly difficult to dismiss as a cultural perversion a social change of such magnitude: by the late 1990s, more than a quarter of all white children were being raised in the home of one parent, and divorce was the leading cause of this trend.

Other, "worrisome," developments had contributed to the rise in single-parent households, namely, the spreading acceptance of premarital sex, the consequent increase of teen pregnancy and illegitimate births among white females, and from an unanticipated source – growing numbers of women who were choosing to conceive and raise children outside of wedlock. Still more trends added to the list of concerns over the status of marriage and family life: a birth rate barely at replacement level; a historically high ratio of adults who have never married; and increasing numbers of couples who choose to cohabit rather than marry. These developments were all the more striking since family life during the two decades after the war had witnessed a seeming return to more tradition-bound patterns of marriage and childrearing. Politicians, policymakers, and some social scientists pointed to these trends with alarm. They declared the end of the family, the decay of the social fabric.

I would like to thank the editors, Jean-Christophe Agnew and Roy Rosenzweig, for their helpful comments on, and close reading of, several earlier drafts of this essay, as well as John Modell and Matthew Broder for their many excellent and timely suggestions.

Historians, more circumspect in their assessments, disagree about the meaning of these changes and even how much change has occurred. Some decry the family's "decline" and argue that the function, form, and feeling of family life have altered irrevocably since World War II. Others have drawn attention to the fact that divorce has replaced death as the primary cause of single-parent headship, the resurgence of "blended families," and step-parenting (Smith, 1995; Ruggles, 1994). Households, moreover, include fewer extended kin and unrelated individuals than at any time in the past (Ruggles and Goeken, 1992). As a site for reproduction, child nurture, and the pooling of economic resources, some historians argue, the family has demonstrated tremendous elasticity in its ability to accommodate changing economic and social relations. Compared with the social and behavioral sciences, however, the historical literature on family life in the postwar period is relatively thin and uneven. Whereas interpersonal and social relations have been key concerns of the behavioral and social sciences for more than a century, historians have been latecomers to the widening discourse on family life in the United States and did not fully turn to the study of family and kinship until the late 1960s. Contemporary historical study of family life was initiated by Philippe Ariès in 1960, but the earliest full-length studies of family and kinship in the United States did not appear until a decade later (Demos, 1970; Greven, 1970). Elemental questions about household structure, life span and cycle, inheritance practices, the functioning of family groups bound together by common (if not mutual) economic and emotional interests, and a host of other concerns that filled people's daily lives from cradle to grave absorbed the attentions of this first wave of scholars in family history. These historians must have felt themselves at the very heart of the movement to compose a comprehensive "history of everyday life" that was ascendant in the early 1970s.

Lost or sidestepped in the effort, however, was a similar accounting for changes in African American family life since World War II. There is no shortage of theory, speculation, and empirical analysis by social scientists of African American family life since 1945, but there remains little scholarship written by historians; and even what little historiography there is displays preoccupations quite remote from those of social scientists concerned with African American families in the same period. The social sciences are "problem"-driven disciplines, which may explain why their attentions have remained riveted to African American group life during the second half of the twentieth century. As social problems are identified in political discourse they become the object of sociological curiosity – and no less the object of scrutiny by economists, political scientists, and even anthropologists. The federal government and philanthropic foundations have an interest in funding such studies because they hold out the promise of a cure for perceived social "ills." As a consequence, most of what histories we have of black families since World War II have been composed by social scientists trying to explain what had transpired before the Moynihan Report or the alleged emergence of a black "underclass" twenty years later, and how each crisis framed current understandings of African American family life.

Two factors, I think, amplify the noticeable silence of historians in this area. First, to those who continued to pursue lines of inquiry established at the renascence of social history in the 1960s, the experience of African American families seemed to follow a different historical trajectory from that of the dominant culture in postwar America and thus to require a different narrative framework and different questions.

Second, the Moynihan Report cast a long shadow across the young field of family history. The Moynihan Report had provoked a storm of protest so devastating that less than a year after its circulation, the issues raised by the report were pronounced "dead" (Rainwater and Yancey, 1967, p. 481). Criticism ranged from ideological objections to quarrels with the methodology and presentation of the data.

Moynihan characterized the black family as a "tangle of pathology" (US Department of Labor, 1965, p. 30). While acknowledging the contribution of white Americans' racism to inequalities between whites and blacks, Moynihan concluded nonetheless that it was the "weakness of family structure" among African Americans that accounted for the many problems that prevented blacks from gaining an equal footing in American social and economic life. Drawing upon E. Franklin Frazier's research on the African American family in the 1920s and 1930s and Stanley Elkins's historical analysis of slavery, Moynihan explained the legacy of the black family's "weakness" as a product of African enslavement, which had broken the family's back, established women at its head, and trapped generations of children in a cycle of poverty, disorganization, and dysfunction, uninterrupted since emancipation (US Department of Labor, 1965, p. 17; Frazier, 1940; Elkins, 1959).

To a much greater degree than perhaps has been appreciated, historians have actively avoided study of black families in the postwar period precisely because they were at a loss to explain what appeared to be a deepening of the very trends identified and condemned by Moynihan. Given the degree of criticism provoked by the report, it was clear that it was politically hazardous to undertake such a study (Rainwater and Yancey, 1967). But what is more, family historians faced an intellectual *cul-de-sac* in studying African American family life. The questions they asked presumed too much about how intimate relations are (or ought to be) configured – between husbands and wives and parents and children in particular – to be able to think about other ways that people might conduct caring, committed relationships that counted as "family" and were infused with meaning and purpose over time.

The absence of a historiography of contemporary African American family and kinship represents a grave shortcoming in any effort to comprehend the variety of family life since World War II. Nonetheless, it is a period full of drama – drama heightened by the confluence of attitudes and behaviors that yielded its most remarkable feature, the "baby boom." The baby boom between 1945 and 1964 was an extraordinary demographic event, not because the birth rate climbed to unprecedented levels – it did not. The birth rate at the beginning of the century surpassed the highest level achieved during the baby boom at its peak. Rather, it was the coalescence of a sustained, elevated birth rate with other demographic features and a reinforcing ideology of pronatalism that made the era distinctive.

During the peak years of the baby boom, social theorist Talcott Parsons argued that the isolated nuclear family represented an ideal social "adaptation" to the conditions of modern life. Parents and their dependent children, living in a dwelling apart from their own families of orientation, economically independent, and subsisting "from the occupational earnings of the husband-father," he observed, was the " 'normal' arrangement" in American society (Parsons and Bales, 1955, p. 10). Moreover, since the roles of the conjugal pair were specialized by temperament, biology, and aptitude, parents, it was proposed, operated most effectively when they worked together as the family's "leadership element" while clearly dividing the tasks to which their different natures inclined them. Complementary to the father-husband's instrumentalist function as family task leader was the mother's "expressive," nurturing role – a role cemented by the "bearing and early nurturing of children" (Parsons and Bales, 1955, p. 23). Unencumbered by responsibilities for the education and care of the sick, disabled, and aged, the modern, nuclear family, according to Parsons, had one primary purpose: the socialization of its children.

Although the nuclear family took root as a widespread social ideal after World War II, its components were in evidence well before mid-century. "Companionate marriage," the notion that men and women formed an egalitarian partnership in marriage based on friendship, mutual respect, and a breadwinner/homemaker division of labor in the family, was popularized in American cinema and other media by the mid-1920s (E. May, 1980; L. May, 1980). The passage of federal prohibitions against child labor, as well as the enforcement of compulsory school attendance laws throughout the nation, sent the family wage economy into permanent decline by the onset of the Great Depression. This meant that children, rather than contributing labor or income to their households, were to be the beneficiaries of mother's attention – the objects of both affection and vigilant, conscientious correction (Zelizer, 1985; Lassonde, 1998). Simultaneously, Social Security enhanced the possibility of independence for elderly Americans after 1940 (Ruggles, 1994). It was not until after World War II, however, that a majority of Americans began to realize the ideals projected by popular culture and underwritten by the Wagner and Social Security Acts during the New Deal administration. After World War II this legislation, aided by the GI Bill, the expansion of home loans through the Federal Housing Administration, and a wave of unprecedented prosperity, expedited the rise of the isolated nuclear family and subsidized the prodigious birth rate.

Other, associated trends were not firmly established until the middle of the 1950s. Historically high marriage rates and lower ages at marriage, a lower age of entry into motherhood, an increased rate of conception within the first year of marriage, a preference for larger families, a significant rise in homeownership, as well as increased consumer spending and debt all combined to create a distinctive commitment to what John Modell has called the era's "family-building ethos": the belief that the height of personal satisfaction was to be found not just in marriage itself but equally in childrearing (Modell, 1989; May, 1988; Cherlin, 1981; Jackson, 1985). Almost as soon as these trends merged, however, they began to unravel. By the late 1950s, key ingredients of the "family-building" ethos – the stay-at-home mother and marital longevity – were challenged by the increased workforce participation of mothers with young children and the renewed climb of the divorce rate (Davis, 1984; Cherlin, 1981; Easterlin, 1980). While the gender roles prescribed by "family building" continued powerfully to shape women's and men's ambitions, sense of duty to others, and relations to one another for a generation, "family building" began to lose its luster as the decade wore on and the relentlessness of raising so many children, so close together in age, and in so solitary a fashion, took its toll on this resanctified arrangement of coupling, reproduction, and childrearing.

Women who strained under the gendered division of labor approvingly depicted in the mass media and modeled on Parsons's isolated nuclear family – working, divorced, and unwed mothers – appeared to threaten the healthy operation of the family. By infringing on the adult male's role as "family task leader," they were considered deviant and condemned for modeling deviance for their children. In 1963 Betty Friedan voiced the deep, if quiet, discontent that later blossomed into the women's movement. Feminists ultimately rejected the political economy of marriage, reproduction, and the stereotyped family roles cast by the Parsonian model and popular culture. In response to its suffocating narrowness, they called for a broader conception of the forms and functions of family and household.

In 1974 support for this perspective came from Carol B. Stack's ethnography of black working-class Chicago, *All Our Kin*, the first sustained scholarly response to the Moynihan Report. No one until Stack had taken on Moynihan's chief assumption, that the fluidity of familial relations among African Americans and especially the pragmatic substitution of adults to perform "parental" obligations were fundamentally "dysfunctional." For this reason, *All Our Kin* was a pivotal study. Rather than catalogue the relative extent of two-parent households in the black community, Stack showed how African Americans had developed "fictive kin" to satisfy the range of functions that parents fulfill in European American families. She not only interrogated the presumption of the nuclear family model but challenged the normative necessity of male headship and authority. In effect, Stack equipped students of African American family life with a new lens through which to view the function and meaning of family and kinship and simultaneously licensed feminist critics to deconstruct contemporary family history from their own vantage point, by toppling the myth of male authority (Rapp, Ross, and Bridenthal, 1979; Collier, Rosaldo, and Yanigisako, 1992). This is not to say that historians had failed to address the issue of male authority in the family sphere before; this had been a central focus of women's historians and theorists since the founding of women's history as a subfield of social history during the 1960s. Rather, it was not until after Stack that feminist historians of family life examined changes in family structure, operation, and ideology in the postwar years. Stack paved the way for a critical evaluation of patriarchy and the maintenance of the nuclear family ideal during this period.

Christopher Lasch, one of the first scholars to assess the state of postwar family life from a historical perspective, published two widely read books on the family in the space of two years: *Haven in a Heartless World* (1977) and *The Culture of Narcissism* (1978). The first was an extended critique of family sociology and the rise of therapeutic solutions to the perceived decline of male authority in the twentieth century. The second disparaged the "attack on the nuclear family" and the arrogation of the family's right to educate and socialize its children. The theme that united these two works was the assertion that American culture is the worse for the decline of male authority – a decline set into motion decades earlier, to be sure, but precipitated by the feminist critique of the nuclear family.

Social trends extending back to the dawn of industrialism had ripened by the 1920s and 1930s, Lasch wrote, but had begun to rot by the middle of the twentieth century. By the 1950s most of the family's functions had been stripped away. Care for the infirm and aged, education, moral instruction, its economic function, all of these had been overtaken by other institutions. More disturbing in Lasch's estimation, however, were the many incursions into the sole remaining purpose of the family as the seat of human intimacy. Increasingly, from the 1920s forward, psychologists and psychiatrists – experts in infant care, childrearing, marital relations, sibling rivalry, and sexuality – began to impose their own notions of correctness upon every aspect of family relations. The result, by the mid-1950s according to Lasch, was the widespread adoption of "permissive" parenting and the complete absence of the patriarch-father, whose role as family leader was so critical to the Parsonian conception of the evolved nuclear family. It had been difficult enough when father had been physically absented from the home by his work; now his lack of authority in the home meant a lapse in moral standards as well (Lasch, 1978, pp. 172–9).

A second consequence was that the mother attempted to compensate for the husband's absence by indulging her children in every feeling and desire. "In this way," Lasch argued, permissive parents "undermine the child's initiative and make it impossible for him to develop self-restraint or self-discipline" (Lasch, 1978, p. 178). Just as ties between parents and children were weakened by the abdication of parental authority, he suggested, ties between men and women had been frayed by what he called the "cult of intimacy." Predicated upon the increased importance of sexual gratification in conjugal relations as well as the "emotional overloading of personal relations" between husbands and wives, marriages dissolved under the weight of unrealistic expectations (Lasch, 1978, p. 188). Divorce was the result and its unparalleled rise, he concluded, could be laid at the doorstep of feminists who had advanced such improbable demands in the first place and worse, who had called off the tacit truce between men and women and their mutual, "easy-going contempt for the weakness of the other sex" (Lasch, 1978, p. 195). Lasch shared Moynihan's presumptive uneasiness about matriarchy as well as his conviction that the nuclear family offered society's best hope against the pathologies that hinder social progress for the majority of Americans and perpetuate poverty and deprivation among blacks (Lasch, 1977, pp. 157–62, 165; US Department of Labor, 1965, p. 76).

A more even-handed assessment of many of the trends troubling Christopher Lasch was offered by Andrew Cherlin in *Marriage, Divorce, Remarriage* (1981). Cherlin's was a stock-taking enterprise that proposed to puzzle out what he described as the "roller-coaster" patterns of marriage and divorce since World War II. If familial living arrangements were transformed in the decade after the war, they looked radically different again by the last quarter of the twentieth century. Not only was divorce near an all-time high and the birth rate at an all-time low, family configurations, single parenthood, and average age at first marriage all reversed patterns that had emerged immediately after World War II. If Lasch wrung his hands over the state of American family life by the 1970s, Cherlin and others pointed to the 1950s as the anomaly to be explained, for the 1960s and 1970s merely reasserted trends of long standing in marriage, fertility, women's labor force participation, and divorce. For Cherlin the appropriate question to ask was: what happened during the 1950s to create such an exceptional cluster of family-forming behaviors?

Cherlin presented the debate over how to explain the 1950s as dividing into two camps. One, which he characterized as the "period" explanation, posited that the rush to marriage, prolific childbearing, slowed divorce rate, and initial withdrawal of married women from the workforce after the war could best be understood as the product of a specific historical era: a collective, emotional response to the deferral of family formation made necessary by the straitened circumstances of the 1930s and then by the absence of marriageable males during World War II. A competing theory, which Cherlin called the "cohort" explanation, had been championed by Richard Easterlin. The cohort explanation understood the 1950s as a reaction to the generational experience of the men and women who had come of age during the late 1940s and 1950s. Born just before and during the 1930s, they had experienced the deprivations of the Great Depression and thus had low material expectations as they moved into the labor market. Yet because their birth cohort was small and the United States rode a long wave of prosperity in the wake of the war, jobs were abundant and wages were relatively high. Able to meet their standards for material comfort early in their working lives without having to trade comfort for children (which most young couples *must* do), they had children. Cherlin sensibly considered some combination of the two explanations as most plausible. Neither cohort size nor the catastrophes of depression and war could alone explain the extraordinary convergence of low age at first marriage, high birth rate, the tendency for newly married women to give birth in their first year of marriage, a stabilizing divorce rate, and an all-time-high ratio of men and women marrying (95 percent).

Cherlin's was one of the first attempts to unravel the complex and baffling puzzle of the baby boom and its aftermath. Yet his characterization of the debate as it stood in 1980 could not anticipate the shape of future historical interpretations of the demographic and political "events" of postwar America. Since the publication of *Marriage, Divorce, Remarriage*, historians have struggled not just with behavioral patterns but with the attitudes that informed these behaviors and with the discourse about family life, attempting to understand parents and children as agents of change as well as continuity. I will examine some of these studies below, but Richard A. Easterlin's *Birth and Fortune* (1980), which, as Cherlin pointed out, had the "virtue of theoretical simplicity" in its modeling of postwar social trends, exemplified an approach to historical change that aspires to a kind of scientistic rigor absent in most of the studies undertaken since.

The industrial revolution, Easterlin pointed out, made possible continued increases in living levels for the masses in every society experiencing its upheavals beginning during the eighteenth century. However, industrialization also introduced tremendous volatility into individuals' financial fortunes and social status. In the United States, the Employment Act of 1946 addressed the worst consequences of industrial capitalism's cyclical growth and contraction. Because the federal government gained the ability to dampen the effects of economic downturn, the economic recessions of the postwar period were, he argued, "hardly enough to ruin a start on a working life for large numbers of young people" (Easterlin, 1980, p. 146). The lone determinant of one's relative prosperity or want, he illustrated repeatedly, was the size of the generation one was born into. The ways women and men organized their personal lives, from cohabitation to reproduction, are accordingly arrayed by the generational hand one is dealt. A bad hand is one in which the birth cohort is large. A lucky one is small. For the large cohort, employment will be relatively scarce and wages correspondingly low, whereas for the diminutive cohort, jobs will be abundant and remuneration generous. And while it has ever been so, according to Easterlin, this phenomenon stood as the single factor with sway over an economy whose cycles have been comparatively flattened out since World War II.

All of us, it seems, make a kind of internal estimate of what we need materially to be happy and then work, as couples, to support that calculus. We reproduce, or not, to the extent that children interfere with our combined capacity to reach our cultural target–family size. The argument is at once compelling (in his rendering, if not mine) and depressing: while none of us chooses our parents and hence the socio-economic status or race we are born into, neither do we choose the size of our birth cohort. Whether or not we believe that women should have the power to decide to carry a pregnancy to term, that women and men should equitably divide the burdens of income earning, housework, and childcare, or whether the nation's social policy should assist or punish parents based on their marital status matters little in the face of factors beyond the individual's control. It is the marrying kind who decide what the fate of the next generation will be and those decisions are made twenty years before anyone looking for work can do anything about them (Easterlin, 1980, p. 56). Despite his unabashed demographic determinism, Easterlin's approach keenly illustrates the difference between the aims of historical demography, which is a tool to predict future reproductive behavior, and social/cultural history, which is a tool for understanding the way people acted and understood themselves, their choices, and their world.

Sociologist David Popenoe, like Lasch, has bemoaned the inevitable decline that he predicts will accompany the swells of change unleashed by the 1960s and that had been already partly realized by the end of the 1980s. *Disturbing the Nest*, which appeared in 1988, views divorce and a number of other indicators as leading the world's "advanced" societies into decline. Popenoe's comparative study of family life in Sweden, the United States, Switzerland, and New Zealand concluded that the collection of trends witnessed in Sweden since World War II is coming to America. These trends portend a shift from what he called the "bourgeois nuclear family" to the "postnuclear family." Early sexual experience, late age at first marriage, low marriage rates, rock-bottom fertility, high divorce rates, high rates of nonmarital cohabitation, serial monogamy (but an increase of sexual polygamy among the married), blended families, and increased reliance on nonfamilial childcare have all resulted in the post-nuclear family. Sweden, he wrote, has become a society dominated by single-person and "nonfamily" households, households with "pair-bonded" adults with no children, and households with children but only one adult. The extended family household with two generations of adults has been driven virtually out of existence and the "traditional" two-parent family "became a small fraction of the total" (Popenoe, 1988, p. 298). If the bourgeois nuclear family had been guilty of greatly restricting women's freedom of association, access to education and wealth, exposing women and children to physical abuse, and contributing to social inequality (by placing a premium on the family's ability to control and inherit wealth), it had the virtue at least, according to Popenoe, of placing the welfare of children at the center of its purpose. The hallmark of the bourgeois nuclear family was child-centeredness – the willingness of parents to forego personal gratification to satisfy children's needs for security, emotional nurturance, and the development of competence and autonomy – even at the cost of happiness in one's marriage, job, and social relations. The post-nuclear family, by contrast, was "adult-centered" and individualistic, and the form of individualism it championed, he asserted, was a "relative newcomer on the world scene" (Popenoe, 1988, p. 329).

Published the year after Popenoe's study, John Modell's *Into One's Own* examined an important consequence of this newly discovered individualism by tracing the structural bases for the experience of adolescence and youth during the middle decades of the twentieth century. While postwar "youth culture" had been flamboyantly individualistic in the very manner that so worried Popenoe, it was also anti-authoritarian in its postures, which openly parodied the adult world projected by Popenoe's postnuclear family. *Into One's Own* bridged work by historians who have explored the rise of youth culture in the postwar era and family history, which exist intuitively as interrelated topics but which have developed nonetheless as separate subfields in social and cultural history. Other studies on postwar youth culture, such as James Gilbert's *Cycle of Outrage* (1986) or William Graebner's *Coming of Age in Buffalo* (1990), neatly complemented Modell's study by describing adolescents' efforts to define themselves in response to and *against* official, "adult" culture. However, these works are more concerned with understanding the effect of mass media on postwar teen life, the fascination with juvenile delinquency during the 1950s, or the variety of subcultures that evolved from, or in defiance of, emerging national symbols of youth culture than in demonstrating the rising influence of peers over family and parents.

Modell analyzed the forces – demographic, economic, and sociocultural – that created this cultural space for adolescents and youths in the first place. He examined long-term change in the way young people organized – or properly, were enabled to organize – their assumption of both the pleasures and responsibilities of adulthood. Modell was concerned with the series of "events" that occur in each young person's development from his or her dependence upon parents, family, and kin to eventual autonomy and the establishment of a family. These events consist of school-leaving, workforce entry, moving out of the parental household, marriage, and parenthood. During the late nineteenth century in the middle class and by 1920 across the US social structure, the combination of these events was imposed upon the "life course" of every young person. *Into One's Own* told the story of how the management of the life course evolved from an adult-controlled, tightly sequenced series of stages with little overlap, to the postwar regime, which was made possible by the spreading affluence enjoyed by the majority of Americans, giving young people more freedom to arrange the order in which they passed through life-course events.

Unfettered by demands to support the family economy, young people could elect to extend their schooling, work at the same time, even establish their own households, marry, and start their own families. The barriers – economic and social – for doing so were much lower than at any time in the past, and the result was both more choice in their sequencing and higher anxiety as a consequence. Much of what young people experience as adolescent angst today, in Modell's view, may stem from having the liberty to choose how to organize and pass through these stages. Of all the historical studies of family relationships during the latter half of the twentieth century in the United States, Modell alone provided a comprehensive analysis of the changing structure of youth – the way growing up is now organized by the interplay of institutions and the people who pass through them.

While Modell made sense out of young people's daring embrace of adult responsibility just after World War II, in *Homeward Bound* (1988) Elaine Tyler May looked beneath the sheen and apparent calm of 1950s family experience to explore the emotional lives of the women who had helped erect the ethos of family building. The most compelling part of the story May told centers on a longitudinal survey of couples' satisfaction with their marriages, which revealed the deep ambivalences women experienced as housewives. Most of the women in the study cited by May had had some college education and had left school to marry early and begin families. While the majority did so willingly, they only realized over time the price exacted by the sublimation of their aspirations and autonomy to their husbands' careers. The full-time responsibility of raising children turned out for many to be more wearying and tedious than satisfying. Some worked the "double shift" that would become so common during the 1980s and afterward. In order to support a higher standard of living (and spending) for their families, they took low-paying, unfulfilling jobs to "help out" with bills and debt while continuing the full-time maintenance of household and children. About the majority of women in the study May concluded that "[t]hey all resented their husbands' unquestioned authority in the home, wished for more attention to their own needs, and chafed against the subordination that was expected of them. Yet they also protested that they loved their husbands, were satisfied with their marriages, and blamed themselves frequently for their discontent" (May, 1988, pp. 199–200).

The most pointed defense of the kinds of changes in family life that nagged Lasch and Popenoe has been mounted by Stephanie Coontz. Coontz reminds scholars, policymakers, and average citizens that change in the organization of familial relations has been eternal and that functional variety, not uniformity, has ever been the rule. *The Way We Never Were* (1992) was written to counter a pervasive cultural myth that the 1950s were years when the lived experience of the majority of Americans approximated the televised rendering of the family circle. Coontz not only exposed the falseness of this image but documented the social costs of nurturing its memory. As a result of this "nostalgia trap," as she called it, girls and boys came of age during the 1960s and afterward believing that the average family has two parents, that the father is the family's sole provider, and that the mother devotes herself exclusively to housework and childrearing, which consist of cooking hearty meals, attending PTA meetings, dispensing timely advice to her children and consolation when they meet with disappointment. Soulmate to her husband, she is his personal sanctuary from the daily rat race that affords a new home, a suburban school system, a new car every few years, and all the pleasures of the highest standard of living in the world. For her, marriage offers both sexual intimacy and the companionship of equals, even if she contributes nothing to the family's income and her husband pays all the bills. In sum, the family is a harmonious ensemble, ever caring, gentle in its expressions of rebuke or affection, and the source of consideration and respect for others (Coontz, 1992).

The least malignant outcome of this myth, Coontz suggested, is that Americans have grown up believing that their own families were, and are, dysfunctional because they so little resemble the image of family life cultivated by the media. They consider themselves failures as parents, just as they have come to believe that their own parents have failed them. More insidious, she added, is the effect of this image on policymakers, who have allowed such distortions to blind them to the sources of continuing social inequality – capitalism, racism, and sexism.

In contrast to Easterlin and even Cherlin, Coontz was ardent in her conviction that the social changes Popenoe, Lasch, and others lamented were brought about not by impersonal demographic and economic forces but by the determination of dissidents in American culture to challenge the unequal treatment of women, consumer conformity, and the "sentimentalization of family life as the final culmination of the search for personal fulfillment" (Coontz, 1992, p. 173). And while critics of contemporary family life were apt to blame the flight from personal and social obligations on nontraditional families and particularly the women's movement for fostering women's independence and spawning divorce, in fact, Coontz argued, it was consumerism that was "eating away at family time, neighborhood cohesion, and public solidarities" (Coontz, 1992, p. 179).

This last observation has had many echoes. Indeed, if there is a unifying idea in historians' judgments about family life over the last half-century, it is that affluence and the expanding consumption it has supported have accelerated the kind of self-seeking that has shaped family life for the majority of Americans since World War II. Moynihan's *The Negro Family* was a product of the same bonanza that expanded the middle class, suburbanized the American landscape, and financed the very consumerism that historians from Lasch to Coontz have worried about. However misguided and racist its analysis, the impulse to "fix" the black family could only have arisen at a time when both the political will and economic clout to fund family support services on a massive scale existed side by side. While the clamorous failure of *The Negro Family* as a policy report seems to have stimulated social science research, it has had the opposite effect on historical studies of postwar African American families – an impact all the more lamentable for the fact that the Moynihan Report had been at the same time the first "history" of postwar African American family life. Bringing up to the present data on African American family structure, male unemployment, educational attainment, illegitimacy, teen pregnancy, AFDC (Aid to Families with Dependent Children) enrollment, fertility, female headship, "broken homes," juvenile delinquency, and drug abuse, Moynihan catalogued every conceivable index of urban "pathology" imaginable, back-lit against the tableaux of slavery, the Great Migration, and the urban ghetto.

At first it seemed that reaction to the document might generate significant historical scholarship. Herbert G. Gutman and his students began researching Moynihan's (and Frazier's) claims about familial headship, marital longevity, and employment among blacks during the nineteenth and early twentieth centuries – an initial outpouring that produced several article-length collaborations and Gutman's tome, *The Black Family in Slavery and Freedom* (1976). But Gutman's study ended chronologically where Frazier's sociology of the African American family had begun in the 1920s. The first historian to push some of the issues raised by Gutman into the postwar period was Jacqueline Jones, whose *Labor of Love, Labor of Sorrow* (1985) surveyed the history of African American women from slavery to the 1980s.

Jones showed that the reign of postwar prosperity in the United States, which stimulated such remarkable and pervasive social change in white America, reestablished a family economy for most African Americans that was all too familiar. Unlike the majority of American women (who retreated from the workforce immediately after World War II), African American women were unremitting as family breadgivers even as veterans reclaimed their jobs in the peacetime economy. One reason they returned so readily to their prewar occupations was that their own husbands, brothers, fathers, and sons confronted the same discriminatory hiring practices after the war that they had suffered before the conflict (Jones, 1985, p. 261). Another was that the kinds of jobs that black women resorted to as the wartime economy cooled were beneath the notice of returning (white) heroes. While white women were as apt to lose their jobs to returning soldiers as to economic recession, the aftermath of war forced black women back into low-paid, demeaning domestic work by "mass firings and layoffs, separate seniority lists based on race and sex, [and] union harassment of women who fought desperately to retain their blue-collar wages" (Jones, 1985, pp. 256–7). This "redomestication" of African American women, as Jones has called it, also meant an accompanying decline in wages relative to white women, whose average earnings doubled those of black women just one year after the war had ended. Yet in stark contrast to white women, says Jones, married black women were much more likely to work than their white "sisters," as "work seemed to form an integral part of the [black] female role" (Jones, 1985, pp. 261, 269).

Andrew Billingsley's *Climbing Jacob's Ladder*, published in 1992, considered the impact of these and other changes on the entire class structure of African Americans since World War II. Where Jones emphasized the profound influence of racism on gender roles in family life, Billingsley analyzed the long-term effects on family structure of deindustrialization and the simultaneous expansion of the black middle class. Deindustrialization had had two major consequences for African Americans, he found. Just as black males gained a foothold in industrial occupations during and after World War II, the proportion of all workers employed in white-collar jobs in the United States surpassed those engaged in manufacturing. Because African Americans did not participate in this shift to white-collar employment to the same degree and with the same frequency as other Americans, however, their entry into the middle class was forestalled. While the black middle class expanded during the 1960s (from 13 percent to 25 percent of the black population between 1960 and 1970), the resultant "lag" in their entry into the white-collar workforce meant that as the US economy was increasingly dominated by its service sector, manufacturing jobs were lost. African Americans were hit hardest by the permanent disappearance of industrial occupations (Billingsley, 1992, p. 139). Already by 1954, African Americans were out of work at twice the rate of whites – a trend interrupted just once over the next three decades.

The consequent decline of the black working class had a devastating impact on the organization of family life. Its diminution, Billingsley observed, was "the single most important force responsible for the decline in the nuclear-family structure over the second half of the twentieth century, from a high of 78 percent in 1960 to 44 percent by 1990" (Billingsley, 1992, p. 138). On one hand, Billingsley lauded the diversity of African American family structure, which is a tribute, he maintained, to the adaptability and ingenuity of African Americans in the face of adverse circumstances. On the other hand, he intimated that the interests of black children would be better served by the two-parent family model. "For the hundred year period between the end of slavery and the aftermath of World War Two," he noted, "the structure of African-American family life was characterized by a remarkable degree of stability . . . the core of the traditional African-American Family system has been the nuclear family composed of husband and wife and their own children" (Billingsley, 1992, p. 36). By 1990, just 39 percent of black families were headed by married couples, a downward trend, he predicted, that was "likely to continue into the future" (Billingsley, 1992, pp. 36–7). Billingsley approvingly cited the research of other scholars to show that the single-parent, female-headed black family is an adaptive strategy to which African American families have resorted in response to joblessness, racism, and the collapse of the welfare state. The single-parent family did not evolve "because of forces internal to . . . [African American] culture," he argued, "but from forces in the wider society" (Billingsley, 1992, p. 35). The key feature of the nuclear family model, he suggested, is the consistency of concern, support, and involvement that it makes possible. While this support has been replicated by other means (by the active engagement of adults in the lives of other people's children, for example), such alternatives are a less dependable form of fostering the development of children (Billingsley, 1992, pp. 381–5).

In *Black Picket Fences* (1999), Mary Pattillo-McCoy offers an ethnography of black middle-class families in a neighborhood on Chicago's South Side. She explores the meaning of what it is to be African American and middle class in postwar America, and the reasons why the children of the "new" black middle class have had such difficulty repeating gains made by their parents. Like most work on African Americans during the latter half of the twentieth century, *Black Picket Fences* was not conceived as an historical study, but it employs history as a way of understanding the current state of black family life in the United States.

Pattillo-McCoy considers the role of geography on the interaction of African Americans across the social structure. Spatial mobility – or its absence – she argues, has dangerously compromised the aspirations and competencies of black children who grow up in middle-class homes. As their numbers swelled after the 1960s, middle-class blacks began leaving the inner city much as white ethnics had done before and just after World War II. However, they could not get very far, as housing covenants and red-lining hemmed them into first-ring suburbs. While black suburbanites had been able to leave the areas of *most* violent crime and drug abuse – of broken-down schools, ineffective law enforcement, and other impotent institutions – they remained to their detriment interwoven into the fabric of the urban black community. Their proximity to "blighted, poor neighborhoods," Pattillo-McCoy shows, exposed middle-class black children to the same influences as children whose parents' means were slender. Thus, compared with white middle-class children, their ability to avoid drug abuse, gang involvement, prison, and violence was hampered. Pattillo-McCoy is less apprehensive than Billingsley about the decline of the black two-parent, nuclear family, however, noting that middle-class African American families have adopted the extended family model of impoverished blacks to good advantage in order to cope with an "increasingly precarious economic context." A good portion of the families she interviewed, she says, "flourished only because of the combined time and money resources and emotional help of many families, sometimes all in one house and sometimes spread out across the neighborhood and city" (Pattillo-McCoy, 1999, p. 213).

Like Pattillo-McCoy, but in contrast to much of the work on African American family life today, Andrew T. Miller has trumpeted the virtues of the extended family in all its forms. The problem with discourse on family life and social policy since the Great Society, Miller argues, has been its assumption that the African American family model is badly flawed. The black family of the late twentieth century was not merely an outcome of adaptation to cruelties wrought by slavery, institutionalized racism, or industrial capitalism but an extension of the folkways of societies ravaged for the New World slave trade. What has been overlooked, he says, is that the African American family is itself a worthy design for living based on traditions that extend far into regions of sub-Saharan Africa, where "fosterage" continues to thrive. Fosterage is the practice of placing children in others' homes – usually but not necessarily those of relatives – where they can be nurtured more easily or advantageously than by their own parents (Miller, 1993, pp. 277–80).

Miller's essay, "Social Science, Social Policy, and the Heritage of African-American Families," turns the Parsonian paradigm on its head, arguing that the upwardly mobile European American family, far from offering a template for family life on which to base social policy, is itself a "tangle of pathology." "Euro-Americans," he says, "show high levels of living alone, have much higher levels of family violence and abuse, . . . abandon children and the elderly to a greater degree, . . . much more often support the practice of abortion, . . . label certain children illegitimate, will not get involved in the family problems of others, and condemn alternative living arrangements" (Miller, 1993, p. 284). While child-centeredness is usually defined by the degree to which parents invest time, money, and other resources in their children, Miller argues that, considering the constraints under which the African American family has long labored, it has proven far more "child-centered" than the isolated nuclear family of Parsons's description. If the modernity of the family form is derived from its concentration of attention and resources upon the child, he suggests, then the African American family may be considered better adapted and more "modern" than those of the majority of European Americans. While for European Americans, family life is defined by the legal union of two heterosexual adults, for African Americans, he points out, it is the creation of the child itself that brings a family into being. This crucial distinction, he argues, is symbolic of very real differences in the ways that children are regarded and cared for.

Miller's table-turning is at points simplistic and polemical, but it highlights the most admirable aspects of African American family life and importantly rejects the kind of defensiveness that has characterized so much of the "underclass" debate since the 1980s. Richard A. Davis's *The Black Family in a Changing Black Community* (1984) shares this quality and yet muddies the waters by emphasizing the emerging ethnic variety of the US black population, which has added to the complexity of the search for the "origins" of attitudes toward childrearing. Identifying the streams of cultural influence on contemporary African American family life will no longer be so simple, he suggests. Or more acutely, he predicts that the necessary vagueness of gestures to the influences of the "African Genesis" will fail to stand up in the face of future contributions to the history of black family life in the United States. As migration from the Caribbean continues – as well as immigration from parts of Africa itself – and infuses black culture with a wealth of influences new and ancient, it will be difficult to be satisfied with the search for remnants of "Black Africa" in the folkways of African American family life.

In 1982, in the tenth-anniversary volume of *Reviews in American History*, Mary P. Ryan surveyed the historiography of family life in the United States in an article entitled "The Explosion of Family History." There, she discussed the major works of a decade that had witnessed the rise and maturation of the study of family history. Only three of the works she cited were histories of the postwar era. As I have already indicated, most of this postwar work appeared after Ryan's review – during the late 1980s. Ryan was convinced that family history was only at the beginning of a boom – that its growth as a subfield in historical studies was mostly ahead of it. However, family history faltered over the next decade and seems to have declined as a unifying field of inquiry for historians. While aspects of human experience within the domain of family history, such as sexuality, gender, or childhood, have flourished in the last several years (spawning their own journals and scholarly organizations), interest in the history of family life per se has failed to attract new scholars at the same pace. Indeed, when *Reviews in American History* published its twenty-fifth-anniversary volume in 1998, it did not even devote a chapter to the history of family life (Masur, 1998). Components of family history as conceived during its formative years – gender in particular, but also motherhood, housework, and sexuality – are mentioned, but the history of family life is nowhere in evidence.

While it is beyond the scope of this essay to explore the reasons for this fragmentation, the results have been twofold. First, there is a dearth of historical studies not only of African American family life in postwar America, but of Chicanos, Puerto Ricans, and peoples who have migrated during the last thirty-five years from Central and South America, the Caribbean, the Indian subcontinent, East Asia, and the Pacific Rim. Second, historians have yet to come to terms with the impact of postwar affluence on values in American culture. Part of what has been purchased with Americans' changing consumer behavior and attitudes is the luxury to expect more from their personal lives. Throughout the twentieth century divorce was increasingly a remedy for marital unhappiness. Once the province of the wealthy or the desperate, divorce became a refuge for those unprotected from the abusive exercise of male authority and physical and economic domination. Desperate women often traded one kind of subordination for another: male control and abuse for destitution. The stimulus to divorce in the United States, nonetheless, has been the consequence not of disillusionment with marriage, but its opposite – the heightened promise of fulfillment through intimacy (E. May, 1980). For white middle-class America, then, the last generation's luxury has become its own necessity. Divorce, single parenthood, and remarriage have become accepted alternatives to time-worn forms of oppression at the hands of convention and fear of social stigma. And yet, there is a certain irony – or hypocrisy, depending on one's politics – about the transforming impact of divorce and single parenthood on family life since World War II. As growing numbers of Americans choose to raise children as single parents, it becomes increasingly difficult to scapegoat minority single-parent families for "weakening" the foundations of family life when the prerogatives of race and class enable the white middle class to do so in the pursuit of happiness.

REFERENCES

Anderson, Michael: *Approaches to the History of the Western Family, 1500–1914* (London: Macmillan, 1980).

Ariès, Philippe: *L'Enfant et la vie familiale sous l'ancien régime* (Paris: Plon, 1960); trans. Robert Baldick, *Centuries of Childhood: A Social History of Family Life* (New York: Alfred A. Knopf, 1962).

Billingsley, Andrew: *Climbing Jacob's Ladder: The Enduring Legacy of African-American Families* (New York: Simon and Schuster, 1992).

Cherlin, Andrew: *Marriage, Divorce, Remarriage* (Cambridge, Mass.: Harvard University Press, 1981).

Collier, Jane, Rosaldo, Michelle Z., and Yanigisako, Sylvia: "Is There a Family? New Anthropological Views," in Barrie Thorne with Marilyn Yalom (eds.), *Rethinking the Family: Some Feminist Questions* (New York: Longman, 1992), 31–48.

Coontz, Stephanie: *The Way We Never Were: American Families and the Nostalgia Trap* (New York: Basic Books, 1992).

Davis, Kingsley: "Wives and Work: The Sex Role Revolution and Its Consequences," *Population and Development Review*, 10 (1984): 397–417.

Davis, Richard A.: *The Black Family in a Changing Black Community* (New York: Garland, 1993).

Demos, John: *A Little Commonwealth: Family Life in Plymouth Colony* (New York: Oxford University Press, 1970).

Easterlin, Richard A.: *Birth and Fortune: The Impact of Numbers on Personal Welfare* (New York: Basic Books, 1980).

Elkins, Stanley M.: *Slavery: A Problem in American Institutional and Intellectual Life* (Chicago: University of Chicago Press, 1959).

Frazier, E. Franklin: *The Negro Family in the United States* (Chicago: University of Chicago Press, 1940).

Gilbert, James: *A Cycle of Outrage: America's Reaction to the Juvenile Delinquent in the 1950s* (New York: Oxford University Press, 1986).

Graebner, William: *Coming of Age in Buffalo: Youth and Authority in the Postwar Era* (Philadelphia: Temple University Press, 1990).

Greven, Jr., Philip J.: *Four Generations: Population, Land, and Family in Colonial Andover, Massachusetts* (Ithaca, NY: Cornell University Press, 1970).

Gutman, Herbert G.: *The Black Family in Slavery and Freedom, 1750–1925* (New York: Pantheon, 1976).

Hacker, Andrew: "The War Over the Family," *New York Review of Books*, 44 (December 4, 1997): 34–5.

Jackson, Kenneth T.: *Crabgrass Frontier: The Suburbanization of the United States* (New York: Oxford University Press, 1985).

Jones, Jacqueline: *Labor of Love, Labor of Sorrow: Black Women, Work, and the Family from Slavery to the Present* (New York: Basic Books, 1985).

Kammen, Michael: "An Americanist's Reprise: The Pervasive Role of *Histoire Problème* in Historical Scholarship Concerning the United States Since the 1960s," in Louis P. Masur (ed.), *Reviews in American History, Special Issue: The Challenge of American History*, 26 (1998): 1–25.

Kutler, Stanley I. and Katz, Stanley N., eds.: *Reviews in American History, The Promise of American History: Progress and Prospects*, 10 (1982).

Lasch, Christopher: *Haven in a Heartless World: The Family Besieged* (New York: Basic Books, 1977).

Lasch, Christopher: *The Culture of Narcissism: American Life in an Age of Diminishing Expectations* (New York: W. W. Norton, 1978).

Lassonde, Stephen A.: "Should I Go or Should I Stay? School Attainment, Adolescence and Parent–Child Relations in Italian Immigrant Families of New Haven, 1900–1935," *History of Education Quarterly*, 38 (1998): 37–60.

Masur, Louis P., ed.: *Reviews in American History, Special Issue: The Challenge of American History*, 26 (1998).

May, Elaine Tyler: *Great Expectations: Marriage and Divorce in Post-Victorian America* (Chicago: University of Chicago Press, 1980).

May, Elaine Tyler: *Homeward Bound: American Families in the Cold War Era* (New York: Basic Books, 1988).

May, Lary: *Screening Out the Past: The Birth of Mass Culture and the Motion Picture Industry, 1896–1929* (New York: Oxford University Press, 1980).

Miller, Andrew T.: "Social Science, Social Policy, and the Heritage of African-American Families," in Michael B. Katz (ed.), *The Underclass Debate: Views from History* (Princeton, NJ: Princeton University Press, 1993), 254–89.

Modell, John: *Into One's Own: From Youth to Adulthood in the United States, 1920–1975* (Berkeley: University of California Press, 1989).

Parsons, Talcott and Bales, Robert F., eds.: *Family, Socialization and Interaction Process* (Glencoe, Ill.: Free Press, 1955).

Pattillo-McCoy, Mary: *Black Picket Fences: Privilege and Peril Among the Black Middle Class* (Chicago: University of Chicago Press, 1999).

Popenoe, David: *Disturbing the Nest: Family Change and Decline in Modern Societies* (New York: Aldine de Gruyter, 1988).

Rainwater, Lee and Yancey, William L., eds.: *The Moynihan Report and the Politics of Controversy* (Cambridge, Mass.: MIT Press, 1967).

Rapp, Rayna, Ross, Ellen, and Bridenthal, Renate: "Examining Family History," *Feminist Studies*, 5 (1979): 174–200.

Ruggles, Steven: "The Transformation of American Family Structure," *American Historical Review*, 99 (1994): 103–28.

Ruggles, Steven and Goeken, Ron: "Race and Multigenerational Family Structure, 1900–1980," in Scott J. South and Stewart F. Tolnay (eds.), *The Changing American Family* (Westport, Conn.: Greenwood Press, 1992), 15–42.

Ryan, Mary P.: "The Explosion of Family History," *Reviews in American History*, 10 (1982): 181–95.

Smith, Daniel Scott: "Recent Change and the Periodization of American Family History," *Journal of Family History*, 20 (1995): 329–46.

Stack, Carol B.: *All Our Kin: Strategies for Survival in a Black Community* (New York: Harper and Row, 1974).

United States Department of Labor, Office of Policy Planning and Research: *The Negro Family: The Case for National Action* (Washington, DC: US Government Printing Office, 1965).

Zelizer, Viviana: *Pricing the Priceless Child: The Changing Social Value of Children* (New York: Basic Books, 1985).

CHAPTER TWO

The Power of Place: Race, Political Economy, and Identity in the Postwar Metropolis

ROBERT O. SELF AND THOMAS J. SUGRUE

Over the course of the late twentieth century, urban America was a shifting and contested terrain of power, politics, and meaning. By the mid-twentieth century, the United States was an overwhelmingly urban nation. Sixty-three percent of Americans lived in cities by 1950, nearly half in places with a population greater than 25,000. Many of the nation's leading elected officials hailed from urban areas; their constituencies were greatly affected by a plethora of public policies that remade the geography and economy of major metropolitan areas. At the same time, cities were reshaped by two of the most extensive internal migrations in American history: the great migration of rural, southern blacks to the cities of the Northeast, Midwest, and West, and the mass movement of whites to the suburbs. Accompanying these population shifts was a remapping of American capitalism, as the commerce and manufacturing that drove postwar consumerism grew increasingly mobile. The combination and interaction of political, demographic, and economic change turned cities and suburbs into battlegrounds over the most pressing and unresolved issues of twentieth-century American history: race and economic power. The story of metropolitan America is thus central to our narratives of postwar American history.

The history of postwar cities and suburbs allows for a stitching of the fragmented historiography of modern America, using place as the thread to sew together grassroots and top-down political history, economic history, and the history of culture and identity that often are told separately. Bounded communities have given shape to and constrained economics, politics, culture, and identities in ways that have far-reaching consequences for our understanding of postwar American history as a whole. For a full account, we must, as Thomas F. Jackson (1993, p. 407) has suggested, "synthesize the elements of racial subordination, economic relations, political power, and cultural change." It is a task to which urban history is becoming well suited.

The most provocative work in postwar urban history narrates the disaggregation of the urban industrial system of the first half of the century and the simultaneous decline of liberal political culture. Both processes were racialized in ways that shaped political economy, political movements, and life chances. This literature connects the culture and social ecology of local places – cities, suburbs, and their metropolitan areas – with formal and informal politics and the federal state. Such work "brings the state back in" without losing sight of social relations and experience. The battles over class, opportunity, race, and property that created the postwar city and suburban periphery produced more than ghettoes and middle-class oases. They gave birth to a new political culture and new centers of power. A history of the interaction between race and liberalism provides a compelling framework for the study of metropolitan American after 1945. It is not the only framework, however. In this essay, we offer an argument about metropolitan history that regards race and political economy as the most salient lenses through which to view the broad story of postwar urban and suburban places. But we also suggest ways that new and rapidly emerging work on culture, gender, sexuality, region, and globalism simultaneously informs our narrative and charts entirely new directions for future scholarship in the field.

The genesis of postwar urban history lies at the intersection of three wide-ranging literatures. The first follows Arnold Hirsch (1983) in examining postwar cities as products of racial conservatism. Du Bois (1899) and Drake and Cayton (1945) pioneered such approaches early in the century, but Hirsch and, more recently, Thomas Sugrue (1996) have powerfully underscored the limitations of post-1945 American cities as sites of racial equality. This work and the new projects it has inspired synthesize urban social science research – on such topics as industrial location, demographic trends, and employment – and social history, particularly labor history. The second literature, influenced most sharply by Kenneth Jackson (1985), frames postwar suburbanization in terms of the growth of a state-subsidized middle class. Suburban development became a vehicle for accelerated and consolidated forms of middle-class consumption underwritten by an activist, liberal federal state. A third literature, from African American studies, has joined the other two at this crossroads of urban history. Here, influenced by historians such as Manning Marable (1984) and Robin Kelley (1994) and sociologists like Michael Omi and Howard Winant (1986), recent work situates African American political culture simultaneously in both national histories of the state and in the context of community-based struggles over culture, identity, and power. Though urban historians have yet fully to embrace African American history and race studies more generally (to their detriment), work in these latter fields has become indispensable to the synthetic approach urbanists increasingly seek. Together, the three literatures bring the history of class and race out of the shopfloor and neighborhood case study and into conversation with postwar urban development and cities as broadly conceived political spaces.

Place and Political Economy

At the core of American urbanism are questions of economy. Metropolitan areas are shaped in large part by economics, modes of production, and structures of accumulation. Cities have long been places of production and consumption and of the generation of capital and labor. There is nothing fixed and unchanging about the economic role of cities, however. American metropolitan areas underwent a profound transformation beginning in the mid-twentieth century as industrial capitalism made and then threatened to unmake urban America. Once regarded as the engines that drove American economic growth, cities found themselves at mid-century subject to an increasingly fluid and turbulent national and multinational economy, vulnerable to industrial downsizing and dispersal as the structures of capital accumulation shifted (Sugrue, 1993).

Economic restructuring came first in the industrial cities of the Northeast and the Midwest and some of the heavy industrial and port cities of the South and West. In the aftermath of World War II, manufacturing firms of all sizes began to decentralize production, relocating operations to suburban areas and, increasingly, to the low-wage regions of the rural Midwest and the South where industrial and trade unions were weak. In addition, the introduction of labor-saving, automated machinery in the 1940s and 1950s disproportionately affected workers in older, urban factories. Politics also rewrote the geography of American industry. The military-industrial complex, which had been concentrated in large urban centers during World War II, began to decentralize, prompted by Cold War fears of nuclear attack and the growing clout of congressional delegations from the South and West. In addition, federal tax policy and public works expenditures, particularly on highways and airports, facilitated industrial dispersion. Local and state governments also encouraged capital mobility by recruiting firms with advertisements about their comparative advantages such as low taxes and low wages (K. Jackson, 1985; Schulman, 1990).

As capital decentralized, manufacturing firms left behind these older industrial centers and port cities. The textile and clothing makers of Providence, Trenton, and Philadelphia moved to small towns in the upper South and, by the 1960s, to the Caribbean and Latin America. Detroit's automakers and related manufacturers of plastic parts, glass, machinery, and stampings opened new plants in small cities and suburbs of the Midwest and the South (Sugrue, 1996). Pittsburgh, Chicago, Gary, Camden, and St. Louis all suffered from the impact of automation in electronics manufacturing, meatpacking, and steelmaking (Bensman and Lynch, 1987; Cumbler, 1989; Scranton 1992; Horowitz, 1997; Cowie, 1999). Shipbuilding waned in nearly every port city, except those that were home to major defense installations. Railroads declined as significant freight haulers, and ports on both coasts modernized, containerized, and eliminated tens of thousands of longshore and warehouse jobs. One should not idealize the urban industrial system of early twentieth-century America. But technological changes, state and federal regulations, and unionization made industrial work more secure and stable in the first half of the twentieth century than ever before. Yet that security and stability were short-lived as postwar capital restructuring eroded the hard-won gains of urban industrial labor (Bluestone and Harrison, 1982).

The economic fate of postwar American cities was intimately intertwined with federal policy. As Mark Gelfand (1975) has observed, prior to the New Deal federal intervention in urban affairs was minimal. But the expansion of federal urban policies from the Depression through the 1960s had a dramatic impact on the economic geography of the United States. A lion's share of federal spending in the post-New Deal years benefited suburban and formerly rural areas. Federal funds were disproportionately channeled to the hitherto underdeveloped South and West. The stronghold that southerners had over congressional committees greatly benefited the Sunbelt (Schulman, 1990). Federal defense spending favored cities in Texas, California, and Washington at the expense of the former "arsenals of democracy" in Illinois, Michigan, and Pennsylvania (Markusen, 1991; Lotchin, 1992). Federal highway funding, most notably in the wake of the Interstate Highway Act of 1956, encouraged the further decentralization of industry (M. Rose, 1979). As the Sunbelt expanded economically, it became a magnet for migrants, usually whites from the Northeast and Midwest. The flow of population to the Sunbelt further expanded the electoral clout of the South and West, enhancing the ability of elected officials to divert even greater federal resources to their regions.

At the same time that the federal government fostered economic decentralization, it also subsidized the mobility of population and commerce. Suburbanization, like industrial decentralization, was a process well underway in the early twentieth century. But the scale and pace of suburban growth accelerated rapidly after World War II. New Deal and wartime programs, administered by the Home Owner's Loan Corporation, the Federal Housing Administration, and the Veterans' Administration, reconstructed the home mortgage market, subsidized large-scale housing construction, and provided strong incentives for homeownership (Freund, 1999; Nicolaides, 2002). These federal housing policies favored new construction in racially homogeneous areas outside central cities. Indeed, the entire postwar architecture of housing finance, underwritten by the federal government and directed by private industry, enforced a virtual racial apartheid on the American metropolis (Massey and Denton, 1993). Construction firms, which before the New Deal had generally been small and family-owned enterprises, consolidated their operations and dramatically expanded the scope and scale of housing development. The most successful, like William Levitt of Levittown fame or Henry Kaiser in suburban Los Angeles, adapted mass production techniques to build standardized houses quickly and cheaply. The result was a dramatic expansion in rates of homeownership, largely among whites. In 1930, fewer than one-third of Americans owned their own homes; by 1960, nearly two-thirds did (Wright, 1981; K. Jackson, 1985; Hise, 1997).

These two trends, regional industrial dispersal and suburbanization, came together powerfully in the postwar rise of the Sunbelt. Stretching from California across the Southwest through Texas and on to Florida, the Sunbelt experienced decades of rapid population growth and exhibited patterns of urbanization that looked, to observers from other parts of the nation, like suburbanization. Following a distinctly twentieth-century pattern of development, these new metropolitan areas were characterized by highly dispersed, low-density neighborhoods and decentralized commerce and industry. Most Sunbelt cities lacked the densely populated downtowns of older cities; many grew up along interstate highways rather than on the waterways and railways that had shaped nineteenth-century urbanization. Low property taxes, anti-union right-to-work laws, and cheap land, in addition to federal military-industrial investment, provided the structural basis for a postwar industrial boomlet in many parts of the region (Abbott, 1981; Lotchin, 1992; Self, forthcoming-b).

The decentralization of industry, massive federal and state expenditures on road improvement and highway construction, and the sprawl of housing all converged to remake the commercial landscapes of metropolitan America. Downtown shopping districts declined as investors turned to suburban sites. Department stores opened new suburban branches that anchored shopping malls surrounded by acres of parking. Developers hastily constructed commercial strips alongside busy highways and near major intersections to provide car-friendly shopping. Tax policies gave incentives to the architects of new suburban shopping malls to build on open land on the periphery of metropolitan areas (Isenberg, 1995; Hanchett, 1998; Dyer, 2000). Suburbia became ground zero of the postwar consumer culture, while urban shopping districts began to fade and decay (Cohen, 1996).

To be sure, the federal government did not wholly ignore central cities. Urban governments became more dependent on federal spending after the New Deal than ever before. Urban voters were a key part of the liberal electoral coalition that brought Franklin D. Roosevelt and the Democratic Congresses of the early 1930s to power, and the New Deal legislative agenda rewarded urban supporters with a variety of social programs. Most important were federal grants-in-aid for welfare, low-income housing, and public works (Gelfand, 1975; Mohl, 1996). The Social Security Act of 1935 significantly reduced rates of urban poverty among the elderly, the disabled, and widowed and unmarried mothers and their children. Rates of poverty in major cities fell significantly during the postwar years, in large part because of federal transfer payments (Stern, 1993). In addition, most major cities constructed public housing for workers and the poor, although it did not make a major dent in urban housing markets. Underfunded and unpopular among middle-class homeowners, public housing remained a second-tier federal program that struggled for funding and legitimacy for most of its history (Radford, 1996). Though uneven, contested, and not universally popular, New Deal policy set the stage for an expansion of the federal urban role in the postwar decades.

Federal involvement in urban development took a new turn with the creation of urban renewal initiatives from the late 1940s through the 1960s. As Jon Teaford (1990) has explained, the "rough road to renaissance" for postwar American cities was paved with federal dollars. Federal grants established the pattern for revitalizing urban core areas across the nation after 1949, the year of the first postwar federal housing legislation. Cities bulldozed working-class, disproportionately minority neighborhoods adjacent to central business districts (leading to the bitter adage that "urban renewal equals Negro removal") and replaced "blight" with office complexes, middle- and high-income apartments and condominiums, and civic institutions like new university campuses, medical centers, and symphony halls. By the 1960s, urban renewal had grown increasingly controversial. Leading urbanists, ranging from Jane Jacobs on the left to Martin Anderson on the right, railed against the hubris of modernist planning. On the grassroots level, community organizations began to mobilize against "the federal bulldozer," demanding greater citizen participation in urban renewal planning. Elected officials began to turn their attention to "public–private partnerships," providing tax breaks and financial incentives for downtown redevelopment projects such as malls and stadiums, while gradually withdrawing from large-scale efforts to redevelop residential neighborhoods (Frieden and Sagalyn, 1989; Teaford, 1990; Thomas, 1997).

As postwar urban redevelopment came under siege, the federal government shifted its energies to social welfare projects that targeted poor urban residents. Liberal social policy initiatives in the 1960s, particularly War on Poverty programs of the Office of Economic Opportunity, the Community Action Program, and Model Cities defined urban problems primarily in terms of the cultural and educational deficiencies of individuals, rather than as products of the restructuring of urban labor markets, racial discrimination, and urban capital disinvestment (Katz, 1989; T. Jackson, 1993; O'Connor, 2001). Particularly controversial were the War on Poverty's programs to encourage the "maximum feasible participation" of poor people in social programs.

By channeling federal funds directly to community organizations, the Office of Economic Opportunity (OEO) threatened urban mayors and political machines that had depended on federal grants for patronage (Self, 2000). Fears of poor people's control of federal spending were largely unfounded. OEO programs were not well funded, and in many cities mayors quickly gained control over Community Action agencies. In the meantime, the greater portion of Great Society expenditures (such as spending for disadvantaged children under the Elementary and Secondary Education Act) was channeled to suburban communities, disproportionately benefiting middle-class Americans (T. Jackson, 1993). The few programs targeted specifically to cities faced harsh cutbacks as the Vietnam War escalated. The result was a "skirmish" on poverty that had little long-term impact on the fortunes of American cities and their impoverished populations (Kelley, 1997).

The dramatic expansion of the federal role in cities left the governing structures of metropolitan America largely intact. Federal programs did not address the fragmented nature of metropolitan politics and the relative autonomy of local governments. By 1960, the United States had 91,186 local governments (Doherty and Stone, 1999). In most parts of the United States, localities controlled education, public works, and social services and paid for goods and services through local taxes. Municipal governments also controlled land use through zoning laws and other local regulations (Briffault, 1990; Frug, 1999). The fragmentation of government reinforced inequalities by race and class. Municipal boundaries determined access to fundamental public goods and services. As population, commerce, and industry fled central cities, these older communities saw their tax bases diminish, while their suburban counterparts were flush with new tax revenue. The interconnection between local government, property taxes, and public goods created a feedback loop that compounded urban disadvantage. Depopulation and decentralization ravaged urban property tax bases, which in turn lowered the quality of city services and education, which spurred further population loss and capital flight. As a consequence, by the 1960s and 1970s many major cities teetered on the brink of bankruptcy, while their suburban neighbors prospered. Cleveland and New York declared fiscal collapse in the mid-1970s, while their adjoining suburbs boasted of world-class school districts, lush municipal golf courses, and low expenditures on social services for the poor and elderly (Mollenkopf, 1983; Swanstrom, 1985).

Not all suburbs were green utopias and not all central cities were hollow and struggling. But postwar metropolitan areas on the whole were characterized by profound racial resegregation, economic inequality, and industrial restructuring that created if not the "two Americas" described by the Kerner Commission in 1968, at least a broadly divided racial opportunity structure that sifted and sorted life chances. The emergence of the "second ghetto" and the preservation of the race line in housing and hiring would, alone, have dealt a powerful blow to postwar dreams of racial equality and economic opportunity. But coupled with industrial automation, decentralization, and the shift from manufacturing to services within the national economy, these developments proved crippling to a generation of the urban working poor. The crises and adjustment faced by cities in the second half of the twentieth century were not merely epiphenomena of market economic pressures, but products of shifting political interests and commitments, especially within the federal government. In its haste to underwrite the expansion of an inclusive white middle class and to unfetter capital from wartime constraints, the federal government helped to exclude the urban poor, increasingly large numbers of whom were black and Latino, from the cycles of occupational mobility and personal and familial capital accumulation that define life chances in American society.

Race, Rights, and Taxes: Transforming Political Culture

As economic changes and public policy remade metropolitan America after 1945, so too did American cities and suburbs remake American politics. Metropolitan transformations drove three broad political realignments in the postwar United States: the decline and reconfiguration of mid-century liberalism, the rise of the New Right, and the emergence of African American electoral power. Cities and suburbs were the battlegrounds where the major political issues of the postwar period were contested. The outcome of urban and suburban political struggles redefined the meanings of race and citizenship in modern America and led to a major political realignment along the lines of race, place, and region. Urban America had been the crucible of the New Deal. By the 1970s, as cities faced growing economic problems and racial conflict, suburban America became the crucible of the New Right.

All three political transformations crested in the late 1960s and early 1970s. Viewed through the traditional prism of national politics, the 1960s look like the pivotal years. But through the prism of urban history, each transformation emerges as the product of a dialectic between local and national political arenas across several decades. While the 1960s remain important, they are no more pivotal than the late 1940s – when urban liberals retreated (or acceded) as the second ghetto gained its foothold – or the mid-1950s – when industrial relocation and urban renewal combined to ravage older neighborhoods, prompting protest and political mobilization. Indeed, the signal contribution of post-1945 urban historiography has been to rework postwar political narratives by seeing local places as the central sites, not peripheral phenomena, of post-Depression battles over the extension and legacy of the New Deal.

The fate of liberalism hung in the balance in a postwar struggle over rights, racial identity, and taxation. The New Deal promised a broad social wage for the American working class – including old age pensions, a welfare safety net, and the right to organize trade unions – and a more democratic distribution of social resources. At the same time, the state fostered a growth politics that, it was argued, would stimulate economic opportunity while creating a stable class of citizen consumers. Roosevelt's Declaration of Rights and Four Freedoms grounded mid-century liberal social policy in a language of rights, while the policies themselves aimed at broadening consumer demand by getting money and capital into the hands of ever larger numbers of people. By the 1950s, New Deal liberalism had been incorporated into the growth economics of the Cold War, but economic opportunity and class stability remained the pillars of liberal-modernist faith in abundance. For workers and their liberal allies that abundance, properly directed by the state, promised good jobs, high rates of employment, and affordable homes, the latter at the core of the postwar consumer economy.

However coherent it appeared, New Deal liberalism was riven by deep fissures. Liberalism was not merely an abstract discourse about rights. It was a constant process of political production, incorporation, and contestation in which class, race, geography, and property coexisted in profound tension. The local implementation of federal legislation often compromised broader public aims. Local elected officials, for example, capitulated to the demands of white homeowners and confined public housing on marginal land or in predominantly African American neighborhoods (Hirsch, 1983; Bauman, 1987; Sugrue, 1996). Urban renewal policy became an engine for the removal and displacement of poor communities, not their revitalization. Anti-poverty programs aimed too few resources at service provision and virtually none at job creation. At the same time, the United States lacked a systematic economic policy to deal with the largest contributor to urban problems after 1945 – the dispersal of industry from central cities. In a political climate that celebrated "free enterprise," the freedom of capital to move at will was left largely unchecked (Sugrue, 1995; Cowie, 1999). Mid-century liberal state formation in the United States, then, was intimately, and problematically, linked to the transformation of urban America.

White workers and homeowners placed substantial brakes on liberalism in the postwar years. White resistance to African American mobility in the workplace and neighborhoods fractured and constrained liberalism long before Black Power and Vietnam tore it asunder in the late 1960s. Based on a fragile alignment of organized labor, northern African Americans, southern whites, and urban machine voters, the New Deal coalition held out to white workers the promise of class security and to black workers the promise of racial equality (Katznelson, 1981; Freeman, 2000; Sugrue, 2001). Already compromised in countless legislative skirmishes between the northern liberal and southern segregationist wings of the Democratic Party, these dual promises clashed violently in the shopfloors and neighborhoods of America's major cities. In the local context, white workers and homeowners understood their "rights" as propertyholders and union labor to exclude African Americans from communities, jobs, schools, and apprenticeships, thus perpetuating segregated communities and a dual labor market. For urban black Americans, immediate postwar priorities included the extension of liberal state protections to include fair employment and housing laws which would, in theory, sink northern Jim Crow. Differently and unevenly empowered by the American welfare state, white and black workers and homeowners battled over the very meaning of the New Deal state, even as groups like the National Association for the Advancement of Colored People (NAACP) and the Congress of Industrial Organizations (CIO) enthusiastically cooperated as cornerstones of the New Deal coalition (Brown, 1999).

By the 1960s, the debate about liberalism turned on a larger discussion of poverty and welfare policy. Concerns about delinquency, crime, and growing urban unrest led policymakers, social scientists, politicians, and social movement activists to turn their attention to impoverished African Americans (and in some cities Latinos). Great Society liberals embraced a social services approach to poverty that stressed inadequate individual preparation for the job market, but by the late 1960s nearly all of the federal government's modest anti-poverty programs were embroiled in an increasingly divisive debate with heavy stakes. On the left, grassroots activists and their political allies called for more money, more local control, and better programs aimed at job creation (the latter was the major theme of Martin Luther King, Jr.'s Poor People's Campaign). The most vocal critics of the War on Poverty, Frances Fox Piven and Richard Cloward (1971), viewed Johnson's programs as an attempt to mollify black protest, while leaving the underlying problems of poverty and disfranchisement largely untouched.

The left critique of the War on Poverty was quickly shunted to the margins by a coherent and increasingly popular conservative anti-welfare movement that grew in influence after the 1970s (Katz, 2001). Scholars and activists on the right, such as Charles Murray (1984) and Myron Magnet (1993), blamed the Great Society for the persistence of urban poverty and called for the complete elimination of federal anti-poverty programs. Welfare, they contended, gave perverse incentives to the poor, discouraging them from working while rewarding family dissolution and out-of-wedlock pregnancy. Other academic conservatives such as Fred Siegel (1997) found in the coincidence of the War on Poverty and urban riots seemingly irrefutable evidence of the failure of liberalism. In addition many conservatives viewed urban anti-poverty agencies as insurgent political strongholds (Self, 2000). The War on Poverty under siege, liberals went on the defensive. In her important analysis of poverty policy, Alice O'Connor (2001) argues that fights over "ideas about culture, race, and poverty" left liberals without "an alternative agenda of political and economic reform." In the 1970s, urban liberals fought desperately to keep the welfare safety net unfrayed rather than developing innovative policies to deal with the combined effects of economic restructuring and racial inequality. Meanwhile, the conservative critique of welfare became a central theme in the political insurgency of the New Right. By the early 1970s, American liberalism was in retreat, its major tenets weakened, transformed, or without broad public support (Fraser and Gerstle, 1989).

Battered on the local level by disputes over race and housing, poverty and welfare, liberalism came under attack in the 1960s by a newly assertive right wing. The rise of the New Right originated in the disaffection and savvy political mobilization of a generation of white American metropolitan residents who believed that taxes were too high, that civil rights had gone too far, and that the liberal state had created, not ameliorated, the problems of core cities by catering to the poor. New Right politics did not always draw upon uniquely urban/suburban matters – evidenced in particular by the right's anti-communism, evangelical religious culture, and ardent nationalism – but postwar conservatives mobilized a constituency whose politics were shaped by the spatial and social disaggregation of the postwar American metropolis. The mass migration of tens of millions of white Americans to suburban areas realigned American politics. By 1970, a plurality of American voters lived outside of central cities and largely withdrew from a polity that included urban residents. Animated by what Lisa McGirr (2001) has called "suburban warriors," the postwar right challenged liberalism, grafting the politics of racial resentment onto older strains of religious and anti-statist conservatism (Rieder, 1989).

For many conservative white Americans, civil rights was an abstract, even at times noble, proposition. But equally large numbers of whites perceived the demand for racial equality as a threat to a more cherished set of perceived rights: in property, school choice, and hiring. In response to civil rights reforms beginning in the late 1940s, many whites began to assert the primacy of their own claims on social resources, a set of claims that had cohered by the late 1960s into a major pillar of New Right politics. Among the most important of these were property rights, especially the freedom to sell and rent property without state regulation. In states like

California, fair housing laws faced steep challenges in the 1950s and 1960s on the grounds that state-enforced anti-discrimination measures violated private property rights. Similarly, court-ordered school desegregation plans outraged whites who asserted a right to attend schools based on residential proximity (Formisano, 1991). Fair employment measures also met with counterassertions that hiring and promotion were private rights protected by managerial prerogative and union contracts. In southern cities, resistance to racial liberalism was often couched in the unapologetic language of Jim Crow, but throughout the North and West, such resistance found public expression in the language of private rights. In the mid-1960s, national politicians such as George Wallace, Spiro Agnew, and Richard Nixon fashioned a political rhetoric that brought together white northerners and southerners through a shared resentment over the perceived excesses of civil rights (Carter, 1996; Durr, 1996).

No single issue laid the foundation for the emergence of a revived and reinvigorated American right more comprehensively than taxes. In taxation, especially property taxation, the right identified a point of resistance to liberalism in which race, residence, private property, and suburbanization overlapped in potent combination. Though California's Proposition 13 inaugurated the tax revolt in 1978, postwar tax fights dated to the 1940s, when the burst of suburban city-building held out to homeowners the promise of an escape from the high tax burden of older industrial cities (Self, forthcoming-b). Federal underwriting of homeownership gave rise to a new middle class whose concerns revolved around private property and the extent to which it could and should be harnessed to the provision of social resources. Suburban homeowners were content to fund local schools and municipal services through property taxes, but balked when county taxes increased to fund welfare programs and when city taxes ballooned as property values rose (Sears and Citrin, 1982). Regionally, the Sunbelt emerged as a low-tax haven for both corporate and individual propertyholders fleeing the upper Midwest and Northeast where the combination of New Deal-inspired social programs, large numbers of low-income residents, and an aging infrastructure translated into high property taxes. If increasing numbers of metropolitan Americans understood race through the lens of property rights in the postwar decades, they too measured the legitimacy of the social and political order against the demands placed by the state on their private property in the form of taxes. As the New American Right built a grassroots conservative movement below the national radar in the 1950s and 1960s, the metropolitan dynamics of race and taxes proved exceptionally fertile soil. By the time that Ronald Reagan took advantage of regional and metropolitan political realignments to capture the presidency in 1980, high taxes, and their symbolic identification with liberal "big government" social programs, had a proven track record as a core conservative issue (Haas, 1991; Edsall and Edsall, 1992; Kazin, 1992; McGirr, 2001).

An important parallel shift in national political culture came from the heart of American cities after 1945 – the rise of organized African American political capacity. Political historians have documented the sweeping movement of the northern black electorate into the Democratic Party beginning with the election of 1936, a historic reversal of African American voting patterns that made northern blacks a crucial, if undervalued, part of the New Deal coalition (Sitkoff, 1978; Weiss, 1983). The second great migration of blacks from the South (from World War II through the 1960s) increased the northern African American electorate by hundreds of thousands, encouraging Democratic Party organizations to incorporate black voters into governing or opposition coalitions (Katznelson, 1981; Marable, 1983; Countryman, 1998). Determined to transform numbers into real influence, African American political entrepreneurs, organizations, and grassroots activists worked both within and outside of established networks of power to reconstitute governing regimes in dozens of major American cities between the end of the war in 1945 and the 1970s. But northern blacks did not gain political power uniformly. In some cities, like Chicago and Philadelphia, black voters were co-opted into political machines; in others, like Detroit, black voters allied with unionists and formed dissenting coalitions in local Democratic politics (Grimshaw, 1992; Kusmer, 1996). The majority of these efforts focused on mayoral races, but the agendas of urban black political movements extended beyond the election of municipal figureheads to the passage of local fair employment and housing ordinances, the establishment of civic civil rights and race relations commissions, police department reform, school board elections and school desegregation, and, in places like Oakland, Newark, Detroit, and Cleveland, to a broad vision of political change that ranged from calls for a progressive urban tax structure to demands for separate, Afrocentric urban institutions (Kusmer, 1996; Woodard, 1999; Self, forthcoming-a).

Recent scholarship on urban black politics complicates conventional narratives of the relationship of civil rights to Black Power. In the North and West, black politics challenged the facile story of a decline from integration to separation. And the struggle for racial justice in the urban North was neither derivative of the southern movement nor a dénouement to the struggle against Jim Crow (Horne, 1995; Gregory, 1998; Arnesen, 2001; Thompson, 2001; Countryman et al., forthcoming). By the early 1960s, African American-led political movements in the urban North and West had grown impatient with racial liberalism. Local activists targeted liberal mayors and city councils, rallied against urban renewal, challenged workplace discrimination, and fought for incorporation on school boards, city councils, union headquarters, and on social welfare and social service agencies. In particular, a combination of protest politics, grassroots mobilizations, traditional Democratic Party-building, and political street theatrics orchestrated by groups as diverse as the Brotherhood of Sleeping Car Porters, the Congress of Racial Equality (CORE), the National Welfare Rights Organization, and the Black Panther Party successfully built both a black electoral base and a political leadership class that would reshape city governments throughout the North and West. At the same time, a new generation of grassroots African American insurgents took to the streets in hundreds of violent uprisings or riots (still greatly understudied by historians) during the "long hot summers" from 1964 to 1968, further undermining confidence in liberalism on both the left and right (Fine, 1989; Horne, 1995). In this developing narrative, northern cities are understood not as places where civil rights organizing failed, but as places where the postwar black freedom movement took unique forms and trajectories and where African American politics overlapped with the logic of race-inflected urban industrial and postindustrial capitalism.

Urban history nonetheless lacks an interpretive paradigm that situates postwar African American politics in the larger frame of traditions in urban American political culture. An agenda of unanswered questions still animates the field. If an ethnic succession model is inadequate for understanding the rise of urban black political

capacity, what is an appropriate approach? Are urban African American political projects best understood as dimensions of the black freedom struggle and black liberation or, as Adolph Reed (1999) has provocatively argued, an essentially conservative
expression of class differentiation within urban communities? How should we theorize the federal government's role in the process of building black political power,
especially in the 1960s – as a crucial, if largely inadvertent, ally or as a neutralizing
force of co-optation (Gregory, 1998)? Recent work strongly suggests that useful
interpretive paradigms lie in synthetic studies that refuse the typical polarization of
African American history into reified competing "opposites": civil rights and Black
Power, integration and nationalism, de facto and de jure segregation, North and
South, classes and masses, armed resistance and nonviolence (Biondi, 2003; Countryman et al., forthcoming). An urban historical approach to black political mobilization will require attention to social movement organizing, scales of political power
and political mobilization, and the relationship of both to everyday black life and
culture (Kelley, 1994).

However conceived, studies of postwar African American urban politics must confront the issue of urban decay. "The postwar city had to compete in the public consciousness with the robust city of the 1920s," Robert Beauregard has observed, "and
suffered in comparison with the great potential of the industrial cities of the turn of
the century" (Beauregard, 1993, p. 4). Urban decline was more than a matter of
perception, however. In cities like Cleveland, Chicago, Detroit, Washington, DC,
Oakland, Gary, Newark, Baltimore, and New Orleans, African American-led political movements inherited municipal power at exactly the moment in the 1960s and
1970s when American cities reached a historical nadir – measured in terms of employment, tax revenue-generating capacity, and crime. In popular parlance, whites had
"abandoned" the city for the suburban periphery, leaving the governance of urban
wastelands to African Americans. Indeed, black urban electoral victories in the 1960s
and 1970s could seem like the "hollow prize" described by one late-1960s urban
commentator, given the fragmentation of metropolitan power in dozens of centers
within any given region and the economic woes of cities plagued by massive depopulation and disinvestment (Kusmer, 1996). But white suburbanization also opened
unforeseen opportunities for urban blacks. It spurred the relatively rapid growth of
an African American middle class based in government services and brought black
communities into the system of municipal governance.

Together, these three broad shifts in political culture redefined the meaning of
race and citizenship in America. Increasingly, in a variety of contexts race came to be
defined spatially and embedded in the structural inequalities of urban America, even
as the nation as a whole embraced civil rights laws. African Americans, especially those
in the North, had long claimed that full citizenship required economic opportunity,
not simply civil equality. Postwar urban black political movements, from the Brotherhood of Sleeping Car Porters to the Black Panther Party, continued to articulate this
message, albeit with different ideological and strategic accents. Among whites, a sometimes unspoken, sometimes explicit racial identity and set of privileges coalesced
around property rights, taxes, and the spatial exclusion of black people from whole
spheres of social and political activity. These developments had roots in older American racial politics that focused on biological and cultural notions of racial hierarchy,
but they quickly developed a powerful life of their own in the second half of the

twentieth century. Race was coded in the language and structures of metropolitan access, opportunity, and space, rather than in the paranoia of miscegenation or the brutal rhetoric of Jim Crow and cultural inferiority. But the new arrangements proved no less onerous and taxing – on American cities, public and political culture, and individual lives.

Shaping Identities, Interests, and Power

The contest for political power was one important manifestation of a larger struggle over group and individual identity that played out in twentieth-century metropolitan America. But other contests were equally consequential. By the 1930s and 1940s, it had become a social scientific orthodoxy that the United States could easily absorb and overcome group differences. A capacious Americanism would easily absorb members of formerly distinct ethnic and racial groups; a generous "American creed" militated against irrational prejudice and gave marginalized groups a claim on full citizenship. Chicago School sociologists promoted an assimilationist modernism in which successive immigrant and migrant groups were understood to leave behind "traditional" beliefs and customs after contact with modernity and the urban milieu. Scholars and journalists alike turned their attention to questions of assimilation and acculturation, and looked to metropolitan America as evidence of a "melting pot" of identity. Proponents of mid-century liberalism absorbed much of this approach, as they articulated a class politics they believed to be so expansive that it would subsume differences of race, gender, sexual orientation, and national origin. But in the hands of American liberals, class ultimately proved too narrow a paradigm of social experience and cultural life. By the 1970s, most scholars had jettisoned the naive pluralism of postwar social science, and did so in large part because the experience of metropolitan America belied easy generalizations about integration and assimilation.

Urban historians and urbanists from other disciplines have also long since abandoned the assimilationist assumptions of Robert Park and his Chicago School contemporaries in favor of social constructionist approaches pioneered by sociologist Peter Berger (1967). More recently, influenced by cultural studies and racial formation scholarship, urbanists have begun to investigate the production of group and individual identity, alongside their longstanding interest in intergroup relationships and conflict (Lewis, 1991; Sánchez, 1993). But variations of Marxism have also found a following in the field, especially among scholars influenced by social theorists in geography and political science, such as David Harvey (1989), Manuel Castells (1983), Edward Soja (1989), and Ira Katznelson (1981). While a single narrative of cultural change and urban ecology has yet to emerge from these various literatures, two highly suggestive plot lines have coalesced around consumption and identity. First, the celebration of the empowered consumer citizen by mid-century liberals – and manifest in consumption-oriented New Deal legislation like the Social Security Act and in programs like those of the Federal Housing Administration – accentuated an existing American doctrine of individualism and underwrote a vast privatization of the postwar landscape. Second, prompted by the challenge of Black Power, but drawing on cultural roots that extended into the nineteenth century, Americans of various backgrounds began to articulate identities and interests – from Puerto Rican nationalism to gay liberation – that liberal modernism neither anticipated nor could subsume.

Postwar US urban history is dominated by dramatic narratives of racial succession, conflict, and violence. But other forms of identity, along lines of gender and class especially, shaped urban and suburban cultural patterns and landscapes, especially those organized around consumption, equally profoundly. Reconversion from World War II and domestic anti-communism fueled a prescriptive suburban domesticity and retreat into a private sphere where production was hypermasculinized and contrasted to the feminized realm of consumption and reproduction (Eisler, 1986; Rupp and Taylor, 1987; May, 1988). The private values and single-family homeownership encouraged by suburbanization and Cold War containment profoundly configured gender identities in the postwar period for both men and women. "Organization men" and child-bearing housewives were lionized in popular media, even as a few critical social scientists lamented the price of widespread conformity. As the definitive center of American consumption and national identity in the two decades after the war, the homeowning suburban family became a site of fixation and anxiety, the suburban landscape a synthesis of nuclear family values and consumerism. The suburban home, particularly its expanded kitchens, newly-named "family rooms," and requisite attached garages became vessels for the new consumer durables – dishwashers, toasters, televisions, cars – that defined domestic life (Spigel, 1992).

Middle-class forms of domesticity and consumption reconfigured both public and private space in the American metropolitan landscape. In the first half of the twentieth century cities became sites of civic sociability and an increasingly democratic culture of urban leisure (Peiss, 1986; Gilfoyle, 1998). After 1945, however, marked shifts in the elaboration of urban and suburban private spaces privileged isolated units of dwelling, controlled access to commercial districts, and fragmented arenas of living, working, and shopping unconnected by public transportation and wholly dependent on the private automobile. Privatization took retail from its cradle in the public spaces of American downtowns and installed it within commercial complexes on the edges of cities (Cohen, 1996) or within the enclosed walls of central city arcades (Findlay, 1992; Longsreth, 1997). But malls and their offspring were merely one symptom of a much deeper social transformation. Forms of residence (like "lifestyle communities," retirement complexes, and entire suburban districts), entertainment (from Disneyland to Sea World), and municipal governance all yielded in the postwar decades to various formulas of private design and management (M. Davis, 1990; Findlay, 1992; McKenzie, 1994; S. Davis, 1997). This was a national process, but led regionally by Sunbelt entrepreneurs who invented entire cityscapes from whole cloth (Abbott, 1993) and created vast horizontal urban expanses served by little or no public transportation.

And yet despite such prescriptions, suburban domesticity was idealized in a period when gender identities, even in suburbs themselves, were increasingly contested (Meyerowitz, 1994; Baxandall and Ewen, 2000). For the millions of women wage workers, work, home, and neighborhood could be sites of empowerment or oppression, politics or silence, escape or danger, in overlapping ways that have yet to be fully explored (S. Murray, 1994). Further, postwar suburban and urban communities were not solely landscapes of privacy. In urban settings, among African American northern migrants women's roles as paid and unpaid laborers, as primary agents of neighborhood sociability, as coordinators of informal local economies and migration streams, and as public political figures in a variety of organizations from the PTA to the NAACP made the black public sphere a space of gender negotiation and female opportunity rather than strictly of conformity (Lemke-Santangelo, 1996; Williams, 1998). Masculinity, too, was subject to competing and unstable meanings. Among New York youth gangs in the 1950s, class-based masculine identities remained out of reach for large numbers of young men and boys excluded from the city's declining blue-collar economy. They found alternative definitions of manhood in the ritualized public displays of violence, virility, and turf defense that were hall-marks of 1950s gang culture (Nightingale, 1998; Schneider, 1999). For both adults and children, the suburban ideal and ideology of the white nuclear family never fully embraced the range of actual familial experience in the postwar decades – especially among single urban mothers and divorced urban and suburban parents, two groups whose numbers grew staggeringly as the postwar period progressed (Coontz, 1992).

If privatization, sprawl, and the decline of public space were unintended legacies of mid-century liberalism's consumption ethos, the rise of cultures of reform, resist-ance, and community identity struck directly at the heart of liberal modernism's paeans to economic growth and idealized social pluralism. By the 1960s, a wide range of urbanites and suburbanites began to challenge the assumption that unchecked eco-nomic growth was a social good. In major cities throughout the United States, urban-ites formed coalitions to oppose highway construction and urban renewal projects. In places as diverse as Roxbury in Boston, Greenwich Village in New York, San Francisco and Baltimore, major urban expressway projects were abandoned in the face of concerted grassroots resistance. In suburbia, a nascent environmental movement challenged the "suburban bulldozer," demanding the setaside of open space, the cre-ation of park and recreation land, and the regulation of heavy industry (Stephenson, 1997; Rome, 2001). While these grassroots movements were not always successful (suburban sprawl continued, even if some land was set aside; urban expressways and redevelopment projects were often constructed over the opposition of local critics), they nonetheless signaled the rise of a new politics of citizen participation.

The politics of citizen participation set its deepest roots in urban communities. Even as the walls of formal segregation were slowly falling, African Americans, His-panics, and Asians, as well as gays and lesbians, began to celebrate the separateness of their communities from "mainstream" urban and suburban America. They began to mobilize politically, often through nonpartisan organizations such as legal defense funds, social service organizations, and informal networks of affinity. Urban ethnic and racial communities became, in part, sites of cultural autonomy, places where groups as diverse as African Americans, Chicanas, and gay men enjoyed a sociability and erected an economy outside of, and in some cases in resistance to, dominant white institutions (Trotter, 1985; Broussard, 1993; Taylor, 1994; Moore, 2001). Such urban enclaves also served to help individuals negotiate between the norms and oppressive racial codes of mainstream America and the personal, gender, and class patterns and traditions of their own community.

Much has been written about pre-World War II black communities, but the post-1945 period typically emerges either as epilogue to earlier periods of community-building, or as the capstone, through civil rights politics, to traditions of struggle

(Trotter, 1985; Lewis, 1991; Broussard, 1993). Recent studies of postwar urban African American communities, however, have moved into the last half of the twentieth century by looking at processes of racial formation, internal community dynamics, and cultural production. Led by Robin D. G. Kelley (1994) and George Lipsitz (1994), an influential group of scholars has found an everyday politics of resistance in popular culture and communal institutions ranging from radical trade unions to storefront churches. They emphasize the transgressive and liberatory potential of infrapolitical and leisure activities in the face of economic marginalization and racism. Within this framework, other scholars have turned their attention to black business entrepreneurs from numbers runners to "race business" owners (Wolcott, 1997; Green, forthcoming), African American suburbanites (Wiese, forthcoming), and on black music from Motown to hip-hop (T. Rose, 1994; Smith, 1999).

The literature on racial identity in postwar US urban history nonetheless remains in its infancy. The community- and ghetto-formation approach still dominates, and though local community studies are invaluable for the "thick description" they offer, the field is still searching for alternative frameworks. Latino and Asian American urban history has yet to complicate fully the internal colonial model developed in the 1970s, though works on police–Chicano relations, on the transnational identity of Puerto Rican immigrants, and Los Angeles automobile culture have offered exciting new interpretive possibilities (Escobar, 1999; Whelan, 2001, Avila, forthcoming). Among the multiple challenges that remain, three stand out. First, urban historians of racial identity must work to connect identity with the formation of interests (personal, community, and institutional) and the articulation of both with modes of power. Identities are not experienced or expressed under circumstances in which power – whether within or outside of the boundaries of defined communities – is absent or an unimportant variable. Second, comparative, multi-site, and broadly interpretive studies are increasingly necessary to counteract the tendency of work on identity to reify local experiences, institutions, and culture. And third, urban history must begin to incorporate and theorize the multiracial/ethnic urban landscape to complement the black/white paradigm that remains the normative blueprint for studying race-making. A strictly biracial analysis does not do justice to cities like Los Angeles, San Francisco, Chicago, New York, Phoenix, Denver, and Miami, particularly in the wake of the post-1965 immigrations from Asia, Latin America, and the Caribbean.

Gay, lesbian, bi-, and transsexual communities also reshaped the geography and politics of the postwar US city. Patrolled by police, classified as deviant, and subject to myriad laws and ordinances regulating behavior, gays and lesbians constructed protected and accessible spaces in self-conscious assertion of their legitimate place in civic life (Chauncey, 1994; Bérubé, 1996; Beemyn, 1997; Stein, 2000). Urban gays (and to a lesser degree lesbians) also played a crucial role in the gentrification and economic redevelopment of core city neighborhoods. The urban gay enclaves that they created – San Francisco's Castro, New York's West Village, Chicago's Boystown, Boston's South End – fostered a place-based sense of gay male identity. As rents climbed in these neighborhoods, and as gay men increasingly dominated street culture, lesbians often looked for more friendly terrain, establishing networks of businesses, residence, and leisure that often stood outside of both mainstream urban culture and gay male culture (Kennedy and Davis, 1993). Gay and lesbian communities challenged and transgressed dominant notions of gender identities and sexual orientation and, in the process, redrew the political, social, and cultural geography of the postwar American city.

Urban historians have stretched and enlivened the study of postwar American history in ways that will continue to reverberate into the foreseeable future. But the field has shortcomings and an unfinished agenda to accompany its proud accomplishments. A mere laundry list of deficiencies and recommendations does an injustice to the ongoing work of scholars currently plumbing the archives, but we should preface our conclusion with at least a brief tour through the territory that remains to be explored. Among the major challenges facing the field is incorporating the provocative neo-Marxist geography (Castells, 1983; Harvey, 1989; Lefebvre, 1991) that has so influenced the traditional social sciences in the last two decades. The "LA School" of urban studies, among the most self-conscious proponents of the new geography, has prompted many urban scholars to "reinsert space" into analysis of social processes (Soja, 1989). But the LA scholarship has a tendency to reproduce rhetorically the fragmented, postmodern abstractions of Southern California itself, and few careful historical works have emerged from this literature. Such criticisms notwithstanding, important efforts are underway to historicize spatial analysis and to think systematically about Los Angeles as a paradigmatic – rather than pathological – American urban city on a par with Chicago and New York (Dear et al., 1996; Abu-Lughod, 1999). The field of postwar urban history has also yet to address systematically the connections between the physical city and the city of lived experience; studies too frequently isolate the built environment from human context and social relations from the physical-spatial patterns of metropolitan change. Few architectural historians or historians of city planning have told their story "from the bottom up," and few urban social and cultural historians have fully integrated the history of planning and public policy into their narratives. The divide between scholars who emphasize "structure" (economics, built environment, and public policy) and those who emphasize "agency" (everyday resistance, popular culture, community formations) has been breached by relatively few urbanists.

The research agenda in postwar urban history thus remains full, with vast areas of yet untapped subject matter. We have discussed above the virtually untouched question of gender, culture, and power in urban history after 1945. This is perhaps the most pressing direction for new work, but a few additional subjects warrant mention. The great postwar migration of African American and white southerners to northern and southern cities awaits its historian. This migration, one of the great demographic transformations of the twentieth century – and as important as earlier urban immigrations – remains in the literature largely a macro-social phenomenon, understood strictly in broad terms. Only Nicolas Lemann's (1992) impressionistic, frequently ahistorical, interpretation of postwar migration to Chicago has attempted a local social analysis. The cultural and social dimensions of white suburban flight also remain poorly documented and understood, even as historians evoke "suburbanization" to explain a variety of phenomena. New work on both types of migration will enrich the field by placing the urban crisis literature in a fresh context, perhaps modifying the crisis paradigm's reliance on violence as a controlling metaphor. Finally, if urban historians of the first two postwar decades have traced the relationship between political economy and race in the context of the deindustrializing city and African American freedom movement, historians of the post-1965 period surely will find a natural epilogue in the emerging multiracial global American city. Post-1965 immigration transformed the American metropolis again, bringing enormous new waves of immigrants from Latin America and Asia who have remapped neighborhoods, commerce, and politics in both city and suburb. Likewise, globalization and accompanying reorganizations of capital accumulation on national and transnational scales have brought new stresses and opportunities to the American metropolitan system. Exploring the narratives of these changes must be part of any new research agenda in urban history.

Space and political culture unite the history of postwar American cities and suburbs – together, the metropolis, that surging, sprawling conglomerate that became the definitive urban formation of the second half of the twentieth century. At the heart of the postwar metropolis lay an epochal transformation in American political life: the eclipse of the labor-centered urban political culture of the New Deal and World War II era by a metropolitan, increasingly suburban, political culture rooted in property and the organization and distribution of spatial resources, from taxes to industrial land. In this transformation, race, politics, and urban development have been mutually constitutive. Indeed, shifts in the ideological and institutional content of race itself drove much of urbanization across the second half of the century. After 1945, with the United States a more urban nation than ever before, cities and their metropolitan peripheries emerged as the dramatic coliseums in which conflicts over race and economic power were enacted. Metropolitan areas mattered in the second half of the twentieth century as terrains of contestation and as the subjects of nearly unending debate in a long narrative of political economic evolution.

But as local places, cities are more than mere stages of dramatic action or abstract objects of argument. Cities are far more than containers or empty vessels. Neither are they sets of teleological processes and impersonal structures. Cities are less static containers of action than constitutive historical subjects that act on and through the social and political landscape of the nation. Metaphorically, they work less as stages or containers and more as multidimensional terrains, simultaneously produced by, shaping, and constraining political and economic options and choices. As the historiography of postwar America continues to develop, urban historians have helped to explode artificial boundaries between varieties of history – from labor, planning, and political to cultural, gender, and African American – that are accustomed to telling stories separately. Continuing to push past those boundaries, to reveal the power of place within the landscape of national history, will enrich and invigorate both urban and twentieth-century history.

REFERENCES

Abbott, Carl: *The New Urban America: Growth and Politics in Sunbelt Cities* (Chapel Hill: University of North Carolina Press, 1981).

Abbott, Carl: *The Metropolitan Frontier: Cities in the Modern American West* (Tucson: University of Arizona Press, 1993).

Abu-Lughod, Janet: *New York, Chicago, Los Angeles: America's Global Cities* (Minneapolis: University of Minnesota Press, 1999).

Arnesen, Eric: *Brotherhoods of Color: Black Railroad Workers and the Struggle for Equality* (Cambridge, Mass.: Harvard University Press, 2001).

Avila, Eric: *Chocolate Cities and Vanilla Suburbs: Popular Culture in the Age of White Flight* (Berkeley: University of California Press, forthcoming).

Bauman, John J.: *Public Housing, Race, and Renewal: Urban Planning in Philadelphia, 1920–1974* (Philadelphia: Temple University Press, 1987).

Baxandall, Rosalyn and Ewen, Elizabeth: *Picture Windows: How the Suburbs Happened* (New York: Basic Books, 2000).

Beauregard, Robert A.: *Voices of Decline: The Postwar Fate of U.S. Cities* (Cambridge, Mass.: Blackwell, 1993).

Beemyn, Brett, ed.: *Creating a Place for Ourselves: Lesbian, Gay, and Bisexual Community Histories* (New York: Routledge, 1997).

Bensman, David and Lynch, Roberta: *Rusted Dreams: Hard Times in a Steel Community* (New York: McGraw Hill, 1987).

Berger, Peter L.: *The Social Construction of Reality: A Treatise in the Sociology of Knowledge* (Garden City, NY: Doubleday, 1967).

Bérubé, Allan: "The History of the Bathhouses," in Dangerous Bedfellows (eds.), *Policing Public Sex: Queer Politics and the Future of AIDS Activism* (Boston: South End Press, 1996).

Biondi, Martha: *To Stand and Fight: The Civil Rights Movement in Postwar New York City* (Cambridge, Mass.: Harvard University Press, 2003).

Bluestone, Barry and Harrison, Bennett: *The Deindustrialization of America: Plant Closings, Community Abandonment, and the Dismantling of Basic Industry* (New York: Basic Books, 1982).

Briffault, Richard: "Our Localism: Part I – The Structure of Local Government Law," *Columbia Law Review*, 90 (1990): 1–115.

Broussard, Albert S.: *Black San Francisco: The Struggle for Racial Equality, 1900–1954* (Lawrence: University Press of Kansas, 1993).

Brown, Michael K.: *Race, Money, and the Welfare State* (Ithaca, NY: Cornell University Press, 1999).

Carter, Dan T.: *From George Wallace to Newt Gingrich: Race in the Conservative Counterrevolution, 1963–1994* (Baton Rouge: Louisiana State University Press, 1996).

Castells, Manuel: *The City and the Grassroots: A Cross-Cultural Theory of Urban Social Movements* (Berkeley: University of California Press, 1983).

Chauncey, George: *Gay New York: Gender, Urban Culture, and the Makings of the Gay Male World, 1890–1940* (New York: Basic Books, 1994).

Cohen, Lizbeth: "From Town Center to Shopping Center: The Reconfiguration of Community Marketplaces in Postwar America," *American Historical Review*, 101/4 (1996): 1050–81.

Coontz, Stephanie: *The Way We Never Were: American Families and the Nostalgia Trap* (New York: Basic Books, 1992).

Countryman, Matthew: "Civil Rights and Black Power in Philadelphia, 1940–1971" (Ph.D. diss., Duke University, 1998).

Countryman, Matthew, Theoharis, Jeanne, and Woodard, Komozi, eds.: *Freedom North: Black Freedom Struggles Outside the South, 1940–1980* (New York: St. Martin's, forthcoming).

Cowie, Jefferson: *Capital Moves: RCA's Seventy-Year Quest for Cheap Labor* (Ithaca, NY: Cornell University Press, 1999).

Cumbler, John T.: *A Social History of Economic Decline: Business, Politics and Work in Trenton* (New Brunswick, NJ: Rutgers University Press, 1989).

Davis, Mike: *City of Quartz: Excavating the Future in Los Angeles* (London: Verso, 1990).

Davis, Susan G.: *Spectacular Nature: Corporate Culture and the Sea World Experience* (Berkeley: University of California Press, 1997).

Dear, Michael J., Schockman, H. Eric, and Hise, Greg, eds.: *Rethinking Los Angeles* (Thousand Oaks, Calif.: Sage Publications, 1996).

Doherty, Kathryn M. and Stone, Clarence N.: "Local Practice in Transition," in Martha Derthick (ed.), *Dilemmas of Scale in America's Federal Democracy* (Cambridge: Woodrow Wilson Center Press and Cambridge University Press, 1999), 154–86.

Drake, St. Clair and Cayton, Horace R.: *Black Metropolis: A Study of Negro Life in a Northern City* (Chicago: University of Chicago Press, 1945).

Du Bois, W. E. B.: *The Philadelphia Negro* (Philadelphia: University of Pennsylvania Press, 1899).

Durr, Kenneth: "When Southern Politics Came North: The Roots of White Working-Class Conservatism in Baltimore, 1940–1964," *Labor History*, 37/3 (1996): 309–31.

Dyer, Stephanie: "Markets in the Meadows: Department Stores and Shopping Centers in the Decentralization of Philadelphia, 1920–1980" (Ph.D. diss., University of Pennsylvania, 2000).

Edsall, Thomas Byrne and Edsall, Mary D.: *Chain Reaction: The Impact of Race, Rights, and Taxes on American Politics* (New York: W. W. Norton, 1992).

Eisler, Benita: *Private Lives: Men and Women of the Fifties* (New York: Franklin Watts, 1986).

Escobar, Edward: *Race, Police, and the Making of a Political Identity: Mexican Americans and the Los Angeles Police Department, 1900–1945* (Berkeley: University of California Press, 1999).

Findlay, John: *Magic Lands: Western Cityscapes and American Culture After 1940* (Berkeley: University of California Press, 1992).

Fine, Sidney: *Violence in the Model City: The Cavanaugh Administration, Race Relations, and the Detroit Riot of 1967* (Ann Arbor: University of Michigan Press, 1989).

Formisano, Ronald P.: *Boston Against Bussing: Race, Class, and Ethnicity in the 1960s and 1970s* (Chapel Hill: University of North Carolina Press, 1991).

Fraser, Steve and Gerstle, Gary, eds.: *The Rise and Fall of the New Deal Order* (Princeton, NJ: Princeton University Press, 1989).

Freeman, Joshua B.: *Working-Class New York: Life and Labor Since World War II* (New York: New Press, 2000).

Freiden, Bernard J. and Sagalyn, Lynne B.: *Downtown, Inc.: How America Rebuilds Cities* (Cambridge, Mass.: MIT Press, 1989).

Freund, David: "Making it Home: Race, Development, and the Politics of Place in Suburban Detroit, 1940–1967" (Ph.D. diss., University of Michigan, 1999).

Frug, Gerald E.: *City Making: Building Communities Without Building Walls* (Princeton, NJ: Princeton University Press, 1999).

Gelfand, Mark: *A Nation of Cities: The Federal Government and Urban America, 1933–1965* (New York: Oxford University Press, 1975).

Gilfoyle, Timothy: "White Cities, Linguistic Turns, and Disneylands: The New Paradigms of Urban History," *Reviews in American History*, 26/1 (1998): 175–204.

Goings, Kenneth and Mohl, Raymond A., eds.: *The New African American Urban History* (Thousand Oaks, Calif.: Sage Publications, 1996).

Green, Adam: *Selling the Race: Cultural Production and Notions of Community in Black Chicago, 1940–1955* (Chicago: University of Chicago Press, forthcoming).

Gregory, Stephen: *Black Corona: Race and the Politics of Place in an Urban Community* (Princeton, NJ: Princeton University Press, 1998).

Grimshaw, William J.: *Bitter Fruit: Black Politics and the Chicago Machine, 1931–1991* (Chicago: University of Chicago Press, 1992).

Haas, Lisbeth: "Grass-Roots Protest and the Politics of Planning: Santa Ana, 1976–1988," in Rob Kling, Spencer Olin, and Mark Poster (eds.), *Postsuburban California: The Transformation of Orange County Since World War II* (Berkeley: University of California Press, 1991).

Hanchett, Thomas W.: *Sorting Out the New South City: Race, Class, and Urban Development in Charlotte, 1875–1975* (Chapel Hill: University of North Carolina Press, 1998).

Harvey, David: *The Urban Experience* (Baltimore: Johns Hopkins University Press, 1989).

Hirsch, Arnold R.: *Making the Second Ghetto: Race and Housing in Chicago, 1940–1960* (New York: Cambridge University Press, 1983).

Hise, Greg: *Magnetic Los Angeles: Planning the Twentieth-Century Metropolis* (Baltimore: Johns Hopkins University Press, 1997).

Horne, Gerald: *Fire This Time: The Watts Uprising and the 1960s* (Charlottesville: University Press of Virginia, 1995).

Horowitz, Roger: *"Negro and White, Unite and Fight": A Social History of Industrial Unionism in Meatpacking, 1930–90* (Urbana: University of Illinois Press, 1997).

Isenberg, Alison: "Downtown Democracy: Rebuilding Main Street Ideals in the Twentieth-Century American City" (Ph.D. diss., University of Pennsylvania, 1995).

Jackson, Kenneth T.: *Crabgrass Frontier: The Suburbanization of the United States* (New York: Oxford University Press, 1985).

Jackson, Thomas F.: "The State, the Movement, and the Urban Poor: The War on Poverty and Political Mobilization in the 1960s," in Michael B. Katz (ed.), *The "Underclass" Debate: Views from History* (Princeton, NJ: Princeton University Press, 1993).

Katz, Michael B.: *The Undeserving Poor: From the War on Poverty to the War on Welfare* (New York: Pantheon, 1989).

Katz, Michael B., ed.: *The "Underclass" Debate: Views from History* (Princeton, NJ: Princeton University Press, 1993).

Katz, Michael B.: *The Price of Citizenship: Redefining the American Welfare State* (New York: Metropolitan Books, 2001).

Katznelson, Ira: *City Trenches: Urban Politics and the Patterning of Class in the United States* (Chicago: University of Chicago Press, 1981).

Kazin, Michael: "The Grass-Roots Right: New Histories of U.S. Conservatism in the Twentieth Century," *American Historical Review*, 97 (February 1992): 136–55.

Kelley, Robin D. G.: *Race Rebels: Culture, Politics, and the Black Working Class* (New York: Free Press, 1994).

Kelley, Robin D. G.: *Yo Mama's Disfunktional: Fighting the Culture Wars in Urban America* (Boston: Beacon Press, 1997).

Kennedy, Elizabeth Lapovsky and Davis, Madeline D.: *Boots of Leather, Slippers of Gold: The History of a Lesbian Community* (New York: Routledge, 1993).

Kusmer, Kenneth: "African Americans in the City Since World War II: From the Industrial to the Postindustrial Era," in Kenneth Goings and Raymond Mohl (eds.), *The New African American Urban History* (Thousand Oaks, Calif.: Sage Publications, 1996).

Lefebvre, Henri: *The Production of Space* (Cambridge, Mass.: Blackwell, 1991).

Lemann, Nicolas: *The Promised Land: The Great Black Migration and How It Changed America* (New York: Vintage, 1992).

Lemke-Santangelo, Gretchen: *Abiding Courage: African American Migrant Women and the East Bay Community* (Chapel Hill: University of North Carolina Press, 1996).

Lewis, Earl: *In Our Own Interests: Race, Class, and Power in Twentieth-Century Norfolk, Virginia* (Berkeley: University of California Press, 1991).

Lipsitz, George: *Rainbow at Midnight: Labor and Culture in the 1940s* (Urbana: University of Illinois Press, 1994).

Lipsitz, George: *The Possessive Investment in Whiteness: How White People Profit from Identity Politics* (Philadelphia: Temple University Press, 1998).

Longsreth, Richard: *City Center to Regional Mall* (Cambridge, Mass.: MIT Press, 1997).

Lotchin, Roger: *Fortress California, 1910–1961: From Warfare to Welfare* (New York: Oxford University Press, 1992).

McGirr, Lisa: *Suburban Warriors: The Origins of the New American Right* (Princeton, NJ: Princeton University Press, 2001).

McKenzie, Evan: *Privatopia: Homeowner Associations and the Rise of Residential Private Governments* (New Haven, Conn.: Yale University Press, 1994).

Magnet, Myron: *The Dream and the Nightmare: The Sixties Legacy to the Underclass* (New York: William Morrow, 1993).

Marable, Manning: "How Washington Won: The Political Economy of Race in Chicago," *Journal of Intergroup Relations*, 11 (1983): 56–81.

Marable, Manning: *Race, Reform, and Rebellion: The Second Reconstruction in Black America, 1945–1982* (Jackson: University Press of Mississippi, 1984).

Markusen, Ann et al.: *The Rise of the Gunbelt: The Military Remapping of America* (New York: Oxford University Press, 1991).

Massey, Douglas S. and Denton, Nancy A.: *American Apartheid: Segregation and the Making of the Underclass* (Cambridge, Mass.: Harvard University Press, 1993).

May, Elaine Tyler: *Homeward Bound: American Families in the Cold War Era* (New York: Basic Books, 1988).

Meyerowitz, Joanne, ed.: *Not June Cleaver: Women and Gender in Postwar America, 1945–1960* (Philadelphia: Temple University Press, 1994).

Mohl, Raymond A.: "African Americans in the City: The Industrial Era, 1900–1950," in Kenneth Goings and Raymond A. Mohl (eds.), *The New African American Urban History* (Thousand Oaks, Calif.: Sage Publications, 1996).

Mollenkopf, John H.: *The Contested City* (Princeton, NJ: Princeton University Press, 1983).

Moore, Shirley Ann Wilson: *To Place Our Deeds: The African American Community in Richmond, California, 1910–1963* (Berkeley: University of California Press, 2001).

Murray, Charles: *Losing Ground: American Social Policy, 1950–1980* (New York: Basic Books, 1984).

Murray, Sylvie: "Suburban Citizens: Domesticity and Community Politics in Queens, New York, 1945–1960" (Ph.D. diss., Yale University, 1994).

Nicolaides, Becky: *My Blue Heaven: Life and Politics in the Working-Class Suburbs of Los Angeles, 1920–1965* (Chicago: University of Chicago Press, 2002).

Nightingale, Carl: "The Global Inner City: Toward a Historical Analysis," in Michael B. Katz and Thomas J. Sugrue (eds.), *W. E. B. DuBois, Race, and the City: The Philadelphia Negro and Its Legacy* (Philadelphia: University of Pennsylvania Press, 1998).

O'Connor, Alice: *Poverty Knowledge: Social Science, Social Policy, and the Poor in Twentieth-Century U.S. History* (Princeton, NJ: Princeton University Press, 2001).

Omi, Michael and Winant, Howard: *Racial Formation in the United States: From the 1960s to the 1980s* (New York: Routledge, 1986).

Peiss, Kathy: *Cheap Amusements: Working Women and Leisure in Turn-of-the-Century New York* (Philadelphia: Temple University Press, 1986).

Piven, Frances Fox and Cloward, Richard: *Regulating the Poor: The Function of Public Welfare* (New York: Pantheon, 1971).

Radford, Gail: *Modern Housing for America: Policy Struggles in the New Deal Era* (Chicago: University of Chicago Press, 1996).

Reed, Adolph: *Stirrings in the Jug: Black Politics in the Post-Segregation Era* (Minneapolis: University of Minnesota Press, 1999).

Rieder, Jonathan: "The Rise of the 'Silent Majority,'" in Steve Fraser and Gary Gerstle (eds.), *The Rise and Fall of the New Deal Order, 1930–1980* (Princeton, NJ: Princeton University Press, 1989).

Rome, Andrew: *The Bulldozer in the Countryside: Suburban Sprawl and the Rise of American Environmentalism* (New York: Cambridge University Press, 2001).

Rose, Mark: *Interstate: Express Highway Politics, 1941–1956* (Lawrence: University Press of Kansas, 1979).

Rose, Tricia: *Black Noise: Rap Music and Black Culture in Contemporary America* (Hanover, NH: Wesleyan University Press, 1994).

Rupp, Leila and Taylor, Verta: *Survival in the Doldrums: The American Women's Rights Movement, 1945 to the 1960s* (New York: Oxford University Press, 1987).

Sánchez, George J.: *Becoming Mexican American: Ethnicity, Culture, and Identity in Chicano Los Angeles, 1900–1945* (New York: Oxford University Press, 1993).

Schneider, Eric C.: *Vampires, Dragons, and Egyptian Kings: Youth Gangs in Postwar New York* (Princeton, NJ: Princeton University Press, 1999).

Schulman, Bruce: *From Cotton Belt to Sunbelt: Federal Policy, Economic Development and the Transformation of the South, 1938–1980* (New York: Oxford University Press, 1990).

Scranton, Philip: "Large Firms and Industrial Restructuring in the Philadelphia Region, 1900–1980," *Pennsylvania Magazine of History and Biography*, 116 (October 1992): 421–65.

Sears, David and Citrin, Jack: *Tax Revolt: Something for Nothing in California* (Cambridge, Mass.: Harvard University Press, 1982).

Self, Robert O.: " 'To Plan Our Liberation': Black Power and the Politics of Place in Oakland, California, 1965–1977," *Journal of Urban History*, 26/6 (September 2000): 759–92.

Self, Robert O.: *American Babylon: Class, Race, and Power in Postwar California* (Princeton, NJ: Princeton University Press, forthcoming-a).

Self, Robert O.: "California's Industrial Garden: Remaking Postwar Oakland and the Greater Bay Area," in Jefferson Cowie and Joseph Heathcott (eds.), *Beyond the Ruins: Deindustrialization and the Meanings of Modern America*, with a foreword by Barry Bluestone (Ithaca, NY: Cornell University Press, forthcoming-b).

Siegel, Fred: *The Future Once Happened Here: New York, D.C., L.A., and the Fate of America's Big Cities* (San Francisco: Encounter Books, 1997).

Sitkoff, Harvard: *A New Deal for Blacks: The Emergence of Civil Rights as a National Issue* (New York: Oxford University Press, 1978).

Smith, Suzanne E.: *Dancing in the Street: Motown and the Cultural Politics of Detroit* (Cambridge, Mass.: Harvard University Press, 1999).

Soja, Edward W.: *Postmodern Geographies: The Reassertion of Space in Critical Social Theory* (London: Verso, 1989).

Spigel, Lynn: *Make Room for TV: Television and Family in Postwar America* (Chicago: University of Chicago Press, 1992).

Stein, Marc: *City of Sisterly and Brotherly Loves: Lesbian and Gay Philadelphia* (Chicago: University of Chicago Press, 2000).

Stephenson, R. Bruce: *Visions of Eden: Environmentalism, Urban Planning, and City Building in St. Petersburg, Florida, 1900–1995* (Columbus: Ohio State University Press, 1997).

Stern, Mark: "Poverty and Family Composition Since 1940," in Michael B. Katz (ed.), *The "Underclass" Debate: Views from History* (Princeton, NJ: Princeton University Press, 1993).

Sugrue, Thomas J.: "The Structures of Urban Poverty: The Reorganization of Space and Work in Three Periods of American History," in Michael B. Katz (ed.), *The "Underclass" Debate: Views from History* (Princeton, NJ: Princeton University Press, 1993).

Sugrue, Thomas J.: " 'Forget About Your Inalienable Right to Work': Deindustrialization and its Discontents at Ford, 1950–1953," *International Labor and Working-Class History*, 48 (1995): 112–30.

Sugrue, Thomas J.: *The Origins of the Urban Crisis: Race and Inequality in Postwar Detroit* (Princeton, NJ: Princeton University Press, 1996).

Sugrue, Thomas J.: "Breaking Through: The Troubled Origins of Affirmative Action in the Workplace," in *Color Lines: Affirmative Action, Immigration, and Civil Rights Options for America* (Chicago: University of Chicago Press, 2001), 31–52.

Swanstrom, Todd: *The Crisis of Growth Politics: Cleveland, Kucinich, and the Challenge of Urban Populism* (Philadelphia: Temple University Press, 1985).

Taylor, Quintard: *The Forging of a Black Community: Seattle's Central District, From 1870 Through the Civil Rights Era* (Seattle: University of Washington Press, 1994).

Teaford, Jon C.: *The Rough Road to Renaissance: Urban Revitalization in America, 1940–1985* (Baltimore: Johns Hopkins University Press, 1990).

Thomas, June Manning: *Redevelopment and Race: Planning a Finer City in Detroit* (Baltimore: Johns Hopkins University Press, 1997).

Thompson, Heather Ann: *Motor City Breakdown: The Politics of Race and Liberalism on the Streets and Shopfloors of Postwar Detroit* (Ithaca, NY: Cornell University Press, 2001).

Trotter, Joe William: *Black Milwaukee: The Making of an Industrial Proletariat, 1915–1945* (Urbana: University of Illinois Press, 1985).

Weiss, Nancy J.: *Farewell to the Party of Lincoln: Black Politics in the Age of FDR* (Princeton, NJ: Princeton University Press, 1983).

Whelan, Carmen: *From Puerto Rico to Philadelphia: Puerto Rican Workers and Postwar Economies* (Philadelphia: Temple University Press, 2001).

Wiese, Andrew: *Places of Our Own: African American Suburbanization Since 1916* (Chicago: University of Chicago Press, forthcoming).

Williams, Rhonda Y.: "Living Just Enough in the City: Change and Activism in Baltimore's Public Housing, 1940–1980" (Ph.D. diss., University of Pennsylvania, 1998).

Wolcott, Victoria W.: "The Culture of the Informal Economy: Numbers Runners in Inter-War Black Detroit," *Radical History Review*, 69 (1997): 46–75.

Woodard, Komozi: *A Nation Within a Nation: Amiri Baraka (LeRoi Jones) and Black Power Politics* (Chapel Hill: University of North Carolina Press, 1999).

Wright, Gwendolyn: *Building the Dream: A Social History of Housing in America* (Cambridge, Mass.: MIT Press, 1981).

CHAPTER THREE

American Religion Since 1945

JAMES T. FISHER

In a 1997 assessment of the historiography of twentieth-century American religion, historian Richard Fox wrote bleakly of the state of the field: "It may be that religious history of any sort will be unable for a long time to mount the main waves of twentieth-century historiography." "For the time being," he added, "we may have to rely on journalists, religionists, and anthropologists for probing analyses of the culture of twentieth-century American religion, and on theologians for studies of twentieth-century American religious ideas" (Fox, 1997, p. 398). The paucity of historical works on American religion since 1945 is even more glaring than that of the first half of the century. In the absence of a "field" (or even a "subfield") in postwar religious history, any account of the subject must rely on elements drawn from a wide variety of disciplines. There is certainly no shortage of material on American religion in the postwar period: some of the most influential works of American scholarship produced since 1945 directly concern religious issues. Several figures from the worlds of theology and the social sciences emerged during the era to exert great influence on the culture as a whole. One form of religious revival or another can be located at virtually every stage in postwar life, marking the period as distinctive, if not unique, in American history.

The Postwar Revival

American religious leaders and religion in general enjoyed a striking upsurge in cultural authority in the years immediately following World War II. In 1951 historian H. Stuart Hughes proclaimed: "religion is now the latest thing." By contrast he noted that "no self-respecting intellectual would have been caught dead with a religious interpretation of anything" in the prewar years (McCarraher, 2000, pp. 101–2). The revival of religion extended far beyond the intellectual class and was partly rooted in the response of religious leaders to the war itself. Haunted by memories of the "holy crusade" imagery championed by the churches during World War I and anxious to avoid a reprise of that fiasco, religious leaders appraised World War II, explained historian Gerald L. Sittser, "slowly and soberly" (Sittser, 1997, pp. 48, 81). Many religious figures viewed the war not as a crusade for civilization but as a sign of God's judgment on a sinful nation, "a time for sackcloth and ashes," in the words of the Jesuit Francis X. Talbot. The renowned Protestant theologian Reinhold Niebuhr characteristically sensed the limitations of this position, in asserting that "the democratic traditions of the Anglo-Saxon world are actually the basis of a just world order." Yet Niebuhr balanced this view with a conviction, according to Sittser, that churches "must provide a transcendent perspective to keep America from becoming proud and ambitious" (Sittser, 1997, pp. 55, 97).

Though a few religious figures pressed denominational agendas during the war, this prevailing consensus of humility led church leaders to offer a relatively united critique of the internment of Japanese Americans in concentration camps while promoting "fellowship among the races" with unprecedented vigor. Despite condemnations of Nazi anti-Semitism, however, America's leading Christians did not succeed in arousing the conscience of the public at large on behalf of European Jews and other victims of the Holocaust. This grave failing did not arouse much attention at the time. Overall, the measured response of religious figures to World War II greatly enhanced the prestige of organized religion in the immediate postwar years.

Accounts of the postwar religious revival have tended to move quickly past the period 1945 to 1949, focusing instead on the spectacular growth in public piety witnessed between 1950 and 1955. It is easy to see why: membership in churches grew at more than twice the rate of the nation's population growth during this period. In 1953 the figure stood at 59.5 percent, easily the highest rate in American history. Between 1949 and 1953 "the distribution of Scripture in the United States increased 140 percent." More than 80 percent of American adults described the Bible as "the revealed word of God" rather than simply a "great piece of literature" (Herberg, 1955, p. 14). Yet the theological dimension of the postwar revival has often been overshadowed by critiques of its "therapeutic" and "consensual" character. The Reverend Norman Vincent Peale became an especially attractive magnet for critics who viewed the postwar revival as a fatuously optimistic excuse for self-indulgence and political paralysis. In 1952 Peale, the pastor of New York City's Marble Collegiate Church, published *The Power of Positive Thinking*, a sequel to his 1948 work, *A Guide to Confident Living*. The latter volume had thrived amid the growing market for inspirational literature, but *The Power of Positive Thinking* would enjoy success beyond measure, with over 2 million hardcover copies sold and many millions more in perennial paperback editions (Meyer, 1980; George, 1993).

Peale's theology was not very challenging. Historians Douglas Miller and Marion Nowak (1977, p. 96) have argued that "much of Peale's appeal was blatantly materialistic." They equated the prophet of positive thoughts with the spirit of the age, when "an optimistic, shallow, non-sectarian religion undoubtedly eased many personal tensions in the age of Korea, McCarthy and Sputnik" (p. 97). Donald B. Meyer (1980) provided a more subtle analysis of Peale's popularity, tracing his sources to the New Thought movement of the early twentieth century – with its focus on the power of mind over matter – and to the psychoanalytic thought of such figures as Peale's erstwhile collaborator, Dr. Smiley Blanton. Like many scholars, Meyer viewed the postwar influence of psychology on religion with ambivalence, a stance grounded in at least two enduring intellectual traditions. The first exalted the transcendent dimension of religion, while the second emphasized the role of faith in promoting a critique of culture. The apparent absence of these themes in the postwar revival ensured that the creative and sometimes unsettling aspects of American religious life between 1945 and 1950 went largely overlooked. Yet the specter of nuclear apocalypse greatly heightened the appeal of an "existential" religious discourse that earlier generations would likely have dismissed as excessively personal if not morbid.

The first postwar spiritual bestseller – and a book often dismissed as a forerunner to the religion-as-therapy movement – was Joshua Loth Liebman's *Peace of Mind* (1946). Liebman, a rabbi and popular radio preacher who employed sophisticated Freudian concepts in his treatise on spiritual wellbeing, offered little comfort to those anxious for a return of an omnipotent God following the "whirlwind of national tragedy" the war had wrought. "We have to grow up," he counseled, "to learn that God is not a magician who changes everything in the twinkling of an eye. Maturity in the religious realm means surrendering our childish view of God and of under-standing that He, too, in building a predictable world, governed by law, voluntarily surrenders something of his sovereignty" (Liebman, 1946, p. 161). Liebman was intent on discovering "A New God for America," characterized by Martin Marty (1996, p. 315) as a "benign affirmer," designed for a civilization increasingly suspi-cious of dominant paternal figures.

Donald B. Meyer (1980) acknowledged that *Peace of Mind* "was only unfairly lumped into the postwar spate of books teaching 'faith-in-faith'" (p. 328). The same fate befell Bishop Fulton J. Sheen's *Peace of Soul* (1948), a work often characterized as a Catholic rejoinder to Liebman's volume. Readers looking for reassuring apolo-getics, however, were surely disappointed. "There is no such thing as the problem of the atomic bomb," Sheen wrote. "There is, rather, the problem of the man who makes and uses it. Only men and nations whose personalities were already atomized could join forces with external nature to use an atomic bomb in an attack on human existence" (p. 202). Though Sheen clearly differed with Liebman on the causes and treatment of spiritual disorders and was disdainful of Freudianism, his approach to the psychology of religion was fairly complex. For all his grounding in neoscholasti-cism (the philosophical system of Thomas Aquinas, whose revival dominated Catholic thought beyond mid-century), Sheen's writings followed the "existential turn" of postwar religious thought. Still, Sheen's celebrity incarnation as host of the extraor-dinarily popular television show, *Life is Worth Living* (which first aired in 1952), made him an easy target for caricature.

Thomas Merton was never seen on television or heard over the radio, but that did not prevent the Trappist monk's 1948 autobiography, *The Seven Storey Mountain*, from ascending the bestseller lists. Merton proffered a blistering critique of con-sumerism and materialism in this conversion story of an Ivy League rake who found God in 1938, became a Catholic, and entered a Kentucky monastery three days after the Japanese attack on Pearl Harbor. Readers who viewed *The Seven Storey Mountain* as a triumphalist work overlooked the desire Merton expressed in its final pages to be as "the Christ of the burnt men" (Merton, 1948, p. 423). This allusion to nuclear holocaust echoed a theme of *Figures for an Apocalypse*, a collection of Merton's poetry published several months prior to *The Seven Storey Mountain* (Mott, 1984).

A central topic of the popular religious literature of 1945–50 was *work*, though this motif is absent from scholarly accounts of the period. Spiritual and psychologi-cal self-awareness required diligent effort and vigilance, as did the work of conver-sion. Thomas Merton wrote of sleeping on a straw mat in an unheated room and rising at 2 a.m. to begin his unchanging routine of prayer and manual labor. Soon monasteries across the nation were erecting Quonset huts to house the waves of men who found themselves suddenly attracted to just such a regimen. That was hardly a recipe for escape. The religious revival also performed highly significant cultural work in relation to postwar sexual attitudes. When Alfred Kinsey published *Sexual Behavior in the Human Male* in 1948, many religious figures responded in conventional fashion. The president of New York's Union Theological Seminary, for example, declared that the book revealed "a prevailing degradation of American morality approximating the worst decadence of the Roman era." Others, however, took the trouble to think seriously about the implications of Kinsey's work. Psychiatrist Karl Stern, a convert to Catholicism, feared that the logic of totalitarianism was seeping into intimate human relationships. "If someone attempted," he wrote in *Commonweal*, "to set the stage for a dehumanized, depersonalized society – for the great beehive – he would start out with things like the Kinsey Report." Reinhold Niebuhr accused Kinsey of never "calling attention to the uniquely human characteristics of man's sexual life" (Morantz, 1977, pp. 575, 580–1). With the rise of a "personalist" existentialism, religious thinkers in the immediate postwar period took on many of the cultural tasks that had been the province of secular humanists for much of the century (McCarraher, 2000).

Reinhold Niebuhr was the most celebrated figure of the early postwar religious revival. Niebuhr was a politically active theologian who sought to reverse a half-century of liberal Protestant accommodation to the gospel of unlimited human progress. In 1935, in his *Introduction to Christian Ethics*, Niebuhr had sharply criticized "the illusion of liberalism that we are dealing with a possible and prudential ethic in the gospel." "The ethic of Jesus," he argued, "does not deal at all with the immediate moral problem of every human life . . . It transcends the possibilities of human life . . . as God transcends the world" (Ahlstrom, 1975, p. 437). Niebuhr became associated with neo-orthodoxy, a theological movement within Protestantism that revived an appreciation of the doctrine of original sin. In the 1940s *Time–Life* magnate Henry Luce grew intrigued by Niebuhr's thought and his works were featured regularly in stories written by Whittaker Chambers, though in *Time* fashion these generally appeared without a byline. As Niebuhr biographer Richard Fox (1985) noted, in the 1940s Chambers made the common error of equating "Niebuhrian" thought with "pessimism." "Meanwhile," Fox explained, "Niebuhr was working beyond endurance in one cause after another to help mold the fate that was supposedly beyond molding" (p. 202). The subheading for a March 8, 1948 cover story on Niebuhr celebrating *Time*'s twenty-fifth anniversary proclaimed: "Man's story is not a success story." Chambers did acknowledge in his text that "Niebuhr's gloomy view of man and history does not inhibit his belief that man should act for what he holds to be the highest good (always bearing in mind that sin will dog his action" ("Faith for a Lenten Age," p. 76).

The Luce empire was less impressed with Niebuhr's role in co-founding Americans for Democratic Action (ADA), an influential liberal anti-communist group that shouldered the ideological burdens of the Cold War without illusions as to the limitations and even the sinfulness of its own vision. Niebuhr's conviction that evil means must sometimes be used to forestall a much greater evil was highly appealing to chastened ex-leftists and assorted figures now drawn to his Christian existentialism. As Richard Fox (1997) explained, "by depicting and validating Christianity as a no-nonsense

realism, Niebuhr erected no-nonsense realism as a standard of ultimate judgment."
This was a vision even purer than secularism, which was seen as "too sentimental,
too contaminated by dreamy complacency" (pp. 404–5). The intensity of Niebuhr's
commitment may have only hastened the decline of liberal Protestantism, but it
attracted a cohort of tough-minded realists seeking to transcend the conventional
prewar ideological dichotomies. Fellow ADA member Arthur Schlesinger, Jr., said of
Niebuhr in 1956: "No man has had as much influence as a preacher in this generation; no preacher has had as much influence in the secular world" (Bingham, 1961,
p. 360). Given his background as a democratic socialist (in 1930 he ran for a Manhattan congressional seat on the Socialist Party ticket), Niebuhr drew the ire of those
who viewed the postwar revival of religion as symptomatic of a "failure of nerve"
(McCarraher, 2000, p. 102). Skeptics alluded to "fellow travelers" of the revival in
language that evoked the Popular Front of the 1930s and 1940s. In 1950 the distinguished sociologist David Riesman identified a "united front" of intellectuals and
theologians bent on immunizing religion from criticism (Silk, 1988, p. 31).

There may indeed have been a desire in the late 1940s to construct a "spiritual
front" to counter if not supplant the left-wing "cultural front," historian Michael
Denning's more inclusive term for the Popular Front era. If so, the effort was crippled by mutual suspicions that reignited denominational and cultural warfare in the
late 1940s and early 1950s. Paul Blanshard's bestselling critiques of Catholic power
were like scripture for many Protestant liberals who were also contemptuous of the
methods of Senator Joe McCarthy, a conspicuously Catholic figure. Perhaps even
more significantly, mainline Protestants were deeply disdainful of conservative evangelicals. In 1950, for example, Niebuhr expressed his dismay at "the evidence of
'mass' conversions under the ministrations of popular evangelists who arouse the religious emotions and elicit religious commitments with greater success than at any time
since the days of Billy Sunday" (Marty, 1996, pp. 346–7).

The popular evangelist Niebuhr had in mind was Billy Graham, fresh from a spectacular revival in Los Angeles in the autumn of 1949. As the tent meeting at the
corner of Washington and Hill Streets commenced in September, Graham was just
another earnest southern evangelist working a competitive circuit. The dramatic conversion in October of local radio personality and horseman Stuart Hamblen resulted
in lavish coverage of the crusade in William Randolph Hearst's *Los Angeles Exam-
iner*, to the degree that historian Mark Silk could call Graham "Hearst's last gift to
the American people" (Silk, 1988, p. 55). Hordes of curious spectators began appearing at the nightly revival and Graham soon reaped a rich harvest of souls (he even
came close to saving gangland figure Mickey Cohen). Graham followed up his
triumph in Los Angeles with an even more unlikely scorched-earth revival in New
England. The *Boston Post*, a paper with a predominantly Irish-Catholic readership,
devoted its front page to coverage of Graham's swing through the region in late 1949
and early 1950. Unlike such prominent evangelists as Harold Ockenga – pastor of
Boston's powerful Park Street Church – who regularly lamented the transformation
of New England into a Catholic stronghold, Graham curried favor with Catholic
leaders and was rewarded with a "Bravo, Billy!" editorial in the *Boston Pilot*, the arch-
diocesan weekly (Martin, 1992).

Billy Graham was the hardest-working man in the religion business. He was the
leading figure in a burgeoning evangelical movement culture that until recently has

been ignored by most historians. Such ambitious programs as Youth for Christ (where Graham launched his career in 1945) and a network of new seminaries led by Pasadena's Fuller Theological Seminary provided a foundation for Graham's spectacular takeoff in 1949 (Marsden, 1987). The National Association of Evangelicals (NAE), founded in 1943, fostered a seemingly paradoxical "fundamentalist ecumenism," a conviction that evangelicals could agree on basic doctrines without splintering into separatist movements like that of Carl McIntire's American Council of Churches (Carpenter, 1997). Billy Graham was all but red-baited by McIntire in the 1950s just as he struggled to overcome the derision with which mainstream Protestants viewed his movement. Graham had a disastrous White House meeting with President Harry S. Truman just weeks after the US entry into the Korean War in June 1950. Truman was a southern Baptist like Graham but – with many of his generation – he was extremely uneasy with public displays of piety and objected mightily when Graham and four colleagues knelt on the White House lawn following their meeting with the president. Things would be very different with President Dwight D. Eisenhower and every president who succeeded him, including the nation's first Roman Catholic president, who golfed with Graham if he did not pray with him. Yet as late as 1957 – when Graham conquered Manhattan in a revival puffed by the city's leading gossip columnist – Niebuhr continued to view the evangelist, in his biographer's words, as "fundamentally unserious, a hick and a huckster whose prime aspiration was to graze with presidents on lush fairways" (Fox, 1997, p. 400).

Graham's transformation from hayseed to wise man has never been fully accounted for in studies of American religion or the 1950s, despite his deep embrace of the culture of celebrity and his mastery of electronic communications. The hard work of revivalism was both a cultural and a theological triumph. Graham's 1953 bestseller, *Peace With God*, was an uncompromising tract on the necessity of rebirth in Christ as the only means to salvation. Graham was a friend of Fulton J. Sheen; the book was a kind of stern evangelical companion volume to earlier works by the bishop and Joshua Loth Liebman. Along with these figures, Graham was rarely taken seriously by religious intellectuals in the 1950s, and certainly not by Will Herberg, the man who made the "triple melting pot" of America's three historic faiths nearly a household term.

No religious document "worked" in more ways in the postwar era than Will Herberg's landmark 1955 study, *Protestant–Catholic–Jew*: a ringing jeremiad and national character study that virtually invented the modern sociology of religion in the United States, despite Herberg's lack of a college degree. *Protestant–Catholic–Jew* showed how the highly diverse ethnic nationalism (the term "ethnicity" was not yet widely used) of previous immigrant generations had been transmuted into a tripartite denominational scheme. Herberg argued that the "triple melting pot" model lent full legitimacy to members of the nation's two historic "minority" faiths. Herberg was a second-generation Jewish American and former communist who first encountered Reinhold Niebuhr's thought in the late 1930s, at a time when "my Marxist faith had collapsed under the shattering blows of contemporary history." Herberg was deeply moved by "the paradoxical combination of realism and radicalism that Niebuhr's 'prophetic' faith made possible" (Bingham, 1961, p. 189). After they became friends Niebuhr helped convince Herberg to deepen his Jewish faith rather than convert to Christianity. Herberg soon "thought of himself as the Jewish

Reinhold Niebuhr" (Hudnut-Beumler, 1994, p. 109); his spiritual existentialism animated *Protestant–Catholic–Jew* just as it had his earlier important study, *Judaism and Modern Man* (1951). Herberg was particularly dismayed by the facile quality of public piety and the tendency of the postwar American scene to foster "a religiousness without religion, a religiousness with almost any kind of content or none, a way of sociability or 'belonging' rather than a way of reorienting life to God" (Herberg, 1955, p. 276).

As a "national character study" *Protestant–Catholic–Jew* was a religious counterpart to such works as David Riesman's *The Lonely Crowd* (1950) and Louis Hartz's *The Liberal Tradition in America* (1955), and like them it yielded myriad readings in its function as an "event." As a jeremiad the work evoked Perry Miller's celebrated 1952 essay, "Errand into the Wilderness." Miller argued that New England Puritans in the 1660s and 1670s ritually lamented their declension from the heroic piety of the founding generation as a backhanded tribute to their own adaptation to new conditions. Like Miller, Herberg's influence nearly transcended criticism since all analyses of postwar religion had to contend with *Protestant–Catholic–Jew*. Herberg understood why the consensual, classless rhetoric of postwar interfaith harmony was a cause for celebration in many quarters. His concern that the prophetic dimension of spirituality be preserved as a source of cultural critique was a sign that religion had substantial work to perform in the place of a previous generation's secularist ideological mission. Above all, Herberg's insistence that "there is a religious revival" generated tremendous cultural authority. As Martin Marty explained, "because so many people believed that to be the case, in a way, there was" (1996, p. 293). Finally, theologian James Hudnut-Beumler observed that although *Protestant–Catholic–Jew* depended heavily on the works of earlier social scientists, the book "was original in the breadth of material it attempted to synthesize. For the average reader it talked about religion in ways that were wonderfully new and yet made perfect sense" (1994, p. 129).

American Religion After Herberg

Will Herberg's portrait of the triple melting pot was so convincing that it quickly became – and remained for decades – the central text in accounts of postwar American religion, especially as a companion guide to the suburban diaspora (Hudnut-Beumler, 1994). Martin Marty's (1996) analysis of the "centripetal tendency" of postwar religion echoed Herberg's focus on the consensual character of interreligious dialogue. At the same time, Herberg's theologically grounded critique of the Religion of the American Way of Life was ambivalent in a manner that reflected broader uneasiness among intellectuals with the legitimacy of the religious revival. As historian Eugene McCarraher has put it, Herberg "vouched for the authenticity of postwar spiritual striving," but "his undisguised contempt for the crassness of popular piety – epitomized for him in Jane Russell's image of God as 'a livin' Doll' – foreclosed any serious engagement with the desires for self-transformation and beloved community that accompanied the glitter and banality" (McCarraher, 2000, p. 107). Herberg's approach thus preserved the transcendent and critical functions of religion in a manner that intellectuals could appreciate.

Protestant–Catholic–Jew was also extremely significant for the subsequent study of religion itself in the United States at a time when divinity schools remained the primary source of authority on matters religious. Herberg's work inspired numerous empirical studies in the late 1950s and 1960s, including studies of ethnic and religious communities that tested his hypotheses and also revived the traditions of inquiry originated in Europe by Max Weber and Emile Durkheim early in the century (Lenski, 1961). Though he was an "amateur" social scientist, Herberg's influence prompted a much wider range of inquiry in the fledgling field of religious studies (Capps, 1955). Herberg's heirs focused almost exclusively on white ethnicity, neglecting, as he had, both the evangelical tradition and the vital role of the African American church.

Ironically, it was just months after the publication of *Protestant–Catholic–Jew* that Rosa Parks's refusal to move to the rear of a Montgomery bus ignited a movement grounded in the kind of prophetic spirituality Herberg found sorely lacking. Like Herberg, Martin Luther King, Jr., the young pastor of Montgomery's Dexter Avenue Baptist Church, had undergone a spiritual and intellectual conversion after reading Reinhold Niebuhr's *Moral Man and Immoral Society*. The influence of Niebuhr's neo-orthodoxy on King's thought and the role of the black church in the early days of the civil rights movement have been treated in detail by historians and biographers (Branch, 1988; Wilmore, 1998), while literature scholar Hortense J. Spillers (1998) has provided a detailed analysis of King's rhetorical indebtedness to the traditions of African American preaching.

The remarkable story of the links between civil rights figures and a virtually underground postwar network of radical communitarians – many with a spiritual orientation – is much less well known. Rosa Parks, for example, had attended a workshop on desegregation at the Highlander Folk School in eastern Tennessee in June 1955. Highlander was notorious as a rural bastion of the Popular Front, but the school's co-founder and animating spirit – Myles Horton – was yet another protégé of Reinhold Niebuhr, who lent his prestige to the fledgling school in the 1930s. In 1946 students at Highlander were taught an adaptation of a traditional Baptist hymn that became – in its incarnation as "We Shall Overcome" – the anthem of the civil rights movement. In 1956 Highlander hosted an interracial camp sponsored by Koinonia farm of Americus Georgia, an interracial Christian community led by Baptist preacher Clarence Jordan and besieged by local segregationists. Jordan's translation of the New Testament into "Cotton Patch Gospels" represented a kind of liberation theology in a southern rural idiom. In 1957 prominent Christian radical pacifists David Dellinger and Dorothy Day traveled separately to Koinonia to offer a witness of peace and justice. Shots were fired into a car carrying Day but she was unharmed (Branch, 1988; K'Meyer, 1997).

Dellinger and Day represented different if occasionally overlapping branches of the communitarian movement that was the main bridge between the 1940s and the spiritual and political radicalism of the 1960s. Dellinger was a postwar rarity: a Protestant (and former Union Seminary student) who rejected Niebuhrian irony in favor of the straightforward tradition of militant witness inspired by such figures as A. J. Muste. A founder of a Christian socialist community in Newark, Dellinger moved with his family after the war to a farm commune at Glen Gardner, New Jersey, where he also operated the Liberation Press. Glen Gardner was influenced by a tradition of Catholic Worker farm communes stretching back to the mid-1930s, not long after Day and Peter Maurin founded their movement in New York City. This model of "Christian colony," as Dellinger called it, was emulated by such figures as

Staughton and Alice Lynd, who lived at the Macedonia Cooperative community in Georgia in the mid-1950s. The Lynds shared "a common religious experience," Staughton Lynd recalled, "that different persons might use quite different words to describe" (McCarraher, 2000, p. 116). A few scholars have followed Dorothy Day's lead in applying the term "personalism" to the spiritual politics that animated the communitarians and other religious radicals of the 1950s. Personalism was a coinage of the French Catholic philosopher Emmanuel Mounier, leader of a group centered at the offices of the journal *Esprit*. Ironically, the French personalists turned sharply toward the Marxian left after the war, while American personalists eschewed sectarianism and frustrated most efforts to contain the movement within any discernible tradition (Fisher, 1989; Farrell, 1998; McCarraher, 2000).

Religious radicals established vital links in the 1950s with insurgents of the secular cultural underground. Dorothy Day, for example, shared a jail cell for a day in the late 1950s with Judith Malina after they were both arrested for protesting New York City's mandatory public air raid drill. Malina was co-founder with Julian Beck of the Living Theater, an avant-garde company with close ties to John Cage, Merce Cunningham, and other architects of what Daniel Belgrad (1998) has called the "culture of spontaneity." Postwar cultural radicals generally eschewed the "rationalist" consciousness associated with the Old Left in favor of modes associated with everything from Native American spirituality to Zen Buddhism to "Gestalt" psychology. In this constellation of forces, scholars have recently discovered, lay the seeds of both the New Left and the preoccupation with themes of "transformation" that dominated the cultural and religious landscape of the 1960s and 1970s. In the Port Huron Statement, the foundational document of Students for a Democratic Society (SDS), Tom Hayden cited the personalist language of Pope John XXIII's encyclical *Pacem in Terris*. Hayden's mentor Michael Harrington was both a veteran of the Catholic Worker movement (a plus in the minds of the young radicals) and the anticommunist sectarian left (a decided minus) (Farrell, 1998).

Historian Doug Rossinow has traced the origins of the influential Texas branch of SDS to the Christian existentialism fostered at the University Y in Austin. The "Christian Faith and Life" community in Austin also figured prominently as "one of those robust experiments in community intellectual living" that transformed students on campuses across the nation. Members of the New York Catholic Worker community were the first radicals to publicly defy the ban on draft card burning in 1965. When television viewers witnessed the assault on civil rights marchers at Selma's Edmund Pettis Bridge in March of that year, many were shocked to discover the clerical collars and nun's habits on prominent display. Yet this was really just one conspicuous demonstration of the impact of the "spiritual front," a force that had been growing since the 1940s and was the single most important link between postwar radicalism and the civil rights movement and New Left (Rossinow, 1998).

Martin Luther King experienced some of his greatest disappointment not in the South but in northern cities such as Chicago. The religious dimension of the great migration of African Americans to northern cities in the twentieth century has been treated episodically, but even less attention has been paid to the postwar period (Lincoln and Mamiya, 1990). The rise of the Nation of Islam (Lincoln, 1994) and the emergence of black liberation theology (Wilmore and Cone, 1979; Wilmore, 1989) are topics that have received some attention from scholars. A greater understanding of King's urban travail has emerged in recent works linked tangentially to the emergence of "whiteness studies." In the late 1980s and 1990s a number of American historians began to explore the "racialized" dimension of identity formation among old-stock white Americans, and especially among immigrant groups arriving from Europe in the late nineteenth and early twentieth centuries. This approach focuses less on the actual relationships between whites and blacks than on the ways in which attitudes about race shape worldviews (Jacobson, 1998).

Inspired partly by these works, a scholarly frontier has opened on the historical boundaries separating African Americans from their white urban neighbors in the postwar period, especially Catholics and Jews. In *Parish Boundaries* (1996), John McGreevy argued that Catholic parishes were configured as sacred space by their members, especially first-, second-, and third-generation European Americans. Because of the juridical authority of local bishops, parishes stayed put when Protestant and Jewish congregations moved to the suburbs under pressure from racially changing neighborhoods. The resistance of ethnic Catholics to integration won them a reputation for racism and the scorn of many third-generation Catholic reformers, who led a campaign against parish-centered spirituality in the 1960s and 1970s, viewing the urban parish as an incubator for tribalism. The central role of the parish in Catholic life was undermined for several decades but enjoyed a revival in the 1990s.

In a comparative study of Catholic and Jewish responses to urban change in postwar Boston, Gerald Gamm (1999) confirmed the validity of McGreevy's model. The religious dimension of ethnic migration more broadly construed was deftly handled by Deborah Dash Moore (1994) in her study of northern Jewish resettlement in postwar Miami and Los Angeles. Moore found that religious identity – as evidenced in membership in Hadassah and similar voluntary organizations – was heightened by the experience of uprooting from immigrant neighborhoods to the new "golden cities." This approach revised the standard view that geographical mobility tended to weaken ties to inherited religious traditions. The focus on the reconstruction of religious identity was characteristic of much scholarship in American religious studies in recent years (Moore, 1994).

The Turn to Religious Studies

The prominence of works on religious and ethnic migration since the late 1980s is attributable in large part to the extraordinary impact of Robert A. Orsi's study of Italian immigrants in East Harlem (Orsi, 1985). Though Orsi's story concludes in 1950, his account of the *festa* of Our Lady of Mt. Carmel – an enduring communal tradition – won widespread acclaim among students of contemporary religion and popularized techniques rooted in the phenomenological study of religious experience. Orsi was a product of a religious studies graduate program, like many of his contemporaries whose work blended a historical focus with attentiveness to the spiritual and theological dimensions of their topics as well. Religious studies programs began to emerge in the 1960s both at public institutions and at private universities whose divinity programs were links to these institutions' denominational origins. Though religion programs had thrived at elite private universities and liberal arts colleges between 1945 and 1965, they depended heavily on the cultural prestige associated with such figures as Reinhold Niebuhr and Paul Tillich, a German émigré theologian who popularized a variety of Christian existentialism in the postwar period. According to historian D. G. Hart, the "study of religion was linked more to the spiritual side of Protestant conceptions of higher education than to sturdier scholarly ideals" (Hart, 1999, p. 132). By the early 1960s the "sectarian" dimension of religious scholarship came under harsh attack and many religious studies programs were secularized in response. In 1964, for example, the National Association of Biblical Instructors was transformed into the American Academy of Religion, an umbrella organization encompassing a plethora of disciplinary and religious orientations.

In the early days of the post-sectarian religious studies movement, the influence of the Romanian émigré scholar Mircea Eliade of the University of Chicago was deeply felt. Eliade, a pioneer in the study of comparative religions, employed an historical method designed to uncover patterns and structures that linked disparate traditions. His work tended to inspire the kind of comparative mythology associated with such controversial if popular figures as Joseph Campbell rather than empirical historical studies. By the 1980s, however, religious studies had embraced a wider range of historically grounded approaches, making possible community studies that, like Robert Orsi's, were very deeply grounded in their social and economic contexts. Though academic historians took some time to discover this new literature, the field of religious studies produced some of the most innovative scholarship in American religious history, especially in studies devoted to the recent past.

The rise of religious studies coincided with the emergence of the women's movement, the "human potential" movement, and the "cult" scare, phenomena centered in varying ways on themes of personal transformation. The women's movement made a tremendous impact on American religion beginning in the early 1970s as well as on the ways in which religion was studied. The theologian Paul Tillich remained an extremely influential figure in religious studies circles in the 1960s. His conviction that "revelatory experiences are uniquely human" was grounded in a notion of consciousness that focused on the process of self-discovery (Capps, 1995). Similarly the cultural feminism that emerged in this same period focused on the transformation of women's consciousness and often employed explicitly religious language. The writer Vivian Gornick, for example, asserted in 1970 that a conversion to feminism was "exactly the same" as a religious conversion experience. "The excitement, the energy, the sheer voluptuous sweep of the feminist ideology is almost erotic in its power to sway me. Feminism has within it the seed of a genuine worldview," she argued (Rosen, 2000, p. 199). The theologian Mary Daly was a tremendously important figure among radical feminists. Beginning in the 1960s Daly's efforts to dismantle the rhetorical structures of a patriarchal church were emulated and adapted by many secular feminists. Daly's influence has been treated both by historians of radical feminism as well as scholars in religious studies (Echols, 1989; Campbell, 2000; Rosen, 2000). Studies of religion and gender that are historically informed are still rare, though Margaret Bendroth's work on gender and fundamentalism provides a good model (Bendroth, 1993).

The Age of Bellah and Beyond

Robert Bellah's 1967 essay, "Civil Religion in America," was the single most influential document in American religious studies since Herberg's *Protestant–Catholic–*

Jew (Bellah, 1991). Bellah's focus on the nondenominational symbols that affirmed "the religion of the American way of life" echoed Herberg's preoccupation with the consensual character of American religion. The civil discord generated by the Vietnam War, however, soon resulted in a sharp break with this tradition. By the early 1970s Bellah offered a lamentation over the "broken covenant." "Today," he concluded, "the American civil religion is an empty and broken shell" (Bellah, 1975, p. 142). In two subsequent decades Bellah and his students exerted extraordinary influence in the search to discover grounds for reassembling a genuine American community, if not a spiritual front. Bellah protégés such as Steven M. Tipton focused on communities broken and reconstituted (devotees of the self-help program EST, for example, were depicted as getting "saved" from the 1960s) (Tipton, 1982). Bellah, Tipton, and three colleagues wrote a runaway bestseller, *Habits of the Heart*, in 1985. They found that the covenant was still broken and that many Americans were content with a religion of the self (or "Sheilaism" in a famous illustration they provided of one subject's theology). The authors' willingness to restrict their study to the experience of middle-class whites only served as further evidence of the futility of a "covenant" model as a vehicle for reclaiming "common ground" for an increasingly diverse society.

Though Robert Bellah achieved prominence in American religious studies for his analysis of the forces that spiritually united the nation, his influence was most deeply felt in studies exposing the increasing diversity and fractiousness of the religious marketplace. By the 1980s the sociological approach seemed particularly well suited for evaluating the proliferation of "cults" (new religious movements) and various manifestations of the "human potential movement" and New Age spirituality. Such a relatively obscure group as the Children of God received serious scholarly attention in a study utilizing a participant-observer methodology (Van Zandt, 1991). A similar approach was employed in studies of firewalking (Danforth, 1989), Vodou (Brown, 1991), serpent handling (Kimbrough, 1995), and other "esoteric" religious practices that had received scant attention from scholars. In the 1980s sociologists David G. Bromley and Anson D. Shupe, Jr., were especially active in the effort to defuse anti-cult "hysteria" by providing balanced, comparative accounts of new religious movements (Bromley and Shupe, 1981). The violent events at Jonestown in 1978 and Waco in 1993 have received much greater attention from journalists than from historians. The People's Temple, the Branch Davidians, and other cults and new religions were finally placed in a deep historical context by Philip Jenkins in *Mystics and Messiahs* (Jenkins, 2000). The impact of leading "televangelists" of the 1980s was treated by Anson Shupe and sociologist Jeffrey K. Hadden in a study published in the wake of controversies involving Oral Roberts and Jerry Falwell and the scandal that toppled the empire of Jim and Tammy Faye Bakker (Hadden and Shupe, 1988). The authors argued that televangelists reflected a very widespread turn toward conservative Christianity, notwithstanding prominent secular critics who belittled Falwell, Pat Robertson, and other religious broadcasters as slick, latter-day Elmer Gantrys.

The Subjective Mode and the Marketplace of the Spirit

In 1988 sociologist of religion Robert Wuthnow produced a major revision of the Herberg thesis. In *The Restructuring of American Religion* Wuthnow argued that divisions within major religious denominations were more significant than differences between them, so that liberal Catholics, for example, were more akin in some ways to liberal Jews and Protestants than to conservative Catholics. Wuthnow became the dominant figure in the study of American religion in the 1990s. In *After Heaven* (1998), he proposed that Americans had shifted since the 1950s from a "spirituality of dwelling" to a "spirituality of seeking."

In the 1990s many scholars in religious studies mingled narratives of their own "seeking" with traditional forms of scholarship. Similar moves were made in other fields but there was something particularly gripping about the autobiographical turn in religious studies, especially in works on traditions conventionally viewed as outside of the religious "mainstream." Historian Randall Balmer, for example, employed a semi-autobiographical mode in his examination of the "evangelical subculture" of the United States, a search that was also documented for a PBS television series (Balmer, 1989). Harvard theologian Harvey Cox caused a stir in 1995 with the publication of a sympathetic account of Pentecostal spirituality (Cox, 1995). The author of *The Secular City* and a figure once associated with "death of God" theology, Cox offered a qualified endorsement of Pentecostalism, a tradition grounded in the belief that an individual may continue to receive effusions of the Holy Spirit after a conversion experience (Synan, 1997). Cox's change of heart was significant mainly because of his stature as a figure of the post-Protestant religious establishment. Randall Balmer – like Cox a professor at an Ivy League university – described evangelicalism as "the most influential religious and social movement in American history" (Balmer, 1999, p. 111), a view that was perhaps taken seriously for the first time by secular intellectuals in the 1990s.

At the same time, evangelical intellectuals began to openly criticize elements of their own tradition, a genre launched by historian Mark Noll in his "cri de coeur on behalf of the intellectual life," *The Scandal of the Evangelical Mind* (Noll, 1994, p. ix). The remarkable upsurge in public and scholarly attention afforded evangelicalism in the 1990s temporarily obscured the large gaps in recent historical scholarship on the tradition. There is still no full-scale interpretive study of evangelicalism in the period since the 1960s, for example. Such highly popular and influential figures as Francis Schaeffer remain unknown to many practitioners of American religious studies. Yet the lack of a "master narrative" treating evangelicalism may itself reflect the diversity of the field in the "postmodern" era. Scholars such as Belden C. Lane produced works that defied categorization by genre or tradition. In his books on sacred landscapes (1988) and mountain and desert spirituality (1998), Lane blended elements of Catholic mysticism, personal narrative (including appreciative brief accounts of his childhood experience of fundamentalism), and nature writing with traditional scholarship.

Albert J. Raboteau, a leading scholar of African American religious history, concluded a volume of reflections on that tradition with a powerful account of his own spiritual journey from a Roman Catholic youth in the segregated South to his initiation into the Christian Orthodox tradition. A collection of personal and scholarly essays by younger Catholic scholars (published initially in the journal *South Atlantic Quarterly*) helped to launch the lively field of American Catholic cultural studies in the mid-1990s (Ferraro, 1997). Working within and without a tradition viewed as deeply authoritarian if not rigidly formalistic, these authors demonstrated the wide variety of contexts in which Catholicism was adapted and interpreted by scholars in the post-Vatican II period. Though American Catholic historiography was deeply influenced by the events of the postwar period – from the celebration of consensus in the 1950s and the triumph of John F. Kennedy, to the liberal reforms of the Second Vatican Council and the ensuing disillusionment that hastened the collapse of the Catholic subculture – few studies examined the period after 1945 in depth. In addition to the work of John McGreevy cited above, important contributions were made by Patrick Allitt (1993), especially in his study of postwar conservative Catholic intellectuals. James T. Fisher (1997) explored Catholic anti-communism and popular culture as part of his study of Thomas A. Dooley, a folk hero as nonsectarian medical missionary to Southeast Asia. Robert A. Orsi's study of popular devotions to St. Jude Thaddeus (1996) reaffirmed the vitality of approaches grounded in the phenomenology of religion and methods informed by the social sciences.

In the 1990s a related field of inquiry emerged in religious studies, spurred perhaps by the robust economy and the maturation of the baby boom generation. Various market models were employed by sociologists of religion to interpret the dynamics of religious affiliation (Finke and Starke, 1992). Other scholars focused intensively on the religious behavior of Americans born between 1945 and 1965 (Roof, 1993, 1999). They found, not surprisingly, that this cohort was much more intent than the previous generation on embracing modes of religious expression tailored to their tastes and worldviews. Religious historian Colleen McDannell's study of *Material Christianity* (1995) – though only partially focused on the postwar era – showed how neatly the market for Christian merchandise mirrored broader trends in consumer culture.

The market for "spiritual" if not "religious" literature since the 1970s helped sustain numerous publishing houses, including trade firms accustomed to producing wholly secular lists. The spiritual recovery movement alone accounted for a vast chunk of the nation's popular literature market, and gurus and sages abounded. Ordinary folk also proved capable of generating fervent audiences for narratives of personal spirituality. The northern California author Anne Lamott – previously known for her works of fiction and an account of her son's early childhood years – produced a bestseller in 1999 devoted to her relatively newfound Christian faith (Lamott, 1999). Lamott worshipped with a working-class, largely African American Presbyterian congregation in Marin County, one of the countless sites of spiritual renewal that dotted the landscape at the end of the millennium.

American Religion in 2000 and Beyond

The habit of baby boomers and younger Americans to construct their spiritual identities from an eclectic mix of world religious traditions was only partly linked to a phenomenon that was often overlooked until the final years of the twentieth century. A reform of the nation's immigration policies in 1965 resulted in a dramatic upsurge in new arrivals from Asia and other underrepresented parts of the world. While roughly half of these newcomers were Christians (with Filipinos making up the largest Catholic group and Koreans the Protestant), many belonged to traditions that had not previously been well known in the United States. In the late 1990s an estimated 650,000 Americans of Indian descent practiced Hinduism, while 500,000 to 750,000 immigrants and their children from Laos, Cambodia, Thailand, Sri Lanka, and Myanmar (Burma) followed the traditions of Theravada Buddhism. Buddhism had been practiced in the United States since the nineteenth century by Chinese and Japanese Americans as well as by European Americans drawn to the contemplative traditions of Asian religions. Some Buddhist temples "house parallel congregations of Asian immigrant Buddhists and American-born practitioners drawn to Buddhism's philosophy and meditation practice" (Eck, 2001, p. 17). Though the early history of Buddhism in America has been treated in detail (Fields, 1981; Tweed and Prothero, 1999), the religious history of the post-1965 Asian immigrants of all religious traditions has yet to be written. Their experience confirms the observation of Thomas A. Tweed that "after the 1960s diversity had become not just one feature of the American religious landscape; it was the major one" (Tweed and Prothero, 1999, p. 9).

By the year 2000 American Muslims were more numerous than members of the Episcopal and Presbyterian churches. This extraordinarily diverse community was similar in size to the American Jewish community (roughly 6 million strong). American Muslims ranged from African Americans with deep roots in the United States to recent immigrants from Middle Eastern nations and a growing number of European American converts. Of the nearly 1,500 mosques found in the United States, more than 1,200 had been established during the past twenty-five years. The sudden and visible emergence of Muslim, Buddhist, and Hindu communities was unsettling to those who were certain that America was preordained as a Christian nation. Violent if isolated attacks on Hindu and Muslim temples recalled the "nativist" era of the mid-nineteenth century – when Catholic churches and converts were often besieged – with racial hostility added to the volatile mix. Members of non-European religious traditions also confronted state and local ordinances that were not designed with diversity of religious practice in mind. In 1994, for example, a Minnesota Muslim woman was arrested in the Mall of America for wearing a *hijab*, a scarf that partially obscured her face. A local law banned the wearing of "disguises." Similar issues involving religious freedom for unfamiliar practices were increasingly negotiated in courts, city councils, and zoning boards (Eck, 2001).

These and other conflicts involving members of non-Western religious communities did not attract much national attention at a time when controversies over "religion and politics" tended to focus on such longstanding issues as abortion and prayer in public schools. Those Americans who continued to insist that there was no place for religion in politics overlooked the experience of four centuries, which saw religious convictions shape political discourse in myriad and ever-changing ways. In the 1960s and 1970s conservatives charged that the "wall of separation" between church and state had grown higher than the nation's founder intended. By the 1990s some prominent liberals agreed (Carter, 1993). As fears of the political clout of the "religious right" abated somewhat toward the end of the decade, politicians of all persuasions and other public citizens began to speak openly of the relationship between their faith and their values (Dionne, Jr., and DiIulio, Jr., 2000).

In February 2001 President George W. Bush named University of Pennsylvania political scientist John J. DiIulio head of the newly created White House Office of Faith-Based and Community Initiatives. The president hoped that the program could find ways to provide public funding for successful projects that were grounded in religious and voluntary organizations and treated poverty, addiction, homelessness, and other social ills. Civil libertarians raised concerns over the constitutionality of the program while it was still in the planning stages, while some church leaders warned that government funding of faith-based programs might compromise religious freedom. DiIulio resigned his position in August 2001, frustrated by political and theological wrangling over numerous issues, including the criteria by which an organization might be deemed "faith-based." The fledgling program continued to arouse vigorous and well-informed debate in the Congress and the public arena, evidence of the ongoing influence of religious conviction in the life of the nation.

REFERENCES

Ahlstrom, Sydney E.: *A Religious History of the American People*, 2 vols. Vol. 2 (Garden City, NY: Image Books, 1975).

Allitt, Patrick: *Catholic Intellectuals and Conservative Politics in America, 1950–1985* (Ithaca, NY: Cornell University Press, 1993).

Ausmus, Harry J.: *Will Herberg: From Right to Right* (Chapel Hill: University of North Carolina Press, 1987).

Balmer, Randall: *Mine Eyes Have Seen the Glory: A Journey into the Evangelical Subculture in America* (New York: Oxford University Press, 1989).

Balmer, Randall: *Blessed Assurance: A History of Evangelicalism in America* (Boston: Beacon Press, 1999).

Belgrad, Daniel: *The Culture of Spontaneity: Improvisation and the Arts in Postwar America* (Chicago: University of Chicago Press, 1998).

Bellah, Robert: *The Broken Covenant: American Civil Religion in a Time of Trial* (New York: Seabury Press, 1975).

Bellah, Robert: "Civil Religion in America" (1967), in *Beyond Belief: Essays on Religion in a Post-Traditionalist World* (Berkeley: University of California Press, 1991), 168–89.

Bellah, Robert N. and Greenspahn, Frederic E., eds.: *Uncivil Religion: Interreligious Hostility in America* (New York: Crossroad, 1987).

Bellah, Robert, Madsen, Richard, Sullivan, William B., Swidler, Ann, and Tipton, Steven M.: *Habits of the Heart: Individualism and Commitment in American Life* (New York: Harper and Row, 1985).

Bendroth, Margaret Lamberts: *Fundamentalism and Gender, 1875 to the Present* (New Haven, Conn.: Yale University Press, 1993).

Bingham, June: *Courage to Change: An Introduction to the Life and Thought of Reinhold Niebuhr* (New York: Charles Scribner's Sons, 1961).

Boyer, Paul: *When Time Shall Be No More: Prophecy Belief in Modern American Culture* (Cambridge, Mass.: Harvard University Press, 1992).

Branch, Taylor: *Parting the Waters: America in the King Years, 1954–63* (New York: Simon and Schuster, 1988).

Bromley, David G. and Shupe, Jr., Anson D.: *Strange Gods: The Great American Cult Scare* (Boston: Beacon Press, 1981).

Brown, Kathleen McCarthy: *Mama Lola: A Vodou Priestess in Brooklyn* (Berkeley: University of California Press, 1991).

Campbell, Debra: "Be-ing is Be/Leaving," in Marilyn Frye and Sarah Lucia Hoagland (eds.), *Feminist Interpretations of Mary Daly* (University Park: Pennsylvania State University Press, 2000), 164–93.

Capps, Walter H.: *Religious Studies: The Making of a Discipline* (Minneapolis: Fortress Press, 1995).

Carpenter, Joel: *Revive Us Again: The Reawakening of American Fundamentalism* (New York: Oxford University Press, 1997).

Carter, Stephen L.: *The Culture of Disbelief: How American Law and Politics Trivialize Religious Devotion* (New York: Basic Books, 1993).

Cox, Harvey: *Fire from Heaven: The Rise of Pentecostal Spirituality and the Reshaping of Religion in the Twenty-First Century* (Reading, Mass.: Addison Wesley, 1995).

Cuddihy, John Murray: *No Offense: Civil Religion and Protestant Taste* (New York: Seabury Press, 1978).

Danforth, Loring M.: *Firewalking and Religious Healing: The Anastenaria of Greece and the American Firewalking Movement* (Princeton, NJ: Princeton University Press, 1989).

Dionne, Jr., E. J. and DiIulio, Jr., John J.: *What's God Got to Do With the American Experiment?* (Washington, DC: Brookings Institution, 2000).

Echols, Alice: *Daring to Be Bad: Radical Feminism in America, 1967–1975* (Minneapolis: University of Minnesota Press, 1989).

Eck, Diana L.: *A New Religious America: How a "Christian Country" Has Now Become the World's Most Religiously Diverse Nation* (San Francisco: HarperSanFrancisco, 2001).

"Faith for a Lenten Age," *Time* (March 8, 1948): 70–9.

Farrell, James J.: *The Spirit of the Sixties: The Making of Postwar Radicalism* (New York: Routledge, 1998).

Ferraro, Thomas J., ed.: *Catholic Lives/Contemporary America* (Durham, NC: Duke University Press, 1997).

Fields, Rick: *How the Swans Came to the Lake: A Narrative History of Buddhism in America* (Boulder, Colo.: Shambhala Publications, 1981).

Finke, Roger and Stark, Rodney: *The Churching of America, 1776–1990: Winners and Losers in Our Religious Economy* (New Brunswick, NJ: Rutgers University Press, 1992).

Fisher, James T.: *The Catholic Counterculture in America, 1933–1962* (Chapel Hill: University of North Carolina Press, 1989).

Fisher, James T.: *Dr. America: The Lives of Thomas A. Dooley* (Amherst, Mass.: University of Massachusetts Press, 1997).

Fox, Richard: *Reinhold Niebuhr: A Biography* (New York: Pantheon, 1985).

Fox, Richard: "Experience and Explanation in Twentieth-Century American Religious History," in Harry S. Stout and D. G. Hart (eds.), *New Directions in American Religious History* (New York: Oxford University Press, 1997), 394–416.

Gamm, Gerald: *Urban Exodus: Why the Jews Left Boston and the Catholics Stayed* (Cambridge, Mass.: Harvard University Press, 1999).

George, Carol V. R.: *God's Salesman: Norman Vincent Peale and the Power of Positive Thinking* (New York: Oxford University Press, 1993).

Graham, Billy: *Peace With God* (New York: Pocket Books, 1953).

Hadden, Jeffrey K. and Shupe, Anson: *Televangelism: Power and Politics on God's Frontier* (New York: Henry Holt, 1988).

Hart, D. G.: *The University Gets Religion: Religious Studies in American Higher Education* (Baltimore: Johns Hopkins University Press, 1999).

Herberg, Will: *Protestant–Catholic–Jew: An Essay in American Religious Sociology* (Garden City, NY: Doubleday, 1955).

Hudnut-Beumler, James: *Looking for God in the Suburbs: The Religion of the American Dream and Its Critics, 1945–1965* (New Brunswick, NJ: Rutgers University Press, 1994).

Jacobson, Matthew Frye: *Whiteness of a Different Color: European Immigrants and the Alchemy of Race* (Cambridge, Mass.: Harvard University Press, 1998).

Jenkins, Philip: *Mystics and Messiahs: Cults and New Religions in American History* (New York: Oxford University Press, 2000).

K'Meyer, Tracy Elaine: *Interracialism and Christian Community in the Postwar South* (Charlottesville: University Press of Virginia, 1997).

Kimbrough, David L.: *Taking Up Serpents: Snake Handlers of Eastern Kentucky* (Chapel Hill: University of North Carolina Press, 1995).

Lamott, Anne: *Traveling Mercies: Some Thoughts on Faith* (New York: Pantheon, 1999).

Lane, Belden C.: *Landscapes of the Sacred: Geography and Narrative in American Spirituality* (Mahwah, NJ: Paulist Press, 1988).

Lane, Belden C.: *The Solace of Fierce Landscapes: Exploring Desert and Mountain Spirituality* (New York: Oxford University Press, 1998).

Lenski, Gerhard: *The Religious Factor: A Sociological Study of Religion's Impact on Politics, Economics and Family Life* (Garden City, NY: Doubleday, 1961).

Liebman, Joshua Loth: *Peace of Mind* (New York: Simon and Schuster, 1946).

Lincoln, C. Eric: *The Black Muslims in America* (Trenton, NJ: Africa World Press, 1994).

Lincoln, C. Eric and Mamiya, Lawrence H., eds.: *The Black Church in the African-American Experience* (Durham, NC: Duke University Press, 1990).

McCarraher, Eugene: *Christian Critics: Religion and the Impasse in Modern Social Thought* (Ithaca, NY: Cornell University Press, 2000).

McDannell, Colleen: *Material Christianity: Religion and Popular Culture in America* (New Haven, Conn.: Yale University Press, 1995).

McGreevy, John T.: *Parish Boundaries: The Catholic Encounter with Race in the Twentieth-Century Urban North* (Chicago: University of Chicago Press, 1996).

Marsden, George: *Reforming Fundamentalism: Fuller Seminary and the New Evangelicalism* (Grand Rapids, Mich.: William B. Eerdmans, 1987).

Martin, William: *The Billy Graham Story: A Prophet with Honor* (London: Hutchinson, 1992).

Marty, Martin E.: *Modern American Religion*, 3 vols. Vol. 3: *Under God, Indivisible* (Chicago: University of Chicago Press, 1996).

Massa, Mark S.: *Catholics and American Culture: Fulton Sheen, Dorothy Day and the Notre Dame Football Team* (New York: Crossroad, 1999).

Merton, Thomas: *The Seven Storey Mountain* (New York: Harcourt Brace, 1948).

Meyer, Donald B.: *The Positive Thinkers: Religion as Pop Psychology, from Mary Baker Eddy to Oral Roberts* (New York: Pantheon Books, 1980).

Miller, Douglas T. and Nowak, Marion: *The Fifties: The Way We Really Were* (Garden City, NY: Doubleday, 1977).

Moore, Deborah Dash: *To the Golden Cities: Pursuing the American Jewish Dream in Miami and L.A.* (New York: Free Press, 1994).

Moore, R. Laurence: *Selling God: American Religion in the Marketplace of Culture* (New York: Oxford University Press, 1994).

Morantz, Regina Markell: "The Scientist as Sex Crusader: Alfred C. Kinsey and American Culture," *American Quarterly*, 24 (Winter 1977): 563–89.

Mott, Michael: *The Seven Mountains of Thomas Merton* (Boston: Houghton Mifflin, 1984).

Noll, Mark A.: *The Scandal of the Evangelical Mind* (Grand Rapids, Mich.: W. B. Eerdmans, 1994).

Orsi, Robert A.: *The Madonna of 115th Street: Faith and Community in Italian Harlem, 1880–1950* (New Haven, Conn.: Yale University Press, 1985).

Orsi, Robert A.: *Thank You, St. Jude: Women's Devotion to the Patron Saint of Hopeless Causes* (New Haven, Conn.: Yale University Press, 1996).

Raboteau, Albert J.: *A Fire in the Bones: Reflections on African-American Religious History* (Boston: Beacon Press, 1995).

Roof, Wade Clark: *A Generation of Seekers: The Spiritual Journeys of the Baby Boom Generation* (San Francisco: Harper SanFrancisco, 1993).

Roof, Wade Clark: *Spiritual Marketplace: Baby Boomers and the Remaking of American Religion* (Princeton, NJ: Princeton University Press, 1999).

Roof, Wade Clark and McKinney, William: *American Mainline Religion* (New Brunswick, NJ: Rutgers University Press, 1987).

Rosen, Ruth: *The World Split Open: How the Modern Women's Movement Changed America* (New York: Viking, 2000).

Rossinow, Doug: *The Politics of Authenticity: Liberalism, Christianity, and the New Left in America* (New York: Columbia University Press, 1998).

Sheen, Fulton J.: *Peace of Soul* (Garden City, NY: Doubleday, 1948).

Silk, Mark: *Spiritual Politics: Religion and America Since World War II* (New York: Simon and Schuster, 1988).

Sittser, Gerald L.: *A Cautious Patriotism: The American Churches and the Second World War* (Chapel Hill: University of North Carolina Press, 1997).

Spillers, Hortense J.: "Martin Luther King and the Style of the Black Sermon," in Jon Butler and Harry S. Stout (eds.), *Religion in American History: A Reader* (New York: Oxford University Press, 1998), 469–85.

Synan, Vinson: *The Holiness-Pentecostal Tradition: Charismatic Movements in the Twentieth Century* (Grand Rapids, Mich: William B. Eerdmans, 1997).

Tipton, Steven M.: *Getting Saved from the Sixties: Moral Meaning in Conversion and Cultural Change* (Berkeley: University of California Press, 1982).

Tweed, Thomas A. and Prothero, Stephen: *Asian Religions in America: A Documentary History* (New York: Oxford University Press, 1999).

Van Zandt, David E.: *Living in the Children of God* (Princeton, NJ: Princeton University Press, 1991).

Wilmore, Gayraud S., ed.: *African American Religious Studies: An Interdisciplinary Anthology* (Durham, NC: Duke University Press, 1989).

Wilmore, Gayraud S. and Cone, James H., eds.: *Black Theology: A Documentary History, 1966–1979* (Maryknoll, NY: Orbis Books, 1979).

Wuthnow, Robert: *The Restructuring of American Religion: Society and Faith Since World War II* (Princeton, NJ: Princeton University Press, 1988).

Wuthnow, Robert: *After Heaven: Spirituality in America Since the 1950s* (Berkeley: University of California Press, 1998).

FURTHER READING

Burrow, Jr., Rufus: *James H. Cone and Black Liberation Theology* (Jefferson, NC: McFarland, 1994).

Davidman, Lynn: *Tradition in a Rootless World: Women Turn to Orthodox Judaism* (Berkeley: University of California Press, 1991).

Ellwood, Robert: *The Sixties Spiritual Awakening: American Religion Moving from Modern to Postmodern* (New Brunswick, NJ: Rutgers University Press, 1994).

Ellwood, Robert: *The Fifties Spiritual Marketplace: American Religion in a Decade of Conflict* (New Brunswick, NJ: Rutgers University Press, 1997).

Ellwood, Robert: *1950: Crossroads of American Religious Life* (Louisville, Ky.: Westminster John Knox Press, 2000).

Friedland, Michael: *Lift Up Your Voice Like a Trumpet: White Clergy and the Civil Rights and Antiwar Movements, 1954–1973* (Chapel Hill: University of North Carolina Press, 1998).

Fulop, Timothy E. and Raboteau, Albert J., eds.: *African-American Religion: Interpretive Essays in History and Culture* (New York: Routledge, 1997).

Keller, Rosemary Skinner and Ruether, Rosemary Radford, eds.: *Women and Religion in America: A Documentary History*, 3 vols. Vol. 3: *1900–1968* (San Francisco: Harper and Row, 1990).

Keller, Rosemary Skinner and Ruether, Rosemary Radford, eds.: *In Our Own Voices: Four Centuries of American Women's Religious Writing* (San Francisco: HarperSanFrancisco, 1995).

Marsden, George, ed.: *Evangelicalism and Modern America* (Grand Rapids, Mich.: William B. Eerdmans, 1984).

Morris, Charles R.: *American Catholic: The Saints and Sinners Who Built America's Most Powerful Church* (New York: Times Books, 1997).

Polner, Murray and O'Grady, Jim: *Disarmed and Dangerous: The Radical Lives and Times of Daniel and Philip Berrigan* (New York: Basic Books, 1998).

Tweed, Thomas A.: *Our Lady of the Exile: Diasporic Religion at a Cuban Catholic Shrine in Miami* (New York: Oxford University Press, 1997).

Wilmore, Gayraud S.: *Black Religion and Black Radicalism: An Interpretation of the Religious History of African Americans* (Maryknoll, NY: Orbis Books, 1998).

CHAPTER FOUR

Time Out: Leisure and Tourism

SUSAN G. DAVIS

The scholar who ventures into a historiography of late twentieth-century leisure and tourism must first acknowledge how work on earlier periods shapes the questions being asked today. At the same time, he or she must notice the relative scarcity of historical work on the years since World War II. More than two decades of creative historical work have given these different but related dimensions of culture a history, yet most of the major problems for the history of postwar leisure and tourism have been defined by scholars who have worked on the nineteenth and early twentieth centuries. Post-World War II leisure and tourism are relatively new historical subjects. The historian researching the way Americans have learned to play will have to travel outside his or her home discipline into the interpretive and ethnographic social sciences.

In this essay I want to highlight three major developments. The first is the discovery of leisure time and recreation themselves as topics with rich implications for historians. Related to this is the discovery of leisure as a social problem in the postwar period, and the shifting ways social observers and scholars have examined it. Over the past fifty years, scholars have moved away from seeing leisure as a question of too much time needing to be morally and meaningfully filled, that is, an overabundance, to uncovering a shortage of time and leisure. A second issue is that in each stance there is a concern with leisure's relationship to commerce and the mass media (see chapter 5 by Susan Douglas in this volume). The location of leisure in the critique of mass culture is a much more complex topic than I can treat in one essay, but it inflects nearly all discussions of free time in the late twentieth century. A third topic synthesizes the first two: the scholarly discovery of tourism as a commercially organized way of using free time, and the elaboration of ways to study a cultural practice that has quickly become a major international industry.

What John Clarke (in Butsch, 1990) has called the populist–pessimist divide in the approach to commercial popular culture applies to leisure and tourism: how much do people control the resource of leisure, and to what extent can they turn the mass industry of tourism to their own uses in the twenty-first century?

According to the pessimistic approach, tourism perfectly exemplifies mass commercial recreation. It is the most highly rationalized, corporate-dominated, alienated form of leisure in a thoroughly commodified world. From the populist vantage, tourism exemplifies choiceful play and cross-cultural meaning-making in a postmodern, postnational world. These conflicting attitudes toward commercial leisure deeply inflect the ways scholars write about late twentieth-century tourism.

In the last four decades, scholars have recognized with great enthusiasm that leisure is more than just fun. An important component of the experience of all human beings, leisure is a physical resource, a time for rest and recuperation from work, but it is also a social and cultural medium – a temporal structure that people turn to varied uses, from play to self-education and political organizing. Leisure is a cultural space that people can fill with activities that collectively transmit shared meanings, history, and memory. But social historians have discovered that as labor processes and working hours have histories, so too do free time and recreation. Along with ethnographers, they have investigated phenomena as disparate as the history of baseball, hobbies, automobile clubs, television soap operas, fan clubs, nightlife, and theme parks, to give only a few examples (Butsch, 1990; Gelber, 1999).

Taking modern leisure and recreation seriously originates in recent work on the eighteenth, nineteenth, and early twentieth centuries. The groundbreaking work of Edward P. Thompson (1963) and Herbert Gutman (1976) focused attention on the difficulty of separating labor and leisure for most of human history. For example, the American artisans Gutman wrote about read aloud, ate, drank, sang, told stories, and discussed politics while they worked in small shops. The industrial revolutions and wage labor, Gutman and Thompson pointed out (following Marx), were assaults on older ways of using time on the job. In *Labor and Monopoly Capitalism* (1974), sociologist Harry Braverman studied the theory and effects of scientific management or "Taylorism," spurring historians to look at the effects of the attempt to sever labor from the rest of life in the early twentieth century. These studies provoked interest in what laboring men and women did in their time off the job. Roy Rosenzweig, for example, pioneered exploration of the ways Americans fought for and organized free time under wage labor (Rosenzweig, 1983).

Labor historians have been particularly interested in workers' fights to shorten the working day and build free-time activities of their own choosing (Rosenzweig, 1983; Hunnicutt, 1988; Roediger and Foner, 1989). Cross (1993) has unpacked American and European intellectual disputes over the meaning of leisure and the cultural effects of the tradeoff of time for money, debates which continued until mid-century in the United States, and persist today in more heavily unionized Europe.

A basic question about the postwar period is the shape and definition of American leisure time. Has leisure been scarce or abundant? Historians agree that hours of work fell dramatically in the first half of the twentieth century. Persistent political agitation resulted in the eight-hour workday, the forty-hour workweek (encoded for many workers in the Fair Labor Standards Act of 1938), and the two-day weekend. Although working hours were unequal across sectors, they hit historical lows immediately after the war, in some industries reaching a thirty-five-hour week. Hours soon began to rise after 1946. Unionized workers, affected by massive unemployment during the Depression, often chose steady work and high wages over time for recreation or education. Contracts increasingly specified holidays, extra pay for weekend and overtime work, and the first paid vacations for the working class, rather than shorter days or weeks. (Vacations had been invented by the professional middle class by the turn of the twentieth century; see Aron, 1998.) Thus began the typical American pattern of distributing leisure in "lumps," rather than spreading free time out more evenly. This leisure was only for the unionized, and it was scant compared to the short workweeks and long vacations achieved in Europe. Federal intervention and McCarthyism stalled the growth of free time. The Taft-Hartley Act, for example, limited union organizing, the closed shop, and regulated strike actions in favor of employers. The forty-hour week became the minimum below which nothing could be imagined, rather than a benchmark of progress toward more autonomous time (Roediger and Foner, 1989; Cross, 1993). Meanwhile, vacations became a common expectation across the population.

Whereas the postwar critics of mass culture worried about whether leisure would be wholesome, in the context of the 1980s and 1990s the questions were: who has leisure, and how is free time distributed across the population? Do the majority have enough time for life outside work? Since the middle 1970s, the upward creep of hours has had less to do with industrial growth than with inflation and economic stagnation. As deindustrialization and, later, the North American Free Trade Agreement (NAFTA) dismantled older industrial sectors of the American economy, high-paying, unionized, and traditionally male blue-collar jobs became scarce (Bluestone and Harrison, 1982). Women, especially women with young children, moved into the paid workforce in record numbers, often to help the family make ends meet. Low-paying, nonunionized service jobs, and part-time, seasonal jobs increased dramatically after the 1970s as employers looked for ways to cut the costs of health, unemployment, and retirement benefits.

Among the impressive features of the last thirty years are increases not only in unemployment and poverty in the United States (despite declines in official federal unemployment counts), but also in the number of employed Americans holding down more than one job (Miringoff and Miringoff, 1999). Blue- and white-collar workers alike are working longer days, for wages that have stagnated or fallen since the middle 1970s. Working-class Americans, especially women, are also laboring for longer parts of their lives, and women's hours of work have grown more quickly than those of men. Wages have risen mainly for the professional and technical classes, and among high-level managers (Roediger and Foner, 1989; Robinson and Godbey, 1997), and it is only some of these workers who can realize the widespread dream of early retirement.

Economist Juliet Schor (1991) argues that Americans are working more hours per week, and more weeks per year than at any time since World War II, as much as an extra month of forty-hour weeks per year. Sociologist Arlie Hochschild (1989) underscores the gendered dimension of overwork that she calls "the second shift." Although jobs give women important autonomy and power, because they have added new hours of paid work to unpaid housework, childcare, eldercare, and community participation, women carry the heaviest burden of hours. The suburbs, with their dispersed, automobile-based chores and long drives to work, and the reduction of social support services for families and children (such as low-cost day care, recreation centers, and afterschool care) have added new time and financial pressures, to the great disadvantage of the social fabric of the United States and the lives of children (Schor, 1991; Hochschild, 1989).

Although Schor's findings have been contested on methodological grounds (for example, by Robinson and Godbey, 1997), the preponderance of evidence seems to uphold her view that at century's end, Americans were working longer than the citizens of any other advanced, industrialized country. Postwar Americans, including teenagers and retirees, have increased their labor force participation since the 1970s.

Yet it appears to make more sense to talk about multiple polarizations in work and leisure than to speak of an average American workweek or an average number of working hours. The childless and the retired wealthy may have a great deal of free time (Robinson and Godbey, 1997; Scott, 1999). Early retirement, an important trend in the 1980s and 1990s, is likely to be voluntary for the wealthy, but "leisure" seems a misnomer for the free time of the involuntarily retired, the laid-off, and the unemployed, disabled, or ill. Much of the rest of the population, and especially those with young children, are overworked. Some of the best paid, a relatively small proportion of the professional and technical class, may work the most. But, Hochschild points out, these professionals are able to "outsource" everyday chores (such as chauffeuring, caring for children, preparing meals, and laundry). They purchase frequent, expensive, and intensive bouts of leisure, prominently from the travel and tourism industries.

The question of what is done with the time that is available for leisure brings us to the pleasures and problems of mass culture. The history of the commercialization of leisure over the last one hundred years traces the intensified commodification of what had previously been either free, or provided by small businesses (Butsch, 1990). By the end of the twentieth century, multinational industries had commercialized much of leisure and people purchased a wide variety of recreations. For this same century, public intellectuals fought over whether commercial cultural forms were worthwhile, moral, or safe. This question was sparked by the collision of struggles for free time with the culture industries that grew up with the twentieth century's mass industrial employment. America's first culture industries, the nickelodeons, movies, dance halls, amusement parks, dime museums, and professional sporting events, all were built on the new wages and freed time of young, urban, industrial workers (Ewen and Ewen, 1982; Nasaw, 1993). Some of the early versions of the arguments over mass leisure expressed deeply antagonistic attitudes toward culture that appealed to workers and youth (Ewen, 1985; Peiss, 1985; D. Schiller, 1996). Some contemporary polemics, most notably those over rock and rap music, continue the same tendency today (Rose, 1994; Kelley, 1997).

Post-World War II debates over mass-produced commercial culture need to be seen in part as arguments about the value of leisure in a society that intellectuals predicted would only become more affluent (Rosenberg and White, 1957; Larrabee and Myerson, 1958). Mass culture, by definition, emanated from a profit-driven center. From comic books to rock and roll, it was seen as degrading of consumers, partly because it threatened the moral authority of "high" culture and partly because it displaced more intellectually sound and challenging activities. It mattered to liberals, conservatives, and a few radicals that the commercial products were increasingly aimed at youth. As James Gilbert (1986) has shown, initial postwar affluence, more time, and young peoples' fads and fashions refocused the mass culture debate into panics about juvenile delinquency, recycling older worries about cultural control. The argument continues today in alarms over the dangers of children's entertainment, for example, violent videogames. The mass culture debates among intellectuals, the problem of women's and youth's relationship to commercial recreation, the introduction of new entertainment technologies and genres, the reinvention by ethnic minorities of their own leisure and art forms, all have attracted historians' attention.

If the public commentaries on leisure have remained hostile, in general, the dominant scholarly assessment has shifted from pessimistic to positive. Some analyses of the postwar period see workers' loss of control in the workplace as redeemed by the pleasures and potentially anti-hegemonic meanings found in mass culture. George Lipsitz, notably, writes about the displacement of workers' struggles for justice and autonomy from the workplace, and their reassertion in the realm of popular culture, especially music (Lipsitz, 1990, 1994). But a more negative view persists, insisting that loss of control over work processes and time is part of a fifty-year trajectory of the weakening of popular democracy. An intensifying commercialization recognizes little outside itself, and straps consumers more tightly into the harness of getting and spending. In this view, leisure becomes as alienated as labor (Marcuse, 1964; H. Schiller, 1973; Schor, 1991; Cross, 2000). In a half-century in which stark inequalities of wealth reemerged, who can afford what kind of leisure? How much space is there for free or noncommercial leisure?

By contrast to the flowering of studies of leisure activities, there have been few studies of the postwar problem of workers' rights to time itself. Perhaps this is because later twentieth-century developments such as deindustrialization have forced discussions of workplace issues back nearly one hundred years, to questions of wages, health and safety, the right to organize, and the right to strike. The early twentieth-century free-time debate differs from its current incarnation because today, people tend to ask questions about time in terms of what private individuals can do to find more time (share the housework? telecommute?), rather than what collective and political solutions would allow for real leisure.

Tourism, an industry rather than a social movement, organizes free time in order to capitalize on it. Studied as both leisure and as mass culture, tourism engages questions of the cultural definitions and uses of time, especially modernity's bifurcation of work and play (Lofgren, 1999). Travel remains a central expression of the promise of affluence for the US working and middle classes; tourism succeeds by offering this formerly upper-class luxury on a mass basis.

Tourism's boosters and critics claim that it is the largest industry in the world (A. Wilson, 1992). It does not produce leisure but industrializes it, churning out experiences and things at the same time – memorable visions, new sights, relaxation, but also hotels, theme parks, cruise ships, low-wage jobs, and an endless array of photos and souvenirs. Late twentieth-century tourism has been studied most often as a structure of sensations. Sociologists have focused on its postmodern play of surfaces and spectacles (Urry, 1990), but neglected the ways the industry reworks cities, ways of life, and economies. One exception is the work of Susan G. Davis, which provides a careful study of the corporate production of tourist experiences in one theme park, connecting political and economic rationales to performances and landscapes (Davis, 1996, 1997).

Historian Daniel Boorstin gave tourism its first modern scholarly notice in *The Image: A Guide to Pseudo-Events in America* (1961), where he described what he saw as the increasingly superficial nature of America's reality. Boorstin distinguished between the tourist, a consumer of manufactured realities, and the traveler, whose experiences were thoughtful, independent, and real. He wrote his critique just as vacations, tours, expanded transport, and a resort building boom made travel, formerly an elite practice, available to many more Americans.

A more sophisticated account appeared at about the same time: Earl Pomeroy's *In Search of the Golden West: The Tourist in Western America* (1957). As a western historian, Pomeroy noticed how deeply the settlement of the far West was intertwined with real estate boosterism and travel promotion. Pomeroy's work stands today as one of the most creative discussions of tourism because he refused to separate the developing leisure industries from empire building. Just as railroads depended on the shipments of agricultural goods, they also needed pleasure travelers, and they helped design sites for travelers to visit. Pomeroy also emphasized the role of mass media – magazines, newspaper accounts, guidebooks, and posters – in building both settlement and markets for travel. Current work on tourism in the West (most of it on the pre-1946 years) follows Pomeroy's lead, underlining how the attraction business has shaped the western landscape (Weigle, 1992; Rothman, 1998).

Historians of postwar tourism must also draw on the work of anthropologists, folklorists, geographers, sociologists, postmodern theorists, museum studies scholars, and writers of regional cultural criticism. Most interdisciplinary work has taken off from the claims staked by sociologist Dean MacCannell. In *The Tourist: A Theory of the New Leisure Class* (1976), MacCannell argued that tourism is a ritual structure revealing the deepest premises of modern life, concepts so central they may be called sacred. MacCannell traced a round of obligatory sites and the ways in which they are constructed, authenticated, and paid homage, in order that people may fully partake of modern citizenship. An example of this is the belief that we cannot truly be American families without visiting Disneyland, a view that the most recent immigrants share.

MacCannell helped interest cultural historians in tracing the construction of regional and nationalist meanings through the invention and promotion of attractions. America's sacred places, the places with historical, literary, patriotic, or religious resonances, were actively developed from early in the nineteenth century (Sears, 1989; Brown, 1995). Niagara Falls, Yellowstone, and Yosemite are celebrated examples. The origins of summer resorts and vacation customs for the wealthy and, later, the middle class also run deep in the nineteenth century (Belasco, 1979; Aron, 1998). But like leisure, tourism has been better studied for this earlier period.

Sociological, anthropological, and literary theorists have generally explored tourism as a process of the collective encoding and decoding of cultural meanings (Culler, 1992); more recently, tourism is seen as an unfolding of multinational contact that causes cultural change. Many anthropologists approach tourism as a process of cultural negotiation, stressing the face-to-face interactions of visitors and performers in, for example, a cultural festival or a guided tour. Yet the colonial and national ideological structures in tourism are seen as enduring (Pratt, 1992, García Canclini, 1995).

Tourism has a complex obligation to the authentic and to the process of constructing national cultural identity. Inventing and laying down really-real roots and "heritage" for an inherently unstable society is one of tourism's key jobs (MacCannell, 1992; Lowenthal, 1997; Kirshenblatt-Gimblett, 1998). Many tourist attractions depend on authentication of specimens of other cultures that are familiar to but different from our "modern" world, and so define it. Yet authenticity is a paradox, as tourists in search of the really real sometimes wind up in a "hyperreality," a world where tourism has bled out into everything else, where everyday life mimics the spectacular attraction, rather than the other way around (Debord, 1970; Eco, 1986; Baudrillard, 1988).

This better-than-real reality is now mass-produced and mass-distributed through the theme park. Since the opening of Disneyland in 1956, large numbers of Americans (by some estimates, the entire population) have been able to explore destinations that have been carefully constructed to deliver familiar surprises on a predictable, routinized, and carefully test-marketed basis (Fjellman, 1992; Davis, 1997). The theme park, some critics argue, is now a model for American cities and towns, and the safe, conflict-free theme park has become a social ideal. The corporate rebuilding of Times Square in Manhattan is held up as the prime example (Sorkin, 1992; Hannigan, 1998). But this process of producing safe realities takes place in the former colonies and poorer fringes of the United States as much as in Orlando and New York. Tourism scholars have noted that, in a typical twist, standardized realities give rise to more urgent searches for authenticity – in, for example, ecotourism and adventure tourism. As the track becomes more beaten, tourists demand to be further "off the beaten track."

Although there has been plenty of work on tourism as a meaning-making or meaning-decoding process, there has been less attention to the ways in which meanings are selected and built into tourist attractions (for exceptions, see Davis, 1997; Handler and Gable, 1997). Here historians have a point of entry and special skills. They ask how we can assess tourism's obsession with turning the past into an attraction, and arrive at a critical definition of authenticity. Historians should inquire into what happens to our research-based knowledge about the past, as it is worked into museums and living history displays, and especially into theme parks like Disneyland (Benson et al., 1986; Wallace, 1996; Handler and Gable, 1997).

No historian has yet described the development of infrastructure that enabled postwar tourism. But the picture looks roughly like this: postwar affluence supported new, commercial forms of play. Although the work ethic of the nineteenth century had been wearing away for decades, Americans were now being told with more urgency, through more pervasive mass media, to live it up and consume more (Cross, 2000). Like home and automobile ownership, recreational travel away from home was becoming a middle-class standard and a working-class dream.

But if the tourism economy was to succeed, people had to be moved, housed, fed, and entertained on a huge scale. Investment in highways and urban development and redevelopment schemes played a crucial part in tourism's growth in the 1950s and 1960s (Jakle, 1985). The expansion of air travel and integrated services (credit cards, travel and booking agencies) made long-distance travel available to a much wider swath of Americans. Federal intervention was especially important in the greater West where interstate highways, bus lines, and airports made previously out-of-the-way places much more accessible (Rothman, 1998). National, state, and municipal tourism bureau promoted travel as a form of civic education (Shaffer, 1996). In turn, federal investment in infrastructure spurred the long post-1946 economic boom, encouraging large companies and small entrepreneurs to expand into tourism. The interstates, for example, encouraged the updating of the old cabin court into the motel, and then into the franchised chain motel (Luxenburg, 1985). Similarly, the postwar expansion of the National Parks and National Monuments and their facilities is a prime example of public spending to create mass attractions, public places that could be turned to myriad recreational uses and infused with complex nationalistic sentiment (Runte, 1997; Rothman, 1998).

Despite its dramatic expansion, the tourism boom did not touch all Americans equally. Indeed, travel to commercial destinations was a white, middle-class, nuclear family ideal. Most white and nonwhite families traveled only to visit kin, or search for work. The migration and mobility of African Americans through the corridors from the deep South to the industrial North, or of Mexicans to El Norte, in search of better jobs and living conditions may count as travel but not, usually, as tourism. Discrimination and segregation have given travel entirely different shapes and meanings for different races and ethnic groups. Well into our period it was common for buses and trains, roadside restaurants, hotels, and motels to formally discriminate against nonwhite customers. Transport, lodging, and amusements had to be desegregated along with schools and workplaces during the civil rights era; this project is still incomplete. The leisure patterns of minorities and their vacation and travel expectations need examination by historians, and not just by marketing specialists. On one hand, minority middle classes appear to have attracted the attention of tourism and convention marketers relatively recently. On the other hand, older patterns of exclusion have persisting effects: a recent study of the National Parks showed that minority group members do not regard these favored vacation spots as pleasurable or welcoming to them (Clifford, 1994).

Tourism is intertwined with postwar urban history. Western cities grew enormously with the help of tourist and recreational industries. Las Vegas, Los Angeles, and San Diego experienced recreational and hotel-building booms, drawing visitors who settled down to become permanent residents (Davis, 1997; Rothman, 1998). Entrepreneurs conjured new conurbations – Las Vegas, Aspen, Vail, Steamboat Springs, Santa Fe, Orlando, Miami, and the Georgia Sea Islands – more or less out of whole cloth. In the process, business and civic leaders planning for tourists on a grand scale have rewritten local cultural landscapes and identities (Wilson, 1997; Rothman, 1998; Joyner, 1999).

From the 1960s, many city governments added convention tourism to their economic mix. Gatherings of professionals, associations, and unions could flood a city with "visitor dollars." The scale of convention profits pushed the tourism industry to depend more heavily on massive, standardized accommodations, charter flights, theme parks, and the careful management of the destination's image. The flourishing, tax-funded convention and visitors' bureaux are semi-public agencies representing private interests and shaping local economic strategies.

Whether one considers tourism as the standardized, industrial production of leisure experiences, or the democratization of pleasure, its postwar growth depended on an expanding economy, a surge of promotional media, and the integration of services. And it depended on the premise that leisure time – or at least vacations – was increasing. Yet, because leisure shrank from the 1970s for the majority of Americans, by the 1990s tourism marketers were concentrating their efforts on smaller niche markets. For example, in the late 1990s, Disneyland and Walt Disney World aimed to attract the affluent "time-starved." Their expanded attractions are designed for people who need to squeeze a two-week vacation into five days.

Tourism creates exactly the sort of jobs that typify the new services economy, in which both free time and wealth are unequally distributed, yet only a few scholars have looked at the labor relations on which the industry depends. Low-wage, benefit-free, seasonal, temporary, and part-time nonunion jobs dominate tourism (Davis, 1997, 1999a). Jane Kuenz (1995) describes bleak employment conditions even at unionized Walt Disney World and EPCOT in South Florida. In Orlando in 1997, full-time entry-level theme park employees earned $10,319 per year, more than $5,000 under the federal poverty level for a family of four (Service Employees' International Union, 1997). Hochschild's provocative 1983 study of "emotional labor" (producing moods and feelings among customers) in the deregulated airline industry suggests that much more qualitative work on labor in tourism needs to be undertaken.

The late twentieth-century tourism boom is an important facet of the economic restructuring of postwar America. Tourism's effects on local economies and politics, labor rights, wage levels, and the environment need historical analysis. There are many prejudices for and against tourism, but few clearly told stories. Historians who investigate the recent past and the present of tourism will need to understand the local and national shape of economic and governmental mechanisms, including tax policies that privilege hotel and attraction development over other kinds of investment. Tourism's historians will find help from anthropologists and geographers who look at whether tourism development is "sustainable" in an international context (Barry et al., 1984; Patullo, 1996).

Few historians have assessed the impact of tourism on local economies. The initial tourism boom of the 1950s and 1960s took place in the context of relative affluence, and tourism's effects on the patterns of local life may have been felt as part of a general rising prosperity and modernization. But mass tourism and the explosion of gambling have taken place in the context of deindustrialization in the "Rustbelt," and population growth combined with fiscal austerity in the "Sunbelt." Cuts in federal spending on cities and domestic social programs have encouraged governments to turn to tourism as a solution to economic crisis. Bed taxes are offered as a panacea for job loss and declines in military spending. But tourism as a "growth machine" may be driven more by large property owners' need to profit from real estate than from meaningful plans for revitalization; defining tourism as economically critical helps rationalize public subsidies for private investment (Logan and Molotch, 1987). The conversion of whole regional economies from industry or agriculture to tourism has dramatically changed the life chances of local young people. Yet most analysts agree that tourism alone does not create a long-term, equitable economic base. Indeed, hotels and casinos may be risky public investments (Goodman, 1995; Stokowski, 1996). Rothman (1998) points to an exception: Las Vegas is now one of the most unionized cities in the United States, and restaurant, casino, and entertainment jobs there are among the few remaining stable, high-paying, and long-term blue-collar careers in the United States. Conversion to an economy even partly dependent on tourism usually means placing the fate of a community in the hands of enormous, multinational leisure consortia, rarely subject to local or state control. Since tourism spending and travel are by definition discretionary, a flourishing future rests on the assumption of someone else's continuing prosperity.

Because culture and difference are the bases of tourist attractions, scholars must probe the experience of the toured as well as the tourist. As MacCannell asked early on, what happens when a people and their way of life become a tourist attraction?

Scholars and critics ask whether tourism undermines local culture, helps preserve it, or changes it in ways unavoidable in a mobile, postnational world (V. Smith, 1977; MacCannell, 1992; García Canclini, 1995). Some argue that communities are objectified and people made to "museumize" their own lives in static displays (Leong, 1989). Others claim that tourism is a more complex social process than this, creating new intercultural expressions, arts, and information (Graeburn, 1976). Some feminists argue that tourism stiffens racial, gender, and class boundaries, rarely providing new opportunities for the previously excluded (Sinclair, 1997; Patullo, 1996). While there is evidence that in some places tourism has given women new entrepreneurial roles and independence (Kinnaird and Hall, 1994), in other cases it helps keep poor, rural, and minority women at the bottom of the economy (M. Smith, 1989).

Such questions are even more pressing and complex when we look at tourism as a global industry that sends the wealthy and powerful to poor and "exotic" places in search of novel experiences. Scholars disagree whether a flood of American and European tourists reproduces imperial relations or creates strange new zones of cultural contact (Pratt, 1992; Schwartz, 1997). Historical-ethnographic studies of what happens when a place becomes a destination are sorely needed.

In the same way that historians of leisure need to examine the distribution of time as a resource alongside the uses people have made of it, historical analysis of tourism as experience must be combined with an analysis of tourism as the result of economic, political, and social choices. Historians have much to add by bringing the problem of human agency to the fore. They can probe the balance between ordinary people's ability to act and determine, and the forces that constrain collective action. Thus far, the literature suggests that the ways in which tourists and the toured shape their experiences vary from case to case, in part because tourism is such a diverse global industry. The degree of political control over the local economy and whether tourists and the toured meet on equal or exploitative gender, racial, class, and national terms will shape the answers. Without doubt, the relative equality between sides will be mediated by local business people and global industries. The "meeting grounds" on which tourism unfolds are far from empty: they have already been shaped by the past, by the history of power relationships between city and country, employers and workers, core and periphery, and first and third world, as well as by long-held ideas and images.

REFERENCES AND FURTHER READING

Aron, Cindy S.: *Working At Play: A History of Vacation in the United States* (New York and Oxford: Oxford University Press, 1998).

Barry, Tom, Wood, Beth, and Preusch, Deb: *The Other Side of Paradise: Foreign Control in the Caribbean* (New York: Grove Press, 1984).

Baudrillard, Jean: *America* (London and New York: Verso, 1988).

Belasco, Warren: *Americans On the Road: From Autocamp to Motel: 1910–1945* (Cambridge, Mass.: MIT Press, 1979).

Benson, Susan Porter, Brier, Stephen, and Rosenzweig, Roy: *Presenting the Past: Essays on History and the Public* (Philadelphia: Temple University Press, 1986).

Bluestone, Barry and Harrison, Bennett: *The Deindustrialization of America: Plant Closings, Community Abandonment, and the Dismantling of Basic Industry* (New York: Basic Books, 1982).

Boorstin, Daniel: *The Image: A Guide to Pseudo-Events in America* (New York: Atheneum, 1961).

Braverman, Harry: *Labor and Monopoly Capitalism* (New York: Monthly Review Press, 1974).

Brown, Dona: *Inventing New England: Regional Tourism in the Nineteenth Century* (Washington, DC: Smithsonian Institution Press, 1995).

Butsch, Richard, ed.: *For Fun and Profit: The Transformation of Leisure into Consumption* (Philadelphia: Temple University Press, 1990).

Clarke, John: "Pessimism vs. Populism: The Problematics of Popular Culture," in Richard Butsch (ed.), *For Fun and Profit: The Transformation of Leisure into Consumption* (Philadelphia: Temple University Press, 1990), 28–44.

Clifford, Frank: "Opening Parks to All of America," *Los Angeles Times* (November 24, 1994): A1, A34–A35.

Cross, Gary: *Time and Money: The Making of Consumer Culture* (New York and London: Routledge, 1993).

Cross, Gary: *An All-Consuming Century: Why Commercialism Won in Modern America* (New York: Columbia University Press, 2000).

Culler, Jonathan: "The Semiotics of Tourism," in Diane George (ed.), *Reading Culture* (New York: Harper Collins, 1992), 153–67.

Davis, Susan G.: "Theme Park: Global Industry and Cultural Form," *Media Culture and Society*, 18/3 (1996): 399–422.

Davis, Susan G.: *Spectacular Nature: Corporate Culture and the Sea World Experience* (Berkeley: University of California Press, 1997).

Davis, Susan G.: "Landscapes of Imagination: Tourism in Southern California," *Pacific Historical Review*, 68/2 (1999a): 173–92.

Davis, Susan G.: "Space Jam: Media Conglomerates Build the Entertainment City," *European Journal of Communication*, 14/4 (1999b): 435–59.

Debord, Guy: *Society of the Spectacle* (Detroit: Black and Red, 1970).

Eco, Umberto: *Travels in Hyperreality: Essays* (San Diego: Harcourt Brace Jovanovich, 1986).

Ewen, Elizabeth: *Immigrant Women in the Land of Dollars: Life and Culture on the Lower East Side, 1890–1925* (New York: Monthly Review Press, 1985).

Ewen, Stuart and Ewen, Elizabeth: *Channels of Desire: Mass Images and the Shaping of American Consciousness* (New York: McGraw Hill, 1982).

Fjellman, Stephen: *Vinyl Leaves: Walt Disney World and America* (Boulder, Colo.: Westview Press, 1992).

García Canclini, Néstor: *Hybrid Cultures: Strategies for Entering and Leaving Modernity*, trans. Christopher L. Chiappari and Silvia L. López (Minneapolis: University of Minnesota Press, 1995).

Gelber, Steven M.: *Hobbies: Leisure and the Culture of Work in America* (New York: Columbia University Press, 1999).

Gilbert, James: *A Cycle of Outrage: America's Reaction to the Juvenile Delinquent in the 1950s* (New York: Oxford University Press, 1986).

Goodman, Robert: *The Luck Business: The Devastating Consequences and Broken Promises of America's Gambling Explosion* (New York: Free Press, 1995).

Graeburn, Nelson H. H., ed.: *Ethnic and Tourist Arts: Cultural Expressions from the Fourth World* (Berkeley: University of California Press, 1976).

Gutman, Herbert S: *Work, Culture, and Society in Industrializing America: Essay in American Working-Class and Social History* (New York: Alfred A. Knopf, 1976).

Handler, Richard and Gable, Eric: *The Old History in a New Museum: Creating the Past at Colonial Williamsburg* (Durham, NC: Duke University Press, 1997).

Hannigan, John: *Fantasy Cities: Pleasure and Profit in the Post-Modern Metropolis* (London and New York: Routledge, 1998).

Hochschild, Arlie Russell: *The Managed Heart: The Commercialization of Human Feeling* (Berkeley: University of California Press, 1983).

Hochschild, Arlie Russell: *The Second Shift* (New York: Viking, 1989).

Hunnicutt, Benjamin Kline: *Work Without End: Abandoning Shorter Hours for the Right to Work* (Philadelphia: Temple University Press, 1988).

Jakle, John A.: *The Tourist in Twentieth-Century North America* (Lincoln: University of Nebraska Press, 1985).

Joyner, Charles: *Shared Traditions: Southern History and Folk Culture* (Urbana and Chicago: University of Illinois Press, 1999).

Kelley, Robin D. G.: *Yo Mama's Disfunktional: Fighting the Culture Wars in Urban America* (Boston: Beacon Press, 1997).

Kinnaird, Vivian and Hall, Derek, eds.: *Tourism: A Gender Analysis* (New York and Toronto: John Wiley, 1994).

Kirshenblatt-Gimblett, Barbara: *Destination Culture: Tourism, Museums and Heritage* (Berkeley: University of California Press, 1998).

Kuenz, Jane: "Inside the Mouse: Work and Play at Disney World," in The Project on Disney (Durham, NC: Duke University Press, 1995).

Larrabee, Eric and Myerson, Rolf, eds.: *Mass Leisure* (Glencoe, Ill.: Free Press, 1958).

Leong, Wai-Teng: "Culture and the State: Manufacturing Traditions for Tourism," *Critical Studies in Mass Communication*, 6/4 (1989): 355–75.

Lipsitz, George: *Time Passages: Collective Memory and American Popular Culture* (Minneapolis: University of Minnesota Press, 1990).

Lipsitz, George: *Rainbow at Midnight: Labor and Culture in the 1940s* (Urbana and Chicago: University of Illinois Press, 1994).

Loewen, James: *Lies Across America: What Our Historic Sites Get Wrong* (New York: New Press, 1999).

Lofgren, Orvar: *On Holiday: A History of Vacationing* (Berkeley: University of California Press, 1999).

Logan, John R. and Molotch, Harvey L.: *Urban Fortunes: The Political Economy of Place* (Berkeley: University of California Press, 1987).

Lowenthal, David: *The Heritage Crusade and the Spoils of History* (New York: Penguin Books, 1997).

Luxenburg, Stan: *Roadside Empires: How the Chains Franchised America* (New York and London: Penguin, 1985).

MacCannell, Dean: *The Tourist: A Theory of the New Leisure Class* (New York: Schocken Books, 1976).

MacCannell, Dean: *Empty Meeting Grounds: The Tourist Papers* (New York and London: Routledge, 1992).

Marcuse, Herbert: *One-Dimensional Man: Studies in the Ideology of Advanced Industrial Society* (Boston: Beacon Press, 1964).

Miringoff, Marc and Miringoff, Marque-Luisa: *The Social Health of the Nation: How America is Really Doing* (New York and Oxford: Oxford University Press, 1999).

Nasaw, David: *Going Out: The Rise and Fall of Public Amusements* (New York: Basic Books, 1993).

Patullo, Polly: *Last Resorts: The Cost of Tourism in the Caribbean* (London: Cassell, 1996).

Peiss, Kathy: *Cheap Amusements: Working Women and Leisure in New York City, 1880 to 1920* (Philadelphia: Temple University Press, 1985).

Pomeroy, Earl: *In Search of the Golden West: The Tourist in Western America* (Lincoln: University of Nebraska Press, 1957).

Pratt, Mary Louise: *Imperial Eyes: Travel Writing and Transculturation* (London and New York: Routledge, 1992).

Robinson, John P. and Godbey, Geoffrey: *Time for Life: The Surprising Way Americans Use Their Time* (University Park, Pa.: Penn State University Press, 1997).

Roediger, David R. and Foner, Phillip S.: *Our Own Time: A History of American Labor and the Working Day* (New York: Greenwood Press, 1989).

Rose, Tricia: *Black Noise: Rap Music and Black Culture in Contemporary America* (Hanover, NH: University Press of New England, 1994).

Rosenberg, Bernard and White, David Manning, eds.: *Mass Culture: The Popular Arts in America* (Glencoe, Ill: Free Press, 1957).

Rosenzweig, Roy: *Eight Hours for What We Will: Workers and Leisure in an Industrial City, 1870–1920* (Cambridge and New York: Cambridge University Press, 1983).

Rothman, Hal: *Devil's Bargains: Tourism in the Twentieth Century West* (Lawrence: University Press of Kansas, 1998).

Runte, Alfred: *National Parks: The American Experience*, 3rd ed. (Lincoln and London: University of Nebraska Press, 1997).

Schiller, Dan: *Theorizing Communication: A History* (New York: Oxford University Press, 1996).

Schiller, Herbert I.: *The Mind Managers* (Boston: Beacon Press, 1973).

Schor, Juliet B.: *The Overworked American: The Unexpected Decline of Leisure* (New York: Basic Books, 1991).

Schwartz, Rosalie: *Pleasure Island: Tourism and Temptation in Cuba* (Lincoln: University of Nebraska Press, 1997).

Scott, Janny: "Working Hard, More or Less," *New York Times* (July 10, 1999): A15 and A17.

Sears, John: *Sacred Places: American Tourist Attractions in the Nineteenth Century* (Oxford and New York: Oxford University Press, 1989).

Service Employees' International Union, "Big Shots vs. Working Folks," *What the *#?!*, 1/2 (December, 1997): 3.

Shaffer, Marguerite S.: "Negotiating National Identity: Western Tourism and See America First," in Hal K. Rothman (ed.), *Reopening the American West* (Tucson: University of Arizona Press, 1996), 122–51.

Sinclair, Thea M., ed.: *Gender, Work and Tourism* (London and New York: Routledge, 1997).

Smith, Michal: *Behind the Glitter: The Impact of Tourism on Rural Women in the Southeast* (Lexington: Southeast Women's Employment Coalition, 1989).

Smith, Valene, ed.: *Hosts and Guests: The Anthropology of Tourism* (Philadelphia: University of Pennsylvania Press, 1977).

Sorkin, Michael, ed.: *Variations On a Theme Park: The New American City and the End of Public Space* (New York: Hill and Wang, 1992).

Stokowski, Patricia A.: *Riches and Regrets: Betting on Gambling in Two Colorado Mountain Towns* (Niwot: University Press of Colorado, 1996).

The Project on Disney: *Inside the Mouse: Work and Play at Disney World* (Durham, NC: Duke University Press, 1995).

Thompson, E. P.: *The Making of the English Working Class* (New York: Vintage Books, 1963).

Urry, John: *The Tourist Gaze: Leisure and Travel in Contemporary Societies* (London: Sage Publications, 1990).

Wallace, Michael: *Mickey Mouse History and Other Essays on American Memory* (Philadelphia: Temple University Press, 1996).

Weigle, Marta: "Exposition and Mediation: Mary Colter, Erna Ferguson, and the Santa Fe Harvey Popularization of the Native Southwest, 1902–1940," *Frontiers: A Journal of Women's Studies*, 12/3 (1992): 117–50.

Wilson, Alexander: *The Culture of Nature: North American Landscape from Disneyland to the Exxon Valdez* (Malden, Mass.: Blackwell, 1992).

Wilson, Chris: *The Myth of Santa Fe: Creating a Modern Regional Tradition* (Albuquerque: University of New Mexico Press, 1997).

CHAPTER FIVE

Mass Media: From 1945 to the Present

SUSAN J. DOUGLAS

If this were, say, 1958 instead of the early twenty-first century, one thing would be very different about the volume you now hold in your hands: there would be no essay about the mass media. Despite the fact that magazines, newspapers, and national advertising began powerfully reshaping American culture in the 1880s and beyond, or that 40 million Americans all tuned in at the same time to listen to *Amos 'n' Andy* or President Roosevelt on the radio in the early 1930s, or that 90 million Americans went to the movies each week in the 1940s, historians shunned this topic. Why?

For years, at most elite colleges and universities, it was considered preposterous to study the mass media, and this was especially true immediately after World War II. In the minds of tweedy types, the media were either the purveyors of the most mindless, insignificant drivel ever laid before the viewing and listening public or, worse, the agents of intellectual narcotization who deliberately turned thinking people into lobotomized robots programmed to talk to the Tidy Bowl man rather than vote or read a book.

There were some exceptions to this consensus. Beginning in the early 1940s at a few places like Columbia and the University of Iowa, for example, scholars began studying how people listened to the radio and how they responded to government efforts to boost morale and patriotic fervor during World War II. The study of public opinion emerged. So did essays on the political stupefaction and cultural degradation produced by radio, films, comics, and television. But this work occurred in journalism schools or sociology departments, not in history (Rogers, 1994).

In most of this work, the notion that the researcher himself (and yes, they were mostly men) might actually *enjoy* media fare, and might himself be implicated in the guilty pleasures the media offered – well, this was simply unspeakable. As the prominent critic Dwight Macdonald wrote in the 1950s, popular culture is "a debased, trivial culture that voids both the deep realities (sex, death, failure, tragedy) and the simple, spontaneous pleasures. The masses, debauched by several generations of this sort of thing, in turn come to demand trivial and comfortable cultural products" (Rosenberg and White, 1957, p. 72). The German émigrés Theodor Adorno and Max Horkheimer, in a famous screed against what they called the "culture industries," wrote that consumers "fall helpless victims of what is offered them" (Adorno and Horkheimer, 1972, p. 133) and emphasized the "stunting of the mass-media consumer's powers of imagination and spontaneity" (p. 126). "The triumph of advertising in the culture industry," they concluded, "is that consumers feel compelled to buy and use its products even though they see through them" (Adorno and Horkheimer, 1972, p. 167). Newton Minow, the chairman of the Federal Communications Commission (FCC), famously referred to television in 1963 as "a vast wasteland." With the tube dominated by shows like *Mr. Ed* (about a talking horse) or *My Favorite Martian* (self-explanatory), these pessimists could hardly be blamed for their dismissal of the mass media.

At the same time, communication scholars had produced studies in the late 1930s and 1940s showing that the mass media had only limited effects on people's political behavior and consumer choices: the influence of family, friends, and community was much more important. What historian was going to study something that was allegedly both banal and inconsequential?

These attitudes were especially pronounced in the humanities until the early 1970s; historians primarily studied presidents and wars, and English professors stuck to the symbolism of *Heart of Darkness*. But in the late 1960s and 1970s there was a sea change in the study of American history, with a new focus on the working classes, on African Americans, on women, on families, and on communities and neighborhoods. Many historians became committed to studying America's past from the bottom up, not just from the top down. And young historians, who had come of age in the 1960s and had witnessed first-hand the enormous impact of the mass media on the civil rights movement, the Vietnam War, attitudes toward women, romantic notions of the family, and on American politics, challenged the elitist biases against studying the mass media. Media history, in fact, allowed for the interplay between bottom-up and top-down history.

Many of us who decided that the history of advertising, or radio, or television, or film was actually consequential faced derision from our elders. In 1974, when I proposed teaching a course on the history and impact of popular culture, a prominent senior historian sneered, "What are you going to do, sit around and read comic books all day?" I was not alone. And those of us who sought to develop courses in this area had very few readings to draw from. Possibly the most famous was Marshall McLuhan's 1964 bestseller *Understanding Media*, which argued, in part, that the form and inherent properties of each medium were more important than their actual content ("the medium is the message"), and which sought to divide the various media into those he deemed "hot" and those he deemed "cool" (a schema many of us found unconvincing). Because the book virtually ignored media content, because it failed to embed the media within larger systems of political and economic power, and because it relied on a highly arbitrary history of communications that emphasized "revolutions" rather than continuities (and suggested that machines, pretty much by themselves, made history), many of us found the book exasperating, at best, and by the late 1970s McLuhan's thesis had fallen into widespread disfavor. Now, thirty years later, not only are there numerous, first-rate books on the history of the various mass media, but also there are lively debates among us about the influence of the mass media during different historical eras. Scholars have learned that some media audiences were not the passive, mindless dupes that Dwight Macdonald said they were, but instead often interacted quite assertively with the flickering images on the nickelodeon screens or boycotted advertisers if they did not like the radio programs they were sponsoring.

Our debates have clustered around three main questions. First, how much power and influence do media institutions and media content have on American society and culture? Second, how much power do audiences have to shape media content (primarily through their choices as consumers) and to resist and talk back to mainstream media images and messages? And third, what have been the major, recurring images and messages of these media? What kinds of stories have they circulated repeatedly over time, what kinds of heroes and villains have they presented, how have these stories and archetypes changed, and what kind of ideological work do these stories perform in our culture?

First, we need to review how the mass media grew and evolved after World War II. All the media had played a central role in selling the war at home and boosting morale overseas. The Office of War Information, the government agency that coordinated and promoted our government's propaganda activities, worked with filmmakers, radio producers, advertising agencies, newspapers, and magazines to produce a variety of media texts that would persuade women to work in war-related industries, encourage rationing and other forms of sacrifice at home, and remind Americans that the Nazis and "the Japs," as they were consistently referred to, were evil incarnate. These propaganda campaigns were highly effective: over 6 million women, for example, took up war work, often in jobs traditionally held by men. Frank Capra, a filmmaker already famous for movies like *It Happened One Night* and *Mr. Smith Goes to Washington*, joined the army and made his famous "Why We Fight" documentary series, highly flattering, patriotic visions of the essential, inherent goodness of America. Once the war was over, and female war workers were no longer needed, a new media campaign told them it was time to return to their "natural" duties, like cleaning house and having babies (Field, 1981; Koppes, 1990).

So interestingly, after the war, there were mixed assessments of the power of the mass media. On the one hand, various researchers had suggested that their effects were limited, mediated, as they were, by educational background, friends and family, income level, and so forth. On the other hand, evidence of the success of various propaganda campaigns during the war revived the notion that people were easily swayed by media images and messages, especially those that were powerful and inflammatory. These warring notions coexisted in the 1950s (Rosenberg and White, 1957).

With the advantage of historical hindsight, scholars in the 1980s started thinking more critically about the real ideological achievement of the 1950s, the triumphal rise of consumerism as our national religion. Certainly the pleasure of buying and owning things – lots of things – as a central defining element of Americanism took firm root by the 1920s, but it was disrupted by the Depression and the war, both of which required sacrifice and an emphasis on communalism and mutual support. After 1945, the ability to consume what you wanted, when you wanted, as the central tenet of the "American Dream," as the foundation of happiness and success, became part of the common sense about what made America great.

But this did not happen in a vacuum. The mass media – advertising, magazines, radio, and especially television – which relied on American consumerism to survive, drove this message home not only through advertisements but also through news stories, celebrity profiles, and television shows. The scholar George Lipsitz, in a highly influential 1986 article called "The Meaning of Memory," analyzed how early television shows that featured working-class or ethnic families – *I Remember Mama* (1949–56) or *The Goldbergs* (1949–54) – specialized in stories in which the older members of the family who had learned to be thrifty, to work hard, and to defer gratification during the Depression and the war now had to learn, often through their children, the "new ways" which involved spending and immediate gratification. Sometimes a commodity itself, like a new stove, was one of the central characters of the show's plot. So media studies scholarship looking back at this period began, in the 1980s, to move beyond descriptions of what happened in the media to analyses of what kinds of ideological frameworks they conveyed to millions of Americans.

The major change in America's media landscape in the 1950s was, of course, the rise of television. First publicly demonstrated at the 1939 World's Fair in New York City, television's adoption was delayed by the war. In 1949, for example, only 2.3 percent of American households owned a television set. Just five years later, that number had soared to 55.7 percent, and by 1962, 90 percent of households had at least one television. Highly popular network radio shows, such as *The Jack Benny Show*, *Burns and Allen*, and *Abbott and Costello*, to name a few, moved to television, taking their prime-time audiences with them. New shows developed specifically for television, like *I Love Lucy* and *Texaco Star Theater* with Milton Berle (nicknamed "Mr. Television"), which exploited sight gags and physical slapstick, became huge hits. The consequences seemed obvious. "Within three years," proclaimed NBC president Niles Tramell in 1949, "the broadcast of sound or ear radio over giant networks will be wiped out" (Douglas, 1999, p. 220).

But radio did not die. In fact, it became more profitable than ever, with advertising revenues jumping from $571 million in 1949 to $692 million in 1960. Radio stations, which had been grouped into four national networks, disaffiliated from these networks. They went local in the 1950s, promoting local DJs and talk-show hosts and featuring local advertisers. Many of them also discovered new audiences: African Americans, and young people. Some of them started playing rhythm and blues, and then rock and roll. While television, after a brief period of experimentation, offered overly cautious, homogenized, white, upper-middle-class renditions of American life as exemplified by *Leave It To Beaver* and *Father Knows Best*, radio stations provided auditory outposts where people could listen, through music and patter, to something a bit more rebellious and nonconformist. Lying in their beds at night with small transistor radios or, increasingly, driving around in cars, teenagers could listen to Chuck Berry, Elvis Presley, or The Shirelles, whose music resonated with sexual longing and youthful defiance against middle-class mores (Douglas, 1999; Smith, 2000).

It was a concern about such rebellion and the influence the media might have, especially, on the morals of young people that prompted several media panics in the 1950s. One of the most highly publicized centered around comic books, which prompted the same kinds of worries that violent videogames do today. Frederic Wertham, a psychologist, wrote *Seduction of the Innocent* (1954), which attacked the increase in crime comics and "headlight" comics (so named because of the exaggerated anatomical features of many of the female characters) and charged that reading such comics contributed to juvenile delinquency. While such charges may seem silly to us today, a look at some of these comics is indeed sobering, as they specialized in the often sadistic torture and threatened sexual abuse of women, or in just plain gore. In one, for example, a woman was tied up and threatened with a branding iron; in another, human innards like intestines were used to lay out a baseball diamond. The US Senate held highly publicized hearings in 1955 and 1956 on juvenile delinquency, and Wertham's charges about the violence and sadism of comics forced the comic book industry to adopt a code of self-censorship that limited the depiction of crime and violence (Gilbert, 1988; Nyberg, 1998).

There were also panics about the alleged pernicious influence of rock and roll on teenagers. Rock and roll was filled with sexual energy, the lyrics at times sexually suggestive or defiant of middle-class norms about work and decorum, and a variety of public figures, from religious leaders to Frank Sinatra, denounced the music as demonic, cannibalistic, or just plain bad. Of course, for white America, the main threat posed by rock and roll was that so much of it was inspired, written, or performed by African Americans, meaning that black music, language, and culture were infusing the very identities of white kids as they listened to their radios or played their phonographs.

Such reactions led to the payola scandals of the late 1950s and early 1960s, when congressional hearings on corruption in television and radio revealed that some DJs had gotten liquor, money, or sex in exchange for playing certain songs by particular record labels on the air. The practice of currying favor with band leaders, or the hosts of radio shows, in order to ensure that certain songs were played on the air had gone on for decades, but in the anti-rock and roll environment, and with the public shock around the quiz show scandals on television, many disc jockeys lost their jobs, and the decision about what to play on the air was taken away from many DJs and given to the station's music director. Alan Freed, the self-proclaimed "Father of Rock'n'Roll," who had pioneered in playing rhythm and blues and many black-authored rock and roll songs on the air, first in Cleveland and then in New York, had his career ruined because of the payola scandal (Douglas, 1999).

Which medium was safe from cheating and manipulation? Even when you went to the movies, according to Vance Packard in his bestselling exposé about advertising, *The Hidden Persuaders* (1957), theater owners would flash images of an ice-cold Coke on the screen, too fast for you to see consciously but embedded on your retina, and powerful enough to make you want to go to the concession stand to buy a Coke (Horowitz, 1994). Not only were Americans being bombarded by dancing cigarette boxes, a genie named Mr. Clean, and other advertising ploys they could see, they also were being hit by subliminal messages, too quick or well hidden to register consciously, but stealthy enough to invade and conquer their unconscious. How could they resist what they could not even see?

The panics over comics, rock and roll, and advertising centered on longstanding fears about the media's power to affect the attitudes and behaviors of the young. The quiz show scandals reactivated another kind of fear about the media: that under the guise of being a "mirror" of reality, of presenting us with the truth, they actually presented us with distortions and lies. Shows like *The $64,000 Question*, which debuted on television in 1955, soared to number one in the ratings and, not surprisingly, spawned a host of imitators. One of these was *Twenty-One*, which in 1957 featured Charles Van Doren, a professor at Columbia University, as a contestant. Van Doren kept winning and became so popular he landed a job on *The Today Show*. But in 1959 charges circulated that several of these quiz shows had been rigged, and Van Doren eventually admitted complicity in cheating. Such revelations increased cynicism about television's push to increase ratings no matter what, reaffirmed for some that Americans really were mindless dupes of the media, and confirmed for others that television was incapable of showing anything remotely realistic and unstaged (Stone and Yohn, 1992).

Behind the scenes, more so in television than in radio, another panic about media influence powerfully shaped what Americans did – and did not – get to see and hear in the 1950s: charges of communist infiltration of the media. At the time, with the Cold War raging and anti-communism at a level of near-hysteria, many Americans saw possible communist infiltration of American institutions as a real concern. Today, media studies scholars analyze how the right wing, with considerable help from a cowed media, manufactured and profited from such hysteria. As the cultural historian Michael Denning documented in *The Cultural Front* (1996), a variety of playwrights, poets, musicians, and performers sought, during the Depression, to produce radio shows, plays, novels, and music that attacked fascism and promoted progressive politics. After the war, conservatives determined to silence these artists.

One of the right's most effective strategies was to encourage blacklisting: to threaten a network with boycotts of any product that sponsored a TV show allegedly written, directed, produced by, or starring an alleged communist. Because broadcasters were terrified of losing or alienating advertisers, they usually acquiesced and refused to hire those on the list. Careers and lives were ruined. Through their publication *Red Channels*, which listed alleged communists working in the broadcast industry, right wingers cited Philip Loeb, who played a character on *The Goldbergs*, as a communist. Loeb was dropped from the show, could not find other work, and committed suicide.

The power of this kind of censorship to shape television programming, which in turn powerfully constructs – or reconstructs – people's memory of a particular era, is evident when we see how such media-framed histories help determine public policy. Conservative politicians and pundits in the 1980s, from Ronald Reagan and Dan Quayle to Bill Bennet and Allan Bloom, harked back to the whitewashed version of American life shown on *The Donna Reed Show* and *The Adventures of Ozzie and Harriet* when they demanded a return to "family values," which meant a return to the nuclear family in which dad worked outside the home and mom did not, and in which dad allegedly knew best. Scholars like Stephanie Coontz have sought to remind people, however, that only a tiny fraction of America ever lived the way the Cleaver family had, and that it was preposterous and destructive to millions of families to judge people against a media-produced and artificial norm.

But media studies scholars, especially from the 1980s onward, also began to emphasize the often enormous contradictions in the mass media, even in the 1950s and early 1960s. In 1963, for example, television viewers could see, during prime time, westerns, variety shows, or utterly unrealistic sitcoms like *The Beverly Hillbillies*. But when they turned on the news, which had expanded that year from fifteen minutes to half an hour, they saw cops in Birmingham, Alabama, attacking black children with German shepherd dogs and using the full force of fire hoses to knock them down. Photographs of these and similarly revolting events during the civil rights movement also circulated in newspapers and magazines. So the media were presenting something more than escapist fantasies to Americans; they were also bringing life and death political struggles into their living rooms. Studies showed that television footage of the civil rights movement, especially of Birmingham in 1963, shocked many Americans and propelled public opinion toward support of civil rights legislation. Intermixed with *The Flintstones*, *The Addams Family*, and *I Dream of Jeannie*, Americans saw President Kennedy, Martin Luther King, and Robert Kennedy shot on television; they saw men in combat in Vietnam and corpses coming home in body bags; they saw increasing numbers of people in the streets demonstrating against the war; they saw the chemical-filled Cayahoga River self-ignite.

It is not surprising that scholars who grew up surrounded by such wildly divergent media imagery would, in the 1970s and 1980s, emphasize that the media are not monolithic. It is also not surprising that many would repudiate a "limited effects" model of media influence and instead emphasize the media's enormous power, not necessarily to get us to vote for one candidate (or product) over another, but rather to shape how we view the broader contours of politics, of who deserves to be heard and who does not, of what is legitimate to say and what is not, of which challenges to the status quo are deemed reasonable and which ones deemed beyond the pale.

One of the first media conceits that these new scholars exposed was the notion that the news media were, and had always been, "objective." They challenged the supposed omniscience, neutrality, and inclusiveness trumpeted by the news media in slogans like the *New York Times*'s "All the News That's Fit to Print" or Walter Cronkite's famous sign-off every night on CBS News, "That's the way it is." As Daniel Schiller (1981) and Michael Schudson (1978) documented, newspapers in the late eighteenth and early nineteenth centuries were highly partisan, tied as they were to political parties or to political movements like the abolition of slavery, and competing editors sometimes came to blows in the streets. Objectivity – an unattainable but theoretically conceivable condition of an absence of bias – took years to take hold as a professional standard in the press, and even when it did, its emphasis on "both sides" (and usually *only* two sides) of a story, its dependence on official government sources and spokespersons, and its equal reliance on elites or leaders meant that many voices, stories, and perspectives remained left out of the journalistic record. Herbert Gans, in his seminal ethnographic study of journalism, *Deciding What's News* (1980), further unpacked the media framework known as "objectivity" and described it instead as a "paraideology," filled with normative assumptions about the superiority of America's political and economic system, the goodness and purity of small-town life, and the importance of rugged individualism to American society. The worldview the news promoted was, according to Gans, white, male, and upper-middle-class.

Todd Gitlin took this critique one step further to the left. In one of the most important media history books of the late twentieth century, *The Whole World is Watching* (1980), Gitlin asked how media coverage of a progressive activist organization, Students for a Democratic Society (SDS), and of the anti-war demonstrations it organized, shaped public perceptions of the anti-war movement and the size and structure of SDS itself. Gitlin documented how the *New York Times* and CBS News, as examples of the mainstream media, often trivialized the demonstrators by focusing on their clothes and hair, understated their numbers and influence, suggested their politics were out of step with the majority of Americans, and exaggerated accounts of internal dissension within the anti-war movement. At the same time, of course, news coverage of demonstrations brought thousands more people into SDS and the anti-war movement. Because newsworthiness in the United States is defined by conflict and disorder, the news media emphasized arrests, clashes with police, and acts of violence over the substance of the movement and the processes by which it hoped to effect change. Gitlin's work showed the advantages and costs of media visibility to social movements, and dramatized the interplay between a powerful news media and an increasingly vocal, oppositional social movement that needed the media, and loathed their tactics at the same time. Most important, his case study documented the news media's powerful role in maintaining the status quo, in part by symbolically incorporating, taming, or discrediting opposition. Here, Gitlin was drawing from the theoretical work of Antonio Gramsci, whose *Prison Notebooks*, written in the 1920s and 1930s, were finally translated into English in 1970. Gramsci's notion of "ideological hegemony," the process through which elites gain the consent of nonelites to support an inequitable political and economic system that benefits, primarily, the elites, became enormously influential in the 1980s and beyond, in part because Gitlin showed how the concept could be used to great effect in media studies. Gitlin's book opened up still ongoing debates about the extent to which the news media, by merely airing social protests, help advance social change or whether, by marginalizing these protests during their coverage, they thwart and stunt the possibilities for such change.

By the mid-1970s, with the power of the news media more fully acknowledged, and with the recognition that, like it or not, television, advertising, movies, popular music, and radio had shaped the attitudes, behaviors, and memories of millions of Americans, in some cases since the nineteenth century, scholars sought to exhume this neglected history of the media's role in American culture. And many brought with them not a contempt for mass culture, but a deep, and often conflicted, attachment to it that made them sympathetic to its allure while still critical of its banalities. Paul Buhle, who became one of the preeminent historians of the left (1987a, 1987b, 1990), in the early and mid-1970s fused media criticism with cultural analysis in one of the earliest journals on popular culture and the media, *Cultural Correspondence*. Buhle's emphasis on the relationships between politics and culture as expressed through – and drawn from – popular culture inspired many fledgling media scholars and anticipated the themes and frameworks of British cultural studies (Buhle, 1987b).

There remained in the 1970s and 1980s ongoing disagreements about exactly how much power to ascribe to the mass media. Since many of us had a background in or affinity with New Left politics, we naturally saw the mass media as industries central to the sustenance of advanced capitalism and the persistence of asymmetrical power relations. But many of these same scholars also saw the liberating and subversive potential of many entertainment and media texts, from Yiddish humor in vaudeville to the skits on *The Smothers Brothers' Comedy Hour*, and struggled constantly (as we still do) to juggle our optimism with our pessimism. Our pessimistic sides welcomed Stuart Ewen's *Captains of Consciousness* (1976), his Marxist analysis of how the advertising industry sought to create needs and desires among the population in the 1920s and to use visions of consumerism to effect social control, particularly of the working classes. But our optimistic sides wondered where those same active audiences we were learning about in film history or theater history were in this story (Nye, 1970; Jowett, 1976). Wasn't this Adorno and Horkheimer *redux*, with an all-knowing culture industry manipulating a passive and monolithic audience? Surely people, even in the 1920s, resisted and made fun of ads, and surely some of these ads spoke to people's hopes, fears, and desires, however socially constructed. Our suspicion of how the media sustain corporate power, coupled with our experience that the media could at times promote social change and our understanding that you did not have to be a Ph.D. candidate to see through the mass media, compelled many of us to take the only stance we could toward our object of study: ambivalence, with an emphasis on contradictions within media texts and audience members.

By the mid-1980s, those of us who had felt so lonely in 1970 now found ourselves surrounded by new studies of the media's past. Daniel Czitrom in *Media and the American Mind* (1982) reviewed Americans' utopian and, later, dystopian reactions to seemingly miraculous forms of communication like the telegraph, film, and radio, which people at first hoped would eliminate loneliness and bring about world peace. T. J. Jackson Lears noted how advertising played a central role in displacing a producer ethos, based on hard work, thrift, and deferred gratification, with a consumer ethos, based on a celebration of leisure, spending, and instant gratification. His identification of what he called "the therapeutic ethos" in early twentieth-century advertising – the promise of physical and psychic rejuvenation through the consumption of products – helped historians in the classroom relate past advertising to the present.

This new work included studying popular entertainments as well, as John Kasson did in his elegant analysis of the amusement parks at Coney Island, *Amusing the Million* (1978). As was typical of this new work, Kasson did not just provide a descriptive history of the rise and fall of Coney Island. Rather, he noted how amusement parks in the late nineteenth and early twentieth centuries were tied to the growth of cities and increased leisure time for workers, and, with their fast, often hair-raising rides, to people's love and fear of new technologies during a period of rapid industrialization. Most important, Kasson pointed out how Coney Island, and the often negative reactions against it from "the educated bourgeoisie," exemplified ongoing struggles over how leisure time should be spent and, indeed, what "culture" should be. The educated bourgeoisie believed that leisure time should be dedicated to uplift, contemplation, and education. Coney Island was devoted to stimulating the senses, to instant gratification, and to abandoning decorum. Who was right, and who got to decide what were legitimate entertainments and leisure activities? And what if young women were attending such amusements?

Kasson reminded us that the answers to these questions were not pat: such entertainments *did* appeal to the emotions and sensations over the intellect, they *did* divert people from political engagement, but they also challenged class hierarchies (although not racial ones), provided working people with pleasure and escape, and gave young women a chance to break free from Victorian constraints that delimited where they could go and who they could mix with in public. Kathy Peiss, in *Cheap Amusements* (1986), focused especially on the liberatory potential of public entertainments for young working women, who went to the movies or amusement parks and gloried in their freedom while reformers railed against public immorality. Likewise, in *Eight Hours for What We Will* (1983), Roy Rosenzweig, in his study of working-class cultures and conflict in Worcester, Massachusetts, sought to step outside the confines of narratives focused on union organizing and union busting. Rosenzweig argued that cultural practices and locales, from large public parades to tiny backroom bars, were crucial to the consolidation of working-class cultures and politics, and to the ethnic divisions among workers. Just as Americans were, in the 1980s, witnessing struggles over who got to define whether the lyrics to rock music were corrupting or not, or whether rap music was dangerous and misogynist, media historians were also revealing the roots of such struggles in the past. And we were insisting that cultural practices, leisure time, and popular entertainments were not marginal to our understanding of American history; they were, in fact, central.

At the same time that so many of us were happily discovering that we now actually had an intellectual community of our own, we were also coming to terms with differences among our interpretations and analytical frameworks. Christopher Lasch, in *The Culture of Narcissism* (1978), brilliantly portrayed the role that the media, and especially advertising, played in constituting the "narcissistic personality of our time," a person utterly reliant on the approval of others, desperate to make a good first impression, filled with a deep self-loathing, terrified of aging and death, and having no core, independent self. But Lasch consistently used the pronoun "he" to describe this person when women were much more frequently the targets of media messages and advertising than men. Worse, as Lasch looked back longingly to some Edenic time when such influences were not ubiquitous, he blamed feminism for the collapse of traditional communities that supposedly protected people from the blandishments of narcissism (but not, I might note, from the strictures of patriarchy). Many scholars who found this book crucially important had to cannibalize it, drawing from the acute observations in the beginning, ignoring or attacking those at the end.

In fact, one question that began to emerge in the 1980s was whether there was some unspoken hierarchy of what we could study: maybe old radio or cinema was OK, but what about soap operas, or those women's films known as "the weepies," or girl group music (as opposed to James Dean or "the King")? This was an unspoken hierarchy left over from the 1950s that feminists quickly challenged. Janice Radway (1984), for example, in a pathbreaking book, decided to study a popular culture text utterly ridiculed by most of the mainstream media: the romance novel. The prevailing image of romance novel readers was of utterly passive women who were gulping down trash novels that encouraged them to accept their own oppression and the dominance of men. But in a careful study of a group of such readers, *Reading the Romance*, Radway found deep contradictions in women's uses of these books. Reading them allowed the women to escape from their domestic duties as wives and mothers. And the stories replayed a rather compelling fantasy: a strong, smart, independent heroine meets an initially aloof, insensitive man whom, over the course of the novel, she succeeds in turning into a more nurturing, caring man. While the novels did indeed reaffirm the dominance of men and the importance of women conforming to the demands of patriarchal marriages, they also offered an image of women humanizing patriarchy. It was these kinds of contradictions that exist in media texts, and in the subjectivities of the audience members who consume them, that reshaped the writing of media history.

Likewise, in *Where the Girls Are* (1994), I challenged the assumption that popular culture aimed at women and girls from the 1950s on was uniformly sexist trash and/or irrelevant to women's history. It was important to me to dethrone the conceit that James Dean mattered but The Shirelles did not, and to help women see how the mainstream media had simultaneously ridiculed feminism while giving feminist activists and ideas a national platform that would change gender roles radically. Robert Allen, in addition to other work, took two benighted forms, the soap opera and burlesque, and examined their gender politics and subversive potentials (Allen, 1985, 1991).

African American scholars too wanted to dethrone white, male-authored (or attended) media and entertainments as the primary objects of research. In fact, media studies and media history began to assume greater significance outside the academy because political battles, especially those around race and gender, were being fought out through cultural representations in the media. For example, when ABC aired the mini-series *Roots* in January 1977 and scored record-breaking ratings – as many as 80 million viewers – the saga of African American history and the indictment of the ravages of slavery were a crucial corrective to decades of media stereotyping of blacks as inferior to whites. Yet by the mid-1980s, when conservative politicians and pundits used the media to attack affirmative action as unfair, welfare as promoting a "cycle of dependency," and used the image of Willie Horton, a black convict, to attack the policies of Democratic presidential candidate Michael Dukakis, African Americans (and many whites) saw the power of cultural politics to shape right-wing public policy, and to dress up old racial stereotypes in distracting and even seductive new clothes. Black filmmakers, comedians, and musicians fought back. Herman Gray, in *Watching Race* (1994), analyzed this "struggle to define blackness," and emphasized both the power of political and media elites to magnify and reinforce persistent stereotypes as well as the power and determination of black artists, and audiences, to defy, repudiate, and reconfigure such imagery. After all, this was the decade when *Cosby* was the number one sitcom in the country, when rap music went mainstream, when Spike Lee became one of the nation's most preeminent directors, and when a shameless stereotype of black male criminality played a central role in electing George Bush president, all at the same time.

The history of racial stereotyping in the media also became more nuanced. Minstrelsy – the practice of blacking up one's face and performing the stereotype of the black man as stupid, childlike, lazy, and happy-go-lucky – dates back to the 1830s, and initially historians denounced these portrayals as stemming from and reinforcing white racism. But scholars like Eric Lott (1995) and Michael Rogin (1996) emphasized that minstrelsy was also about whites' desire to embrace the sensuality and freedom they thought they saw in black culture, and about covert white longing for interracial exchange and comity. Lott and Rogin both insist that minstrelsy was not some marginal entertainment form, but was instead central to the evolution of American media culture. In fact, they argue, one of the ways that many white immigrants – Irish, Jewish, and Eastern and Southern European – came to feel more included in that category "American" was to watch white performers put on, and then take off, blackface, a symbolic rite of passage from ridiculed outsider to accepted American (Roediger, 1999). Again, in this work, it has been crucial to analyze how media representations could be contested, loved, and reviled, and could be, simultaneously, both politically progressive and deeply reactionary. Correspondingly, the new emphasis on how gender and race were, and are, socially constructed has prompted scholars like Michael Kimmel (1996), Gail Bederman (1995), Richard Dyer (1997), and others to see masculinity, and whiteness, as social constructions too, as masquerades of gender and race that people learn how to put on and wear.

By the 1980s, there was a name for this work that sought to embed media texts within broader social and cultural practices, and to blend an acknowledgment of the power of the mass media to shape and even define the overarching discourses of culture with an appreciation of audiences' abilities, at times, to see through, resist, and influence these discourses. That name was cultural studies. Emerging in Britain in the 1960s, and then influenced by intellectual trends in France, what came to be known as cultural studies began as an effort to overturn top-down elite histories, and instead to study history from the bottom up. Studies of working-class history had led to studies of working-class cultures, including the often oppositional youth sub-cultures that appeared in the 1960s and 1970s. Cultural studies drew from Marxist analyses of the power of the media to reinforce the privileged position of elites, but also emphasized the multiple ways in which audience members resisted or talked back to that power. "Culture" did not refer to some province of aesthetic excellence, like museums or symphonies, but rather was understood to include the texts and prac-tices of everyday life. And culture was characterized by struggle and conflict: women, white male elites, the working classes, young people, people of color, all fought over what culture should be and over who the proper arbiters of "good" culture should be as well. Cultural studies was never a coherent discipline with one method, but as an intellectual movement it prompted media historians to foreground certain themes, especially those that confronted the relationships between knowledge and power.

No scholar was more important in translating and distilling the ideas that emerged from this Birmingham–Paris axis than Stuart Hall, one of the founders of the Birmingham School. Hall's articles emphasized the importance of studying the media as the primary storytellers of our time whose narratives – whether fictional or repor-torial – contained dominant ideological themes that justified and reinforced state power, corporate power, and unequal economic relations. But in one of his most influential articles, "Encoding and Decoding" (1980), Hall also reminded us that not all viewers sit in their living rooms and buy the dominant set of meanings embed-ded in the news or a crime show. Rather, some read against the grain, taking excep-tion to particular versions of reality, while others reject the whole message outright. It was the elegance with which Hall continued to lay out the push and pull between media power and viewer resistance to that power that served as a model to so many of us struggling, still, to understand how different historical eras shaped the balance of power between these forces.

But cultural studies has also been controversial and resisted by many historians suspicious of an overemphasis on the discourses of texts instead of on the details of social, political, and economic history. Robert McChesney, an eminent historian of broadcasting and the media, has expressed concern that emphasis on the interpreta-tions of media texts and the supposed agency of the audience simply lets the culture industries off the hook, especially in an age of unprecedented mergers. In *Rich Media, Poor Democracy* (1999), for example, McChesney placed the political economy of the mass media, from an unabashedly Marxist perspective, front and center and effec-tively said, "It's consolidation, stupid," as he documented how the new media giants limit the range of political discourse and divert attention from their own growing power.

McChesney – and he was not alone – was also reacting to the work of John Fiske, probably the scholar most closely associated with the notion that audiences were active media consumers who talked back to their televisions, ripped their jeans to protest mass consumption and conformity, and appropriated media texts as their own by doing, say, "gay readings" of *Star Trek* or subversive readings of *Hart to Hart*. While Fiske's highly influential work was an important antidote to the kind of Frankfurt School view of media audiences as docile, stultified, and indoctrinated, many felt that Fiske went too far, seeing resistance everywhere.

The pendulum had indeed swung in the 1970s and 1980s from seeing media power as overwhelming to seeing it as highly resistible by savvy, defiant audiences. So the broadest challenge in our field remains that of assessing the enormous power of the media megaliths to colonize our inner selves, our very consciousness, and our daily practices while not losing sight of the fact that the nation is filled with different interpretive communities, some of whom swallow the media's versions of reality hook, line, and sinker, with others yelling obscenities at FOX-TV and defacing the ads in *Cosmopolitan*. While media studies scholars still appreciate that audience members do talk back to their televisions, radios, and magazines, they have also backed away from this, at times, overly optimistic view of audience power and resistance. At this point in media historiography there is hardly consensus about how much power the media have, but most scholars agree that the media, in the past and the present, have considerable ability to define what is and is not important and what should or should not be on the national agenda. The news media frequently set the agenda for political debate. The media constantly reaffirm what kinds of women deserve admiration and which kinds do not. In a still largely segregated society, they feature more African Americans than they used to while still accentuating the differences and conflict between blacks and whites and restricting African Americans to roles as comics or criminals. A few TV programs and films portray gays and lesbians, but the TV talk shows still present them as freaks. Most importantly, scholars are now noting the media's central role in advancing market ideology: the notion that "the market" is the best arbiter of social and political problems.

The biggest challenge we face as college professors is what media studies scholars call "the third person effect": the belief that others (too often, in my experience, referred to as "Joe Sixpack") are influenced by the media but we sophisticated college types are not. Too many students, in other words, see working- and lower-class audiences as passive and manipulable while seeing the educated classes – themselves – as impervious to the blandishments of the media. So getting students to view themselves as both active and passive media consumers, as filled with contradictory relationships to the media, as sucked into media discourses yet cynical about many of them, is to get them to internalize the last twenty years of work in cultural studies. And I will testify that that is often not easy.

Another major theme in our field is thinking about the evolution, which began in earnest in the 1970s, from a mass, national audience to niche markets based on demographics. In the 1970s and early 1980s, a host of new communication technologies redefined the scope of what people got to see in their living rooms, as well as the speed with which they saw it, and also gave them more control over what they watched and when. Videotape, which was much cheaper than film and did not need to be developed, brought news events more rapidly to viewers, and also led to some really ridiculous innovations like "Copter Cam," which showed news events from a chopper. Communications satellites also meant that images could be transmitted almost instantly from one continent to another; no more waiting for film footage to be flown in to the networks. In 1975, there was only one cable service that relied on satellite transmission; by 1985, the number had soared to sixty-five. In 1980, only 1.1 percent of TV homes had videocassette recorders; eight years later, 58 percent had them. In 1970, 7.6 percent of homes had cable service; in 1985, 43 percent did. The proliferation of cable channels and the rise of home movie-viewing took viewers away from the networks. But these trends also accelerated market segmentation, the dividing up of a formerly national audience into niches increasingly defined by age, gender, race, education, and socioeconomic rank. Media scholar Joseph Turow, in *Breaking Up America* (1997), documents this trend and argues that advertisers are exacerbating social divisions in America by producing "segment-making media" instead of "society-making media." Historians have only begun to examine these sea changes in the 1970s and 1980s and their impact, not just on a sense of nationhood, but also on Americans' sense of their connections to the rest of the world, on the tensions Americans feel between belonging to a nation, belonging to a locale, and belonging to a demographic group, and on their increasingly cynical attitudes to the media that assault them ever more aggressively with interlocking marketing campaigns. What does the dividing up of the country into ever finer demographic niches do to our notions of national identity, of sharing in a common culture, of needing to understand one another across racial, gendered, and generational divides? Turow suggests that this heightened perception of social division is now, through the media, being built into the very structures that shape people's lives, from the gated communities where many live to the separate media spheres in which they learn about and make sense of the world (Sunstein, 2001).

In fact, one of historians' major concerns is the extent to which consumerism, media saturation, and marketing ideology eradicate people's understanding of and appreciation for history itself. In a society in which shopping has become the number one cultural activity, in which people are constantly urged to abandon and forget the old in favor of the new and improved, and in which history is distorted or not presented at all in the mainstream media, Americans are repeatedly urged to disregard all histories except those of popular culture. So we go to a movie theater and see slides quizzing us about famous lines in movies, or watch quiz shows steeped in pop culture trivia. With history safely sequestered on "The History Channel" (nicknamed "The Hitler Channel" because of its repeated airings of World War II documentaries), Americans learn all too little about their own past, a trend the media have promoted and profited from. And when they do see media versions of history, as in the 2001 special effects blockbuster *Pearl Harbor*, historians who know what actually happened, but will never have that kind of storytelling apparatus at their disposal, are left to cry in their beers as they deplore what Americans do and do not learn about their own past (Kammen, 1991; McChesney, 1999).

One assumption the media reinforce when they retell their own history is that commercial support through advertising was really the only sensible way to support broadcasting. Radio historians like Robert McChesney (1993), Susan Smulyan (1994), and myself (1987) have taken on this notion that a commercially supported system of broadcasting was somehow inevitable. Silted under the media versions of broadcast history are stories of fierce opposition in the 1920s and 1930s to commercial domination of the airwaves. As Smulyan shows, even advertisers themselves were wary of radio, afraid of alienating customers by invading their homes with unwanted sales pitches. And in the late 1920s and early 1930s, as McChesney shows, there was a coordinated effort to reserve at least some small portion of the airwaves for noncommercial uses, an effort that failed in the face of equally fierce corporate lobbying. Media historians often find that their students, who are themselves relatively cynical about advertising, are nonetheless unaware that alternative forms of financing American broadcasting were even imagined, no less debated. It is when people do not know about this kind of history that they fail to imagine alternatives to the present system.

Historians will have to confront and understand better the rise of market segmentation in the media since the 1970s which has led, in part, to racial segregation in the television-viewing practices of blacks and whites. They will also need to assess the rise of celebrity journalism, increased sensationalism and reliance on "spin" in the news media, and the emergence of what Neal Gabler (1998) has called "the lifies": real-life dramas like the O. J. trial or the life and death of Princess Diana that become ongoing soap operas for weeks, months, or years. As people share fewer fictional programs in common, these sensationalized lifies have become the media glue that binds Americans in a common experience, but one that is riddled with political divisions (Gamson, 1994).

Although there has been a quantum change since 1970 in the sheer amount and high quality of media history being written, there is still so much we do not know. And, of course, it is exceedingly difficult to ascertain what past audiences made of the media that surrounded them, given that we have so few accounts of those reactions. Nonetheless, historians persist in trying to locate new sources and new stories. A resurgence in radio history, for example, has uncovered the rise of black radio in America, the importance of women's programming, and how discourses about gay men got woven into radio comedy and drama (Doty, 1994; Hilmes, 1998). Much still needs to be done on local radio stations and their relationship to social and cultural changes in cities and regions. Roland Marchand, in his magisterial *Advertising the American Dream* (1985), analyzed the modes of address, morality tales, and gender and racial codes of advertising in the 1920s and early 1930s. Thomas Frank, in *The Conquest of Cool* (1997), studied the revolution in advertising styles in the 1960s. But we still need more histories of advertising, especially in the postwar period, that consider the complicated and contradictory visual and textual appeals that have colonized Americans' imaginations. Tricia Rose, in *Black Noise* (1994), her study of the rise and significance of hip hop culture, showed how discourses quite at odds with those in the mainstream media – about police violence or inner-city poverty – circulated powerfully through music and constituted "hidden transcripts," a phrase borrowed from political anthropologist James Scott to describe alternative accounts of reality rarely heard on the nightly news. Likewise, in *Just My Soul Responding* (1994), Brian Ward showed how rhythm and blues and soul music gave sustenance to and also drew from the energy and politics of the civil rights movement. These are important beginnings, as the relationships between music and social change, including social movements, require much more work (Smith, 2000).

With the rise of media studies and media history has come a renewed denigration of that work: jokes in the press about how ridiculous it is to study Elvis, exposés of entire courses devoted to Oprah Winfrey, and so forth. But media history, virtually nonexistent thirty years ago, is here to stay, because the media themselves have become so central to people's everyday rituals and routines, and to their understandings of who they are and what in life is important. College students, in many ways quite sophisticated about the media, still hunger for a critical language and an historical framework that can give voice and shape to their perceptions. And the Internet, which has made possible all sorts of improbable communications while also morphing into an on-line strip mall, will confound and challenge a whole new generation of historians. Like my generation, they will look to the events of their own lives, ignore the nay sayers, and chart out a new scholarship that helps us understand how the media, with all their contradictions, burrow into our very hearts and minds, reconfiguring history in the process.

REFERENCES

Adorno, Theodor and Horkheimer, Max: *The Dialectic of Enlightenment* (New York: Herder and Herder, 1972).

Allen, Robert C.: *Speaking of Soap Operas* (Chapel Hill: University of North Carolina Press, 1985).

Allen, Robert C.: *Horrible Prettiness: Burlesque and American Culture* (Chapel Hill: University of North Carolina Press, 1991).

Anderson, Karen: *Wartime Women* (Westport, Conn.: Greenwood Press, 1981).

Bederman, Gail: *Manliness and Civilization* (Chicago: University of Chicago Press, 1995).

Blum, John: *V Was For Victory: Politics and American Culture During World War II* (New York: Harcourt Brace Jovanovich, 1976).

Buhle, Paul: *Marxism in the U.S.: Remapping the History of the American Left* (London: Verso, 1987a).

Buhle, Paul: *Popular Culture in America* (Minneapolis: University of Minnesota Press, 1987b).

Buhle, Paul: *Encyclopedia of the American Left* (New York: Garland, 1990).

Coontz, Stephanie: *The Way We Never Were* (New York: Basic Books, 1992).

Czitrom, Daniel: *Media and the American Mind: From Morse to McLuhan* (Chapel Hill: University of North Carolina Press, 1982).

Denning, Michael: *The Cultural Front* (New York: Verso, 1996).

Doty, Alexander: *Making Things Perfectly Queer* (Minneapolis: University of Minnesota Press, 1994).

Douglas, Susan: *Inventing American Broadcasting, 1899–1922* (Baltimore: Johns Hopkins University Press, 1987).

Douglas, Susan: *Where the Girls Are: Growing Up Female with the Mass Media* (New York: Times Books, 1994).

Douglas, Susan: *Listening In: Radio and the American Imagination* (New York: Times Books, 1999).

Dyer, Richard: *White* (New York: Routledge, 1997).

Field, Connie: *The Life and Times of Rosie the Riveter* (film, 1981).

Fiske, John: *Understanding Popular Culture* (Boston: Unwin Hyman, 1989).

Fiske, John: *Media Matters: Everyday Culture and Political Change* (Minneapolis: University of Minnesota Press, 1994).

Fox, Richard Wightman and Lears, T. J. Jackson: *The Culture of Consumption* (New York: Pantheon, 1983).

Gabler, Neal: *Life: The Movie* (New York: Alfred A. Knopf, 1998).

Gamson, Joshua: *Claims to Fame: Celebrity in Contemporary America* (Berkeley: University of California Press, 1994).

Gans, Herbert: *Deciding What's News* (New York: Vintage, 1980).

Gilbert, James B.: *A Cycle of Outrage: America's Reaction to the Juvenile Delinquent in the 1950s* (New York: Oxford University Press, 1988).

Gitlin, Todd: *The Whole World is Watching* (Berkeley: University of California Press, 1980).

Gramsci, Antonio: *Selections from the Prison Notebooks*, trans. Quintin Hoare and Geoffrey Nowell Smith (New York: International Publishers, 1971).

Gray, Herman: *Watching Race* (Minneapolis: University of Minnesota Press, 1994).

Hall, Stuart: "Encoding and Decoding," in Stuart Hall et al., *Culture, Media, Language* (London: Hutchinson, 1980).

Hall, Stuart: "Notes on Deconstructing the Popular," in R. Samuel (ed.), *People's History and Socialist Theory* (London: Routledge and Kegan Paul, 1981).

Hall, Stuart: "The Rediscovery of Ideology," in Michael Gurevitch et al., *Culture, Society and the Media* (London: Methuen, 1982).

Hilmes, Michele: *Radio Waves* (Minneapolis: University of Minnesota Press, 1998).

Horowitz, Daniel: *Vance Packard and American Social Criticism* (Chapel Hill: University of North Carolina Press, 1994).

Jowett, Garth: *Film: The Democratic Art* (Boston: Little, Brown, 1976).

Kammen, Michael: *Mystic Chords of Memory: The Transformation of Tradition in American Culture* (New York: Vintage, 1991).

Kasson, John: *Amusing the Million* (New York: Hill and Wang, 1978).

Kimmel, Michael: *Manhood in America* (New York: Free Press, 1996).

Koppes, Clayton R.: *Hollywood Goes to War: How Politics, Profits and Propaganda Shaped World War II Movies* (Berkeley: University of California Press, 1990).

Lasch, Christopher: *The Culture of Narcissism: American Life in an Age of Diminishing Expectations* (New York: W. W. Norton, 1978).

Lears, T. J. Jackson: *Fables of Abundance* (New York: Basic Books, 1994).

Lipsitz, George: *Time Passages* (Minneapolis: University of Minnesota Press, 1980).

Lott, Eric: *Love and Theft* (New York: Oxford University Press, 1995).

McChesney, Robert: *Telecommunications, Mass Media and Democracy* (New York: Oxford University Press, 1993).

McChesney, Robert: *Rich Media, Poor Democracy* (Urbana and Chicago: University of Illinois Press, 1999).

McLuhan, Marshall: *Understanding Media* (New York: Signet, 1964).

Marchand, Roland: *Advertising the American Dream* (Berkeley: University of California Press, 1985).

Nyberg, Amy Kiste: *Seal of Approval: The History of the Comics Code* (Jackson: University Press of Mississippi, 1998).

Nye, Russel: *The Unembarrassed Muse: The Popular Arts in America* (New York: Dial Press, 1970).

Packard, Vance: *The Hidden Persuaders* (New York: D. McKay, 1957).

Peiss, Kathy: *Cheap Amusements: Working Women and Leisure in Turn-of-the-Century New York* (Philadelphia: Temple University Press, 1986).

Radway, Janice: *Reading the Romance* (Chapel Hill: University of North Carolina Press, 1984).

Roediger, David R.: *Wages of Whiteness: Race and the Making of the American Working Class*, rev. ed. (New York: Verso, 1999).

Rogers, Everett: *A History of Communication Study: A Biographical Approach* (New York: Free Press, 1994).

Rogin, Michael: *Blackface, White Noise* (Berkeley: University of California Press, 1996).

Rose, Tricia: *Black Noise: Rap Music and Black Culture in Contemporary America* (Hanover, NH: Wesleyan University Press, 1994).

Rosenberg, Bernard and White, David Manning: *Mass Culture: The Popular Arts in America* (New York: Free Press, 1957).

Rosenzweig, Roy: *Eight Hours for What We Will* (New York: Cambridge University Press, 1983).

Schiller, Daniel: *Objectivity and the News* (Philadelphia: University of Pennsylvania Press, 1981).

Schudson, Michael: *Discovering the News* (New York: Basic Books, 1978).

Smith, Suzanne E.: *Dancing in the Street: Motown and the Cultural Politics of Detroit* (Cambridge, Mass.: Harvard University Press, 2000).

Smulyan, Susan: *Selling Radio* (Washington, DC: Smithsonian Institution Press, 1994).

Stone, Joseph and Yohn, Tim: *Prime Time and Misdemeanors: Investigating the 1950s TV Quiz Scandal* (New Brunswick, NJ: Rutgers University Press, 1992).

Sunstein, Cass: *Republic.com* (Princeton, NJ: Princeton University Press, 2001).

Turow, Joseph: *Breaking Up America* (Chicago: University of Chicago Press, 1997).

Ward, Brian: *Just My Soul Responding: Rhythm and Blues, Black Consciousness, and Race Relations* (Berkeley: University of California Press, 1998).

CHAPTER SIX

What the Traffic Bares: Popular Music "Back in the USA"

ALLEN TULLOS

"Of books on American popular music there seems to be no end," wrote David Ewen, the author of many by his seventieth year, as he delivered his nimble-toed, eight-hundred-page *All the Years of American Popular Music*, promising an "entire world ... in all its varied facets within a single volume" (Ewen, 1977, p. vii). In "attempting what no book so far has attempted," Ewen sketches musical milieus, song-writers, and singers from the congregations of colonial New England to the soul of Aretha Franklin and James Brown. Most comfortable chronicling Tin Pan Alley, musical theater, and Hollywood soundtracks, Ewen dutifully follows the left political culture of the 1930s into the 1950s Folk Revival. An open ear to oncoming sounds and a curiosity about commodity forms set him grappling with LPs, 45s, radio DJs, television dance parties, and the rock and roll juggernaut with which teen culture supplanted the centrality of show tunes, swing bands, and croony ballads. It's all requisite and too much, with still so much unexamined. Bo Diddley's 1959 warning that "you can't judge a book by looking at the cover" goes unsung in the now out-of-print *All the Years of American Popular Music*.

Meanwhile, crusty Carl Sandburg's help-yourself collection of tunes and lyrics, *The American Songbag* (first published in 1927), still thrives, as do similar compilations by various Lomaxes and Seegers, all manner of hymnals and gospel softbacks, key-board fake books, Sousa march scores, as well as Dixieland and ragtime how-to's. Old musics for new covers. Seedbeds of song waiting to sprout wings and fly.

"If there is a single feature which both characterizes and defines American music," concludes David Nicholls (1998, p. xiii), editor of *The Cambridge History of American Music*, "it is diversity." Susan McClary, a crossover musicologist tracing the currents of European classical music while coming to terms with American popular repertories, agrees, arguing for tributaries and channels, but "no single main stream" (2000, p. 32). American music has found many rivers to cross, skate away on, dive into, roll on, or be washed or drowned in. The murmurings of these streams entrance children, punch their way out of juke boxes, mingle with the glow of dashboard lights, transport sinners, conjure melancholy and memory, get squeezed into elevators, and are downloaded by college students until the bandwidth chokes and the campus servers crash again.

The author would like to thank Cynthia Blakeley, Tim Dowd, Walt Reed, and Nick Spitzer for their readings and helpful suggestions.

All of these musical flows and popular traffickings have chroniclers and critics. "There are probably already more anthologies devoted to jazz than to any other twentieth-century musical genre," prefaces Robert Walser in his excellent jazz history reader, *Keeping Time* (1999, p. ix). Bookshelves sag with the weight of the blues, with rock paeans, with lives and times of country and western stars, with biographical regards to Broadway, and encyclopedias of pop. Late twentieth-century scenes such as punk, rap, and metal quickly attracted journalists and doctoral students. Hipper-than-thou critics, along with determined producers of specialized albums and CDs, harvest reviews and liner notes into published collections. Writing or listening, who can keep afloat, sort the hype, check out the venues and CD bins, count the money, assess the talent on myriad labels and formats bundled together and hustled mainly by a handful of global entertainment corporations? Any pretense of commanding the liquid landscape of American popular music perches on an eroding watchtower while dissidents laugh and spray graffiti in broad daylight before clearing away a site for, say, the Lounge Music Hall of Fame.

Unchained Melodies

In the years immediately following World War II, as the decline of big band swing gave way to finger-snapping pop vocalists doing their renditions of melodic "standards" and novelty songs from the handful of major record companies, a domestic climate settled in that complemented the Truman foreign policy of containment. "The values of the white middle class," argues Elaine Tyler May (1988, p. 13), "shaped the dominant political and economic institutions that affected all Americans. Those who did not conform to them were likely to be marginalized, stigmatized, and disadvantaged as a result." Mainly from the young and the marginal, in late-night dance clubs and juke joints, on upstart labels and regional radio stations ushering in the golden age of the disk jockey, came the speeding, noisy musics which rattled the wheels off the vehicles of domesticated, sentimental tunes and shook up America's sexual, racial, and class conventions.

"As was the case with television and film," notes George Lipsitz (1994, p. 304), attuned to the American cultural rainbow and the working-class origins of rock and roll, "industrial modes of production, commodity form, monopoly control, private censorship, and state regulation all narrowed the range of what could be done within popular music." Yet, he adds, "for all of its shortcomings, commercial popular music in the postwar period emerged as one site where the blasted hopes and utopian aspirations of working-class life found expression." Russell and David Sanjek's indispensable *Pennies From Heaven* (1996), which tracks the business of popular music throughout the twentieth century, notes the flowering of hundreds of small record companies by the mid-1950s (see also Gillett, 1970).

Reading the postwar alternatives can begin with the move from swing to bebop as expressive of shifting racial and professional possibilities for musicians in the city, across the generations, and on the road between gigs. It has taken time, however, to assemble the complexities. First came books placing the music and its players in history and on a lasting map. These extend from Rudi Blesh's retrospective *Shining Trumpets* (1946), Leonard Feather's *Inside Be-Bop* (1949) and *The Encyclopedia of Jazz* (1955), to Nat Hentoff's *The Jazz Life* (1961), Martin Williams's *The Jazz*

Tradition (1970), and many, many others. While blowing jazz's horn, US writer-aficionados frequently neglected discussion of the cash nexus. "One of the most striking aspects of the writing on jazz," observes Scott DeVeaux, "is a reluctance to relate the history of the music to the messy and occasionally sordid economic circumstances of its production."

> Many of the most prolific proselytizers for jazz – Leonard Feather, Martin Williams, Dan Morgenstern, Stanley Dance, John Hammond, Gene Lees, Gunther Schuller – have been intimately familiar with the business side of music. . . . These experiences, however, seem to have made them more determined than ever to present jazz as something other than a form of entertainment shaped by mass consumer preferences. (DeVeaux, 1997, pp. 12, 13)

Characteristic of the best new writing about popular music, DeVeaux's *The Birth of Bebop* is a dust-settled revisiting that wrestles the legendary while gauging the social, personal, economic, and musical pressures present at a form's creation.

A suggestive list of recent jazz books reveals the formats through which American writers continue to deepen the scrutiny of key practices and performers. Paul F. Berliner's *Thinking in Jazz* (1994) combines oral history, music theory, and cultural interpretation to delve into learning, transmission, and making it up as you go. Veteran critic Gary Giddens's *Visions of Jazz* (1998) moves among over eighty major American performers exploring the distinct, yet intertwined, stylistics of each. Mark Tucker (1993) anthologizes the sole subject of Duke Ellington. From the Institute for Research in African American Studies at Columbia University comes Robert G. O'Meally's *The Jazz Cadence of American Culture* (1998), an essential collection of some three dozen wide-ranging essays featuring writers such as Zora Neale Hurston, Olly Wilson, Albert Murray, and Hazel Carby. Narrating from style to style, Ted Gioia's *The History of Jazz* (1997) offers a synthesis of the music that, as Louis Armstrong put it, is never played the same way once. Preston Love's *A Thousand Honey Creeks Later* (1997) invites readers into the life and times of a working, thoughtful instrumentalist who played the full range of African American musics.

In the territory between jazz and pop, many wonderful singers – a partial list includes Ella Fitzgerald, Peggy Lee, Nat "King" Cole, Sarah Vaughan, Bing Crosby, Frank Sinatra, Barbra Streisand, and Tony Bennett – are the subjects of biographies and autobiographies, but are missing the kind of historicized grouping and cultural analysis such as Angela Y. Davis (1998) has given Billie Holiday in her book about classic blues women, or Richard Peterson (1997) has given to country music stars. Margo Jefferson's brief essay on Sinatra (1998), for example, has more smart things to offer than a whole shelf of filiopietisms. Having said that, however, readers will enjoy Henry Pleasants's *The Great American Popular Singers* (1974) as an instance of an appreciative, ungushing narrative. Charles L. Granata's *Sessions with Sinatra* (1999), a chronological close study of representative studio sessions, combines interviews with Sinatra collaborators (musicians, engineers, producers, executives) and unedited studio discs and tapes to develop a (still overly reverent) musical biography alongside a fifty-year history of recording technology and music industry trends.

The situation is similar when it comes to the theatrical musical, despite Broadway's presence at the crossroads of American entertainment, commerce, song and dance, and dress-up fantasy. Readers might begin with Joseph P. Swain's *The Broadway Musical* (1990), then venture on to Geoffrey and Fred Block's *Enchanted Evenings* (1997), and veteran writer Gerald Martin Bordman's *American Musical Theatre* (2001). D. A. Miller's meditation on homosexuality and Broadway, *A Place for Us* (2000) opens new possibilities for engagement with the musical. Two aptly titled works, Roy Pendergast's *Film Music: A Neglected Art* (1992) and Laurence E. MacDonald's *The Invisible Art of Film Music* (1998), present another major popular form that has yet to draw sufficient historical-critical analysis.

Remarkable in his ability to listen with equivalent urgency, concern, and excitement to Broadway's Sondheim, alongside John Cage, Philip Glass, Laurie Anderson, Ornette Coleman, Eddie Palmieri, Neil Young, and other selected worthies of "composition," classically honed critic John Rockwell welcomes the prospects for an *All American Music* (1983) increasingly ecumenical, catholic, technologically sophisticated, and open to world influences.

Blues People

Books which take the blues as their main subject begin with Samuel Charters's *The Country Blues* (1959) and Paul Oliver's *Blues Fell This Morning* (1960). *Blues People* (1963) by Amiri Baraka [LeRoi Jones] remains one of the most provocative and important works in its seeking of the social meanings of the blues and jazz, and in connecting African American music with the African diaspora. Charles Keil's *Urban Blues* (1966) is an impassioned, personalized effort at depicting roles of black masculinity through the figure and context of the bluesman. With the widening realization of the blues' expressive nuances and emotional power, and its inflection upon twentieth-century popular music of all stripes, has come a continuous river of writing. Paul Oliver's edited series of blues paperbacks for Stein and Day/Studio Vista in the early 1970s enabled a number of young American, British, and European students of the form (David Evans, Bill Ferris, Bruce Bastin, Tony Russell, Bengt Olsson, et al.) to publish research and fieldwork that extended from Mississippi to West Africa.

Outstanding ethnomusicological studies include Jeff Todd Titon's *Early Downhome Blues* (1977), Evans's *Big Road Blues* (1982), and Alan Lomax's *The Land Where the Blues Began* (1993). Richard Wright's *Black Boy/American Hunger* (1945/1991) tells how it felt to have the hellhound on your trail. Lawrence Levine's influential *Black Culture and Black Consciousness* (1977) synthesized generations of work by song collectors, anthropologists, historians, and folklorists in showing how African Americans shaped the contours of West African culture in New World situations, creating such forms as the spiritual, blues, jazz, gospel, Bad Man ballads, toasts, and dozens. Robert Palmer's *Deep Blues* (1981) pursues the origins of the Delta sound and the move up Highway 61 to Chicago and electrification. Nadine Cohodas's *Spinning Blues into Gold* (2000) is a thorough accounting of the immigrant Polish Jewish Chess Brothers and their legendary label.

From the restless moment in which young, white, British men of the late 1950s and early 1960s transformed the blues and the bluesman into terms expressive of their own needs for satisfaction, McClary has pointed to "an ideology of noncommercial authenticity" as a major constituent of the rebellious self-images of performers such as John Mayall, Eric Clapton, and Mick Jagger. Reminiscent of DeVeaux's commentary on writers about jazz, she suggests that this ideology "continues to inform many of the rock critics who emerged . . . as the historians, theorists, and arbiters of popular taste" (McClary, 2000, p. 60).

As a revision of writers who have had difficulty hearing or knowing what to do with the anomalous but unforgettable women consigned to the "classic blues," feminist scholars have placed singers such as Gertrude "Ma" Rainey, Bessie Smith, Ida Cox, and Billie Holiday in a complex racial entertainment milieu. Sustained through a commercial nexus of vaudeville, jazz, Tin Pan Alley, club dates, and recordings, these blues women sought strategies of survival and creativity, which included the voicing of their own expressions of sexuality. Central to this perspective are Carby (1998 [1986]), Daphne Duval Harrison's *Black Pearls* (1988), and Davis's *Blues Legacies and Black Feminism* (1998).

American Routes

Decades-long efforts by scholars and fieldworkers, small-label record producers, specialized journals, and cultural institutes have led to a deepening knowledge of American roots musics such as Cajun and zydeco, jazz, Appalachian vocal and instrumental traditions, conjunto and orquesta, gospel, and occupational and protest song. Serge Denisoff's *Great Day Coming* (1971), an examination of the use of folk music by the political left, and Archie Green's *Only a Miner: Studies in Recorded Coal-Mining Songs* (1972) were the first two of many books in the ongoing Music in American Life series (guided by the general editorship of Judith McCulloh) from the University of Illinois Press. This consistently thoughtful and well-researched series has ranged across genres such as doowop, Piedmont blues, railroad song, Texas swing, and sixties rock.

Religious music, which may be the most frequently heard and widely performed of American popular musics, persists and permutates in urban, suburban, and grass-roots places, yet there are precious few books devoted to the subject. Major singers and styles in the African American gospel tradition are discussed in Anthony Heilbut's standard work, *The Gospel Sound* (1971, 1997), and in Clarence Boyer's *How Sweet the Sound* (1995). Activist-scholar-performer Bernice Johnson Reagon's edited collection, *We'll Understand It Better By and By* (1992), offers perspectives upon a variety of gospel composers, while Michael Harris fleshes out the mighty, singular example of Thomas Dorsey (1992). Recent work on American sacred music tends toward close, particular studies such as those by Jeff Todd Titon (1988) and Beverly Bush Patterson (1995) in Southern Appalachia, Kip Lornell (1988) and Alan Young (1997) in Memphis and environs, Ray Allen (1991) in New York City, and Jacqueline DjeDje and Eddie Meadows in California (1998). As part of their general concern with music and social change, Brian Ward (1998) and Craig Werner (1999) take up the influence of African American religious song upon the freedom struggle. An exemplary ethnography of the black gospel service as form and experience is Glenn Hinson's *Fire in My Bones* (2000).

Through an inquiry into invented traditions such as the fiddle convention and the folk school, and introduced instruments such as the dulcimer, David Whisnant's *All*

That Is Native and Fine (1983) provides essential background to politics of culture and the role of outside interveners in the formation of modern Appalachian identity. In her exhaustive field and archive-based project, Cecelia Conway (1995) runs down the Afro-Celtic nexus in Appalachia by means of the banjo. Folksong revivalism, and the many meanings and purposes to which the "folk" have been put, are pursued in Norm Cohen (1990), Robert Cantwell's *When We Were Good* (1996), Peter Goldsmith's *Making People's Music* (1998), Greil Marcus's hyperdramatized and Dylan-obsessed *Invisible Republic* (1997), and Benjamin Filene's *Romancing the Folk* (2000). Charles Wolfe and Kip Lornell's *The Life and Legend of Leadbelly* (1992) locates the most well-known African American folksinger within cultural history. By tracing a lineage from Walt Whitman through Woody Guthrie and Bruce Springsteen, Bryan Garman's *A Race of Singers* (2000) uncovers potentials and limits of the working-class hero.

The study of Latin music's influence and its relation to changing US politics and demography has grown from pathbreaking works by Américo Paredes (1958, 1976), John D. Robb (1980), and Manuel Peña (1985) to John Storm Roberts's overview, *The Latin Tinge* (2nd ed., 1999), which extends from old forms in the Southwest, to Afro-Cuban inflected styles, through tango, rhumba, and mambo eras, to New York salsa and Latinized jazz. Steven Loza's excellent *Barrio Rhythm* (1993) searches out Mexican American music in Los Angeles since the mid-1940s. In *Tito Puente and the Making of Latin Music* (1999), Loza carries readers from mambo to salsa via the long creative life and legacy of a major figure and popularizer.

The first books to consider how the white, working-class, honky tonk milieu (as expressed in steel guitar-based amplified music and cheating songs) met the pressures and temptations, pushes and pulls of farm to city migration, the changing ways of work, and new sexual situations include Robert Shelton and Burt Goldblatt's *The Country Music Story* (1966), and Bill Malone's landmark *Country Music U.S.A.* (1968). Across many years, Charles K. Wolfe has proved himself country music's most authoritative grassroots-based chronicler. On the other hand, Cecelia Tichi (1994) leaps geographies, eras, and literary and artistic canons in connecting a personal vision of "country" with transcendent "American" themes. More helpful is her anthology, *Reading Country Music* (1998). Cantwell (1984) and Neil Rosenberg (1985) delve into the roots and leaves of bluegrass. Loretta Lynn's *Coal Miner's Daughter* (1976) tells candidly of the life and career of a major singer-songwriter whose experiences span country's history. Gerald Haslam's *Workin' Man Blues* (1999) considers country music in California, while Nicholas Dawidoff's *In the Country of Country* (1997) is an evocative geocultural foray.

Richard Peterson's indispensable *Creating Country Music: Fabricating Authenticity* (1997) follows the music's institutionalization from its hillbilly Opry era through several stages of reinvention. *The Encyclopedia of Country Music* (1998), edited by Paul Kingsbury, is the genre's most helpful reference book. More often than not, writing about country fails to address the music's chronic reactionary politics, its sexism, jingoism, and racism. Glimpses of the possible are raised in Mary Bufwack and Robert Oermann's compendium on women in country music, *Finding Her Voice* (1993). Dorothy Allison's novel *Bastard Out of Carolina* (1992) powerfully conveys how country and gospel were felt and put to use in fantasy and everyday life at one site of their reception during the 1950s.

Highways Revisited

As for all those rock and rollers stirring out of the mid-1950s and early 1960s, books since Charlie Gillett's *The Sound of the City* (1970) have visited and revisited the primal scenes out of which rhythm and blues, rockabilly, and gospel propelled the emergence of a music that threatened to transform everything in its path. Greil Marcus, whose unequivocal commentaries and analysis began in the 1960s and continue into the post-punk, dead Elvis years, remains most widely known for *Mystery Train* (1976), a regularly revised milestone-millstone of rock and roll origins that spins insight and casts hard-to-break spells. Peter Guralnick's years of intrepid labor in, around, and out of the cradle of Memphis make for required reading in *Sweet Soul Music: Rhythm and Blues and the Southern Dream of Freedom* (1986); *Last Train to Memphis: The Rise of Elvis Presley* (1994); and *Careless Love: The Unmaking of Elvis Presley* (1999).

Ed Ward, Geoffrey Stokes, and Ken Tucker's *Rock of Ages* (1986) remains a valuable source for the 1950s through the early 1980s. Craig Morrison (1996) lays down the definitive rockabilly tract. Reebee Garofalo's *Rockin' Out: Popular Music in the USA* (1997) is a readable catalogue of industry trends, bands, and stars during the last half of the twentieth century. Important for understanding soul music are Guralnick (1986), Rochelle Larkin (1970), Gerri Hirshey's *Nowhere to Run* (1984), and Robert Pruter's *Chicago Soul* (1991). Through a focus upon black radio and record companies, Nelson George, in *The Death of Rhythm and Blues* (1988), bemoans assimilationist practices in the music entertainment business. Timothy White's *The Nearest Faraway Place* (1994) almost does what it should in connecting the Beach Boys and the emergence of the California sound with our worst family secrets, but ultimately fails to link the smiley smile of white Americans to the surf of Southeast Asia. Rickey Vincent (1996) brings the funk. The irrupting vitality of punk and post-punk, amid new rounds of British invaders, is thrashed about, along with an eyeful of spit aimed at MTV, in Marcus's *Ranters and Crowd Pleasers* (1993). Both musicologist Walser (1993) and sociologist Deena Weinstein (2000) bring seriousness to the study of metal's performers, audience, and ethos.

Stepping back at the end of the 1990s to survey aspects of African American music in the post-World War II history, Ward (1998), Werner (1999), and Suzanne E. Smith (1999) examine how shifts in the popularity of musical forms and the development of markets relate to struggles for desegregation, empowerment, and social justice. "The most popular black musical styles and artists of the past forty years," observes Ward, "have achieved their popularity precisely because they have dramatized and expressed, but also helped to shape and define, a succession of black consciousnesses" (1998, p. 15).

Ward reconstructs emblematic scenes of the 1950s and 1960s that reveal the disparity between white responses to, and white understanding of, black music. He notes that black music was "enthusiastically admired" when it fulfilled romanticized white expectations about black grace and ease with leisure, pleasure, sex, and style. "But this," Ward insists, "required no real consideration of, or empathy with, the frequently unromantic circumstances from whence those qualities in black culture emerged" (p. 360). Through her study of Motown, Smith reveals how the music of black Detroit engaged the issues of African Americans in that center of industrial worker migration. Beyond Motown's relationship to the cultural politics of Detroit, her work is a demonstration that "place matters – that productive social, cultural, economic, and political changes emerge from distinctive communities" (1999, p. 259). Ranging more broadly in space and time than Smith, Mark Anthony Neal's *What the Music Said* (1999) is a strongly argued, passionately felt articulation of music and the politics of resistance proceeding on the assumption that, from bebop to hip hop, "the black popular music tradition has served as a primary vehicle for communally derived critiques of the African-American experience" (p. xi).

Rock and roll writing seldom presses social justice to the fore as urgently as the tradition linking Jones [Baraka], Keil, Werner, Ward, Smith, Rose, and Neal. One recent attempt is Michael Bertrand's *Race, Rock, and Elvis* (2000). But with rock, there is always scads of money to track. Steve Chapple and Garofalo (1977) bring venerable muckraking tools to bear, while, despite its too-contrived categories, Philip Ennis's *The Seventh Stream* (1992) keeps the economic as well as stylistic constituents of rock in mind. Fred Goodman lays out the schemes and ambitions of managers and promoters in *The Mansion on the Hill* (1997). John Jackson's *American Bandstand* (1997) meticulously trails Dick Clark's pocket-lining as well as his central role in mediating rock and roll to an emerging mass television audience. Tired of simplistic arguments over whether "production determines consumption or whether audiences can subvert the power of corporate controlled production," Keith Negus moves "to consider some of the ways that popular music is mediated by a series of technological, cultural, historical, geographical and political factors" (1996, p. 65).

Important as deep background for the artistic resources and survival practices needed to understand rap are Roger D. Abrahams's study of the toasts and dozens in Philadelphia, *Deep Down in the Jungle* (1964, 1970), and Henry Louis Gates's theorizing of the speakerly text in *The Signifying Monkey* (1988). Alan Light's *The Vibe History of Hip Hop* (1999) offers an introduction to a subcultural style gone very large. Nelson George's *Hip Hop America* (1998) is helpful, despite George's slighting women performers and gender politics. Straight outta the Music/Culture Series of Wesleyan University Press comes Tricia Rose's exemplary *Black Noise* (1994), a study of how rap's reportage emerged to represent the South Bronx in the 1970s. Rose tackles many difficult things head on, including the sexual politics, critiquing limitations in white feminism while arguing that "black women rappers have effectively changed the interpretive framework for the work of male rappers" (p. 182).

A major assemblage of women's music criticism is *Rock She Wrote* (1995), edited by Evelyn McDonnell and Ann Powers. Here, gathered in one place, but not of one mind, are Ellen Willis from the 1960s, Patti Smith from the 1970s, Thulani Davis from the 1980s, bell hooks from the 1990s, and many others forgotten or separated in the library stacks. Also not to be missed is McClary's take on Madonna the musician in *Feminine Endings* (1991). The most significant and sustained exploration of the interplay between feminist issues and musical cultures is Sheila Whiteley's *Women and Popular Music* (2000).

Building upon lessons learned from British cultural studies, an exciting new approach to popular music takes the interplay of instrumentation, creative longing, capitalist marketing, and the changing values ascribed to sonority as its subject. In *Any Sound You Can Imagine*, Paul Théberge pursues the hybridity of digital music-making and sound reproduction since the early 1980s as a way of studying not only the effects of high tech on popular music, but of examining the tension "between the desire to create, communicate, and consume" in which musicians simultaneously define themselves and in which they find themselves caught (1997, p. 255). Extending Théberge, but fundamentally inspired by the French musicologist Jacques Attali (1985), Steve Waksman's *Instruments of Desire* combines a history of the electric guitar with a study of modes of musical practice that emphasizes musicians' engagement with particular ways of shaping sound (1999, p. 8). As Waksman shows in a series of case studies, noisy new instruments and reorganizations of musical practice by no means guarantee "progressive or liberatory" reconceptualizations of "social and political differences through music" (p. 12).

Dangerous Crossroads

By the mid-1980s, writes David Sanjek, "while record companies and retailers exerted a stranglehold on the music business, consumers began to purchase an increasingly diverse body of music." Much as rhythm and blues, and rock and roll, had done beginning in the mid-1940s, emerging genres such as punk, new wave, women's music, rap, and heavy metal appeared first on small independent labels which the A&R staffs of the majors treated "as farm teams, waiting to see which of their artists found a constituency and then offering them lucrative contracts" (Sanjek and Sanjek, 1996, p. 657).

Echoing Sanjek, but from deep within the rhetorical thicket thrown up in *Dancing In Spite of Myself* (1997), Lawrence Grossberg announces that the "rock formation" which "emerged in the 1950s to become the dominant cultural formation of youth (if not of the United States) from the 1960s until the mid-1980s" had, by the end of the 1980s, been replaced by a new dominant formation of "eclecticism and hybridity," "a network of scenes," that, for better *and* worse, "willingly and simultaneously embraces the global megastar and the local rebel" (p. 21). Grossberg ponders how rock has tangled with alienation, powerlessness, and boredom to provide "strategies of survival and pleasure for its fans." Selectively combining approaches of two British scholars, he extends a Simon Frith functionalism "on the ways rock and roll produces the material context within which its fans find themselves" into a concern with fans' "affective investments."

Invoking and revising Dick Hebdige, Grossberg treats "rock and roll as a set of practices, but practices of strategic empowerment rather than of signification" (pp. 30–2). Claiming that rock only rarely challenged the major dimensions of American ideology, he argues that, at best, it "sought to change the possibilities – the rhythms – within everyday life itself," projecting "a world in which every moment could be lived as Saturday night" (pp. 99, 115). Here, Grossberg's assessment recalls Susan Douglas's revelatory rereading of the "girl groups" of the late 1950s and early 1960s. "The main purpose of pop music," she writes, "is to make us feel a kind of euphoria that convinces us that we can transcend the shackles of conventional life" (1994, p. 98). Whether or not euphoria best locates Jimi Hendrix's imagined footsoldier humping it through Vietnamese rice paddies to the tune of "Machine Gun," or Kurt Cobain nailing the lid on his "Heartshaped Box," suggests that just as there is no mainstream, perhaps there is no main purpose.

McClary presses further, proposing a Raymond Williams-like assignment: "We need to be able to grasp present-day musical culture in all its complexity. And that means being prepared to recognize the structures of feeling underlying many different repertories, as well as their processes of dynamic change and their strategic fusions." Musicians, whatever their various situations, are "concerned with performing some active negotiation with the cultural past for the sake of the here and now" (McClary, 2000, p. 168).

How it is possible to grasp, for a shimmering moment, these contingent, strategic fusions is on the order of learning more from a three-minute record than you ever learned in school. Try the koans of quick-take artist par excellence Robert Christgau (1990, 1998, 2000) and a pith-dense text like his *Grown Up All Wrong*. Or stretch with the anti-essentialist potential of popular music "as a site for experimentation with cultural and social roles not yet possible in politics," as proposed and examined by Lipsitz in *Dangerous Crossroads* (1997, p. 17).

Certainly the slackening riptide of rock and the rising waters of postmodernity have loosed a flood of musical forms, reappreciations, and cross-influences including, in the United States, assertions and celebrations of ethnicity in the klezmer and polka revivals (Henry Sapoznik, 1999; Victor Greene, 1992), and the resurgence of regional musics from south Louisiana (Nicholas Spitzer, 1985; Jason Berry, Jonathan Foose, and Tad Jones, 1986; Barry Ancelet, Jay Edwards, and Glen Pitre, 1991) to Hawaii (George Kanahele, 1979). College radio and standing-room venues featuring upstart bands with passionate devotees have spawned musical movements from Athens to Austin to Seattle. Places continue to turn up all over, and more compelling books than can be mentioned here to accompany them. A few suggestive examples would include the richness and diversity in African American music described in the anthology *California Soul* (1998), edited by DjeDje and Meadows; various Los Angeles scenes (Barney Hoskyns, 1996); Nathan Pearson's *Goin' to Kansas City* (1987); and Rick Koster's *Texas Music* (1998). There is also the ecstatic realm of the dance floor with its techno, rave, and electronica presided over by DJs in many materializations (Simon Reynolds, 1998; Bill Brewster and Frank Broughton, 2000). And, unearthed for those with ears to see, is the humdrum, everyday world's dialectic with "the sheer wonderland of the cosmo drama" via John Szwed's illumination of Sun Ra (1997, p. 288).

As the millennium turns, the sounds of the wider world increasingly come through on US airways, in the streets, and across the pipes of the Worldwide Web. "It would be difficult," writes Philip V. Bohlman, "to take a taxi in any large American city without experiencing an immigrant music on the radio, Pakistani or Nigerian music in Chicago, or Haitian or Ukrainian in Baltimore" (1998, p. 280). But differences that make any difference often get lost in hearing, dancing around, appropriating, or reprocessing the life experiences, historical cultures, and social pressures carried through cultural sounds and rhythms. By placing the power of US music within a critique of globalization, George Lipsitz in *Dangerous Crossroads* scrutinizes practices such as Paul Simon's and David Byrne's collaborations with South African and South American musicians. North American pop stars frequently

define delight in difference as a process organized around exotic images from overseas, with no corollary inspection of their own identities. Their escapes into postmodern multi-culturalism, however well-motivated, hide the construction of "whiteness" in America – its privileges, evasions, and contradictions. (1997, p. 63)

Instead of searching for somewhere to run to, somewhere to hide, Lipsitz urges us to consider "how our identities have been constructed and at whose expense" and "how we can pay back the debts we incur as examples from others show us the way out of the little tyrannies of our own parochial and prejudiced backgrounds" (p. 64).

Intent on mixing a new bohemia from the juices of indie rock, hip hop culture, and gay rights activism, music critic Ann Powers's coming-of-age tale, *Weird Like Us* (2000), locates the cultural spaces out of which came the wrenching, chilling, electrifying, introspective, raving music and alternative social possibilities in the 1980s and 1990s. "The average person may not see herself in the pierced and tattooed body and black leather pants of the stereotypical freak," Powers writes, "but she may be surprised to discover that this wild creature's reinventions of kinship, the work ethic, consumerism, and even desire . . . intersect with her own quandaries and solutions" (p. 37). Add Lipsitz's poetics of place, multiply Powers's numbers, and that sounds about right. For now.

REFERENCES

Abrahams, Roger D.: *Deep Down in the Jungle* (Hatboro, Pa.: Folklore Associates, 1964; rev. ed., Chicago: Aldine, 1970).

Allen, Ray: *Singing in the Spirit* (Philadelphia: University of Pennsylvania Press, 1991).

Allison, Dorothy: *Bastard Out of Carolina* (New York: Dutton, 1992).

Ancelet, Barry Jean, Edwards, Jay, and Pitre, Glen: *Cajun Country* (Jackson: University Press of Mississippi, 1991).

Attali, Jacques: *Noise: The Political Economy of Music* (Minneapolis: University of Minnesota Press, 1985).

Baraka, Amiri [LeRoi Jones]: *Blues People* (New York: William Morrow, 1963).

Bastin, Bruce: *Red River Blues* (Urbana: University of Illinois Press, 1995).

Berliner, Paul F.: *Thinking in Jazz* (Chicago: University of Chicago Press, 1994).

Berry, Jason, Foose, Jonathan, and Jones, Tad: *Up from the Cradle: New Orleans Music Since World War II* (Athens: University of Georgia Press, 1986).

Bertrand, Michael T.: *Race, Rock, and Elvis* (Urbana: University of Illinois Press, 2000).

Blesh, Rudi: *Shining Trumpets: A History of Jazz* (New York: Alfred A. Knopf, 1946).

Block, Geoffrey and Block, Fred L.: *Enchanted Evenings: The Broadway Musical from Show Boat to Sondheim* (New York: Oxford University Press, 1997).

Bohlman, Philip V.: "Immigrant, Folk, and Regional Musics in the Twentieth Century," in David Nicholls (ed.), *The Cambridge History of American Music* (New York: Cambridge University Press, 1998).

Bordman, Gerald Martin: *American Musical Theatre* (New York: Oxford University Press, 2001).

Boyer, Horace Clarence: *How Sweet the Sound* (Washington, DC: Elliott and Clark, 1995).

Brewster, Bill and Broughton, Frank: *Last Night a DJ Saved My Life* (New York: Grove Press, 2000).

Bufwack, Mary A. and Oermann, Robert K.: *Finding Her Voice: The Saga of Women in Country Music* (New York: Crown, 1993).

Cantwell, Robert: *Bluegrass Breakdown* (Urbana: University of Illinois Press, 1984).

Cantwell, Robert: *When We Were Good: The Folk Revival* (Cambridge, Mass.: Harvard University Press, 1996).

Carby, Hazel V. "'It Jus' Be's Dat Way Sometime': The Sexual Politics of Women's Blues," *Radical America*, 20 (1986): 9–24; rpt. in Robert G. O'Meally, *The Jazz Cadence of American Culture* (New York: Columbia University Press, 1998).

Chapple, Steve and Garofalo, Reebee: *Rock and Roll Is Here to Pay* (Chicago: Nelson Hall, 1977).

Charters, Samuel: *The Country Blues* (New York: Rinehart, 1959).

Christgau, Robert: *Christgau's Record Guide: The '80s* (New York: Da Capo, 1990).

Christgau, Robert: *Grown Up All Wrong: 75 Great Rock and Pop Artists from Vaudeville to Techno* (Cambridge, Mass.: Harvard University Press, 1998).

Christgau, Robert: *Christgau's Consumer Guide: Albums of the '90s* (New York: St. Martin's, 2000).

Cohen, Norm: *Long Steel Rail: The Railroad in American Folksong* (Urbana: University of Illinois Press, 1981).

Cohen, Norm: *Folk Song America* (Washington, DC: Smithsonian Collection of Recordings, 1990).

Cohodas, Nadine: *Spinning Blues into Gold* (New York: St. Martin's, 2000).

Conway, Cecelia: *African Banjo Echoes in Appalachia* (Knoxville: University of Tennessee Press, 1995).

Davis, Angela Y.: *Blues Legacies and Black Feminism: Gertrude "Ma" Rainey, Bessie Smith and Billie Holiday* (New York: Pantheon, 1998).

Dawidoff, Nicholas: *In the Country of Country* (New York: Pantheon, 1997).

de Toledano, Ralph: *Frontiers of Jazz* (New York: O. Durrell, 1947).

Denisoff, R. Serge: *Great Day Coming: Folk Music and the American Left* (Urbana: University of Illinois Press, 1971).

DeVeaux, Scott: *The Birth of Bebop* (Berkeley: University of California Press, 1997).

DjeDje, Jacqueline Cogdell and Meadows, Eddie S.: *California Soul: Music of African Americans in the West* (Berkeley: University of California Press, 1998).

Douglas, Susan: *Where the Girls Are: Growing Up Female with the Mass Media* (New York: Times Books, 1994).

Ellison, Ralph: *Shadow and Act* (New York: New American Library, 1966).

Ennis, Philip H.: *The Seventh Stream: The Emergence of Rocknroll in American Popular Music* (Hanover, NH: Wesleyan University Press and the University Press of New England, 1992).

Evans, David: *Big Road Blues* (Berkeley: University of California Press, 1982).

Ewen, David: *All the Years of American Popular Music* (Englewood Cliffs, NJ: Prentice Hall, 1977).

Feather, Leonard G.: *Inside Be-Bop* (New York: J. J. Robbins and Sons, 1949).

Feather, Leonard G.: *The Encyclopedia of Jazz* (New York: Horizon Press, 1955).

Ferris, William: *Blues from the Delta* (London: Studio Vista, 1970).

Filene, Benjamin: *Romancing the Folk: Public Memory and American Roots Music* (Chapel Hill: University of North Carolina Press, 2000).

Frith, Simon: *Sound Effects* (New York: Pantheon, 1981).

Frith, Simon: *Performing Rites: On the Value of Popular Music* (Cambridge, Mass.: Harvard University Press, 1996).

Frith, Simon, Goodwin, Andrew, and Grossberg, Lawrence, eds.: *Sound and Vision: The Music Video Reader* (London: Routledge, 1993).

Garman, Bryan: *A Race of Singers* (Chapel Hill: University of North Carolina Press, 2000).

Garofalo, Reebee: *Rockin' Out: Popular Music in the USA* (Boston: Allyn and Bacon, 1997).

Gates, Jr., Henry Louis: *The Signifying Monkey* (New York: Oxford University Press, 1988).

George, Nelson: *The Death of Rhythm and Blues* (New York: Pantheon, 1988).

George, Nelson: *Hip Hop America* (New York: Viking, 1998).

Giddens, Gary: *Visions of Jazz* (New York: Oxford University Press, 1998).

Gillett, Charlie: *The Sound of the City: The Rise of Rock and Roll* (New York: Outerbridge and Dienstfrey, 1970; rev. ed., New York: Da Capo, 1983).

Gioia, Ted: *The History of Jazz* (New York: Oxford University Press, 1997).

Goldsmith, Peter D.: *Making People's Music: Moe Asch and Folkways Records* (Washington, DC: Smithsonian Institution Press, 1998).

Goodman, Fred: *The Mansion on the Hill* (New York: Times Books, 1997).

Granata, Charles: *Sessions with Sinatra* (Chicago: A Cappella, 1999).

Green, Archie: *Only a Miner: Studies in Recorded Coal-Mining Songs* (Urbana: University of Illinois Press, 1972).

Greene, Victor: *A Passion for Polka* (Berkeley: University of California Press, 1992).

Grossberg, Lawrence: *Dancing in Spite of Myself* (Durham, NC: Duke University Press, 1997).

Guralnick, Peter: *Sweet Soul Music: Rhythm and Blues and the Southern Dream of Freedom* (New York: Harper and Row, 1986).

Guralnick, Peter: *Last Train to Memphis: The Rise of Elvis Presley* (Boston: Little, Brown, 1994).

Guralnick, Peter: *Careless Love: The Unmaking of Elvis Presley* (Boston: Little, Brown, 1999).

Harris, Michael W.: *The Rise of Gospel Blues* (New York: Oxford University Press, 1992).

Harrison, Daphne Duval: *Black Pearls: Blues Queens of the 1920s* (New Brunswick, NJ: Rutgers University Press, 1988).

Haslam, Gerald W., with Alexandra Haslam Russell and Richard Chon: *Workin' Man Blues* (Berkeley: University of California Press, 1999).

Hebdige, Dick: *Subculture: The Meaning of Style* (London: Routledge, 1979).

Heilbut, Anthony: *The Gospel Sound* (New York: Simon and Schuster, 1971; 5th ed., New York: Limelight, 1997).

Hentoff, Nat: *The Jazz Life* (New York: Dial Press, 1961).

Hinson, Glenn: *Fire in My Bones: Transcendence and the Holy Spirit in African American Gospel* (Philadelphia: University of Pennsylvania Press, 2000).

Hirshey, Gerri: *Nowhere to Run* (New York: Penguin, 1984).

Hoskyns, Barney: *Waiting for the Sun: Strange Days, Weird Scenes and the Sound of Los Angeles* (New York: St. Martin's, 1996).

Jackson, John A.: *American Bandstand: Dick Clark and the Making of a Rock 'n' Roll Empire* (New York: Oxford University Press, 1997).

Jefferson, Margo: "Sinatra, Not a Myth but a Man, and One Among Many," *New York Times* (June 1, 1998).

Kanahele, George S., ed.: *Hawaiian Music and Musicians* (Honolulu: University of Hawaii Press, 1979).

Keil, Charles: *Urban Blues* (Chicago: University of Chicago Press, 1966).

Kingsbury, Paul, ed.: *The Encyclopedia of Country Music* (New York: Oxford University Press, 1998).

Koster, Rick: *Texas Music* (New York: St. Martin's, 1998).

Larkin, Rochelle: *Soul Music* (New York: Lancer, 1970).

Levine, Lawrence W.: *Black Culture and Black Consciousness* (New York: Oxford University Press, 1977).

Light, Alan, ed.: *The Vibe History of Hip Hop* (New York: Three Rivers Press, 1999).

Lipsitz, George: *Rainbow at Midnight* (Urbana: University of Illinois Press, 1994).

Lipsitz, George: *Dangerous Crossroads: Popular Music, Postmodernism and the Poetics of Place* (New York: Verso, 1997).

Lomax, Alan: *Folk Song, U.S.A.* (Garden City, NY: Doubleday, 1960).

Lomax, Alan: *The Land Where the Blues Began* (New York: Pantheon, 1993).

Lornell, Kip: *"Happy in the Service of the Lord": Afro-American Gospel Quartets in Memphis* (Urbana: University of Illinois Press, 1988).

Love, Preston: *A Thousand Honey Creeks Later: My Life in Music from Basie to Motown* (Hanover, NH: Wesleyan University Press and University Press of New England, 1997).

Loza, Steven: *Barrio Rhythm: Mexican American Music in Los Angeles* (Urbana: University of Illinois Press, 1993).

Loza, Steven: *Tito Puente and the Making of Latin Music* (Urbana: University of Illinois Press, 1999).

Lynn, Loretta, with George Vecsey: *Coal Miner's Daughter* (Chicago: Regnery, 1976).

McClary, Susan: *Feminine Endings: Music, Gender, and Sexuality* (Minnesota: University of Minnesota Press, 1991).

McClary, Susan: *Conventional Wisdom: The Content of Musical Form* (Berkeley: University of California Press, 2000).

MacDonald, Laurence E.: *The Invisible Art of Film Music* (New York: Ardsley House, 1998).

McDonnell, Evelyn and Powers, Ann, eds.: *Rock She Wrote: Women Write about Rock, Pop, and Rap* (New York: Delta, 1995).

Malone, Bill C.: *Country Music, U.S.A.* (Austin: University of Texas Press, 1968).

Marcus, Greil: *Mystery Train* (New York: Dutton, 1976).

Marcus, Greil: *Ranters and Crowd Pleasers* (New York: Doubleday, 1993).

Marcus, Greil: *Invisible Republic* (New York: Henry Holt, 1997).

May, Elaine Tyler: *Homeward Bound: American Families in the Cold War Era* (New York: Basic Books, 1988).

Miller, D. A.: *A Place for Us* (Cambridge, Mass.: Harvard University Press, 2000).

Morrison, Craig: *Go Cat Go!* (Urbana: University of Illinois Press, 1996).

Neal, Mark Anthony: *What the Music Said: Black Popular Music and Black Public Culture* (New York: Routledge, 1999).

Negus, Keith: *Popular Music in Theory* (Hanover, NH: Wesleyan University Press and University Press of New England, 1996).

Nicholls, David: "Preface," in David Nicholls (ed.), *The Cambridge History of American Music* (New York: Cambridge University Press, 1998).

O'Meally, Robert G.: *The Jazz Cadence of American Culture* (New York: Columbia University Press, 1998).

Oliver, Paul: *Blues Fell This Morning* (London, Cassell, 1960).

Oliver, Paul: *Savannah Syncopaters: African Retentions in the Blues* (New York: Stein and Day, 1970).

Olsson, Bengt: *Memphis Blues and Jug Bands* (London: Studio Vista, 1970).

Palmer, Robert: *Deep Blues* (New York: Viking, 1981).

Paredes, Américo: *With His Pistol in His Hand* (Austin: University of Texas Press, 1958).

Paredes, Américo: *A Texas-Mexican Cancionero* (Urbana: University of Illinois Press, 1976).

Patterson, Beverly Bush: *The Sound of the Dove: Singing in Appalachian Primitive Baptist Churches* (Urbana: University of Illinois Press, 1995).

Pearson, Nathan W.: *Goin' to Kansas City* (Urbana: University of Illinois Press, 1987).

Peña, Manuel: *The Texas-Mexican Conjunto: History of a Working-Class Music* (Austin: University of Texas Press, 1985).

Pendergast, Roy M.: *Film Music: A Neglected Art*, 2nd ed. (New York: W. W. Norton, 1992).

Peterson, Richard A.: *Creating Country Music: Fabricating Authenticity* (Chicago: University of Chicago Press, 1997).

Pleasants, Henry: *The Great American Popular Singers* (New York: Simon and Schuster, 1974).

Powers, Ann: *Weird Like Us* (New York: Simon and Schuster, 2000).

Pruter, Robert: *Chicago Soul* (Urbana: University of Illinois Press, 1991).

Reagon, Bernice Johnson: *We'll Understand It Better By and By* (Washington, DC: Smithsonian Institution Press, 1992).

Reynolds, Simon: *Generation Ecstasy* (Boston: Little, Brown, 1998).

Riesman, David: "Listening to Popular Music," in Bernard Rosenberg and David Manning White (eds.), *Mass Culture: The Popular Arts in America* (Glencoe, Ill.: Free Press, 1957).

Robb, John D.: *Hispanic Folk Music of New Mexico and the Southwest* (Norman: University of Oklahoma, 1980).

Roberts, John Storm: *The Latin Tinge: The Impact of Latin American Music on the United States*, 2nd ed. (New York: Oxford University Press, 1999).

Rockwell, John: *All American Music: Composition in the Late Twentieth Century* (New York: Alfred A. Knopf, 1983).

Rose, Tricia: *Black Noise: Rap Music and Black Culture in Contemporary America* (Hanover, NH: Wesleyan University Press and University Press of New England, 1994).

Rosenberg, Neil V.: *Bluegrass* (Urbana: University of Illinois Press, 1985).

Russell, Tony: *Blacks, Whites, and Blues* (New York: Stein and Day, 1970).

Sandburg, Carl: *The American Songbag* (New York: Harcourt Brace, 1927).

Sanjek, Russell and Sanjek, David: *Pennies From Heaven: The American Popular Music Business in the Twentieth Century* (New York: Da Capo, 1996).

Sapoznik, Henry: *Klezmer! Jewish Music from Old World to Our World* (New York: Schirmer Books, 1999).

Shelton, Robert and Goldblatt, Burt: *The Country Music Story* (Indianapolis: Bobbs Merrill, 1966).

Smith, Suzanne E.: *Dancing in the Street: Motown and the Cultural Politics of Detroit* (Cambridge, Mass.: Harvard University Press, 1999).

Southern, Eileen: *The Music of Black Americans*, 2nd ed. (New York: W. W. Norton, 1983).

Spitzer, Nicholas, ed.: *Louisiana Folklife* (Baton Rouge: Moran, 1985).

Swain, Joseph P.: *The Broadway Musical* (New York: Oxford University Press, 1990).

Szwed, John F.: *Space Is the Place: The Lives and Times of Sun Ra* (New York: Pantheon, 1997).

Théberge, Paul: *Any Sound You Can Imagine* (Hanover, NH: Wesleyan University Press and University Press of New England, 1997).

Tichi, Cecelia: *High Lonesome* (Chapel Hill: University of North Carolina Press, 1994).

Tichi, Cecelia, ed.: *Reading Country Music* (Durham, NC: Duke University Press, 1998).

Titon, Jeff: *Early Downhome Blues* (Urbana: University of Illinois Press, 1977).

Titon, Jeff: *Powerhouse for God: Speech, Chant, and Song in an Appalachian Baptist Church* (Austin: University of Texas Press, 1988).

Tucker, Mark, ed.: *The Duke Ellington Reader* (New York: Oxford University Press, 1993).

Vincent, Rickey: *Funk* (New York: St. Martin's Griffin, 1996).

Waksman, Steve: *Instruments of Desire: The Electric Guitar and the Shaping of Musical Experience* (Cambridge, Mass.: Harvard University Press, 1999).

Walser, Robert: *Running With the Devil: Power, Gender, and Madness in Heavy Metal Music* (Hanover, NH: University Press of New England, 1993).

Walser, Robert: *Keeping Time: Readings in Jazz History* (New York: Oxford University Press, 1999).

Ward, Brian: *Just My Soul Responding: Rhythm and Blues, Black Consciousness, and Race Relations* (Berkeley: University of California Press, 1998).

Ward, Ed, Stokes, Geoffrey, and Tucker, Ken: *Rock of Ages: The Rolling Stone History of Rock and Roll* (New York: Summit Books, 1986).

Weinstein, Deena: *Heavy Metal* (New York: Da Capo, 2000).

Werner, Craig: *A Change Is Gonna Come: Music, Race and the Soul of America* (New York: Plume, 1999).

Whisnant, David E.: *All That Is Native and Fine* (Chapel Hill: University of North Carolina Press, 1983).

White, Timothy: *The Nearest Faraway Place* (New York: Henry Holt, 1994).

Whiteley, Sheila: *Women and Popular Music* (New York: Routledge, 2000).

Williams, Martin: *The Jazz Tradition* (New York: Oxford University Press, 1970; 2nd rev. ed., 1993).

Wolfe, Charles K.: *Tennessee Strings* (Knoxville: University of Tennessee Press, 1977).

Wolfe, Charles K.: *Kentucky Country* (Lexington: University of Kentucky Press, 1982).

Wolfe, Charles K.: *A Good-Natured Riot: The Birth of the Grand Ole Opry* (Nashville: Country Music Foundation, 1999).

Wolfe, Charles K. and Lornell, Kip: *The Life and Legend of Leadbelly* (New York: Harper, 1992).

Wright, Richard: *Black Boy* (New York: Harper, 1945); restored in 1991 as *Black Boy/American Hunger* by the Library of America.

Young, Alan: *Woke Me Up This Morning: Black Gospel Singers and the Gospel Life* (Jackson: University of Mississippi Press, 1997).

FURTHER READING

Baker, Jr., Houston: *Blues, Ideology, and Afro-American Literature* (Chicago: University of Chicago Press, 1984).

Bangs, Lester: *Psychotic Reactions and Carburetor Dung* (New York: Alfred A. Knopf, 1987).

Bayles, Martha: *Hole in Our Soul* (New York: Free Press, 1994).

Bennett, Tony, Frith, Simon, Grossberg, Lawrence, Shepherd, John, and Turner, Graeme, eds.: *Rock and Popular Music* (New York: Routledge, 1993).

Bergreen, Laurence: *Louis Armstrong* (New York: Broadway Books, 1997).

Brown, James, Tucker, Bruce, and Marsh, Dave: *James Brown*, rpt. ed. (New York: Thunder's Mouth Press, 1997).

Cohen, John and Seeger, Mike, eds.: *The New Lost City Ramblers Songbook* (New York: Oak Publications, 1964).

Courlander, Harold: *Negro Folk Music, U.S.A.* (New York: Columbia University Press, 1963).

Denisoff, R. Serge and Peterson, Richard A.: *The Sounds of Social Change* (Chicago: Rand McNally, 1972).

Draper, Robert: *Rolling Stone Magazine* (New York: Doubleday, 1990).

Feather, Leonard G. and Gitler, Ira: *The Biographical Encyclopedia of Jazz* (New York: Oxford University Press, 1999).

Guthrie, Woody: *Bound for Glory* (New York: E. P. Dutton, 1943).

Hebdige, Dick: *Cut 'n' Mix: Culture, Identity and Caribbean Music* (London: Routledge, 1987).

Hobsbawm, Eric: *The Jazz Scene*, rev. ed. (New York: Pantheon, 1993).

Holiday, Billie, with William Dufty: *Lady Sings the Blues* (New York: Doubleday, 1956).

Jackson, Bruce: *Wake Up Dead Man: Afro-American Worksongs from Texas Prisons* (Cambridge, Mass.: Harvard University Press, 1972).

Klein, Joe: *Woody Guthrie* (New York: Alfred A. Knopf, 1980).

Lomax, Alan: *Mister Jelly Roll* (1950; rpt., Berkeley: University of California Press, 1973).

Lomax, John A. and Lomax, Alan: *Our Singing Country* (New York: Macmillan, 1941).

McAllester, David P.: "North America/Native America," in Jeff Todd Titon (ed.), *Worlds of Music* (New York: Schirmer, 1992).

Macy, Laura, ed.: *New Grove Dictionary of Music and Musicians* (New York: Macmillan, 2001).

Miller, James: *Flowers in the Dustbin* (New York: Simon and Schuster, 1999).

Murray, Albert: *Stomping the Blues* (New York: McGraw Hill, 1976).

Palmer, Robert: *Rock and Roll: An Unruly History* (New York: Harmony Books, 1995).

Pareles, Jon and Romanowski, Patricia, eds.: *The Rolling Stone Encyclopedia of Rock and Roll* (New York: Rolling Stone, 1983).

Proulx, E. Annie: *Accordion Crimes* (New York: Scribner, 1996).

Ramsey, Frederic: *Been Here and Gone* (New Brunswick, NJ: Rutgers University Press, 1960).

Santoro, Gene: *Dancing in Your Head: Jazz, Blues, Rock, and Beyond* (New York: Oxford University Press, 1994).

Santoro, Gene: *Stir It Up: Musical Mixes from Roots to Jazz* (New York: Oxford University Press, 1997).

Schuller, Gunther: *The Swing Era* (New York: Oxford University Press, 1989).

Shaw, Arnold: *Honkers and Shouters: The Golden Years of Rhythm and Blues* (New York: Collier, 1978).

Southern, Eileen: *The Music of Black Americans* (New York: W. W. Norton, 1971; 2nd ed., 1983).

Tucker, Sherrie: *Swing Shift: "All-Girl" Bands of the 1940s* (Durham, NC: Duke University Press, 2000).

Van der Merwe, Peter: *Origins of the Popular Style* (New York: Oxford University Press, 1989).

CHAPTER SEVEN

The Visual Arts in Post-1945 America

ERIKA DOSS

In 1949 art historian Oliver Larkin ended his Pulitzer Prize-winning survey, *Art and Life in America*, with this optimistic statement: "Nowhere . . . is there more brilliant artistic technique, more latent creative talent, than here" (Larkin, 1949, p. 478). Larkin's paeans to America's cultural exceptionalism were not atypical in the immediate post-World War II era. Indeed, in 1948, influential critic Clement Greenberg proclaimed "how much the level of American art has risen in the last five years, with the emergence of new talents so full of energy and content as Arshile Gorky, Jackson Pollock, David Smith." "The main premises of Western art," he added, "have at last migrated to the United States, along with the center of gravity of industrial production and political power" (Greenberg, 1948, p. 215).

For many historians and critics, the second half of the twentieth century has meant the cultural and economic dominance of America's visual arts. Notions of cultural nationalism, first championed in the 1910s and 1920s and supported during the Great Depression by various New Deal arts programs, remained strong in the immediate postwar years. A steady progression of new American art styles, from Pollock's postwar brand of Abstract Expressionism to later movements such as Neo-Dada, Pop art, Minimalism, Conceptual art, Feminist art, and Neo-Expressionism, whetted critical appetites, fed historical understandings of native creativity, and piqued art market interests, nationally and internationally. If European strains of modern art, especially those of French avant-garde artists such as Picasso and Matisse, had previously commanded the attention of collectors and curators, the post-World War II era saw a surge of interest in an American avant-garde, and American culture in general.

By mid-century, New York had clearly replaced Paris as the world capital of modern art – the culmination of aesthetic, social, and economic trends decades in the making – and modern art had become widely understood as "American" art. During the 1940s, many universities added courses in American art to their curriculum; a decade later, the first dissertations in American art and "the systematic filling of academic and museum positions with Ph.D.s in American art history began to take place" (Johns, 1984, p. 342). In 1951, the first training center specifically focused on the study of American art and culture was established at the Henry Francis Dupont Winterthur Museum (Delaware); in 1952, the editors of *Partisan Review* organized a benchmark symposium, "Our Country and Our Culture"; in 1954, the Metropolitan Museum of Art mounted the twenty-four-gallery exhibition, *Two Centuries of*

American Painting; in 1956, *Time* magazine championed American art in an eight-page cover story (Stich, 1987, p. 8); in 1958, the Museum of Modern Art circulated a major survey of contemporary art, *The New American Painting*, throughout Europe. Even at the end of what was termed the "American century," American art remained triumphant: celebrated in the much-touted 2000 Whitney Museum of American Art Biennial and commanding new art market records in gallery sales and auctions.

Surveys of American art, from Oliver Larkin's landmark historiography (Wallach, 2001) to texts by art historians (Wilmerding, 1976; Taylor, 1979; Baigell, 1984; W. Craven, 1994; Bjelajac, 2000; Doss, 2002) and critics (Rose, 1967; Hughes, 1997), detail the evolution of art styles and important cultural moments. Yet many accounts of post-1945 American art have been shaped by "histories" outside the academy: by critics and theorists who wrote for art journals and magazines; by museum curators who organized exhibitions; and by artists who found their voice in manifestos and interviews. In the years after World War II, American art emerged, evolved, and was repeatedly redefined in artists' studios, galleries, museums, and classrooms, and by institutions such as the College Art Association (CAA, the primary professional organization for art teachers and art historians in higher education, numbering 14,000 members in 1997). The art press and mainstream media played major roles in articulating the artistic agenda, shaping cultural tastes, and contributing to larger public discourses about American art. Moreover, since the mid-1970s, the historiography of America's postwar visual arts has been informed by revisionist sensibilities which recognize that earlier versions of the story of modern American art were frequently biased and exclusive, overlooking much of the art and many of the artists of the postwar period. Shifting understandings of modernism, and of modern art, are central to an understanding of postwar art, as are shifting understandings of national identity; indeed, much of post-1945 American art, and its historiography, has repeatedly focused on recreating and redefining modernism as well as notions of modern American identity.

From Regionalism to Abstract Expressionism: New Notions of American Modernism

During the 1940s, a remarkable shift occurred in American art as the representational American Scene, Social Realist, and Regionalist styles dominant during the Great Depression were eclipsed by new strains of abstract painting and sculpture. As one critic observed in 1944: "There's a style of painting gaining ground in this country which is neither Abstract nor Surrealist, though it has suggestions of both, while the way the paint is applied – usually in a pretty free-swinging spattery fashion, with only vague hints of subject matter – is suggestive of the methods of Expressionism." "Jackson Pollock, Lee Hersch, and William Baziotes are of this school," he added, "in addition to some forty other contemporaries" (Coates, 1944, p. 50).

The new modern art was called Abstract Expressionism, and alternately "action painting" and the "New York School" because most of its artists lived and worked in New York City, and because postwar American critics deliberately aimed to contrast it with the "School of Paris" abstractions of Picasso and Matisse. Jackson Pollock's *Autumn Rhythm: Number 30, 1950* (plate 1), a huge 8 × 17-foot canvas

Plate 1 Jackson Pollock, *Autumn Rhythm*, 1950. Oil on canvas, 105 × 207″.

densely covered with intersecting lines and splashes of paint, is emblematic of the Abstract Expressionist style that dominated post-World War II American art, and typical of the "drip" compositions the artist pursued from 1947 to 1950. A foremost student of Regionalist artist Thomas Hart Benton in the 1930s, Pollock rejected his mentor's commitment to "art for the millions" and social reform, concentrating instead on personal expression and social alienation (Doss, 1991). As Pollock remarked, "My work with Benton was very important as something against which to react very strongly" (Pollock, 1944, p. 14). Postwar artist Adolph Gottlieb similarly echoed: "It was necessary for me to destroy . . . the concept of what constituted a good painting at that time" (Sylvester, 1990 [1963], p. 265).

Explanations of Abstract Expressionism's emergence and cultural dominance prevail in postwar American art history. Indeed, Abstract Expressionism remains the most discussed and debated movement in twentieth-century American art: inspiring more scholarship and speculation (history surveys, artist biographies, museum exhibitions); commanding some of the highest prices in the art market (a 1956 painting by Mark Rothko sold for $13 million at Sotheby's in spring 2000); and dramatically influencing subsequent generations of artists. Abstract Expressionism, in other words, remains the measure of success against which modern and contemporary American art is judged – as art, as art history, as blue-chip goods. Indeed, in the late 1970s, when a younger generation of artists including Julian Schnabel aimed to "become" art historical, they imagined themselves as the new Pollocks, fashioned an audacious style similarly full of drips and splashes (although Schnabel's "drips" were broken plates), and called their grand scale art "Neo-" Expressionism.

The romance of Abstract Expressionism began with this historical narrative: in post-World War II America there emerged an heroic band of avant-garde artists, rebels whose cause was to overthrow various representational styles of art and the political agenda they embodied in order to create a culture more in keeping with the "American Century" that magazine publisher Henry Luce prophesied in *Life* magazine in 1941. Arguably one of the most important twentieth-century declarations of national purpose and identity, Luce's manifesto urged the nation to embrace a "vision of America as a world power which . . . will guide us to the authentic creation of the 20th Century – our Century" (Luce, 1941, p. 65).

A decade later, in an equally influential *Art News* essay titled "The American Action Painters," critic Harold Rosenberg lionized the typical Abstract Expressionist artist as an American loner, "heir of the pioneer and the immigrant," a "vanguard painter [who] took to the white expanse of the canvas as Melville's Ishmael took to the sea." Rosenberg also constructed the standard history of the movement, noting: "Many of the painters were 'Marxists' (WPA unions, artists' congresses) – they had been trying to paint Society. Others had been trying to paint Art (Cubism Post-Impressionism) – it amounts to the same thing. The big moment came when it was decided to paint. . . . Just *TO PAINT*. The gesture on the canvas was a gesture of liberation, from Value – political, aesthetic, moral" (Rosenberg, 1982 [1952], p. 30). Such accounts mythologized the Abstract Expressionists as heroic avant-garde rebels, the art world equivalents of brooding 1950s movie stars like Marlon Brando and James Dean, or teen idols like Elvis Presley.

The look of their painterly gestures ranged from Pollock's drips to Rothko's luminous fields of color, and the loose brushstrokes and spontaneous forms of an all-male Abstract Expressionist "club" that included Willem de Kooning, Robert Motherwell, Barnett Newman, and Clyfford Still. The subjects of their monumental canvases embodied the artists' profound disaffection with both earlier modes of American art and political culture (whether New Deal Regionalism or radical left Social Realism), and with the changed political climate of consensus and Cold War. As Motherwell remarked, the "rebellious, individualistic, unconventional, sensitive, irritable" paintings of the Abstract Expressionists "arose from a feeling of being ill at ease in the universe." "Nothing as drastic an innovation as abstract art could have come into existence," he added, "save as the consequence of a most profound, relentless, unquenchable need. The need is for felt experience – intense, immediate, direct, subtle, unified, warm, vivid, rhythmic" (Motherwell, 1951, p. 12). While physically powerful and energetic, Abstract Expressionist art betrays a palpable sense of uneasiness. Feeling caught in a trap of reactionary consensus politics and Cold War tensions, Pollock and other postwar avant-garde artists responded with highly individualized "signature" styles expressing personal and social alienation. In this respect, Abstract Expressionism embodied artistic yearnings for self-determination and struggles to relegitimize the transgressive possibilities of the avant-garde. As Pollock observed in 1956, "Painting is a state of being . . . painting is self-discovery. Every good artist paints what he is" (Rodman, 1961, p. 82). Pollock's pictures were revolutionary attempts to liberate himself, and the larger American culture, from the alienating conformity and pathological fears of the postwar era.

Avant-garde interests in synthesis and integration – abiding characteristics of American modernism since the early twentieth century – converged with interests in myth, in the universal symbols and heroes of both Western antiquity and "primitive" cultures. These interests were equally pervasive among the New York School and mainstream US culture: indeed, Mark Rothko called his fellow Abstract Expressionists "a small band of myth-makers" (Rothko, 1946), and James Frazer's classic book of mythology, *The Golden Bough* (1922), was a postwar bestseller (Polcari, 1991, p. 38). Convinced of the bankruptcy of previously dominant styles and subjects, postwar artists searched for new forms of identity. Many valorized the myths and symbols of diverse premodern cultures, feeling they best embodied a universal language that expressed essential truths about the human condition.

Abstract Expressionism was inherently ambiguous and unresolved, an open-ended modern art unbeholden to any particular ideology and committed to liberation through personal "acts" of expression. Pollock, in particular, was idolized as a postwar rebel: "the embodiment of our ambition," wrote artist/critic Allan Kaprow, "for absolute liberation" (Kaprow, 1958, p. 24). Yet precisely because of its rebellious and utopian appeal to personal expression and autonomy, Abstract Expressionism represented an enormous threat in Cold War America. Recognizing this, and taking advantage of its core ambiguity, many postwar critics deliberately misrepresented the movement.

The misconstruction began with Abstract Expressionism's consolidation as a "school" and a "canon" of art. By the mid-1950s, the movement had gained national and international currency, becoming "the" style to master in postwar America's booming universities and art schools and inspiring a "second generation" of improvisational artists, including color-stain painters Helen Frankenthaler and Morris Louis. Willem de Kooning had argued that Abstract Expressionism "implies that every artist can do what he thinks he ought to – a movement for each person and open for everybody" (de Kooning, 1951, p. 12). But many commentators reduced this multifaceted phenomenon of individual expression to a single art movement and ignored assertions of personal autonomy and cultural liberation. Instead, postwar critics emphasized Abstract Expressionism's *formal* qualities: its rejection of shading, modeling, and realistic perspective; its avoidance of representational subjects.

Because its emergence was concurrent with US global ascendancy in politics and industrial production, Abstract Expressionism was championed throughout the Cold War as evidence of American cultural superiority by critics such as Clement Greenberg and hailed as an art of uniquely American individualism by scholars such as Irving Sandler, who titled his 1970 history of the movement *The Triumph of American Painting*. If Pollock was ridiculed by some as "Jack the Dripper," *Life* magazine presented him as "the greatest living painter in the United States," intimating that the style of Abstract Expressionism best met the terms of Henry Luce's prophesied "American Century" (Seiberling, 1949, p. 42).

Greenberg was one of the leading critics to shape the postwar response to Abstract Expressionism and to modern art in general. His influential essay, "Avant-Garde and Kitsch," prescribed the rigid separation of modern art from kitsch, or popular and mass culture. Kitsch, Greenberg explained, was not only escapist and debased but politically dangerous: "the official tendency of culture in Germany, Italy, and Russia ... another of the inexpensive ways in which totalitarian regimes seek to ingratiate themselves with their subjects" (Greenberg, 1939, p. 35). Only an avant-garde art free of popular subjects and mass politics was appropriate to the modern culture he envisioned. Greenberg later elaborated on these ideas, asserting that the rejection of realism, a tendency toward "flatness," and the reduction to "pure" form was the inevitable path for modern painting, and that modern sculpture should similarly strive for self-referentiality: referring only to its particular medium (steel, bronze, etc.) and to the individual aims of its artist-maker (Greenberg, 1940, 1965).

Critical renunciation of popular and representational styles exemplified the general, postwar, intellectual backlash against "the masses." Liberals and leftists who had earlier placed their faith in collective reform, including figures like Clement Greenberg, Harold Rosenberg, Hannah Arendt, Arthur Schlesinger, Jr., and Daniel Bell, now condemned mass political and cultural movements, fearing their links to totalitarianism. Reneging on a previous generation's trust that humanity was rational and reformable, these postwar intellectuals held that humankind was intrinsically irrational, even evil – as the horrific circumstances of World War II had shown. Abandoning notions of human and historical progress, they now advocated the conservative and cautious concept of a "vital center" – the title of Schlesinger's influential yet contradictory 1949 book, which insisted on the importance of individuality but also advocated conformity, or consensus. Their new mandate was to promote modern cultural forms – such as Abstract Expressionism – which embodied these conflicted qualities. Consequently, the meaning of modern art profoundly shifted during these years, from a movement associated with social reform and cultural pluralism to an art viewed as the apolitical abstraction of individual, and especially male, artists.

In recent decades, more fully contextualized accounts of Abstract Expressionism's patronage and position in Cold War culture have emerged. Although Abstract Expressionism addressed issues of postwar disaffection and proposed personal, individualist modes of autonomy, historical and critical analyses of postwar art and politics explain how the movement became a weapon in the Cold War: championed by critics and museums in the United States and abroad as a powerful symbol of American individuality, as an emblem of the creative and personal freedoms denied communist artists and others behind the Iron Curtain (Kozloff, 1973; Mathews, 1976). One of the most debated books in this regard was Serge Guilbaut's *How New York Stole the Idea of Modern Art: Abstract Expressionism, Freedom, and the Cold War* (1983), which provided a sharply critical analysis of the institutional contributions to the cultural history of the 1940s and 1950s (by the Museum of Modern Art, for example) but was curiously indifferent to a discussion of the art itself. Other revisionist narratives explained how deep-felt desires by postwar artists to break away from and "destroy" the modern art styles of an earlier era were grounded in a larger political and cultural transition: from the New Deal to the burgeoning of a "Cold War" between the United States and the Soviet Union (Doss, 1991).

Issues of race and gender have further shaped the ongoing revision of Abstract Expressionism, as have accounts of its appropriation of "primitive" myths and "glyphs" and its postcolonial lineage (Leja, 1993; Belgrad, 1998; D. Craven, 1999). If formerly reduced to limited formalist descriptions and cast as a small "club" of white male artists, revisionist histories such as Ann Gibson's *Abstract Expressionism: Other Politics* (1997) demonstrate that the postwar avant-garde was actually very diverse, consisting of many women and nonwhite artists including Lee Krasner, Norman Lewis, and Sonia Sekula. Reasons for their exclusion from the Abstract Expressionist canon relate in part to the formalist New Criticism practiced by Greenberg, Roland Barthes, Michel Foucault, Michael Fried, and Rosalind Krauss. Intending to foster "objective" analyses of art, formalist criticism suppressed the intentionality, subjectivity, and biography of the artist. Barthes's influential 1968 essay, "The Death of the Author," insisted that only the work of art – not the author/artist, and not the audience for art – was important (Barthes, 1977 [1968]). Subsequent generations of artists, critics, and historians would repeatedly challenge these limited formalist understandings of American modern art, many addressing the manner in which postwar art and its early historiography reinscribed larger cultural understandings of racism and sexism.

Modernist Sensibilities: 1950s–1970s

In the mid- to late 1950s, British critic Lawrence Alloway began writing about growing artistic interests in mass media and popular culture. As he noted, "Acceptance of the mass media entails a shift in our notion of what culture is. Instead of reserving the word for the highest artifacts and the noblest thoughts of history's top ten, it needs to be used more widely as the description of 'what a society does.'" Once this was done, Alloway added, "unique oil paintings and highly personal poems as well as mass-distributed films and group-aimed magazines can be placed within a continuum rather than frozen in layers in a pyramid" (Alloway, 1988 [1959], p. 30).

Alloways's critical insights were a far remove from Greenberg's insistence on the hierarchical superiority of fine art over kitsch. During the later 1950s and throughout the 1960s, formalist New Criticism continued to dominate art discourse, dramatically influencing the development of certain styles of postwar painting and sculpture, from hard-edge abstraction to Minimalism. Yet critical and artistic recognition of postwar consumerism and commercialism, inspired in part by Marshall McLuhan's theories of mass media and new technologies, was also pervasive (McLuhan, 1964).

McLuhan's idea that the "medium is the message" became a mantra of sorts for a new generation of artists who were especially stimulated by mass culture's visual vocabulary and broader cultural meanings. Around 1958, Lawrence Alloway coined the term "Pop art" to describe a burgeoning postwar visual art movement based on the subjects of mass media and popular culture – from comic books and advertisements to magazines, movies, television programs, and product packaging. Tom Wesselmann's 1963 *Still Life #30* (plate 2), a collage painting featuring a kitchen table laden with brand-name foods (Dole pineapple, Kellogg's Rice Krispies), a pink General Electric refrigerator showcasing 7-Up bottles, and a small framed reproduction of Picasso's *Seated Woman*, captures Pop art's attention to middle-class consumerism. Pop art "cannot be separated from the culmination of affluence and prosperity during the post-World War II era," art historian John Wilmerding remarked in 1976. By the early 1960s, "America had become a ravenously consuming society, packaging art as well as other products, indulging in commercial manipulation, and celebrating exhibitionism, self-promotion, and instant success." Pop art "seized on these elements and exploited them," said Wilmerding, "with a brazenness that seemed offensive both for its discomforting insinuations and for its assault on the elevated hegemony of abstract expressionism" (Wilmerding, 1976, p. 222). Intrigued by and occasionally disgusted with the manner in which middle-class consumerism and conformity had become the primary forms of American identity,

Plate 2 Tom Wesselmann, *Still Life #30*, 1963. Oil, enamel, and synthetic polymer paint on composition board with collage of printed advertisements, plastic artificial flowers, refrigerator door, plastic replicas of 7-Up bottles, glazed and framed color reproduction, and stamped metal, 48.5 × 66 × 4″. The Museum of Modern Art, New York. © Tom Wesselmann/VAGA, New York/DACS, London 2002.

postwar Pop and Neo-Dada artists forged an anti-aesthetic focused on cultural commodification and on the divide between fine art and popular culture.

In the later 1950s and 1960s, American artists and critics no longer worried about competing with Europe: the "triumph" of Abstract Expressionism and the authority of the New York art market proved the cultural and economic superiority of postwar American art. Yet some remained uneasy with the terms of this postwar triumph and worried that American art had become too personalized and autobiographical. Others criticized Abstract Expressionism's appropriation as a political symbol of American "freedom" and as a widely copied signifier of sophisticated modern taste in advertising and interior decoration. By 1960, in other words, the revolutionary and liberating art of Abstract Expressionism had become thoroughly commodified as political pawn, lucrative investment, and cultural prop. A new generation of postwar artists, recognizing this manipulation, challenged the heroic individualism and art world dominance of Abstract Expressionism, and the art market's rapacious appetite for the avant-garde, with new styles that emphasized a nonhierarchical and fundamentally conceptual aesthetic.

Ironically, their efforts paralleled that of a flourishing New York gallery scene and art market. The number of major collectors swelled from two dozen in 1945 to 200 in 1960, and 2,000 by 1970. Sales of postwar American art skyrocketed after the Metropolitan Museum of Art purchased Pollock's *Autumn Rhythm* for $30,000 in 1957. In 1960, gallery dealer Leo Castelli sold Jasper Johns's *Painted Bronze* for $960; in 1973, the same sculpture sold for $90,000. Likewise, a Pop art painting by Roy Lichtenstein that sold for $1,200 in 1962 sold for $40,000 in 1967. The 1950s and 1960s also saw the dramatic growth of other modern art institutions: university art programs and schools; art museums and American art collections; the creation in 1966 of the National Endowment for the Arts (NEA); and an art press focused especially on postwar American visual arts. Tensions between the marketing and meaning of art, and changing definitions of modernism and the avant-garde, would preoccupy American artists as well as critics throughout these decades. Philosopher Arthur Danto, for example, addressed those tensions in the highly influential essay "The Artworld" (1964), which considered why Andy Warhol's *Brillo Box* was "art" and the boxes of Brillo in the supermarket were not, and concluded that "participation in the discourses of the artworld, mastery of some of its theories, and knowledge of its relevant history" determined the making and meaning of "art" (Danto, 1998, p. 23).

A new generation of "Neo-Dada" artists emerged in the mid-1950s and worked throughout the 1960s, inspired by artist/theorist Marcel Duchamp (who had pioneered the international movement of Dada in the 1910s). Intrigued by Duchamp's primary interest in the conceptual – not visual – underpinnings of art, Neo-Dada artists merged painting and sculpture in experimental hybrids that revamped postwar understandings of modern art and artmaking. Jasper Johns and Robert Rauschenberg worked with banal and often unexamined images and objects (maps, alphabets, flags, advertisements), reusing them in nonreferential ways. Claes Oldenburg and Allan Kaprow similarly challenged Greenberg's strict separation of media and his hierarchical readings of "art" versus popular culture with ephemeral performances – called "Happenings" – that aimed at eliminating borders between art and audience (Kirby, 1966; Banes, 1993).

Collage-like, collaborative, and carnivalesque, Happenings further challenged art market understandings of modern culture, as did Beat and Funk "assemblage" artworks produced by Robert Arneson, Bruce Conner, Jay DeFeo, Edward Kienholz, and Betye Saar, and experimental films made by Stan Brakhage and Ken Jacobs (Seitz, 1961; Phillips, 1995). Finding inspiration in found objects and urban detritus, these artists claimed the marginal and debased as their primary subjects, emphasizing process over product and subverting cultural commodification with willfully ugly and highly perishable "junk" sculptures and noncommercial films.

By deconstructing the meaning of modern art – especially its dominant postwar meaning as highly personalized and increasingly collectable forms of Abstract Expressionism – these avant-garde artists aimed to return postwar art to issues and problems of representation and perception and to redirect artmaking toward a broader engagement with social subjects and mass culture. Such impulses did not go unnoticed. "Contemporary artists such as Robert Rauschenberg have become fascinated by the patterns and textures of decaying walls with their torn posters and patches of damp," commented art historian Ernst H. Gombrich. "Though I happen to dislike Rauschenberg," he added, "I notice to my chagrin that I cannot help being aware of such sights in a different way since seeing his paintings" (Gombrich, 1982, p. 31).

The possibilities of different ways of seeing preoccupied multiple postwar artists – Neo-Dada, Pop, Minimalist, and Conceptual alike. What linked them was a changed aesthetic sensibility of "cool detachment," a shift from "subjectivity to objectivity, from interpretation to presentation, from symbol to sign – to seeing things as they literally are and 'saying it like it is'" (Sandler, 1988, p. 61). Pop artists including Wesselmann, Andy Warhol, and Roy Lichtenstein violated traditional art standards of personal execution, craftsmanship, and originality and mimicked the detached and depersonalized character of mass culture. Culling images from mass media – stills of movie stars, tabloid newspaper photographs of car crashes – Warhol employed a photo-silkscreen process and a staff of artists who "made" his art (sometimes as many as eighty paintings a day) in assembly-line fashion at a New York studio he named "The Factory." As Warhol remarked in 1963, "I think it would be so great if more people took up silk screens so that no one would know whether my picture was mine or somebody else's" (Swenson, 1997 [1963], p. 104).

Pop's deadpan imagery and ambivalent intentionality initially provoked heated controversy as critics debated its artistic merits, and whether it was even art. Following its earlier nod to Jackson Pollock, *Life* featured Pop artist Roy Lichtenstein in a 1964 article headlined: "Is He the Worst Artist in the U.S.?" (Seiberling, 1964, p. 79). Soon, however, critics began assessing Pop in terms of its formal qualities, identifying its reliance on flat, unmodulated color, simple forms, and an impersonal, machine-like surface (Rosenblum, 1965; Russell and Gablik, 1969). Although Pop artists selected representational and mass media subjects to critique the separation of high and low culture, their art was ironically "embraced under the formalist umbrella" (Stich, 1987, p. 4) until the advent of revisionist art historical approaches in the 1970s. These later accounts placed Pop in its postwar historical, economic, and political contexts, delineating its relationship with American mass culture, the art market, and issues of gender (Kozloff, 1973; Roth, 1977; Mamiya, 1992; Whiting, 1997).

The historiography of Minimalist art is similar. A style of painting and sculpture that emerged in the mid-1960s, Minimalism was particularly preoccupied with the literal, physical presence of art. "Increasingly the demand has been for an honest, direct, unadulterated experience in art," art historian Eugene Goossen noted in 1966, "minus symbolism, minus messages, and minus personal exhibitionism" (Goossen, 1966, p. 31). Opposed to artifice and emotionalism, Minimalism's reductive style was especially informed by the theoretical framework of structuralism and semiotics. Shifting attention from Abstract Expressionism's existential individuals to the "systems" of modern society, Minimalist art adopted a machine-like, industrial style of geometric abstraction and elementary forms. Subverting painting's traditional role as a mode of representation, or as bearer of artistic feelings, Frank Stella's canvases were inherently objects: their content was their form. "My painting is based on the fact that only what can be seen there *is* there," Stella remarked in 1964. He added: "If the painting were lean enough, accurate enough, or right enough, you would just be able to look at it. All I want anyone to get out of my paintings, and all I ever get out of them, is the fact that you can see the whole idea without any confusion. . . . What you see is what you see" (Battcock, 1968, p. 158). Likewise, the large-scale "object sculptures" of Minimalists Don Judd, Sol LeWitt, and Carl Andre, made of

Plate 3 Robert Morris, *Untitled (L-Beams)*, 1965. Stainless steel in 3 parts. Dimensions variable: a) L Beam (flat) 24 × 96 × 96"; b) L Beam (upright) 96 × 24 × 24"; c) L Beam (on both ends) 86 × 136 × 24". Collection of Whitney Museum of American Art. Gift of Howard and Jean Lipman. 76.29a–c. Photograph © 2001 Whitney Museum of American Art. © ARS, NY and DACS, London 2002.

industrial materials and based on elementary geometric shapes, were distinguished by "no more than a literal and emphatic assertion of their existence," noted critic Barbara Rose in 1965. Minimalist sculpture was "not supposed to be suggestive of anything other than itself" (Rose, 1965, p. 66).

In his widely read polemic, "Art and Objecthood," critic Michael Fried attacked Minimalist sculpture because of its "theatricality," or its emphasis on the role of the spectator, the "beholder" (Fried, 1967). Indeed, as Minimalist artist Robert Morris argued: "The better new work takes relationships out of the work and makes them a function of space, light, and the viewer's field of vision. The object is but one of the terms in the newer aesthetic" (Morris, 1966). Although critics such as Fried aimed to narrowly classify Minimalism as the logical extension of a reductive aesthetic formalism, Minimalist sculptors were more broadly interested in the phenomenological underpinnings of modern art, in the links between objects, audiences, and the spaces they occupied. Andre, for example, placed his "plains" of metal plates on gallery floors and encouraged audiences to walk on them, while Morris arranged and rearranged L-shaped beams (plate 3, *Untitled*, 1965) and other "unitary forms" in galleries, considering how the variables of light, space, and the human body articulated the "meaning" of art objects.

Like the Pop artists, Minimalists mimicked the banal designs of mass production and further appropriated their construction methods, usually hiring industrial fabricators to assemble their plans. Eradicating their personal touch or "hand," Minimalists raised fundamental questions about who was an artist, and whether sculpture made by factory technicians qualified as "art." Too large for most homes and art galleries, Minimalism's monumental industrial forms suited more the huge headquarters of corporations and government buildings, and the sober "white cubes" of modern museums (O'Doherty, 1986). In the 1980s and 1990s, historians and critics concluded that Minimalism's inherently institutional aesthetic was deeply embedded in "the cultural authority of the markers of industry and technology" (Chave, 1990, p. 44) and that its forceful and domineering aesthetic evoked the (male) authority of the late 1960s: the authority of corporate capitalism and the defense industry (Wallis, 1983; Foster, 1996). Despite efforts otherwise, Minimalism recapitulated Abstract Expressionism's historical trajectory.

Challenging the formalist stranglehold on modern art and the avant-garde, many Minimalist and Conceptual artists devoted much of their creative energies to theoretical issues traditionally left to historians and critics. Indeed, the 1960s and 1970s saw an eruption of artist-driven critical theory, and journals like *Artforum*, *October*, and *Art in America* gained increasing authority as sites of art theory distribution and debate. In 1967, *Artforum* published Sol LeWitt's "Paragraphs on Conceptual Art," which argued that the "idea or concept is the most important aspect of the art" and "what the work of art looks like isn't too important" (LeWitt, 1967). This manifesto paralleled Joseph Kosuth's 1970 statement that Conceptual art was "the investigation of the function, meaning, and use" of art (Lippard, 1973, p. 261).

Indebted as it was to Marcel Duchamp, to linguistic philosophy, to Thomas Kuhn's articulation of "paradigm shifts" in *The Structure of Scientific Revolutions* (1962), and to worldwide destabilizing social, political, and economic conditions and movements (including student and worker revolts in the late 1960s in France, Japan, Mexico, Eastern Europe, and the United States), Conceptual art focused on issues of cultural production, distribution, and reception. Aiming to radically unsettle the institutional frameworks of modern art, Conceptual artists bought space in newspapers and magazines to "exhibit" their work, made "mail art," and generated their own theories – thereby eliminating the need for galleries, museums, and art criticism. Some critics embraced Conceptual aesthetics as the next step in the evolution of the postwar avant-garde, while others denounced its "politicization" of art (Kramer, 1970). Until recently, Conceptual art was largely ignored in the history of postwar American visual arts, an ironic gap given its tremendous influence on subsequent artistic developments and on critical understandings of postmodernism (Alberro and Stimson, 2000, p. xiv).

Feminism and Postmodernism

In 1971, art historian Linda Nochlin's highly influential essay entitled "Why Have There Been No Great Women Artists?" appeared in *Art News* (Nochlin, 1971). Nochlin argued that notions of "greatness" (artistic and otherwise) were constructed rather than natural or innate, and that critics, historians, and art institutions had consistently ignored and undervalued women's art. As Nochlin pointed out, the very question she posed of the supposed lack of female "greatness" betrayed these abiding patriarchal conceits. Her provocative analysis of art and authority was one of many feminist volleys fired in the early 1970s. Angered by their exclusion from art history (H. W. Janson's popular survey, *The History of Art*, first published in 1962, failed to include a single female artist), and from the art world (only eight women, of 143

Plate 4   Judy Chicago, *The Dinner Party*, 1974–79. Painted porcelain and needlework, 576 × 576 × 36″. Collection of the artist. © Judy Chicago 1979. Photo © Donald Woodman.

artists, were included in the 1969 Whitney Museum of American Art Annual exhibition), Feminist artists aimed to raise consciousness, invite dialogue, and transform cultural attitudes about women (Lippard, 1995 [1980]). A touchstone in the Feminist art movement was *The Dinner Party* (plate 4), a monumental, multi-media project (organized by Judy Chicago) that celebrated the lives and achievements of over 1,000 women and mythical female figures (from the Primordial Goddess to Georgia O'Keeffe), and featured porcelain plates shaped in labial-butterfly forms that asserted the value and integrity of female sexuality.

A core issue in early Feminist art was female identity, and the ways in which images shape and direct identity. In 1975, filmmaker and theorist Laura Mulvey published "Visual Pleasure and Narrative Cinema," a groundbreaking essay that introduced notions of the "male gaze" and linked the power relations of "looking" and being "looked upon" to the construction of male and female identity, and to patriarchal ideologies (Mulvey, 1975). Recognizing the long history of demeaning representations of the female body as a passive object to be gazed upon and desired – a history repeatedly reinscribed in art, mass media, and advertising – Feminist artists sought to reclaim the female body as a *subject*. Some artworks resisted the male gaze by parodying its visual stereotypes, while other projects, such as *The Dinner Party*, subverted and revised traditionally masculinist historical narratives by highlighting female identity and new understandings of female sexuality.

Inspired by the activism of civil rights, the anti-war movement, and Women's Liberation, artists' collectives proliferated during the 1970s, challenging the longstanding exclusion of women and nonwhite artists. At the same historical moment that formalist New Criticism theorized the death of the author, Feminist and black artists, among others, reclaimed marginalized female and minority voices and redirected postwar American art along more expansive and pluralistic pathways. Feminist art programs were developed across the United States; by 1974, over 1,000 US colleges offered women's studies courses. New journals were published (*Feminist Art Journal*, *Woman's Art Journal*, *Heresies*), aimed at "excavating the buried history" of women artists (Rickey, 1994, p. 120). Likewise, in the late 1960s, African American artists attuned to issues of black nationalism formed groups, organized gallery and museum exhibitions, directed community mural projects, and debated notions of a modern black aesthetic (Campbell, 1985; Patton, 1998). Protests against racial and ethnic stereotypes and limiting and monolithic assumptions of American identity found further resonance among Native American and Chicano artists.

Egalitarian aspirations and protest aesthetics infused new revisionist practices in American art history; scholars "chafed at the narrow definition of their field" and "rebelled against the elitism and restrictiveness of a canon that privileged male artists and high art masterpieces" (Corn, 1988, p. 96). Marxist, feminist, postcolonialist, psychoanalytic, and semiotic approaches, among others, provided new interpretive and interdisciplinary strategies for the new art history and destabilized myopic or fixed understandings of art. Art history surveys expanded to include non-Western works and visual cultures once considered unworthy of academic study (such as advertising, tabloid journalism, comics, movies, and self-taught art); panels and professional papers at the College Art Association were increasingly attentive to theoretical debates and issues of class, race, gender, ethnicity, and sexual difference; the CAA's flagship quarterly, *Art Bulletin*, began to feature articles on commercial illustrators such as Norman Rockwell; and the CAA itself took an active role as an advocate for First Amendment rights for artists and historians.

Reckoning with the contradictions and complexities of American history and identity, artists, historians, and critics deconstructed earlier postwar assumptions of cultural and national exceptionalism. They challenged limited formalist understandings of modernism that had centered on individual (and mostly white male) artists, discrete media, and stylistic innovation. Some went so far as to pronounce the "end of art" (Danto, 1984) and the "death of modernism" (Foster, 1984), lauding instead diverse and often conflicted forms of "postmodernism" and interdisciplinary analyses of cultural relationships.

Critic Craig Owens described postmodernism as "a crisis of cultural authority, specifically of the authority vested in Western European culture and its institutions" (Owens, 1992 [1983], p. 166). Battles over cultural authority raged in the 1980s and 1990s, as various political, social, and artistic factions struggled for recognition and power. Neoconservative political figures and religious demagogues attacked art, artists, and art organizations as a "moral cancer in our society" (Selcraig, 1990, p. 24). Art museums and government funding agencies such as the NEA were indicted for exhibitions some found offensive, including Robert Mapplethorpe's photographs of gay men and Andres Serrano's critiques of Catholic religious symbols. Angry protests against public art, including the *Vietnam Veterans Memorial* (1982) and the

Minimalist sculpture *Tilted Arc* (1981–9), and fierce arguments over freedom of expression and public funding for art heightened the era's contentious mood (Doss, 1995). The overnight success of the Neo-Expressionists, a group of young, male, and heavily promoted New York painters determined to become the "new" Pollocks, provoked bitter debates about artistic "quality" and "merit" in the art world (Buchloh, 1981).

Issues of power and authenticity dominated postmodern criticism and art in the 1980s, evident in Mark Tansey's 1984 painting, *Triumph of the New York School* (plate 5), which used the military liberation of France as a cultural metaphor to satirize perceived historical notions of the French avant-garde ceding modern art to Clement Greenberg and Abstract Expressionism. Borrowing subjects and styles from multiple sources – especially advertising, photojournalism, and television, but also earlier genres of art – "appropriation" artists such as Tansey, Barbara Kruger, Sherry Levine, and Jeff Koons raised questions about the originality and institutional framework of art and art history. Levine copied photographs by Walker Evans and paintings by Miró, "representing someone else's work as her own," wrote critic Thomas Lawson, "in an attempt to sabotage a system that places value on the privileged production of individual talent" (Lawson, 1981, p. 45). Kruger quoted mass media images and words to expose the cultural dominance of advertising. Koons displayed Hoover vacuum cleaners and Spalding basketballs in heavily promoted exhibitions, selling his art for extremely high prices and exposing the ways in which art, artists, and notions of taste are manufactured.

In the 1990s, postmodern cultural analyses centered especially on the complexities of contemporary identity: race, class, gender, ethnicity, and sexual difference. The decade opened with *The Decade Show: Frameworks of Identity in the 1980s*, a collaborative project of three New York art institutions (the Museum of Contemporary Hispanic Art, the New Museum of Contemporary Art, and the Studio Museum in Harlem) that highlighted social and cultural understandings of difference. It closed with the Whitney Museum's "Millennial Biennial," an exhibition that showcased new visual media (such as video and electronic imagery) and revealed a robust multiplicity of artmaking practices and cultural identities at the end of the "American Century."

Issues of difference were especially dominant in the 1990s, as artists and museums wrestled with the nation's conflicted and abiding history of multiculturalism. Earlier artistic affirmations of race, ethnicity, and gender as art subjects were now complicated by more sophisticated understandings of the hybridic or syncretic realities of contemporary American cultural identities. Jaune Quick-to-See Smith's *Trade (Gifts for Trading Land with White People)* (plate 6, 1992), conveys the kaleidoscopic dimensions of contemporary Indian – and all-American – identity. Her humorous but pointed critique draws on Abstract Expressionist and Neo-Dada styles, and features sports souvenirs of the Cleveland Indians and Washington Redskins as trinkets to "trade back" to whites for stolen Indian lands.

"Despite the dispiriting statistics on race, poverty, crime, and the 'culture wars' that bedevil America, there is scarcely another country more obsessed with the rights of minorities and the recognition of cultural diversity," critic Homi Bhabha wrote in 1999. "It has infused the American century with a spirit of freedom and equality embodied in civil rights, women's rights, the needs of and obligations toward AIDS

Plate 5 Mark Tansey, *Triumph of the New York School*, 1984. Oil on canvas, 74 × 120″. Collection of Whitney Museum of American Art. Promised gift of Robert M. Kaye. P. S. 84. Photograph © 2001 Whitney Museum of American Art.

Plate 6   Jaune Quick-to-See Smith, *Trade (Gifts for Trading Land with White People)*, 1992. Oil, collage, mixed media on canvas with objects, triptych, 60 × 170″. The Chrysler Museum, Norfolk, Virginia.

communities, the freedom of cultural and artistic expression, the care of the environment, and much else" (Phillips, 1999, p. 337).

Toward the Future

In the early twenty-first century, a "new" art history shaped from multiple theoretical horizons – social history, feminism, queer theory, psychoanalysis, semiotics, postcolonialism, poststructuralism, intertextuality – is clearly in place. An interdisciplinary hybrid called visual culture studies has emerged, focused on the genealogy, practice, and experience (reception) of modern visual culture – from art, advertising, and mass media to new technologies of holography, lasers, computer graphics, digital imagery, robotics, the Internet, and virtual reality (Mirzoeff, 1999). Recognition of the varieties of visual interpretation – "no interpretation can be privileged over any other" – has "decentered" knowledge (Bal and Bryson, 1991, p. 207), much as postwar notions of a monolithic "American Century" have shifted to those of a more expansive American multiculturalism. Some historians protest this state of affairs: the Association for Art History, a group "interested in traditional approaches to art history," formed in the mid-1990s as an alternative to the College Art Association; and Rosalind Krauss, a professor of art history at Columbia University and an editor of the theoretical journal *October*, is among those "frankly suspicious" of art history's "flirtation" with visual culture. "Students in art history graduate programs don't know how to read a work of art," she remarked in 1996. "They're getting visual studies instead – a lot of paranoid scenarios about what happens under patriarchy or under imperialism" (Heller, 1997, p. 105).

Still, revisionist narratives assessing race, gender, ethnicity, class, and sexuality continue to inform American art scholarship today, and new accounts of the visual culture of American religions and issues of spirituality challenge the predominantly secular focus of postwar historiography (Morgan and Promey, 2001). One can only speculate about the look and shape of visual culture in the future, but clearly, revised perspectives regarding the nature of art and the meaning of American history will continue to inform our knowledge of the field.

REFERENCES

Alberro, Alexander and Stimson, Blake: *Conceptual Art: A Critical Anthology* (Cambridge, Mass.: MIT Press, 2000).

Alloway, Lawrence: "The Long Front of Culture," *Cambridge Opinion*, 17 (1959); rpt. in *Modern Dreams: The Rise and Fall and Rise of Pop* (Cambridge, Mass.: MIT Press, 1988), 30–3.

Baigell, Matthew: *A Concise History of American Painting and Sculpture* (New York: Harper and Row, 1984).

Bal, Mieke and Bryson, Norman: "Semiotics and Art History," *Art Bulletin*, 73 (1991): 174–208.

Banes, Sally: *Greenwich Village 1963: Avant-Garde Performance and the Effervescent Body* (Durham, NC: Duke University Press, 1993).

Barthes, Roland: "The Death of the Author" (1968), in *Image-Music-Text*, trans. Stephen Heath (New York: Hill and Wang, 1977).

Battcock, Gregory, ed.: *Minimal Art: A Critical Anthology* (New York: E. P. Dutton, 1968).

Belgrad, Daniel: *The Culture of Spontaneity: Improvisation and the Arts in Postwar America* (Chicago: University of Chicago Press, 1998).

Bjelajac, David: *American Art: A Cultural History* (Upper Saddle River, NJ: Prentice Hall, 2000).

Buchloh, Benjamin: "Figures of Authority, Ciphers of Regression," *October*, 16 (Spring 1981): 39–68.

Campbell, Mary Schmidt: *Tradition and Conflict: Images of a Turbulent Decade, 1963–1973* (New York: Studio Museum in Harlem, 1985).

Chave, Anna: "Minimalism and the Rhetoric of Power," *Arts Magazine* (January 1990): 44–63.

Coates, Robert M.: "Assorted Moderns," *New Yorker* (December 23, 1944): 50–1.

Corn, Wanda: "Coming of Age: Historical Scholarship in American Art," *Art Bulletin*, 70/2 (June 1988): 188–207.

Craven, David: *Abstract Expressionism as Cultural Critique: Dissent During the McCarthy Period* (New York: Cambridge University Press, 1999).

Craven, Wayne: *American Art: History and Culture* (Madison: Brown and Benchmark, 1994).

Danto, Arthur: "The End of Art," in Berel Lang (ed.), *The Death of Art* (New York: Haven Publishers, 1984).

Danto, Arthur: "The Artworld," *Journal of Philosophy* (October 15, 1964): 571–84; rpt. in Steven Henry Madoff (ed.), *Pop Art: A Critical History* (Berkeley: University of California Press, 1997), 269–78.

Danto, Arthur: "The Artworld and Its Outsiders," in *Self-Taught Artists of the 20th Century: An American Anthology* (New York: Museum of American Folk Art, 1998), 18–27.

de Kooning, Willem: "What Abstract Art Means to Me," *Museum of Modern Art Bulletin* (Spring 1951): 12–13.

Doss, Erika: *Benton, Pollock, and the Politics of Modernism: From Regionalism to Abstract Expressionism* (Chicago: University of Chicago Press, 1991).

Doss, Erika: *Spirit Poles and Flying Pigs: Public Art and Cultural Democracy in American Communities* (Washington, DC: Smithsonian Institution Press, 1995).

Doss, Erika: *Twentieth-Century American Art* (Oxford: Oxford University Press, 2002).

Foster, Hal: *Art After Modernism: Rethinking Representation* (New York: New Museum of Contemporary Art, 1984).

Foster, Hal: *The Return of the Real: The Avant-Garde at the End of the Century* (Cambridge, Mass.: MIT Press, 1996).

Fried, Michael: "Art and Objecthood," *Artforum* (June 1967): 12–23.

Gibson, Ann: *Abstract Expressionism: Other Politics* (New Haven, Conn.: Yale University Press, 1997).

Gombrich, Ernst H.: *The Image and the Eye: Further Studies in the Psychology of Pictorial Representation* (London: Phaidon Press, 1982).

Goossen, Eugene C.: "Distillation: A Joint Showing," *Artforum* (November 1966): 31–3.

Greenberg, Clement: "Avant-Garde and Kitsch," *Partisan Review* (Fall 1939): 34–49.

Greenberg, Clement: "Toward a Newer Laocoön," *Partisan Review* (July/August 1940): 296–310.

Greenberg, Clement: "The Decline of Cubism," *Partisan Review* (March 1948): 369.

Greenberg, Clement: "Modernist Painting," 1961, Radio Broadcast Lecture 14 of *The Voice of America Forum Lectures: The Visual Arts*, published in revised form in *Art and Literature*, 4 (Spring 1965): 193–201.

Guilbaut, Serge: *How New York Stole the Idea of Modern Art: Abstract Expressionism, Freedom, and the Cold War* (Chicago: University of Chicago Press, 1983).

Heller, Scott: "What Are They Doing to Art History?" *Art News* (January 1997): 102–5.

Hughes, Robert: *American Visions: The Epic History of Art in America* (New York: Alfred A. Knopf, 1997).

"Jackson Pollock," *Arts and Architecture* (February 1944): 14.

Johns, Elizabeth: "Histories of American Art: The Changing Quest," *Art Journal*, 44/4 (Winter 1984): 338–44.

Kaprow, Allan: "The Legacy of Jackson Pollock," *Art News* (October 1958): 24–6, 55–7.

Kirby, Michael: *Happenings: An Illustrated Anthology* (New York: E. P. Dutton, 1966).

Kozloff, Max: "American Painting During the Cold War," *Artforum* (May 1973): 43–54.

Kramer, Hilton: "Show at the Modern Raises Questions," *New York Times* (July 2, 1970): 26.

Larkin, Oliver: *Art and Life in America* (New York: Rinehart, 1949).

Lawson, Thomas: "Last Exit: Painting," *Artforum* (October 1981): 40–7.

Leja, Michael: *Reframing Abstract Expressionism: Subjectivity and Painting in the 1940s* (New Haven, Conn.: Yale University Press, 1993).

LeWitt, Sol: "Paragraphs on Conceptual Art," *Artforum* (June 1967): 79–83.

Lippard, Lucy, ed.: *Six Years: The Dematerialization of the Art Object from 1966 to 1972* (New York: Praeger, 1973).

Lippard, Lucy: "Sweeping Exchanges: The Contribution of Feminism to the Art of the 1970s" (1980), rpt. in Lippard, *The Pink Glass Swan: Selected Feminist Essays on Art* (New York: New Press, 1995), 171–82, 328–9.

Luce, Henry: "The American Century," *Life* (February 17, 1941): 61–5.

McLuhan, Marshall: *Understanding Media* (New York: Signet, 1964).

Mamiya, Christin: *Pop Art and Consumer Culture: American Super Market* (Austin: University of Texas Press, 1992).

Mathews, Jane de Hart: "Art and Politics in Cold War America," *American Historical Review*, 81 (1976): 762–87.

Mirzoeff, Nicholas: *An Introduction to Visual Culture* (New York: Routledge, 1999).

Morgan, David and Promey, Sally, eds.: *The Visual Culture of American Religions* (Berkeley: University of California Press, 2001).

Morris, Robert: "Notes on Sculpture," *Artforum* (February 1966): 42–4.

Motherwell, Robert: "What Abstract Art Means to Me," *Museum of Modern Art Bulletin* (Spring 1951): 12–13.

Mulvey, Laura: "Visual Pleasure and Narrative Cinema," *Screen* (Autumn 1975): 6–18.

Nochlin, Linda: "Why Have There Been No Great Women Artists?" *Art News* (January 1971): 22–39.

O'Doherty, Brian: *Inside the White Cube: The Ideology of the Gallery Space* (Santa Monica, Calif.: Lapis Press, 1986).

Owens, Craig: "The Discourse of Others: Feminists and Postmodernists" (1983), rpt. in Owens, *Beyond Recognition: Representation, Power, and Culture* (Berkeley: University of California Press, 1992), 166–90.

Patton, Sharon F.: *African-American Art* (Oxford: Oxford University Press, 1998).

Phillips, Lisa: *Beat Culture and the New America, 1950–1965* (New York: Whitney Museum of American Art, 1995).

Phillips, Lisa: *The American Century: Art and Culture, 1950–2000* (New York: Whitney Museum of American Art, 1999).

Polcari, Stephen: *Abstract Expressionism and the Modern Experience* (New York: Cambridge University Press, 1991).

Rickey, Carrie: "Writing (and Righting) Wrongs: Feminist Art Publications," in Norma Broude and Mary D. Garrard (eds.), *The Power of Feminist Art: The American Movement of the 1970s, History and Impact* (New York: Harry N. Abrams, 1994), 120–9.

Rodman, Selden: "Jackson Pollock" (interview conducted 1956), in *Conversations with Artists* (New York: Capricorn Books, 1961), 76–87.

Rose, Barbara: "ABC Art," *Art in America* (October/November 1965): 57–69.

Rose, Barbara: *American Art Since 1900* (New York: Praeger, 1967; rev. and expanded ed., 1975).

Rosenberg, Harold: "The American Action Painters" (1952), in *Tradition of the New* (Chicago: University of Chicago Press, 1982), 25–35.

Rosenblum, Robert: "Pop Art and Non-Pop Art," *Arts and Literature* (Summer 1965): 80–93.

Roth, Moira: "The Aesthetic of Indifference," *Artforum*, 16 (November 1977): 46–53.

Rothko, Mark: "Introduction," in *Clyfford Still* (New York: Art of This Century, 1946).

Russell, John and Gablik, Suzi: *Pop Art Redefined* (New York: Praeger, 1969).

Sandler, Irving: *The Triumph of American Painting: A History of Abstract Expressionism* (New York: Harper and Row, 1970).

Sandler, Irving: *American Art of the 1960s* (New York: Harper and Row, 1988).

Schlesinger, Jr., Arthur: *The Vital Center: The Politics of Freedom* (Boston: Houghton Mifflin, 1949).

Seiberling, Dorothy: "Jackson Pollock: Is He the Greatest Living Painter in the United States?" *Life* (August 8, 1949): 42–5.

Seiberling, Dorothy: "Roy Lichtenstein: Is He the Worst Artist in the U.S.?" *Life* (January 31, 1964): 79–83.

Seitz, William C.: *The Art of Assemblage* (New York: Museum of Modern Art, 1961).

Selcraig, Bruce: "Reverend Wildmon's War on the Arts," *Sunday New York Times Magazine* (September 2, 1990): Sec. 6, 22–5, 43, 52–3.

Stich, Sidra: *Made in U.S.A.: An Americanization in Modern Art, The '50s and '60s* (Berkeley: University of California Press, 1987).

Swenson, G. R.: "What is Pop Art? Part I, Interview with Andy Warhol" (1963), in Steven Henry Madoff (ed.), *Pop Art: A Critical History* (Berkeley: University of California Press, 1997), 103–5.

Sylvester, David: "Adolph Gottlieb: An Interview" (1963), in David Shapiro and Cecile Shapiro (eds.), *Abstract Expressionism: A Critical Record* (New York: Cambridge University Press, 1990), 264–9.

Taylor, Joshua: *The Fine Arts in America* (Chicago: University of Chicago Press, 1979).

Wallach, Alan: "Oliver Larkin's *Art and Life in America*: Between the Popular Front and the Cold War," *American Art*, 15/3 (Fall 2001): 80–9.

Wallis, Brian: "Notes on (Re)Viewing Don Judd's Work," in *Donald Judd: Eight Works in Three Dimensions* (Charlotte, NC: Knight Gallery, 1983).

Whiting, Cecilé: *A Taste for Pop: Pop Art, Gender, and Consumer Culture* (New York: Cambridge University Press, 1997).

Wilmerding, John: *American Art* (Harmondsworth: Penguin, 1976).

Wright, William: "Radio Interview with Jackson Pollock," The Springs, Long Island, 1950; transcript published in Francis V. O'Connor and Eugene V. Thaw, *Jackson Pollock: A Catalogue Raisonné of Paintings, Drawings, and Other Works*, vol. 4 (New Haven, Conn.: Yale University Press, 1978), 248–51.

CHAPTER EIGHT

American Intellectual History and Social Thought Since 1945

PATRICK N. ALLITT

American intellectual historians sometimes complain that their subfield has declined in visibility and importance since the 1950s when it enjoyed the services of giants – Richard Hofstadter, Merle Curti, Perry Miller, and Henry Steele Commager. The complaint is misleading. Intellectual history may have suffered a relative decline beside the new social history, but it is practiced more intelligently and by more people than ever before. In the decades after 1960 intellectual history opened itself to the insights of the social sciences and literary theory, feminism and multiculturalism, without being disabled by them; to the contrary, it became more rigorous in research techniques and more guarded in the making of facile generalizations than ever before. Historians came to appreciate the need to consider the social location and cultural characteristics of intellectuals as a group. Their ability and willingness to contextualize their subjects showed an unquestionable advance over the work of their predecessors. Intellectual history in the last five decades has wrestled with a range of philosophical questions, including: the power of ideas as instruments of social change; the ability of influential writers to shape and change the course of government policy; and the benefits and drawbacks of social advocacy in the guise of historical study. It has done so in an often lively and imaginative way, ensuring it an important place in the broader context of American historical study.

Intellectual historians were both participants in, and analysts of, the era's social debates and controversies. They bore witness to the climax and decline of liberalism, the rise of "new" and "neo" conservatism, the short but intense impact of the New Left, the rise of feminism, and the long debate about American poverty. In those years America's intellectual infrastructure, the research universities, grew vast and prompted fears of an academic overspecialization that would close out all but highly trained specialists from participation. Further complicating matters, the insights of postmodernism and literary theory began to cast doubt on the relationship between social realities and intellectuals' analysis of them. Issues previously confined to the philosophy department's epistemology specialists began to appear at the heart of debates over race, gender, and poverty.

In the late 1940s and early 1950s intellectual historians doubling as liberal social analysts dominated the landscape. Miller, Curti, and Commager saw themselves as defenders of American civilization against the threat of communism from the left and the threat of philistine McCarthyism from the right. Curti's *The Growth of*

American Thought (1943), Miller's *The New England Mind* (1939/1953), and Commager's *The American Mind* (1950) all assumed, as their titles suggest, that there was something identifiably American about a certain kind of thinking. Their characterization of this national style as processual, indebted to scientific method, but pragmatic and oriented to everyday affairs, was prescriptive as well as descriptive. By the standards of their successors, these historians were insensitive to variation and contradiction within the traditions they explored. They had no time to spare for ethnic variation or the literature of minority groups, and they scarcely glanced at female authors (Perry, 1984; Pells, 1985; Novick, 1988).

These historians wrote under the shadow of the Cold War, and it is clear in retrospect that they were defining the "American Mind" as the antithesis of the "Soviet Mind." Americans, said Daniel Boorstin, another postwar liberal luminary, were experimental, tolerant, open-minded, democratic, and entrepreneurial; all these qualities were desirable. No wonder, then, that communism had made so little headway in America; its "Mind" was closed, dogmatic, tyrannical, and bureaucratic. America's intellectual spokesmen were nevertheless anxious. Marxists, after all, believed that socialism was destined sooner or later to take over all industrial economies in accordance with the laws of history. Werner Sombart had published *Why Is There No Socialism in the United States?* back in 1906 and the question had remained implicit in most discussions of political economy ever since. Socialists asked it with impatience; anti-communists asked it with dread. Not until the Reagan/Thatcher/Gorbachev years of the 1980s could historians relinquish the question and begin to see socialism as a vital episode in the history of Western intellectual, economic, and political development, but *not* as their inevitable destiny.

Arthur Schlesinger, Jr. (*The Vital Center*, 1949) and Reinhold Niebuhr (*The Irony of American History*, 1952) were also prominent figures in the liberal camp. Fearing ideological contamination from left and right, they tried rhetorically to position themselves and America at the heart of Western civilization. They denied the conservative claim that liberalism lacked solid intellectual or religious foundations; indeed Niebuhr was the era's leading Protestant theologian (Fox, 1987). They also denied the socialist claim that liberalism was merely a fig leaf of decency for rapacious capitalism. Instead Schlesinger and Niebuhr argued that American liberalism's dedication to progress, freedom, equality, and minority rights made liberalism the heart and soul of American history. A like-minded liberal economist, John K. Galbraith, gave a name to the era with *The Affluent Society* (1958), in which he argued that America's incredible economic growth had not yet been matched by an equitable distribution, and that the society must now strive for "social balance." Galbraith's subsequent work, strongly consonant with the New Deal heritage, argued for a powerful central government as counterweight to the power of corporations (Waligorski, 1997; Okroi, 1998).

The defense of New Deal liberalism also underlay what is remembered as the "consensus" school of American historiography, whose character was nicely encapsulated at the time in John Higham's *History* (1965), which is today equally useful as a primary and as a secondary source. Richard Hofstadter was a key figure in this school and his books *The American Political Tradition* (1948) and *The Age of Reform* (1955) are among its principal documents. Almost equally important was Louis Hartz, who argued that a homogeneous political and intellectual culture of liberalism had characterized the nation's relatively conflict-free past, because it had been spared the ordeal of feudalism. Schlesinger's hefty trilogy on the New Deal era, published between 1957 and 1960, is a classic work in this idiom, though with lingering debts to the Progressive historical tradition in which he had been raised.

Schlesinger went on to become an adviser to President John F. Kennedy and Niebuhr made it onto the cover of *Time* magazine, while other liberal celebrities of the era, like Walter Lippmann, continued to play the role of "public intellectuals" (Steel, 1980; Riccio, 1994). The rise of academic hyperspecialization since then has led a more recent generation of critics to fear that the age of great public intellectuals, the brilliant generalists, has ended (Jacoby, 1987). The postwar baby boom and the increasing need for technologists and experts fed an immense expansion of universities in the years 1945–65. Their story has been told in various ways. David Hollinger (1996) is most attentive to the faculty's cosmopolitan and scientific ideals, and to the way in which the American academy became increasingly hospitable to Jews. Several recent collections discuss the distortion of research priorities engendered by the Cold War itself. Weapons research preoccupied the physicists, not surprisingly, but even fields ostensibly more remote, such as anthropology and psychology, were drawn in by the lure of big research dollars for work on how to demoralize an enemy or how to influence peasant groups' behavior in Indo-China (Montgomery, 1997; Simpson, 1998). Moreover the universities themselves were swept by McCarthyism, showing academic freedom to be a weak reed and jeopardizing the livelihood of all who had been communists or "fellow travelers" (Schrecker, 1986). Hofstadter's *Anti-Intellectualism in American Life* (1963) investigated the paradox of a nation suspicious of experts nevertheless training more of them and depending on them more than any other society in history.

Among the groups destined to make a big mark on American social thought were the "New York Intellectuals" gathered around *Partisan Review, Commentary,* and later *Dissent* (Bloom, 1986; Wald, 1987). Mainly second-generation Jews in revolt against their families' religious heritage, and inspired by ideals of universal liberation, these critics had been attracted to the political left during the Great Depression but, in most instances, had revolted against the political brutality and cultural philistinism of Stalinism by 1940. Leading figures included Morris Cohen, Sidney Hook, Irving Howe, Philip Rahv, Irving Kristol, Lionel Trilling, Alfred Kazin, Nathan Glazer, Daniel Bell, William Barrett, and Seymour Martin Lipset. Peripheral figures included Hofstadter (who was half-Jewish and half-Lutheran), the great literary critic Edmund Wilson (an old WASP), and the novelist Mary McCarthy (a lapsed Catholic). Historians Michael Denning (1996) and Paul Gorman (1996) explore the rich cultural life of the era in which this group was politicized and explain its allure. Some of the New Yorkers, as Kristol later (1983) recalled, had dabbled in Trotskyism, which for a time had seemed to represent communism with a human face. By the postwar years, however, most of these figures had abandoned what they regarded as a repressive political left and had begun to make peace with American institutions – and then to enjoy the rewards the nation had to offer. This discovery that America was happy to have them is cleverly depicted in *Commentary* editor Norman Podhoretz's autobiography, *Making It* (1967), whose smug tone enraged his detractors.

The New York "family" divided over an appropriate response to McCarthyism, the more or less official attempt between 1947 and 1955 to purge American communists and their sympathizers from public life. Irving Kristol, by then an editor of CIA-subsidized *Encounter*, regarded Stalinism as so vicious that he could not work up much ire against the Wisconsin demagogue. Others in his circle, particularly Irving Howe, editor of *Dissent*, saw McCarthy's threats and smears as an attack on American civil liberties; the dispute drove a deep wedge into the group's allegiances (Howe, 1968).

Unlike the liberal anti-communists and the New York "family," members of the New Conservative intellectual movement were strident anti-communists and often outright defenders of McCarthy. One of the biggest shifts in the intellectual historiography of recent decades has been the recognition that these conservatives (whom Bell [1955] and Hofstadter [1965] once casually brushed aside with social-psychological insults) played as important a role in American life as their liberal counterparts (Nash, 1975; Miles, 1980; Hoeveler, 1991; Allitt, 1993). Some of these New Conservatives, including James Burnham, Will Herberg, Whittaker Chambers, and Max Eastman, were ex-communists, now convinced that nothing was deadlier to the future of the world than communism (Diggins, 1975; Weinstein, 1978; Tanenhaus, 1997). The New Conservatives were led by William F. Buckley, Jr., whose journal, *National Review*, founded in 1955, became the intellectual center of the movement on the East Coast while Russell Kirk's *Modern Age* was its midwestern standard-bearer. Richard Weaver's *Ideas Have Consequences* (1948), Buckley's *God and Man at Yale* (1951), and Kirk's *The Conservative Mind* (1953) were the movement's first big statements. Edmund Burke and Cardinal Newman played the same role for these conservatives that John Locke and Thomas Jefferson had played for the liberals. The New Conservatives provided an intellectual justification of American civilization, by arguing the close connection between a free society, a market economy, anti-communism, and freedom of religion. Their economics gurus were Friedrich von Hayek, Ludwig von Mises, and later Milton Friedman, and they recognized a theoretical debt to such European émigrés as Leo Strauss and Eric Voegelin (Nash, 1975; McAllister, 1996).

Liberals and conservatives alike owed transatlantic debts. In the nineteenth and early twentieth centuries, American intellectuals had felt distinctly inferior to their European counterparts and, as studies by James Kloppenberg (1986) and Daniel Rodgers (1998) have shown, American reform and social policy ideas drew heavily on European models. Even world dominance after World War II and an unrivaled institutional support for intellectuals in a thriving and expanding university system were not enough to banish this sense of inferiority. Dependence on external intellectual blood transfusions persisted. First came the Frankfurt School (founded 1923), a body of mainly Jewish German intellectuals on the left whose Institute for Social Research had had to be disbanded with the election of Hitler in 1933 but had been refounded in New York as a branch of Columbia University (M. Jay, 1973). These intellectuals made no pretense of being "objective" or value-neutral; they intended, rather, to understand society with an eye to transforming it. Their leading figures, Max Horkheimer, Leo Lowenthal, Walter Benjamin, Theodor Adorno, Hannah Arendt, Erich Fromm, and Herbert Marcuse practiced what they called "interdisciplinary materialism," trying to take advantage of the growing sophistication of the social sciences' empirical techniques and linking them to Marxist theoretical foundations. They were also among the first social theorists to incorporate Freudian psychoanalysis into Marxism (systems which, as Jay shows, had previously seemed antithetical).

Completely unsentimental about the proletariat (unlike Denning's "popular front" Marxists of the 1930s), they were sharply critical of American "mass culture." They were no more willing to celebrate it than the Spanish conservative Ortega y Gasset, whose *The Revolt of the Masses* (1930), a classic statement of patrician distaste for the common people, also enjoyed a vogue among American intellectuals in the 1950s and 1960s. Adorno's *The Authoritarian Personality* (1950) drew on developments in social psychology to state his theme with bleak clarity – it argued that lower-middle-class Americans were susceptible to fascism. Adorno's book, and Arendt's *The Origins of Totalitarianism* (1948), arguing the essential similarity of Nazism and Stalinism, owed a debt to another Frankfurt classic, Fromm's *Escape from Freedom* (1941). Marcuse's *Eros and Civilization* (1955) and *One Dimensional Man* (1964) similarly argued that the apparent freedoms of affluent America were illusory – his phrase was "repressive desublimation" – and became compulsory reading for members of the early New Left (Gitlin, 1987; Isserman, 1987).

Psychology and psychiatry played an increasingly prominent role not just among these émigrés but more broadly in postwar American social thought (Lunbeck, 1994; Herman, 1995). A vast literature debated ideas about the human individual, the nature of "selfhood," and the relationship between self and society (McClay, 1994). Psychological warfare studies and dismaying revelations about the inability of American prisoners of war in Korea to stand up to communist "brainwashing" suggested that psychological pressures had created a feeble new character type in America. *The Lonely Crowd* (1950) by David Riesman, Nathan Glazer, and Reuel Denney argued that the tradition-oriented personality of earlier epochs had been displaced, first by the hard-driving, "inner-directed" personality of early capitalism, then by the weak "other-directed personality" of the modern corporation. Riesman's other-directed personality (similar to what William Whyte called "the organization man" in a book of the same name) lacked the strong inner gyroscope to guide him single-mindedly through the world in pursuit of his goal. He depended instead on the validation and reassurance of his friends, neighbors, and colleagues.

Members of the "lonely crowd" comprised the "conformist" suburbanites, now much stereotyped in younger historians' accounts of the 1950s. They amused themselves with "middlebrow" culture and got heavily criticized for it by Dwight Macdonald, around whom a vigorous scholarly debate has raged in recent years. Biographer Stephen Whitfield (1984) describes Macdonald as a shallow but engaging contrarian while Michael Wreszin (1994) and Gregory Sumner (1996) both portray him as a more impressive figure of lasting intellectual significance. Offsetting Macdonald's critical approach to popular culture was the enthusiastic embrace of it by a younger generation, reared on movies, radio dramas, and now television. Several distinguished American writers had already tried their hand at movie reviewing, notably James Agee, the author of *Let Us Now Praise Famous Men* (1941). Thanks in part to the work of Robert Warshow in the 1950s, film began to enjoy the status of art, deserving of the same kind of critical scrutiny and respect as poetry and theater. In the 1960s, moreover, "Pop" artists like Andy Warhol, Roy Lichtenstein, and Robert Rauschenberg would seek out and artistically transfigure such everyday objects as Campbell's soup cans, boys' war-story comics, and fast foods. Far from condemning them as products of a decadent middlebrow world, like Macdonald, however, they celebrated them. Warhol did as much as anyone to erase the lines between high and pop culture and the 1960s was the decade in which the idea of the avant-garde – art whose shock value paved the way for a new sensibility – expired in a welter of styles, forms, and artistic theories (Hughes, 1981; Wolfe, 1985; Hobbs, 1997).

The social upheavals of the 1960s transformed the intellectual landscape in count-less other ways, making it the most ideologically contentious decade in America since the 1930s. Students politicized in the civil rights, voter registration, anti-war, and anti-draft movements grew up to analyze their own generation's work according to standards their parents would have shunned. The 1960s itself bore witness to a great deal of intellectual parricide. The "sixties" sensibility of the New Left made it reluc-tant to admit debts to any ancestors. Denigrating the rigidity of the old communists by contrast with their own flexibility was a good way for New Left leaders to estab-lish their credentials. In reality, guidance from Michael Harrington, Irving Howe, Max Schachtman, and other alumni of the Old Left was of lasting value. Maurice Isserman's study (1987) of these connections is convincing. New Left historians, like their predecessors, found inspiration in Europe. Their intellectual godfather was the English historian E. P. Thompson, whose *The Making of the English Working Class* (1963) is a twentieth-century historiographical classic. Its subtle analysis of class for-mation as a continuous process and its insistence on the agency of working men and women in shaping their own way of life had the short-term effect of pushing intel-lectuals to the historical margins. In the long run, however, historians of the left learned from Thompson to place their intellectuals in a fuller social context. Almost equally influential was the Italian Marxist and cultural theorist Antonio Gramsci, whose ideas were first and most brilliantly adapted to the American historical setting by Eugene Genovese in his studies of slavery. Gramsci's notion of class hegemony, supported by what he called "organic intellectuals," was a starting point for New Left historians analyzing what to them was the vexing durability of American capitalism.

Another development in left historiography, as in the New Left itself, was the ten-dency to downplay the study of institutions and to take existential revolutionaries like Che Guevara as heroes in preference to organizational leaders like Lenin. Just as the New Left drew recruits from middle-class college students rather than from the working class, so historians under its influence tended to scant the importance of trade unions and formal parties (Socialist, Communist) in their study of the radical past. Staughton Lynd's *Intellectual Origins of American Radicalism* (1968), for example, had nothing to say about the labor struggles of the 1930s, seeking instead for inspiration from Tom Paine and nineteenth-century middle-class abolitionists.

The New Left transformed the mood and priorities of American radicalism. It also midwifed the birth of modern feminism. As countless "sixties" memoirs now attest, women in "the Movement" found that their menfolk expected them to have sex, shop, cook, and clean up the mess, without showing much respect for their political views (Evans, 1979; Echols, 1989; Shulman, 1999). Stephen Buechler (1990) paints a useful, schematic picture of feminist intellectual developments and, like Isserman, points to continuities with earlier movements, showing analogies with the branches of early twentieth-century feminism. Rose-Marie Tong's *Feminist Thought* (1998) explores the central ideas in more detail, while Alice Echols and Sara Evans make an effective case for the transformation of the personal into the political among New Left women.

Liberal feminism, handily symbolized by Betty Freidan's *The Feminine Mystique* (1963) and the National Organization for Women (NOW), argued that women were psychologically damaged by being confined to the role of housewives and mothers after enjoying a wide-ranging liberal education. As a matter of individual human rights they should, rather, be free to fulfill the hopes roused by their teachers and enjoy all the career options open to men, especially since most middle-class careers made few demands on physical strength. The second strand of feminist thinking – "women's liberation" – was more radical: identifying men as the antagonists of women, it argued for something analogous to the old Marxist call for class struggle, substituting "women" for proletariat and "men" for bourgeoisie. As described by Shulamith Firestone, Kate Millett, and later Andrea Dworkin, men were forever persecuting women, who in turn had to learn to ally with one another and then fight back against the patriarchal foe. A more muted reaction followed, in which Jane Alpert, Carol Gilligan, and others argued for feminism not on the grounds of men's and women's similarities but *because* of their differences. Women's propensity for nurture, according to this argument, made even those who were not actually mothers approach the world, each other, and whatever difficulties they faced in a sharing, cooperative, maternal way (Rosenberg, 1992).

Feminists early developed an interest in the past and began to show how incomplete all prior histories had been. A mawkish early phase of seeking inspirational "foremothers" quickly gave way to a profounder analysis of the distinction between biological "sex" and socially created "gender" (Scott, 1988; Kerber, 1997). Uncomfortably aware that "feminism" itself was predominantly a white, middle-class phenomenon, white feminists were eager to include the insights of poor and minority women. Black women writers like Toni Morrison and Alice Walker, along with Asian Americans (Maxine Hong Kingston, Amy Tan), Native Americans (Mary Crow-Dog), and Hispanics (Vicki Ruíz), all emphasized the contrast between men's and women's historical experiences. As the feminist intellectual historian Rosalind Rosenberg wrote (1992, p. 235): "Because they knew first hand the protective power of female bonds in a racist society, these minority women tended to value gender and cultural differences more positively than many white feminists did. To them, equality did not necessarily mean the erasure of difference."

One point on which feminists of all types could agree was that women were economically vulnerable. To be an unmarried woman, a divorcee or a widow, even in the affluent society, was to be at risk of poverty. Indeed the "feminization of poverty" was one of the principal women's policy issues of the post-1970 era. Some poverty analysts, like Daniel Patrick Moynihan, argued that female dominance contributed to the pathological dysfunction of black families by denying black children any familiarity with hard-working, self-disciplined, male role models. Others, like Carol Stack in *All Our Kin* (1974), argued that female kin networks were one of few sources of strength available to poor women in the face of implacable economic circumstances.

Poverty in general, not just its gender aspect, was the subject of an energetic debate from the 1960s onwards. A relatively minor issue in the social thought of the 1940s and 1950s, it came into sharp focus for academics through the work of the anthropologist Oscar Lewis, and for the general public through Michael Harrington's surprise bestseller, *The Other America* (1962). Lewis believed that a "culture of poverty" was passed along from generation to generation and that its characteristics were present orientation, fatalism, and machismo. (This worldview was memorably and sympathetically depicted in Elliott Liebow's *Talley's Corner* [1967], describing the difficult lives of a group of men on a Washington, DC street corner.) Lewis also believed, however, that collective movements such as the Cuban Revolution or the American civil rights movement could energize the poor and bring them out of their passivity and dependency (Patterson, 1981; Katz, 1989). President Johnson's "War on Poverty" programs aimed to overthrow this culture of poverty and found intellectual reinforcement in John Rawls's theory of distributive justice. In line with Lewis's ideas about the transformative powers of activism, moreover, the War was premised on the idea that the poor should actually run their own programs; there should be, in the language of the legislation, "maximum feasible participation." The programs, however, soon ran into difficulties, because they coincided with the inner-city riots of the mid-1960s and the abandonment of nonviolence by influential sections of the civil rights movement.

Stephen Steinberg's *Turning Back: The Retreat from Racial Justice in American Thought and Policy* (1995), a vigorous blend of intellectual history and advocacy, asserts that the real issue in the poverty debate all along was not the culture of poverty or the heritage of prejudice, as many participants alleged, but structural racism. Systematic job discrimination, as Steinberg tells it, was always more important than questions of individual psychology. He reminds readers that the 1963 March on Washington itself was largely about the very practical matter of jobs for black men. In a series of bravura passages Steinberg annihilates Nathan Glazer's argument that African Americans would eventually follow the upward path of other immigrant groups, Moynihan's family-breakdown model, and William Julius Wilson's argument that African American disadvantages were principally a matter of class rather than race. The issue *is* race, Steinberg insists, and only a massive commitment to affirmative action in the all-important arena of jobs could begin to set things right. Steinberg's muscular prose makes invigorating reading but his polemic is too blunt, and he is unable to make awkward evidence contradicting his thesis disappear.

Daniel P. Moynihan's *The Negro Family* (US Department of Labor, 1965), mentioned above, was the most controversial of his many contributions to the poverty debate. Working for the Johnson administration, influenced by Lewis, and sympathetic to the aims of the civil rights and anti-poverty programs, Moynihan was dismayed to find that his remarks about "a tangle of pathologies" had put him in the center of a furor; he felt he was unjustly accused of racism. Another Moynihan book, *Maximum Feasible Misunderstanding* (1969), written in the wake of that controversy, can now be seen as the debut of "neoconservatism," the era's most important new trend among political and policy intellectuals. Neoconservatives were, according to Irving Kristol, another of their standard-bearers, "liberals who have been mugged by reality." Kristol, an alumnus of the New York "family" and an increasingly voluble supporter of America's role in the Cold War, shaped the new movement's distinctive blend of analysis and advocacy (Steinfels, 1979). Like Kristol, neoconservatives often originated in the anti-Stalinist left of the New Deal era, and then flourished in the social sciences professoriate in the 1950s and 1960s; by the early 1970s many of them had concluded that their optimism about the possibilities of social and political engineering had been misplaced. The "long hot summers" of the 1960s were the decisive experience that disabused them of their earlier optimism. The urban riots, after all, came not in the dark night of Jim Crow and economic depression but at a time of improved civil rights and in the middle of an economic boom. Neoconservatives' meditations on this paradox led them to argue that government poverty programs unwittingly did more harm than good, creating incentives against work, draining away billions of taxpayers' money, and nurturing grievance constituencies (Gerson, 1997).

The development of neoconservative ideas can be traced closely in the pages of *The Public Interest*, a policy affairs journal run by Nathan Glazer and Daniel Bell through the 1960s and 1970s. Edward Banfield's *The Unheavenly City* (1970) was a classic statement of their outlook. Cities, as this pessimistic Harvard urbanologist told it, were concentrations of crime, idleness, dishonesty, and dysfunctional families, made all the worse by the meddling of liberal ideologues armed with government dollars. Among his and other neoconservatives' targets were social science and policy wonks, the bureaucratic intellectuals, professors, and journalists to whom they gave the name "the new class." New class intellectuals, as they told it, claimed value-neutrality for their studies while surreptitiously feathering their own nests by justifying the continued expansion of the federal government and the appropriation of funds to support their research. Whether "the new class" really *was* a class in the old sense was doubtful. After all, the neoconservatives were usually professors, journalists, and bureaucrats too, in a very similar structural situation. Were they part of the new class, or did their opinions exempt them?

Neoconservatives like Jeanne Kirkpatrick entered the conservative administrations of Ronald Reagan and George Bush, Sr. If the emphasis of Great Society programs had been on nurturing equality, the watchword of the neoconservative 1980s was on nurturing entrepreneurs. Milton Friedman, George Gilder, and Michael Novak were among the writers on economics to argue that entrepreneur-driven growth benefits everyone and that its good effects trickle, or even flow, down to the poor (Dorrien, 1993). Their work also enjoyed the highbrow support of philosopher Robert Nozick, a leading critic of Rawls's *Theory of Justice* (1971) whose own influential book, *Anarchy, the State and Utopia* (1974), made a powerful theoretical case for the minimal state. The most controversial neoconservative book of the 1980s was Charles Murray's *Losing Ground* (1984), which condemned the entire legacy of the Great Society programs, arguing that urban poverty, crime, and family disarray were worse than they would have been if the federal government had done nothing at all. Intellectual historians had long pondered the relationship between social thought and public policy. Did intellectuals' ideas ever get put into practice? Yes. Murray's example (like Michael Harrington's in an earlier round of the poverty debate) suggested that a writer who hit the right note at the right moment could have a big impact. By 1994, when a new edition of *Losing Ground* was published, America's entire welfare apparatus was being dismantled by Congress, with no author more frequently cited by the politicians than Murray.

The combative Murray further outraged academic conventions in the 1990s with *The Bell Curve* (1994), co-written with psychologist Richard Herrnstein. Moving beyond the culture-of-poverty idea, indeed beyond cultural categories altogether – the hallmark of nearly all American social science of recent decades – the two authors introduced what to many observers was an ominous appeal to biological evidence. They argued that American social scientists had for too long relied on cultural explanations of human difference. Accumulating evidence, they believed, pointed to differences between whites' and blacks' overall levels of intelligence, with blacks less well represented at the high end (Fraser, 1995; Fischer, 1997). Carl N. Degler's *In Search of Human Nature* (1991), a controversial work of intellectual history, also broke the "biological" taboo. It showed how social Darwinism, dominant in the social sciences at the end of the nineteenth century, had yielded to cultural explanations in anthropology, sociology, history, and psychology in the early twentieth century. Now, Degler argued, improvements in scientific methods and striking findings by such biologists as E. O. Wilson were reviving the plausibility of biological explanations of social phenomena. This book, too, occasioned a lot of grumbling, but Degler, one of the grand old men of American historiography, was clearly no ignorant "biology-is-destiny" type.

Liberal intellectuals felt that if anyone was losing ground in the 1980s it was themselves, as Reagan's brand of conservatism became mainstream. Liberals could hardly avoid admitting to themselves and each other that the aftermath of the Great Society had been a sobering disappointment. It had sustained a succession of withering attacks from the right and found no champions to match the caliber of its old heroes (Matusow, 1984). Liberalism lacked a single animating force because its advocates no longer agreed even about the central importance of economic growth or the meaning of social justice. Some liberal writers had been influenced by the 1970s "ethnic" movement and the new multicultural ideal, which contradicted the earlier commitment to a colorblind, individualistic society. Others had been influenced by environmentalism, a movement that shifted from the margins to the mainstream almost as rapidly as Reagan-style conservatism. Environmentalists, preoccupied with the hazards of pollution, overpopulation, species extinction, and an allegedly deteriorating quality of life, queried whether economic growth, long central to liberal thought, could any longer be thought of as a good thing, and whether social justice goals should be pursued at the risk of environmental sustainability. The mood of liberal impotence is ably embodied in the work of economist Lester Thurow, the inheritor of Galbraith's mantle as the preeminent liberal economist. His *The Zero-Sum Society* (1980), with its sober description of the economic paralysis of the late 1970s and the high political cost of effecting any changes, stands in dramatic contrast to the swashbuckling tone of neoconservative manifestos from the same years.

Among liberal intellectuals, ironically, declining political energy correlated with growing theoretical sophistication. As they appropriated the anthropological definition of culture and took the principle of cultural relativism more seriously than hitherto, they found it more difficult to be confident that policies aimed at social progress were justifiable. In the late 1970s the Carter administration's investigation of the problems of American families found itself unable to reach agreement about what a "family" was. At the same time a collection of essays on *New Directions in American Intellectual History* (1979), peppered with references to Mary Douglas, Clifford Geertz, Victor Turner, and cultural symbol-systems, shied away from the confident generalizations that had been the hallmark of liberal intellectual historiography earlier in the century. In his contribution, for example, Lawrence Veysey wrote that "generalizations, . . . to be credible, must be extremely hard-earned. They require far more arduous preparation, far more careful spadework, far closer attention to logic, than many of our predecessors a generation ago were aware" (Higham and Conkin, 1979, p. 23). Gordon Wood wrote in the same collection that intellectual historians needed to learn from the anthropologists how to contextualize their subjects. "If we are to write fully satisfying intellectual history we will need a kind of zoom lens that will enable us to move easily back and forth from the small, close-up world of unique events and individual volition where men try to use ideas for their own particular purposes to the larger aggregate and deterministic world of cultural conventions and collective mentalities where ideas control men" (Higham and Conkin, 1979, p. 37). The contributors, notably Wood and David Hollinger, were also more acutely aware than pre-1960 intellectual historians that there is a *culture* of intellectual life and that intellectuals have to be regarded not just as thinking individuals but also as a social group, and sometimes as representatives of particular social classes.

Two intellectual descendants of liberalism, as it unraveled, were multiculturalism and postmodernist theory. Drawing on the American tradition of pluralism and mutual tolerance and the anthropological ideal of cultural relativism, multicultural-ism emphasized that an individual's starting point, the "subject position," in a par-ticular time, place, and community will vitally affect how he or she understands the world, as will the starting point, community, gender, class position, and race of each reader. This perception could sometimes be invigorating, but it raised the hazard of solipsism.

Meanwhile, postmodernists intensified a long-developing attack on the idea that there was an historical *truth* to be discovered by patient research and impartial pres-entation of evidence. Literary theorists in the decades after 1970 pointed to the remoteness between an event and the language used to describe or explain it. Language itself could no longer be regarded simply as the medium through which historical truth was passed along from author to reader. Historians had long been aware of the significance of style and rhetoric in reinforcing the effectiveness of an histo-rian's argument – Carl Becker and Charles Beard had been debating the point back in the 1920s and 1930s – but many had continued to assume that history was a form of writing that, if done right, really could tell readers the truth about what happened in the past. Surely meticulous archival research and careful weighing of evidence in accordance with time-honored procedures and rules would make it possible to describe what the past was like, especially in an arena where numerous historians were constantly correcting each others' work in an atmosphere of constructive rivalry. Otherwise there was little difference between real history and mere historical fiction, in which "real" and imaginary characters were jumbled together indiscriminately. Such confidence became harder to sustain as the influence of Foucault and Roland Barthes began to be felt. Hayden White's books *Metahistory* (1973) and *Tropics of Discourse* (1978) were, for historians in America, particularly influential bearers of the bad news.

Although the effects of the "linguistic turn" were felt less heavily among histori-ans than among scholars of literature, the fact that there were effects at all caused alarm to those who held to the old positivist and objectivist ideal. John Diggins, for example, lamented the theoretical turn taken by the "Academic left" of the post-1970 generation (Diggins, 1992). Previously, he noted, the left and its intellectuals had been confident that their methods provided them with incontrovertible truths about society and a recipe for changing the world. Now, bogged down in literary theory and philosophical quibbles over language, left intellectuals had lost the ability to communicate with and inspire the working class, or anybody else. In dismay Diggins pointed out to his colleagues and erstwhile comrades that there could be no political substance to a movement that did not even claim to know the single truth about a single reality out there in the world. Similarly, in *Denying the Holocaust* (1993), Deborah Lipstadt addressed the dangers of devaluing the idea of a single definite historical truth at a time when certain writers were denying that the Holocaust had ever taken place.

It is impossible to read Diggins, Lipstadt, and others without sympathizing. But then, neither is it possible to read the theoretical objections to them without admitting their plausibility too (Hayden White was, after all, a forceful and convincing stylist who knew how to make the best of a good case!). A related complaint, voiced frequently in the 1980s and 1990s, was that the technical language in which these linguistic issues were debated was hard to follow without an advanced degree in the appropriate field. Russell Jacoby, another acerbic critic on the left, decried the unintelligibility of academic prose and the disappearance of "public intellectuals" comparable to Lewis Mumford, Edmund Wilson, and Walter Lippmann in an earlier generation. Not only were today's intellectual leaders unreadable, he concluded (offering the example of Fredric Jameson), they had also committed themselves to an academicism of the most sterile kind, further severing their connections to whatever sources of radical activism might be out there in the world. A systematic discussion of these language and overspecialization problems can be found in Peter Novick's superb and far-ranging book, *That Noble Dream: The Objectivity Question and the American Historical Profession* (1988). Novick shows in convincing detail how the traditional claim of writing "objective" history had already become incoherent by the time of the linguistic debates of the 1970s and 1980s, even as it was passionately defended by a new generation of "hyperobjectivists."

Russell Jacoby's *The Last Intellectuals* (1987) can be seen, in retrospect, as part of the "culture wars" debate of the late 1980s and 1990s. The debate began with the firing of a few conservative salvos, notably Allan Bloom's *The Closing of the American Mind* (1987), E. D. Hirsch's *Cultural Literacy* (1987), and Roger Kimball's *Tenured Radicals* (1990). These books deplored what their authors saw as the growing ignorance, illiteracy, and immorality of young Americans and the perversion of intellectual life by former countercultural militants who had risen to positions of power and influence on American campuses. Closely related to these attacks was a series of laments for the decline of traditional religion and religious values, including Richard Neuhaus's *The Naked Public Square* (1984) and former Education Secretary William Bennett's *De-Valuing America* (1994).

In 1992 the National Endowment for the Humanities invited UCLA professor Gary Nash and a group of California historians to write national guidelines for the study of history in schools. To the scholars' dismay, they found their draft proposal attacked by cultural conservatives as an example of all that was wrong with contemporary education. Nash defended his group while other academic historians tried to rebut other aspects of the attack (Levine, 1996; Lucas, 1996; G. Jay, 1997; Nash et al., 1997). Lawrence Levine, the ablest of these respondents and a Macarthur-winning superstar of American cultural history, was able to show in convincing detail that American higher education had always been an arena of debate and controversy

and that many of the so-called "traditional" curriculum items favored by conservatives had in fact been regarded as dangerous novelties at the surprisingly recent time
of their introduction.

A jargon phrase in the culture wars debate was "paradigm shift," used by writers
on both sides to give the impression of fundamental changes in the order of things.
It originated in Thomas Kuhn's *The Structure of Scientific Revolutions* (1962), one
of the most important books of the post-World War II era. Kuhn, an historian and
philosopher of science, studied crucial intellectual turning points from the past and
discovered they were marked by an entirely new conception of the universe. These
rare moments he referred to as "paradigm shifts" and they were successful, he argued,
when accumulations of evidence previously adduced in support of the old view were
shown to be even more effective when adapted to the new one. The Copernican revolution, the subject of another of his books, was a case in point; its paradigm shift
took scientists from the assumption of an earth-centered universe to the assumption
of one centered on the sun.

References to paradigm shifts are littered through recent historiography too. The
importance of Kuhn to historians can be illustrated by consideration of George
Marsden, the era's foremost intellectual historian of religion, who has knowingly used
the idea of paradigm shifts to good effect, first in *Fundamentalism and American
Culture* (1980), later in *The Soul of the American University* (1994). Marsden knows
how to make familiar things suddenly look strange. At a time when other historians
of religion were consigning fundamentalism to the dustbin of history on the grounds
that it was anti-intellectual, he showed, to the contrary, that it was a highly intellec-
tualized system, but loyal to a pre-Darwinian scientific paradigm. And while they
were marveling at the exceptional persistence of religion in America (unlike the other
Western industrialized nations), Marsden was lamenting its catastrophic decline on
university campuses.

Marsden felt a responsibility to reach out beyond a strictly academic audience to
intelligent laity in the evangelical world from which he came, as did his colleagues
Mark Noll, Grant Wacker, Joel Carpenter, and Nathan Hatch. A few other intellectual historians, fighting against hyperspecialization, also tried to reach a broader
reading public. The feminist movement, which by the 1980s was divided into a highly
theoretical academic branch and a hands-on activist side, found a high-caliber intellectual who could bridge the gap: Barbara Ehrenreich. The daughter of a Butte,
Montana, copper miner, she had earned a Ph.D. in biology but abandoned academic
life for work as a freelance writer. She drew admiring reviews from academics who
recognized her books as real contributions to intellectual history. She proved that
her feminist socialist ideas (she was also a leader of Democratic Socialists of America)
could, with the right presentation, enjoy a wide and admiring audience. In *The Hearts
of Men* (1983), *Re-Making Love* (1987), *Fear of Falling* (1989), and nine other
books, she showed a gift for critical summary of trends in "expert" literature on family
life, middle-class existence, psychology, the feminization of poverty, and sexuality.
Her scorching satire, her gift for debunking, and her shrewd advocacy writing
demonstrated a method of highly engaged and polemical intellectual history rarely
found inside the faculty club.

Her male counterpart was Christopher Lasch, a public intellectual whose
book *The Culture of Narcissism* (1978) became a classic statement of the sour

post-Vietnam, post-Watergate mood. Lasch had been a graduate student at Columbia under William Leuchtenburg and Richard Hofstadter, and Hofstadter's use of psychological and social-psychological models ("status anxiety," the "paranoid style") had influenced his own work on the therapeutic character of Progressive-era radicalism (Lasch, 1965). In his view, every society has its own characteristic pathology. Whereas in Freud's day obsessional neuroses had been common, America in the 1970s exhibited, instead, the diffuse anxiety characteristic of pathological narcissism. The typical "seventies" American, he claimed, was "facile at managing the impressions he gives to others, ravenous for admiration but contemptuous of those he manipulates into providing it; unappeasably hungry for emotional experiences with which to fill an inner void; terrified of aging and death" (1978, p. 82). The book, a surprise bestseller despite its psychoanalytical language and its bleak view of the world, found signs of narcissism in every American trend – even the introduction of the designated hitter in the American League! In the 1980s Lasch became ever more of a Cassandra, lamenting the decline of civic virtue, the family, and the republic. He turned to religion for consolation, becoming a regular contributor to the *New Oxford Review* (an intellectually stimulating journal run by a group of ex-Episcopalian converts to Catholicism). His last book, *The Revolt of the Elites and the Betrayal of Democracy* (1995), argued that selfish meritocratic elites were poisoning the republic. Far from working to promote social justice, they sought to isolate themselves from the masses and turned their backs on the all-important civic world. Lasch's books drew strong critical reactions but there was no question that he, like Ehrenreich, had found a way to engage serious social issues that could hold the attention of wide audiences within and beyond academia.

Other figures bridging the wide gulf between academia and the general educated middle class included Cornel West, the most distinguished in a recent generation of African American scholars, and Garry Wills. Wills claimed to be a conservative but had an outlook and offered policy proposals that had a "left-of-center-Democrat" flavor (Wills, 1979). Vastly learned, he never regained the wounding brilliance he had attained with *Nixon Agonistes* (1971), but his Pulitzer-prize-winning book on Jefferson, and penetrating studies of Madison, Washington, Lincoln, and Reagan, attested to his continuing sharpness.

American intellectual historians in the second half of the twentieth century participated regularly in the major scholarly journals, the *American Historical Review* and the *Journal of American History*, but did not create a journal of their own, apart from the annual *Intellectual History Newsletter*. Founded in 1979 in the wake of a 1977 conference on the condition of intellectual history, its editors feared that intellectual history was in danger of disappearing, partly in the face of the great vogue for social history, and partly as a consequence of intensive specialization among historians of science, law, anthropology, and other detailed subspecialties. The *Newsletter* has monitored developments in the field since then and still serves as a guide to the main directions and interests of intellectual historians. As the twentieth century ended, moreover, cultural and intellectual historians began to write summary narrative histories of the era, outlining its main characteristics and the central debates. Among them Richard Pells's *The Liberal Mind in a Conservative Age* (1985) and Stephen Whitfield's *The Culture of the Cold War* (1991) make ideal introductions to the postwar years, while Howard Brick's *The Age of Contradiction* (1998) and David

Hoeveler's *The Postmodernist Turn* (1996) do a comparable job for the 1960s and 1970s. Such surveys, along with *Reviews in American History* and the *Journal of the History of Ideas* (for issues in the philosophy of history), are probably the most useful media by which to make contact with, and keep track of, developments in intellectual history, whose overall wealth and fertility can only be hinted at in a brief introductory review.

REFERENCES

Adorno, Theodor et al.: *The Authoritarian Personality* (New York: Harper, 1950).

Allitt, Patrick: *Catholic Intellectuals and Conservative Politics in America: 1950–1985* (Ithaca, NY: Cornell University Press, 1993).

Arendt, Hannah: *The Origins of Totalitarianism* (1948; New York: Harcourt Brace, 1951).

Banfield, Edward: *The Unheavenly City: The Nature and Future of Our Urban Crisis* (Boston: Little, Brown, 1970).

Bell, Daniel, ed.: *The New American Right* (New York: Criterion, 1955).

Bell, Daniel: *The Cultural Contradictions of Capitalism* (New York: Basic Books, 1976).

Bender, Thomas: *New York Intellect* (New York: Alfred A. Knopf/Random House, 1987).

Bloom, Alexander: *Prodigal Sons: The New York Intellectuals and Their World* (New York: Oxford University Press, 1986).

Bloom, Allan: *The Closing of the American Mind* (New York: Simon and Schuster, 1987).

Boorstin, Daniel: *The Americans: The Democratic Experience* (New York: Random House, 1973).

Brick, Howard: *The Age of Contradiction: American Thought and Culture in the 1960s* (New York: Twayne, 1998).

Buckley, Jr., William F.: *God and Man at Yale: The Superstitions of Academic Freedom* (Chicago: Henry Regnery, 1951).

Buechler, Stephen: *Women's Movements in the United States: Woman Suffrage, Equal Rights and Beyond* (New Brunswick, NJ: Rutgers University Press, 1990).

Commager, Henry Steele: *The American Mind* (New Haven, Conn.: Yale University Press, 1950).

Curti, Merle: *The Growth of American Thought* (New York: Harper and Row, 1943).

Degler, Carl N.: *In Search of Human Nature: The Decline and Revival of Darwinism in American Social Thought* (New York: Oxford University Press, 1991).

Denning, Michael: *The Cultural Front: The Laboring of American Culture in the Twentieth Century* (New York: Verso, 1996).

Dickstein, Morris: *Gates of Eden: American Culture in the 1960s* (New York: Basic Books, 1977).

Diggins, John: *Up From Communism: Conservative Odysseys in American Intellectual History* (New York: Harper and Row, 1975).

Diggins, John: *The Rise and Fall of the American Left* (New York: W. W. Norton, 1992).

Dorrien, Gary: *The Neoconservative Mind* (Philadelphia: Temple University Press, 1993).

Echols, Alice: *Daring to Be Bad: Radical Feminism in America, 1968–1975* (Minneapolis: University of Minnesota Press, 1989).

Ehrenreich, Barbara: *The Hearts of Men: American Dreams and the Flight from Commitment* (Garden City, NY: Anchor Doubleday, 1983).

Ehrenreich, Barbara: *Fear of Falling: The Inner Life of the Middle Class* (New York: Pantheon, 1989).

Ehrenreich, Barbara, with Elizabeth Hess and Gloria Jacobs: *Re-Making Love: The Feminization of Sex* (Garden City, NY: Doubleday, 1987).

Evans, Sara: *Personal Politics: The Roots of Women's Liberation in the Civil Rights Movement and the New Left* (New York: Alfred A. Knopf/Random House, 1979).

Farber, David, ed.: *The Sixties: From Memory to History* (Chapel Hill: University of North Carolina Press, 1994).

Fischer, Claude: *Inequality by Design: Cracking the Bell-Curve Myth* (Princeton, NJ: Princeton University Press, 1997).

Fox, Richard W.: *Reinhold Niebuhr: A Biography* (San Francisco: Harper and Row, 1987).

Fraser, Steve: *The Bell-Curve Wars: Race, Intelligence, and the Future of America* (New York: Basic Books, 1995).

Friedman, Milton: *Capitalism and Freedom* (Chicago: University of Chicago Press, 1962).

Fromm, Erich: *Escape from Freedom* (New York: Rinehart, 1941).

Galbraith, John Kenneth: *The Affluent Society* (Boston: Houghton Mifflin, 1958).

Gerson, Mark: *The Neoconservative Vision: From the Cold War to the Culture Wars* (New York: Madison Books, 1997).

Gitlin, Todd: *The Sixties: Years of Hope, Days of Rage* (New York: Bantam, 1987).

Gorman, Paul: *Left Intellectuals and Popular Culture in 20th-Century America* (Chapel Hill: University of North Carolina Press, 1996).

Graebner, William: *The Age of Doubt: American Thought and Culture in the 1940s* (New York: Twayne, 1991).

Harrington, Michael: *The Other America: Poverty in the United States* (New York: Macmillan, 1962).

Hartz, Louis: *The Liberal Tradition in America* (New York: Harcourt Brace, 1955).

Herman, Ellen: *The Romance of American Psychology: Political Culture in the Age of Experts* (Berkeley: University of California Press, 1995).

Higham, John: *History: Professional Scholarship in America* (Baltimore: Johns Hopkins University Press, 1965).

Higham, John and Conkin, Paul, eds.: *New Directions in American Intellectual History* (Baltimore: Johns Hopkins University Press, 1979).

Hirsch, E. D.: *Cultural Literacy: What Every American Needs to Know* (Boston: Houghton Mifflin, 1987).

Hobbs, Stuart: *The End of the American Avant Garde* (New York: New York University Press, 1997).

Hoeveler, J. David: *Watch on the Right: Conservative Intellectuals in the Reagan Era* (Madison: University of Wisconsin Press, 1991).

Hoeveler, J. David: *The Postmodernist Turn: American Thought and Culture in the 1970s* (New York: Twayne, 1996).

Hofstadter, Richard: *The American Political Tradition and the Men Who Made It* (New York: Alfred A. Knopf, 1948).

Hofstadter, Richard: *The Age of Reform: From Bryan to FDR* (New York: Alfred A. Knopf, 1955).

Hofstadter, Richard: *Anti-Intellectualism in American Life* (New York: Alfred A. Knopf, 1963).

Hofstadter, Richard: *The Paranoid Style in American Politics and Other Essays* (New York: Alfred A. Knopf, 1965).

Hollinger, David: *Postethnic America: Beyond Multiculturalism* (New York: Basic Books, 1995).

Hollinger, David: *Science, Jews, and Secular Culture: Studies in Mid-Twentieth-Century American Intellectual History* (Princeton, NJ: Princeton University Press, 1996).

Hollinger, David and Capper, Charles: *The American Intellectual Tradition*, 4th ed. (New York: Oxford University Press, 2001).

Howe, Irving: "The New York Intellectuals: A Chronicle and a Critique," *Commentary* (October 1968).

Hughes, Robert: *The Shock of the New* (New York: Alfred A. Knopf, 1981).

Hughes, Robert: *The Culture of Complaint: The Fraying of America* (New York: Oxford University Press, 1993).

Isserman, Maurice: *If I Had a Hammer: The Death of the Old Left and the Birth of the New Left* (New York: Basic Books, 1987).

Isserman, Maurice: *The Other America: The Life of Michael Harrington* (New York: Public Affairs Press, 2000).

Jacoby, Russell: *The Last Intellectuals: American Culture in the Age of Academe* (New York: Basic Books, 1987).

Jacoby, Russell: *Dogmatic Wisdom: How the Culture Wars Divert Education and Distract America* (Garden City, NY: Doubleday, 1994).

Jay, Gregory: *American Literature and the Culture Wars* (Ithaca, NY: Cornell University Press, 1997).

Jay, Martin: *The Dialectical Imagination: A History of the Frankfurt School and the Institute of Social Research, 1923–1950* (Boston: Little, Brown, 1973).

Katz, Michael: *The Undeserving Poor: From the War on Poverty to the War on Welfare* (New York: Pantheon, 1989).

Kerber, Linda: *Toward an Intellectual History of Women* (Chapel Hill: University of North Carolina Press, 1997).

Kimball, Roger: *Tenured Radicals* (New York: Harper and Row, 1990).

Kirk, Russell: *The Conservative Mind* (Chicago: Henry Regnery, 1953).

Kloppenberg, James T.: *Uncertain Victory: Social Democracy and Progressivism in European and American Thought, 1870–1920* (New York: Oxford University Press, 1986).

Kloppenberg, James T. and Fox, Richard W.: *A Companion to American Thought* (New York: Cambridge University Press, 1995).

Kristol, Irving: *Two Cheers for Capitalism* (New York: Basic Books, 1978).

Kristol, Irving: "Memories of an Ex-Trotskyist," in *Reflections of a Neoconservative* (New York: Basic Books, 1983), 3–13.

Krupnick, Mark: *Lionel Trilling and the Fate of Cultural Criticism* (Evanston, Ill.: Northwestern University Press, 1986).

Kuhn, Thomas: *The Structure of Scientific Revolutions* (Chicago: University of Chicago Press, 1962).

Lasch, Christopher: *The New Radicalism in America, 1889–1963: The Intellectual as a Social Type* (New York: Alfred A. Knopf, 1965).

Lasch, Christopher: *The Culture of Narcissism: American Life in an Age of Diminishing Expectations* (New York: W. W. Norton, 1978).

Lasch, Christopher: *The Revolt of the Elites and the Betrayal of Democracy* (New York: W. W. Norton, 1995).

Levine, Lawrence: *The Opening of the American Mind: Canons, Culture, and History* (Boston: Beacon Press, 1996).

Lipstadt, Deborah: *Denying the Holocaust: The Growing Assault on Truth and Memory* (New York: Free Press, 1993).

Lucas, Christopher: *Crisis in the Academy: Rethinking Higher Education* (New York: St. Martin's, 1996).

Lunbeck, Elizabeth: *The Psychiatric Persuasion: Knowledge, Gender, and Power in Modern America* (Princeton, NJ: Princeton University Press, 1994).

Lynd, Staughton: *Intellectual Origins of American Radicalism* (New York: Pantheon, 1968).

McAllister, Ted: *The Revolt Against Modernity: Leo Strauss, Eric Voegelin and the Search for a Postliberal Order* (Lawrence: University Press of Kansas, 1996).

McClay, Wilfred: *The Masterless: Self and Society in Modern America* (Chapel Hill: University of North Carolina Press, 1994).

Marcuse, Herbert: *Eros and Civilization* (New York: Vintage, 1955).

Marcuse, Herbert: *One Dimensional Man* (Boston: Beacon, 1964).

Marsden, George: *Fundamentalism and American Culture* (New York: Oxford University Press, 1980).

Marsden, George: *The Soul of the American University: From Protestant Establishment to Established Nonbelief* (New York: Oxford University Press, 1994).

Matusow, Allen: *The Unraveling of America: A History of Liberalism in the 1960s* (New York: Harper and Row, 1984).

Miles, Michael: *The Odyssey of the American Right* (New York: Oxford University Press, 1980).

Miller, Perry: *The New England Mind: From Colony to Province* (Cambridge, Mass.: Harvard University Press, 1939, 1953).

Montgomery, David: *The Cold War and the University: Toward an Intellectual History of the Postwar Years* (New York: New Press, 1997).

Moynihan, Daniel P.: *Maximum Feasible Misunderstanding: Community Action in the War on Poverty* (New York: Free Press, 1969).

Murray, Charles: *Losing Ground: American Social Policy, 1950–1984* (New York: Basic Books, 1984).

Murray, Charles, with Richard Herrnstein: *The Bell Curve: Intelligence and Class Structure in American Life* (New York: Free Press, 1994).

Nash, Gary et al.: *History on Trial: Culture Wars and the Teaching of the Past* (New York: Alfred A. Knopf/Random House, 1997).

Nash, George: *The Conservative Intellectual Movement in America Since 1945* (New York: Basic Books, 1975).

Neuhaus, Richard: *The Naked Public Square* (Grand Rapids, Mich.: Eerdman's, 1984).

Niebuhr, Reinhold: *The Irony of American History* (New York: Scribner, 1952).

Novak, Michael: *The Spirit of Democratic Capitalism* (New York: Simon and Schuster, 1982).

Novick, Peter: *That Noble Dream: The Objectivity Question and the American Historical Profession* (New York: Cambridge University Press, 1988).

Nozick, Robert: *Anarchy, the State and Utopia* (New York: Basic Books, 1974).

Okroi, Loren: *Galbraith, Harrington, Heilbroner: Economics and Dissent in an Age of Optimism* (Princeton, NJ: Princeton University Press, 1998).

Patterson, James: *America's Struggle Against Poverty* (Cambridge, Mass.: Harvard University Press, 1981).

Pells, Richard: *The Liberal Mind in a Conservative Age: American Intellectuals in the 1940s and 1950s* (New York: Harper and Row, 1985).

Perry, Lewis: *Intellectual Life in America: A History* (New York: Franklin Watts, 1984).

Plotke, David: *Building a Democratic Political Order: Reshaping American Liberalism in the 1930s and 1940s* (New York: Cambridge University Press, 1996).

Podhoretz, Norman: *Making It* (New York: Random House, 1967).

Rainwater, L. L. and Yancey, William: *The Moynihan Report and the Politics of Controversy* (Cambridge, Mass.: MIT Press, 1967).

Rawls, John: *A Theory of Justice* (Cambridge, Mass.: Belknap Press of Harvard University Press, 1971).

Riesman, David, Glazer, Nathan, and Denney, Reuel: *The Lonely Crowd* (New Haven, Conn.: Yale University Press, 1950).

Riccio, Barry: *Walter Lippmann: Odyssey of a Liberal* (New Brunswick, NJ: Transaction, 1994).

Rodgers, Daniel: *Atlantic Crossings: Social Politics in a Progressive Age* (Cambridge, Mass.: Belknap Press of Harvard University Press, 1998).

Rosenberg, Rosalind: *Divided Lives: American Women in the Twentieth Century* (New York: Hill and Wang, 1992).

Schlesinger, Jr., Arthur: *The Vital Center: The Politics of Freedom* (Boston: Houghton Mifflin, 1949).

Schlesinger, Jr., Arthur: *The Age of Roosevelt*, 3 vols. (Boston: Houghton Mifflin, 1957–60).

Schrecker, Ellen: *No Ivory Tower: McCarthyism and the Universities* (New York: Oxford University Press, 1986).

Scott, Joan: *Gender and the Politics of History* (New York: Columbia University Press, 1988).

Shulman, Alix K.: *A Good Enough Daughter* (New York: Schocken, 1999).

Simpson, Christopher, ed.: *Universities and Empire: Money and Politics in the Social Sciences During the Cold War* (New York: New Press, 1998).

Stack, Carol B.: *All Our Kin: Strategies for Survival in a Black Community* (New York: Harper and Row, 1974).

Steel, Ronald: *Walter Lippmann and the American Century* (Boston: Little, Brown, 1980).

Steinberg, Stephen: *Turning Back: The Retreat from Racial Justice in American Thought and Policy* (Boston: Beacon Press, 1995).

Steinfels, Peter: *The Neoconservatives: The Men Who Are Changing America's Politics* (New York: Simon and Schuster, 1979).

Sumner, Gregory: *Dwight MacDonald and the Politics Circle* (Ithaca, NY: Cornell University Press, 1996).

Tanenhaus, Sam: *Whittaker Chambers* (New York: Random House, 1997).

Thompson, E. P.: *The Making of the English Working Class* (London: Gollancz, 1963).

Thurow, Lester: *The Zero-Sum Society* (New York: Basic Books, 1980).

Tong, Rose-Marie: *Feminist Thought: A More Comprehensive Introduction* (Boulder, Colo.: Westview Press, 1998).

United States Department of Labor, Office of Policy Planning and Research: *The Negro Family: The Case for National Action* (Washington, DC: US Government Printing Office, 1965).

Wald, Alan: *The New York Intellectuals: The Rise and Decline of the Anti-Stalinist Left from the 1930s to the 1980s* (Chapel Hill: University of North Carolina Press, 1987).

Waligorski, Conrad: *Liberal Economics and Democracy: Keynes, Galbraith, Thurow, and Reich* (Lawrence: University Press of Kansas, 1997).

Weaver, Richard: *Ideas Have Consequences* (Chicago: University of Chicago Press, 1948).

Weinstein, Allen: *Perjury: The Hiss–Chambers Case* (New York: Alfred A. Knopf, 1978).

West, Cornel: *Race Matters* (Boston: Beacon Press, 1993).

White, Hayden: *Metahistory: The Historical Imagination in 19th-Century Europe* (Baltimore: Johns Hopkins University Press, 1973).

White, Hayden: *Tropics of Discourse: Essays in Cultural Criticism* (Baltimore: Johns Hopkins University Press, 1978).

Whitfield, Stephen: *A Critical American: The Politics of Dwight Macdonald* (Hamden, Conn.: Archon Books, 1984).

Whitfield, Stephen: *The Culture of the Cold War* (Baltimore: Johns Hopkins University Press, 1991).

Wills, Garry: *Nixon Agonistes: The Crisis of the Self-Made Man* (Boston: Houghton Mifflin, 1971).

Wills, Garry: *Confessions of a Conservative* (Garden City, NY: Doubleday, 1979).

Wilson, William Julius: *The Declining Significance of Race: Blacks and Changing American Institutions* (Chicago: University of Chicago Press, 1978).

Wolfe, Tom: *The Painted Word* (New York: Farrar, Straus, and Giroux, 1985).

Wreszin, Michael: *A Rebel in Defense of Tradition: The Life and Politics of Dwight Macdonald* (New York: Basic Books, 1994).

PART II

People and Movements

CHAPTER NINE

American Political Culture Since 1945

RICHARD H. KING

Though the United States has enjoyed an unprecedented run of economic prosperity as it enters the new millennium, its political culture is full of contradictions, some fruitful and others merely frustrating. Conventional wisdom has it that America is the country of the future, yet American politics is in many respects more conservative than it was in 1945. On a crude calculation, the amount of economic and personal freedom is greater than ever before; but while equality has become a fact of political and legal life over the half-century since World War II, social and economic equality are ever more elusive. American culture in general seems to lurch between the postmodern and the premillennial, between globalism and localism. No wonder its political culture presents so many contradictions and has more shapes than Proteus.

It may be that, as Seymour Martin Lipset has argued recently, American political culture represents the wave of the future (Lipset, 2000). With the end of communism, the United States seems to be the model for the postmodern polity, one in which the emphasis falls upon: economic growth; identity and/or single-issue politics; the loss of master narratives or comprehensive ideologies to guide political thinking; and the end of the politics of revolution and emancipation in some deep transformational sense. Indeed, such a politics bears a family resemblance to that suggested by "end of ideology" thinkers of the late 1950s such as Daniel Bell and Lipset (Bell, 1960; Lipset, 1963; Lyotard, 1984; Feher and Heller, 1991). Though Lipset identifies this new politics as a form of American "exceptionalism," it is rather that America often stands at the cutting edge of historical change and plays a "vanguard," not an "exceptionalist," role in its political responses to the contemporary world.

Still, such sweeping generalizations make too many rough places smooth and overlook too many unintended consequences. There is no inexorable link between the "end of ideology" and the "end of history," except that champions of both positions were probably wrong in their general claims. No comprehensive narrative of political development can explain how all this has come to pass, including why there can be no comprehensive narrative of political development. When viewed through the lens of Fredric Jameson's Marxist account of "the cultural logic of late capitalism," or of the liberal exceptionalist position of Bell–Lipset, or of the Kojevean conservatism of Francis Fukuyama's "end of history" position, the whole development seems all too inevitable. Such was not at all the case (Jameson 1991; Fukuyama 1992).

One way to complicate the picture is to break the half-century plus since the end of World War II roughly at 1970, with the decade of the 1960s standing as the hinge of recent history. It was this long decade, running from the 1960 presidential election of John F. Kennedy by a whisker to the overwhelming reelection of Richard Nixon to the presidency in 1972, that saw American politics disrupted, turned upside down, and threatened with revolution (Jameson, 1988; Dionne, 1991; Isserman and Kazin, 2000). When the dust had settled on the 1960s, the most startling change in American political culture was the ascendancy of what Kevin Phillips called the "emerging Republican majority," underpinned by a reinvigorated conservative movement and ideology (Phillips, 1969; Nash, 1996). In the same decade, the American left failed to make its challenge to the political status quo stick, or to perpetuate itself in coherent organizational or ideological form (Gitlin, 1987). Despite the increased political visibility of African Americans, women, and ethnic and sexual minorities, the terms of political debate were increasingly shaped by conservatives, while constraints upon political and social change were dictated by an unstable, but at times real, Republican majority. In sum, the 1960s were not the confirmation but the end of the left-of-center political culture regnant since the early 1930s.

Any form of political analysis must confront the problem of how to reconcile historical change with the persistence of political ideologies and structures. This essay is no exception. In what follows, I want to track the fate of three very broad ideological positions – liberalism, conservatism, and radicalism – over the course of the half-century after 1945. To do this I will focus on a cluster of concerns – the role of the state, the nature of politics, and the idea of citizenship as they evolved within each of these positions over time. My focus will fall on American political culture since 1945 and will move back and forth among formal political thought, political institutions and traditions, and political behavior, while relating those phenomena to historical and cultural changes (Almond and Verba, 1963; Rodgers, 1987).

The Vital Center

If Franklin D. Roosevelt's New Deal continued to shape most of the domestic policies of mainstream liberalism between 1945 and the late 1960s, the ideological ethos of liberalism was less ebullient, its domestic vision more constrained, and its global outlook more contained (Brinkley, 1998). Characterized by the oxymoronic label "The Vital Center" of historian Arthur Schlesinger, Jr., American liberalism threaded its way warily between a new conservatism enlivened by the Cold War climate of suspicion and an increasingly beleaguered radicalism (Schlesinger, 1949; Nash, 1996; Denning, 1997; Cuordileone, 2000). Moreover, the master concept, and great fear, of the period was totalitarianism, "the great mobilizing core and unifying concept of the Cold War" (Gleason, 1995, p. 3; Arendt, 1958), a phenomenon that stood at the intersection of crass Cold War demagoguery and sophisticated political theory. And thus the politics of "the vital center," a.k.a. "consensus politics" or "liberal pluralism," was geared to countering the totalitarian impulse on all fronts, while trying to retain a core of concern with social and political change. First, "real" politics was "about" the pursuit of concrete social and economic interests, as opposed to the "symbolic" politics of identity and status, with its disruptive cultural issues and moral claims (Hofstadter, 1964). Politics was a complex game of bargaining among party and interest-group elites, with the "countervailing power" of government, business, and labor keeping each other in check (Galbraith, 1956; Schumpeter, 1962). In a political situation where there were no permanent friends or enemies, the premium was upon pragmatic flexibility rather than ideological consistency, the morality of the half-loaf rather than the dogmatism of the whole one. Second, the role of the citizen in the liberal conception of politics was limited primarily to periodic assent to the actions and agreements of elites (Dahl, 1961; Almond and Verba, 1963). Cold War liberals frowned upon mass participation in politics as a threat to political stability and civility. It was all too reminiscent of the totalitarian mobilization of the populations in Nazi Germany and the Soviet Union. Finally, liberal politics reflected what Daniel Bell famously referred to as the "end of ideology" in which a rough ideological consensus, not conflict, was the source and destination of healthy politics (Bell, 1960).

Underlying this new liberalism were a long-range and a short-range perspective on American political culture. First, a whole literature, what might be called "the School of Tocqueville," took the long view by stressing the way that American political culture had been, and still was, dominated by what Louis Hartz (1955) called the "liberal tradition" of individual liberties, the contractarian view of society and representative government. The implication of Hartz's position was that the post-World War II consensus informing American politics was always already there at the beginning of the republic. It was no mere product of Cold War conformity. Though Hartz was decidedly ambivalent about the hegemonic role of liberalism, others, such as historian Daniel Boorstin (1953), located – and celebrated – the "genius of American politics" as precisely the absence of ideological compulsions or utopian visions in American political culture. Ironically, Boorstin illustrated Hartz's more subtle point quite strikingly: it was not the absence of ideological politics but the pervasive hegemony of liberalism that most clearly marked American political culture, past and present. Where Swedish social scientist Gunnar Myrdal had identified the shared values of the "American Creed" as an instrument for resolving the nation's racial "dilemma" in the mid-1940s, liberalism by the mid-1950s seemed much more a bulwark of the status quo (Myrdal, 1944; Mills, 1956; Rogin, 1967; Hodgson, 1976; Novick, 1988).

Yet the new chastened liberalism was far from at ease with itself. Though seen by its conservative adversaries as a social and economic leveler, postwar liberalism significantly downplayed the importance of equality as an economic or social value. The Keynesian emphasis upon economic growth rather than redistribution assumed, as President Kennedy put it, that "the rising tide lifts all the boats" (Galbraith, 1956; Lekachman, 1966). But, as was later pointed out, in an advanced capitalist economy there was no way to equalize "positional" goods (Hirsch, 1978); and thus affluence, ironically, stimulated as much as it quieted status anxieties. For every celebration of American democracy – and economic affluence – there were anxious voices bemoaning the rampant conformity of postwar American society and culture. Books of popular social criticism served as secular jeremiads against "the lonely crowd," "the organization man," and "the status seekers." Why in the midst of affluence did juvenile delinquency flourish, and why did popular music fall to what seemed to be the antinomian impulses of rock and roll? In this postwar cultural mood of diminished confidence, liberalism had become more timid and less self-assured, a defender of an attenuated New Deal legacy at home and champion of the containment of communist expansion abroad. Schlesinger was ironically right on target when he referred to postwar liberalism as the vital "Center," not as a mature "Left."

Yet the 1960s saw developments that both redirected and diffused the thrust of liberalism, in theory and in practice. American liberalism had never exactly been a crusading force for racial equality. Franklin Roosevelt's New Deal shied away from the issue for fear of alienating its white southern support, while Adlai Stevenson, the Democrats' candidate in 1952 and 1956 and darling of sophisticated liberals, was a "moderate" on the issue. Yet liberalism became, willy-nilly, the (white) mainstream champion of black civil rights after World War II. Indeed, the race issue put some of the moral fervor back into an ideologically pragmatic liberalism in the wake of the 1954 *Brown v. Board of Education* decision of the Supreme Court. Shaped both by Myrdal's overly optimistic assessment of white America's commitment to racial fairness and by a new postwar confidence in the capacity of American society to assimilate diverse ethnic groups, the liberal assumption was that, if and when the Jim Crow system of segregation and disfranchisement could be gradually dismantled in the South, African Americans there, and in the rest of the country, could be incorporated into the American consensus without major social or institutional change (Woodward, 1955; Moynihan and Glazer, 1963; Gerstle, 1995).

By the mid-1960s, however, strains within the liberal consensus were beginning to become more apparent. Liberals themselves tended to divide on the political morality and/or wisdom of the civil rights movement's commitment to direct action. For some liberals, the revival of popular action was to be welcomed. For others, the idea that citizens could be political by marching as well as voting came as something of a shock. In reaction to an expanded notion of citizen participation in politics and to the introduction of clear moral issues into what was supposedly a politics of pragmatic accommodation, some liberals began moving to the center over the course of the 1960s, and then to the right thereafter. For them, the new politics, which bypassed existing political elites and established institutions, threatened the delicate workings of American political institutions. Indeed, many northern liberals missed the significance of Martin Luther King, the most important single political figure of the decade and perhaps of the half-century. But by the mid-1960s, even King adviser and one-time black radical Bayard Rustin was calling for the civil rights movement to leave off "protest" and reenter normal "politics." Only in that way could the momentum generated by successful challenges to disfranchisement and segregation be channeled into support for President Lyndon Johnson's "Great Society" and its attempt to revitalize the New Deal politics of economic and social improvement through a "war on poverty" (Rustin, 1971 [1965]; Carson, 1981; Garrow, 1986).

Overall, a crucial political and historical effect of the civil rights revolution was to marry the cause of African Americans with that of the Democratic Party, the party of liberalism. In terms of political alignments, the Republican Party lost – or handed over – the black vote to the Democrats from the 1960s on. The process of attrition that had begun in the 1930s became a rout by the end of that decade. But the Republican loss of the African American vote was more than balanced by the "southern strategy" adopted by presidential candidate, and then President, Nixon. According to the latter, Republicans increasingly picked up the support of the white South, both middle class and blue collar, and of those white Americans generally who were motivated by racial prejudice and/or fear of what was perceived as an alarming growth of "crime in the streets" and the decline of "law and order." Inside and outside the South, the hemorrhaging of crucial blue-collar and white ethnic support away from liberalism was proceeding apace. Most importantly, it meant that conservatism exited the 1960s with a new popular (and populist) base. Race was by no means the only cause of the reconfiguration of American party politics and the reshaping of its political culture. But it stood somewhere very near the center of those political-historical trends (Phillips, 1969; Bartley, 1995; Carter, 1995).

A second major development growing out of the civil rights movement and massive public demonstrations against the Vietnam War was the growing centrality of "rights talk" to the rhetorical and political agenda of one wing of liberalism. As legal theorist Ronald Dworkin announced in the title of his 1977 book, it was time that Americans began "taking rights seriously." Yet, as recently as the 1930s, liberalism had been very wary of the politics and jurisprudence of rights. Historically, American conservatives had been much more prone to appeal to rights, primarily in defense of private property and freedom from state regulation, while progressive forces, informed by the hard-headed jurisprudence of legal realism and with confidence in popular support, looked to the decisions of popularly elected bodies, for example the Congress, not to the court system to right social wrongs. But the civil rights revolution had revealed that the Congress would rarely initiate significant measures against racial discrimination; and thus the appeal to rights, not interests, in the court system became the first resort for racial change rather than the last resort against it.

The effects of the rights revolution – not only on blacks but on women, gays, and the disabled – were hugely significant, though not entirely positive. The "judicialization" of liberalism meant that the more court rulings to enforce the rights of African Americans or women or any minority group were handed down, the more liberalism lost the support of crucial sectors of the white population. Whether it was Alabama's George Wallace's railing against bureaucrats and "pointy-headed intellectuals" in the 1960s and early 1970s, or Richard Nixon's appeals to "middle America," or successive presidential candidates of both parties running "against" Washington, a sure-fire vote winner in the wake of the 1960s seemed to be an attack on the courts and the federal bureaucracies in Washington (Edsall and Edsall, 1991; Carter, 1995). Liberalism was identified with issues – busing, affirmative action, the failed Equal Rights Amendment, abortion rights – that inevitably offended this or that sector of its former (white and European ethnic) constituency and seemed to indicate that it was captive to the minorities and "special interests." By the 1980s, liberalism, helped along by conservative special pleading, was increasingly seen to be out of touch with "the people" and dominated by a "new class" of elite intellectuals, academics, and policymakers located in Washington (Kristol, 1983).

As the 1990s hove into view, blue-collar and working-class Americans, largely white and largely male – those who had illogically come to be called the "middle class" – were fed up with feeling overtaxed and underappreciated (Edsall and Edsall, 1991). The sense of focused anger that George Wallace had mobilized in the 1960s had now become a free-floating irritability permeating mainstream politics. For some socially oriented liberals, American social democrats as it were, a renewed emphasis upon social and economic issues over racial, ethnic, and cultural differences seemed to be the best way to recreate the New Deal coalition and to halt liberalism's precipitous decline. If, as sociologist William Julius Wilson maintained, class had replaced race as the prime obstacle to black progress, then perhaps a new coalition could be formed across racial and ethnic lines (Wilson, 1978; Gitlin, 1995; Sleeper, 1997). "Justice as fairness," to evoke political philosopher John Rawls's resonant phrase, still had a certain hold on the liberal imagination. The more viable, centrist alternative was for liberalism to adopt much of the conservative rhetoric celebrating market forces, encouraging economic innovation and trimming bloated government, while trying to keep this leaner federal government responsive to its core constituency. Above all, claimed journalist E. J. Dionne in the early 1990s, liberalism had to break the conservative stranglehold on the political-ideological agenda by shifting the political debate away from the 1960s arguments about race, culture, and communism (Dionne, 1991).

Still, for all the efforts to find a "Middle" or "Third Way," post-1960s liberalism was riven by a tension between a social liberalism, which itself was divided between its commitment to ethnic, racial, and sexual minorities and to a still potent industrial working-class population, and a rights-oriented liberalism that stressed the judicial and bureaucratic route to a more just society. There was no logical or conceptual incompatibility between social and rights liberalism. But, in actual fact, these two orientations stretched liberalism nearly to the breaking point. What kept this tension manageable was the general run of economic success of the two Clinton administrations in the 1990s. In power, liberals became centrists after the Clintons' failure to pass a comprehensive medical care bill. That, along with the president's support for conservative-initiated welfare reform, meant that liberalism in power had come to depend upon the continued growth of the economy to bail it out of trouble. And even that failed to guarantee a Democrat victory, as shown by the 2000 election.

Up From Traditionalism

If liberalism was placed on the defensive by the Cold War and McCarthyism, those phenomena were the making of post-World War II conservatism. And if liberalism spent the rest of the century trying to live down the failures – and sometimes the successes – of the 1960s, this was because post-1960s conservatism placed a dogged hostility to the 1960s at the core of its ideological vision. It is a startling fact that American conservatism flourished over the last three decades of the century, despite having backed the "wrong" side in the four major political crises of the three decades after World War II – McCarthyism, civil rights, Vietnam, and Watergate.

Not surprisingly, political and intellectual historians disagree as to the essence of American conservatism. Where some see a considerable overlap with the liberal tradition, others, particularly conservatives, suggest that it is best seen as a coalition of anti-communists, traditionalists, libertarians, and, after the 1960s, neoconservatives and a religious right based on certain shared values and on a common enemy, liberalism (Allitt, 1995; Nash, 1996; Brinkley, 1998). The contrasts with liberalism on the communism issue are instructive. Where anti-communist liberals considered the conflict with the Soviet Union to be a political one, conservatives saw it as a Manichean conflict, a metahistorical face-off between "the Free World" and what President Reagan later referred to as the totalitarian "evil empire" of the Soviet Union and its satellites. The contrast between the liberal rhetoric of "containment" and the conservative goal of "rolling back" communism spoke volumes about the differences in vision.

Still, postwar conservatives could differ widely from one another. Traditionalist conservatives, whether of Catholic, southern, or European provenance, saw modernity as a period of inexorable decline, a long twilight struggle, not just against communism and liberalism but against what these secular ideologies represented – rationalism and secularism, materialism and egalitarianism. At the other end of the conservative spectrum, libertarian conservatives stressed freedom over order and competition over traditional institutions. Where traditionalists bemoaned the materialism and license of modernity, libertarians deified the workings of the market and often sounded as though their *raison d'être* was to make the world safe for profit-making. Still, these disparate strands of conservatism were brought together by William F. Buckley, Jr., whose magazine, *National Review*, founded in the mid-1950s, became the respectable mouthpiece for the broad church of American conservatism. On the vital issues of the 1950s and 1960s – race and civil rights, decolonization, President Johnson's Great Society, opposition to the Vietnam War, the counterculture and the New Left – conservatism spoke a "No – in Thunder" (Buckley, 1959; Judis, 1988).

But what united practically all conservatives was (and remains) a firm opposition to the state. In this, conservatives drew liberally upon a persistent "anti-governmentalist" strain in American political culture. Thus, there was practically no tradition of strong-state, "one-nation" conservatism in America, in contrast with, say, Britain. Many conservatives, particularly those south of the Mason-Dixon line, deployed traditional states' rights doctrine to argue against federal civil rights measures in the 1960s. Libertarians considered the *dirigiste* state as a force that stifled rather than encouraged the most productive functioning of the economy and as responsible for restrictions on individual freedoms (Friedman, 1962). Though traditionalist conservatives might doubt the beneficent effect of market forces on settled practices and received institutions, they could unite with libertarians in opposing (federal) government intervention where race or economics were concerned. For conservative refugee intellectuals, anti-statism grew quite naturally out of their experience with totalitarianisms of the left and right in Europe (Hayek, 1944). Thus where New Deal and Great Society liberals saw the state as a valuable instrument of social policy, conservatives sought to bolster the strength of the core institutions of civil society and of the household. All roads led to serfdom in conservative attitudes toward the state.

Another area where conservatives differed significantly from liberalism and radicalism was in the rank ordering of equality, freedom, and order. Not surprisingly, order rather than liberty and certainly not equality was the first principle of conservatism. Conservative narratives of the origins of the American republic stressed the priority of the Constitution over the Declaration of Independence and often interpreted Jefferson's document as a defense of the rights of British subjects, not as a charter of inalienable (human) rights and the right to revolution (Kendall, 1988). Thus, the rights discourse of post-1960s liberalism fell on deaf conservative ears. In a broad sense, conservatives were for restrictions on individual freedom where it threatened the general authority of the state or seemed to undermine the institutions of marriage and the family, heterosexuality, and traditional roles for women. In no way were conservatives First Amendment champions or devotees of civil disobedience. While liberalism sought to strengthen individual liberty in matters of conscience and taste, conservatives sought to create a moral consensus about personal morality and artistic choice that would provide a firm foundation for a properly ordered society. In this sense, conservatives privileged order above freedom and equality.

Yet, in the economic sphere, most conservatives sought to maximize market freedoms, while restricting regulatory and redistributionist measures to achieve a greater economic and social equality as traditionally advocated by New Deal and Great Society liberalism (Brinkley, 1998). Indeed, the basic conservative assumption was that, aside from basic moral equality and equal civil and political rights, equality was neither possible nor desirable. If the market were allowed to operate in unfettered fashion, as Friedmanite theory and Reaganite practice asserted, then individuals, whatever their creed or color or gender, would assume the social and economic position appropriate to their talent and virtue. More so than with liberals, citizenship was for conservatives a call to patriotism, an obligation to support traditional morality and institutions, and the imperative to become politically involved when conservative positions were threatened. But neither conservatives nor liberals had a strong participatory notion of citizenship as a good in its own right.

The post-1960s social and cultural development that most benefited conservatives was a religious revival among evangelical, pentecostal, charismatic, and fundamentalist Protestants, while the traditional denominations stagnated. As a social phenomenon, it confounded sociologists of religion in several ways. First, it exploded the static, trinitarian division of Americans into simple categories of "Protestant–Catholic–Jew" suggested by Will Herberg in the 1950s. Second, it also fragmented the liberal political consensus, which was already coming unglued in the social and political turmoil of the 1960s, by challenging what Robert Bellah had called the American "civil religion," a rather bland, vaguely liberal, political religion which assumed that all Americans agreed on the spiritual underpinnings of their political institutions. Third, and most surprisingly, the revival discredited the assumption that the modernization of America would see the waning of religious belief and observance (Herberg, 1955; Bellah, 1970; Cuddihy, 1978; Putnam, 2000).

In retrospect, it was too easy to identify these new Christian groups with a hostility to modernity, due to their post-1960s emphasis upon traditional family values and their tendency to "moralize" all political issues (Lienisch, 1993), for they readily embraced the latest (post)modern technologies to spread their message. Most importantly, this new Great Awakening became, contrary to most precedents, political with a vengeance. From the early 1970s to the early 1980s, a new religious/Christian right emerged, drawing many of its members from traditional Democratic constituencies in the rural and small-town South and Southwest and moving them into the Republican column, particularly in presidential elections. Thus the popular base of American conservatism was radically expanded not only by "dissenters" from the civil rights revolution, but also by those who rejected the new hedonistic and "secular humanist" lifestyle identified with the 1960s counterculture and its heirs (Hunter, 1983; Lienisch, 1993).

Finally, the Reagan Revolution of the 1980s was aided by the addition of a new grouping to the ranks of conservative intellectuals – the so-called neoconservatives (Steinfels, 1980; Nash, 1996). The core neoconservative intellectuals were one-time liberals and Old Left radicals from the talented group of New York intellectuals who had set the agenda for high culture from 1945 to the mid-1960s. During the Cold War, several of them began a long odyssey across the political spectrum. In the wake of the 1960s, they rejected the cultural antinomianism and the "triumph of the therapeutic" marking that decade. Underpinning the conservative cultural critique was the assumption that the health of the nation's political values and institutions was bound up closely with its personal, expressive, and intellectual culture. A culture of hedonism and liberal "openness" mistook vacuity for tolerance, while moral relativism undermined the cultural traditions that provided foundations for political as well as cultural institutions (Rieff, 1966; Bell, 1976).

But the neoconservatives were also reacting against what they saw as the failure of liberal social policies and programs. Conventional liberal measures, they argued, increased rather than decreased personal dependency on the state, particularly among African Americans. Neoconservatives, and also some older liberals, opposed the emerging federally mandated policy of affirmative action and the shift from what they saw as the principle of "equality of opportunity" to one of "equality of result" (Bell, 1972). Though such figures as Daniel Bell and Daniel Patrick Moynihan tacked back toward liberalism by 1980, there is no doubt that American conservatism gained considerably in intellectual credibility from the defection of these one-time liberals to its side.

Ronald Reagan's great political achievement was to unite, for a time, the various strands of the postwar conservative tradition in one great conservative moment (Wills, 1987; Himmelstein, 1990; Kazin, 1992). Perhaps the first "postmodern" president insofar as he was a creation of the entertainment industry and a quintessential product of image politics, Reagan built his ideology on anti-communism abroad and anti-statism at home, except in the area of national defense, where there was a vast expansion in the 1980s driven by a kind of military Keynesianism. Otherwise, the economy was ostensibly run on "supply-side," free-market principles, a triumph for the libertarian wing of conservatism, while the traditional morality of the Christian right set the terms for behavior in the private sphere. But as Reagan's successors discovered, it was no easy task to keep the conservative coalition together. As with liberalism, turn-of-the-millennium conservatism was as much a set of tendencies in search of a unifying ideology as it was a coherent vision of the world, particularly in the wake of the collapse of the Soviet Union and its Eastern European empire.

Democracy Was in the Streets

If liberalism was placed on the defensive, political radicalism was fatally damaged by the Cold War and the anti-communist atmosphere after World War II. On the face of it, the left was in a very strong position at the conclusion of the war. Union membership was at its peak; the New Deal still had considerable strength; and the Cold War had not yet become a fact of life. By 1948, however, radicalism was in tatters. The loose but powerful "cultural front" identified by Michael Denning as made up of left-leaning New Dealers, the CIO unions, and the Communist Party, along with "progressive" writers and intellectuals, never recovered from the internecine strife within the CIO (Congress of Industrial Organizations) over the issue of communism; the onset of the second Red Scare in 1947; and the rout of the Progressive Party in 1948. As millions of white and black southerners streamed north after 1945, the composition of the northern working class itself changed drastically and its progressive political orientation was significantly diluted. Neither white nor black southerners had much in common with the left-wing culture of the prewar northern working class (Denning, 1997).

Yet the decimation of the Old Left cleared the way for what came to be called the New Left, energized by the emerging civil rights movement in the South after 1954 and in some cases taking its cue from the British New Left. If the nascent New Left agreed on anything, it was the need to find a new agency or carrier of radical change to replace the classical proletariat. As C. Wright Mills asserted in 1959, the left should jettison its "labor metaphysic" (Mills, 1963 [1960]). As the 1960s unfolded, this search for a new proletariat was to identify and then drop as possible candidates young people, intellectuals, African Americans, even a new middle class, and finally, the traditional proletariat again.

Indeed, this issue was symptomatic of the wide organizational, ideological, and experiential gap between the Old Left and the New Left. Yet the gap should not be taken as an abyss, since the intellectual and political progenitors of the New Left were veterans of the Trotskyist movement, the Communist Party, Garveyite Black Nationalism, the Progressive intellectual tradition, anarchist and peace movements, and European émigré radicalism identified with the Frankfurt School of Social Research (King, 1972; Jay, 1973; Breines, 1982; Isserman, 1987; Miller, 1987). Small political journals such as Dwight Macdonald's *Politics*, Irving Howe's *Dissent*, *Liberation*, *Studies on the Left*, and *Freedomways* constituted a bridge between the 1930s and the 1960s (Isserman, 1987).

As it shaped up in the early 1960s, the New Left ideology divided between a critique of American political, social, and economic reality and a positive vision of a new form of politics. While some still used Marxist terms such as "monopoly capitalism," it was more common to indict "advanced industrial society" or "the Power Elite," the "Organized System" or "the Technocracy" (Mills, 1956; Goodman, 1960; Marcuse, 1964; Roszak, 1969). Significantly, it was not so much economic exploitation as it was the system's political and cultural domination that attracted most New Left attention. This of course was another salient difference from the Old Left. New Left intellectuals also attacked the liberal elite, especially so-called "NATO" intellectuals such as Arthur Schlesinger, Jr., and Daniel Bell, who, it was claimed, existed to justify American anti-communism and defense of the status quo (Mills, 1963 [1960]; Marcuse, 1964; Chomsky, 1969). With the escalation of the Vietnam War by the Johnson administration, this critique of the American system came to seem increasingly persuasive.

Yet the New Left was not without a positive vision of politics, as expressed in two slogans – "participatory democracy" and "the personal is political" (SDS, 1966; Miller, 1987). Participatory democracy had a complex genealogy, but in the immediate context of the 1960s it originated in the radical student wing of the civil rights movement as it organized rural and small-town black communities (not industrial workers) throughout the South (Payne, 1995). Leaders of the Students for a Democratic Society (SDS) such as Tom Hayden had experience in the early civil rights movement; and SDS became committed to participatory democracy within its own organization, while encouraging it in the northern working-class communities and among the university students it sought to organize (Sale, 1973; Breines, 1982). Participatory democracy entailed a rejection of conventional party politics and representative institutions and an embrace of consensus rather than majority rule in its own organizations. Most importantly, neither leadership nor issues were to be imposed on a community by radical organizers; rather, people had the right to make the decisions that affected their lives.

In particular, three aspects of the ideology of participatory politics challenged mainstream liberalism. Energized by the civil rights movement and the anti-war movement, the New Left insisted that moral and ideological issues were an essential part of politics and not to be eschewed as somehow nonpolitical. Second, the New Left was often as hostile to the activist state as conservatives were, particularly the militantly libertarian Young Americans for Freedom in the 1960s (Berman, 1996). That said, the New Left was certainly no champion of free-market economics. A cooperative commonwealth or communitarian socialism was its model in the first half of the decade, while there was even a relapse into Marxism by the end of the decade.

Third, the New Left's emphasis upon participatory politics placed the issue of citizenship at the heart of (its) political vocabulary. Southern blacks spoke movingly of the empowering effects of voting and participation in politics as a citizen (King, 1992; Payne, 1995). At about this same time, young New Left historians aimed to write early American history "from the bottom up," to focus on the people and not political elites when writing political history (Lemisch, 1968). In addition, what was known as the "republican synthesis" emerged by the mid-1970s to challenge the Hartz thesis concerning the hegemonic role of liberalism in American political culture (Bailyn, 1967; Wood, 1969; Pocock, 1975). Hannah Arendt's *On Revolution* (1963) apotheosized certain forgotten aspects of the era of the American Revolution – namely, Jefferson's ward system and its attempt to institutionalize citizen participation in politics. For Arendt this was an alternative revolutionary tradition to the Old Left's Jacobin–Bolshevik one. Thus Arendt, the German Jewish refugee, gave to participatory politics a very powerful and important native pedigree (Arendt, 1963).

In retrospect, the republican historiography and Arendt's political theory of participatory freedom clearly prefigured the emergence of communitarianism in the 1980s as an alternative to rights-based, procedural liberalism. In *Habits of the Heart* (1985), the sociologist Robert Bellah and his colleagues reached for biblical and republican traditions as communitarian antidotes to the individualistic tendencies of mainstream American politics and culture. At the heart of the communitarian vision stood the active citizen, schooled in the political virtues of democratic discussion and action. Indeed, the term "community" had shifted meaning between the 1960s and the 1980s. Where 1960s radicalism conceived of community in terms of "intentionalist" utopian projects, by the 1980s it referred more to actually existing ethnic/racial, religious, or even gender communities. Community was not something to be consciously created *de novo* by casting off older commitments. Rather, it was to be rediscovered and nurtured in already existing sites and groups, though a considerable degree of choice of one's political and cultural identity was assumed (Lenz and Ling, 2000).

The other big political idea generated by the New Left was "the personal is the political." It was particularly important for the more radical, activist sector of a burgeoning second-wave feminism, referring as it did both to a personal style of political practice and to the need to develop a political analysis of the family and of intimate relations (Evans, 1979). That is, the personal or private sphere – the site of intimate relations between men and women, husbands and wives, and parents and children –

was political to the extent that its functioning was linked to the larger structures of power (Elshtain, 1981; Pateman, 1989). "Patriarchy," to use the term radical feminist Kate Millet put into circulation, was the glue that held together the macro- and micro-levels of political, social, economic, and cultural life (Millet, 1970). Carol Gilligan's *In a Different Voice* (1982) was a moderate-sounding book with radical implications for the development of "difference" feminism, since it rooted two distinct modes of ethical thinking in the quite different early childhood experiences of boys and girls. Indeed, the two styles – an ethic of care and responsibility versus an ethic of rights and autonomy – captured something essential about the difference between communitarianism and liberalism.

Still, for all the genuine theoretical advances made, what was striking about feminist politics in the post-1960s period was that the focus fell not on transforming economic and political institutions, but in addressing the way personal issues – access to birth control and abortion, for example – had to become part of a public political debate. The great political setback of the 1970s and early 1980s for the women's movement was the defeat of the Equal Rights Amendment (ERA). Indeed, according to some analysts of the issue, the failure of the ERA was linked to the failure of the women's movement to do the kind of grassroots organizing that the civil rights movement had done (Berry, 1986; Mansbridge, 1986).

A final political legacy of the 1960s derived from the intertwined successes and failures of the civil rights movement. With the passage of the two great pieces of civil rights legislation in 1964 and 1965, the face of southern society and polity was on its way to being transformed. (That the movement itself encompassed elements of all three positions on the political spectrum may provide one clue to its eventual triumph.) But the disillusionment with white society that followed in the wake of the movement helped generate another important new idea – that African Americans were a distinct community of history, tradition, and culture. The theme of black *difference*, along with the impossibility and undesirability of assimilation into American society, was the great message of Malcolm X, who, until just before his death in February 1965, worked to reawaken the nationalist tradition among black Americans (Malcom X, 1965; Cruse, 1967). Taken up in various ways by black political and cultural nationalists, along with groups such as the Black Panthers, the idea of organizing around cultural differences spread to other groups. Indeed, in almost every post-1960s social movement, including the women's movement, an emerging gay and lesbian subculture, and among America's rapidly growing Hispanic population, an initial stage in which the goal was integration and assimilation rapidly gave way to the cultivation of group cultural and political consciousness in opposition to mainstream culture and politics. Thus the origins of, and template for, "identity politics," the "new social movements," and eventually "multiculturalism" in the 1980s lay in the trajectory of 1960s racial politics as the civil rights movement gave way to Black Power and Black Consciousness, including an early version of Afrocentrism (Van Deburg, 1992). Indeed, an important semantic shift in the meaning of "pluralism" took place between the 1950s and the 1980s. While pluralism in liberal political discourse referred primarily to the economic and social differences the political system existed to mediate, by the 1980s, pluralism referred more often to the variety of cultural, that is, ethnic, racial, linguistic, and gender traditions among America's increasingly diverse population.

Two important issues in cultural politics were raised by multiculturalism as it surfaced in the 1980s. First, what was it exactly that the "politics of recognition" wanted (Taylor, 1992; Hollinger, 1995)? It was perfectly rational to debate affirmative action, bilingual education, Afrocentric educational curricula, gender or ethnic racially based schools if the needs and interests of new, post-1960s immigrant groups from Latin America as well as from Asia were to be accommodated. Yet the politics of recognition seemed also at times to entail explicit legal recognition and protection for cultural differences. Again, a semantic shift had occurred since the 1960s. Where rights in the liberal tradition referred to powers and protections adhering to individuals, the politics of multiculturalism tended to conceive of rights in group terms and as belonging to individuals by virtue of their membership in that group. Where the assumption of moral universalism was once considered a major achievement of early post-World War II political and legal developments, universalism and liberal humanism were by the 1980s regularly denounced as an ideological smokescreen for white, middle-class, Western male domination.

Opposition to multiculturalism was not hard to predict. Conservatives suddenly emerged as firm defenders of a colorblind Constitution and, along with traditional liberals, vigorously defended "equality of opportunity not results" (Thernstrom and Thernstrom, 1997). Indeed, a growing cadre of black conservatives joined their white counterparts in opposing affirmative action and racial preferences (Sowell, 1984; Loury, 1995). Not surprisingly, liberals were often bitterly divided over the politics of difference, affirmative action, and the political implications of multiculturalism. One effect of the debate was to push some liberals to a kind of cultural nationalist position. According to this position, there was a common American culture of shared values and commitments to basic institutions, and without that common culture the political health of the nation would be hard to maintain. More positively, a coherent political culture was worth preserving and strengthening, not straining to the breaking point. Thus, on the view of liberal nationalists such as Arthur Schlesinger, Jr., and Michael Lind, the destination of multiculturalism was likely to be a cultural – and political – balkanization, even apartheid (Schlesinger, 1992; Lind, 1995; Sleeper, 1997).

And yet, for all the heat – and light – generated by 1960s radicalism and its spin-offs over the ensuing decades, changes in the political culture and basic political institutions of the country were surprisingly circumscribed. The political-legal recognition of African Americans and women was a major, and long overdue, accomplishment. But no radical political party survived the 1960s; nor was there an independent movement of the left that regularly influenced national elections. More surprisingly, ecological-environmental forces, potentially the most significant political contribution of the countercultural wing of 1960s radicalism, never developed the political coherence or power of European Green parties. By the new millennium, political activity in this area lagged far behind, though demonstrations against the World Bank and the International Monetary Fund (IMF) in Seattle, Washington, and Washington, DC, in 2000 promised a more active future. And with communism and socialism discredited, what had always been a weakness in post-World War II radicalism – the inability to conceive of alternative forms of economic organization – was even more glaring than it had been in the 1960s. By privileging the political and cultural as the crucial areas for radical analysis and action, radicalism lost what base it had in the white working class and never regained it. The result was, and is, an impoverishment of American political culture.

Coda: Salem Without the Witches?

Taking the collective temperature of the United States is a longstanding tradition in the nation's intellectual history. The latest effort to examine the basic political and social institutions of the nation, including its political culture, is Robert Putnam's massively documented and often fascinating study, *Bowling Alone* (2000). Though he describes himself as a member of the "declensionist" tradition of American Studies (Putnam, 2000, p. 25), his work is nevertheless the gentlest of jeremiads. "State of the nation" studies, since Tocqueville, have tended to divide into two broad camps. One post-World War II tradition, which includes works such as Christopher Lasch's *The Culture of Narcissism* (1978) and Bellah et al.'s *Habits of the Heart* (1985), focuses on the dangers of excessive individualism, while the other tradition, exemplified in the work of Erik Erikson and David Riesman, warns of the tyranny of the majority. Putnam, whose central thesis is that since the 1960s almost every sphere of American social and political life has seen a decline in participation and in "social capital," clearly belongs in the anti-individualism, pro-community tradition. Declensionist though he may be, Putnam is also an optimist. The subtitle of his book is: "The Collapse and Revival of American Community"; the ideal of the revival being something like "Salem Without the Witches" (Putnam, 2000, p. 354).

Though Putnam's work reveals much about what ails the nation's political culture, particularly the low voter turnout in local, state, and national elections, his main concern is with the rise of civic disengagement since the 1950s. (This in itself is a far cry from the liberal pluralists who feared too much political participation in the early years after World War II.) Putnam's research led him to identify several factors that explain this decline. They include new patterns of work, which incorporate women into the workforce; the suburbanization of the society; and the baleful influence of television. But the chief cause of the decline, he contends, is generational. Something in the experience of those born after World War II, a population cohort encompassing the "baby boomers" and the "Generation Xers," led them to withdraw from social, religious, cultural, economic, and political organizations. To unpack the title: it is not that people no longer go bowling, suggests Putnam. It is that they no longer bowl as a team. Hence: "bowling alone."

Before concluding, a few comments by way of critique of Putnam are in order. Though Putnam is extremely thorough in exploring the implication of his data, there are certain conceptual weaknesses in *Bowling Alone*. Putnam clearly distinguishes between political and civic/social participation, but his chief emphasis falls upon the latter. Perhaps for that reason, he fails to conceptualize the relationship and/or differences between the two spheres. For instance, he accepts the Tocquevillean assumption that there is a positive correlation between civic and political participation. Yet one has to wonder why, if American civic participation is still as high or higher than that of most European countries, its political participation, as measured by voting, is significantly lower. Second, there are several respects in which Putnam's taxonomy of civic participation remains unsatisfactory. Theda Skocpol has, for instance, suggested an important distinction between organizations where people "do for" others and those where people "do with" their fellow participants (Skocpol, 1999, p. 8). A distinction between institutions that seek to maintain the status quo and those that seek to reform or transform it might also have been of use in refining his analysis.

But most importantly, Putnam seriously slights the importance of the power differentials among social and political institutions. There may be cultural trouble "out there" on Main Street; but, if John Judis and others are correct, the more serious problem lies in the concentration of economic and political power along the K Street corridor of Washington, DC. Put another way, it is not just the habits of the heart but the depths of corporate pockets and the decimation of American unions that have contributed to the decline of political participation (Vallely, 1996, p. 1; Judis, 2000; Robin, 2001, p. 3). Interestingly, such a critique of Putnam echoes C. Wright Mills's critique of American political culture in *The Power Elite* in 1956. Mills too noted the loss of what he called "publics" and thus a certain massification of political and social life. But his more important point, one which Putnam neglects, was that the crucial, life-and-death decisions affecting the nation were not made in the middle-range political institutions, including the US Congress, which citizen mobilization might influence. Thus, it is not clear what difference increased citizen participation would make in the operation or impact of large national and global economic-financial institutions. Whatever the case, it is an area of concern that Putnam largely avoids.

Finally, Putnam's book helps make the point that the 1960s were truly the hinge of postwar American political life. It also confirms that that decade was not the beginning of a "new politics" but the last gasp of the "old politics" created by what Putnam calls "the long civic generation" born between 1910 and the early 1940s. This historical irony is underscored by the fact that the most vital political movements surviving – and flourishing – after the 1960s have tended to be conservative rather than radical. As Putnam suggests, it is "among evangelical Christians, rather than among the ideological heirs of the sixties, that we find the strongest evidence of an upwelling of civic engagement against the ebb tide" (Putnam, 2000, p. 162). On the plus side, the most important single achievement of that decade – the dismantling of institutional racism and sexism – has been reenforced since then by rising tolerance of diversity. Putnam is nothing if not honest in admitting that an increase in social capital itself is not always an unalloyed good. The emergence in the 1950s and 1960s of White Citizens' Councils in the South testified to emerging white grassroots political activity, while the organization of violence-prone movements of the radical right in the 1990s also increased the fund of social capital in American society. But generally, Putnam claims, an increase in civic participation can be correlated with an increase in social tolerance.

Overall, Putnam seems to offer a deterministic decline narrative, one in which nothing any individual or group could have done would have reversed the trend toward privatism. But the micro-explanations for political withdrawal can range very widely and the reader of *Bowling Alone* might have hoped for more along these lines. If politics is seen as essentially concerned with the satisfaction of economic interests, as it is in the standard liberal and conservative models of politics, it is hardly surprising that politics can seem superfluous in times of general prosperity. Those who do vote vote for the party/ideology which promises to minimize state interference and maximize personal and economic liberty, though which of these two factors – economic wellbeing or state interference – trumps the other is not clear. Nor, in such a situation, is it surprising that symbolic politics – issues dealing with self-respect and recognition, the spiritual fate of the nation, cultural decline – and "log-jam" issues such as abortion, gun control, and affirmative action seem to dominate political discourse. Such issues are not ones that generally originate in regular party organizations; nor do they tend to be resolvable through "rational" compromise, since they derive from overarching worldviews, not concrete economic interests. If the election of 2000 shows anything, it is that it is stupid to think it is ever "just the economy, stupid."

Finally, Putnam's study, instructive and genuinely interesting as it is, fails to illuminate what it meant to be political in the 1960s or in the year 2000, from any position along the political spectrum. How much of the withdrawal from civic and political engagement has been linked to the deep disappointment with and alienation from "the System" experienced by the politically active in the 1960s? Or was it that the New Left was less an aberration from, than an accentuation of, certain American traits that diminished civic and political participation? The New Left's anti-institutional and anti-ideological bias seems, in retrospect, to be fundamentally at odds with its "project" of democratizing American life. Where the New Right, suggests Putnam, used church organizations or soon created new ones, a major bulwark of the left, the union movement, was crippled by the postwar Red Scare, and the changing nature of the economy militated against the continued growth of the traditional working class. The left never found anything or anyone to replace it. On the other hand, post-1960s racial, ethnic, and gender groupings have been too divided to create stable political coalitions or to develop a politics of the public interest. One lesson of the 1960s and since may be that the particularism of identity politics makes it very difficult to build coalitions, much less to develop a coherent ideology; and emphasizing "the personal" can undermine, as much as it contributes to, a vital politics.

As for the future, the long-term political effects of information technology and the Internet remain to be seen. The range of, and the speed with which, political ideas and images can be transmitted have increased tremendously. But whether this will fundamentally change the nature of politics, facilitating the emergence of an "electronic republic" or merely encouraging the "soundbite" politics already so prevalent, is anyone's guess. Yet, a global, public realm created by television and the Web emerges periodically, as in 1989 and coverage of the events in China, in Eastern Europe, and in the Soviet Union. But for every example of the revival of the politics of participation, there are just as many cautionary tales of massive invasions of the private sphere and attenuation of individual or group freedoms through surveillance to make anyone wary of predicting new forms and possibilities for democratic politics in America or around the globe.

REFERENCES

Allitt, P.: *Catholic Intellectuals and Conservative Politics in America, 1950–1985* (Ithaca, NY: Cornell University Press, 1995).

Almond, G. and Verba, S.: *The Civic Culture: Political Attitudes and Democracy in Five Nations* (Princeton, NJ: Princeton University Press, 1963).

Arendt, H.: *The Origins of Totalitarianism*, 2nd ed. (Cleveland and New York: Meridian Books, 1958).

Arendt, H.: *On Revolution* (New York: Viking Press, 1963).

Bailyn, B.: *The Ideological Origins of the American Revolution* (Cambridge, Mass.: Belknap Press of Harvard University Press, 1967).

Bartley, N.: *The New South, 1945–1980* (Baton Rouge: Louisiana State University Press, 1995).

Bell, D.: *The End of Ideology and Other Essays* (Glencoe, Ill.: Free Press, 1960).

Bell, D., ed.: *The Radical Right* (Garden City, NY: Anchor, 1964).

Bell, D.: "Meritocracy and Equality," *Public Interest*, 29 (Fall 1972): 29–68.

Bell, D.: "The Sensibility of the Sixties," in *The Cultural Contradictions of Capitalism* (New York: Basic Books, 1976), 120–45.

Bellah, R.: *Beyond Belief* (New York: Harper and Row, 1970).

Bellah, R. et al.: *Habits of the Heart: Individualism and Commitment in American Life* (Berkeley: University of California Press, 1985).

Berman, P.: *A Tale of Two Utopias: The Political Journey of the Generation of 1968* (New York: W. W. Norton, 1996).

Berry, M.: *Why ERA Failed: Politics, Women's Rights and the Amending Process of the Constitution* (Bloomington: Indiana University Press, 1986).

Blumenthal, S.: *The Rise of the Counter-Establishment: From Conservative Ideology to Political Power* (New York: Times Books, 1986).

Boorstin, D.: *The Genius of American Politics* (Chicago: University of Chicago Press, 1953).

Breines, W.: *Community and Organization in the New Left, 1962–1968: The Great Refusal* (New York: Praeger, 1982).

Brinkley, A.: *Liberalism and Its Discontents* (Cambridge, Mass.: Harvard University Press, 1998).

Buckley, Jr., W. F.: *Up From Liberalism* (New York: Hillman Books, 1959).

Carmichael, S. and Hamilton, C.: *Black Power* (New York: Vintage, 1967).

Carson, C.: *In Struggle: SNCC and the Black Awakening in the 1960s* (Cambridge, Mass.: Harvard University Press, 1981).

Carter, Dan T.: *The Politics of Rage: George Wallace, The Origins of the New Conservatism and the Transformation of American Politics* (New York: Simon and Schuster, 1995).

Chomsky, N.: *American Power and the New Mandarins* (New York: Pantheon, 1969).

Cruse, H.: *The Crisis of the Negro Intellectual* (New York: William Morrow, 1967).

Cuddihy, J. M.: *No Offense: Civil Religion and Protestant Taste* (New York: Seabury Press, 1978).

Cuordileone, K. A.: " 'Politics in an Age of Anxiety': Cold War Political Culture and the Crisis in American Masculinity, 1949–1960," *Journal of American History*, 87 (2000): 515–45.

Dahl, R.: *Who Governs? Democracy and Power in an American City* (New Haven, Conn.: Yale University Press, 1961).

Denning, M.: *The Cultural Front: The Laboring of American Culture in the Twentieth Century* (London: Verso, 1997).

Dionne, E. J.: *Why Americans Hate Politics* (New York: Touchstone Books, 1991).

Dworkin, R.: *Taking Rights Seriously* (Cambridge, Mass.: Harvard University Press, 1977).

Edsall, T. B. and Edsall, M. D.: *Chain Reaction: The Impact of Race, Rights and Taxes on American Politics* (New York: W. W. Norton, 1991).

Elshtain, J. B.: *Public Man, Private Woman: Women in Social and Political Thought* (Princeton, NJ: Princeton University Press, 1981).

Evans, S.: *Personal Politics* (New York: Random House, 1979).

Feher, F. and Heller, A.: *The Postmodern Political Condition* (Oxford: Polity Press, 1991).

Friedman, M.: *Capitalism and Freedom* (Chicago: University of Chicago Press, 1962).

Fukuyama, F.: *The End of History and the Last Man* (New York: Free Press, 1992).

Galbraith, J. K.: *American Capitalism* (Boston: Houghton Mifflin, 1956).

Garrow, D.: *Bearing the Cross* (New York: William Morrow, 1986).

Gerstle, G.: "Race and the Myth of Liberal Consensus," *Journal of American History*, 82 (1995): 579–86.

Gilligan, C.: *In a Different Voice* (Cambridge, Mass.: Harvard University Press, 1982).

Gitlin, T.: *The Sixties: Years of Hope, Days of Rage* (New York: Bantam Books, 1987).

Gitlin, T.: *The Twilight of Common Dreams: Why America is Wracked by Cultural Wars* (New York: Henry Holt, 1995).

Gleason, A.: *Totalitarianism: The Inner History of the Cold War* (New York: Oxford University Press, 1995).

Goodman, P.: *Growing Up Absurd* (New York: Vintage, 1960).

Hartz, L.: *The Liberal Tradition in America* (New York: Harcourt Brace and World, 1955).

Hayek, F.: *The Road to Serfdom* (Chicago: University of Chicago Press, 1944).

Herberg, W.: *Protestant–Catholic–Jew: An Essay in American Religious History* (Garden City, NY: Doubleday, 1955).

Himmelstein, J. L.: *To the Right: The Transformation of American Conservatism* (Berkeley: University of California Press, 1990).

Hirsch, F.: *The Social Limits to Growth* (Cambridge, Mass.: Harvard University Press, 1978).

Hodgson, G.: *American in Our Time. From World War II to Nixon: What Happened and Why* (Garden City, NY: Doubleday, 1976).

Hofstadter, R.: "The Pseudo-Conservative Revolt," in Daniel Bell (ed.), *The Radical Right* (Garden City, NY: Doubleday, 1964).

Hollinger, D.: *Postethnic America: Beyond Multiculturalism* (New York: Basic Books, 1995).

Hunter, J. D.: *Conservative Religion and the Quandary of Modernity* (New Brunswick, NJ: Rutgers University Press, 1983).

Isserman, M.: *If I Had a Hammer: The Death of the Old Left and the Birth of the New Left* (New York: Basic Books, 1987).

Isserman, M. and Kazin, M.: *America Divided: The Civil War of the 1960s* (New York: Oxford University Press, 2000).

Jameson, F.: "Periodizing the 1960s" (1984), in *The Ideologies of Theory ("The Syntax of History")*, vol. 2 (London: Routledge, 1988), 178–200.

Jameson, F.: *Postmodernism* (Durham, NC: Duke University Press, 1991).

Jay, M.: *The Dialectical Imagination* (Boston: Little, Brown, 1973).

Judis, J.: *William F. Buckley, Jr.: Patron Saint of Conservatives* (New York: Simon and Schuster, 1988).

Judis, J.: *The Paradox of American Democracy: Elites, Special Interests, and the Betrayal of Public Trusts* (New York: Pantheon, 2000).

Kazin, M.: "The Grass-Roots Right: New Histories of U.S. Conservatism in the Twentieth Century," *American Historical Review*, 97 (1992): 136–55.

Kazin, M.: "The Agony and Romance of the American Left," *American Historical Review* (1995): 1488–1512.

Kendall, W.: "Equality and the American Political Tradition," in W. Buckley and C. Kesler (eds.), *Keeping the Tablets* (New York: Harper and Row, 1988).

King, R. H.: *The Party of Eros* (Chapel Hill: University of North Carolina Press, 1972).

King, R. H.: *Civil Rights and the Idea of Freedom* (New York: Oxford University Press, 1992).

Kristol, I.: *Notes of a Neoconservative* (New York: Basic Books, 1983).

Lasch, C.: *The Culture of Narcissism: American Life in an Age of Diminishing Expectations* (New York: W. W. Norton, 1978).

Lekachman, R.: *The Age of Keynes* (New York: Random House, 1966).

Lemisch, J.: "The American Revolution Seen from the Bottom Up," in Barton Bernstein (ed.), *Towards a New Past: Dissenting Essays in American History* (New York: Pantheon, 1968), 3–45.

Lenz, G. and Ling, P., eds.: *Transatlantic Encounters: Multiculturalism, National Identity and the Uses of the Past* (Amsterdam: Free University Press, 2000).

Lienisch, M.: *Redeeming America: Piety and Politics in the New Christian Right* (Chapel Hill: University of North Carolina Press, 1993).

Lind, M.: *The Next American Revolution: The New Nationalism and the Fourth American Revolution* (New York: Free Press, 1995).

Lipset, S. M.: *Political Man: The Social Bases of Politics* (Garden City, NY: Doubleday Anchor, 1963).

Lipset, S. M.: "Still the Exceptional Nation?" *Wilson Quarterly* (Winter 2000): 1–21 (on-line).

Loury, G.: *One by One from the Inside Out: Essays and Reviews on Race and Responsibility in America* (New York: Free Press, 1995).

Lyotard, J.-F.: *The Postmodern Condition: A Report on Knowledge* (Minneapolis: University of Minnesota Press, 1984).

Malcolm X and Haley, A.: *The Autobiography of Malcolm X* (New York: Grove Press, 1965).

Mansbridge, J.: *Why We Lost the ERA* (Chicago: University of Chicago Press, 1986).

Marcuse, H.: *One-Dimensional Man* (Boston: Beacon Press, 1964).

Miller, J.: *"Democracy is in the Streets": From Port Huron to the Siege of Chicago* (New York: Simon and Schuster, 1987).

Millet, K.: *Sexual Politics* (New York: Doubleday, 1970).

Mills, C. W.: *The Power Elite* (New York: Oxford University Press, 1956).

Mills, C. W.: "The New Left" (1960), in *Power, Politics and People* (New York: Oxford University Press, 1963), 247–59.

Moynihan, D. and Glazer, N.: *Beyond the Melting Pot: The Negroes, Puerto Ricans, Jews, Italians, and Irish of New York City* (Cambridge, Mass.: MIT Press, 1963).

Myrdal, G.: *An American Dilemma: The Negro Problem and Modern Democracy* (New York: Harper, 1944).

Nash, G.: *The Conservative Intellectual Movement in America Since 1945* (Wilmington, Del.: Intercollegiate Studies Institute, 1996).

Novick, P.: *That Noble Dream: The Objectivity Question and the American Historical Profession* (Cambridge: Cambridge University Press, 1988).

Pateman, C.: *The Disorder of Women* (Oxford: Polity Press, 1989).

Payne, C.: *I've Got the Light of Freedom: The Organizing Tradition and the Mississippi Freedom Struggle* (Berkeley: University of California Press, 1995).

Phillips, K.: *The Emerging Republican Majority* (New Rochelle, NY: Arlington House, 1969).

Pocock, J. G. A.: *The Machiavellian Moment* (Princeton, NJ: Princeton University Press, 1975).

Putnam, R. D.: *Bowling Alone: The Collapse and Revival of American Community* (New York: Simon and Schuster, 2000).

Rieff, P.: *The Triumph of the Therapeutic* (New York: Harper and Row, 1966).

Robin, C.: "Missing the Point," *Dissent* (Spring 2001): 1–5 (on-line).

Rodgers, D.: *Contested Truths: Keywords in American Politics Since Independence* (New York: Basic Books, 1987).

Rogin, M. P.: *The Intellectuals and McCarthy: The Radical Spector* (Cambridge, Mass.: MIT Press, 1967).

Roszak, T.: *The Making of the Counter-Culture* (Garden City, NY: Doubleday Anchor, 1969).

Rustin, B.: "From Protest to Politics" (1965), in A. Meier et al. (eds.), *Black Protest Thought in the Twentieth Century* (Indianapolis and New York: Bobbs Merrill, 1971), 444–60.

Sale, K.: *SDS: Ten Years Toward a Revolution* (New York: Random House, 1973).

Schlesinger, Jr., A.: *The Vital Center* (Boston: Houghton Mifflin, 1949).

Schlesinger, Jr., A.: *The Disuniting of America* (New York: W. W. Norton, 1992).

Schumpeter, J.: *Capitalism, Socialism and Democracy* (New York: Harper Torchbooks, 1962).

Skocpol, T.: "Associations Without Members," *American Prospect*, 10 (July 1–August 1, 1999): 1–20 (on-line).

Sleeper, J.: *Liberal Racism* (New York: Viking Press, 1997).

Sowell, T.: *Civil Rights: Rhetoric or Reality* (New York: William Morrow, 1984).

Steinfels, P.: *The Neoconservatives: The Men Who Are Changing American Politics* (New York: Touchstone Books, 1980).

Students for a Democratic Society (SDS): *The Port Huron Statement* (Chicago: SDS, 1966).

Taylor, C.: *Multiculturalism and "The Politics of Recognition"* (Princeton, NJ: Princeton University Press, 1992).

Thernstrom, S. and Thernstrom, A.: *America in Black and White: One Nation Indivisible* (New York: Simon and Schuster, 1997).

Vallely, R.: "Unsolved Mysteries: The Tocqueville Files," *American Prospect*, 7 (March 1–April 1, 1996): 1–2 (on-line).

Van Deburg, W. L.: *New Day in Babylon: The Black Culture Movement and American Culture, 1965–1975* (Chicago: University of Chicago Press, 1992).

Whitfield, S.: *The Culture of the Cold War*, 2nd ed. (Baltimore: Johns Hopkins University Press, 1996).

Wills, G.: *Reagan's America: Innocents at Home* (New York: Doubleday, 1987).

Wills, G.: *A Necessary Evil: A History of American Distrust of Government* (New York: Simon and Schuster, 1999).

Wilson, W. J.: *The Declining Significance of Race: Blacks and Changing American Institutions* (Chicago: University of Chicago Press, 1978).

Wood, G.: *The Creation of the American Republic, 1776–1787* (Chapel Hill: University of North Carolina Press, 1969).

Woodward, C. V.: *The Strange Career of Jim Crow* (New York: Oxford University Press, 1955).

Young, I. M.: *Justice and the Politics of Difference* (Princeton, NJ: Princeton University Press, 1990).

CHAPTER TEN

Hyphen Nation: Ethnicity in American Intellectual and Political Life

MATTHEW FRYE JACOBSON

Few today would identify Nathan Glazer and Patrick Moynihan's *Beyond the Melting Pot* as an inaugurating text of the late twentieth-century "culture wars," but the book does embody the critical elements that would characterize American discussions of diversity – left *and* right – in ensuing decades. "This is a beginning book," the authors wrote portentously in 1963, and indeed it was. On the one hand, their fundamental premise presaged a number of key developments in the United States for the balance of the twentieth century – the centrality of ethnic and racial differences to our conception of the nation, the tenacity of ethnic identity among the children and grandchildren of earlier European immigrants, the evolution of what would later be known as "multiculturalism." "The notion that the intense and unprecedented mixture of ethnic and religious groups in American life was soon to blend into a homogenous end product has outlived its usefulness, and also its credibility," they declared. "The point about the melting pot . . . is that it did not happen" (Glazer and Moynihan, 1971 [1963], p. xcvii). Indeed, the homogenizing trope of the melting pot rapidly fell from grace in public discussion, though only a few years earlier sociologists like Will Herberg had confidently dismissed cultural pluralism as the irrelevant fantasy of "backward-looking romantics" (Herberg, 1960 [1955], p. 20).

But if Glazer and Moynihan's death knell for assimilationism augured the eventual rise of multiculturalism on the left, so did their tenacious Eurocentrism predict the tenor of the *anti*-multicultural right. In *Beyond the Melting Pot* Glazer began to formulate what he later called the "ethnic pattern" of American social development, a presumed group-by-group succession of "newcomers" to the scene for whom the voluntary European immigrant stood as the prototype. As in John F. Kennedy's rendition a few years earlier, Glazer's America was "a nation of immigrants," with all the celebrations and erasures that that image entailed. The historical weight of incorporation by conquest or by slavery was of relatively little account in this model, as any group could expect to proceed along roughly the same lines of acceptance, mobility, and success as had the great waves of European immigrants beginning in the 1840s. If the black experience in New York looked markedly different from the Italian, say, it was only because "the Negro immigrant" had not been there as long. This highly Eurocentric formulation of American pluralism was to leave a profound imprint on American conservatism.

American politicians have long recognized the importance of ethnicity in organizing the American polity, as have ethnicity's chief theorists, Glazer and Moynihan included. But current understandings of ethnicity as a highly flexible, situational mode of self-identification, rather than a "primordial" ancestral bond, suggest not merely that ethnicity *may* occasionally become politically significant (shaping voting blocs, coalitions, or interest groups), but that in a deep sense ethnicity *is* politics. It is not just that ethnic groups mobilize around this civic question or that; but political circumstances can conjure and consolidate wholly new "ethnic" groups (like present-day Latinos, once a congeries of Puerto Ricans, Mexicans, Dominicans, and Cubans), or can call older ones out of retirement (like the third- and fourth-generation European Americans who suddenly became Greek, Polish, or Irish in the civil rights era).

The very concept "ethnicity" and its scholarly uses are tightly aligned with the political movements of recent history. Anyone wanting to trace the analyses of "ethnicity" in the academic disciplines could do no better than to borrow the chronological framework of American political history: World War II (when ethnicity presented an appealing conceptual alternative to "race" during the nation's "war against racism"); the early Cold War (when, as an emptied and innocuous category, it bolstered the language of democracy and offered proof of American openness); and the civil rights and post-civil rights eras (when its uses responded to the acknowledgment that US political culture was organized around *group* experience after all). Contrariwise, the best roadmap for a summary of ethnicity and its influence in the nation's political life is the progression of benchmark works in the social sciences: Lloyd Warner and Leo Srole's *Social Systems of American Ethnic Groups* (1945) and Will Herberg's *Protestant–Catholic–Jew* (1955) endorsed the prevailing assimilationist paradigm of the melting pot; Glazer and Moynihan's *Beyond the Melting Pot* (1963) announced that perhaps assimilation was not taking place after all; Stephen Steinberg's *Ethnic Myth* (1981), Micaela di Leonardo's *Varieties of Ethnic Experience* (1984), and Mary Waters's *Ethnic Options* (1990) all challenged or fine-tuned what was by then a prevailing *pluralist* paradigm; and David Hollinger's call for a *Postethnic America* (1995) and Nathan Glazer's concession that *We Are All Multiculturalists Now* (1997) spoke to the utter triumph of group identity in American political life. Titles like David Reimers's *Still the Golden Door* (1985), meanwhile, indicated that the resurgence in immigration was further complicating the national mosaic.

This essay charts the strange career of "ethnicity" in both the scholarly and political realms in the latter twentieth century, establishing an intellectual history of "ethnicity" as a social scientific idea, with very close reference to those shifting political imperatives that have governed the discourses of diversity and "difference" since World War II. When Glazer and Moynihan noted that the notion of a melting pot did not "grasp what would happen in America," they were challenging habits of scholarly inquiry that had reigned for a generation (Glazer and Moynihan, 1971 [1963], p. 13). So were they noting something important about the behavior of their largely "Americanized" subjects. But when they set family values and familial arrangements at the center of their study – contrasting "strong" Italian families with "problem" black families and "confused" Puerto Rican families – they were advancing a formulation that would exert tremendous influence on the politics of civic reliability and belonging for decades to come (pp. 197, 89, 50). The social sciences *reflect* the major developments of our political life, to be sure; but so do they *participate* in our political life in powerful ways. By the phrase "hyphen nation" I mean to communicate the view from the early twenty-first century in both arenas: current academic thinking about US diversity, and the manner in which millions of Americans have laid claim to "Americanness" by the very virtue of their ethnic particularity.

Ethnicity, Assimilation, and Mid-Twentieth-Century Liberalism

Although by the late twentieth century "ethnicity" was almost always invoked as a means of emphasizing *particularity*, at the moment of its ascendance in social scientific thought the concept carried quite the opposite connotation. As against the biological, fixed traits connoted by the term "race," "ethnicity" stressed culture – an ideational outlook rather than a condition of birth, a cultural affiliation rather than a bloodline, a set of sensibilities and associational habits that would ultimately be subject to the forces of "assimilation," in sharp contrast to the stubborn inheritances of "race." The ascendance of "ethnicity" as an analytic category is best understood as one element in a broader tendency toward universalism in American social thought at mid-century, an effort to revise away the concept of heritable "difference" wherever possible, and to posit (or to celebrate) the vast assimilative capacities of American culture.

David Hollinger has summarized the movement in latter twentieth-century American thought as a steady shift "from species to ethnos" – from a paradigm of human unity to one of ethnic particularity (Hollinger, 1995). He invokes a range of mid-century titles to indicate the powerful impulse toward the universal: Wendell Willkie's *One World* (1943); Joseph Campbell's *Hero with a Thousand Faces* (1949); Alfred Kinsey's *Sexual Behavior in the Human Male* (1948) and *Sexual Behavior in the Human Female* (1953); and Edward Steichen's *The Family of Man* (1955). Jacob Bronowski's *Ascent of Man* (1973), a notable latecomer in this tradition, seems the last gasp of what by the 1970s was a dying universalist viewpoint.

For a brief moment in the 1930s and early 1940s, there had appeared an alternative to this universalizing tendency: a pluralist approach to American diversity articulated in works like Carey McWilliams's *Brothers Under the Skin* (1942) and Louis Adamic's *Nation of Nations* (1944). But their view was not to prevail: a near consensus on universalism between World War II and the 1960s – and an attendant emphasis on "culture," "ethnicity," and "assimilation" – was woven of many threads. The common embrace of "ethnicity" in the mid-century social sciences in part reflected a longer-term ascendance of the "culture concept," beginning earlier in the century with thinkers like Franz Boas and Robert Park. But this thinking began to take on a certain urgency in the 1930s, as events in Nazi Germany rendered the "race concept" increasingly unpalatable in liberal American thought. Figures like Boas, Ruth Benedict, and Ashley Montagu now sought to expunge "race" from social analysis wherever possible. Ashley Montagu labeled race "man's most dangerous myth," self-consciously promoting the term "ethnic group" precisely because "the conventional stereotype of 'race' is so erroneous, confusing, and productive of injustice and cruelties without number" (Montagu, 1946, pp. 262–4). As a corrective to "race," in this context, "ethnicity" accomplished far less as a species of distinction than it did as a partial erasure of "difference" – a universalizing appeal to the underlying "sameness" of humanity and to the assimilative powers of American culture.

Initially "ethnicity" applied only to European immigrants and their children; and, just as the concept's ascendance marks a homogenizing of *whiteness*, a lessening of the presumed difference separating an earlier era's "Hebrews," "Celts," and "Anglo-Saxons" (who indeed turned out to be "brothers under the skin"), so does it mark a deepening of the presumed difference separating these former white races from peoples of color. The concept was born precisely as the American colorline was sharpening in new ways – the "Negro Problem," as Stephen Steinberg writes, "had migrated from South to North" (Steinberg, 1981, p. 24). Nothing marks this development as well as the appearance of Gunnar Myrdal's *American Dilemma* (1944), which celebrated America's universalizing "creed" of openness, egalitarianism, and tolerance, even as it documented the massive violations of these ideals on the basis of race.

Nationalist imperatives during World War II and the Cold War, too, required unifying narratives of universalism. The nation's touted "war against racism" could not admit of deep divisions or particularities within the American populace; nor could the coming war against communism tolerate anything that undermined the notion of pure "Americanism." Ethnicity, then, was among the symbolic building blocks of American national unity; and ethnic particularism, diluted as it was, became an idiom of universalized American nationality. In popular culture the universalizing and nationalizing gestures of "ethnic diversity" are best captured in the multi-ethnic platoon of the Hollywood war movie. The Irish soldier, the Jew, the Pole, all working together and defending one another – *this* is America. One popular wartime song expressed impatience for the day "when those little yellow bellies / meet the Cohens and the Kelleys."

Lloyd Warner and Leo Srole's *Social Systems of American Ethnic Groups* (1945) was among the first studies to advance "ethnicity" as an alternative to what had earlier been America's white "races." Warner and Srole did not entirely escape the biological concept of "race": their delineation of "ethnic" groups conspicuously breaks down along the line of "light Caucasians" (like the Irish) and "dark Caucasians" (like Sicilians and "dark-skinned" Jews) (p. 294). The ease with which these groups assimilate in American life falls out predictably according to the differentiations of color. But even if the traces of race are still thick in this conception of "ethnicity," Warner and Srole's treatment does reflect the waning of the "white racial" paradigm and the waxing of culturally based "ethnicity"; and in its overall attention to the prospects of assimilation, the book shares a universalizing perspective with other works of the period. Any group whose differences were "minor" (meaning "ethnic") could expect to be fully assimilated into the nation's core culture; and indeed, the authors predicted that the future of white ethnic groups *as* self-conscious groups was limited.

In *Protestant–Catholic–Jew* (1955) Will Herberg advanced a "triple melting-pot" model, by which diverse Americans assimilated into not one but three distinct groups demarcated by religion. But Herberg, too, demonstrated an astonishing confidence in the disappearance of ethnic or nationality groups on the American scene. "America knows no national or cultural minorities except as temporary, transitional phenomena," he declared. Not only did "the ethnic group [have] no future," but ethnic pluralists were woefully "out of touch with the unfolding American reality" (Herberg 1960 [1955], pp. 38, 20). If this prevailing view at mid-century captured something significant for a generation whose ethnic differences were declining in salience (as

English-language proficiency increased, and as old ethnic neighborhoods dispersed), so did it neatly answer the imperatives of the moment: the moral imperative of revising the race concept in view of Nazism, and the political imperative among both hot and cold warriors of forging national unity by eliding those divisions born of heterogeneity.

Beyond the Melting Pot

Scarcely had the ink dried on Herberg's pronouncements when both scholarly and vernacular assessments of ethnic particularity underwent a sea change. By 1963 Glazer and Moynihan matched Herberg's confidence in assimilation with their own confidence in pluralism – the melting pot "did not happen." A year later, in *Assimilation in American Life*, Milton Gordon noted that although particularity in the realm of *culture* might be fading, "structural pluralism" – ethnicity's influence in shaping residential, occupational, economic, institutional, and organizational life – still prevailed. By 1971 Michael Novak could celebrate *The Rise of the Unmeltable Ethnics*, and by 1981 Thomas Sowell would remark, "The massive ethnic communities that make up the mosaic of American society cannot be adequately described as 'minorities.' There is no 'majority'" (p. 4).

The "ethnic revival," as it has been called, consisted in part of a "discovery" of ethnic roots on the part of earlier immigrants' descendants, including a nascent ethnic pride and a newfound passion for genealogy. But it consisted of a number of other, related developments as well: (1) a new attention to ethnic themes in television, Hollywood, and publishing; (2) a dawning consensus among academics that America was less a "melting pot" than a "mosaic"; (3) a series of institution-building movements across the country on behalf of Italian American, Irish, Jewish, or ethnic studies; (4) the emergence of immigration history as a subfield, and the consequent proliferation of distinct "ethnic" histories; (5) the advent of new "ethnic" merchandise and marketing practices, ranging from shamrock keychains to European "roots" tours arranged by American travel agents; (6) the engagement of the state in the construction and celebration of "ethnic heritage," in projects like the Statue of Liberty/Ellis Island restorations; and (7) a move into the rhetorical spaces created by these developments, on the part of working-class whites who had never exactly "lost" their ethnic identifications and lifeways, but who were quick to mobilize on the basis of this newly legitimated public language. Taken together, these developments constitute a wholly new syntax of nationality and belonging, one which put little stock in "assimilation" as it had been touted in the 1940s and 1950s, and which embraced ethnicity not as a universalizing idiom of commonality, but as a marker of significant and enduring *particularity*.

The "new ethnicity" sprang upon America from many sources. The first, most politically potent source of the ethnic revival was the civil rights movement, which inflected the meaning of ethnic particularism in two ways. First, it introduced a new idiom of group identity and group activism on the American scene – or rather, it legitimated group-based resistance to an older, longstanding reality of group *privilege*. Of course, the history of the republic is replete with instances where rights and privileges were either accorded or denied, not to individuals but to groups: white male propertyholders, blacks, Native Americans, Mexicans, Chinese immigrants, women, Japanese immigrants and their children. But American liberalism has long cherished the notion that "individual liberties" reside at the very core of the nation's political culture and values, and that appeals to *group* rights and protections are profoundly un-American. Never was this insistence more powerful than during the Cold War.

Only upon the civil rights successes of 1964 and 1965 did dominant civic discourse acknowledge the salience of group experience and standing. This acknowledgment's effect was electrifying, not only for people of color, whose racialized experience with society, law, and the market in the United States suggested a political kinship with African Americans, but also for the "unmeltable" white ethnics, whose inchoate social grievances needed only the right vocabulary to become mobilized. There exists "an inner conflict between one's felt personal power and one's ascribed public power," wrote Michael Novak, suggesting the limits of white privilege in a 1974 essay (Novak, 1995, p. 347). If European ethnics were indeed white, according to Novak, in the schemes of American power and economics they were not *that* white. As Irving Howe put it, "even in the mid-twentieth century many American Jews, certainly a good many of those who came out of the east European immigrant world, still *felt* like losers" (Howe, 1976, p. 632). The group-based mobilization of the civil rights movement began to suggest a model for action.

But the civil rights movement influenced white ethnic consciousness in another way, too: the sudden centrality of black grievance to national discussion prompted a rapid move among white ethnics to dissociate themselves from monolithic white privilege. The popular rediscovery of immigrant grandparents became one way of declaring, "We're merely newcomers. The nation's crimes are not our own." Reporting an exchange with a militant Native American speaker who was decrying "what our ancestors did to *his* ancestors," Michael Novak writes, "I tried gently to remind him that *my* grandparents . . . never *saw* an Indian. They came to this country after that. Nor were they responsible for enslaving the blacks (or anyone else)" (Novak, 1971, p. xx). This disavowal is itself open to critique, since it relegated racial injustices to dim national antiquity, glossing over any more recent discriminatory practices which these "newcomers" *did* benefit from, fresh off the boat though they were. Twinned with the emergent idioms of group mobilization, this move to distance one's group from the white monolith of American power could give way to a politics of white grievance that pitted itself against unfair *black* privilege. As Micaela di Leonardo argues, in some manifestations the ethnic revival represented a distinctly post-civil rights brand of mobilization, in which, ironically, "key expressions of white resentment were couched in a language . . . copied from blacks themselves" (di Leonardo, 1994, p. 175).

A second impetus to the ethnic revival was a powerful current of anti-modernism, and the common notion that ethnicity represented a haven of "authenticity," removed from the bloodless, homogenizing forces of mass culture and suburbanization. In the 1920s Horace Kallen had equated assimilation in the American setting with absorption into an undignified and vacuous modern mass. In his view, "ancestral endowments" ennobled the spirit and provided an oasis in the cultural desert of modern, mechanized, mass-produced, and mass-consumed lifeways. Beginning in the 1960s, latterday pluralists likewise sought refuge from the banalities of mass society in the philosophical premodern commune of ethnic particularism. Markers of this tacit connection between ethnicity, "authenticity," and anti-modernism include the Native American and peasant motifs of hippie fashion, the late-1960s vogue for Eastern mysticism, and the explicit appeals to mighty, blood-coursing tradition in productions like *Fiddler on the Roof.*

The nationalist pitch of many ethnic subcultures, too, added impetus to the ethnic revival, as contemporary events in the Old World pulled for an emotional involvement in the fate of those whom the migrating generation had left behind. Soviet anti-Semitism, the "Troubles" in Northern Ireland, the Israeli wars of 1967 and 1973, the "Prague Spring" of 1968, the workers' movement in Poland – such developments captured the attention and the sympathies of (now) overseas ethnic compatriots, whose diasporic cultures had invested homeland causes with considerable interest. Such engagements in Old World affairs may have been symbolic in that American ethnics had no intention of actually "returning"; but they were organic in that the narratives and mythologies of immigrant (and later "ethnic") cultures often posited immigrants and their descendants as "exiled" members of the homeland, uniquely placed to serve its cause. In the wake of the Six Day War, for instance, Jewish Americans from across the country volunteered for Israeli military service – over 2,000 in New York City alone.

And finally, the practices of US historiography were themselves reshaping the national narrative, reintroducing those "underdog elements" – like immigrants – who had vanished at mid-century. In an apocalyptic speech before the American Historical Association (AHA) in 1962, Carl Bridenbaugh had decried "the great mutation" of American historiography as a result of the shifting demographics of the university after the war, particularly as a result of the GI Bill. "Many of the young practitioners of our craft, and those who are still apprentices," he worried, "are products of lower middle-class or foreign origins, and their emotions frequently get in the way of historical reconstructions" (Nash et al., 1997, p. 54).

Bridenbaugh's observation presaged the shift in historiographic focus and theme over the next generation or two – the rise of the "new social history," black studies, immigration history, women's history, and ethnic studies. But the national narrative was already under significant revision. An early signal was Oscar Handlin's famous remark, "Once I thought to write a history of the immigrants in America. Then I discovered that the immigrants *were* American history" (Handlin, 1951, p. 3). By the time Bridenbaugh stood wringing his hands at the podium of the AHA, the emptied universalism of the early Cold War was already in decline. Along with *The Uprooted*, John Higham's *Strangers in the Land* (1955), Barbara Miller Solomon's *Ancestors and Immigrants* (1956), and Maldwyn Allen Jones's *American Immigration* (1960) had established beachheads for a new subfield; the founding of the Immigration History Society was but a stone's throw away (1965); and historians like Rudolph Vecoli, Alice Kessler-Harris, Stephen Thernstrom, and Victor Greene were just over the horizon.

Within a context of overdetermined ethnic consciousness – reinvigorated by civil rights discourse, the anti-modern impulse, the register of overseas events in the diasporic imagination, and the revised historical record – a stream of popular literary and cinematic texts emerged, charting the rise of the new pluralist sensibility. After languishing in neglect for some decades, novels like Abraham Cahan's *Rise of David Levinsky*, Anzia Yezierska's *Bread Givers*, and Ole Rolvaag's *Giants in the Earth* came back into print in popular paperback editions. Fresh literary renditions of the ethnic saga, too, found an eager audience: Mario Puzo's *Fortunate Pilgrim* (1964), Harry Mark Petrakis's *A Dream of Kings* (1966), Chaim Potok's *The Chosen* (1967). Audiences flocked to stage productions like *Zorba the Greek* (1968) and to films like *The Godfather* (1973) and *Hester Street* (1975). And in the realm of social commentary, these years produced Novak's *Rise of the Unmeltable Ethnics* (1971), Richard Gambino's *Blood of My Blood* (1974), and Andrew Greeley's *Ethnicity in the United States* (1974).

If *Beyond the Melting Pot* signaled the demise of assimilationist models, and works like *Blood of My Blood* charted a rising countertradition in the 1970s, then a number of key scholarly works in the 1980s indicated just how thoroughly that pluralist countertradition had triumphed in a relatively short time. In *The Ethnic Myth* (1981), Stephen Steinberg argued that "ethnicity" had too often served as an explanatory device where class would have been more suitable. In *The Varieties of Ethnic Experience* (1984), Micaela di Leonardo, too, argued for a structural and more variegated approach to "ethnic" experience – consideration of factors like gender, class, occupational segregation, and economic stratification – rather than the notions of cultural form and "tradition" that had become common in assessing group histories. Both authors pointed to conceptions such as the "strong Italian family" or the "Jewish passion for education" as developments whose *structural* contexts would fruitfully complicate the picture. And in *Beyond Ethnicity* (1986), Werner Sollors excavated the "ethnic" character of American literature across several centuries as a means of analyzing the tension between "consent" and "descent" in American political culture. Though quite diverse in their orientations, together such works spoke to the hegemony of the pluralist paradigm in the decades after the 1960s.

The ethnic revival was not merely some quirky family romance, then, nor do St. Patrick's Day parades or "Polish and Proud" bumperstickers fully convey its import. Rather, the ethnic revival recast American nationality, and it continues to color our judgment about who "we" Americans are and about who the many would-be Americans are who still knock at our gates.

Ethnic Revival and American Politics – Left and Right

"The 1960s was the decade of gaps," reflected Peter Schrag in 1970, "missile gaps, credibility gaps, generation gaps – when we became, in many respects, a nation of outsiders, . . . the mainstream, however mythic, lost its compelling energy and its magnetic attraction" (Rose, 1972, p. 184). This shift in collective identities did not disrupt the normative racial whiteness that had long held the key to "American" belonging and power relations. It did not cut into the notion of consanguine, "Caucasian" whiteness, in other words. But it did suggest and celebrate a distinctly new set of narratives about who these "Caucasians" were and where they had come from. It revised that normative whiteness from what one might call Plymouth Rock whiteness to *Ellis Island* whiteness. In the years that laid beyond the melting pot there arose a new national myth of origins whose central conceit was the "nation of immigrants." In parsing "ethnicity" both as theory and as politics in the 1960s and after, there is no overestimating the power that the European immigrant saga exerted in American discussion.

First, multiculturalism. In 1977 the *New York Times Book Review* announced the "best" books published in the previous year. Among them were Alex Haley's *Roots*, Maxine Hong Kingston's *Woman Warrior*, and Irving Howe's *World of Our Fathers*. The coincidence and enthusiastic reception of these three landmark publications mark the maturation of a long-term development in American intellectual life, the coalescence of the "ethnic revival" and entry into a new phase in the cultural politics of American diversity.

Multiculturalism is now wholly regarded as an intellectual engagement, for better or worse, among various educators, critics, and cultural producers representing peoples of color. Its prehistory is in Black Power and related movements of the late 1960s; its ascendance is marked by the emergence of black studies, the American Indian movement, Ebonics, Afrocentrism, and bilingual education; its pantheon of heroes (or anti-heroes, depending on one's view) includes figures like bell hooks, Vine Deloria, Frank Chin, Sandra Cisneros, Janice Mirikitani, Ishmael Reed, Leslie Marmon Silko, Ronald Takaki, and Rudolfo Anaya. No Richard Gambinos in this tradition; no Michael Novaks or Irving Howes; no *Blood of My Blood, Unmeltable Ethnics*, or *World of Our Fathers*.

But the concurrent appearance and celebration of *Roots, Woman Warrior*, and *World of Our Fathers* denote a pervasive national thrall, shared across the colorline. In its formative moments, "multiculturalism" was not the exclusive province of peoples of color. Irving Howe's *World of Our Fathers* may have spoken to insular, specifically *Jewish* concerns of peoplehood, collective destiny, and memory, to be sure. But in reckoning with the book's status as a bestseller, the meanings affixed to the book in the *non*-Jewish press may be more useful than contemporary scholarly debates among Jews. *Time* magazine set its review of *World of Our Fathers* beneath the telling banner, "Assimilation Blues," situating Howe's work within the proximate cultural context of *Fiddler on the Roof* and *Portnoy's Complaint*, texts that spoke only imperfectly to the forgotten or distorted – but hungered-for – past of those "many Americans whose non-English-speaking [forebears] were part of the huddled masses that funneled through Ellis Island at the turn of the century." *Business Week* mused upon ethnicity's new status as "a literary and political buzzword," noting that "135 colleges have established ethnic studies programs" before going on to call Howe's "the most impressive of the recent ethnic books." The *Christian Science Monitor* ventured that Howe had captured in his Jewish masses "the archetypes of the immigrant (one wants to say American) experience." This reviewer went on to remark that the greatest Jewish successes in this promised land were reserved not for the immigrants themselves, but "for their children and grandchildren, who moved into the professions and into the suburbs – diaspora." His equation of professionalization and suburbanization with "diaspora" – a dispersion from the "promised land" of immigrant immediacy – says a great deal about the hungers of the second and third generations. As Marcus Klein remarked in the *Nation*, "Everybody wants a ghetto to look back to."

For many white ethnics, initial encounters with books like *World of Our Fathers* may have prompted a moment of ethnocentric romance and introspection; but ultimately such encounters could as easily turn the gaze outward. It was but a small step from Irving Howe's ghetto to the many other ghettoes, barrios, and Chinatowns on the US scene; from the magnetism of Elizabeth Gurley Flynn to that of Ida B. Wells,

Carlos Bulosan, or Raymond Barrio; from the pluralist integrity of Hayim Zhitlovsky's "Yiddishism" to Du Bois's "sorrow songs"; from the recovery of one's own "roots" to the related recovery projects of ethnic studies broadly conceived: "forgotten" texts like John Okada's *No-No Boy*, and "forgotten" chapters in the nation's history – the Trail of Tears, Guadalupe-Hidalgo, the Black Codes, the Chinese Exclusion Act. In short, it was but a small step from *World of Our Fathers* to *Roots* and *Woman Warrior*.

To recall the energy for pluralism among white writers like Puzo, Petrakis, and Helen Barolini is to revise the received wisdom on contemporary multiculturalism. Multiculturalism did not unfurl neatly on one side of the colorline alone, from *The Autobiography of Malcolm X* to black studies, *The Color Purple*, bilingualism, and *The Joy Luck Club*. Though they later became objects of derision for some white critics, initially the racial pride movements and even the separatisms among people of color were not cordoned off from the "ethnic revival." Arthur Schlesinger, Jr., seems closer to the mark when he goes ahead and identifies Michael Novak as "an early and influential theorist of multiculturalism" (Schlesinger, 1998 [1991], p. 47).

But in the context of the United States in the 1960s and after, this usable immigrant past has had many uses indeed. If the invigorated, often epic narratives of European immigration established a renewed "we" for the so-called white ethnics (and one that shares deeply in the impulses now associated with multiculturalism), so did they establish an invigorated "we-and-they" which has informed the *anti*-multicultural agenda. Not only have many influential neoconservative thinkers – Irving Kristol, Nathan Glazer, Norman Podhoretz, Gertrude Himmelfarb, Milton Himmelfarb, Michael Novak – themselves hailed from the old immigrant ghetto, but so has the immigrant saga held a prominent place in neoconservative thought on questions of discrimination, poverty, and social policy.

In an "Afterword" for a 1965 reprint of Mike Gold's *Jews Without Money*, the progressive Michael Harrington distinguished between the "old" and the "new" poverty, quite frankly pointing out America's romance with the old – the experience of "an adventurous poor" seeking "streets paved with gold" (Gold, 1965 [1930], p. 232). Despite Harrington's recognition, in structural terms, that "the poverty of 1960 is not like the poverty before World War One," he noted one element in Gold's narrative that has become characteristic of national debate: "even in [Gold's] dark view of the slum there are those moments of collective action and self-help which ultimately made the old poverty so dynamic" (pp. 232–3).

The imaginative leap from "dynamic poverty" to inherently "dynamic people" has been fairly thorough in national discussion. On the right, the most elaborate treatment of US political culture and diversity through this lens of the European immigrant experience was Nathan Glazer's *Affirmative Discrimination* (1975), a treatise on the liberal state and ameliorative social policy. Here Glazer worked out both the comprehensive history and the policy implications of the "ethnic pattern" of group incorporation he had first articulated in *Beyond the Melting Pot*. His resistance to structural interpretations of racism and the "new" poverty was quite explicit: having enumerated many features of American history which indicated that heterogeneity could be a rocky road indeed (including "the enslavement of the Negro, anti-immigrant and anti-Catholic movements that have arisen again and again in American life, the near extermination of the American Indian, the maintenance of blacks in a subordinated and degraded position for a hundred years after the Civil War, the lynching of Chinese, the exclusion of Oriental immigrants, the restriction of immigration from Southern and Eastern Europe, the relocation of the Japanese and the near confiscation of the property, the resistance to school desegregation, *and so forth*"), Glazer conceded that, were one seeking the single defining characteristic of American society, hierarchy and exclusion might appear a "central tendency." *But*, he concluded in a mighty reversal, "I think this is a selective misreading of American history" (Glazer, 1987 [1975], pp. 6–7, emphasis added).

The alternative reading which Glazer proposed, the "ethnic pattern," derived from three interlacing principles that have informed American political culture over time: (1) that the nation was open to all comers; (2) that any and all groups had to join the political life of the nation rather than nourishing separatisms and establishing new nations of their own; but (3) that in the realms of *culture* and *association* ethnic groups could maintain themselves voluntarily (pp. 3–32). The result has been a thriving and open culture in which "the ethnic group is one of the building blocks of . . . society," and in which "one is required neither to put on ethnicity nor to take it off" (pp. 28, 29). The history of race in this paradigm presents a fairly constant irritant, but it has been neither decisive to American history nor fatally disruptive of the "ethnic pattern."

In Glazer's scheme, then, European immigrants stand as the very exemplars of this "central tendency in American history" – its openness, its premium on diversity, and its *laissez-faire* attitude toward group cohesion and personal identity choices. "We had seen many groups become part of the United States through immigration," he wrote in an introduction to the 1987 edition, "and we had seen each in turn overcoming some degree of discrimination to become integrated into American society. What this process did not seem to need was the active involvement of government, determining the proper degree of participation of each group in employment and education. It had not happened that way in the past, and one should not expect that it would be necessary for it to happen that way in the future" (p. xii).

Neoconservative writings of the 1970s and 1980s exemplify sociologist Richard Alba's observation that a romanticized European ancestral experience now determined "'the rules of the game' by which other groups will be expected to succeed in American society." Alba finds "significant political import" in this tendency to define the European immigrant saga as "a prototypical American experience, against which non-European minority groups, some of long-standing on the American continent and others of recent vintage, are pressured to measure themselves" (Alba, 1990, p. 316). Where the mythic European immigrant experience – complete with its epic struggles and its mythology of self-help – provides the template, newer arrivals and the ghetto's newer residents stake but a weak claim on public sympathies. In this respect the white ethnic revival may have been a protest against assimilationism – even a denial that assimilation had indeed taken place – but so was it a pan-European ethnic celebration of white *assimilability*.

The celebrated "us" and the implied "them" in this era suggest that the politically opposed currents of "multiculturalism" and neoconservatism paradoxically share an intellectual ancestry. The significance of the ethnic revival resides precisely in the *contradictory* political logics of diversity which have borrowed the motifs and symbols of European immigration. The tributaries flowing out of this swelling ethnic consciousness are many: one led to the establishment of ethnic studies or Italian American studies programs across the country; another, to the thin charms of *Crossing Delancey* or the keening for a bygone world in Barry Levinson's *Avalon*; yet another, to green beer and the *faux* "authenticity" of *Riverdance*. But many have been swept by these currents to the politics and the curricular concerns of multiculturalism, and still others to the social conservatism of the so-called Reagan Democrats.

Post-1965 Immigration and the Newest American Nativism

Adding to the passions surrounding American diversity, too, was the massive influx of new immigrants in response to the 1965 Immigration Act. The newest immigration, the largest since early in the century, itself represented a population of staggering diversity. By the 1990 census not only had overall immigration swelled beyond its pre-1965 levels (the foreign-born population in the 1990 census reached some 19.7 million, up from 9.7 million in 1960), but the sources of immigration had also shifted: by the early 1990s Europe was contributing fewer than 15 percent overall – roughly 85 percent of the nearly 1 million immigrants arriving in 1992, for instance, hailed from some thirty Asian countries, seventeen Central and South American countries, thirteen Caribbean countries, and thirteen African countries. Mexico became the single largest sending country, accounting for more immigrants per year than the whole of Europe; and by the year 2000 US Latinos represented the fifth largest "nation" in Latin America. Of the top ten sending countries, only two – the old Soviet Union and Poland – were European. This aroused notice in a context where the word "immigrant" had long *meant* "European."

Clearly JFK did not single-handedly invent and propagate the conceit of the *Nation of Immigrants*, though his 1958 volume by that title helped to popularize the phrase. But both Kennedy and Johnson did rely heavily upon it in selling their liberalized immigration policy, and they reaped some unintended consequences in the bargain. On the one hand, the legislation that finally passed in 1965 resulted in a dramatic increase in immigration rates, and the new immigrants' perceived "difference" from the historic European waves was startling to many. On the other hand, however, the ensuing, decades-long debate on immigration and diversity was all but dominated by the myths about, and romance with, European immigrants that held sway in post-ethnic revival America.

Of central concern has been the immigrants' predilection and capacity for assimilation, qualities in which Europeans are presumed to have cornered the market. Debate over the 1965 immigration bill itself was largely a disagreement between "harsh" Eurocentrists (who opposed the reform) and "mild" Eurocentrists (who – in a logic inherited from Kennedy – supported it). Speaking for the harsh Eurocentrists, Sam Ervin argued that "there is a rational basis and a reasonable basis to give preference to Holland over Afghanistan, and I hope I am not entertaining a highly iniquitous thought when I entertain that honest opinion." The worst charge of discrimination that could be leveled at the existing law, he remarked, "is that it discriminates in favor of the people who made the greatest contribution to America." In defense of the bill, on the other hand, Edward Kennedy averred that "the ethnic pattern of immigration under the proposed measure is not expected to change as sharply as the critics seem to think."

The presumed "assimilability" of the prototypical European – whether figured in racial terms or in cultural-geographical terms – is indispensable to the common understanding of the new, non-European immigrants and their prospects. One common argument poses US nationality as a "family" of consanguine Europeans: "The word 'nation,'" writes Peter Brimelow without apology, "is derived from the Latin *nescare* [*sic*], to be born. It intrinsically implies a link by blood. A nation in a real sense is an extended family" (Brimelow, 1995, p. 203). Closely akin to this trope of familial US nationality is the cultural-geographical construction of a grand "European tradition" that unites white ethnic groups just as surely as it excludes those from Asia, Africa, and the Americas. As one writer commented in the *Conservative Review*, "there is no evidence that the European tradition can or will be transmitted to immigrants of African, Asian and Hispanic origin, or to any other of the Third World immigrants who are now entering the country at an increasing rate." Likewise in *The Path to National Suicide* Lawrence Auster relied upon this common "tradition" as a means of consecrating the earlier waves of US immigration even while deploring the present one: turn-of-the-century immigrants "still had much in common with the earlier Americans; the fact that they were of European descent and came from related cultures within Western civilization made it relatively easy for them to assimilate into the common sphere of civic habits and cultural identity" (Auster, 1990, p. 45).

But this "European tradition" is a recent and uncertain invention, and such assessments of Italian or Slavic immigrants' "related cultures" have far less to do with the actual relationship of these cultures at the time than with a perceived "kinship" only after a century's hindsight and a few generations of distance from the Old World. Indeed, at the time American commentators most often sounded remarkably like Lawrence Auster in their assessments of these incoming "Europeans." According to the New York school superintendent, for instance, "The majority of people who now come to us have little akin to our language; they have little akin to our mode of thought; they have little akin to our customs; they have little akin to our traditions." Senator Henry Cabot Lodge, for his part, judged them "races most alien to the body of the American people"; they "do not promise well for the standard of civilization of the United States." Francis Amasa Walker, the Superintendent of the Census, regarded them as "beaten men from beaten races," who "have none of the ideas and aptitudes which fit men to take up readily and easily the problem of self-care and self-government."

If the first maneuver in recent nativist thinking has consisted of *forgetting* the contemporary reception of European immigrants, the next has consisted of establishing positive myths regarding their traits and their virtues. As Nancy Foner writes, "An elaborate mythology has grown around immigration at the turn of the century, and perceptions of that earlier migration deeply color how the newest wave is seen" (Foner, 2000, p. 2). It is here that the loving, epic-heroic imagery of ethnic-revival cultural production comes into full play – *Fiddler on the Roof*, the History Channel's *Ellis Island*, and even the below-deck scenes from James Cameron's *Titanic*. It is here that the "dynamic poverty" of an earlier era, in Harrington's formulation, gives way to common conceptions of the "dynamic people" who inhabited the turn-of-the-century ghetto.

It is this pan-European revision of white ethnicity that allowed an *immigrant*, Forbes editor Peter Brimelow, to pen the most vociferous "nativist" tract of the

1990s, *Alien Nation*. Nor was it necessarily a contradiction that President Carter began militarizing the US–Mexican border at the very moment that Americans made a bestseller of *World of Our Fathers* and established a national park at Ellis Island. In the years since the great European migration, Walker's "beaten men from beaten races" have been transformed: in memory they have become clean and moral and hugely striving; they have become joint-stockholders in a unified "European tradition" – they have become, in a word, "America."

Conclusion: Race and Ethnicity in the Age of Multiculturalism

Throughout the years since the 1940s, "race" has been the larger body around which the concept of "ethnicity" has quietly revolved, as a moon around a planet. Each turn in the one has caused an adjustment in the other. In the early war years, the culturally based concept of ethnicity may have seemed an alternative to the biologically based "race concept," as Montagu and others suggested. But race and its inheritances have been stubborn indeed: the mid-century's revision of race stopped at the colorline, eradicating "racial" Hebrews and Celts, perhaps, but reifying "racial" blacks. With the advent of the modern civil rights movement, both left and right acknowledged the colorline as a fundamental fact of US social and political life, either to be eradicated or upheld; and among scholars and activists the mid-century paradigm of *prejudice* gradually gave way to root-and-branch interpretations of *racism*, not merely as an individualized problem of bigotry, but as a systemic organizer of power and economics. By the 1980s and 1990s, not only had "ethnicity" failed to displace "race" as an analytic category, but – since race had been etched into social reality and encoded in law – no conception of the vicissitudes of "ethnicity" could hold much explanatory power if it failed to reckon as well with the undergirding realities of "race." This has been apparent in both street-level politics (where ethnic particularism has been among the idioms of white backlash) and in scholarly discourse (where the most sophisticated recent analyses of "ethnicity" have taken up the term *in conjunction* with racialized categories like white, black, Asian, or Latino).

The burgeoning literature on ethnicity between the 1950s and the 1970s was almost exclusively about "white ethnics," though the full significance of the modifier "white" long remained invisible. But as whiteness itself claimed attention, the scholarship took some new turns. In *Ethnic Options*, for instance, Mary Waters warned that the whiteness underlying white ethnicity lent a certain flexibility to the ethnic identity of Jews, Italians, Greeks, or Poles in the United States – they *do* choose their grandparents, to some degree – which has in turn led many to misconstrue the "ethnic" constraints experienced by their counterparts on the other side of the colorline. Richard Alba went further in *Ethnic Identity*, tracing the gradual formation of a "European American" identity for whom Polish, Greek, or Irish specificities may lose all salience, but for whom a generic conception of Old World origin – along with the romance of departure, arrival, and resettlement – is fundamentally defining. Although the passion for ancestral narratives is no longer as visible among the "unmeltable ethnics" as it was in the 1970s, still their familial saga of immigration and civic inclusion remains the template of normative "Americanness."

If heightened attention to racial whiteness informs recent interpretations of "white ethnicity," on the other side of the colorline *ethnicity* has become an indispensable instrument for analyzing the racialized experience of many *nonwhite* groups. Examples include Felix Padilla's *Latino Ethnic Consciousness* (1985) and Ilan Stavans's *Hispanic Condition* (1995), which describe the making of a single, politicized "ethnic" group from an array of distinct nationality groups; Mary Waters's *Black Identities* (1999), which interrogates assumptions about assimilation and mobility by examining West Indians' "assimilation" into American blackness; and Yen Le Espiritu's *Asian American Panethnicity* (1992), which maps the creation of an "Asian American" political identity amid the cultural variety of Japanese and Chinese Americans, South Asians, Koreans, Filipinos, and Pacific Islanders.

As the United States population has become still more diverse in the years since the assimilationist predictions of the 1940s, then, and as race has retained its centrality in American social and political life, the concept of "ethnicity" has become not the "race concept's" *replacement*, as Montagu and Boas had hoped, but its inseparable twin. "Ethnicity" itself has become a term of particularity rather than of universalism, and it is a particularity whose very form and fluctuation are now understood to depend upon the deeper, enduring social structures of "race." And just as the formulation of ethnicity in the 1940s was partly a response to the political imperatives of that historical moment, so this turn in the recent race-*and*-ethnicity scholarship across the disciplines represents a nuanced response to the politics of the post-civil rights period.

"The hyphen *performs*," writes Jennifer DeVere Brody; "it is never neutral or natural" (Ma, 2000, p. 155). Early in the twentieth century the hyphen performed an adopted Americanism that was largely rejected in the majority view. In the 'teens "hyphenated Americanism" amounted to *un*-Americanism, as far as some were concerned; it was the subject of much surveillance and worry. But two generations later, in that political era "beyond the melting pot," the Americanism performed by the hyphen has risen above reproach. The United States has become a veritable hyphen nation; and ethnic hyphenation, if not "neutral," has at least become a most *natural* idiom of national belonging in this "nation of immigrants."

REFERENCES

Alba, Richard: *Ethnic Identity: The Transformation of White America* (New Haven, Conn.: Yale University Press, 1990).

Auster, Lawrence: *The Path to National Suicide* (Monterey, Va.: AICF, 1990).

Brimelow, Peter: *Alien Nation: Common Sense About America's Immigration Disaster* (New York: Random House, 1995).

di Leonardo, Micaela: *The Varieties of Ethnic Experience: Kinship, Class, and Gender Among California Italian-Americans* (Ithaca, NY: Cornell University Press, 1984).

di Leonardo, Micaela: "White Ethnicities, Identity Politics, and Baby Bear's Chair," *Social Text*, 41 (Winter 1994): 165–91.

Espiritu, Yen Le: *Asian American Panethnicity* (Philadelphia: Temple University Press, 1992).

Foner, Nancy: *From Ellis Island to JFK: New York's Two Great Waves of Immigration* (New Haven, Conn.: Yale University Press, 2000).

Gambino, Richard: *Blood of My Blood: The Dilemma of the Italian Americans* (1974; Toronto: Guernica, 1996).

Glazer, Nathan: *Affirmative Discrimination: Ethnic Inequality and Public Policy* (1975; Cambridge, Mass.: Harvard University Press, 1987).

Glazer, Nathan: *We Are All Multiculturalists Now* (Cambridge, Mass.: Harvard University Press, 1997).

Glazer, Nathan and Moynihan, Daniel: *Beyond the Melting Pot: The Negroes, Puerto Ricans, Jews, Italians, and Irish of New York City* (1963; Cambridge, Mass.: MIT Press, 1971).

Gold, Mike: *Jews Without Money* (1930; New York: Avon, 1965).

Gordon, Milton: *Assimilation in American Life: The Role of Race, Religion, and National Origins* (New York: Oxford University Press, 1964).

Greeley, Andrew: *Ethnicity in the United States: A Preliminary Reconnaissance* (New York: Warner, 1974).

Handlin, Oscar: *The Uprooted: The Epic Story of the Great Migrations that Made the American People* (Boston: Little, Brown, 1951).

Herberg, Will: *Protestant–Catholic–Jew: An Essay in American Religious Sociology* (1955; New York: Anchor, 1960).

Higham, John: *Strangers in the Land: Patterns of American Nativism, 1860–1925* (1955; New Brunswick, NJ: Rutgers University Press, 1963).

Hollinger, David: *Postethnic America: Beyond Multiculturalism* (New York: Basic Books, 1995).

Howe, Irving: *World of Our Fathers* (New York: Harper, 1976).

Jones, Maldwyn Allen: *American Immigration* (Chicago: University of Chicago Press, 1960).

Kennedy, John F.: *A Nation of Immigrants* (1958; New York: Harper, 1964).

Ma: *The Deathly Embrace* (Minneapolis: University of Minnesota Press, 2000).

Montagu, Ashley: *Race: Man's Most Dangerous Myth* (New York: Columbia University Press, 1942).

Montagu, Ashley: "What Every Child and Adult Should Know About 'Race,'" *Education* (January 1946): 262–4.

Myrdal, Gunnar: *An American Dilemma: The Negro Problem and Modern Democracy* (New York: Harper, 1944).

Nash, Gary, Crabtree, Charlotte, and Dunn, Ross: *History on Trial: Culture Wars and the Teaching of the Past* (New York: Alfred A. Knopf, 1997).

Novak, Michael: *The Rise of the Unmeltable Ethnics* (New York: Macmillan, 1971).

Novak, Michael: *Unmeltable Ethnics* (New Brunswick, NJ: Transaction, 1995).

Padilla, Felix: *Latino Ethnic Consciousness: The Case of Mexicans and Puerto Ricans in Chicago* (South Bend, Ind.: Notre Dame University Press, 1985).

Reimers, David: *Still the Golden Door: The Third World Comes to America* (New York: Columbia University Press, 1985).

Rischin, Moses: *The Promised City: New York's Jews, 1870–1914* (1962; New York: Harper, 1970).

Rose, Peter I., ed.: *Nation of Nations* (Washington, DC: University Press of America, 1972).

Schlesinger, Jr., Arthur: *The Disuniting of America: Reflections on a Multicultural Society* (1991; New York: W. W. Norton, 1998).

Sollors, Werner: *Beyond Ethnicity: Consent and Descent in American Culture* (New York: Oxford University Press, 1986).

Solomon, Barbara Miller: *Ancestors and Immigrants: A Changing New England Tradition* (Chicago: University of Chicago Press, 1956).

Sowell, Thomas: *Ethnic America: A History* (New York: Basic Books, 1981).

Stavans, Ilan: *The Hispanic Condition: Reflections on Culture and Identity in America* (1995; New York: HarperCollins, 1996).

Steinberg, Stephen: *The Ethnic Myth: Race, Ethnicity, and Class in America* (Boston: Beacon Press, 1981).

Warner, W. Lloyd and Srole, Leo: *The Social Systems of American Ethnic Groups* (New Haven, Conn.: Yale University Press, 1945).

Waters, Mary: *Ethnic Options: Choosing Identities in America* (Berkeley: University of California Press, 1990).

Waters, Mary: *Black Identities: West Indian Immigrant Dreams and American Realities* (Cambridge, Mass.: Harvard University Press, 1999).

CHAPTER ELEVEN

Labor During the American Century: Work, Workers, and Unions Since 1945

JOSHUA B. FREEMAN

Seen from afar, United States labor at the start of the twenty-first century looked much like it did when World War II ended. Work for wages still constituted the dominant form of labor, the basic legal framework for industrial relations remained unchanged, unions continued to represent a significant (if much diminished) minority of the workforce, and by world standards workers and their families lived extremely well. But seen from the point of view of the individual worker, labor had undergone an extraordinary transformation. Where and how workers lived and worked, and how much power they wielded, had changed profoundly.

Work and the working class have been in continual flux since 1945. Automation and economic shifts have changed the content and context of jobs. Massive movements of people and industry, and changed gender roles, have altered the composition of the labor force. But perhaps most revolutionary has been an astonishing rise in the working-class standard of living. Before 1974, increased earnings, pushed upward by robust economic growth and a powerful union movement, accounted for most of the gains. After 1974, wage rates fell, but a growing prevalence of multiple wage earners kept family income fairly steady until the mid-1990s, when it began to rise again.

Until recently, scholars had only sketchy accounts of these developments. Few historians wrote about post-1945 labor, and those who did focused on a small set of topics, primarily industrial relations in basic industry. The 1990s, though, saw an explosion of scholarship on everything from managerial strategies to race relations to deindustrialization. As a result, historians know far more about labor since 1945 than they did just a few years ago. Whereas labor history once was dominated by studies of the nineteenth century and the 1930s, now much of the most exciting work deals with the post-1945 period.

The New Deal Formula

The New Deal has been the touchstone for much of the historiography of labor after World War II. The fifteen years prior to 1945 took labor on a rollercoaster ride. The Great Depression undid the relative prosperity that workers in selected industries, like automobile manufacturing, had enjoyed during the 1920s, and brought deeper misery to those in already depressed industries, like coal mining. The economic crisis, however, created conditions for the emergence of new structures of industrial relations and working-class activity.

Most importantly, union membership soared during the mid-1930s, as a wave of militant strikes allowed organized labor to significantly penetrate, for the first time, major national corporations like General Motors and US Steel. At the forefront of the union surge stood the Congress of Industrial Organizations (CIO), a labor federation that split off from the American Federation of Labor (AFL) in 1935. It organized on an industrial basis, grouping together all workers at particular facilities or in particular industries, regardless of their skill or occupation. (Many AFL unions organized on a craft basis and spurned unskilled, female, and nonwhite workers.) Union membership rose from fewer than 3 million in 1933 to over 10 million by the time the United States entered World War II.

Mass worker mobilization sparked fundamental changes in labor and employment law. The 1935 National Labor Relations Act (or Wagner Act) guaranteed the right of workers to join organizations of their choice without interference by employers, and required companies to negotiate with unions that demonstrated support from a majority of their employees. The Social Security Act, also passed in 1935, established national pension and unemployment insurance systems. The 1938 Fair Labor Standards Act set a minimum wage and capped the workweek, requiring overtime pay after forty hours. While none of these laws was universal in its coverage – they excluded farm and domestic workers, public employees, and others – they brought a new set of benefits, protections, and procedures to the heart of the industrial economy.

Much of the scholarship on post-1945 labor examines how the industrial relations system established under the New Deal operated during the ensuing decades, and why it eventually decayed. More particularly, historians have hotly debated the possibilities and limits of what David Montgomery (1979, p. 161) dubbed "the New Deal formula": "state subsidization of economic growth, the encouragement of legally regulated collective bargaining, and the marriage of the union movement to the Democratic Party."

World War II set the trajectory for the postwar era, as Nelson Lichtenstein showed in *Labor's War at Home: The CIO in World War II* (1982). The industrial demands of total war brought steady work and rising income to workers for the first time in a generation. To ensure uninterrupted production and restrain inflation, the federal government regulated labor relations to an extent only precedented in World War I, checking labor militancy and wage gains while forcing employers to grant concessions on union representation. The result was the continued growth and accelerated bureaucratization of unions, whose combined membership surpassed 14 million by the war's end, equivalent to 35 percent of the nonagricultural workforce, an all-time high. At the same time, a deep labor shortage sparked a resumption of migration by whites and blacks out of the South to industrial centers in the Northeast and Midwest and on the Pacific Coast, a demographic shift that would profoundly affect postwar culture, race relations, and politics. The tight labor market also forced companies to hire women for jobs once reserved for men, a movement that reversed after the war but eventually resumed.

During World War I, workers and unions had made great advances, only to see them soon undone. After World War II, most business leaders sought, again, to roll back at least some of labor's wartime (and New Deal) gains. Union leaders hoped to build on them, both through collective bargaining and legislation expanding the New Deal. Meanwhile, wartime population and employment shifts, along with the democratic rhetoric of the war effort, had raised expectations among African Americans and women that progress would be made after the war toward equal rights, but also stirred fears among whites and men that their advantageous positions in the labor market would be undermined. And overshadowing all else, many people feared that with the conclusion of the war the country would again slide into economic stagnation and mass unemployment. The resolution of these issues defined the core labor experience during the first decades after the great world conflict ended.

Postwar Labor Relations

In November 1948, thirteen-year-old Elvis Presley and his parents moved from Tupelo, Mississippi, to Memphis, Tennessee, hoping to escape chronic poverty and pinched opportunities. Though Vernon Presley found work at a munitions factory and Gladys as a sewing machine operator, the family at first could afford only one room in a boarding house, cooking meals on a hotplate and sharing a bathroom with several other families. Their move a year later to a public housing project felt like a giant step upward. To help maintain the family's new lifestyle, Elvis worked afternoons and evenings at a furniture assembly plant. After graduating high school, he moved on to a machine shop, the munitions factory, and a truck-driving job. When he hit it big, he became so giddy with the experience of wealth after a lifetime of privation that he gave away countless automobiles to friends, family, and even strangers (Guralnick, 1994).

Few Americans rocketed upward as quickly or as far as Elvis, propelled as he was by an explosive mix of black and white music and an emerging culture of rebellious youth. But during the quarter-century after the war, the economic status of labor underwent a transformation nearly as miraculous as that of the "King." At the start of the period, most working-class Americans lived lives of economic marginality. One of the country's leading television shows of the 1940s and 1950s, *The Honeymooners*, comically portrayed the life of a New York City bus driver and his wife. It not inaccurately depicted a barebones existence: a two-room apartment, little furniture, no telephone, television, or modern appliances, and constant squabbling over money (Freeman, 2001, p. 318). Judith Stein (1998, p. 9), in a study of the steel industry, noted that "In 1942, 15 percent of steelworkers . . . lived in homes without running water and 30 percent had no indoor bathroom."

All this changed radically during the decades after World War II. Between 1946 and 1960, average annual earnings, adjusted for inflation, rose by over a third (US Bureau of the Census, 1977). In addition, many workers gained previously rare or unknown employer-financed benefits, such as health insurance and pensions to supplement social security. For southern mill workers, rising income meant indoor plumbing, better clothes, radios, and new furniture (Clark, 1999, p. 151). Jack Metzgar, the son of a Pennsylvania steel worker, recalls in *Striking Steel, Solidarity Remembered* (2000, pp. 38–9) that the 50 percent increase in real hourly wages steel workers won during the 1950s meant that "you had something very few workers had ever had up until then – discretionary income, income that in a sense you didn't need, income that you could *decide* how to spend," be it to buy a car, television, refrigerator, or home, to take a vacation, or to send a child to college, all of which his family did. "If what we lived through in the 1950s was not liberation," wrote Metzgar, "then liberation never happens in real human lives." By the 1970s, there were so many retired New York City transit workers living in Florida that the union representing them set up branches of its retirees' association there.

Historians generally credit unionism, at least in part, for this upgrade of working-class life. After World War II, the United States experienced the greatest strike wave in its history, as business and labor fought to establish the parameters of postwar industrial relations and the relationships among prices, wages, and profits. We still lack a comprehensive study of the postwar strikes, but George Lipsitz recounts the feisty spirit of the strikers in *Rainbow at Midnight: Labor and Culture in the 1940s* (1994), while various historians have chronicled the clashes in particular industries, including electrical equipment manufacturing (Schatz, 1983), automaking (Lichtenstein, 1995), and meatpacking (Horowitz, 1997).

Strike settlements in basic industry, especially steel and auto, set benchmarks for other unionized sectors and even many nonunion firms. Unlike after World War I, unions achieved institutional stability, many gaining union shop agreements that required all covered workers to pay union dues. In addition, they won rising wages (by the 1950s often protected from inflation by automatic cost-of-living adjustments), an ever-growing set of benefits, and some control on the shopfloor through work rules and grievance procedures. Employers, for their part, won greater stability and predictable labor costs through longer contracts and bans on strikes during their course. More important, they succeeded in limiting what matters would be subject to negotiation, generally excluding decisions on investments, products, prices, production methods, and plant locations. Meanwhile, in an increasingly conservative political climate, proposals to expand the New Deal, for example through a federal commitment to full employment or a national health insurance system, went down to defeat.

Leading industrial relations experts, like Derek Bok and John Dunlop (1970), have viewed the postwar industrial relations system favorably, citing the order it brought to the economy, along with greater fairness in the workplace and new benefits for workers. Historians influenced by the New Left have taken a more critical stance. Mike Davis (1986) and Nelson Lichtenstein (1995, 1999), for example, have argued that postwar structural and contractual arrangements reflected union weakness as much as strength. Unions, they contend, survived postwar company offensives and growing political opposition by jettisoning their more radical ideas and modes of activity, including hopes for a social democratic polity and ongoing, shopfloor mobilization. Through collective bargaining, unions did obtain substantial benefits and a degree of workplace security, but only for their members, thereby deepening fissures within the working class.

Many historians see the seeds of labor "containment" in the New Deal itself (Brody, 1993, pp. 135–56). The expansion of state regulation, writes Montgomery (1979, p. 165), "was simultaneously liberating and cooptive for workers." Dependence on state protection, Davis, Lichtenstein, and others contend, pushed the labor movement into a junior partnership with the Democratic Party and left it susceptible to shifting political winds. Legal scholars, including Karl Klare (1978), Katherine Stone (1981), and Christopher Tomlins (1985), argue that the radical potential of the Wagner Act became eclipsed by administrative practices and court decisions that encouraged the substitution of quasi-judicial grievance procedures for direct worker struggle.

Events of the late 1940s and early 1950s accelerated labor's acceptance of an attenuated liberalism. The 1947 Taft-Hartley Act contained a series of business-promoted amendments to the Wagner Act that made organizing more difficult and restricted acts of worker solidarity such as secondary boycotts and sympathy strikes. The law also required officers of federally certified unions to file affidavits affirming that they did not belong to the Communist Party. President Harry Truman's veto of the bill, overridden by Congress, drew many union leaders closer to the Democratic Party. The Communist Party, by contrast, decided in 1948 to back third-party presidential candidate Henry Wallace. The upshot was to accelerate the erosion of the once-influential position of the communist-led left in the labor movement, a process to which historians have devoted a great deal of attention (Cochran, 1977; Levenstein, 1981; Rosswurm, 1992).

Even before Taft-Hartley, many unions placed restrictions on the rights of communists. After the 1948 election, the CIO expelled ten affiliates because of their communist links. Many historians argue that whatever the merits and faults of the communist left, its repression weakened labor, narrowed the range of debate among unionists, and contributed to labor's growing political timidity (Zieger, 1995; Freeman, 2000). Lipsitz portrays working-class initiative, creativity, and "resentment against hierarchy" moving out of the industrial and political arenas, where huge roadblocks had been erected, into such cultural expressions as custom-car-building and rock and roll (1994, p. 330).

The purge of communists ended significant labor debate about foreign policy. By the end of the 1940s, union leaders had all but abandoned the notion that international labor might play an independent role in shaping the postwar world, instead lining up behind the increasingly hardline anti-communism of the Truman administration. From the late 1940s through the 1990s, unions worked with the federal government openly and covertly to battle left-wing unionists abroad (Frank, 1999; Silverman, 2000).

While the "containment" interpretation of postwar labor remains dominant, it has come under challenge. Some scholars, including Metzgar and David L. Stebenne (1996), have assessed the benefits and costs of postwar labor–management arrangements more positively than Davis, Lichtenstein, and other critics. Given the historic weakness of labor in the United States, the enormous strength of the major corporations, and the resurgence of the Republican Party, they believe unions did as well as could have been expected, bringing very substantial material and social benefits to tens of millions of workers and their family members and providing a liberal influence on national politics. They argue that scholars need to appreciate what was accomplished and focus less on what was not. As Daniel J. Clark (1999) noted in his study of a southern textile town, for workers who first unionized after World War II, bureaucratized collective bargaining and grievance procedures represented a major, much-appreciated gain in power at the workplace, not a retreat from a different, perhaps more radical, vision of industrial relations.

Other scholarship suggests that the dominant historiography devotes too much attention to a handful of CIO unions, overstating their importance. In a scathing account of the twentieth-century labor movement, Paul Buhle (1999) sees its central flaws – conservatism, exclusivity, support for imperialist foreign policy, and passivity – primarily stemming not from the degeneration or deradicalization of the CIO, but from the triumph of AFL business unionism, exemplified by George Meany, who became president of the AFL in 1953 and the first head of the AFL-CIO after the two federations merged in 1955.

At all times, the AFL had more members than the CIO, yet historians have yet to chronicle its membership and activities during and after World War II with the same energy and sophistication they have brought to their study of the CIO. When they do, the results may be surprising. Some AFL unions did act as a conservative force within organized labor, but others defy stereotypes. The Teamsters union, though riddled with corruption, more aggressively organized workers than the more politically liberal CIO unions (Russell, 2001). The Hotel Employees and Restaurant Employees, as Dorothy Sue Cobble shows in *Dishing It Out* (1991), used the craft form of organization – usually associated with skilled, male exclusivity – to unionize waitresses, who in many cases, by choice, formed all-female locals. In New York City, AFL unions proved as likely as CIO ones to sponsor innovative benefit programs such as nonprofit cooperative housing projects and comprehensive, prepaid health care (Freeman, 2000).

As historians move toward a more balanced picture of organized labor, they also have begun reassessing the relative importance of the unionized and nonunionized elements of the economy. Sanford M. Jacoby points out in *Modern Manors: Welfare Capitalism Since the New Deal* (1997, pp. 35–6) that while

[l]arge nonunion firms followed wage and benefit patterns established in the union sector, . . . these firms also set patterns (norms of conduct, personnel innovations, models of employee relations) for their unionized counterparts to imitate.

Welfare capitalism, usually associated with the pre-New Deal years, "did not die in the 1930s but instead went underground – out of the public eye and beyond academic scrutiny – where it would reshape itself" (Jacoby, 1997, p. 5). Ultimately, nonunion companies with innovative labor practices derived from welfare capitalism, like Eastman Kodak, Sears Roebuck, and Thompson Products, proved more influential models for the future of industrial relations than unionized giants like General Motors or US Steel.

Regionalism and Race

During the 1930s and 1940s, many corporate executives acquiesced to unionism because they believed they had no choice. Determined to change that after the war, businesses moved to check the power of unions not only through collective bargaining and legal restrictions, but also through extensive public relations campaigns extolling free enterprise and attacking organized labor (Harris, 1982; Fones-Wolf, 1994). They also began a systemic effort to relocate industry to parts of the country where unions were weak and social and political conditions were not conducive to them.

At the end of the 1940s, in spite of two decades of massive union growth, organized labor remained essentially a regional phenomenon. Union membership clustered in the Midwest, Mid-Atlantic, Northeast, and parts of the West Coast, with two-thirds of all union members living in just ten states (Stein, 1998, p. 17). The existence of large, nonunion regions, most notably in the South, undermined labor's strength. First, it made it difficult to establish national wage scales or maintain high wages in unionized sectors of industries that also operated in nonunion zones. Second, it created incentives for companies to build new facilities or relocate old ones in nonunion areas, threatening the jobs of unionized workers. Third, it sustained the social basis for an anti-liberal political bloc in Washington, joining Republicans from the North with conservative Democrats from the South. This cross-party political alliance frustrated efforts, from the late 1930s through the mid-1960s, to pass pro-labor or civil rights legislation.

Soon after World War II, both the CIO and the AFL launched southern organizing campaigns, but neither achieved substantial breakthroughs. Barbara S. Griffith's *The Crisis of American Labor: Operation Dixie and the Defeat of the CIO* (1988) is the only full-length study we have of these campaigns. Griffith blames the failure of the CIO effort on a variety of factors, including southern paternalism, flawed union strategies, and employer propaganda charging the CIO with being communist and integrationist. More than any one factor, though, Griffith argues that it was the totality of the southern social structure, especially employer access to institutions of authority, combined with the CIO's inability to establish its cultural legitimacy, that led to the union defeat.

More recent studies – part of a burgeoning of southern labor history – paint a more complicated picture. In a study of the southern textile industry, Timothy J. Minchin (1997) notes that unions made substantial membership gains in the region during World War II, and that in the immediate postwar years southern workers took part in numerous large strikes, which belies their usual conservative image. In Minchin's view, the CIO's failure to expand its foothold in the textile industry – the key target of its southern drive – reflected the policy of nonunion firms of matching union wages as much as any cultural predilection among workers against unionism.

Race played a role in both the failed southern organizing efforts and the development of the union movement nationally. Not inappropriately, it has been a central concern of historians of post-1945 labor, and the subject of fierce debate. During the first two decades after World War II, every possible system of racial organization could be found within the labor movement, from all-white, racially exclusive unions, common among the railroad brotherhoods and AFL craft groups, to organizations like the International Longshoremen's Association, which had both black and white members but often kept them in separate locals, to a few, virtually all-black unions, like the Brotherhood of Sleeping Car Porters, to racially integrated unions, the model to which the CIO, at least on paper, committed itself. Looking at this complex pattern, scholars have reached contradictory conclusions about whether organized labor served as a progressive force in the struggle for racial equality or primarily as a vehicle for white workers to maintain their privileged position in the labor market.

Local studies have revealed complex interconnections between the labor and civil rights movements. The unionization of large numbers of black workers during the 1940s provided a financial and political base and a degree of self-confidence that enabled African Americans to begin challenging restrictions on voting rights and the segregation of public facilities in both the South and the North (Korstad and Lichtenstein, 1988; Jones, 2000). Michael K. Honey's study of Memphis reconstructs how CIO biracial organizing challenged the widespread denial of basic rights not only to African Americans, but also to white political activists (Honey, 1993). Martha Biondi (1997) and Joshua B. Freeman (2000) show how African American and left-wing unionists launched a multi-fronted attack on racial discrimination in New York City. Joseph E. Wilson (1989) documents the role of the Sleeping Car Porters in civil rights efforts. Taken together, these works portray labor playing a major role in challenging racial injustice during the immediate postwar years.

But even as some scholars were unearthing the ties between labor and civil rights struggles, others were documenting labor resistance to desegregation and racial equality. Herbert Hill put the case most strongly:

> In the development of labor unions in the United States, racist ideas and practices were not occasional expressions of a random, deviant attitude, or of individual malevolence; rather they were a basic characteristic of the social organization of white working class life.

Even in the post-1945 years, Hill believes,

> unless there was a significant concentration of black workers in a specific industry over a long period of time and unless they had established their own leadership in advance of white-led organizations, labor unions would inevitably engage in a broad range of discriminatory practices. (Hill, 1987, pp. 32–3)

While few other historians are as unremitting in their criticism, studies of a range of unions, including ones formally committed to racial equality, have shown how race often marked what Bruce Nelson (2001) calls "the limits of solidarity."

In her steel industry study, Judith Stein (1998) moves beyond the debate over discrimination in trying to understand the experience of black industrial workers. Liberal activists and federal legislation treated black employment as a civil rights issue, but from the point of view of black workers, equal access to industrial jobs meant little if such jobs were disappearing from their communities. And precisely that happened, in both southern industrial centers like Birmingham and the northern manufacturing centers to which so many southern blacks moved. In Stein's view, the failure of postwar liberalism lay not in its approach to reforming race relations, but in its failure to develop economic and foreign policies that sustained sufficient industrial employment opportunities for both white and black workers.

In the steel industry, the great implosion of employment opportunities did not occur until the 1980s, but as studies of Detroit and New York show, blue-collar job loss had begun to undermine the status of workers, especially nonwhites, in northern cities as early as the 1950s (Sugrue, 1996; Freeman, 2000). Industrial relocation to the South became especially attractive once the Taft-Hartley Act gave states the option of outlawing union shops, which many southern states did. Taking advantage of their low labor costs and scarcity of unions, southern states launched aggressive campaigns to lure northern industry, offering tax breaks, publicly built factories, worker-training programs, and other subsidies. Indirectly, the federal government promoted the shift of industry southward and westward by financing the interstate highway system, which made the dispersion of industry practical, and by concentrating military spending in the emerging "Sunbelt" (Friedman, 2001).

"Post-Industrial Society"

While "runaway shops" cost communities some jobs, others were lost to automation and technological change. In the years after 1945, many industries introduced mechanized systems for transferring material or aiding production that dramatically increased productivity. In some sectors, like mining, the workforce shrank absolutely. In others, like manufacturing, roughly the same number of workers produced an ever-greater quantity of goods. Meanwhile, employment in business and personal services mushroomed. The net result was a relative decline in the importance of manual labor.

This change provoked a great deal of discussion among journalists and social scientists. Many followed sociologist Daniel Bell (1973) in celebrating what he called "post-industrial society," which placed an economic and cultural premium on knowledge and brought increased power to the "professional and technical class." As a smaller proportion of the population engaged in blue-collar work, and the union movement increasingly seemed a stodgy, if liberal, element of the establishment, social critics like C. Wright Mills and Herbert Marcuse questioned whether or not labor would continue to function as an agent of social change. Somewhat hesitantly, they pointed to the growing number of skilled white-collar workers, technicians, scientists, and professionals as a potential force for restructuring society and checking the power of business, a line of thinking taken up by elements of the New Left during the 1960s (Miller, 1987).

Discussions of "the new working class" of white-collar and professional workers, and of "post-industrialism," often had an abstract air, floating above lived experience. For many workers, "post-industrialism" concretely meant fewer job opportunities and less security, especially for those with limited education or training living in northern cities. African Americans suffered disproportionately from the decline of goods production, a process that Thomas Sugrue has identified as part of the "origins of the urban crisis" of the 1960s (Sugrue, 1996; Freeman, 2000).

We know less about what "post-industrialism" meant for white-collar workers and the technical-professional class about which so much theorizing took place. Though one theorizer, C. Wright Mills, undertook a pioneering study of such workers, *White Collar* (1951), labor historians have yet to follow his lead. No overall picture has been painted of the political, organizational, and cultural life of the expanding occupations of the post-1945 years and the workers who filled them, for the most part upwardly mobile white men and women.

Public employees form an exception to this scholarly neglect. The postwar years saw a tremendous growth of government employment, which encompassed a broad range of occupations, from clerical to blue-collar to professional. The vast majority of public employees remained unorganized or members of nonunion civil service associations until the 1960s. The next two decades saw a massive wave of public sector unionization, labor's one great post-1945 organizing success. While the full dimensions of this story have yet to be told, a growing number of monographs ably chart the history of public employee unionism among particular groups of workers, such as teachers (Murphy, 1990), or in particular locales, such as New York City (Maier, 1987).

Glory Days

At least on the surface, labor's place in society never seemed more assured than during the 1960s. A growing economy and the organization of public employees brought a steady flow of new members to the union movement, which peaked at over 19 million members in 1970. George Meany's cigar-smoking visage and gruff pronouncements regularly adorned newspaper front pages. With the unemployment rate dropping, in part as a result of the Vietnam War, workers grew increasingly aggressive. By the end of the decade, strikes reached a frequency not seen since the early 1950s.

The AFL-CIO's Committee on Political Education (COPE) gave unions considerable political influence. With an extensive network of volunteers and a huge war chest, COPE provided favored candidates with a ready-made field operation and substantial funding. The Democratic recapture of the White House in 1960, and the massive Democratic congressional victory in 1964, created the greatest opportunity for labor legislative action since the New Deal. After a decade as Washington outsiders, labor leaders and lobbyists found themselves roaming the corridors of power, helping formulate and run a host of federal programs. Much of the clout for the passage of the 1964 Civil Rights Act, the 1965 Voting Rights Act, and the Medicare/Medicaid program came from labor (Brody, 1993, pp. 215–16). Belatedly, at least some elements of labor's postwar political agenda reached fruition.

Ironically, though, as David Brody put it, "the AFL-CIO proved a better champion of the general welfare than of its own narrow interests." During the late 1950s, unions failed to counteract the bad publicity they received from congressional hearings on labor corruption and racketeering. Recognizing political realities, the AFL-CIO reluctantly supported the 1959 Landrum-Griffith Act, which established federal oversight of internal union operations. Then, during the 1960s, several efforts to repeal section 14(b) of Taft-Hartley, which allowed states to outlaw the union shop, went down to defeat (Brody, 1993, pp. 216–18; Boyle, 1995; Stebenne, 1996).

By the late 1960s, the civil rights movement, urban riots, white "backlash," the "counterculture," and the war in Vietnam had shattered the loose bloc of liberal forces within which organized labor operated. On economic issues, union leaders remained committed to a liberal vision of government-managed growth, expanded state benefits, and federal programs to raise the floor of the national standard of living. But on social and cultural issues, many labor leaders moved to the right. Furthermore, no group remained more firmly committed to the country's course in Vietnam than the upper echelons of labor, which shared the deep anti-communism behind the policy. Even many self-styled social democrats, like United Automobile Workers president Walter Reuther, preferred supporting President Lyndon Johnson's actions in Indochina to losing their insider status in Washington (though a minority of unions did join the anti-war movement early on) (Foner, 1989; Levy, 1994; Lichtenstein, 1995).

Labor leaders often found themselves out of touch with their own members. Polls indicated that working-class men and women were more likely to oppose US policy in Vietnam than the economically better off (though many also disliked anti-war protestors). At the same time, some workers began questioning basic tenets of postwar labor–management arrangements, especially the trade of increased wages and job security for a relatively free management hand over the methods and pace of production, and the bureaucratic model of unionism in which elected officers and large staffs "serviced" a demobilized rank and file.

A 1972 strike at General Motors' Lordstown, Ohio, assembly plant brought public and political acknowledgment of the new working-class mood, quickly dubbed by the media "the blue-collar blues." Managers at the Lordstown plant, one of GM's newest, introduced robotic equipment, speeded up the assembly line, and imposed draconian discipline in an effort to boost productivity. The young workforce, which included many Vietnam veterans, revolted. The strikers seemed infused with the anti-authoritarian ethos of the protest movements of the 1960s. Some openly expressed dissatisfaction with the relentless pursuit of "the almighty dollar" (Green, 1980, pp. 218–22).

From the mid-1960s to the mid-1970s, the mood of militancy and dissatisfaction evident at Lordstown manifested itself elsewhere, too, in official and wildcat strikes and efforts to oust incumbent union leaders. Several factors contributed to this wave of worker mobilization, rarely noted in general histories of the period and only beginning to be examined in depth by labor historians. Like the Lordstown strike, some protests stemmed from dissatisfaction with oppressive working conditions, especially in mass-production factories, and the failure of grievance procedures to provide adequate remedies. Others targeted racial discrimination. In the wake of the civil rights movement, African American workers displayed greater impatience with racial inequities in access to jobs and union power. Workers also acted in response to accelerating inflation, which wiped out wage increases, drove up the cost of mortgages, and threatened savings. Finally, many unionists protested what they saw as a lack of union democracy.

The rank-and-file rebellion reached its peak in the early 1970s. In 1970, the largest public employee strike, and quite possibly the largest wildcat strike, in the nation's history took place when New York City postal workers defied a ban on federal employee walkouts to demand higher pay, improved benefits, and the right to strike. Their walkout quickly spread to other cities, until some 200,000 workers were off the job. The strike ended only after the federal government conceded some of the strikers' demands, and President Richard Nixon sent National Guard troops to occupy New York post offices. The telephone, automobile, coal, and trucking industries also were hit by strikes led by rank-and-file activists dissatisfied with deals their national leaders had negotiated. In the United Mine Workers, in 1972 Miners for Democracy managed to oust union president Tony Boyle, who had turned to murder in an effort to maintain power. In the Teamsters, a series of rank-and-file groups formed that eventually coalesced as Teamsters for a Democratic Union and helped eject the union's mob-linked officers (Moody, 1986; Brenner, 1996). Changing economic and political conditions, however, soon brought the labor offensive to a halt.

Recession and Retreat

During the 1960s, a booming economy, growing membership, and militant worker action masked structural weaknesses in the union movement. Since the mid-1950s, the percentage of private sector workers who carried a union card had been dropping, weakening organized labor's ability to set industry-wide wage and benefit standards, and leaving it vulnerable to counterattack. During the 1970s, this trend became brutally obvious. A series of severe recessions, marked by high unemployment and high inflation, a drive by business to lower labor costs, and a conservative turn in national politics sent organized labor into a tailspin, while checking, and in some respects reversing, the advances in living standards and security workers had achieved since 1945.

Each year between 1973 and 1981, the average income of employed workers, adjusted for inflation, fell by at least 2 percent. Nonunion workers were hit hardest. By 1981, the real income of workers was at its lowest level since 1961. All the wage gains workers as a group had made during the 1960s – when they were at the height of their power – were wiped out in less than a decade.

Business took advantage of the changed economic climate by launching aggressive anti-union efforts. Companies resisted organizing drives with new vigor, employing sophisticated psychological measures along with wholesale violations of the law, most notably the firing of union activists. Corporate managers also took very tough stands in negotiations. Rather than the post-World War II norm, in which every contract brought better pay and improved conditions for workers, now businesses saw negotiations as an opportunity to eliminate longstanding work rules, reduce benefits, cut wages, and introduce two-tier wage systems.

Union efforts to resist "give-backs" generally proved ineffective. Employers willingly endured long strikes, or even provoked them, to cripple unions. President Ronald Reagan set the pattern in 1981, when he fired more than 11,000 air traffic controllers who violated federal law by going out on strike. His bold action and willingness to tolerate years of turmoil until a new workforce could be trained, inspired private business to act similarly. Jonathan D. Rosenblum (1995) chronicles how in 1983 the Phelps Dodge corporation used "permanent replacement workers" (a sanitized term for what once had been called "scabs"), protected by the National Guard, to break a strike at its Arizona copper mines and rid itself of long-established unions. Other companies, including Hormel, International Paper, the *Chicago Tribune*, Greyhound, Caterpillar, and several airlines, used similar tactics. In the face of a string of widely publicized union defeats, workers became increasingly reluctant to strike.

Employers also weakened unions, won wage concessions, and disciplined their workforces by using the time-tested tactic of threatening to move or close factories and offices. A massive wave of plant closings during the late 1970s and early 1980s made these threats credible. The number of permanent jobs in the American auto industry fell from 940,000 in 1978 to about 500,000 in 1982. The steel industry suffered a similar downsizing.

Increased transnational mobility of goods and capital contributed to the job losses. Rising foreign competition meant declining sales of domestically made products. Also, many US companies began moving production facilities abroad or buying parts or finished products from foreign manufacturers. Jefferson Cowie's study of RCA

(1999) showed how its establishment of electronics factories in northern Mexico extended its long-established pattern of industrial relocation within the United States in an unremitting search for cheap, pliable labor.

Dana Frank (1999) argues that labor was reaping the harvest of its postwar backing for a US foreign policy that kept anti-communist, anti-labor regimes in power throughout the developing world. Cold War politics created the social and economic infrastructure that enabled US companies to find cheap production alternatives abroad. Unions floundered for a response to the new wave of globalization. A few, including the garment and automobile workers, launched "Buy American" campaigns and called for federal restrictions on imports, but with little success.

The US economy did add millions of new jobs during the 1970s and 1980s. But the typical job created during the Ford–Carter–Reagan years was not making steel or building computers, but cooking French fries at Burger King or selling clothes at the mall. One economist estimated that between 1973 and 1980, 70 percent of all new private sector jobs were in low-paid service and retail areas. Many were temporary or part-time. For working-class Americans, the shift away from manufacturing often meant a move from secure, high-paid, unionized jobs to insecure, nonunion jobs that sometimes paid little more than the minimum wage and lacked benefits or opportunities for promotion.

A series of community studies traces the devastating impact of deindustrialization. William Serrin (1992), David Bensman and Roberta Lynch (1987), and Milton Rogovin and Michael Frisch (1993) document in text, interviews, and photographs the damage caused by the rapid downsizing of the steel industry, which left many once-great centers of steel production, like Youngstown and Buffalo, with few facilities operating. An elegiac mood suffuses these studies, which celebrate the tight-knit working-class communities and high union wages that once characterized centers of basic industry.

Ruth Milkman's sociological comparison of workers who accepted or rejected a buyout offer at a GM factory in Linden, New Jersey, goes against this grain (Milkman, 1997). She found that workers who left the plant expressed few regrets, even when it meant, as it usually did, a decline in income. Both workers who stayed at GM and those who did not reported an intense dislike of the physical demands of auto work and the autocratic behavior of managers. Only African Americans, who because of discrimination found it more difficult than whites to get good new jobs, tended to feel that they had made a mistake in taking the buyout. Milkman's study revealed that the dissatisfactions of the Lordstown era had not disappeared but had merely become less likely to be expressed in the harsher economic climate of the late 1970s and beyond. She concludes that the former GM workers' "lack of nostalgia highlights a sad fact that is all too often forgotten in the age of deindustrialization: factory work in the golden age of mass production was deeply problematic in its own right" (p. 12).

Despite the decline in wages from the early 1970s through the early 1990s, family and per capita income stayed steady or, in the latter case, actually rose. Much of the explanation for this lies in a rise in the percentage of the population that worked for wages. As families got smaller, children made up a smaller percentage of the population, shrinking a group largely outside the workforce. Also, more teenagers began taking jobs, both to help meet family needs and to enable them to buy expensive, youth-oriented products that flooded the market. Finally, and most importantly, the percentage of women who worked for wages rose dramatically.

For most of the twentieth century, female labor force participation had been going up, but the second half of the century saw an acceleration of this trend, with a big jump after 1970. By the latter year, even a majority of women with children under the age of six worked outside the home. As one study noted, "Virtually all of the income gain among white two-parent families in the years after 1967 can be accounted for by the wages of wives and daughters" (Lichtenstein et al., 2000, p. 714).

The prolongation of worktime also contributed to the rise in per capita income, as documented by Juliet Schor in her influential book, *The Overworked American* (1991). Countering both historic trends and developments in other industrial countries, the number of hours Americans worked each year increased from the 1970s on, jumping sixty hours between 1979 and 1998 alone (Mishel et al., 2001, p. 400). Combined with increased female labor force participation, this led to a time crisis, as families struggled to care for children and do domestic chores while working more and more.

A dramatic increase in immigration further transformed the labor market. In 1965, as a result of the civil rights movement and a business desire for more labor, Congress eliminated the racist, national quota system that had heavily favored immigration from Northern and Western Europe and virtually banned it from Asia. Along with changes in the world economy, the result was a dramatic increase in the rate of immigration, with the majority of new arrivals coming from Latin America or Asia, not Europe, as had been the case in the past. Some immigrants filled jobs in emerging, high-tech industries, such as computer programming, sparing employers and the country the cost of training the native born. But most took unskilled, low-paid jobs in service and manufacturing: cleaning homes and hotels, packing meat and preparing food, sewing garments, driving cabs, caring for children. The growing pool of documented and undocumented immigrant workers allowed employers in some industries to set wages, conditions, and benefits at a level below what native-born workers would accept. Labor historians have yet to study the new immigration in depth, but sociologists and anthropologists have portrayed the worklife of recent arrivals in such diverse settings as restaurants in New York, garment shops in Los Angeles, and meatpacking plants in rural Iowa (Kwong, 1987; Fink, 1998; Milkman, 2000).

The combination of economic change, growing female employment, and immigration created a workforce at the end of the twentieth century quite different in composition than when World War II ended. White men no longer constituted a majority of the waged labor force; women made up nearly half of it, while African Americans and Hispanics accounted for one out of every five workers (Zweig, 2000, p. 31). In 1999, manufacturing workers made up only 15 percent of the workforce, down from 24 percent in 1950, while the service industries had ballooned in size. As the twenty-first century began, sales clerks, hospital aides, and schoolteachers were more representative of the working class than the steel workers, coal miners, auto workers, and railroad men who dominated images and notions of twentieth-century labor.

Labor at the New Millennium

By the 1990s, over twenty years of decline had left organized labor in sorry shape. In 2000, just 13.5 percent of the workforce belonged to a union, down from 20.1

percent in 1983. Looking at just the private sector, the situation looked bleaker, since the high rate of government employee unionization drove up the overall rate. With only 9.0 percent of privately employed workers belonging to unions, the labor movement found itself at roughly the same private sector density as before the New Deal.

Organized labor proved slow to respond to its woes. Finally, though, in the mid-1990s, in the face of growing rank-and-file discontent and shrinking economic and political power, a group of union leaders moved to oust AFL-CIO president Lane Kirkland, who had succeeded George Meany in 1979. A contested election for the top AFL-CIO posts resulted, the first in the federation's history, with a new team, led by John Sweeney, victorious. Moving quickly, it reemphasized organizing, beefed up labor's political operations, and began building ties to various groups from which labor had been estranged, including religious leaders, academics, and left-wing activists. All this brought the labor movement a higher profile, a more positive image, and some political payoffs, including the 1996 passage by a Republican-dominated Congress of a higher minimum wage. Union membership gains, though, remained modest, leaving the long-term future of the movement in question (Fraser and Freeman, 1997).

In part because organized labor had become so weakened, workers made only limited gains during the economic boom of the 1990s, as the vast majority of the new wealth went to those already rich. Still, the standard of living of most workers did rise. As the twentieth century ended, two-thirds of all American families owned their own homes, while such items as air conditioners and televisions, rare or unknown in working-class homes a half-century earlier, had become all but taken for granted. Vacations, travel, and college education, though by no means universal, had become common.

While in some respects workers had achieved an enormous amount since 1945, in other respects they had fallen backward, particularly in influencing, as a social group, national social and economic policy. Issues of work and class by no means disappeared. Job discrimination, the need of overtaxed workers for flexible schedules, the desire of companies to be freed of regulations governing working hours and overtime pay, decreased job tenure and security among white-collar workers, and the growing number of workers without health insurance or other basic benefits all received considerable public attention. So did the reemergence of sweatshops in some industries like garment manufacturing, a problem once thought to have been eradicated. Courts, legislatures, trade associations, human rights groups, and even student activists addressed these issues (with limited effectiveness), but workers themselves had little direct say. As the new millennium began, labor remained a social process subject to public concern and contending interests, but workers had become a less visible and influential element of society.

Historians have gone a long way to explain how and why labor gained and lost so much. But to fully understand the transformation of labor, we need to know more, not only about workers but about their relationship to the larger society. This will require investigating such matters as the impact of militarization on work and workers, suburbanization and its effects, working-class culture and its relationship to mass culture, working-class participation in the protest movements of the 1960s and beyond, immigrant workers and their interactions with one another and with the native born, and the changing ways workers and their families have thought about themselves, the nation, and their place in it. Building on what they already have accomplished, labor historians have plenty of fruitful work ahead.

REFERENCES

Bell, Daniel: *The Coming of Post-Industrial Society: A Venture in Social Forecasting* (New York: Basic Books, 1973).

Bensman, David and Lynch, Roberta: *Rusted Dreams: Hard Times in a Steel Community* (New York: McGraw Hill, 1987).

Biondi, Martha: "The Rise of the Modern Black Freedom Struggle: New York City, 1945–1955" (Ph.D. diss., Columbia University, 1997).

Bok, Derek C. and Dunlop, John T.: *Labor and the American Community* (New York: Simon and Schuster, 1970).

Boyle, Kevin: *The UAW and the Heyday of American Liberalism, 1945–1968* (Ithaca, NY: Cornell University Press, 1995).

Brenner, Aaron Michael: "Rank and File Rebellion, 1966–1975" (Ph.D. diss., Columbia University, 1996).

Brody, David: *Workers in Industrial America: Essays on the 20th-Century Struggle*, 2nd ed. (New York: Oxford University Press, 1993).

Buhle, Paul: *Taking Care of Business: Samuel Gompers, George Meany, Lane Kirkland and the Tragedy of American Labor* (New York: Monthly Review Press, 1999).

Clark, Daniel J.: *Like Night and Day: Unionization in a Southern Mill Town* (Chapel Hill: University of North Carolina Press, 1999).

Cobble, Dorothy Sue: *Dishing It Out: Waitresses and Their Unions in the Twentieth Century* (Urbana: University of Illinois Press, 1991).

Cochran, Bert: *Labor and Communism: The Conflict that Shaped American Unions* (Princeton, NJ: Princeton University Press, 1977).

Cowie, Jefferson: *Capital Moves: RCA's 70-Year Quest for Cheap Labor* (Ithaca, NY: Cornell University Press, 1999).

Davis, Mike: *Prisoners of the American Dream* (London: Verso, 1986).

Fink, Deborah: *Cutting into the Meatpacking Line: Workers and Change in the Rural Midwest* (Chapel Hill: University of North Carolina Press, 1998).

Foner, Philip S.: *U.S. Labor and the Vietnam War* (New York: International Publishers, 1989).

Fones-Wolf, Elizabeth A.: *Selling Free Enterprise: The Business Assault on Labor and Liberalism, 1945–1960* (Urbana: University of Illinois Press, 1994).

Frank, Dana: *Buy American: The Untold Story of Economic Nationalism* (Boston: Beacon Press, 1999).

Fraser, Steven and Freeman, Joshua B., eds.: *Audacious Democracy: Labor, Intellectuals, and the Social Reconstruction of America* (Boston: Houghton Mifflin, 1997).

Freeman, Joshua B.: *Working-Class New York: Life and Labor Since World War II* (New York: New Press, 2000).

Freeman, Joshua B.: *In Transit: The Transport Workers Union in New York City, 1933–1966, with a new epilogue* (Philadelphia: Temple University Press, 2001).

Friedman, Tami J.: "Communities in Competition: Capital Migration and Plant Relocation in the U.S. Carpet Industry, 1929–1975" (Ph.D. diss., Columbia University, 2001).

Green, James R.: *The World of the Worker: Labor in Twentieth-Century America* (New York: Hill and Wang, 1980).

Griffith, Barbara S.: *The Crisis of American Labor: Operation Dixie and the Defeat of the CIO* (Philadelphia: Temple University Press, 1988).

Guralnick, Peter: *Last Train to Memphis: The Rise of Elvis Presley* (Boston: Little, Brown, 1994).

Harris, Howell John: *The Right to Manage: Industrial Relations Policies of American Business in the 1940s* (Madison: University of Wisconsin Press, 1982).

Hill, Herbert: "Race, Ethnicity and Organized Labor: The Opposition to Affirmative Action," *New Politics*, 1 (Winter 1987): 31–82.

Honey, Michael K.: *Southern Labor and Black Civil Rights: Organizing Memphis Workers* (Urbana: University of Illinois Press, 1993).

Horowitz, Roger: *"Negro and White, Unite and Fight!" A Social History of Industrial Unionism in Meatpacking, 1930–1990* (Champaign: University of Illinois Press, 1997).

Jacoby, Sanford M.: *Modern Manors: Welfare Capitalism Since the New Deal* (Princeton, NJ: Princeton University Press, 1997).

Jones, William P.: "Black Workers and the CIO's Turn Toward Racial Liberalism: Operation Dixie and the North Carolina Lumber Industry, 1946–1953," *Labor History*, 41 (August 2000): 279–306.

Klare, Karl: "Judicial Deradicalization of the Wagner Act and the Origins of Modern Legal Consciousness," *Minnesota Law Review*, 62 (1978): 265–339.

Korstad, Robert and Lichtenstein, Nelson: "Opportunities Found and Lost: Labor, Radicals, and the Early Civil Rights Movement," *Journal of American History*, 75 (December 1988): 786–811.

Kwong, Peter: *The New Chinatown* (New York: Noonday Press, 1987).

Levenstein, Harvey A.: *Communism, Anticommunism, and the CIO* (Westport, Conn.: Greenwood Press, 1981).

Levy, Peter B.: *The New Left and Labor in the 1960s* (Champaign: University of Illinois Press, 1994).

Lichtenstein, Nelson: *Labor's War at Home: The CIO in World War II* (Cambridge: Cambridge University Press, 1982).

Lichtenstein, Nelson: *The Most Dangerous Man in Detroit: Walter Reuther and the Fate of American Labor* (New York: Basic Books, 1995).

Lichtenstein, Nelson: "American Trade Unions and the 'Labor Question': Past and Present," in Report of the Century Foundation Task Force on the Future of Unions, *What's Next for Organized Labor?* (New York: Century Foundation Press, 1999).

Lichtenstein, Nelson, Strasser, Susan, and Rosenzweig, Roy: *Who Built America? Working People and the Nation's Economy, Politics, Culture and Society.* Vol. 2: *Since 1877* (New York: Worth Publishers, 2000).

Lipsitz, George: *Rainbow at Midnight: Labor and Culture in the 1940s* (Champaign: University of Illinois Press, 1994).

Maier, Mark H.: *City Unions: Managing Discontent in New York City* (New Brunswick, NJ: Rutgers University Press, 1987).

Metzgar, Jack: *Striking Steel, Solidarity Remembered* (Philadelphia: Temple University Press, 2000).

Milkman, Ruth: *Farewell to the Factory: Auto Workers in the Late Twentieth Century* (Berkeley: University of California Press, 1997).

Milkman, Ruth, ed.: *Organizing Immigrants: The Challenge for Unions in Contemporary California* (Ithaca, NY: ILR Press, 2000).

Miller, James: *"Democracy is in the Streets": From Port Huron to the Siege of Chicago* (New York: Simon and Schuster, 1987).

Mills, C. Wright: *White Collar* (New York: Oxford University Press, 1951).

Minchin, Timothy J.: *What Do We Need a Union For? The TWUA in the South, 1945–1955* (Chapel Hill: University of North Carolina Press, 1997).

Mishel, Lawrence, Bernstein, Jared, and Schmitt, John: *The State of Working America 2000/2001* (Ithaca, NY: Cornell University Press, 2001).

Montgomery, David: *Workers' Control in America* (Cambridge: Cambridge University Press, 1979).

Moody, Kim: *An Injury to All: The Decline of American Unionism* (London: Verso, 1986).

Murphy, Marjorie: *Blackboard Unions: The AFT and the NEA, 1900–1980* (Ithaca, NY: Cornell University Press, 1990).

Nelson, Bruce: *Divided We Stand: American Workers and the Struggle for Black Equality* (Princeton, NJ: Princeton University Press, 2001).

Rogovin, Milton and Frisch, Michael: *Portraits in Steel* (Ithaca, NY: Cornell University Press, 1993).

Rosenblum, Jonathan D.: *Copper Crucible: How the Arizona Miners' Strike of 1983 Recast Labor–Management Relations in America* (Ithaca, NY: ILR Press, 1995).

Rosswurm, Steve, ed.: *The CIO's Left-Led Unions* (New Brunswick, NJ: Rutgers University Press, 1992).

Russell, Thaddeus: *Out of the Jungle: Jimmy Hoffa and the Remaking of the American Working Class* (New York: Alfred A. Knopf, 2001).

Schatz, Ronald W.: *The Electrical Workers: A History of Labor at General Electric and Westinghouse, 1923–1960* (Urbana: University of Illinois Press, 1983).

Schor, Juliet B.: *The Overworked American: The Unexpected Decline of Leisure* (New York: Basic Books, 1991).

Serrin, William: *Homestead: The Glory and Tragedy of an American Steel Town* (New York: Times Books, 1992).

Silverman, Victor: *Imagining Internationalism in American and British Labor, 1939–1949* (Urbana: University of Illinois Press, 2000).

Stebenne, David L.: *Arthur J. Goldberg: New Deal Liberal* (New York: Oxford University Press, 1996).

Stein, Judith: *Running Steel, Running America: Race, Economic Policy, and the Decline of Liberalism* (Chapel Hill: University of North Carolina Press, 1998).

Stone, Katherine Van Wezel: "The Post-War Paradigm in American Labor Law," *Yale Labor Journal*, 90 (June 1981): 1509–80.

Sugrue, Thomas J.: *The Origins of the Urban Crisis: Race and Inequality in Postwar Detroit* (Princeton, NJ: Princeton University Press, 1996).

Tomlins, Christopher L.: *The State and the Unions: Labor Relations, Law, and the Organized Labor Movement in America, 1880–1960* (Cambridge: Cambridge University Press, 1985).

US Bureau of the Census: *Historical Statistics of the United States, Colonial Times to 1970*, electronic ed. (New York: Cambridge University Press, 1977).

Wilson, Joseph E.: *Tearing Down the Color Bar: A Documentary History and Analysis of the Brotherhood of Sleeping Car Porters* (New York: Columbia University Press, 1989).

Zieger, Robert H.: *The CIO, 1935–1955* (Chapel Hill: University of North Carolina Press, 1995).

Zweig, Michael: *The Working-Class Majority: America's Best Kept Secret* (Ithaca, NY: ILR Press, 2000).

FURTHER READING

Dubofsky, Melvyn: *The State and Labor in Modern America* (Chapel Hill: University of North Carolina Press, 1994).

Fink, Leon and Greenberg, Brian: *Upheaval in the Quiet Zone: A History of Hospital Workers' Union Local 1199* (Urbana: University of Illinois Press, 1989).

Gabin, Nancy Felice: *Feminism in the Labor Movement: Women and the United Automobile Workers, 1935–1975* (Ithaca, NY: Cornell University Press, 1990).

Gerstle, Gary: *Working-Class Americanism: The Politics of Labor in a Textile City, 1914–1960* (Cambridge: Cambridge University Press, 1989).

Gregory, James N.: "Southernizing the American Working Class: Post-War Episodes of Regional and Class Transformation," *Labor History*, 39 (May 1998): 135–54.

Gross, James A.: *Broken Promise: The Subversion of U.S. Labor Relations Policy, 1947–1994* (Philadelphia: Temple University Press, 1995).

Halle, David: *America's Working Man: Work, Home, and Politics Among Blue-Collar Property Owners* (Chicago: University of Chicago Press, 1984).

Halpern, Rick: *Down on the Killing Floor: Black and White Workers in Chicago's Packinghouses, 1905–1954* (Urbana: University of Illinois Press, 1997).

Hamper, Ben: *Rivethead: Tales from the Assembly Line* (New York: Warner Books, 1991).

Hochschild, Arlie Russell: *The Time Bind: When Work Becomes Home and Home Becomes Business* (New York: Metropolitan Books, 1991).

Hunnicutt, Benjamin Kline: *Work Without End: Abandoning Shorter Hours for the Right to Work* (Philadelphia: Temple University Press, 1988).

Linder, Marc: *Wars of Attrition: Vietnam, the Business Roundtable, and the Decline of Construction Unions* (Iowa City: Fanpihua Press, 1999).

McColloch, Mark: *White Collar Workers in Transition: The Boom Years, 1940–1970* (Westport, Conn.: Greenwood Press, 1983).

Mills, C. Wright: *The New Men of Power: America's Labor Leaders* (New York: Harcourt Brace, 1948).

Sweeney, John J.: *America Needs a Raise: Fighting for Economic Security and Social Justice* (Boston: Houghton Mifflin, 1986).

Walkowitz, Daniel J.: *Working With Class: Social Workers and the Politics of Middle-Class Identity* (Chapel Hill: University of North Carolina Press, 1999).

CHAPTER TWELVE

The Historiography of the Struggle for Black Equality Since 1945

KEVIN GAINES

At the dawn of the twenty-first century, there can be little argument that while the historical study of the black freedom struggle has flourished over the past two decades, the moral authority of the cause of racial justice has been eroded by the ascendancy of the political right. An enumeration of conservative attempts to dismantle the movement's achievements of voting rights, anti-discrimination laws, and affirmative action over the past three decades would require many more pages than this essay contains (Franklin, 1993; Berry, 1994; Guinier, 1998). During the 1990s, historians have fared badly in the national debate over the meaning and legacy of the movement; the best of their work has been drowned out by the inflammatory sound-bites of conservative politicians and pundits. The disfranchisement of thousands of African American voters in Florida in the presidential election of 2000 is only the most recent blow against the legacy of the postwar freedom movement. Issues of voting rights and democracy were slighted by the mass media, which covered the deadlocked election primarily as a matter for adjudication in the courts. It remained for the National Association for the Advancement of Colored People (NAACP), movement veterans, and historians to break this silence, situating this violation of the Voting Rights Act in the context of the South's disfranchisement of blacks and poor whites a century ago. That the majority of Americans have evidently reconciled themselves to such a patently undemocratic electoral process and outcome signals the triumph of conservative revisionists whose skillful merger of racial symbolism and the myth of a colorblind society has compelled historians of the civil rights movement to set the record straight.

Before conservative pundits raised the stakes by hijacking the national discourse on civil rights, the dispute over the interpretation of the movement pitted liberal historians against their radical counterparts. In 1988, Julian Bond criticized what he regarded as the reigning liberal interpretation of the movement. Speaking as both historian and a participant in the Student Nonviolent Coordinating Committee's (SNCC) voting rights campaigns, and referring specifically to the work of Allen Matusow, Bond disputed the tendency to blame SNCC activists for giving up on American liberalism and for their embrace of racial and revolutionary nationalism. In Bond's view, "[w]e didn't abandon liberalism; liberals abandoned [SNCC]." When civil rights and Democratic Party leadership closed ranks at the 1964 Democratic Convention against SNCC's attempt to unseat the all-white Mississippi delegation,

SNCC's already strained relationship with liberalism soured irreparably (Robinson and Sullivan, 1991, pp. 8–9). Bond criticized top-down, elite-centered accounts preoccupied with the collapse of what was considered the triumphant southern phase of the movement. These accounts were silent on the role of SNCC and the movement's antecedents, specifically the role of left-wing groups, including the Communist Party. For Bond, the community forged by SNCC organizers and local people in the lower South warranted further study. He hoped that future scholars would display more interest in the movement's genesis than its demise.

It is sobering to consider Bond's remarks in the aftermath of the Florida debacle. Recent history and historical analyses alike have underscored Bond's view of the betrayal of American liberalism. Experience had taught Bond and his generation of activists that African Americans could not rely on American liberalism and federalism for redress of even the most egregious violations of their rights. Bond's conclusion then (and one inescapable for us today) was that the impetus for democratic change had come principally from the movement itself, from those at the margins of American society who mobilized against the nation's indifference to their plight; hence his call for more study of the contributions of the political left and his interest in the secular and religious circumstances that helped sustain a utopian community of resistance against terrifying odds.

As Bond voiced these views in 1988 in the teeth of the Reagan administration's anti-black agenda and rhetoric (Franklin, 1993) as well as a disturbing increase in incidents of campus racism, other scholars would share Bond's impatience with top-down, legalistic approaches to the movement (Payne, 1995). Central to this prevailing narrative were the responses of the Eisenhower, Kennedy, and Johnson administrations to racial crises, culminating in the passage of the Civil Rights and Voting Rights Acts (Meier and Rudwick, 1973; Brauer, 1977; Burk, 1984). For such scholars as Allen J. Matusow (1984), and later Robert Weisbrot (1990), the unraveling of the liberal consensus for civil rights was attributable to the divisive rhetoric of black militants.

Successive waves of revisionist historians, many of whom came of age during the 1960s, and including a younger generation of scholars radicalized by the unabashed racial retrenchment of the Reagan–Bush era, challenged many of the assumptions of this narrative of liberal good will betrayed by black militancy. Much of the recent scholarship on the movement rejects such triumphalism, doing so in the spirit of Justice Thurgood Marshall's 1987 speech on the occasion of the bicentennial of the Constitution. Marshall punctured the celebratory mood of tributes to the Framers' genius by reminding the nation that the Founding Fathers had produced a "defective" document that had compromised with slavery, "requiring several amendments, a civil war, and momentous social transformation to attain the system of constitutional government, and its respect for the individual freedoms and human rights, we hold as fundamental today." One imagines that if Marshall had witnessed the electoral fraud in Florida, he, too, would have spoken out against the threat it posed to those freedoms and rights. Evidently those freedoms were less cherished than he supposed, certainly among the conservative majority on the Court that handed the Oval Office to George W. Bush.

Having as little patience for liberal triumphalism as Marshall, scholars revising both liberal interpretations and conservative distortions of them have produced narratives structured by the rise and fall of black and interracial movements and projects. Many of these new studies seek to place persistent inequality and continuing attacks on the rights of minorities in historical perspective, and to recover the movement's most far-reaching political and economic challenges to American society. Taken together, these studies have given us a more comprehensive vision of the postwar African American freedom movement, encompassing the North as well as the South, calling into question assumptions about periodization, and exploring the relationship between radical ideologies and agendas and those of civil rights liberalism. Moreover, acknowledging the coexistence of movements for African American and women's rights, scholars have recently incorporated gender and sexuality as important modes of inquiry, fundamentally transforming our understanding of movements, organizational behavior, and leadership. The interest in gender politics has challenged male-centered accounts and granted long-overdue recognition to the contributions of black women to the movement. At the same time, gender analyses have focused attention on the movement's internal tensions. No longer can scholars ignore the gendered aspects of oppression and resistance.

Given their engagement with the ongoing political and ideological struggles over civil rights, academic historians have been participant observers whose research has often been inseparable from the movement and its legacy. To study the movement for black equality, then, is to study the ways in which movement participants and their intellectual allies (including historians), policymakers, and opponents of civil rights employed competing visions of the history of race in America. While the participants may change, the contest within the courts, the mass media, and the academy over the meaning of the racial past and future, as analysis of the complicated racial demographics of the 2000 census proceeds, remains fundamental to American political culture.

With this in mind, I will examine some of the major interpretive trends in the study of the modern black struggle for equality in five interrelated areas. First and foremost, recent scholarship has foregrounded black agency and autonomy, disclosing the movement's foundations in a tradition of African American resistance dating from Reconstruction onward. Second, this recovery of black agency has led scholars to examine the movement's antecedents in the New Deal, liberal–left coalition from the 1930s to World War II, within which the labor movement provided an important social base for civil rights activism. Third, following the spate of studies of the movement and its leadership at the level of national politics, scholars have turned their attention to local and rural sites of the movement, emphasizing the struggle for voting rights and bottom-up organizing for black empowerment. Fourth, scholars have recently explored the international dimensions of the movement. Here, seemingly disparate local and international perspectives have merged in some scholars' accounts of the movement. Indeed, the studies discussed in this section stress the interconnectedness in the minds of movement activists between local, national, and international settings.

Finally, surely some of Julian Bond's misgivings about the field as he saw it stemmed from the absence, despite the proliferation of studies, of the rich milieu of black scholarship and activism that he had known as the son of the social science scholar and president of Lincoln University, Horace Mann Bond. Revisionist writers in the spirit of Bond's challenge have begun to mine the analytical contributions of an earlier generation of pioneering Black Studies intellectuals that were instrumental to freedom struggles. Indeed, these scholars' and creative writers' critiques of liberalism in the urban North during the 1940s and 1950s, along with their indictments of a reactionary segregated South, anticipated certain aspects of the Black Power phase of the movement.

From the Nadir of Segregation and Disfranchisement to the Second Reconstruction

It is impossible to do justice to the reflexive character of historical writing on the postwar movement without reference to the longer history of racial subordination in the South. During the 1960s, the historian C. Vann Woodward termed the modern civil rights movement the Second Reconstruction, noting that its reforms had restored the first Reconstruction's short-lived commitment to voting rights and full national citizenship for African Americans. As a national policy, Reconstruction had ended with the Republicans' withdrawal of federal troops from the South in 1877 as part of the settlement of the disputed presidential election of the previous year. Southern authorities resorted to violence and election fraud to elect Democrats hostile to African American rights throughout the region. The democratic potential of Reconstruction persisted, however, in biracial coalitions of Republicans and Populists, who throughout the 1880s and 1890s achieved electoral successes by promoting an economic agenda responsive to impoverished tenant farmers. The region's ruling class and their political allies put an end to this challenge by disfranchising African Americans through appeals to white supremacy. But the disfranchisement amendments to state constitutions throughout the South between 1890 and 1906 also deprived many poor whites of the vote as well, consolidating the hegemony of powerful whites.

The historian Rayford Logan certainly had disfranchisement in mind in the 1950s when, following the crushing defeat of the wartime struggles for equality, he referred to the post-Reconstruction period as the nadir, or lowest point, of African American history. Logan's term encapsulated the brutal system of racial domination that followed Reconstruction's demise. That system was characterized by disfranchisement, legal segregation, and the widespread practice of lynching – the mob execution of African Americans in absence of the rule of law. Segregation, or its informal designation Jim Crow, described a network of state and local ordinances enforcing strict separation of blacks and whites in all spheres of public life, including schools, restaurants, movie theaters, public restrooms, and even cemeteries. Jim Crow constituted a total system of political, economic, and social domination. Under it, African Americans labored on plantations or in white households under conditions not far removed from slavery. In the South, the courts, juries, and police were controlled by powerful whites, maintaining the racial and economic status quo. To be sure, the North had its own history of racial subordination dating back to the transplanting of Africans as slaves in the colonial period. But by the late nineteenth century, while blacks in the North were plagued by racial and economic discrimination, prohibitions on rights were not as comprehensive, nor as deadly, as in the South.

The legal restrictions on blacks' access to public accommodations were only part of the system of Jim Crow; its endemic violence shadowed the psyches of blacks as well. Under segregation, the white South devised elaborate and mandatory rituals of racial deference to eradicate the spirit of freedom exhibited by blacks during Reconstruction. Terror was intrinsic to the system. The ghastly institution of lynching was the ultimate expression of white dominance. From the 1880s until 1964, it is estimated that almost 5,000 blacks died by mob violence, the overwhelming majority of those deaths occurring in the South. As if to obscure the lynching campaign's political motivation, the white South rationalized its violence by projecting its own history of sexual misconduct onto black men. Statutes outlawing marriage between blacks and whites throughout the South bolstered both lynching and concubinage, the practice by which many white men claimed the rape of black women and girls as their birthright.

In 1896, when the Supreme Court held in *Plessy v. Ferguson* that state laws mandating segregation were "separate but equal" and thus constitutional, nine out of ten African Americans lived in the South. At its height, from the 1890s to 1964, the system of Jim Crow segregation exercised such total dominion over African Americans that for many years their only recourse was migration from the rural South, where poverty and repression were most severe. At the dawn of the modern civil rights movement during the 1950s, it remained for the one half of the nation's population of 15 million African Americans still residing in the South to help usher in the Second Reconstruction that would restore the constitutionally sanctioned citizenship and voting rights destroyed under Jim Crow.

As an illustration of the inseparability of scholarship and activism, W. E. B. Du Bois's landmark study *Black Reconstruction in America* (1935) gave an eloquent defense of African American political participation, challenging the dominant accounts of pro-southern apologists, who, in scapegoating black citizenship, were nakedly propagandizing on behalf of the segregationist status quo. Du Bois's study affirmed the democratic influence of African Americans on southern politics during Reconstruction. While the profession generally dismissed Du Bois's study, a handful of younger historians, including Woodward, communicated their appreciation to its author. While it remained fashionable for consensus historians of the 1950s to disparage the work for its Marxist content, Du Bois had cleared a path not only for the scholarly rehabilitation of Reconstruction by John Hope Franklin and Kenneth Stampp during the 1960s, but also for the subsequent work of Thomas Holt, Nell Irvin Painter, and Eric Foner, all of whom highlighted African American political behavior as central to the era's democratic promise.

Recent studies of the gendered dimension of African American responses to the crisis of Jim Crow have strongly suggested their continuity with modern freedom struggles. As Paula Giddings, Glenda Gilmore, and others have shown, African American women at the turn of the century organized in opposition to racial oppression, their efforts constituting a tradition of struggle linking them to the student sit-in demonstrators who revitalized the movement in 1960. Giddings's groundbreaking work (1984) responded to the lacunae in both African American and women's history that neglected black women's activism. Her work contributed to scholarly investigation of the gender dynamics of the modern freedom movement. Gilmore's work (1996) in particular was informed by some of the innovative work on black resistance to Jim Crow. Gilmore's analysis placed black women suffragists in North Carolina at the vanguard of struggles for equal rights, thereby exposing the limitations of earlier accounts of southern politics that were all too content to exclude marginalized groups who were, in fact, the main catalysts for social transformation.

African American Agency, Black Autonomy, and the Movement

In the 1930s, W. E. B. Du Bois was a lone voice in emphasizing the indispensable contributions of the freedpeople to Reconstruction. Some generations later, with the democratization of the academy after the social movements of the 1960s, Du Bois's vision would be refined by many other scholars. Sociologist Aldon Morris challenged the tendency, even among some progressive scholars, to slight African American agency (Morris, 1984). Against the view of liberal scholars that *Brown* and other external factors initiated the modern civil rights movement, and contrary to radical scholars' claims of the spontaneity of black protest, Morris emphasized "indigenous" organization and the strategic acumen of leadership as enabling the movement to command national attention through disruptive mass protest. Mass mobilization developed within a highly organized, autonomous black public sphere of churches and civil rights organizations, allowing the movement's leadership to draw on a substantial reservoir of spiritual and material resources. Morris argued that the unsuccessful boycott against the segregated bus system in Baton Rouge in 1953 demonstrated that the modern civil rights movement was already underway, predating *Brown*. The ministers who led the Baton Rouge campaign drew up a blueprint that was to be followed by the leaders of the Montgomery bus boycott in 1955. Morris highlighted the sharing of tactical knowledge and resources among civil rights activists in different cities, and the importance of charismatic leadership. At the national level, as well as within the South, black churches were crucial centers for organization and fundraising. The culmination of black churches' involvement was the Birmingham campaign orchestrated by Reverend Martin Luther King and the Southern Christian Leadership Conference (a campaign that captured worldwide attention and compelled a reluctant President Kennedy to endorse sweeping civil rights legislation). In emphasizing the black community's indigenous resources and strategizing, Morris criticized those accounts that focused on external influences and "third parties" (i.e., white liberal support), as well as the federal government, as dominant or determining actors in the movement. By foregrounding black organizational initiative and by calling attention to cross-generational traditions of struggle, Morris laid the foundation for much of what followed in civil rights historiography.

Clayborne Carson's pioneering 1981 study of SNCC inaugurated a deeper interest in the southern radical wing of the movement, based largely in Mississippi, where the forces of white supremacy were arguably the most organized and violent. Carson also redirected attention to the rural sites of movement organizing, challenging the image of the movement as predominantly urban. Where Morris had identified charismatic leadership in the person of King and other ministers as an indigenous asset for the civil rights movement, Carson's SNCC activists saw such charisma as at best double-edged, a power subject to compromise with the establishment, and as a fleeting presence within rural communities continually besieged by segregationist violence. As an alternative to the charisma manifested in the direct action campaigns of King and SCLC, which targeted segregation in selected cities in the hope of amassing public support for federal civil rights legislation, SNCC's grassroots organizing for voting rights sought the direct empowerment of blacks kept at the bottom of southern society. Moreover, a reliance on charismatic leadership clashed with the group-centered leadership philosophy of SNCC and its main exponents, Ella Baker and Robert Moses. In Carson's nuanced account of the demise of SNCC, he argues that the organization's embrace of black separatism pushed aside highly effective women leaders, especially Fannie Lou Hamer and Ruby Doris Robinson. While perhaps inevitable (in the sense that black separatism was imposed on SNCC from the outset, given the totality of white supremacy and racial subordination in Mississippi), the declaration of Black Power displaced SNCC's movement culture, including its Freedom songs, which had been vital in forging community and helping conquer the fear generated by white violence. While Carson's critique was more balanced than most, more sympathetic appraisals of Black Power would have to await scholarly inquiry into northern sites of movement activism.

Labor, the Left, and African American Traditions of Resistance

Aldon Morris's and Clayborne Carson's emphasis on group-centered leadership and rural activism sparked further investigation of traditions of black resistance. Their interest in black agency and the search for pre-*Brown* origins also led to influential work locating the southern movement's beginnings in the progressive liberal–left alliances of the Depression era and World War II. A host of community studies of black politics, including those by Mark Naison (1983), Cheryl Greenberg (1991), Joe William Trotter (1985), and Earl Lewis (1991), rooted black activism in the urban migrations of black working people and their encounters with labor and the left. Many of these studies also highlighted community traditions of independent black politics dating back to Reconstruction. In these traditions of resistance scholars found a precedent for some of the initiatives in the 1930s against lynching and unemployment, including the "don't buy where you can't work" boycotts. The popularity of economic nationalism among African Americans during the Depression enhanced the appeal of trade unions and other left-wing organizations, including the Communist Party, as organizational vessels for African Americans' ongoing agitation for racial and economic justice.

A productive tension developed between these seemingly disparate historical approaches emphasizing either internal or external factors within the study of black activism. The role of organized black workers as harbingers of the southern civil rights movement raised further questions about a black working-class consciousness that predated organizational activity. Precisely who were these people who eventually joined the NAACP, or such working-class organizations as unions and the Communist Party? What cultural practices, family histories, and memories of resistance did working-class African Americans bring with them into these organizations? An emerging synthesis merged community-based studies of the movement, scholarship on the roots of civil rights struggles in the campaigns of black workers and biracial unionism, and careful attention to the historical, cultural, and religious background that informed African American workers' activism (Kelley, 1990; Honey, 1993).

Perhaps reflecting Cold War protocols, most previous scholarship on the movement had devoted cursory attention, if any, to the left and the Communist Party. Or, on those rare occasions when scholars examined the relationship between civil rights and communism, they were unable to imagine African Americans with left-wing affinities as anything but the factotums of world communism (Record, 1951; Cruse, 1967). Such disregard for black agency and the totality of black struggles ensured their misrepresentation or erasure.

Moving beyond a Cold War mindset blind to the autonomy of black activism, Robin D. G. Kelley's study of the Communist Party in Alabama before the Depression demonstrated that the unlettered black working people who joined the party in Alabama brought with them their own histories and cultural practices of resistance. Kelley explored "a culture that enveloped and transformed the Party into a movement more reflective of African American radical traditions than anything else" (Kelley, 1990, p. 99). Kelley noted the divergence between the left literati, the party's proletarian writers whose stories depicted heroic workers in violent showdowns against anti-labor forces, and those pragmatic black communists in Alabama for whom guile and the evasive ways of trickster figures were essential survival tactics against potentially violent adversaries. Similarly, black communists cleaved to African American folk religion, updating traditional church hymns with radical lyrics in a synthesis far more relevant to their lives than party doctrine. Devout black communists thus inhabited an entirely different world than radical musicologists who were determined to extract secular "complaining" folk blues songs from black informants, not to mention those noncommunist black migrants to such northern cities as Detroit or Cleveland who were moved to save memorable editions of the *Daily Worker* or any encouraging news items from the black press. (My grandmother, whose family migrated to Cleveland from Birmingham in the 1940s, preserved several clippings, one of which exulted, upon the demise of the arch-segregationist Mississippi senator, BILBO DEAD!)

In acknowledging the contribution of the left, including such progressive organizations as the Southern Negro Youth Congress (SNYC), in paving the way for subsequent struggles for civil rights, Kelley linked these organizations to an indigenous black culture of resistance dating back to Reconstruction. Kelley's subsequent work drew on the political scientist James Scott's notion of infrapolitics, through which Kelley characterized black working-class resistance in Birmingham since World War II as a hidden transcript of subaltern consciousness that motivated working-class African Americans' sporadic acts of protest. Regardless of whether it dealt with blacks within or outside such organizations as unions or the Communist Party, the concept of infrapolitics brought the matter of black agency to the fore (Kelley, 1994). Kelley's analysis of the ways in which black subjects remade putatively nonblack organizations in their own image was an invaluable advance beyond the simplistic and falsely racialized dichotomy of nationalism versus integration that hobbled both liberal and black nationalist accounts of the movement (Cruse, 1967; Weisbrot, 1990).

Along with Kelley, other scholars working at the crossroads of labor, southern, and African American history were exploring the roots of black struggles in the labor movement. In the late 1980s, Robert Korstad and Nelson Lichtenstein identified the urbanization of black America during the 1940s as the catalyst for the modern civil rights era. Sparked by wartime labor demands, the migration of over 2 million blacks to northern and western cities, and approximately 1 million from farms to cities within the South, fostered a group commitment to channel increased voting strength into demands for equal rights. Within the South the number of black reg-istered voters quadrupled, and membership in the NAACP skyrocketed, growing from 50,000 in 1940 to almost 450,000 in 1946. Drawing on research on urban-ization, voting rights, and labor relations with the federal government, Korstad and Lichtenstein (1988) located black workers in the Congress of Industrial Organiza-tions (CIO) at the vanguard of this early civil rights activism. Members of the alliance between labor unions and civil rights organizations had seized the opening provided by pro-labor New Deal legislation. Led by A. Philip Randolph's March on Wash-ington Movement, black workers had applied the political leverage that elicited Pres-ident Franklin D. Roosevelt's Executive Order 8802 in 1941 calling for fair employment in war industries. But the conservative limits of federalism compelled exponents of this "workplace-oriented civil rights militancy" to push for racial justice against the government's failure to endow the Fair Employment Practices Committee (FEPC) with enforcement powers. Here, as was the case after *Brown*, black activists would bear the burden of implementing the government's anti-discrimination policies.

Korstad and Lichtenstein focused on two local union-based struggles for economic and racial justice, waged by tobacco workers in Winston-Salem, North Carolina, and members of the United Auto Workers (UAW) in Detroit. Just as the war galvanized black aspirations nationwide, so it fostered among Winston-Salem's black workers an expansive vision of struggle that extended beyond workplace issues to voter registration campaigns. Local initiatives produced the election of congressional and local representatives sympathetic to labor and civil rights causes, and the first black city official to be elected against a white opponent in the twentieth-century South. In Detroit, black members of the UAW Local 600 in the River Rouge Ford plant demanded more defense jobs. In 1942, they also defended black occupants of the federal housing facility, the Sojourner Truth Homes, against violent white opposition to integrated housing. Their numbers also swelled the ranks of the Detroit NAACP. After the war, black working-class insurgency was silenced by anti-communist purges, and the adoption by unions and civil rights organizations of a bureaucratic, or legal-administrative civil rights strategy. Korstad and Lichtenstein thus imagined an alternative, counterfactual course for the civil rights movement, an economic agenda linking both the North and South that might have spared the nation the chaos of urban rebellions and the controversy over the domestic war on poverty, whose cost was minuscule compared to the wasteful and catastrophic war in Vietnam. The authors noted that when Martin Luther King and others confronted the issue of economic inequality after 1965, they "were handicapped by their inabil-ity to seize the opportunities of a very different sort of civil rights movement found and lost twenty years before" (Korstad and Lichtenstein, 1988, p. 811).

The result of this work, taken together, was an account of a movement with deeper roots in traditional subcultures of African American resistance and white southern radicalism. In another synthesizing move, Patricia Sullivan highlighted the interac-tion between federal policy and movement activism in her account of the origins of the southern movement (Sullivan, 1996). For Sullivan, the crisis of the Depression and the New Deal's federal relief programs created a wedge against southern states' rights ideology. New Deal pro-labor policies energized southern liberals, and fostered a movement culture of progressive whites and black activists determined to extend the federal government's involvement in the region's economy to a more explicit commitment to civil rights. From the 1930s through the wartime years, progressives and liberals targeted the system of disfranchisement, the denial of voting rights to most blacks and many poor whites, as the bulwark of the economic exploitation of the South's black and white workers. The removal of suffrage restrictions, activists contended, coupled with voter education and registration campaigns, would revolutionize southern economic relationships, replacing conservative officials with representatives sympathetic to organized labor and New Deal reforms. New Deal labor-organizing drives, the democratic ideology of World War II, and such legal victories as *Smith v. Allwright* (1944), in which the Supreme Court declared unconstitutional the whites-only primary election for statewide office, lent momentum to this early incarnation of the southern movement.

By granting voting rights a central place in her narrative, Sullivan illustrated the continuities linking activism in the 1940s with the post-Montgomery movement that had been obscured by *Brown*-centered accounts. In 1944, the South Carolina Progressive Democratic Party elected its own slate of delegates to the Democratic National Convention in a challenge to disfranchisement and that state's all-white delegation. Although it failed, this unprecedented challenge to the national Democratic Party's collusion with Jim Crow was a strategy revisited by SNCC at the 1964 Convention. The guiding wisdom of Ella Baker was evident across generations of struggle. SNCC organizers embraced Baker's group-centered leadership philosophy in their voter registration campaigns. Years before, in 1946, Baker had led an NAACP leadership training workshop that numbered Rosa Parks and E. D. Nixon (known for their involvement in the Montgomery movement in 1955) as participants. Nixon, a Pullman Porter, had become politically active during the New Deal, and during the 1940s led abortive voting rights marches to the Alabama board of registrars (Payne, 1995). Such continuities of struggle remain, however, part of a larger story of the adaptability of white racial hegemony and the fleeting nature of black progress.

With the advent of the Cold War, segregationists regained the upper hand, as the wartime rhetoric of racial inclusion was quickly discarded. The white South added anti-communist hysteria to its litany of racial and sexual epithets and taboos invoked to justify its violent defense of white supremacy. Sullivan concludes with the image of Progressive Party nominee Henry Wallace attempting to shout down hate-filled and menacing crowds while touring the South during his campaign for the presidency in 1948. Despite Truman's verbal support for a civil rights platform in the 1948 presidential campaign, the postwar demands for voting rights raised by African American war veterans and others were thwarted in these years by the white South's own tradition of violence, this time bolstered, in part, by Truman's anti-communism.

International Perspectives on the Movement

Like the interpretation of Korstad and Lichtenstein, Sullivan's work suggests that the Cold War was a major watershed. More than a devastating blow to the movement's labor–left alliance, Cold War anti-communism imposed limits on much of the subsequent language and tactics of civil rights politics. Indeed, by writing against the prevailing Cold War logic, Patricia Sullivan and others revealed the limitations of viewing the movement solely within a liberal or "domestic" analytical frame. The exclusion of left-wing influences impoverished our understanding of not only the movement itself, but the character of American liberalism as well. With recent studies placing African American civil rights struggles in the context of international relations and the Cold War, including those of Gerald Horne (1986), Brenda Gayle Plummer (1996), Penny Von Eschen (1997), and Mary Dudziak (2000), we have a better understanding of black activism, North and South, within the global developments of the Cold War and the decolonization of Asia and Africa.

In her study of the intersections of anti-colonialism, the struggle for civil rights, and the Cold War, Penny Von Eschen vividly recaptured the internationalism that shaped black public culture during the 1940s (Von Eschen, 1997). African American newspapers avidly reported the wartime collapse of European empires and campaigned for victory against Jim Crow in the United States as they supported the allies' struggle against fascism overseas. In addition to a thriving black press, a host of middle-class black institutions, from churches, college fraternities and sororities, and civil rights organizations, supported the cause of African independence. Readers of the nationally circulated *Pittsburgh Courier* and the *Chicago Defender*, as well as a substantial segment of black leadership, were conversant with "the politics of the black diaspora," characterized by the wartime linkage of African and African Americans' movements for freedom. The leading exponent of this politics was the Council on African Affairs (CAA), a lobby publicizing colonial conditions, headed by the renowned singer and actor Paul Robeson, the doyen of black intellectuals W. E. B. Du Bois, and the scholar and activist Alphaeus Hunton. Members of the CAA also included such prominent liberals as Mary McLeod Bethune, president of the National Council of Negro Women, and Walter White, executive director of the NAACP.

This diverse association of independent black radicals and civil rights liberals under the banner of anti-colonialism and desegregation collided head-on with the Cold War, which drastically altered the terms and tactics of civil rights activism. The CAA became a casualty of Cold War repression, which ostensibly targeted communists and their sympathizers, but which had an equally chilling effect on dissent in all forms, even from liberal quarters. Yet it was not anti-communism, per se, that explained the crackdown on the CAA. Rather, that organization and its leaders were targeted for linking US struggles against lynching and Jim Crow to the plight of darker peoples worldwide, an anti-imperialist, anti-capitalist vision that not only challenged the legitimacy of the United States, but also demanded economic and political democracy in America and abroad. Even the fervently anti-communist Richard Wright found that his support for anti-colonial movements, and his similar criticisms of the United States from self-imposed exile in France, made him an enemy of the US state. Paul Robeson had his passport revoked by the State Department, denying him the international forums from which he might have protested ongoing practices of lynching and disfranchisement. To shield the NAACP, and especially the Legal Defense Fund's assault on "separate but equal," from official suspicion, Walter White abandoned the linkage of civil rights to African independence and cleansed the NAACP of such potentially damaging radical voices as Du Bois. In this bulldozed ideological landscape, all that remained was a liberal argument that advocated civil rights reform to rid the nation of the "Achilles heel" of racial segregation that undermined America's claim to leadership of the "Free World." In hoping to bend the repressive situation to their advantage, White and other African American liberals were important architects of

Cold War liberalism. Thus the scholarly emphasis on internationalism highlights the initiative of black protest, including black radicalism, as the catalyst for an essentially reactive, though no less hegemonic, US policy (Von Eschen, 1997; Dudziak, 2000).

The consequences of the Cold War era dismantling of a black radical democratic movement were profound, entrenching the movement's subsequent reluctance to broach issues of economic inequality. That decisive turn of events, coupled with persistent poverty in the urban North exacerbated by deindustrialization and residential segregation, provides an important context, as well, for understanding the urban rebellions of the 1960s.

"Local People" on the National and Global Stage

Several important studies of the desegregation campaigns in local communities, including those by William Chafe (1980) and Robert Norrell (1985), have challenged the grand national narratives of consensus for civil rights, producing a clouded picture of uneven successes, protracted struggles, and the persistence of racism. These studies, along with Carson's work on SNCC, paved the way for work on the local sites of the Mississippi movement that foregrounded voting rights as a direct challenge to Jim Crow. Much of this work was guided by the view that movements predated and created leadership. In addition, the turn away from an emphasis on elite, national leadership and anti-discrimination campaigns, and toward the study of grassroots activism and struggles for voting rights in rural locations, opened up the question of the movement's gender politics. This scholarship raised the long-submerged issue of sexism in the movement, including the male monopoly on leadership and the consignment of women to the invisible labor of clerical work, organizing, and fundraising. That said, this reappraisal of the movement framed by issues of gender has yielded revealing studies of such important and resourceful women leaders as Fannie Lou Hamer, Ella Baker, and Ruby Doris Robinson (Crawford et al., 1993; Lee, 1999). Along with the emphasis on group-centered leadership, the study of the movement's gender politics has challenged the messianism of male-centered narratives that blinded earlier scholars and potential activists to the movement's diversity and egalitarian promise.

For historians earning their doctorates during the 1980s as attacks on civil rights and the welfare state increasingly scapegoated black women, an analysis of the gender contradictions within the freedom movement was essential. In addition, the Reagan–Bush administrations promoted powerful black conservatives disdainful of the movement's achievements (exemplified by Supreme Court Justice Clarence Thomas), and encouraged the divisive conservative rhetoric on race, poverty, and civil rights entering the 1990s, epitomized by Clint Bolick, Dinesh D'Souza, and Stephen and Abigail Thernstrom. Undoubtedly, these polarizing trends informed efforts by Charles Payne, John Dittmer, Vincent Harding, and other revisionist historians to display the movement's moral and political achievements, and universal humanism. Reminding readers of the extraordinary courage with which organizers and local people confronted mortal danger, these historians explored the dynamic relationship between structural, historical, and subjective factors that made numbers of individuals "ready to move" in the face of white terror and intimidation and in defiance of calls from federal authorities and some local black leaders to "go slow."

The confluence of domestic and global affairs in the Montgomery movement, the Little Rock school desegregation crisis, and the independence of several African nations helped spark an act of protest that galvanized black college students throughout the South. On February 1, 1960, four freshmen at North Carolina A&T college in Greensboro, North Carolina, demanded service at the whites-only Woolworth's lunch counter. At Woolworth's blacks could purchase the dime store's merchandise, but were refused service at lunch counters. The students were not served and stayed until closing. Word of this and subsequent protests rapidly spread to black colleges throughout the South, generating hundreds of similar protests against segregated public facilities in southern cities involving over 70,000 students over the next year and a half. In that period over 3,000 were arrested. Prompted by this upsurge in student militancy, Ella Baker, then executive director of SCLC, convened a conference in April 1960 in Raleigh, North Carolina, to aid students in planning future efforts. In the early issues of SNCC's newspaper, the *Student Voice*, young activists linked their demand for an end to segregation to African independence with the mordant observation that Africans would be free before African Americans could have a cup of coffee downtown.

SNCC's involvement with the voting rights struggles of Mississippi sharecroppers and domestic workers was not the inevitable outcome of the student sit-in movement that gave rise to the organization. SNCC's attempts to persuade local people to challenge the system of disfranchisement were guided by activists involved in the voting rights campaigns of the previous generation. Such veteran activists as Mrs. Baker, and Mississippi NAACP leaders Aaron Henry and Medgar Evers, provided indispensable assistance to SNCC's young organizers. Political self-interest lay behind the Kennedy administration's pledge of funds for SNCC, as it preferred behind-the-scenes voter education efforts to direct action protests certain to culminate in mob violence. By supporting SNCC's local organizing, the administration hoped to minimize embarrassing international press coverage of such demonstrations as the Freedom Rides. In 1961, an integrated group of Congress of Racial Equality (CORE) activists staged a bus tour through the South to test a recent federal law desegregating interstate transportation facilities. In Alabama, one of the buses used by the activists was bombed and disabled; later, in Birmingham and Montgomery, riders were attacked and viciously beaten by white vigilantes in collusion with local police.

As Mary Dudziak (2000) has shown, US authorities were acutely sensitive to the adverse effect of racial crises on world opinion. When authorities in Birmingham resorted to the use of water cannon and attack dogs against demonstrators, indignation at home and abroad led Kennedy to champion civil rights reform in a televised address from the Oval Office. Secretary of State Dean Rusk became a leading supporter for civil rights legislation. Yet the patience of SNCC organizers was wearing thin. If anything, the work of Carson (1981), Charles Payne (1995), John Dittmer (1995), Chana Lee (1999), and others shows that historiographical attention to local struggles illuminates the ambiguous (to put it mildly) role of the federal government, specifically, the Kennedy Justice Department's reluctance to commit federal power to the protection of movement organizers or to prosecution of known perpetrators of violence. With the federal government's failure to provide solace to organizers, one can scarcely wonder why local activists embraced internationalism as a balm for their sense of abandonment. As Dittmer and others have shown, this had been the case for some time. Black World War II veterans like Evers had been at the vanguard of voting rights challenges during the late 1940s, seeking to enact at home the global ideals of democracy. Trying to revitalize movement activity as field secretary of the NAACP in Mississippi at the height of massive resistance in the 1950s, Evers (who was slain the day after Kennedy's speech) was sufficiently inspired by the armed struggle of Kenyan nationalists to mull over the prospects of armed self-defense during the lonely struggles of the 1950s against segregationists' reprisals (Dittmer, 1995).

For local people and organizers who bore the brunt of segregationist terror, self-protection militated against their professed commitment to nonviolence. Tim Tyson's work on the Monroe, North Carolina, NAACP leader Robert Williams sheds light on an important yet neglected strain of black leadership, and further illustrates the continuum between the local and the international. Williams, an ex-serviceman who had revived his town's moribund NAACP chapter by organizing an all-black militia to defend the community against Ku Klux Klan raids, was suspended by the NAACP for a statement threatening black retaliation against unpunished white assaults. Williams's ideology of armed self-defense, Tyson argues, was an amalgam of his family's history of armed resistance dating back to Reconstruction, with additional inspiration drawn from anti-colonial and third world revolutions of the day. Williams received material assistance, including guns, from northern black militants who supported Williams in his debate with Martin Luther King over the merits of non-violence. Through Williams, who made speaking and fundraising appearances at a number of northern college campuses, one can discern a connection between the northern and southern movements that warrants further exploration. Significantly, Tyson suggests that the movement's tactical nonviolence was actually a deviation from black southern traditions of armed self-defense. This view of armed self-defense as the norm squares with anecdotal evidence that King himself, amid the cross burnings and bombings during the Montgomery campaign, had to be talked out of keeping his own cache of weaponry by the Gandhian pacifist Bayard Rustin (Branch, 1988, p. 179). Tyson's work demonstrates that Black Power had deeper historical (and even rural southern) roots than suggested by the prevailing wisdom.

There was no room within the movement or American political culture for a militant like Robert Williams. Williams eventually went into exile in Cuba after eluding a federal manhunt on a trumped-up kidnapping charge. He thus joined the ranks of African American expatriates, some of whom had been radical activists in the States. W. E. B. Du Bois had exiled himself, becoming a citizen of Ghana and joining the Communist Party in a final gesture of anti-American defiance. Evading police roadblocks and a federal manhunt, the Harlem novelist Julian Mayfield had accompanied Williams on his flight North. Mayfield fled authorities by relocating to Ghana, as did Preston King, who as a graduate student in England, had his passport revoked after he had defied his local draft board in his hometown of Albany, Georgia, in protest of its racist mistreatment. Williams, Mayfield, and King were, in effect, political refugees from Jim Crow America. Ghana became an expatriate haven for a range of radical and idealistic African Americans. Its president, American-educated Kwame Nkrumah, had invited blacks from the diaspora to lend the new nation their intellectual and technical skills. For those who were pessimistic about the racial situation in the United States, Nkrumah's invitation was a welcome opportunity. Not all black expatriates in Ghana were politically active, but for those who were, they sought political alliances with Ghanaians by exposing the brutal facts of American racism to African audiences. The group of "revolutionary returnees," as one of their number, Maya Angelou, later termed them, staged a demonstration at the US embassy in Accra timed to coincide with the March on Washington in August of 1963. The demonstrators submitted a petition meant for President Kennedy that denounced his administration's broken promises on civil rights. The petition also denounced the administration's foreign policy, including its support for the apartheid regime in South Africa, the failed "Bay of Pigs" invasion of Cuba, and the initial phase of American involvement in Vietnam. The demonstration also became a tribute to Du Bois, who had died the previous evening.

Certain that their enemies resided comfortably within the US government, many of the black expatriates harbored a thorough disillusionment with American racism at home and abroad. The political pressure brought to bear on radicals in SNCC in Atlantic City in 1964, in addition to their isolation in the field, was enough to send many of these local people into exile, as well. From accounts of the relationship between the movement and the FBI, we know that much of the activists' sense of abandonment was justified. FBI Director J. Edgar Hoover's correspondence on civil rights activities suggests that the Bureau's surveillance was motivated as much by racial animosity as by anti-communist ideals (Garrow, 1986; O'Reilly, 1989). Of course, blacks were not the only targets of federal surveillance and suspicion of subversion. Nevertheless, Hoover's surveillance against King, and his determination to prevent the advent of a "black messiah" with the capability of uniting black and student movements, suggests that the Cold War, while central in many accounts, may only partly explain the antagonistic relationship between the government and the movement.

Even as local people, virtually alone, took their stand against segregation and its attendant violence, SNCC leaders were swept up in national and international issues and ideologies. Eric Burner's study (1994) of Robert Moses goes further than most in capturing Moses's linkage of the plight of blacks in Mississippi with the abuses of American military power overseas. Departing from accounts that portray Moses as a dreamy eccentric, Burner credits Moses as a brilliant organizer and gives a trenchant analysis of SNCC's international concerns. By 1965, Moses withdrew from the schisms in the organization and became involved in the anti-war movement. Even before that, SNCC, which had long resisted Cold War dictates, had articulated a more radical vision of foreign policy than the NAACP and SCLC. After the setback at the 1964 Democratic Convention, Moses and other SNCC leaders vacationed in the West African nation of Guinea. There, they observed US propaganda seeking to convince Africans that the terror and voting rights violations SNCC confronted in the South did not exist. Like black anti-colonial activists of the 1940s, and later, Malcolm X, Moses and SNCC activists came to view US domestic and foreign policy as two sides of the same racially oppressive coin. Drafted into the army at the height of the Vietnam War, Moses believed that he was being targeted for his dissent. Moses fled the country with his wife and resided in Tanzania, where other disillusioned and exhausted SNCC workers had exiled themselves. That exile – and assassination – proved to be the common fate of black radicals attests to the magnitude of their indictment of the violence and bad faith inherent in American liberalism. Their marginalization by the government affirmed that their political vision was anything but marginal.

The Recovery of Black Studies and New Perspectives on the Urban Dimension

Throughout the 1990s, racial polarization and the rightward drift of American politics demanded a response from historians of the movement. President Clinton withdrew his nomination of Lani Guinier to head the Civil Rights division in the Justice Department, after conservative opponents branded her "Quota queen." A dedicated and well-organized Christian-right constituency, led by history Ph.D. Newt Gingrich, captured the majority in the House of Representatives in 1994. Discussions of race and inequality reached their nadir with the appearance in that same year of *The Bell Curve* (sponsored by the Pioneer Fund, an extremist group with historical links to Nazi-era racism), whose claims about the genetic inferiority of minorities supported further attacks on the welfare state. The protest tradition of black nationalism associated with Malcolm X (whose legacy had been, by then, mass-mediated and commodified beyond recognition) had culminated in the cathartic, but ephemeral, Million Man March of 1995. The assault against affirmative action and voting rights waged by such conservative revisionists as D'Souza and the Thernstroms continued with public university systems in Texas, California, and Washington State outlawing race-conscious admissions policies.

As the end of the twentieth century approached, historians began to answer the conservatives' fantasy of the end of racism with narratives of the making, through the human agency of public policy, of institutional racism in the urban North (Sugrue, 1996). Such narratives do more than disabuse us of the myth of northern "de facto" segregation; they also challenge longstanding assumptions of liberal consensus and of the essential perfectibility of American institutions. In making such claims, historians sympathetic to the freedom movement have availed themselves of the critical perspectives of an earlier generation of black intellectuals and social science scholars who were participant-observers in the struggle.

In 1945, St. Clair Drake and Horace Cayton wrote that "Negroes are becoming a city people, and it is in the cities that the problem of the Negro in American life appears in its sharpest and most dramatic forms. It may be, too, that the cities will be the arena in which the 'Negro problem' will be finally settled" (Drake and Cayton, 1945, p. 755). In retrospect, this was more prescient than Gunnar Myrdal's influential *An American Dilemma* (1944), whose emphasis on the liberal "American Creed" downplayed black demands for equality and displaced racial and social conflict from the structural to the psychological realm. In their sociological study of race relations in Chicago, *Black Metropolis*, Drake and Cayton situated the northern, urban phase of the struggle within the ferment of World War II, thus anticipating Korstad and Lichtenstein's treatment of a national black-led struggle for economic and racial justice. By contrasting the fates of that city's segregated African Americans with the upward mobility of foreign-born immigrants, Drake and Cayton pioneered an analysis of institutional racism that would become prominent within Black Power and Black Studies discourse. Drake and Cayton provided a language for the structural impediments to African Americans' social mobility in the urban North. The "Job

Ceiling" limited blacks to unskilled and semi-skilled labor, and residential segregation confined blacks to the ghetto. In political and social life, the colorline diminished both human contact between the races and opportunities for advancement.
During World War II, blacks revolted against these barriers, demanding full citizenship at the ballot box, through economic boycotts, and in the courts. Recent work
on black activism since the war by Martha Biondi (2002) on New York City and
Matthew Countryman (Countryman et al., 2002) on Philadelphia demonstrates that
contrary to accounts of the southern-based movement, the northern phase of the
struggle against employment discrimination and institutional racism was underway
long before the emergence of Black Power in 1966.

   Along with many of their contemporaries, Drake and Cayton argued that the war
internationalized the problem of American racism. They emphasized the global
dimension to the plight of African Americans, an implicit condemnation of the
unresponsiveness of liberal reform to the structural barriers facing blacks. Conversely,
the American black population's demands for equal citizenship became central to the
global political contest between Cold War superpowers and the nonaligned movement comprising the nationalist struggles of the colonized world. Drake participated
in National Negro Congress campaigns in Chicago against residential segregation,
served as teacher and, later, a political adviser to the SNCC leader James Forman,
and was an active supporter of African independence from the late 1940s onward.
Drake's career as a member of the founding generation of African and Black
Studies scholars offers a window into the important, and still largely unexplored,
relationship between social activism and knowledge production (Gaines, 2002).

Challenges to Liberalism in Early Black Studies Discourse

Echoing the concerns of Julian Bond, recent explorations of the roots of inequality
in the urban North are at bottom an historical assessment of American liberalism.
Pioneering Black Studies scholars have provided influential critiques of liberalism
through their discussions of racism in the urban North. Drake and Cayton redefined
the American Dilemma by focusing on its significance for black urban dwellers.
For them, the relative freedom of cities heightened the contradiction between the
democratic ideology of free competition and the efforts of real estate firms, insurance companies, and financial institutions to maintain exclusionary racial barriers. As
if to elaborate Drake and Cayton's analysis, black writers of the 1950s – the informal historians of their times – wrote extensively of the alienation of those trapped in
urban ghetto conditions. Frank London Brown's novel *Trumbull Park* (1959) was
based on contemporary struggles for desegregated housing in that Chicago neighborhood. In *Maud Martha* (1953), Gwendolyn Brooks wrote of the deferred dreams
and repressed rage of a black working-class woman struggling to reconcile herself to
the stifling conditions of racism and poverty in Chicago. These themes would be
further explored in Lorraine Hansberry's *A Raisin in the Sun* (1959), which dramatized a black family's attempt to leave their Southside ghetto apartment for an integrated suburb and to confront the likelihood of vigilante violence. Undoubtedly more
searing on the imaginations of many, including northern blacks, was the 1955 lynching of Emmett Till, a fourteen-year-old Chicago youth murdered while visiting relatives in Mississippi. A combination of mass outrage and national and international

press coverage compelled that state to bring the known perpetrators of the crime to trial. An all-white jury swiftly acquitted Till's killers, who then went on to sell their story to a national news magazine.

Arguably one of the most influential texts in African American letters in the second half of the century was the work of a sociologist, E. Franklin Frazier's *Black Bourgeoisie* (1957). At the dawn of the civil rights movement, Frazier's book galvanized middle-class African American youth, who embraced the book's indictment of their elders' apparent acquiescence to segregation and Cold War liberalism. It was the popularity of Frazier's critique of the black middle class that laid an important foundation for Black Power discourse, as well as the Black Arts movement's antibourgeois celebration of black folk culture and scorn for high modernism in African American literature.

Frazier aside, African American writers aspired to much more than exposing an uncommitted black bourgeoisie. Such figures as Hansberry, James Baldwin, and others were taking aim at Cold War liberalism. Baldwin's bestselling essay *The Fire Next Time* (1963) exposed the racist undertones of northern liberalism, particularly the contention that black people had to prove themselves "acceptable" for equal citizenship. As Drake and Cayton had done, Baldwin wrote of the alienating effect of the North's institutional racism on blacks. Northern blacks were increasingly restive and enraged; white liberals willfully blind to the ghetto's corrosive effect on human relationships. Time was running out, Baldwin warned, unless a minority of blacks and whites dedicated themselves to overcoming social and spiritual boundaries.

With the Harlem riot of July 1964, sparked by the police killing of an African American teenager, Baldwin's worst fears had come to pass. Having witnessed many more urban rebellions, the violent repression of the Black Panther Party, the slaughter of thousands of Vietnamese by saturation bombing, and the assassinations of Medgar Evers, Malcolm X, and Martin Luther King, Baldwin issued a bitter indictment of American society in *No Name in the Street* (1972). His harrowing account of the New York criminal justice system's incarceration of his secretary on a homicide charge, despite a complete lack of evidence, is sadly anticipatory of the 1990s' expansion of the prison system and the spiraling incarceration of the poor and people of color. Baldwin defended the Black Panthers, and eulogized Malcolm X against the distortions of the US press upon his death.

The Panthers had furthered Malcolm's legacy in their calls for armed self-defense and in their insistence that racist police, white vigilantes, and the US military were the actual purveyors of violence. Like Malcolm, the Panthers sought the psychological emancipation of the masses of African Americans. Yet Malcolm and the Panthers were undone in large part by the very image that they themselves had cultivated. Despite his reincarnation as an advocate of progressive multiracial coalitions, Malcolm had become a tragic prisoner of his mass-mediated image as the fiery Nation of Islam minister and mouthpiece for Elijah Muhammed's distorted version of Islam. And the Panthers were hopelessly vulnerable against a massive campaign of federal, state, and local surveillance, incarceration, and violence. The sexism and suicidal adventurism prevalent within the organization were criticized by Angela Davis, Toni Cade Bambara, and other black feminist activists and writers whose vision of revolution renounced armed struggle and romantic internationalism, focusing instead on gender relations and local community-building. To their credit, the Panthers were willing to join coalitions with progressive whites and with other social movements, pursuing their vision of an international revolutionary movement, as Malcolm X had attempted after his break with the Nation of Islam.

Scholars are just beginning to study the impact of Black Power in the urban North, and the uneasy coexistence of black cultural nationalism with the establishmentarian electoral politics of urban black regimes. In his discussion of Black Power politics in Newark, and the central leadership role of Amiri Baraka, Komozi Woodard identified Malcolm's support of African and third world revolution as a strong influence on the movement's vision of cultural nationalism. Woodard argued that Baraka's cultural nationalism provided the basis for popular mobilization, not a retreat from activism (though such scholars as Carson and Payne are less positive in their assessment of Black Power; for Payne, it was characterized by younger activists' ill-advised rejection of the guidance of veteran organizers). Insisting that Black Power in the urban North be treated independently from conventional southern civil rights narratives, Woodard emphasized the pragmatism and the experimental nature of the political formation in Newark that sought to rectify overcrowded housing conditions and to end police brutality. Ultimately, these efforts were unsuccessful, owing to the extreme corruption and racism of a white power structure, which easily co-opted black elected officials (Woodard, 1999). An interesting alternative to Woodard's account is the memoir of the Detroit movement activist Grace Lee Boggs. Her partnership with James Boggs, whose radical analyses of American politics and Black Power were rooted in his southern African American heritage and his daily experience as an auto worker, eschewed the internationalism so often characteristic of black radicalism for the concreteness of local struggles for justice and community in Detroit (Boggs, 1998).

The Erosion of Voting Rights and the Abandonment of Liberalism

Advocates of Black Power, which generally marked the shift from the southern to the northern movement, demanded redistributive justice and called for control by African Americans of their communities and the public institutions serving them. Influenced by SNCC's voting rights campaigns, Malcolm X spoke incessantly of African Americans' need to master power politics, and challenged his northern audiences to claim the ballot as a political weapon. But Malcolm spoke only of power. When the phrase "Black Power" exploded onto the national scene in 1966, many white liberals and conservatives – and some black leaders – condemned the term, expressing a deep antipathy toward black aspirations within American and southern politics. Nowhere was this antipathy more evident than after the passage of the Voting Rights Act. From the late 1960s to the 1980s, white-controlled municipal and state governments throughout the South employed redistricting and modified electoral procedures with the goal of diluting black voting strength (Kousser, 1999). During the period of massive resistance to desegregation, Cold War anti-communism had provided segregationists a pretext for maintaining the status quo. But after 1965, the Voting Rights Act and the prospect of political power wielded by newly enfranchised African Americans were themselves sufficient to motivate powerful whites to change the rules in order to prevent blacks from electing representatives of their own choosing.

During the 1890s the demise of the democratic experiment of black political power had been effected by the disfranchisement of African American (and poor white) voters. A century later, redistricting became the primary instrument for diminishing the political influence of African Americans and Latinos. Both processes relied on radical revisions of history, the first discrediting, if not demonizing, black political participation; the second, more recently, by obfuscating the original intent and purpose of the equal protection clause as protector of the rights of African Americans. The Supreme Court's ruling in *Shaw v. Reno* (1993) and subsequent voting rights cases reversed the egalitarian guidelines for redistricting that a coalition of civil rights attorneys and lobbyists, including Lani Guinier, had written into the renewal of the Voting Rights Act by Congress in 1982.

In *Shaw*, the Court allowed whites to sue under the Fourteenth Amendment if race were the "predominant factor" in the drawing of election districts. Justice Sandra Day O'Connor, writing for the majority, penned an opinion so fanciful and at variance with history that J. Morgan Kousser acidly termed it "postmodern equal protection theory." In effect, O'Connor and the court majority reinterpreted the Fourteenth Amendment to protect the interests of powerful whites instead of protecting minorities from discrimination. Plaintiffs were no longer required to demonstrate that they had been harmed, as had been the precedent in vote dilution cases, which was fortunate for them, because as politically advantaged whites, they could not have done so. Nevertheless, Justice O'Connor made the novel argument that "a lasting harm to our society" could be asserted by "white voters (or voters of any other race)" if districting lines suggested a "racial classification." Although she concluded her opinion with a solemn defense of equality before the law, O'Connor's radical reinterpretation of the equal protection clause contained a racial double standard: blacks and other peoples of color had to demonstrate injury; for whites, however, the mere appearance of a racial distinction granted them standing.

Justice O'Connor resorted to ahistorical hyperbole in equating districts drawn to achieve racial balance with the evils of segregation, balkanization, and "political apartheid," even though many of these districts held white majorities, and none were more than two-thirds black. O'Connor asserted that minority-majority districts could be challenged if the boundaries of such districts appeared "irregular" or "bizarre." No proof of discriminatory injury was necessary. O'Connor's criteria in identifying racial gerrymandering solely by the irregular appearance of districts failed to conceal what was, at bottom, a racial and partisan bias. She invented "compactness" or "traditional districting principles" (another fiction conveniently blind to the historical use of racial gerrymandering to diminish black political power) as the standard for legitimate districting schemes that might eliminate any suspicion of racial gerrymandering. Unfortunately for her and what Kousser termed "the revolutionary-conservative majority," not only did O'Connor's vague notion of "compactness" reside in the eye of the beholder, but also, whatever it was, she neglected to make "compactness" a requirement for relieving majority-white districts (whose boundaries occasionally appeared to be as "bizarre" as those of suspect majority-minority districts) from the suspicion of unconstitutional racial gerrymandering. In short, *Shaw* was revolutionary, overturning the settled principles of the Voting Rights Act, undermining the hard-won citizenship rights of the First and Second Reconstructions, and distorting their legacy to achieve a semblance of formal neutrality. The decision enshrined the

Fourteenth Amendment as protector of white privilege rather than minority rights; used egalitarian language to sanction inequality and exclusion; and upheld racial and partisan biases while claiming to be colorblind (Kousser, 1999, pp. 366–485).

The Clinton administration's abandonment of Lani Guinier and the principle of voting rights, and the Court's majority opinion in *Shaw v. Reno*, resuscitated an anti-democratic tradition rooted in the South's century-old history of disfranchisement. In retrospect, Clinton's betrayal of his erstwhile friend, combined with the drumbeat of legal challenges to majority-minority districts, was a portent of the effective disfranchisement of thousands of African Americans in Florida. That event demonstrated how tenuous is the national consensus for the principle of electoral democracy when it is put to the test. Attempts by black leadership and organizations to protest and publicize this undermining of the democratic process received scant media coverage. This disregard also greeted a statement of protest by former SNCC activists. Here is an excerpt from their press release:

> We have increasing documentation of thousands of registered voters being turned away because their names were not listed or because their polls closed while they were waiting on line. These are voting injustices that must not be ignored. We are horrified at the prospect that in the year 2000, we Americans would resign ourselves to the results of an election achieved by questionable and undemocratic means. We urge all Americans who believe in the sacredness of honest elections to support the legal battle for a full and fair counting of the votes in Florida and to demand a Justice Department investigation into incidents of voter irregularities. We must not let this happen again!

The recent setbacks to voting rights represent the most far-reaching challenge to the painstakingly won democratic achievements of the movement for black equality, achievements that were dealt a final, telling blow by the Supreme Court's majority when it invoked the equal protection clause to spare President Bush the harm of further recounts in Florida. Those setbacks insult the memory of those who died working to expand voting rights as the hallmark of American citizenship. Such unabashedly partisan judicial and political attacks on democracy may well galvanize an aroused citizenry to seek true democratic change at the ballot box, as SNCC activists and their forebears had believed. What remains certain is that future scholarship on the movement will derive much of its force and insight from the challenges of the present and future, as well as the lessons and sacrifices of the past.

REFERENCES

Baldwin, James: *The Fire Next Time* (New York: Dial Press, 1963).

Baldwin, James: *No Name in the Street* (New York: Dial Press, 1972).

Berry, Mary Frances: *Black Resistance, White Law: A History of Constitutional Racism in America* (New York: Penguin, 1994).

Biondi, Martha: *"To Stand and Fight": The Struggle for Civil Rights in Postwar New York City* (Cambridge, Mass.: Harvard University Press, 2002).

Boggs, Grace Lee: *Living For Change: An Autobiography* (Minneapolis: University of Minnesota Press, 1998).

Branch, Taylor: *Parting the Waters: America in the King Years, 1954–1963* (New York: Simon and Schuster, 1988).

Brauer, Carl: *John F. Kennedy and the Second Reconstruction* (New York: Columbia University Press, 1977).

Brooks, Gwendolyn: *Maud Martha: A Novel* (Chicago: Third World Press, 1953).

Brown, Frank London: *Trumbull Park: A Novel* (Chicago: Regnery, 1959).

Burk, Robert Frederick: *The Eisenhower Administration and Civil Rights* (Knoxville: University of Tennessee Press, 1984).

Burner, Eric R.: *And Gently He Shall Lead Them: Robert Parris Moses and Civil Rights in Mississippi* (New York: New York University Press, 1994).

Cade, Toni, ed.: *The Black Woman: An Anthology* (New York: New American Library, 1970).

Carson, Clayborne: *In Struggle: SNCC and the Black Awakening of the 1960s* (Cambridge, Mass.: Harvard University Press, 1981).

Chafe, William H.: *Civilities and Civil Rights: Greensboro, North Carolina and the Black Struggle for Freedom* (New York: Oxford University Press, 1980).

Countryman, Matthew, Theoharis, Jeanne, and Woodard, Komozi: *Freedom North: Black Freedom Struggles Outside the South* (New York: Palgrave, 2002).

Crawford, Vicki et al.: *Women in the Civil Rights Movement: Trailblazers and Torchbearers, 1941–1965* (Bloomington: Indiana University Press, 1993).

Cruse, Harold: *The Crisis of the Negro Intellectual* (New York: William Morrow, 1967).

Davis, Angela Y.: *An Autobiography* (New York: Random House, 1974).

Dittmer, John: *Local People: The Struggle for Civil Rights in Mississippi* (Urbana: University of Illinois Press, 1995).

Drake, St. Clair and Cayton, Horace: *Black Metropolis: A Study of Negro Life in a Northern City* (New York: Harcourt Brace, 1945).

Du Bois, W. E. B.: *Black Reconstruction in America* (New York: Harcourt Brace, 1935).

Dudziak, Mary: *Cold War Civil Rights: Race and the Image of American Democracy* (Princeton, NJ: Princeton University Press, 2000).

Franklin, John Hope: *The Color Line: Legacy for the Twenty-First Century* (Columbia: University of Missouri Press, 1993).

Frazier, E. Franklin: *Black Bourgeoisie* (Glencoe, Ill.: Free Press, 1957).

Gaines, Kevin: "Black Studies, Afrocentrism and Coalition-Building: St. Clair Drake's *Black Folk Here and There*," *Black Scholar* (forthcoming, 2002).

Garrow, David J.: *Bearing the Cross: Martin Luther King and the Southern Christian Leadership Conference* (New York: William Morrow, 1986).

Garrow, David J.: *The FBI and Martin Luther King, Jr.* (New York: W. W. Norton, 1991).

Giddings, Paula: *When and Where I Enter: The Impact of Black Women on Race and Sex in America* (New York: William Morrow, 1984).

Gilmore, Glenda E.: *Gender and Jim Crow* (Chapel Hill: University of North Carolina Press, 1996).

Greenberg, Cheryl: *"Or Does it Explode?": Black Harlem in the Great Depression* (New York: Oxford University Press, 1991).

Guinier, Lani: *Lift Every Voice: Turning a Civil Rights Setback into a New Vision of Social Justice* (New York: Simon and Schuster, 1998).

Hansberry, Lorraine: *A Raisin in the Sun* (1959; New York: Vintage Books, 1994).

Harding, Vincent: *Hope and History: Why We Must Share the History of the Movement* (Maryknoll, NY: Orbis Press, 1990).

Holt, Thomas C.: *Black Over White: Negro Political Leadership in South Carolina During Reconstruction* (Urbana: University of Illinois Press, 1977).

Honey, Michael K.: *Southern Labor and Black Civil Rights: Organizing Memphis Workers* (Urbana: University of Illinois Press, 1993).

Horne, Gerald: *Black and Red: W. E. B. Du Bois and the African-American Response to the Cold War, 1944–1963* (Albany: State University Press of New York, 1986).

Kelley, Robin D. G.: *Hammer and Hoe: Alabama Communists During the Great Depression* (Chapel Hill: University of North Carolina Press, 1990).

Kelley, Robin D. G.: *Race Rebels: Culture, Politics and the Black Working Class* (New York: Free Press, 1994).

Korstad, Robert and Lichtenstein, Nelson: "Opportunities Found and Lost," *Journal of American History*, 75 (December 1988): 786–811.

Kousser, J. Morgan: *Colorblind Injustice: Minority Voting Rights and the Undoing of the Second Reconstruction* (Chapel Hill: University of North Carolina Press, 1999).

Lawson, Stephen F.: "Freedom Then, Freedom Now: The Historiography of the Civil Rights Movement," *American Historical Review*, 96 (April 1991): 456–471.

Lee, Chana Kai: *For Freedom's Sake: The Life of Fannie Lou Hamer* (Urbana: University of Illinois Press, 1999).

Lewis, Earl: *In Their Own Interests: Race, Class and Power in Twentieth-Century Norfolk, Virginia* (Berkeley: University of California Press, 1991).

Logan, Rayford: *The Negro in American Life and Thought: The Nadir, 1877–1901* (New York: Dial Press, 1954).

Matusow, Allen J.: *The Unraveling of America: A History of Liberalism in the 1960s* (New York: Harper and Row, 1984).

Meier, August and Rudwick, Elliott: *CORE: A Study in the Civil Rights Movement, 1942–1968* (New York: Oxford University Press, 1973).

Morris, Aldon D.: *The Origins of the Civil Rights Movement: Black Communities Organizing for Change* (New York: Free Press, 1984).

Myrdal, Gunnar: *An American Dilemma: The Negro Problem and Modern Democracy* (New York: Harper and Brothers, 1944).

Naison, Mark: *Communists in Harlem During the Depression* (Urbana: University of Illinois Press, 1983).

Norrell, Robert: *Reaping the Whirlwind: The Civil Rights Movement in Tuskegee* (New York: Alfred A. Knopf, 1985).

O'Reilly, Kenneth: *Racial Matters: The FBI's Secret File on Black America, 1960–1972* (New York: Free Press, 1989).

Painter, Nell Irvin: *Exodusters: Black Migration to Kansas After Reconstruction* (New York: Alfred A. Knopf, 1976).

Payne, Charles: *I've Got the Light of Freedom: The Organizing Tradition and the Mississippi Struggle* (Berkeley: University of California Press, 1995).

Plummer, Brenda Gayle: *Rising Wind: Black Americans and U.S. Foreign Affairs, 1935–1960* (Chapel Hill: University of North Carolina Press, 1996).

Record, Wilson: *The Negro and the Communist Party* (Chapel Hill: University of North Carolina Press, 1951).

Robinson, Armstead L. and Sullivan, Patricia, eds.: *New Directions in Civil Rights Studies* (Charlottesville: University Press of Virginia, 1991).

Stampp, Kenneth: *The Era of Reconstruction, 1865–1877* (New York: Alfred A. Knopf, 1965).

Sugrue, Thomas J.: *The Origins of the Urban Crisis: Race and Inequality in Postwar Detroit* (Princeton, NJ: Princeton University Press, 1996).

Sullivan, Patricia: *Days of Hope: Race and Democracy in the New Deal* (Chapel Hill: University of North Carolina Press, 1996).

Thernstrom, Abigail: *Whose Votes Count? Affirmative Action and Minority Voting Rights* (Cambridge, Mass.: Harvard University Press, 1987).

Trotter, Joe William: *Black Milwaukee: The Making of an Industrial Proletariat, 1915–1945* (Urbana: University of Illinois Press, 1985).

Tyson, Timothy B.: *Radio Free Dixie: Robert F. Williams and the Roots of Black Power* (Chapel Hill: University of North Carolina Press, 1999).

Von Eschen, Penny: *Race Against Empire: Black Americans and Anticolonialism, 1937–1957* (Ithaca, NY: Cornell University Press, 1997).

Weisbrot, Robert: *Freedom Bound: A History of America's Civil Rights Movement* (New York: W. W. Norton, 1990).

Woodard, Komozi: *A Nation Within a Nation: Amiri Baraka, LeRoi Jones, and Black Power Politics* (Chapel Hill: University of North Carolina Press, 1999).

CHAPTER THIRTEEN

Postwar Women's History: The "Second Wave" or the End of the Family Wage?

NANCY MACLEAN

I

A half-century has brought a world of change to women's lives and American ideas about gender. What would have seemed unthinkable fifty years ago is now taken for granted. Today, a majority of women with children under one year are in the labor force. Most children will spend at least some of their years growing up in a single-parent household. Women can be found, sometimes in considerable numbers, in all the occupations that once barred them entry, from medicine to firefighting. Others interpret the Constitution on the Supreme Court or win Pulitzer prizes for their prose. Women serve as conduits to the divine in some religious denominations, and as decorated officers in the armed forces. The culture itself has altered on gender in ways unlikely to be reversed. Lesbianism not only dares to speak its name; it does so in the voices of likeable characters on prime-time television. Wife-beating, rape, and incest, once abetted by public silence, are now popular topics for daytime talk shows as well as award-winning works of literature. Backed by Title IX's guarantee of equal access to sports, young women are growing up with a novel sense of their physical power along with new arenas for their minds.

Of course, much has remained the same, and new obstacles have emerged. The resistance to altering gender roles and widening women's possibilities has been vocal and influential. It has also been subtle and institutional, even badgering and inter-nal. A still sex-segregated labor force and persistent assumptions that housework and childrearing are ultimately women's responsibility, for example, remain heavy anchors of continuity. But to understand women's history since 1945 and the historiography that has arisen to interpret it, the place to start is with an appreciation of just how much has changed – and how rapidly. It is fair to say that we are in the midst of an epochal transformation. "We are witnessing the breakup," the economist Barbara Bergmann declares, "of the ancient system of sex roles under which men were assigned a monopoly of access to money-making and mature women were restricted to the home" (Bergmann, 1986, p. 3).

The surge to prominence of the field of women's history since 1970 is yet another sign of the shifts underway. All but nonexistent in 1945, it has become one of the most vibrant specialties in the discipline, one few departments would do without. The field itself arose from the women's movement, as feminists who were also students and professors of history began to look to the past for bearings. "The recognition that we had been denied our history," recalled Gerda Lerner, the pathbreaking historian of American women, "came to many of us as a staggering flash of insight, which altered our consciousness irretrievably" (Lerner, 1979, p. 159). Not surprisingly given the field's origins, its questions about the postwar years from the outset revolved around aspects of that struggle: its roots, nature, impact, and limitations. Having ties to an ongoing movement for social change gave vitality to women's history and endowed it with broad appeal. Galvanized by practical struggles for gender justice, women's historians unearthed vast riches in the way of primary sources and produced engrossing accounts of myriad aspects of women's lives and gender politics, making their discipline the most magnetic for the early movement.

The themes of the women's liberation movement have also indelibly imprinted the historiography, making for some of its distinctive contributions and also for some of its limitations. Above all, the movement's conviction that "the personal is political" – that personal experiences are shaped by forces in public life and therefore can be altered by changes there – led to new scrutiny of "private life." One sees this in the capacious definition of the "political" that women's historians (and increasingly other scholars as well) employ: it takes in developments in childrearing, romance, household labor, and community networks as well as electoral politics, social movements, and state action. The work of feminist historians has in turn shifted the whole discipline, combining with the efforts of social historians and cultural historians to produce a profound epistemological shift. In seeking to answer new questions, scholars moved beyond the study of elites and began sifting through the artifacts of everyday household life, the ephemera of local movements, the records of hospital medical boards, the lyrics of popular music, trial transcripts, episodes of radio and television shows, and oral histories with individuals from all walks of life.

The movement contributed in another way to a fresh historical literature. Its unprecedented challenge to the sexual division of labor made scholars alert to the prevalence and power of all such boundaries in history. Writing on subjects as varied as occupational distribution and erotic preferences, women's historians have revealed how patterns that Americans had long taken for granted were in fact, as the literature came to put it, "socially constructed." Not only did scholars show how these differences were historically created by human actors and their institutions. The best of the new studies offered insight into the wider cultural and political work such boundaries performed, and thereby made the discipline as a whole aware of, as one title puts it, *U.S. History as Women's History* (Kerber et al., 1995).

Having themselves confronted demeaning gender stereotypes in their era's most radical movements, women's historians were attuned to the subtleties of political language and practice. Some produced works that cumulatively exposed how deeply gender exclusion is built into American political culture. Yet, sharing the movement's vision of people as subjects of their own history as well as victims of others' power, such scholars also recovered women's "agency," as it came to be called, in shaping their lives and finding leverage in the country's political culture for claims of independence, freedom, and equality (Kerber, 1980, 1999; Baker, 1984; Evans, 1989). Movement experience had also imparted a sense of the power of bonding among women – what activists spoke of as "sisterhood" – and of the efficacy of small groups in working for large changes. Building on this, women's historians documented informal women's networks and voluntary organizations, albeit divided by class and race, that grew from sexual divisions of labor even as they reconfigured them. Some analyzed how such networks become radicalized in hard times, as in the cases of the kosher meat boycott of 1902 or the militant housewives' leagues, black and white, nationalist and communist, of the Great Depression (Hewitt, 1994; Hine, 1994; Orleck, 1995).

And yet, for all that it propelled scholarship forward in the first few decades, the continuing strong pull of the women's movement as the ultimate question for the years after 1945 may now be restricting the field's vision. Unlike other eras of women's history, this one has not yet generated overarching interpretive paradigms with which to assess the impressive empirical data scholars have amassed. For the postwar years, there is little to compare with the imaginative breakthroughs of the literature on earlier periods. One thinks, for instance, of Laurel Thatcher Ulrich's creative entry into the world of colonial goodwives; of Nancy Cott's dialectical reading of the bonds of womanhood; of Linda Gordon's recovery of the enigmatic politics of voluntary motherhood; or of Elsa Barkley Brown's incisive critique of the hold of "dichotomous thinking" about race, class, and gender among historians (Ulrich, 1982; Cott, 1978; Gordon, 1976; Brown, 1994, p. 278). Similarly, one could point to the broad literatures and complex debates that have coalesced under the rubrics of "domesticity" for the Victorian era or "maternalism" for early twentieth-century women's politics. Why is there no parallel for the post-1945 years? Perhaps the history itself is simply still too close to acquire the strangeness from which fresh thinking comes. Whatever the reasons, women's historians of the postwar period have not yet generated interpretive frameworks that go beyond looking backward, forward, or sideways from the women's movement.

Yet perhaps now, a quarter-century into the project of recovering women's past, it is time to broaden the field's reach in the post-1945 era, and to ask some different questions of the novel situations in which American women find themselves at the beginning of a new century. These questions may help to make better sense of a paradox of the movement's recent history: despite having produced the world's strongest women's movement and the vastest public policy apparatus to fight sex discrimination, the United States still has one of the largest wage gaps between the sexes. That gap, the labor economists Francine Blau and Lawrence Kahn have demonstrated, is due less to the usual suspect (sex discrimination) than to a rarely imagined culprit: the country's unmatched and ever-widening levels of overall economic inequality. The wage gap remains so large less because of gender, that is, and more because of such things as low unskilled wages generally and low levels of unionization. "American women," explains Blau, "were essentially swimming upstream in a labor market increasingly unfavorable to low wage workers" (Blau, 1993, p. 85; Blau and Kahn, 1996). The pay gap is one instance of a truth that the field might grapple with even more than it has: that women's fate is not decided apart from other forms of inequality but is intimately bound up with them.

In fact, this essay will argue that the story that best anchors the gender history of the greatest number of Americans in the second half of the twentieth century is not the women's movement per se. It is the unraveling of the whole family wage system that was once hegemonic in American culture, law, and social policy, if honored in the breach in real life. Based on the idea of the male breadwinner as provider for dependent wife and children, that system emerged as a jerry-built compromise between social groups with different interests: white male wage earners, their employers, middle-class reformers (women as well as men), and public officials. First articulated by early nineteenth-century trade unionists and reformers, it became possible to growing numbers of households with improved wages in the first half of the twentieth century. Even as a significant share of Americans fell outside of its net – not only widowed and single women but also less-skilled workers in general, and low-wage workers of color in particular – its assumptions structured the political economy they had to navigate in the labor force and the welfare state. "By the advent of the New Deal," the historian Linda Gordon has shown, "the family-wage norm was a dead weight crushing the imagination of welfare reformers" (Gordon, 1994, p. 291).

And yet it persisted. Defining male labor as the norm and female labor as an aberration, it helped to shape a labor market biased toward men (especially white men) and to dictate social welfare policy aimed at shoring up male-dominant households. A myth insofar as it claimed to *describe* rather than *prescribe* behavior, the family-wage norm still served as a grounding principle for what scholars have called the two-track welfare state that took shape in the United States in the Progressive era and the New Deal years. The superior, entitlement track of this system rewarded male wage earning through such policies as workmen's compensation, unemployment insurance, and Social Security; its inferior, means-tested track grudgingly sustained women and children cut off from access to male wages through mothers' pensions and later Aid to Families with Dependent Children (AFDC) (M. May, 1982; Ehrenreich, 1983; Gordon 1990, 1994; Fraser, 1997). That family-wage norm and the policies sustaining it shaped the context in which women would make their own varied histories. A case in point: exclusion from the family-wage system as from the rights of citizenship profoundly affected the lives of most African Americans over these years (Quadagno, 1994).

Always partial and rickety, that family-wage structure has collapsed in the last quarter-century. Once, it was self-reinforcing, as women's lack of good job prospects and of reproductive control combined with the stigmas attached to divorce and homosexuality to bolster the male breadwinner system. Now, however, men's ability to support families on a single wage has broken down just as all those other braces to the system have crumbled. No longer gender-specific, breadwinning has become an almost universal adult role. Any number of signs point to the historic change still underway. Most women now remain in the labor force through their adult lives, and they have access to better jobs. Contraception and abortion are widely available. Marriage is less permanent as divorce has become commonplace. Childcare and domestic labor have increasingly become commodities available for purchase. Norms of male gender in many communities are coming to include responsibility for childcare and housework. And in the wake of the Reagan–Bush administrations and the Clinton-backed welfare "reform" of 1996, the family-wage-based New Deal social policy edifice has itself been renovated in the minimalist style of neoliberalism.

Ultimately, it is this complex process of the breakdown of a family-wage system decades in the making that helps make sense of much recent gender history. It has freed some women for unprecedented achievements while leaving others more vulnerable to old abuses. It is, arguably, behind many other stories as well. It made for sharp disagreements between white feminists and feminists of color over family politics. It furthered the separation of sexuality and reproduction, and increased the visibility of queer life. It anchored the rise and later dismantling of welfare in the form of AFDC, as Marisa Chappell has persuasively demonstrated (Chappell, 2002). It divides women into feminist and anti-feminist camps. It shapes the lives of immigrants as well as of native-born feminists and anti-feminists. It has contributed to an epochal upheaval in ideas about gender in almost every area of human endeavor. And it makes sense of the changing gender history of men along with women.

Why not, then, reexamine the history of women from 1945 to the present in terms of the relationship of different groups to that evolving family-wage system? It is striking, after all, that the white middle-class women made most comfortable by this system were those whose public activity entered "the doldrums" in the years of its greatest power (Rupp and Taylor, 1987). It is also notable that in the family wage's heyday the wage-earning women and women of color excluded from its purview became most active. Experimenting with other tools to protect their interests, above all labor unions and civil rights organizing, they usually, not coincidentally, organized in the company of same-class or same-group men: their life paths, after all, were less distinct from men's than those of white middle-class women. Only later, as the system began to disintegrate, did the latter come to the fore again in large numbers: some to dismantle a system whose constraints now outweighed its benefits for them, others to staff barricades in the embattled system's defense. What will end up replacing the family-wage system in the coming years is still uncertain. Many of our public arguments about gender, family life, and employer and government obligations are about this vacuum and how to fill it (Coontz, 1992; Stacey, 1996). But the family-wage system's demise seems indisputable. This essay surveys the field of post-1945 women's history by addressing first the achievements and arguments of that scholarship on its own terms, and then sketching how a shift in focus to the fate of the family-wage system might bring both broader reach and deeper understanding.

II

One of the first significant works in the field set the terms of debate on postwar women's history that are still in use. They concerned the relationship of the recent past to the women's movement. William Chafe's *The American Woman: Her Changing Social, Economic, and Political Roles, 1920–1970* (1972) looked at the years after woman suffrage became law. Chafe sought to trace popular ideas about women's place through a half-century to see how they fared in upheavals such as depression and war. Offering a behaviorist analysis, he concluded that "only when events made it necessary and desirable for females to assume a new role could there be a realistic chance for modification of women's status" (Chafe, 1972, p. 111). The major such event in his account was World War II. Where "the Depression had fostered a wave of reaction against any change in women's role," the war quickly and "radically transformed the economic outlook of women" (p. 135).

Chafe pointed to many indicators. The number of women in the workforce doubled, as did the number of employed wives. Female union membership quadrupled. Black women, like black men, got better jobs than ever before. Like "Rosie the

Riveter," women entered production and craft occupations that were once male pre-serves. And both the government and the press extolled these developments. The war, Chafe announced, was "a watershed": "a catalyst which broke up old modes of behavior and helped forge new ones" (pp. 136, 247). For a time, it delivered more improvement for women than fifty years of feminist organizing. While spotlighting the drama of sudden alteration on a mass scale, Chafe also stressed that "a perma-nent change in women's economic status . . . required a continued redistribution of sexual roles, a more profound shift in public attitudes, and a substantial improvement in the treatment and opportunities afforded the female worker" (p. 150). None of these, he noted, was forthcoming. Viewing the changes in women's roles as tempo-rary, most Americans saw no reason to abet them. Still, the shifts in behavior and family life implied by married women's employment boded more dramatic equaliza-tion over the long term.

A new field likes nothing better than a target argument, and the notion of World War II as watershed attracted sharpshooters from many sides. Based on careful empir-ical research, the ensuing studies clarified the stakes of different interpretations for understanding modern feminism. Collectively, the challengers disputed the idea that anything fundamental had changed in the war years. The growth in married women's employment started in the Depression, some pointed out, in the service of family need rather than feminist aspirations. Good wartime opportunities and patriotism served as added pulls, but without altering the basic calculus. Moreover, employers, government, and workers alike treated women's entry into once-male preserves as a stopgap and shored up traditional gender thinking by analogies between this labor and housework. As if to make sure that employed women got no wider ambitions, public officials refused to relieve the burden of mothering and domestic labor. Unlike some European nations, the United States built few public childcare centers, nor did it enact any creative policies to ease the load of the double day. As well, discrimina-tion against black women remained pervasive (Clive, 1979; Anderson, 1981; Hine, 1994). Even in the military, women faced sometimes preposterous efforts to maintain Stateside gender norms such as demands that they wear skirts through European winters and the swamps of the Pacific. American women in uniform could not go around "wearing the pants" (Meyer, 1996, p. 155). Providing a richer sense of the wartime years, Chafe's critics made clear how deep the resistance ran even when change in gender arrangements seemed at first sight dramatic.

In 1979, Sara Evans issued what for want of clear challengers still stands as the bookend on the other side of Chafe's work in this historiography. It established the women's liberation movement as the centerpiece of the postwar story. Evans's *Personal Politics* argued what its subtitle pithily declared: *The Roots of Women's Liberation in the Civil Rights Movement and the New Left*. The book was a stunning contribution to historical thinking about what preconditions a social movement requires: in the case of women's liberation, she argued, it was experience in other struggles that made new ways of seeing possible. In the black freedom movement and the campus New Left, young white women who had never before known other possibilities found an ideology to guide and inspire change, experience in organiz-ing, role models of freer womanhood, and networks of communication with which to spread new ideas. They also met with challenges to that newfound sense of self-worth after 1965 in the form of black separatism and white male chauvinism that led them to strike out on their own. "Feminism," in Evans's memorable formulation, "was born in that contradiction – the threatened loss of new possibility" (Evans, 1979, p. 221). Assuming with the movement that "the oppression of most American women centered on their primary definition of themselves as 'housewife,' whether they worked solely inside the home or also outside it," Evans argued that the greatest contribution of the women's liberation movement was its thoroughgoing critique of "personal" life and its challenge to that circumscribed, gender-specific identity. In this, the youth movement was, she said, quite unlike the older, more professional women who gravitated to the National Organization for Women (NOW). Less bothered by the public–private division and arriving at activism by a different path, they concentrated on discrimination in *public* life.

Persuasive in its interpretation of how many white women changed in the 1960s, Evans's work largely accepted the activists' own view of the 1950s as a kind of dystopia. Betty Friedan had first drawn the portrait of egregious gender indoctrination and strictly enforced conformity in her bestselling 1963 manifesto, *The Feminine Mystique*. In recent years, popular works such as Brett Harvey's *The Fifties: A Women's Oral History* enlivened the critique. "In the fifties as in no other decade," Harvey wrote, "the current of the mainstream was so strong that you only had to step off the bank and float downstream into marriage and motherhood" (Harvey, 1993, p. xiii). In Harvey's treatment of topics ranging from "sexual brinkmanship" to the effect on women of the GI Bill, the era became one of stunning regression. In such recountings, which established the standard for the field, the 1950s became at worst a wasteland, and at best an age that rumbled with underground innovations in lifestyles but was incapable of generating political alternatives because it had so systematically suppressed them. Its doomed ideas merely ensured that when change came, it would be explosive. Writing at the end of the 1980s, Elaine Tyler May synthesized earlier accounts to provide a lively interpretation of the whole Cold War era as one in which public and private life converged on the goal of "containment." The familial ideal of the era, she showed, was not an archaic traditionalism, but rather a radically restructured household form. It addressed anxieties from two decades of depression and war, built on the new conditions of suburban life in a mass consumer society, and encouraged expressive individualism in a shrunken emotional universe. In the end, it would be difficult for such families to carry the weight of expectations invested in them (E. May, 1988).

So astutely had Evans anchored women's liberation that few treatments of the largely white sections of the movement since her book have taken issue with it on fundamentals. Even the most recent works on "second-wave" feminism, whether interpretive or collections of fresh primary sources, essentially accept her interpretation while enriching it with new detail. Historians have agreed, for example, that feminism is best understood as an antidote to the 1950s and an outgrowth of the youthful left, black and white, and as one of the most – if not *the* most – influential social movements of modern American history (Wandersee, 1988; Brownmiller, 1999; Baxandall and Gordon, eds., 2000; Rosen, 2000). Some accounts have celebrated the movement's achievements; others, while appreciative, have been more critical. Early on, for example, the activist and political scientist Jo Freeman called attention to problems the women's movement had inherited from the New Left, among them a reliance on personal networks in organizing that effectively excluded women of color and those less advantaged by class and education, and a suspicion of leadership that bred what she called "the tyranny of structurelessness" (Freeman, in Baxandall and Gordon, 2000, pp. 73–5; also Freeman, 1975). Yet most agreed that radical feminism in particular had wrought a conceptual revolution. The edgiest of the era's feminisms, it invented "sexual politics." Under that heading came new understanding of abortion rights as essential to female self-determination, of rape as a political act, of sexist language as an influence on thought, and of wife-beating as a logical outcome of overweening male power (Ferree and Hess, 1985; Echols, 1989).

In this interpretive framework, black feminism appeared *sui generis*. It helped to define a new category, women-of-color feminism, soon enriched by contributions from Latinas, Native Americans, and later Asian Americans. The distance was mutually constructed to some degree: most black women initially suspected that, as the historian Deborah Gray White put it, "woman's liberation was a white woman's bid to share power with white men" (White, 1999, p. 214). Articulating their own feminist politics in contrast, African American women insisted on the irreducible importance of race in American life. They pointed to how it shaped *white* women's experiences, views, and goals as well as black women's. Indeed, some argued that race was most insidious when dominance and privilege rendered it invisible. Black feminist scholars exposed in women's history, as in most currents of feminist activism, what the poet Adrienne Rich called "white solipsism": the propensity "to think, imagine, and speak as if whiteness described the world" (Lerner, 1972; Davis, 1981; Giddings, 1984; Higginbotham, 1995; Guy-Sheftall, 1995; Rich, 1979, p. 299). As the historian Elsa Barkley Brown brilliantly aphorized the inescapable conclusion: "All women do not have the same gender." Nor were the differences static or unconnected: gender and race, it became clear, would best be understood in relational terms (Brown, 1995, p. 43).

Yet the prevailing framework's compulsion to categorize and divide various strands of feminism also hid from view the cross-fertilization among them and their own dynamism. While all variants of black feminism explored the interactions of race and gender in American society, for example, the differences in analysis and vision among black feminists paralleled those among white feminists. Pauli Murray and Shirley Chisholm could thus be said to broadly share the liberal feminist approach; Michele Wallace and Alice Walker the radical or cultural feminist approach; and Angela Davis and the Combahee River Collective the socialist-feminist approach. Whether such categorization was itself the most interesting line of analysis to pursue is an open question, however. At least as interesting was the way Latinas and then Asian American women followed a parallel trajectory of first solidarity with same-group men, then critique of the masculine posturing that often accompanied nationalism, followed by the appropriation and tailoring of feminist ideas to their own purposes (Moraga and Anzaldua, 1981; Garcia, 1997; Asian Women United of California, 1989; Ruíz, 1998). Working-class white women engaged in a similarly selective application of movement principles to their workplaces, families, unions, and communities (Baxandall and Gordon, 1976; Seifer, 1976; O'Farrell and Kornbluh, 1996; MacLean, 1999). Feminism is not and has never been a single entity, these varied genealogies remind us. As Nancy Cott said of another context, it "was an impulse that was impossible to translate into a program without centrifugal results." Just as the forms of gender inequality varied with the conditions of women's lives, so too did women's sources of provocation and inspiration (Cott, 1987, p. 282; Hewitt, 1994).

Other scholars filled in the portrait of the women's movement by examining the wing that women's liberation-based scholars tended to dismiss: so-called liberal feminism. Most of these studies, perhaps fittingly, focused on the public work of their subjects. Cynthia Harrison charted the fate of women in national politics from World War II until the passage of the Equal Pay Act of 1963 and the founding of the President's Commission on the Status of Women by John F. Kennedy. Even in the absence of a large-scale feminist movement, she showed, these largely white and in many ways conventional women won significant policy changes through a shrewd marshaling of scant resources with a sympathetic administration (Harrison, 1988). Susan Lynn documented the groundbreaking interracial work of women in the YWCA and the American Friends Service Committee between the end of the war and the resurgence of protest in the 1960s, alongside their labors for peace and social reform (Lynn, 1992).

Others have since complicated the very idea of liberal feminism. The historian and documentary filmmaker Joyce Follet traced a group of older midwestern feminists, among them trade unionists, public officials, civil rights activists, and others. She showed how their life experiences and ideas defied rigid schemes that claim awareness of the personal dimensions of gender subordination as the unique insight of college-trained youthful radicals (Follet, 1998). Even the division between liberal and radical ideas seems more porous today than it once did. We now know, for example, that Betty Friedan, the best-known voice of mainstream feminism, first learned politics on the left and in the company of militant trade unionists (D. Horowitz, 1998).

Here, then, is the core of the standard narrative that is being taught in schools around the country. It posits a long conservative period from about 1946 to 1960 in which women's aspirations were systematically circumscribed to domestic life. Then, the reawakening of the left side of the political spectrum in the 1960s helped revive feminism. At once inspired and irritated by their male comrades, feminist women constructed a movement composed of two distinct wings, a liberal one of older women in government service, unions, and the professions, and a radical one of younger women's liberationists, themselves divided between self-styled radical feminists (later, cultural feminists), socialist feminists, and feminists of color. Pursuing projects congruent with their analyses, these tendencies endured in ensuing years. Examples of the division of labor would be the Equal Rights Amendment for liberal feminists, rape crisis centers for radical feminists, reproductive rights or support for women's labor activism for socialist feminists, and woman-centered anti-racist initiatives for feminists of color (or "womanists," as some called themselves following the writer Alice Walker). As the wider movements of the 1960s receded and American politics grew more conservative, liberal feminists – always better organized and working nationally as well as locally – became the most visible face of feminism. But that face had altered through dialogue with more radical tendencies, such that ostensibly liberal feminists can now be found working on once-radical issues such as reproductive rights or comparable worth.

This account has much to recommend it. It captures broad trends clearly and economically. It recognizes political differences meaningful to the subjects of the story. It accounts for change over time. Above all, it has acquired the standing that comes with age – the interpretive equivalent of seniority rights. And, yet, the very neatness of the story seems increasingly suspect to some, the present writer included, who believe that its categories bleach out and isolate what should be a vibrant story with many connections to other histories.

III

Without slighting the considerable achievements of the existing literature in postwar women's history, then, I would like to suggest a somewhat different framework for consideration. This one would recognize the historical importance of second-wave feminism, yet would decenter it from its current place so as to make room for other important developments and account for them better. A focus on the waxing and waning of the family-wage system would help not only to better incorporate the revisionist findings of recent years on various topics, but would also bring into view subjects necessarily neglected when a white-dominated movement is assumed to be an era's pivotal development. Ironically, this approach also better captures the truly epochal significance of second-wave feminism: by situating it in the context of the specific social system that it both emerged from and helped to undo – much to the consternation of anti-feminists, who had their own complex relation to that system. The long decade popularly referred to as the 1950s, the years from 1946 to 1960, appears today as both the apex of that family-wage system and the beginning of its decline. And in fact many of the revisions and new visions now emerging in the field concern what exactly was going on in that period.

One question being aired with growing frequency is just how reactionary *were* the 1950s for women and gender? On the one hand, few would gainsay that the period from the late 1940s to the early 1960s was notably conservative. The heyday of the Cold War, it was also a time of domestic reaction. As communists were hounded and their ideas virtually outlawed, progressive Congress of Industrial Organizations (CIO) unions were cut adrift and with them the activists who had pressed hardest for racial and gender justice. Within the federal government, public officials consumed with fear about changes in public and private life purged not only suspected communists but also suspected homosexuals – the latter in much larger numbers (D'Emilio, 1983; E. May, 1988; Johnson, forthcoming). Unorthodox sexuality, like dissent of any kind, became more dangerous than at any time in recent memory. And yet, as true as all of this is, some scholars have come to question the view of the 1950s that came from Friedan's journalistic indictment.

The most obvious way Friedan's now virtually hegemonic view of the 1950s skews understanding is how it made a small minority stand in for women as a group. In Friedan's lexicon, "American wom[a]n" and "suburban wife" served as synonyms (Friedan, 1963, p. 15). The author's primary informants were her fellow Smith College graduates, a far more white, suburban, middle-class and upper-class population than American women at large. Their dissatisfaction with lives restricted to home and motherhood did resonate with women in other groups. Yet for low-income white women and black and Chicana women still living in segregated communities plagued by interlocking forms of discrimination, Friedan's pronouncements about the state of American womanhood seemed at best partial. Some working-class women and women of color also took offense at her prescriptions for change, most notably the idea that her constituency might solve its "problem that has no name" by getting advanced education and "meaningful" jobs and, by implication, hiring other women, presumably less unreasonably stymied, to clean their homes and care for their children. "If the care of a house and children is so unrewarding and unfulfilling to a wife and mother," one woman queried Friedan, "why isn't it so to other women, and why should other women do such work?" What about, asked another, "the poor thing who must tie herself to the bonds of housekeeping in my place? What of her? We must emancipate her too" (Foner, 1998, p. 296).

Even if one restricts the Friedan view of the 1950s to women who were white and middle class, it still impedes understanding of how change occurred. For one, it neglects to consider women's social opposites and how they were changing. One of the first historical studies to examine men as people of gender, Barbara Ehrenreich's *The Hearts of Men*, made the 1950s a much more interesting and internally conflicted age. Creatively surveying sources of male popular culture from the newly launched *Playboy* magazine to social criticism of imperiled manhood in the corporate colossus, Ehrenreich argued that the male breadwinner ideology had begun to come undone in the very years of its heyday. Where after the war, men still expected to grow up, marry, and support their wives and children with their earnings, by the 1970s growing numbers chafed under those responsibilities. Some simply went AWOL or deserted. In Ehrenreich's reading, the male "flight from commitment" was less a response to feminism than a goad to it: women came up with new ways of thinking about and organizing their lives because they *needed* to (Ehrenreich, 1983).

Since then, Friedan's synthesis has suffered a devastating challenge from the historian Joanne Meyerowitz, whose systematic study of the kinds of popular culture sources Friedan used drew quite different conclusions. Those sources were nowhere near as unequivocally hostile to women's aspirations as Friedan made out. Black publications especially, but white ones too, endorsed individual achievement as well as domestic ideals for women. "Friedan," Meyerowitz explained, "drew on mass culture as much as she countered it": "her forceful protest against a restrictive domestic ideal neglected the extent to which that ideal was already undermined" (Meyerowitz, 1994, pp. 232, 250). Even the outlawed abortion of this era appears differently in the light of careful research. Challenging the notion that the Supreme Court or dissenting doctors won legalization, Leslie Reagan has shown how ordinary women were the original and most important source of pressure for reform. "Their demand for abortions, generally hidden from public view and rarely spoken of in public," she writes, "transformed medical practice and law over the course of the twentieth century" (Reagan, 1997, p. 1). Documenting a crackdown on abortion that began in the 1940s, Reagan at the same time uncovered the refusal of women of all classes and contexts to honor a law that would make them bear children against their will. That stance finally convinced doctors to put aside their own professional conservatism and press for legal reform in the interest of their patients. Accounts such as these, more attuned to the complexities of social change, provide a stronger framework for interpreting information long available on how everyday life was changing in the years after World War II.

Seen in hindsight, those data capture the beginning of the end of the family-wage system. As early as 1972, Chafe understood that seemingly dull census numbers were adding up in potentially exciting ways. By now many scholars, especially demographic historians such as Robert Wells, have identified the key trends. The one that received the most attention was the steady rise in employment among married women and, later, women with young children as well: prima facie evidence of the demise of the family wage. Thus, where once the typical female worker was a young woman in the labor force briefly before marriage, now she was an adult with children working to support her family (Weiner, 1985). The rise in women's paid employment both reflected and furthered another trend: the growing use of contraception and abortion as women sought to plan their childbearing and as couples looked to sexuality more for pleasure than for reproduction. Once an economic asset for the labor or wages they could contribute to family support, children were now an economic burden for American parents – especially after Social Security and pensions came to provide financial support in old age. Seen in long-term perspective, the changes are dramatic: from 1800 to 1970, for example, while the birth rate dropped by more than half, life expectancy doubled. For women, it reached seventy-nine years by 1997 – as compared to forty-eight years in 1900. Modern couples thus envision much more time together after their children are gone – and wives can expect many years on their own after their husbands die: developments historians have barely touched. Marriage itself was becoming an increasingly insecure institution in the postwar years, as men and women alike came to *need* it less and to *want* more from it. As divorce rates mounted and "blended" families became the norm, Americans seemed to be redefining the purposes of marriage and family life (Wells, 1982; D'Emilio and Freedman, 1988).

Moreover, while it was barely visible in the census data, the antithesis of a society based on male-dominated households was taking root: a lesbian subculture involving larger numbers of women from more diverse origins than ever before. Its expansion presupposed the spread of female employment and higher education, as these won some women the autonomy to bypass traditional marriage in favor of life paths based on their own sexual orientations. With independent incomes and the relative anonymity of urban life, working-class lesbians in particular had the freedom to create new communities constructed around their own bars as gathering spaces (Faderman, 1992; Kennedy and Davis, 1993). As well, this subculture built on the wartime experiences of lesbians and gay men, who found partners and community in unprecedented numbers while in uniform (Berube, 1990; Meyer, 1996).

But it was not a matter of new behavior leading inevitably or simply to social change. Many people began *thinking* in new ways in the postwar years, or at least creatively appropriating to new purposes ideas then in circulation. One of the first to see this was the labor historian Alice Kessler-Harris. Faced with a booming, inflation-prone economy and a Cold War adversary that employed women workers in huge numbers in challenging work, the United States government came to identify women as an untapped national resource: "Womanpower," as one 1955 White House Conference dubbed their potential. Working women, for their part, turned the government's talk of "the free world" against longstanding discrimination as they called on Americans to practice the meritocracy the United States boasted of to the world. "Complaints of various kinds of discrimination," Kessler-Harris found, "flooded the Women's Bureau" well before sex discrimination on the job became illegal (Kessler-Harris, 1982, p. 308; also Hartmann, 1994). Consumer culture, too, may have prompted changes. Once scorned by Frankfurt School social critics as an anaesthetic if not a tool of capitalist mind control, consumer culture now appears to have been at least partially responsible for drawing more married women into the workforce and so advancing the changes that followed. As old luxuries became necessities and as service industries expanded their labor demands, more women left home to earn the money to buy these things: houses, college educations for their children, cars, refrigerators, and all the rest.

Some have also argued that commercial mass culture in the 1950s and early 1960s was not the mind-numbing force once thought. Looking at popular television shows, movies, and music of the era, the cultural historian Susan Douglas has argued that "growing up female with the mass media" helped bring millions of women to feminism. The media did this not intentionally, but incidentally, through their very contradictions: the mixed messages that at once goaded women to claim equality and told them they were subordinate sex objects. Popular music was another important site of cultural change. When young white teenage women chose rock and roll and rhythm and blues, music grounded in African American culture, they were opening doors to a world their elders hoped to wall off – and thereby in a small but significant way disrupting contemporary constructions of racial difference (Douglas, 1994, p. 7; Breines, 1992).

The long 1950s were also a time of cogent and influential social criticism. C. Wright Mills, Martin Luther King, Jr., Paul Goodman, Margaret Mead, Arthur Miller, and Lorraine Hansberry, among others, all produced popular work with important implications for gender, family, and community. Women read this work as avidly as men, and it deepened what the Beat fellow traveler Joyce Johnson called "the psychic hunger of my generation." Even words that speakers aimed at men landed beyond them. "Never for one minute did I think JFK was talking only to boys," writes Douglas of Kennedy's call to her generation in his inaugural address; "he was talking to me as well" (Ehrenreich, 1983; Breines, in Meyerowitz, 1994, p. 391; Douglas, 1994, p. 23).

When all of these strands are considered together, the long 1950s seem less the killer of major social change than its chrysalis. And the Friedan-inspired view of the 1950s appears as the organizing tool it was: as the sociologist Wini Breines said of women's liberationists, "we learned to understand our own lives as a flight from that time" (Meyerowitz, 1994, p. 383). Certainly it was a time when women of many groups *other* than the white middle and upper classes were doing significant organizing. It hardly seems coincidental that those active in the most creative ways were from groups left out of the family-wage bargain, who therefore had to find other ways of making do.

For black women in particular, the 1950s was hardly "the doldrums"; it was the germinal phase of one of the most significant mass movements in history. Scholars have come to realize how in that struggle, as Charles Payne puts it, "men led, but women organized" (Payne, 1990, p. 156). While women's historians had noted the prominence of black women in grassroots civil rights activism, it was students of the black freedom movement who recovered their work. By now, the biographies and local studies have multiplied. Among the stories best told are those of Jo Ann Gibson Robinson, whose group organized the infrastructure for the Montgomery bus boycott; Fannie Lou Hamer, the Mississippi sharecropper turned freedom fighter who inspired a generation of activists; and Ella Baker, whose profoundly democratic approach to social change continues to captivate scholars and activists alike (Robinson, 1987; Crawford, 1990; Lee, 1999; Grant, 1998).

Nor was it only in the civil rights movement per se that black women worked for change in the 1950s and 1960s. Labor historians have mined rich veins of activism by and for black women in trade unions of this era. The best-documented case is the United Packinghouse Workers of America (UPWA), where Addie Wyatt and others stood up for civil rights and gender equity within the union itself and in contracts with employers. Not coincidentally, the UPWA was a left-led, highly democratic union with a sizable black membership; those in more conservative, bureaucratic unions with a largely white male base would find the struggle less inviting (Halpern, 1997; R. Horowitz, 1997; Fehn, 1998; Follet, 1998).

In fact, the progressive wing of the labor movement was the site of significant organizing among white women as well as black from the late 1940s to the early 1960s. Like the civil rights work, it goes overlooked in the middle-class-derived "doldrums" model. Here, again, the pioneering work was done by those who lived outside the protection of the family-wage norm. The case of the United Auto Workers (UAW) is perhaps best known, thanks to the pioneering research of Nancy Gabin, who has revealed how from the late 1940s onward activists made use of the UAW's democratic ideology to bargain for women's needs with employers and combat the union's internal sexism. "If there had not been a few people like us doing the kinds of things that we have done," one of these women pointed out, "much of what we have seen happen in the women's movement might well not have happened" (Gabin, 1990, p. 188). The UAW was the largest union to host such activity, but it and the UPWA were not alone. The left-wing United Electrical Workers (UE) fought for principles that would still be considered radical today, such as differential pay raises for women to close the gender wage gap. And union men fought alongside union women for such demands. It was in working as a labor journalist for the UE in the 1940s that Betty Friedan first glimpsed feminism in action (Kannenberg, 1993; D. Horowitz, 1998).

Given its scope, such labor organizing suggests a need to rethink postwar women's politics away from the prevailing focus on exclusively female and overtly feminist currents. "If feminism is taken to be a recognition that women as a sex suffer inequalities and a commitment to the elimination of these sex-based hierarchies," the labor historian Dorothy Sue Cobble reasons, "then the struggles of union women for pay equity and for mechanisms to lessen the double burden of home and work should be as central to the history of twentieth-century feminism as the battle for the enactment of the Equal Rights Amendment" (Cobble, 1994, p. 57; also Ruíz, 1987; Rose, 1994). This political work and the victories it won for working-class women are of special interest because of the tendency in much scholarship to give the middle term of "race, class, and gender" less rigorous attention. Such working-class initiatives might offer an alternative historical model to the individualism for which white middle-class feminists are so often criticized. At the least, overlooking such political work leaves the historiography ill-equipped to understand change because it cannot appreciate where it started. As one UE activist told an interviewer: "When I meet younger women in higher jobs, I say 'You're welcome,' because many of them are in their jobs because my generation laid the foundations for them" (Kannenberg, 1993, p. 323).

IV

A new and more flexible framework would help not only in assimilating to a core narrative some of the revisions already appearing in the scholarship. It would also better accommodate the many questions left orphaned by the current approach because they do not fit well within its confines. So much has happened on so many fronts since the grassroots women's movement peaked a quarter-century ago in the mid-1970s that it would seem foolish to retain that movement as the point at which all interpretive lines must converge. Shifting attention away from the white, middle-class women who dominate the existing storyline, a new framework would turn our eyes toward others whose experiences could provide a fuller, richer, and more multilayered understanding of the period.

One area that desperately needs attention, and that fits better with the rise and fall of the family-wage system than with the resurgence of feminism, is gender in the new immigration. American society has been virtually remade by the influx of over 12 million people between the Immigration Act of 1965 and 1990 and more since, large numbers of them women and girls. Yet one would hardly know this from reading the literature on US women's history since 1945. Moreover, like the so-called "new immigrants" at the turn of the twentieth century, many recent immigrants are understood by the white majority to be racially different: somehow Other by appearance or culture, whether Latinos, West Indians, Asians, or Africans. Against the backdrop of global labor flows in an information age and growing fission in racial politics, what distinctive gender dimensions do the various new streams of immigration have?

These immigrants, like those of earlier eras, seem to have experienced tensions between first and second generations based on the rival pulls of the world they have left and the one they are joining. Scholars of early twentieth-century immigration have pointed to the powerful lure exercised on young women by commercial leisure, personal consumption, and the new freedoms perceived to come through these. Outside work, these proved the key means of initiation to an individualistic American culture, a culture about which many nevertheless remained ambivalent (Ewen, 1985; Gabaccia, 1994). One encounters these themes again in the oral histories of parents and the writings of young Asian American and Hispanic women – the rival accusations of being "old-fashioned" and patriarchal and of forfeiting a precious heritage for illusory gains.

But this generation's gender stories are likely to differ from older ones in important ways that deserve attention. What, for example, of Muslims who choose to wear the veil, of women who came as war brides or through arranged marriages (Glenn, 1986; Yuh, forthcoming), or of the sojourners – male and female – who return to their countries of birth with new resources? How do the experiences of highly educated women émigrées, many of them employed in traditionally male professions, differ from their homebound or wage-earning counterparts in 1900 and today? What difference does it make to immigrant women's traditional role in sustaining ethnic identity and imparting it to the next generation that global travel and communication are now so much easier? So far, fiction writers have said more on such questions than historians.

With renewed large-scale immigration and surging native-born female employment has come a revival of the mistress–maid dynamic that historians wrote so well about for the nineteenth century, thinking it largely a finished story by the 1970s. Barbara Ehrenreich, having recently worked as a participant-observer in the trade, has written brilliantly about the many unsettling questions this growth industry poses for feminism, hence women's history: about domestic labor itself, the women doing the work, and the families that employ them. Surely, the breakdown of the family-wage system helps to explain both demand and supply here (Ehrenreich, 2000). The racial dynamics of such service employment, or what Evelyn Nakano Glenn has called "the racial division of reproductive labor," also deserve closer attention from historians in this context (Glenn, 1994).

Scholars of gender might also undertake new kinds of community studies to explore the changing spatial dynamics of postwar US life. As growing numbers of immigrants in varied occupations settle in the suburbs, perhaps these long-stereotyped communities will be reconsidered by historians. Long the fortress of the family wage, suburbs now account for the vast majority of residents in the United States – more than live in cities and rural areas combined. As well, those once excluded from these communities – notably African Americans and immigrants of color – are now settling in established suburbs or creating new ones. In a pioneering treatment of these patterns and of gender in their making, Rosalyn Baxandall and Elizabeth Ewen explored how suburban Long Island residents themselves understood their communities and how the communities changed in the wake of civil rights and women's liberation (Baxandall and Ewen, 2000). This work is an important beginning. Still, historians have yet to produce scholarship on gender and postwar suburbs that rivals the sophistication of colonial and nineteenth-century community studies.

As future women's historians rethink how gender varied and changed over time in urban and suburban settings, they might also look in new ways at the later years of the Great Migration, when so many African Americans (as well as whites) left the South. Although most of the scholarly literature has focused on the population shift in the World War I era, in fact the numbers of black southerners heading North and West grew exponentially with World War II labor shortages and the collapse of the sharecropping system. In the 1940s and 1950s the numbers ran triple their counterparts for the years more studied; in the 1960s, another 613,000 left the South. Did women have distinctive reasons for leaving? Few empirically minded researchers have followed up on Darlene Clark Hine's suggestion that black women may have emigrated as much to escape rape and domestic violence as economic subjugation and Jim Crow (Hine, 1994). The lone study of women's migration from the South in the World War II era, by Gretchen Lemke-Santangelo, uses oral histories with Bay Area migrants to reveal how many managed to build communities of mutual care and sustenance and improve their own lives in the process (Lemke-Santangelo, 1996). Looking only at those who achieved economic security, however, her work bypasses questions about the origins and development of contemporary urban poverty.

More broadly, historians could explore the gender dimensions of the widening class structure among African Americans in the postwar years, with increasingly concentrated poverty at one end and unprecedented occupational mobility after the

1960s on the other. One thing is clear. The in-migration of people from the rural South coincided with the out-migration of living-wage jobs from cities. Weakening prospects for economic security dramatically affected family formation, and so contributed to the steep rise in welfare caseloads since the 1960s. The prominence of race, gender, and sexual themes in the public debate over welfare that has so profoundly shaped national politics in recent years thus has deep roots in the evolving systems of race, gender, and economics (Piven and Cloward, 1971; Stack, 1974; Gordon, 1990; Quadagno, 1994).

With new jobs opening up to blacks from civil rights organizing while old ones disappeared, the 1960s and 1970s would prove a formative time for modern urban black communities and for gender in them. Yet historians have yet to catch up to social scientists in coming to terms with the changes and their meaning. The distinctive qualities of black middle-class life in cities might draw attention, particularly now that the sociologist Mary Pattillo-McCoy has so insightfully captured how young women and men navigate growing up with a unique set of pressures (Pattillo-McCoy, 1999). Indeed, as the number of professional and better-off African Americans grows, scholars will likely pay more attention to the black middle class and the upwardly mobile women in it. Always more cut off than white women from the promises of the family-wage system, black women innovated from the materials at hand to find new ways of combining work, education, family, and community. In the postwar years, for example, black women were earning post-secondary degrees and building professional careers at higher rates than either black men or white women (Giddings, 1984; Jones, 1985). Their experiences and strategies deserve attention along with the more tragic stories of the women condemned to intergenerational poverty and endless frustration by a political economy stacked against them.

Lastly, curiosity about the demise of the family-wage system might bring more historians to probe questions of subjectivity. Perhaps because of the way the women's liberation movement, following the New Left, valued experience and action to the neglect of ideas, the intellectual history of women since 1945 – or even of feminism for that matter – is remarkably thin. The gap is especially puzzling in light of the conceptual revolutions that feminism has wrought in most academic disciplines as it changed the culture at large (DuBois et al., 1987).

Yet there are beginnings. From her ethnography of the Silicon Valley, the sociologist Judith Stacey, for example, has charted connections between socioeconomic change and increasingly complex blended family structures on one side, and New Age religious culture and what she calls postfeminism on the other (Stacey, 1990). Pointing to such diverse developments as the popularity of Robert Bly, the Promise Keepers movement, and the Million Man March as the main nexus of the emerging sex/gender system becomes the mother–child bond, Stacey sees a culture "desperately seeking daddies" (Stacey, 1996). The spread of anorexia nervosa, now afflicting black middle-class girls along with white, can also tell us about gender in contemporary American middle-class culture, according to the historian Joan Jacobs Brumberg. In a time of profound social change and in an economy in which "hedonism and discipline must coexist," this disease that in some ways resembles the fasting of medieval women seeking holiness "appears to be a secular addiction to a new kind of perfectionism, one that links personal salvation to the achievement of an external body configuration rather than an internal spiritual state" (Brumberg, 1988, pp. 260, 7).

Similarly, the surge of spiritual interest in recent years might be usefully explored in light of the ever-more hegemonic therapeutic culture in American life, with its thick gender content and deep but ambivalent connections to feminism. Second-wave feminism is almost unthinkable, after all, without vulgar Freudianism as its prompt and without humanistic psychology as its beacon. Ideas mattered to the emergence of this movement, as did the feelings to which these particular ideas gave legitimacy – namely, concern with "identity," "authenticity," and the realization of individual "human potential" (Herman, 1995; Buhle, 1998). Historians of postwar women, usually secular in their own orientations, might also seek out fresh ways of understanding why millions of American women embrace faith of one kind or another. The United States is the most religious of industrialized countries, after all, and seeking to understand that pattern and its consequences might enrich women's history scholarship – and even shake up what historians *think* they know about ostensibly secular institutions (Fitzgerald, 2001). Some outstanding models of analysis of the fusion of the sacred and the secular in women's lives can be found in African American historical writing. Kimberley Philips, for example, has explored "the braiding of faith and personal agency" and the role of churches as sites of intracommunity contestation, while Charles Payne has rigorously examined how spiritual conviction worked for adult black women in the Mississippi freedom movement (Philips, 1998, p. 230; Payne, 1990). Perhaps one day scholars of gender might even look to the mounting corpus of poststructuralist writing as a mass of primary sources with which to explore the assumptions, anxieties, and altered visions of this transitional era.

There might also be imaginative ways of connecting the gender content of the varied subjectivities of our own era with the demise of the family wage and the rise of a globalizing, information-driven economy. Historians of the post-1945 period could learn much from the rich historiography on the market revolution, the Second Great Awakening, and the remaking of white middle-class gender in the North in the nineteenth century. At the least, we might begin to think about the varied spiritualities of the postwar era in conjunction with its evolving social, political, and cultural divisions. Among white women, for example, we know that the social gospel of liberal Protestantism offered many a way into interracial reform long before it was popular (Evans, 1979; Lynn, 1992). But religion energized the right as well as the left. Conservative female activists in causes ranging from Boston's anti-busing movement to the campaign against the Equal Rights Amendment have drawn strength from Catholicism and certain strains of evangelical Protestantism, a reliance that needs closer historical attention (Mansbridge, 1986; Formisano, 1991). Faith has also tended to play a powerful role in community organizing across the political spectrum. Given the prominence of women as grassroots leaders in such local organizing of all descriptions in the last quarter-century, including in many working-class communities of color, historians have done astonishingly little to document, let alone to analyze, their efforts (Rose, 1994; Kaplan, 1997). A scholarship that explored the workings of faith in such diverse settings might find ways of blending the best of the many subfields that have enlivened recent history. Attuned to political economy and social history, its practitioners could develop a deeper grasp of consciousness and a better-anchored version of cultural studies than that now dominant.

The kind of framework suggested here would also make for better integration of organized *anti*-feminism into the narrative of postwar women's history. Prior to the late 1970s, a kind of teleology about feminism's future went unquestioned, even when the movement was criticized for racial or class chauvinism. The assumption, rarely argued but widely shared, was that once women were aroused, their politics would naturally move in a progressive direction – perhaps now deepened by anti-racism and attention to class inequities. The rise of a mass female anti-feminist movement in the 1980s came as a jolt to that very American faith in progress. Now, suddenly, feminists had to confront living – and loud – evidence that some women *liked* the system feminists aimed to change. At the least, they had to confront what Deirdre English called "the fear that feminism would free men first" (English, 1983).

As the lifelong conservative activist Phyllis Schlafly built a women's movement strong enough to defeat the Equal Rights Amendment, and as tens of thousands of women rallied against abortion rights by the late 1970s, a handful of feminist social scientists tried to understand what was happening. Using ethnographic methods, they found that feminist and anti-feminist activists, despite both camps being broadly middle class and white, tended to live contrasting lives with different values. The sociologist Kristin Luker starkly yet empathetically contrasted the two sides in the abortion conflict, showing how activists' positions emerged from their divergent views about motherhood, ethics, sex, the good society, and the role of government. In effect, each group saw the issue in zero-sum terms: if the government endorsed the values of their opponents, their own way of life would suffer. "Each side," explained the anthropologist Faye Ginsberg, "constitutes itself in dialogue with the 'enemy,' real and imagined" (Luker, 1984; Ginsberg, 1989, p. 196). Historians have yet to contribute their own research to this literature; when they do, a family-wage framework should aid understanding.

It should also help in comprehending men as people of gender in the years after 1945, perhaps the newest frontier for historians. Judith Stacey has argued that "the sort of family values campaign we most urgently need is one to revise popular masculinities" (Stacey, 1996, p. 77). Surely one way to promote such a revision is to dig beneath stereotypes, whether conservative or feminist, and seek to recover the complexities of manhood as idea and lived experience among different groups in the past. Some have already begun this work. The literature in African American studies about black masculinity in different contexts is rich and growing (Liebow, 1967; Harper, 1996; Carby, 1998; Hine et al., 1999). A similar exploration is beginning in Chicano studies, as evidenced by Ramón Gutiérrez's exploration of the gender and sexual politics of the Chicano movement and its historiography, and in Asian American studies, as in Yen Le Espiritu's thoughtful synthesis of how labor conditions and immigration law have structured gender relations among Asian Americans over time (Gutiérrez, 1993; Espiritu, 1997). Among the studies focusing on whites, labor historians have so far produced the most exciting work, such as Joshua Freeman's exposition of the gendered work culture of construction worker "hardhats" in the early 1970s (Freeman, 1993). But this project is just beginning: a great deal remains to be done.

V

The resurgence of feminism in the 1960s and 1970s will necessarily be a big part of the historiography of postwar US women and one of its most exciting objects of analysis. But it need not be the only one, nor the one to which all other developments are forced to speak. Chances are that if we move away from the women's movement story for a time to ask other questions of other groups and other developments in American life, we will come back to that story with fresh eyes. Able to be surprised and more deeply curious about what is in the sources, historians might also conceive more broad-gauged and generative interpretations. Beyond its capaciousness – its ability to embrace the gender histories of American women and men in both public and personal life in all their variety and complexity in the post-1945 years – a framework based on the unraveling of the family-wage system might have other advantages.

For some time now, historians of the 1960s have polarized in their interpretations of the meanings of these struggles. Some, largely but not only white men, argue that the excesses of the later years undermined the New Deal coalition and swelled the ranks of conservatives. Others, including scholars of color and white feminists, see this reading as a profound capitulation to the right that devalues the contributions of feminism, Black Power, and lesbian and gay liberation and that ignores the situations that made independent movements seem necessary to participants. The clash pivots on counter-posing class politics – usually understood as politics agreeable to the officialdom of the labor movement and the Democratic Party – to so-called identity politics. As the quarrels multiply, the rancor deepens. This, the philosopher Nancy Fraser warns, is a hazard characteristic of our age. When oppositions are created between what she calls the politics of recognition and the politics of redistribution, all parties who would benefit from progressive change lose – "stuck," as Fraser puts it, "in the vicious circles of mutually reinforcing cultural and economic subordination" (Fraser, 1997, p. 33).

The case of the anomalous gender wage gap mentioned earlier illustrates this. An inequity experienced by women turns out to build on wider economic inequality, such that it is hard to imagine a solution that does not incorporate both dimensions: recognition and redistribution, gender justice along with class fairness. Indeed, ironically, experts estimate that insofar as the wage gap has narrowed in the United States since the 1980s, over two-thirds of the change comes not from the improvement of women's earnings but from the reduction of blue-collar men's earnings with economic restructuring. The family-wage framework thus offers a way for historians to come to terms with the tensions so pivotal to our politics and so deeply rooted in our history and everyday life, while escaping dead-end debates over them. With the family-wage system as the object of inquiry, we might turn away from the circular firing line and turn our energies toward matters of common concern. We might, that is, approach with more curiosity *both* the current impasse in the politics of redistribution *and* the roots of the appeal of the politics of recognition. Such an approach could more effectively account for the distance women have traveled on so many fronts since 1945, while better illuminating the road ahead. Rather than persist in the bashing of "identity politics" in the name of "class politics" or vice versa, then, we might instead look to one of the core historical institutions that shaped each of these currents and left different groups of Americans with such conflicting feelings about them.

REFERENCES

Anderson, Karen: *Wartime Women: Sex Roles, Family Relations, and the Status of Women During World War II* (Westport, Conn.: Greenwood Press, 1981).

Asian Women United of California: *Making Waves: An Anthology of Writings By and About Asian American Women* (Boston: Beacon Press, 1989).

Baker, Paula: "The Domestication of American Politics," *American Historical Review*, 89 (June 1984): 620–49.

Baxandall, Rosalyn and Ewen, Elizabeth: *Picture Windows: How the Suburbs Happened* (New York: Basic Books, 2000).

Baxandall, Rosalyn and Gordon, Linda, eds.: *America's Working Women: A Documentary History* (New York: Vintage, 1976).

Baxandall, Rosalyn and Gordon, Linda, eds.: *Dear Sisters: Dispatches from the Women's Liberation Movement* (New York: Basic Books, 2000).

Bergmann, Barbara R.: *The Economic Emergence of Women* (New York: Basic Books, 1986).

Berube, Allan: *Coming Out Under Fire: The History of Gay Men and Women in World War Two* (New York: Free Press, 1990).

Blau, Francine D.: "Gender and Economic Outcomes: The Role of Wage Structure," *Labour*, 7 (Spring 1993): 73–92.

Blau, Francine D. and Kahn, Lawrence M.: "Wage Structure and Gender Earnings Differentials: An International Comparison," *Economica*, 63 (1996): S29–S62.

Breines, Wini: *Young, White, and Miserable: Growing Up Female in the Fifties* (Boston: Beacon Press, 1992).

Brown, Elsa Barkley: "Womanist Consciousness: Maggie Lena Walker and the Independent Order of Saint Luke," in Ellen DuBois and Vicki Ruíz (eds.), *Unequal Sisters: A Multicultural Reader in U.S. Women's History*, 2nd ed. (New York: Routledge, 1994), 268–83.

Brown, Elsa Barkley: "'What Has Happened Here?': The Politics of Difference in Women's History and Feminist Politics," in Darlene Clark Hine, Wilma King, and Linda Reed (eds.), *"We Specialize in the Wholly Impossible": A Reader in Black Women's History* (Brooklyn: Carlson, 1995), 39–54.

Brownmiller, Susan: *In Our Time: Memoir of a Revolution* (New York: Dial Press, 1999).

Brumberg, Joan Jacobs: *Fasting Girls: The History of Anorexia Nervosa* (Cambridge, Mass.: Harvard University Press, 1988).

Buhle, Mari Jo: *Feminism and Its Discontents: A Century of Struggle with Psychoanalysis* (Cambridge, Mass.: Harvard University Press, 1998).

Carby, Hazel V.: *Race Men* (Boston: Harvard University Press, 1998).

Chafe, William H.: *The American Woman: Her Changing Social, Economic, and Political Roles, 1920–1970* (New York: Oxford University Press, 1972).

Chappell, Marisa: "From Welfare Rights to Welfare Reform: The Politics of AFDC, 1964–1982" (Ph.D. diss., Northwestern University, 2002).

Clive, Alan: "Women Workers in World War II: Michigan as a Test Case," *Labor History*, 20 (1979): 44–72.

Cobble, Dorothy Sue: "Recapturing Working-Class Feminism: Union Women in the Postwar Era," in Joanne Meyerowitz (ed.), *Not June Cleaver: Women and Gender in Postwar America, 1945–1960* (Philadelphia: Temple University Press, 1994), 57–83.

Coontz, Stephanie: *The Way We Never Were: American Families and the Nostalgia Trap* (New York: Basic Books, 1992).

Cott, Nancy F.: *The Bonds of Womanhood: "Woman's Sphere" in New England, 1780–1835* (New Haven, Conn.: Yale University Press, 1978).

Cott, Nancy F.: *The Grounding of Modern Feminism* (New Haven, Conn.: Yale University Press, 1987).

Crawford, Vicki L. et al., eds.: *Women in the Civil Rights Movement: Trailblazers and Torchbearers, 1941–1965* (Bloomington: Indiana University Press, 1990).

Davis, Angela Y.: *Women, Race and Class* (New York: Random House, 1981).

D'Emilio, John: *Sexual Politics, Sexual Communities: The Making of a Homosexual Minority in the United States, 1940–1970* (Chicago: University of Chicago Press, 1983).

D'Emilio, John and Freedman, Estelle B.: *Intimate Matters: A History of Sexuality in America* (New York: Harper and Row, 1988).

Douglas, Susan J.: *Where the Girls Are: Growing Up Female with the Mass Media* (New York: Times Books, 1994).

DuBois, Ellen Carol, Korsmeyer, Carolyn, and Kelly, Gail P.: *Feminist Scholarship: Kindling in the Groves of Academe* (Urbana: University of Illinois Press, 1987).

Echols, Alice: *Daring to Be Bad: Radical Feminism in America, 1967–1975* (Minneapolis: University of Minnesota Press, 1989).

Ehrenreich, Barbara: *The Hearts of Men: American Dreams and the Flight from Commitment* (New York: Anchor Books, 1983).

Ehrenreich, Barbara: "Maid to Order: The Politics of Other Women's Work," *Harper's Magazine* (April 2000): 59–70.

English, Deirdre: "The Fear That Feminism Will Free Men First," in Ann Snitow et al. (eds.), *Powers of Desire* (New York: Monthly Review Press, 1983), 477–83.

Espiritu, Yen Le: *Asian American Women and Men: Labor, Laws, and Love* (Thousand Oaks, Calif.: Sage Publications, 1997).

Evans, Sara M.: *Personal Politics: The Roots of Women's Liberation in the Civil Rights Movement and the New Left* (New York: Alfred A. Knopf, 1979).

Evans, Sara M.: *Born for Liberty: A History of Women in America* (New York: Free Press, 1989).

Ewen, Elizabeth: *Immigrant Women in the Land of Dollars: Life and Culture on the Lower East Side, 1890–1925* (New York: Monthly Review Press, 1985).

Faderman, Lillian: *Odd Girls and Twilight Lovers: A History of Lesbian Life in Twentieth-Century America* (New York: Penguin, 1992).

Fehn, Bruce: "African-American Women and the Struggle for Equality in the Meatpacking Industry, 1940–1960," *Journal of Women's History*, 10 (Spring 1998): 45–69.

Ferree, Myra Marx and Hess, Beth B.: *Controversy and Coalition: The New Feminist Movement* (Boston: Twayne, 1985).

Fitzgerald, Maureen: "Losing Their Religion: Women, the State, and the Ascension of Secular Discourse," in Margaret Bendroth (ed.), *Women and Twentieth-Century Protestantism* (Urbana: University of Illinois Press, 2001).

Follet, Joyce: "Step by Step: Building a Feminist Movement" (videocassette, Wisconsin Public Television, 1998).

Foner, Eric: *The Story of American Freedom* (New York: W. W. Norton, 1998).

Formisano, Ronald P.: *Boston Against Busing: Race, Class and Ethnicity in the 1960s and 1970s* (Chapel Hill: University of North Carolina Press, 1991).

Fraser, Nancy: *Justice Interruptus: Critical Reflections on the "Postsocialist" Condition* (New York: Routledge, 1997).

Freeman, Joshua B.: "Hardhats: Construction Workers, Manliness, and the 1970 Pro-War Demonstrations," *Journal of Social History* (Summer 1993): 725–44.

Freeman, Jo: *The Politics of Women's Liberation: A Case Study of an Emerging Social Movement and Its Relation to the Policy Process* (New York: David McKay, 1975).

Friedan, Betty: *The Feminine Mystique* (New York: W. W. Norton, 1963).

Gabaccia, Donna: *From the Other Side: Women, Gender, and Immigrant Life in the U.S., 1820–1990* (Bloomington: Indiana University Press, 1994).

Gabin, Nancy F.: *Feminism in the Labor Movement: Women and the United Auto Workers, 1935–1975* (Ithaca, NY: Cornell University Press, 1990).

Garcia, Alma M.: *Chicana Feminist Thought: The Basic Historical Writings* (New York: Routledge, 1997).

Giddings, Paula: *When and Where I Enter: The Impact of Black Women on Race and Sex in America* (New York: William Morrow, 1984).

Ginsberg, Faye D.: *Contested Lives: The Abortion Debate in an American Community* (Berkeley: University of California Press, 1989).

Glenn, Evelyn Nakano: *Issei, Nissei, Warbride: Three Generations of Japanese American Women in Domestic Service* (Philadelphia: Temple University Press, 1986).

Glenn, Evelyn Nakano: "From Servitude to Service Work: Historical Continuities in the Racial Division of Paid Reproductive Labor," in Ellen DuBois and Vicki Ruíz (eds.), *Unequal Sisters: A Multicultural Reader in U.S. Women's History*, 2nd ed. (New York: Routledge, 1994), 405–35.

Gordon, Linda: *Woman's Body, Woman's Right: A Social History of Birth Control in America* (New York: Penguin, 1976).

Gordon, Linda: *Women, the State and Welfare* (Madison: University of Wisconsin Press, 1990).

Gordon, Linda: *Pitied But Not Entitled: Single Mothers and the History of Welfare* (New York: Free Press, 1994).

Grant, Joanne: *Ella Baker: Freedom Bound* (New York: John Wiley, 1998).

Gutiérrez, Ramón A.: "Community, Patriarchy and Individualism: The Politics of Chicano History and the Dream of Equality," *American Quarterly*, 45 (March 1993): 44–72.

Guy-Sheftall, Beverly, ed.: *Words on Fire: An Anthology of African-American Feminist Thought* (New York: New Press, 1995).

Halpern, Rick: *Down on the Killing Floor: Black and White Workers in Chicago's Packinghouses, 1904–54* (Chicago: University of Illinois Press, 1997).

Harper, Phillip Brian: *Are We Not Men? Masculine Anxiety and the Problem of African-American Identity* (New York: Oxford University Press, 1996).

Harrison, Cynthia: *On Account of Sex: The Politics of Women's Issues, 1945–1968* (Berkeley: University of California Press, 1988).

Hartmann, Susan M.: *The Home Front and Beyond: American Women in the 1940s* (Boston: Twayne, 1982).

Hartmann, Susan M.: "Women's Employment and the Domestic Ideal in the Early Cold War Years," in Joanne Meyerowitz (ed.), *Not June Cleaver: Women and Gender in Postwar America, 1945–1960* (Philadelphia: Temple University Press, 1994), 84–100.

Harvey, Brett: *The Fifties: A Women's Oral History* (New York: HarperCollins, 1993).

Herman, Ellen: *The Romance of American Psychology: Political Culture in the Age of the Experts* (Berkeley: University of California Press, 1995).

Hewitt, Nancy: "Beyond the Search for Sisterhood: American Women's History in the 1980s," in Ellen DuBois and Vicki Ruíz (eds.), *Unequal Sisters: A Multicultural Reader in U.S. Women's History*, 2nd ed. (New York: Routledge, 1994), 1–19.

Higginbotham, Evelyn Brooks: "African-American Women's History and the Metalanguage of Race," in Darlene Clark Hine, Wilma King, and Linda Reed (eds.), *"We Specialize in the Wholly Impossible": A Reader in Black Women's History* (Brooklyn: Carlson, 1995), 3–24.

Hine, Darlene Clark: *Hine Sight: Black Women and the Re-Construction of American History* (Bloomington: Indiana University Press, 1994).

Hine, Darlene Clark et al.: *A Question of Manhood: A Reader in U.S. Black Men's History and Masculinity* (Bloomington: Indiana University Press, 1999).

Horowitz, Daniel: *Betty Friedan and the Making of "The Feminine Mystique": The American Left, the Cold War, and Modern Feminism* (Amherst: University of Massachusetts Press, 1998).

Horowitz, Roger: *"Negro and White, Unite and Fight!": A Social History of Industrial Unionism in Meatpacking, 1930–1990* (Urbana: University of Illinois Press, 1997).

Johnson, David K.: *The Lavender Scare: Gays and Lesbians in the Federal Civil Service, 1945–1975* (Chicago: University of Chicago Press, forthcoming).

Jones, Jacqueline: *Labor of Love, Labor of Sorrow: Black Women, Work, and the Family, from Slavery to the Present* (New York: Basic Books, 1985).

Kannenberg, Lisa: "The Impact of the Cold War on Women's Trade Union Activism: The UE Experience," *Labor History*, 34 (Spring/Summer 1993): 309–23.

Kaplan, Temma: *Crazy for Democracy: Women in Grassroots Movements* (New York: Routledge, 1997).

Kennedy, Elizabeth Lapovsky and Davis, Madeline D.: *Boots of Leather, Slippers of Gold: The History of a Lesbian Community* (New York: Routledge, 1993).

Kerber, Linda K.: *Women of the Republic: Intellect and Ideology in Revolutionary America* (Chapel Hill: University of North Carolina Press, 1980).

Kerber, Linda K.: *No Constitutional Right to Be Ladies: Women and the Obligations of Citizenship* (New York: Hill and Wang, 1999).

Kerber, Linda K. et al.: *U.S. History as Women's History: New Feminist Essays* (Chapel Hill: University of North Carolina Press, 1995).

Kessler-Harris, Alice: *Out to Work: A History of Wage-Earning Women in the United States* (New York: Oxford University Press, 1982).

Lee, Chana Kai: *For Freedom's Sake: The Life of Fannie Lou Hamer* (Urbana: University of Illinois Press, 1999).

Lemke-Santangelo, Gretchen: *Abiding Courage: African American Migrant Women and the East Bay Community* (Chapel Hill: University of North Carolina Press, 1996).

Liebow, Elliot: *Tally's Corner: A Study of Negro Streetcorner Men* (Boston: Little, Brown, 1967).

Lerner, Gerda: *Black Women in White America: A Documentary History* (New York: Random House, 1972).

Lerner, Gerda: *The Majority Finds Its Past: Placing Women in History* (New York: Oxford University Press, 1979).

Luker, Kristin: *Abortion and the Politics of Motherhood* (Berkeley: University of California Press, 1984).

Lynn, Susan: *Progressive Women in Conservative Times: Racial Justice, Peace, and Feminism, 1945 to the 1960s* (New Brunswick, NJ: Rutgers University Press, 1992).

MacLean, Nancy: "The Hidden History of Affirmative Action: Working Women's Struggles in the 1970s and the Gender of Class," *Feminist Studies*, 25 (Spring 1999): 43–78.

Mansbridge, Jane J.: *Why We Lost the ERA* (Chicago: University of Chicago Press, 1986).

May, Elaine Tyler: *Homeward Bound: American Families in the Cold War Era* (New York: Basic Books, 1988).

May, Martha: "The Historical Problem of the Family Wage: The Ford Motor Company and the Five Dollar Day," *Feminist Studies*, 8 (Summer 1982): 399–424.

Meyer, Leisa D.: *Creating GI Jane: Sexuality and Power in the Women's Army Corps During World War II* (New York: Columbia University Press, 1996).

Meyerowitz, Joanne, ed.: *Not June Cleaver: Women and Gender in Postwar America, 1945–1960* (Philadelphia: Temple University Press, 1994).

Moraga, Cherrie and Anzaldua, Gloria: *This Bridge Called My Back: Writings by Radical Women of Color* (Watertown, Mass.: Persephone Press, 1981).

O'Farrell, Brigid and Kornbluh, Joyce L.: *Rocking the Boat: Union Women's Voices, 1915–1975* (New Brunswick, NJ: Rutgers University Press, 1996).

Orleck, Annelise: *Common Sense and a Little Fire: Women and Working-Class Politics in the United States, 1900–1965* (Chapel Hill: University of North Carolina Press, 1995).

Pattillo-McCoy, Mary: *Black Picket Fences: Privilege and Peril Among the Black Middle Class* (Chicago: University of Chicago Press, 1999).

Payne, Charles: "Men Led, But Women Organized: Movement Participation of Women in the Mississippi Delta," in Guida West and Rhoda Lois Brumberg (eds.), *Women and Social Protest* (New York: Oxford University Press, 1990), 156–65.

Philips, Kimberley L.: "Making a Church Home: African-American Migrants, Religion, and Working-Class Activism," in Eric Arnesen et al. (eds.), *Labor Histories: Class, Politics, and the Working-Class Experience* (Urbana: University of Illinois Press, 1998), 230–56.

Piven, Frances Fox and Cloward, Richard: *Regulating the Poor: The Functions of Public Welfare* (New York: Pantheon, 1971).

Quadagno, Jill: *The Color of Welfare: How Racism Undermined the War on Poverty* (New York: Oxford University Press, 1994).

Reagan, Leslie: *When Abortion Was a Crime: Women, Medicine, and Law in the United States, 1867–1973* (Berkeley: University of California Press, 1997).

Rich, Adrienne: *On Lies, Secrets, and Silence: Selected Prose, 1966–1978* (New York: W. W. Norton, 1979).

Robinson, Jo Ann Gibson, with David J. Garrow: *The Montgomery Bus Boycott and the Women Who Started It: The Memoir of JoAnn Gibson Robinson* (Knoxville: University of Tennessee Press, 1987).

Rose, Margaret: "Gender and Civic Activism in Mexican American Barrios in California: The Community Service Organization, 1947–1962," in Joanne Meyerowitz (ed.), *Not June Cleaver: Women and Gender in Postwar America, 1945–1960* (Philadelphia: Temple University Press, 1994), 177–200.

Rosen, Ruth: *The World Split Open: How the Modern Women's Movement Changed America* (New York: Viking, 2000).

Ruíz, Vicki L.: *Cannery Women, Cannery Lives: Mexican Women, Unionization, and the California Food Processing Industry, 1930–1950* (Albuquerque: University of New Mexico, 1987).

Ruíz, Vicki L.: *From Out of the Shadows: Mexican Women in Twentieth-Century America* (New York: Oxford University Press, 1998).

Rupp, Leila and Taylor, Verta: *Survival in the Doldrums: The American Women's Rights Movement, 1945 to the 1960s* (New York: Oxford University Press, 1987).

Seifer, Nancy: *"Nobody Speaks for Me!": Self-Portraits of American Working-Class Women* (New York: Simon and Schuster, 1976).

Stacey, Judith: *Brave New Families: Stories of Domestic Upheaval in Late-Twentieth-Century America* (New York: Basic Books, 1990).

Stacey, Judith: *In the Name of the Family: Rethinking Family Values in the Postmodern Age* (Boston: Beacon Press, 1996).

Stack, Carol B.: *All Our Kin: Strategies for Survival in a Black Community* (New York: Harper and Row, 1974).

Ulrich, Laurel Thatcher: *Good Wives: Image and Reality in the Lives of Women in Northern New England, 1650–1750* (New York: Oxford University Press, 1982).

Wandersee, Winifred D.: *On the Move: American Women in the 1970s* (Boston: Twayne, 1988).

Weiner, Lynn Y.: *From Working Girl to Working Mother: The Female Labor Force in the U.S., 1820–1980* (Chapel Hill: University of North Carolina Press, 1985).

Wells, Robert V.: *Revolutions in Americans' Lives: A Demographic Perspective on the History of Americans, Their Families, and Their Society* (Westport, Conn.: Greenwood Press, 1982).

White, Deborah Gray: *Too Heavy a Load: Black Women in Defense of Themselves, 1894–1994* (New York: W. W. Norton, 1999).

Yuh, Ji-Yeon: *Beyond the Shadow of Camptown: Korean Military Brides in America* (New York: New York University Press, forthcoming).

CHAPTER FOURTEEN

Sexuality and the Movements for Sexual Liberation

BETH BAILEY

Even to the casual observer, it seems obvious that profound and fundamental changes have taken place in the realm of sexuality in the last half of the twentieth century. Most prominent among these, one might argue, are changes in sexual behaviors and sexual mores, the role of sex in our popular culture, the increased acceptance of gender equality and reproductive freedoms, and the growing visibility of gay men and lesbians in American society. The evidence of such change is worth recounting in some detail.

In 1950, fewer than four out of one hundred babies were born to unmarried women. In the 1990s, 30 percent of all births were to single women. In 1960, only 17,000 couples were reported to be living together "without benefit of matrimony," as it was described at the time. That number increased 900 percent by the end of the decade and continued to rise until "living together" had become virtually unremarkable.

In 1963, a discussion of "The Sexual Revolution" was pulled from the schedule of a New York City TV station because station executives thought the very topic inappropriate for broadcast television. This was not an aberration: on TV sitcoms, married couples were consigned to twin beds and even the term "pregnant" was not fully acceptable. In 1965, *The Sound of Music* won the Academy Award for best motion picture; in 1999 it was the R-rated film *American Beauty*.

In the 1940s, 1950s, and 1960s, gay men and lesbians were commonly expelled from universities or fired from jobs if discovered to be homosexual. Homosexuality was classified as a mental illness by the American Psychiatric Institute until 1974. In contrast, by the end of the twentieth century many major corporations offered benefits to same-sex domestic partners, most college campuses had active lesbian-gay-bisexual student organizations, and annual gay pride parades drew huge crowds of celebrants throughout the nation. (Gay men and women still were subject to dishonorable discharges from the military and only one state recognized the union – not marriage – of homosexual couples.)

Before the Supreme Court decision *Roe v. Wade* guaranteed a woman's constitutional right to abortion in 1973, women sought often dangerous illegal abortions or attempted the process themselves, resorting to injections of lye, douching with bleach, or inserting coathangers into their uteruses. In the early 1960s, Chicago's Cook County Hospital alone treated more than 5,000 women a year for abortion-related complications, some of which were fatal. Perhaps more surprising is the fact that, before the 1965 *Griswold v. Connecticut* Supreme Court decision, married couples could be denied access to birth control. Before 1972, doctors could legally refuse birth control to unmarried adults – not for medical reasons, but for "moral" ones.

At the beginning of the twenty-first century, Americans disagree about the meaning of such changes. Some see them as signs of progress (even if they are concerned about some of the specifics), while others see them as evidence of the degradation of American society. Historians of sexuality, who by no means represent a cross-section of the American public, tend toward the former.

Political and moral evaluation aside, however, such pieces of historical evidence suggest that the history of sexuality written about postwar America would be a narrative of sexual liberation. To some extent that is true. Historians have tended to focus on change, as historians do, and the "sexual revolution" of the postwar era commands a central position in the historiography. But historians are scarcely unanimous about the meaning of these changes or their causes. Some focus on human agency and trace the political movements for sexual and gender liberation. Others locate the sources of change primarily in large-scale social, economic, and cultural forces. A significant handful believe that the focus on change obscures the continuity of experience of those who had never conformed to middle-class (hetero)sexual mores and who had, for the most part, existed beyond the purview of mainstream society before the "revolution." Some scholars question the validity of a progressive narrative altogether. These historians do not divide into clear and discrete historiographical schools or camps. In scholarly analyses, these positions and focuses overlap, and there is frequently tension (sometimes quite productive) within a single book.

That complexity is further complicated by two other factors. First, there is no agreement about what we write about when we write about "sex." There is a surprisingly small amount of "sex," per se, in these histories. Most of the history of sexuality is at some remove from sex itself, in part because unmediated "sex" is impossible to find. We rely on representations of sex or on discourses about sex. Usually, the closest we get to the physical acts of sex is through records of some form of surveillance, most frequently of those deemed sexually deviant. These records are scarcely an unproblematic source.

Of course, most historians agree that the history of sexuality has a broad scope and that sex is much more than physical acts. Some historians of sexuality write about social movements. Some write about attempts to control sexual behaviors or to define and regulate "sex." Others attempt to understand the construction of sexuality, especially in relation to gender. One group of historians writes about the formations of sexual identities or communities. Another tries to understand the production of sexual norms and conventions. Still others use traditional social history methods to attempt to recover the experience of "ordinary" Americans – in contrast to those who focus on people who most prominently seek sexual freedom or "revolution." Once again, these categories are not rigid or exclusionary. Most historians of sexuality do not restrict themselves to a single focus within the field. The clearest topical division in the field is based on sexual orientation; another, less important division is gender-based. There is a large literature exclusively on gay/lesbian/queer Americans; a small literature focused exclusively on heterosexual experiences; and a somewhat larger set of works that address both or analyze the construction of these binary categories.

Finally, a second complicating factor stems from the origins of the field itself. The very notion of a history of sexuality emerged in the postwar years, and the field was shaped by the very events it attempts to analyze. The history of sexuality is one of the newest fields in American history, and the portion of the field focusing on postwar America is among the most rapidly changing and inchoate areas in American historiography. For those reasons, it is not possible or even especially useful to lay out an orderly set of schools and interpretations. Instead, this essay will discuss the origins of the field and the historiographical implications of those origins. Following that discussion I will offer a chronological overview of the history of sexuality in America beginning in World War II. Within that history I will address specific historiographical debates and controversies.

Origins and Issues

The history of sexuality in America is, in many ways, a field just coming into its own. One might, arguably, trace its origins as a self-conscious field to 1988, with the publication of John D'Emilio and Estelle Freedman's pathbreaking *Intimate Matters: A History of Sexuality in America*. Certainly, many historians had been writing about sexuality before that; *Intimate Matters* was, in fact, a synthesis of existing scholarship. D'Emilio and Freedman, both of whom had written previously about sexuality, cited 283 books and articles in their selected bibliography – hardly suggesting a virgin field. However, most of the historians upon whom they relied did not define themselves as historians of sexuality. They fit, usually fairly comfortably, in existing fields: social or cultural history; the history of women (with a few using the term gender) or of the family; histories of science and medicine. It was not until 1992 that American history's premier journal, the *Journal of American History*, began to list recent scholarly publications under the category "sexuality."

At the beginning of the twenty-first century, the history of sexuality is a boom field – it has become "sexy," in the informal jargon of the academy. Presses ranging from the University of Chicago to Routledge not only have series on sexuality, but devote considerable editorial and promotional resources to them. College courses on the history of sexuality are commonplace. Dissertation students eagerly embrace topics relating to sexuality and assume the legitimacy – even the necessity – of using sexuality as a category of historical analysis.

Yet for all its contemporaneity and its youth, the history of sexuality shows clear signs of its parentage. The field emerged from the "new" histories created in the social and political upheavals of the 1960s and 1970s. As Americans struggled over issues such as the Vietnam War, the African American civil rights movement, and feminism, historians (themselves Americans caught in the turmoil of the time) found models of American unity and consensus ever-less compelling. "New" social historians focused on the divisions in American society and asked questions about power relations. Strongly influenced by the era's movements for social justice, they wrote about the poor, the marginalized, the oppressed, recasting American history by shifting its focus.

Many of the men and women who wrote these first, controversial, histories intended them not only as scholarship but as activism. Recovering the history of women, African Americans, and workers gave those groups voice, historians argued, framing their projects as acts of empowerment. While this claim was critically important to the early works of "new" women's history (often concerning sexuality), it also provided the basis for early work on the history of gay men and lesbians. Jonathan Katz, who in 1976 published the first collection of historical documents on the experience of gay men and lesbians in America, wrote in his introduction: "We have been the silent minority, the silenced minority – invisible women, invisible men. . . . For a long time we were a people perceived out of time and place – socially unsituated, without a history." In an activist voice, Katz argued: "Knowledge of Gay history helps restore a people to its past, to itself; it extends the range of human possibility, suggests new ways of living, new ways of loving" (Katz, 1976, pp. 1, 14).

The "new" histories' activist intent and concern with the marginalized and oppressed have continued into the next scholarly generation. Those who write histories of sexuality are, in the main, highly conscious of the possible political import of their work and continue in the desire that historical knowledge may improve contemporary society. Many are often fairly explicit about political commitments and/or activist intentions. For example, Leslie Reagan concludes her excellent study *When Abortion Was a Crime: Women, Medicine, and Law in the United States, 1867–1973* by arguing for continued legal abortion in the United States. "Making abortion hard to obtain will not return the United States to an imagined time of virginal brides and stable families," she writes, "it will return us to a time of crowded septic abortion wards, avoidable deaths, and the routinization of punitive treatment of women by state authorities and their surrogates" (Reagan, 1997, p. 250). Her statement of advocacy follows almost 250 pages of immensely careful and nuanced historical analysis, but a feminist concern for women's reproductive choice animates the entire book. In a different tack, John Howard begins his equally impressive *Men Like That: A Southern Queer History* with the claim that "in today's movements for economic and social justice, we benefit from recounting and scrutinizing historical events." "Without apology," he states, "I concede that my academic explorations of the past are informed by my activist's will for social change in the present" (Howard, 1999, p. xxii).

Also in keeping with the practice of their fields of origin, current historians of sexuality continue to focus on those who have been historically oppressed and marginalized. Today it is easier to find excellent histories of "queer" experience than of heterosexual lives; we know more about the sexualities of heterosexual women than of heterosexual men; more about those who challenged gender/sexual norms than about those who lived by them.

Of course, many of those currently writing histories of sexuality are a scholarly generation – or even two – removed from the new social historians of the 1960s and 1970s, to whom they owe so much, and have moved in different directions from what was once called "history from the bottom up." The development of the history of sexuality has been influenced by a range of theoretical formulations most fully articulated or disseminated in the final decades of the twentieth century. In general, American historians have been notably resistant to theoretical enthusiasms. That is at least in part because grand theory often appears totalizing and ahistorical. Historians of sexuality (along with historians of gender and of race) have been somewhat more interested in cultural theory than most Americanists, but tend to treat "theory" as a toolbox, selecting useful ideas in a fairly eclectic fashion and jettisoning the aspects that fit uneasily with the specificity of historical analysis. The most important concepts that have shaped the historiography of sexuality include the general notion of social constructionism and the more specific understandings of power and of sexuality set forth by Michel Foucault in work that appeared in the English language in the 1970s.

First and most fundamentally, most historians of sexuality have treated both gender and sexuality as socially (and historically) constructed. Rather than positing a set of timeless, inherent, and *essential* differences between the sexes, they have argued that basic biological differences are given meaning – or constructed – in and by specific cultures. Through the 1980s, most would make a distinction between the term "sex" (used to describe the basic biological "facts" of maleness and femaleness) and the term "gender" (the socially constructed categories of male and female, masculine and feminine, through which those biological differences were given meaning). Later theorists would raise questions about the givenness of the body itself, suggesting that biological sex was also constructed. Few historians have traveled very far down that path, but in general they are increasingly careful about assuming the givenness of any definitional category.

Not surprisingly, those who attempt to write histories of sexuality tend to be constructionists, for the very idea that sexuality has a history presumes that sexuality is not stable, essential, timeless, or universal in its manifestations and meanings. Constructionists begin with the premise that sex and sexuality are subject to historical forces and do indeed change over time and across cultures. Of course, there is probably very little that has changed over time in the physical acts of sex; human bodies have been coming into contact with one another for many thousands of years, and even allowing for unbounded creativity there are still a relatively limited number of possible physical permutations. The meaning of those acts, however, both to participants and to the cultures in which they are situated, has varied greatly over time and place.

Within the field of the history of sexuality in America, debates over social construction versus essentialism have only been truly significant in gay and lesbian history. Some historians, most prominently Europeanist John Boswell but to some extent Jonathan Katz in his 1976 documentary collection, *Gay American History*, have written about "gay people" or about "Lesbians and Gay men" in the distant past. Most historians agree that same-sex sex (and the confusion inherent in the terms is worth noting) has always existed, but was not defined through categories like "gay," "homosexual," or "lesbian." In most Western cultures, while sexual acts such as sodomy were often illegal and punishable by extreme means, an individual's identity – whether to him/herself or to the society at large – was not based upon the sort of sexual acts in which he or she engaged. The categories "homosexual" and "heterosexual" themselves did not exist, nor did such modern notions of identity. Historians date the emergence of a possible homosexual identity differently, but most agree that by the late nineteenth century categories of homosexuality and heterosexuality had been consolidated and often structured the experiences and meanings of sex.

As this essay focuses on the history of sexuality in postwar America, such debates about pre-twentieth-century categories seem irrelevant. However, they have more significance than one might imagine. The first historians who sought a history of gay people did so to demonstrate the legitimacy of such identity: we are everywhere; we have always been here. As I have already argued, many historians of sexuality still write from a desire to promote social justice; they are aware of the political implications of their work. And since the 1970s, much has been invested in the public claim that sexual orientation is, in some fundamental way, essential – not a choice, not a "sickness," not an "identity," just a simple and unalterable fact. While social-constructionist analysis does not dispute the existence of same-sex desire, dealing, instead, with the ways in which such desire has been given meaning and constituted within a set of binary categories of identity, scholarly notions about the construction of "homosexuality" fit uneasily with arguments for the civil rights of gay, lesbian, bisexual, and transgendered people. Scholarly nuances do not necessarily translate very well in the public arena (Epstein, 1987).

The dilemma is somewhat similar to that faced by scholars who reject the existence of biological categories of "race" but who, in what might seem a paradox, seek race-based remedies to social inequality. Very much aware that people's lives are structured in and through historically-socially constructed racial categories, whether or not biological races "really" exist, some advocate a "strategic essentialism." Few historians of gay/lesbian/queer Americans find themselves in such troubled waters, but they often must walk a fine line in their treatments of identity and desire.

After the notion of social construction, the work of Michel Foucault probably influenced the development of the field more than any other theoretical approach. That is not to say that Foucault's theories were carefully and systematically applied by historians; there were few strict Foucauldian analyses of the history of sexuality in America. Nonetheless, his influence was powerful and widespread. In a way, just as one might distinguish between Freud's work and a more general Freudianism, one might think of Foucault and a more general Foucauldianism.

Perhaps most important was Foucault's insistence that power was multiple, deployed and coordinated through a multiplicity of discourses, not located in a single, identifiable, external site. Thus humans are not caught between the poles of freedom and repression, liberation and domination, but instead are enmeshed in webs of power. Such understandings, even though not fully accepted or articulated by historians, helped to undermine the dominance of a "progressive" narrative of the history of sexuality, in which the forces of liberation struggle against – and gradually triumph over – repression. In fact, John D'Emilio and Estelle Freedman, on the very first page of their introduction to *Intimate Matters*, disavow the progressive narrative: "The history of American sexuality told in the following pages is not one of progress from repression to liberation, ignorance to wisdom, or enslavement to freedom. Indeed, the poles of freedom and liberation are not the organizing principles of our work" (p. xi).

A suspicion of the progressive narrative did, in fact, shape much writing on the history of sexuality in America. At the same time, the pull of the freedom narrative is and has been extraordinarily strong in the scholarship on *postwar* American history. Studies of movements for social justice and liberation tend to accept a framework of justice and liberation, especially as a full generation of historical scholarship was written by those who had been part of those struggles and felt strongly enough about them to continue to attempt to understand their successes and failures. Experientially, intuitively, and analytically, these scholars believed that movements for civil rights, against the Vietnam War, and for social justice and equality were meaningful and progressive, even if sometimes flawed and incomplete.

Historiographically, scholarship on the history of postwar sexuality is probably as closely related to the scholarship on "the Sixties" or "the Movement" as to the larger field of the history of sexuality. That is not surprising, as few historians would argue that a topic can be studied in isolation from its time. Our historiographical under-standings of society and politics in the colonial era are scarcely absent from histories of sexuality in colonial America. Nonetheless, a field that owes much both to narra-tives of liberation and to Foucauldian notions of power must contend with some important tensions.

Histories of Sexuality in Postwar America

Though this volume focuses on the period from 1945 forward, a historiography of sexuality demands the inclusion of World War II as well. World War II is a watershed in the history of sexuality in twentieth-century America, but not for the obvious reasons. Yes, as young men and women faced separation "for the duration" with the knowledge that death might come sooner than victory, they did things they might not otherwise have done: have sexual intercourse; get married; explore desires they had been told were not "normal." These changes in sexual behavior and the strug-gles over them are undeniably significant. But World War II was significant to the history of sexuality for many other reasons, some of which had very little to do with sex.

World War II changed the United States. This was a war not confined to the mil-itary, but one in which the civilian population was mobilized as well. The demands of such a war put people into motion. More than 13 million Americans served in the armed forces and more than 15 million civilians moved to another county or another state, most for defense-related work. People who had never traveled more than a hundred miles from their homes found themselves across the country or across the world, living in close proximity to people from very different backgrounds and with very different cultural expectations.

It is important to remember how provincial much of America was in 1941. Regional differences were much more pronounced then than now; racial segregation much more complete; mechanisms of national culture, whether the media or educa-tional institutions, were much weaker. As David Farber and I argue in *The First Strange Place: The Alchemy of Race and Sex in World War II Hawaii* (an argument upon which I build in *Sex in the Heartland*), World War II changed the cultural geog-raphy of the nation. During the war, more than ever before, Americans found them-selves in close and often enforced contact with others not like themselves. These contacts were not always pleasant or easy, especially under the difficult circumstances of war, but they were disruptive. These disruptions and the dislocations brought about by the war created new spaces for contestation and change in American society. They opened new arenas of possibility, created cracks and fissures in which social change – including changes in sexual behaviors and mores – would take root (Bailey and Farber, 1992).

Changes brought about by the war were not only demographic, but structural. During World War II the federal government assumed an unprecedented role in the life of the nation. The needs of the wartime state, as defined by the federal government, often conflicted with local custom. In administering the war, the federal government often undermined the control of local elites and created new sites of power and authority which ultimately tied local communities and their citizens more closely to an increasingly powerful national culture. In terms of sex, most of the institutions through which the federal government attempted to manage sex – departments of public health focused on VD control, the military itself – took actions that would be difficult to characterize as progressive. Yet these institutions would have a different long-term effect. And in some ways, what is most important is that they disrupted local control and local hierarchies of power. These disruptions, like the demographic ones, would create the ground on which the sexual revolution would eventually be staged.

Historians who write about sex and sexuality during World War II are divided on the question of whether the new freedoms of wartime or the new mechanisms of surveillance and control were most significant. Those who write about sexuality in general terms, focusing explicitly or implicitly upon majority experiences, tend to stress new freedoms. Those who focus on the experiences of "minority" populations – gay men and lesbians; people of color; the working class; even women – are more aware of mechanisms of control that were employed to counter possible freedoms. These different interpretations reflect the critical divisions that existed among groups in American society during the war years.

For example, John Costello, in his engaging work on sexuality in Britain and the United States during the war, *Virtue Under Fire*, suggests that the intense experience of the war itself "enhanced intimacy and the expression of love that liberated many people from traditional inhibitions" (Costello, 1985, p. 2). Costello argues, in a progressive vein, not only that the war accelerated the process of social change and so helped to liberalize moral attitudes, but also that sexual liberalization was inextricably linked to improvements in women's economic and social status brought about, in large part, by the war.

In contrast, Allan Bérubé's emotionally powerful *Coming Out Under Fire: The History of Gay Men and Women in World War II*, paints a deeply ambivalent picture of sexuality in wartime America. Surveillance and control are a central part of this history. In an attempt to forge the most effective fighting force, Bérubé explains, the military tried to screen out those whom military officials believed might somehow compromise morale or effectiveness in combat. According to Bérubé, psychiatrists introduced the idea that the "homosexual [was] a personality type unfit for military service and combat" to the armed forces and, in introducing screening procedures to detect and disqualify gay men, helped to create an "administrative apparatus" that relied heavily on surveillance, interrogation, mass indoctrination, and discharge from service (Bérubé, 1990, p. 2).

At the same time, Bérubé finds much evidence that wartime mobilization "relaxed the social constraints of peacetime" and made it possible for many gay men and lesbians to escape lives of isolation and silence. "Gathered together in military camps," he writes, "they often came to terms with their sexual desires, fell in love, made friends with other gay people, and began to name and talk about who they were." Bérubé is not simply documenting the existence of both repression and liberation. Instead, he sees World War II as an arena of struggle and negotiation, in which "a dynamic power relationship developed between gay citizens and their government and . . . transformed them both" (Bérubé, 1990, p. 7).

Among the most interesting works on sexuality during the war is Leisa Meyer's *Creating GI Jane: Sexuality and Power in the Women's Army Corps During World War II*. Meyer focuses on constructions of sexuality rather than on the experiences of women in the WAC, analyzing the ways in which such constructions were deployed in attempts to "create a place for women without disrupting contemporary definitions of 'masculinity' and 'femininity'" (Meyer, 1996, p. 2). Meyer's attention to the importance of race in constructions of sexuality and to the sexual agency of both heterosexual women and lesbians makes her study especially useful.

In the years following the end of World War II, "sex" became increasingly visible in America's public culture. The new pulp paperback industry relied on sexually sensationalist covers to sell books, and comic books contained enough sex to prompt a congressional investigation. As Joanne Meyerowitz argues, this sexualization of mass culture was largely a matter of redrawing boundaries of respectability (Meyerowitz, 1996), as such material had long been available in an under-the-counter fashion. However, as *Playboy* magazine (begun in 1953) and cheap paperbacks promising tales of lesbian love were set out on newsstands alongside the *Ladies' Home Journal*, it seemed to many Americans that something significant had changed.

The publication of what were popularly known as "the Kinsey reports" (on men in 1948 and women in 1952) made sex a topic of public debate as they revealed to the American public that contemporary notions of sexual morality and normality did not come close to matching the actual sexual behavior of Americans. Subsequent historical scholarship on Kinsey and on sexology, or the scientific study of sex, analyzes the ways in which Kinsey and other scientists constructed "sex" in their research (Morantz, 1977; Robinson, 1989; Bullough, 1994; Jones, 1997; Terry, 1999; Gathorne-Hardy, 2000), but it is critical that Kinsey's data were presented to millions of Americans in the 1940s and 1950s as a *scientific* depiction of actual sexual behavior.

Finally, as historians of lesbian and gay American experiences have shown, some people built on the consolidation of gay identities in World War II to establish gay communities in cities throughout the nation. "Teen" identity was also consolidated in this era, and the highly visible cultures of young Americans seemed to center around sexually charged issues, whether the practice of going steady or the emergence of rock and roll (Bailey, 1988).

These trends were accompanied by heightened public concern about sex and sexuality, and the 1950s can scarcely be characterized as an era of sexual liberation. Many histories of this period, in fact, focus on issues of sex control. In general, "the Fifties" are a complicated era in the historiography of sexuality because they fall between "the War" and "the Sixties." How to explain the powerful (re)claiming of "traditional" gender roles and the accompanying emphasis on sexual control after the war? How to explain the relation of this decade to the sexual revolution that followed?

Some historians situate the repressive aspects in or around Cold War politics. Elaine Tyler May, in her influential *Homeward Bound* (1988), employs the foreign policy term "containment" to describe Americans' relation to sexuality during the postwar era. Sex was understood to be a powerful force which, if "contained" within the proper spheres of heterosexual marriage and home, could strengthen family and nation alike. Both Jennifer Terry (1999) and Michael Rogin (1987) draw even more explicitly on Cold War politics in their discussions of sexuality. In Terry's words, "The Cold War period was characterized by a large-scale tendency toward demonizing particular groups of people . . . and particular forms of sexually taboo behavior, though commonly practiced among average Americans, were attributed by conservative isolationists and anti-communists to external and evil forces outside the healthy mainstream of the nation" (Terry, 1999, pp. 329, 331). Moving beyond the Cold War paradigm, Rickie Solinger considers the ways in which unmarried pregnant girls and women were incorporated into the political arena, divided by race, and used to "explain and present solutions for a number of [domestic] social problems" in the postwar era (Solinger, 1992, p. 3).

Some of the more interesting new works on homosexuality or gay and lesbian experiences explicitly reject "the assumption that the 1950s were a universally bleak and homophobic decade" (Beemyn, 1997, p. 5). These works, in a tradition that goes back to John D'Emilio's *Sexual Politics, Sexual Communities* (1983), demonstrate that gay life in America did not begin with the riot at the Stonewall Inn in 1969. Works like Elizabeth Lapovsky Kennedy and Madeline Davis's *Boots of Leather, Slippers of Gold* (1993), Esther Newton's *Cherry Grove, Fire Island* (1993), Marc Stein's *City of Sisterly and Brotherly Loves* (2000), and (though covering an earlier era) George Chauncey's *Gay New York* (1994) document the existence of strong and viable gay and lesbian communities stretching back well before the sexual revolution and gay liberation. As Brett Beemyn notes in his anthology, *Creating a Place for Ourselves* (1997), many of these community studies contradict longstanding assumptions that outside a few major metropolises gay, lesbian, and bisexual Americans existed in sexual and cultural wastelands. Instead, works such as these demonstrate the richness of gay life in the pre-Stonewall era.

Most of the earlier works also emphasize the repressive nature of the larger society and stress the ways in which these communities survived against great odds. In Kennedy and Davis's words, members of these communities "supported one another for survival in an extremely negative and punitive environment" and also "boldly challenged" those repressive aspects of American society. Some recent works shift that emphasis. For example, in *Men Like That*, John Howard argues that the "quiet accommodation of difference" that existed in rural and small-town Mississippi during the 1940s and 1950s ended in the "'free love sixties'" with "strident, organized resistance to queer sexuality" (Howard, 1999, pp. xvii, xv), due in part to the visible role queer Mississippians played in the civil rights movement during the 1960s and to a subsequent crackdown on homosexuality. In a further difference from the studies above, Howard's study is not of community-building, and it is not identity-focused. He writes about "queer sex" and gender nonconformity, thus including men who did not claim a gay identity and focusing on the "meanings, practices, and regulations" of sex and gender in specific times and spaces (Howard, 1999, p. xviii).

While increasing numbers of historians find continuities between the 1950s and the 1960s, "the sexual revolution" still commands the central position in the historiography. As I argued above, the historiography of the sexual revolution is closely related to the historiography of "the Sixties." Much historical writing about the sexual revolution is not about sexuality alone but is instead embedded in histories of movements for equality and social justice. For example, both Terry Anderson's *The Movement and the Sixties* (1995) and Todd Gitlin's *The Sixties: Years of Hope, Days of Rage* (1987) incorporate the sexual revolution into "the Movement."

In keeping with that understanding, a "first wave" of writing about the sexual revolution treated it primarily as a social movement. For example, D'Emilio and Freedman define the sexual revolution broadly in *Intimate Matters*, ranging from *Playboy* to communes in their discussion, but find its heart in movements for social justice. In the 1960s, they argue, "sexuality emerged more clearly than ever as an issue of power and politics," as "women's liberation and gay liberation each presented a wide-ranging critique of deeply held assumptions about human sexual desire, its place in social life, and the hidden purposes it served. In particular, both movements analyzed the erotic as a vehicle for domination which, in complex ways, kept certain social groups in a subordinate place in society" (D'Emilio and Freedman, 1988, p. 308).

Liberation movements provide the framework for many of the early treatments of the sexual revolution and its prehistory. Historians who were particularly aware of the importance of sex in the emergence of the women's movement include Sara Evans, who describes the complex role of sex in women's experiences of activism and liberation in the early 1960s in *Personal Politics: The Roots of Women's Liberation in the Civil Rights Movement and the New Left* (1979). Although in different ways, both Wini Breines (1992) and Susan Douglas (1994) look to the cultural messages about sexuality that pervaded 1950s-era girlhood for the seeds of feminist consciousness.

The gay liberation movement likewise provided both site and impetus for discussion of the sexual revolution. Some, such as sociologist Laud Humphreys's *Out of the Closets: The Sociology of Homosexual Liberation* (1972) and Jonathan Katz's anthology, *Gay American History* (1976), were fundamentally part of the movement they analyzed. Later scholarly works such as John D'Emilio's influential *Sexual Politics, Sexual Communities* (1983) continued to focus on activism, tracing activist struggles before the rebellion at the Stonewall Inn symbolically launched the gay liberation movement. (A more recent narrative history by journalists Dudley Clendinen and Adam Nagourney, *Out for Good: The Struggle to Build a Gay Rights Movement in America* [1999], offers a carefully researched and very readable history of the movement from 1969 through the 1980s.)

As historians began to write more directly about the sexual revolution in a "second wave" that overlapped with the first, several framed their work around the notion of revolution itself. Had there really been a sexual revolution? Some historians (usually in brief asides in books on other topics) treated sexual desire as a constant force, which, once the Pill freed women from fear of pregnancy, flowered into revolution. Others took more complex positions, conceding the magnitude of change in the realm of sex, but asking whether changes in the sexual landscape simply worked to accommodate the existing power structure and ideological organization of sex. Was the sexual revolution "only [male] libertinage by another name" (Grant, 1994, p. 13)? Was it "little more than a male fling and a setback for women," to whom the sexual revolution offered only "deepening objectification . . . as potential instruments of male pleasure" (Ehrenreich et al., 1986, p. 1)?

Barbara Ehrenreich, Elizabeth Hess, and Gloria Jacobs, in *Re-Making Love: The Feminization of Sex* (1986), firmly reject the notion that the sexual revolution was simply a "male fling." They argue that much of what commonly passes for sexual revolution – *Playboy*, wife-swapping – represents the *men's* sexual revolution, a superficial set of changes that were hardly revolutionary. The *women's* sexual revolution – which they find everywhere from "Beatlemania" to fundamentalist Christian Marabel Morgan's *Total Woman* – was another matter entirely. In this interpretation, the winners of the revolution were not men, but women, who realized a new realm of sexual rights and expressions.

Linda Grant's study of the British and American sexual revolutions, *Sexing the Millennium*, begins like *Re-Making Love*, with a dichotomy between male and female sexual revolution. Grant, however, moves to a less completely gender-based opposition. "The sexual revolution," she writes, "has its origins in the struggles of those who fought not to explore the crevices of their own desires, but to change the world." One sexual revolution is "the seediness of swinging and the disintegration of group marriages", the other a millenarian movement, a desire to re-make not only sex but society (Grant, 1994, pp. 26, 17).

In *Romantic Longings*, Steven Seidman rejects not only the idea of dual sexual revolutions (male and female/good and bad), but the very notion of revolution. He argues that the changes attributed to the 1960s-era sexual revolution actually stemmed from an early twentieth-century "cultural rebellion against Victorianism" (Seidman, 1991, pp. 122–4). Dismissing the revolution as "more rhetoric than reality," he nonetheless finds revolutionary potential in a movement to uncouple sex from love. While the dominance of the love–sex nexus never wavered even during the "free love" 1960s, he argues, rejections of the belief that sex must be justified by love constituted an important countercultural stance that was most fully articulated in what he describes as the community-building role of casual sex in gay male communities.

Recent works on the sexual revolution – what might be described as a "third wave" of scholarship – tend to manage the question of the revolutionary nature of the revolution not by positing dual revolutions (male/female; libertine/millenarian), but by accepting the long-term, evolutionary nature of social-sexual change while still insisting on the importance of purposeful revolutionaries. The debate among these authors is not explicit, but implicit. They look in different places for "the sexual revolution," and so find different revolutions.

At least superficially, the most similar books are James Peterson's popular survey, *A Century of Sex: Playboy's History of the Sexual Revolution, 1900–1999* (1999), which was commissioned by Hugh Hefner, and David Allyn's *Make Love, Not War: The Sexual Revolution: An Unfettered History* (2000). Both center on the usual suspects – national figures like Hugh Hefner, Alfred Kinsey, and sex researchers Masters and Johnson, all of whom undoubtedly helped to change the sexual culture of the United States. In so doing, each treats the sexual revolution as a set of struggles against repression, engaged in by people who, in Allyn's words, "devoted their lives to challenging society's views about sex" (Allyn, 2000, p. 7).

What Wild Ecstasy: The Rise and Fall of the Sexual Revolution (1997), by former *Penthouse* "Forum" editor John Heidenry, leaves behind the usual suspects to focus on sex's most ardent enthusiasts. Heidenry paints a portrait of the most extreme parts of America's sexual culture and, rather oddly, calls it the sexual revolution. This sexual revolution took place in Plato's Retreat and New York SM clubs like Hellfire; the heroes of this revolution were people like Hellfire's Annie Sprinkle and Marco Vassi, a self-described "meta-sexual" who boasted that he had had sex with 5,000 women and 10,000 men.

On the other end of the spectrum is my work, *Sex in the Heartland* (1999), which portrays the sexual revolution in Lawrence, Kansas. While the sexual revolution would have looked much different without the "heroes" identified by Peterson, Allyn, and Heidenry, I argue, the acts of sexual revolutionaries do not, in themselves, constitute a revolution. It is when revolutionary beliefs and practices (though perhaps less ardently embraced or strenuously practiced) are taken up by those who have *not* devoted their lives to sexual revolution that we see a sexual revolution rather than a set of sexual subcultures or bohemian lifestyles.

The sexual revolution I describe is a mainstream revolution, born of widely shared values and beliefs. It develops from major transformations in the structure of American society, such as the greater inclusiveness of America's civil society that was created in part by federal interventions into local cultures in the years following World War II. It is made possible by people who had absolutely no intention of fostering sexual freedom, such as policymakers who promoted birth control as a solution to the "population explosion" and college administrators who supported the end of parietal rules as a way to develop student "responsibility." Only after significant changes had already taken place in American culture was this nascent revolution engaged by purposeful revolutionaries.

Their revolution, however, was not a singular, unified movement. Even the committed sexual revolutionaries had radically divergent ideas about what sort of revolution they sought and how it might be achieved. In the 1960s and early 1970s, "living together" was quite different from "free love," which was not the same thing as "wife-swapping," which was different from "the [SM] Scene," though all were, arguably, part of "the revolution." The violent and misogynistic sexual images that some members of America's counterculture used as weapons against "straight" society did not seem liberating to everyone. Many self-styled sexual revolutionaries were openly hostile to gay and lesbian struggles. Prominent feminists described the role of sex in women's oppression; social movements splintered over the proper role of sex in movements for liberation. It is critically important to untangle the various strands of the sexual revolution, for a movement that encompasses both "The Playboy Philosophy" and "The Myth of the Vaginal Orgasm" is obviously not a coherent whole. At the same time, we must remember that most people did not experience these enormously diverse phenomena as separate and discrete. The world seemed in revolution because of the combined force of all these changes, not because of a single set of acts or beliefs.

Very little *history* has been written about sexuality in the last two decades of the twentieth century. The field has been left primarily to sociologists, polemicists, and to cultural studies scholars. There are, however, three relatively recent developments that seem especially significant for the study of sexuality in postwar America.

First are the feminist struggles over sex and its meaning. These debates were played out most conspicuously in the "pornography wars" or "sex wars" that peaked in the 1980s, and then in the controversial 1990s analyses of the "woman as victim" model that some critics identified as the cornerstone of "second-wave" feminism (MacKinnon, 1987; Roiphe, 1993). Sociologist Lynn Chancer, in *Reconcilable Differences: Confronting Beauty, Pornography, and the Future of Feminism* (1998), argues that a troublesome divide has emerged in contemporary feminism, in which pro-sex and anti-sexism positions have come to seem mutually exclusive, even oppositional. She analyzes the way in which this fragmentation frames several debates in contemporary feminism, including the contests over pornography, rape, and the "beauty myth."

Second is the emergence of popular "men's movements" that range from Robert Bly's *Iron John*-inspired programs to the Promise Keepers and the Million Man March. They coincide with the recent growth of the scholarly field focused on the history of masculinity and of men. Historical sociologist Michael Kimmel is one of the few scholars who writes at the nexus of these movements, and the relationship between histories of men and masculinity and of the men's movement is nowhere near so close as between women's history and the women's movement. Nonetheless, it seems plausible that the development of both popular and scholarly movements will influence the writing of the history of sexuality in the future.

Finally, the relatively new field of cultural studies, not surprisingly, has found sex an enticing subject. Queer theory, which rejects the notion of stable and clear-cut sexual identities, has already influenced the writing of the history of sexuality (Howard, Terry), and may well continue to complicate assumptions about identity that underlie even avowedly social-constructionist scholarship. Some cultural studies work is appallingly ahistorical, but there is much good work – such as Judith Halberstam's *Female Masculinity* (1998) and Erica Rand's *Barbie's Queer Accessories* (1995) – that should be of interest to historians. Since cultural studies scholars are claiming the same historical topics as historians, the historians of sexuality will need to come to terms with their theoretical claims and their specific analyses.

While it is difficult to predict what directions future scholarship will take in such a new and rapidly growing field, I will end with a few recommendations. Studies of "queer" acts and identities promise to continue to complicate the homosexual–heterosexual binary in which much scholarship is based and I hope it will prompt useful discussions about how historians employ notions of identity in our scholarship. Greater attention to the role of race/ethnicity both in constructions of sexuality and in sexual behaviors is critically important; there is surprisingly little history of postwar American sexuality that does not focus on white Americans. More works that carefully examine relations between sex(uality) and gender would be most welcome. Socially conservative understandings of sexuality and opposition to changes in America's sexual landscape both deserve scholarly attention. And, finally, normative heterosexuality needs more of a history.

I, like many historians of sexuality, hope that the field's current focus on historically oppressed or marginalized groups will help to challenge the heterosexism and sexism that still exist in contemporary American society. At the same time, such focus on sexual rebels or on marginalized groups creates a rather odd mapping of the historical landscape of American sexuality. The problem is in part that majoritarian experiences are downplayed, leaving a significant gap in our historical understanding. It is also that they are rendered invisible. Just as the equation of "race" with African Americans in historical scholarship worked to render "whiteness" natural and invisible, or as the equation of "gender" with women obscured the constructions of masculinity, so the equation of sexuality with homosexuality or sexual transgression tends to suggest that "mainstream" heterosexuality is timeless, natural, and universal.

Early in the twenty-first century, the history of sexuality is one of the most intellectually exciting fields in recent US history. It is volatile and incoherent, but that is perhaps a strength, allowing for new and vital combinations of topic and method in our attempts to write about something as elusive as "sex."

REFERENCES

Allyn, David: *Make Love, Not War: The Sexual Revolution: An Unfettered History* (New York: Little, Brown, 2000).

Anderson, Terry: *The Movement and the Sixties* (New York: Oxford University Press, 1995).

Bailey, Beth: *From Front Porch to Back Seat: Courtship in Twentieth-Century America* (Baltimore: Johns Hopkins University Press, 1988).

Bailey, Beth: *Sex in the Heartland* (Cambridge, Mass.: Harvard University Press, 1999).

Bailey, Beth and Farber, David: *The First Strange Place: The Alchemy of Race and Sex in World War II Hawaii* (New York: Free Press, 1992).

Beemyn, Brett, ed.: *Creating a Place for Ourselves: Lesbian, Gay, and Bisexual Community Histories* (New York: Routledge, 1997).

Bérubé, Allan: *Coming Out Under Fire: The History of Gay Men and Women in World War II* (New York: Free Press, 1990).

Boswell, John: *Christianity, Social Tolerance, and Homosexuality: Gay People in Western Europe from the Beginning of the Christian Era to the Fourteenth Century* (Chicago: University of Chicago Press, 1980).

Breines, Wini: *Young, White, and Miserable: Growing Up Female in the Fifties* (Boston: Beacon Press, 1992).

Bullough, Vern L.: *Science in the Bedroom: A History of Sex Research* (New York: Basic Books, 1994).

Chancer, Lynn: *Reconcilable Differences: Confronting Beauty, Pornography, and the Future of Feminism* (Berkeley: University of California Press, 1998).

Chauncey, Jr., George: "The Postwar Sex Crimes Panic," in William Graebner (ed.), *True Stories from the American Past* (New York: McGraw Hill, 1993).

Chauncey, Jr., George: *Gay New York: Gender, Urban Culture, and the Making of the Gay Male World, 1890–1949* (New York: Basic Books, 1994).

Clendinen, Dudley and Nagourney, Adam: *Out for Good: The Struggle to Build a Gay Rights Movement in America* (New York: Simon and Schuster, 1999).

Costello, John: *Virtue Under Fire: How World War II Changed Our Social and Sexual Attitudes* (Boston: Little, Brown, 1985).

D'Emilio, John: *Sexual Politics, Sexual Communities: The Making of a Homosexual Minority in the United States, 1940–1970* (Chicago: University of Chicago Press, 1983).

D'Emilio, John and Freedman, Estelle: *Intimate Matters: A History of Sexuality in America* (New York: Harper and Row, 1988).

Douglas, Susan: *Where the Girls Are: Growing Up Female with the Mass Media* (New York: Times Books, 1994).

Ehrenreich, Barbara, Hess, Elizabeth, and Jacobs, Gloria: *Re-Making Love: The Feminization of Sex* (New York: Doubleday, 1986).

Epstein, Steven: "Gay Politics, Ethnic Identity: The Limits of Social Constructionism," *Socialist Review*, 17 (May/August 1987): 9–54.

Evans, Sara: *Personal Politics: The Roots of Women's Liberation in the Civil Rights Movement and the New Left* (New York: Alfred A. Knopf, 1979).

Faderman, Lillian: *Odd Girls and Twilight Lovers: A History of Lesbian Life in Twentieth-Century America* (New York: Columbia University Press, 1991).

Foucault, Michel: *The History of Sexuality.* Vol. 1: *An Introduction,* trans. Robert Hurley (New York: Vintage Books, 1978).

Freedman, Estelle: "Uncontrolled Desires: The Response to the Sexual Psychopath, 1920–1960," in Kathy Peiss and Christina Simmons (eds.), *Passion and Power* (Philadelphia: Temple University Press, 1989), 199–225.

Gathorne-Hardy, Jonathan: *Sex the Measure of All Things: A Life of Alfred C. Kinsey* (Bloomington: Indiana University Press, 2000).

Gitlin, Todd: *The Sixties: Years of Hope, Days of Rage* (New York: Bantam, 1987).

Grant, Linda: *Sexing the Millennium: Women and the Sexual Revolution* (New York: Grove Press, 1994).

Halberstam, Judith: *Female Masculinity* (Durham, NC: Duke University Press, 1998).

Heidenry, John: *What Wild Ecstasy: The Rise and Fall of the Sexual Revolution* (New York: Simon and Schuster, 1997).

Howard, John: *Men Like That: A Southern Queer History* (Chicago: University of Chicago Press, 1999).

Humphreys, Laud: *Out of the Closets: The Sociology of Homosexual Liberation* (Englewood Cliffs, NJ: Prentice Hall, 1972).

Jones, James Howard: *Alfred C. Kinsey: A Public/Private Life* (New York: W. W. Norton, 1997).

Katz, Jonathan: *Gay American History: Lesbians and Gay Men in the U.S.A.* (New York: Avon Books, 1976).

Kennedy, Elizabeth Lapovsky and Davis, Madeline D.: *Boots of Leather, Slippers of Gold: The History of a Lesbian Community* (New York: Routledge, 1993).

Kinsey, Alfred C., Pomeroy, Wardell B., and Martin, Clyde E.: *Sexual Behavior in the Human Male* (Philadelphia: W. B. Saunders, 1948).

Kinsey, Alfred C. and Staff of the Institute for Sex Research, Indiana University: *Sexual Behavior in the Human Female* (Philadelphia: W. B. Saunders, 1952).

May, Elaine Tyler: *Homeward Bound: American Families in the Cold War Era* (New York: Basic Books, 1988).

Meyer, Leisa D.: *Creating GI Jane: Sexuality and Power in the Women's Army Corps During World War II* (New York: Columbia University Press, 1996).

Meyerowitz, Joanne: "Women, Cheesecake, and Borderline Material: Responses to Girlie Pictures in the Mid-Twentieth-Century U.S.," *Journal of Women's History,* 8 (1996): 9–35.

Morantz, Regina Markell: "The Scientist as Sex Crusader: Alfred C. Kinsey and American Culture," *American Quarterly,* 29 (1977): 563–89.

Newton, Esther: *Cherry Grove, Fire Island: Sixty Years in America's First Gay and Lesbian Town* (Boston: Beacon Press, 1993).

Peterson, James: *A Century of Sex: Playboy's History of the Sexual Revolution, 1900–1999* (New York: Grove Books, 1999).

Rand, Erica: *Barbie's Queer Accessories* (Durham, NC: Duke University Press, 1995).

Reagan, Leslie: *When Abortion Was a Crime: Women, Medicine and Law in the United States, 1867–1973* (Berkeley: University of California Press, 1997).

Robinson, Paul: *The Modernization of Sex: Havelock Ellis, Alfred Kinsey, William Masters, and Virginia Johnson* (1976; Ithaca, NY: Cornell University Press, 1989).

Rogin, Michael: "Kiss Me Deadly: Communism, Motherhood, and Cold War Movies," in *Ronald Reagan, the Movie and Other Episodes in Political Demonology* (Berkeley: University of California Press, 1987), 236–71.

Roiphe, Katie: *The Morning After: Sex, Fear, and Feminism on Campus* (Boston: Little, Brown, 1993).

Rosen, Ruth: *The World Split Open: How the Modern Women's Movement Changed America* (New York: Viking, 2000).

Seidman, Steven: *Romantic Longings: Love in America, 1830–1980* (New York: Routledge, 1991).

Solinger, Rickie: *Wake Up Little Susie: Single Pregnancy and Race Before Roe v. Wade* (New York: Routledge, 1992).

Stein, Marc: *City of Sisterly and Brotherly Loves: Lesbian and Gay Philadelphia, 1945–1972* (Chicago: University of Chicago Press, 2000).

Terry, Jennifer: *An American Obsession: Science, Medicine, and Homosexuality in Modern Society* (Chicago: University of Chicago Press, 1999).

A Movement of Movements: The Definition and Periodization of the New Left

VAN GOSSE

Historians and Reconstructions

To write the history of Cold War radicalism – of the New Left – is exciting and risky. The events, movements, organizations, crises, polemics, and persons involved are so near at hand that anger, nostalgia, and unresolved disputes hang over the historiography like a cloud.

In key respects, the successive narratives of "the Sixties" and the New Left resemble the historiography of the Civil War in the late nineteenth and early twentieth centuries, when many participants were still alive. At first, the sharp-eyed contemporary reporting of the war and Reconstruction was forgotten, as northern whites turned their back on the politics of racial equality. After a period of silence, scholarly histories appeared, offering a new consensus based in commonsense truths regarding black political incapacity, scalawag rapacity, and Reconstruction's disorder, which went unchallenged for decades among whites, and even many blacks. Eventually, however, radically different perspectives confronted that consensus.

The historiography of the New Left follows a parallel, if compressed, trajectory: extensive political journalism in the 1960s, followed by an exhausted pause during the 1970s, then a first wave of scholarship in the 1980s, offering a compelling, insistently tragic account of declension, which in turn provoked a proliferation of counternarratives in the 1990s. To capture this evolution, and because many of the earliest accounts retain a surprising utility, this essay will examine both scholarship from the post-New Left era and certain contemporary books.

To some, it may seem presumptuous to compare the New Left, posited here as the totality of the overlapping social movements for radical democracy and social justice in the post-1945 era, to the defining events in United States history – the Civil War and Reconstruction. But if one puts the black freedom struggle and the passage from First to Second Reconstructions at the narrative's center, the analogy becomes not only apt, but unavoidable, as Manning Marable (1991) and Maurice

Thanks to Max Elbaum, Jeffrey Escoffier, Eric Foner, and Lise Vogel for critical readings which greatly improved this essay.

Isserman and Michael Kazin (2000) have suggested in different ways. At a minimum, one can usefully compare the "unfinished" character attaching to two periods of greatly divisive, revolutionary social change that remained unacceptable to much of the body politic for generations after. It remains to be seen whether the New Left "failed" as a social revolution, a quarter of a century after the concluding events in its trajectory, given that most revolutionary movements fail in the short term, as they are overturned, betrayed, or made redundant.

This essay seeks answers to three major questions about the New Left: *what and who was it?* (which movements and organizations should be included); *when did it function?* (its beginning and ending); *what did it achieve?* As we shall see, the first and second questions are intimately related – by "starting" the New Left sooner rather than later, in the mid-1950s or earlier, one is compelled to include a much wider range of groups and constituencies. Similarly, by extending its history well into the 1970s, one must contend with new movements and trends, a challenge few scholars have met.

Conversely, if one defines the New Left through the personal memories and engaged scholarship of veterans, its history becomes compressed into the 1960s, and takes on the contours of a youth revolt, more specifically, the white student movement, especially the Students for a Democratic Society (SDS). This briefer, contained New Left begins fortuitously in 1960 with the wave of southern sit-ins and the renaming of the Student League for Industrial Democracy as SDS, and concludes equally neatly in 1969–71 with that organization's self-destruction and the putative waning of anti-war protest. In effect, one has a self-reinforcing syllogism, whereby the New Left equals "the Sixties" in a literal sense, and political developments before or after are shoehorned into the silent Fifties or the hedonistic Seventies, leaving "the Sixties" alone, pure and isolated. That mass movements and cultural watersheds rarely conform to abstract chronological boundaries should not require underscoring; such is the power of old-fashioned narrative and the "presidential synthesis," since scholars who equate the New Left with the 1960s usually invoke John F. Kennedy's victory as heralding a new, youthful era – a prospect that escaped many then, given his manipulative centrism.

The distinction between a broader, larger, more diverse, and longer-lasting New Left, and one tightly defined by age, race, the moment, and a particular organizational identity, marks the central axis of historiographical argument. If one presumes a single, coherent New Left of white youth led by SDS, then other movements and struggles can be treated as influences, points of origin, schismatic developments, and after-effects. The campaigns, organizations, and mobilizations led by African Americans, Puerto Ricans, Chicanos, Native Americans, Asian Americans, women, gays and lesbians, poor people, prisoners, pacifists, anti-imperialists, and others are perforce something other than "the left." Traditional liberal historians (and some former New Leftists) claim one or another of these movements as dissenting species of liberalism that ultimately returned to the fold. Most recently, they are described as evidence of "identity politics," outside of and detrimental to the left. Of course, these struggles are not omitted from history itself, but they are either captured in isolation – a social movement here, a social movement there – or pushed to the margins and deprived of agency, portrayed as either precursors (the civil rights movement) or legatees (women's liberation) of the student New Left at the Sixties' center. This makes for a tidy, but profoundly limited, narrative.

The alternative to this privileged vision of a generationally based white New Left is necessarily much more provisional, as it encompasses "all of the above," and resists closure, or absolute clarity about where liberalism, or just particularism, leaves off and radicalism begins. The pluralist thesis of a "movement of movements," a framing once ubiquitous and since forgotten, requires investigating a constant efflorescence of sub-movements, temporary coalitions, breakaway factions, and organizational proliferation over several decades. It is wary of permanent demarcations between "old" and "new" lefts, since often the latter required the incorporation of the former, whether pacifist, religious, or Marxist. But accepting the challenge of making sense of this chaos, with its confusions, political contradictions, ideological richness, multiplicity of organizational forms, and great regional and local variety, will ultimately provide a more accurate view of that fractionated left that reemerged publicly in the later 1950s and was genuinely "new."

To clear the ground, we need a history of the various histories. This will take two forms. First, I describe the rise of the canonical narrative focused on SDS from the mid-1960s to late 1980s, indicating how one particular story moved to the foreground, pushing many others to the side. Second, I argue that an alternative account developed simultaneously, ceding the use of the term "new left," but demonstrating a more complete grasp of Cold War radicalism by examining varieties of political experience not limited to the campus, or by race, gender, or a particular ideological configuration – the exceptional scholarship on the civil rights movement, and to lesser extents on women's and gay liberation, the anti-Vietnam War movement, and Black, Brown, and Red Power. Finally, I discuss the major gaps in the historiography.

Whose New Left?

From its earliest days in the late 1950s, problems of subjectivity, self-definition, naming, and ambiguity about "newness" have surrounded the New Left. More than forty years ago, C. Wright Mills wrote his famous "Letter to a New Left" in the British *New Left Review*, adopting the self-identification of former English communists after Khrushchev's 1956 denunciation of Stalin. Mills hailed a new generation of international youth, unafraid to challenge orthodoxy and untainted by socialism's "labor metaphysic." Since then, the assertion of that newness has remained a rallying cry, a place to stand upon, to speak from, and, not infrequently, to denounce. Even those who adopt the elegiac pose, evoking the New Left as a dream stillborn, do so to damn contemporary varieties of political action (Gitlin, 1995; Tomasky, 1996).

The political cartography of the New Left, setting boundaries and defining frontiers, has three major phases.

During the 1960s, most writing about the "new radicalism" was inclusive and eclectic, defining it as a multiracial "movement of movements." All writers recognized how the black freedom movement catalyzed the reemergence of visible activism among students, women, white liberals, and other racial and ethnic groups (Jacobs and Landau, 1966; Newfield, 1966; Long, 1969). Early documentary collections with "New Left" in their titles were highly pluralist, linking Herbert Marcuse and Stokely Carmichael, the anti-war movement and Freedom Riders, radical pacifism and Berkeley's Free Speech Movement (Long, 1969; Oglesby, 1969; Teodori, 1969).

Other than some tendentious sociology reflecting outrage at students' lack of deference (examined in Breines, 1989), there was little scholarship on the New Left during the years of its rise and influence upon national politics. Among historians, one exception is a dissertation by James O'Brien (1971), which traced the revival of northern student activism through sympathy pickets of chainstores during the 1960 sit-ins that birthed the Student Nonviolent Coordinating Committee (SNCC) and a surge in disarmament activism via the Student Peace Union, all preceding SDS's development. Equally important was August Meier and Elliot Rudwick's (1975) dense organizational history of the Congress for Racial Equality (CORE), outstanding for its linking of grassroots activism against de facto Jim Crow in the North with the better-known southern mobilizations, demonstrating how "Black Power" grew up organically within civil rights organizing. In that same year, the political scientist Jo Freeman, a pioneer of women's liberation, published a still useful account of its genesis and rapid evolution. Otherwise, writings from this period that remain influential are theoretical and autobiographical. Three stand out: a powerful narrative of SNCC by its Executive Secretary James Forman (1972), and two books acerbically dissecting black nationalism and radicalism by Harold Cruse (1967, 1968), which remain highly influential for anyone seeking to unravel the rise of Black Power.

The early 1970s marked a major shift in the popular and then academic definitions of the New Left. The waning of the vast anti-war coalition that was its common ground, the emergence of new movements after 1968, increasingly sharp political differences between constituencies, the implosion of SDS in 1969–70, and the movement of many radicals into the Democratic Party via the McGovern campaign exploded the old understanding of a collective, pluralist New Left. Within a few years, that term came to mean only white student radicals – or even, just their self-conscious leadership in SDS.

This new understanding emerged with lasting impact in Kirkpatrick Sale's (1973) history of SDS. Working directly from its papers microfilmed in neat chronological order, Sale constructed a dramatic, coherent, and ultimately mythic narrative of ascension and declension compressing or eliding the history of many organizations into a single group. African Americans, the women's and anti-Vietnam War movements, Marxist organizations, seasoned "old left" and pacifist activists who actually led many coalitions and campaigns – all became external actors while subjectivity was granted to a select group of heroic youth. Key to the book's success was its "historical" style, as events and personalities evolved over time. In a larger sense, Sale's account succeeded precisely because of its embrace of "newness," with clean beginnings and endings, as specific individuals made personal choices, versus the methodology of historical scholarship emphasizing multiple origins, contradictions and continuities, the significance of larger impersonal or "overdetermined" processes constraining individual agency, and long-term causality rather than immediate effects.

Writing when the shibboleth of the silent, McCarthyized 1950s was universal, Sale had little to say about the complex roots of "new" leftism, which germinated long before SDS's halting emergence. Nor did he assay the New Left's practical political effects, then evident all around him in the flowering women's movement, the advent of black electoral power, thousands of young organizers in multiracial "party-building" formations, shifts to the left in US foreign policy, and much more. Instead, the reader follows a thrilling, hermetic account that foretells the 1970 self-immolation of Weatherman bombers in a New York townhouse, and casts that minor disaster as the nadir of a downward spiral – a tragic *finis* to what was finally more of a romance than a history, yet one that spoke to many white radicals in the 1970s, because it made sense of their own lives, living in an unromantic time.

After Sale, little appeared for more than a decade, with two outstanding exceptions underlining for a new generation of activists and scholars how the New Left's axis was the black movement in the American South. Sara Evans's (1979) justly admired examination of how the women's liberation movement germinated in SNCC and SDS remains one of the few works focused on links between the segmented parts of the larger radical movement, tying black liberation to the young whites' radicalization, with SDS as a transmission belt. Clayborne Carson's (1981) model study of SNCC's evolution focused on its intensive organizing practice, and the complex ideological responses to its role in spurring the constitutional milestone embodied in the Civil Rights and Voting Rights Acts. By reminding readers of how the arc of organizing that led up to and then out of the Mississippi Freedom Summer was the mainspring of 1960s radicalism, Carson and Evans established a touchstone. (Though more sociological than historical, Todd Gitlin's [1980] analysis of the distorting effects of media attention upon SDS, published at the same time, has remained highly influential.)

The next major historiographical phase came in the later 1980s, at the height of the Reagan Revolution. Three books by James Miller, Maurice Isserman, and Todd Gitlin (1987, all) expanded upon and reinforced Sale's prescription for a white student New Left defined by SDS. While offering valuable insights, each presumes the exceptional importance of that particular organization, in terms of its ideological insights, unrealized promise, and the belief that its 1969 disappearance heralded the "end" or "death" of the New Left. Collectively, these authors (aided by Tom Hayden's memoir, appearing the next year) established a new consensus, which reinforced powerful political currents defining the New Left's legacy as a severe hindrance to new progressive initiatives (Hayden, 1988; Edsall and Edsall, 1991; Gitlin, 1995; Tomasky, 1996; Sleeper, 1990).

Isserman's book has the greatest explanatory value, because it offers a nuanced excavation of seedbeds for the white New Left in 1945–60: the 1956–8 crisis of the Communist Party, when a majority declared its commitment to an American road to socialism, and then departed *en masse*; Shachtmanite Trotskyism advocating a "third camp" position between East and West; the powerful trend of direct-action pacifism dating from World War II, heralding how pacifists like A. J. Muste and Dave Dellinger would act as a center of gravity in the subsequent decade. After Isserman, no one could write as if the New Left emerged spontaneously as a literal break with the "Old." Though the influence of *Dissent* and similar anti-communist socialist projects is exaggerated, and the "death" of the communist (more accurately, Popular Front) left considerably overstated, it remains foundational.

On its own terms, Miller's history of SDS as an intellectual project to reestablish democratic radicalism in modern America is equally definitive. No one interested in that organization, with its talismanic significance for certain white radicals, can ignore it. As an organizational narrative of one important group, it is a model history, akin to Carson's work on SNCC, if ultimately different in that SDS achieved so much less. The problem is the claim, once again, to speak for all – the unblinking insistence that the New Left's definitive manifesto and birth-moment is the 1962 Port Huron Statement, and that the New Left as a whole flamed out in the "siege of Chicago" at the 1968 Democratic Convention and the October 1969 Days of Rage.

This claim to primacy has unfortunate consequences. Though his narrative is replete with examples of how SDS responded to and attempted to emulate the formidable organizing practice of SNCC and the larger, southern-based "human rights movement," Miller never draws the appropriate conclusion, to study SDS not in isolation, but as a heterogeneous and unstable wing of the larger white student left that rose up in solidarity with the civil rights movement and then turned to its own liberation, even self-preservation, during the Vietnam War (that much campus radicalism operated outside of SDS is rarely acknowledged here or elsewhere).

Of all these books, Gitlin's is the most problematic, and its great public resonance is linked to its flaws. As acknowledged at the outset, he blended two different genres: the scholarly work, and the memoir. Gitlin had been president of SDS in 1962, and a well-connected member of its "Old Guard" for the next decade. In his sweeping but always accessible account, he moves back and forth from the largest panorama of radical change to his own witnessing of, and personal responses to, many events. By detailing his own standpoint, both then and later in hindsight, Gitlin presents an "auto-critique" which brings controversies much closer than they would normally seem. This tone of immediacy and critical self-consciousness combined with an elegiac tone, and its moderate political stance, explains the book's popularity with the public and many intellectuals as a comprehensive résumé of what "the Sixties" changed in America, and what went wrong – that the left failed is the bedrock frame and argument of the book.

So far, so good, if indeed this was recognized as just a personal account and polemic. But Gitlin insists upon the legitimacy of his own narrative, interwoven seamlessly with events he neither participated in nor even observed (like civil rights, Black Power, women's and gay liberation), as a or even *the* general narrative for all social change during "The Sixties," as his title claims. Ultimately, after various qualifications, the reader is led to the conclusion that the experience of early SDS leaders like Gitlin and Hayden was at the center of this period of mass movements and state crisis, and the book's memoiristic character naturalizes that narrow vision: the movement that Gitlin remembers begins to gear up in 1960–2 as he goes to college, hits a series of high points defined by SDS's episodic engagement with the larger "Movement," and winds down precipitously with the author's estrangement from the post-1968 radicalization of the anti-war movement and allied groups like the Black Panther Party, a final stage he consigns to history's dustbin as a "death culture" of nihilism and self-destruction.

The enduring power of these three books illustrates the power of agreement among able scholars to define a consensus that shapes and contains subsequent scholarship: Isserman and Miller also posit a fatal decline in 1968–70, tied to the war and SDS's collapse. Like Gitlin, they see no need to engage with the rise of new social movements that defy any narrative of collapse – the women who built "second-wave" feminism into a mass movement melding radical and liberal currents, ascending throughout the 1970s; the gay and lesbian movement that dates its symbolic founding from 1969, for which the 1970s constituted a mass "coming out" into visible politics; the wave of Black Power leading up to the Gary Convention of 1972, and successful electoral campaigns in cities from Cleveland (1967) to Newark (1970) to Detroit (1973).

This new consensus regarding who constituted the New Left, when it came into existence, and when and why it failed (or died, or declined) has come under sharp attack. Wini Breines's (1988) review in the *Journal of American History* asking "Whose New Left?" is repeatedly cited, since she pointed out the organizational affinities of these authors (Isserman had been in SDS like Gitlin, and Miller counted himself as a partisan), disputing their assumption that a handful of white male SDS intellectuals were the leaders of radical change, and the positing of a "good" New Left in the early 1960s that was betrayed by the revolutionary fantasies of a later "bad" New Left.

Subsequently, Alice Echols and I published studies that, falling outside the "short Sixties" posited by Gitlin, Miller, and Isserman, suggested a wider frame of reference, and critiqued the declensionism of their books. I investigated a broad current of support for the Cuban Revolution, first among liberals rather than leftists in 1957–8 when Fidel Castro led a guerrilla movement, and then in 1959–61, when the Fair Play for Cuba Committee linked the widest array of proto-New Left forces, from old-style conscience liberals to Robert F. Williams, the North Carolina National Association for the Advancement of Colored People (NAACP) leader who advocated armed self-defense. My argument was that this early instance of the New Left was clearly multiracial, and not limited to students. I also showed that disgust with US government backing of right-wing dictatorships, and willingness to take sides in solidarity with the third world, existed long before the ground war in Vietnam (Gosse, 1993). At the decade's other end, Echols (1989) investigated the intense internal life of radical feminism during the 1968–75 high tide, before women's liberation diffused into a "cultural feminism" that ceded political leadership to liberal feminists in the National Organization for Women (NOW). While not all scholars and veterans see this downturn, Echols caught the explosive excitement of those years of consciousness-raising and theoretical innovation in "small groups" like New York Radical Women, Redstockings, The Feminists, Cell 16, and The Furies. Most recently, in a dissection of the premises of Gitlin, Miller, and Isserman's work, Allen Smith (2000) argues that the epochal influence claimed for the Port Huron Statement is based mainly on assertions repeated over decades by its partisans, undergirding a larger body of myths about SDS.

An alternative approach to the New Left examines how radicalism germinated at flagships of revolt during "the Sixties": the University of California at Berkeley, the University of Wisconsin at Madison, the University of Texas at Austin. At two of these, SDS played little or no role; at all three, the emergence of a visible "New Left" began well before 1960, and mainstream city and state politics (two are capitals) were directly connected to on-campus organizing. W. J. Rorabaugh's (1989) study of Berkeley connects local civil rights struggles for open housing and an end to job discrimination to the development of student insurgency, leading to the 1964 Free Speech Movement, then mass anti-war mobilization and pitched battles with Ronald Reagan's administration. He also sketches how Berkeley's radicalism became institutionalized, via a takeover of city government and Ron Dellums's election to Congress. Paul Buhle's (1990) book about Madison from 1950 to 1970 is more modest – a collective memoir with some documents by a large group associated with the History Department that played a central role in revolutionizing the study of history in the U.S. It provides an excellent feel for how people rethought radicalism at the Cold War's height, and how their politics evolved. Douglas Rossinow's (1998) rich exploration of Austin's campus left and larger counterculture, centered by a Texas-style SDS chapter based in Christian radical and civil-libertarian populist traditions, is the most ambitious. While still identifying the New Left with white student radicalism, he sharply contests other historians of SDS, decrying the dismissal of indigenous American radical traditions and ideological elitism he sees reproduced in their scholarship. Taken together, these geographically distinct case studies – "beginning" early and "ending" late or not at all, cutting across any single issue, with national organizations playing a secondary role – indicate the work needed for an appropriately complex picture of the New Left as a whole.

Despite these counterarguments, the SDS-centered accounts continue to shape the definition and periodization of the New Left, establishing a cul-de-sac that blocks systematic efforts to contextualize the new radicalism that gathered force from 1955 on, surged to national prominence in 1960–5, accelerated in tandem with the war in 1965–8, reached a crest of disruption in 1968–71, and diffused into separate currents of change in the mid-1970s. The most common route out of this blind alley has been to avoid theorizing "the New Left" as a general phenomenon and instead, following Gitlin's lead, address social change via the trope of "the Sixties" (Morgan, 1991; Farber, 1994; Steigerwald, 1995; Anderson, 1996; Isserman and Kazin, 2000). Of these studies there have been many – perhaps too many, for while all have their virtues, and their differences are productive, none offers a coherent narrative of the era's radicalism. Indeed, William Chafe's general history of the post-1945 United States has a more nuanced reading of the social movements' relationship to power and policy than any of the above (Chafe, 1999). As syntheses, they remain bound by the limitations of current scholarship. All suffer from the unexamined premise that the New Left was defined by youth; all insist that "the Sixties" (and therefore the New Left) must literally parallel the decade itself; all give short shrift to a host of significant radical leaders, organizations, and even whole movements whose chronology, age, or politics does not fit the established pattern, so that the Berrigan brothers and Dorothy Day, A. J. Muste and Dave Dellinger, Corky Gonzalez and Reies Tijerina, James and Grace Lee Boggs, LeRoi Jones (Amiri Baraka) and Robert F. Williams, Shulamith Firestone and Bella Abzug, are absent or barely noted, along with many, many others. It is to those ellipses, and the possibility of a new narrative embracing all of the movements, that we now turn.

Historians, "The Movement," and the Movements

While the New Left's historiography became narrower and more exclusive, scholars focusing on each of the postwar social movements, without preconceptions regarding "the Sixties," put the building blocks for a competing, grander synthesis in place.

The sharpest challenge to assertions that the New Left was defined by SDS, and came crashing down with that organization's demise in 1969, can be found in the extraordinarily rich writing on black politics and the civil rights movement (for a key historiographical review, see Lawson, 1991; also the bibliographical essay in Payne, 1995, which critiques top-down, white-inflected history ignoring poor and working-class people, the women who were the backbone of local organizing, and radicalism).

Much of this scholarship has focused on the organizations and leaders identified with the great campaigns of 1955–65. Besides the works on CORE and SNCC already cited, David Garrow (1986, 2001), Taylor Branch (1988, 1998), and Adam Fairclough (1987) have authored significant treatments of Dr. Martin Luther King, Jr. and the Southern Christian Leadership Conference (SCLC), and Nancy Weiss (1989) has analyzed the most moderate wing of the movement, the National Urban

League, via its head, Whitney Young. Various historians have offered overviews, notably Manning Marable, whose sweeping narratives of twentieth-century black politics are notable for their attention to nationalist and radical currents, and almost alone in extending the narrative forward into the 1970s and 1980s, when "black power" became a reality (Marable, 1985, 1991; Weisbrot, 1990; Sitkoff, 1993; McAdam, 1999). Further studies emphasizing the continuity of the struggle to regain political rights include those by Steven Lawson, the historian of black electoralism (1985, 1997, 1999), and Aldon Morris (1984), examining incubators of the movement that surged in the 1950s. Also important in uncovering origins are Patricia Sullivan's (1996) study of New Deal liberalism in the South, Irwin Klibaner's (1989) little-known history of the Southern Conference Educational Fund, carrier of the Popular Front legacy into the later era, and Michael Honey's (1993) sophisticated unpacking of interracial working-class politics in Memphis during the 1940s.

The framework for interpreting the history of civil rights was laid during the 1980s. Recently, powerful local studies have deepened this account, questioning the emphasis on leadership exercised by national organizations, including exceptional books by Charles Payne (1995) and John Dittmer (1994) on Mississippi, crucible of the movement. Both are notable for their attention to the fabric of rural organizing, and their insistence that understanding the civil rights movement requires looking at the trajectory since Reconstruction. Similarly, in his study of the struggle to overturn Jim Crow in Louisiana, Adam Fairclough (1995) goes back to 1915, and disfranchisement's immediate aftermath. Exceptional in this framework is George Lipsitz's (1995) investigation of "a life in the struggle" by one unsung St. Louis activist who helped hold the local movement together. All of these works suggest, again, the need to rethink "the Sixties" as a radical break. The most evident new direction in studies of civil rights organizing, however, is the tide of books, collections and memoirs focused on women's leadership, effectively rewriting a very male-centered narrative. These include general histories (Crawford, Rouse, and Woods, 1993; Olson, 2001), biographies of key figures in SNCC, such as Joanne Grant's study of Ella Baker (1998), Cynthia Griggs Fleming's recovery of Ruby Doris Smith Robinson (1998), and biographies of Fannie Lou Hamer by Kay Mills (1993) and Chana Kai Lee (1999), a collective memoir by white women activists (Curry et al., 2000), and a study of Jewish women who "went south" (Schultz, 2001).

The impressive histories of civil rights organizing contrast sharply with the limited historiography on Black Power. Only in the late 1990s did scholars begin examining specific instances of this politically fragmented but culturally pervasive movement, and the concomitant reorientation of black activists toward electoral politics. Many aspects of Black Power, or simply black politics and culture after 1965, are still unexplored. Until recently, other than Forman and Cruse's accounts and Carson's tracing of SNCC into the later 1960s, readers had to rely on contemporary texts and a handful of crucial contemporary analyses, including two accounts of the key nationalist-Marxist formation, Detroit's League of Revolutionary Black Workers (Georgakas and Surkin, 1975; Geschwender, 1977) and Frank Kofsky's (1970) essays on revolutionary nationalism and the jazz avant-garde led by John Coltrane. One standout is Essien Essien-Udom's (1962) study of the Nation of Islam, written when a mass revival of black nationalism seemed outlandish, still the best work on that subject. Amiri Baraka's (1997) autobiography is also invaluable.

Professional historians have had little to say. Besides Marable's essential overviews, a lone standout is William Chafe's (1980) exploration of Greensboro, North Carolina, across the 1950s and 1960s, demonstrating the bitter, very partial character of civil rights victories, and Black Power's organic relation to earlier efforts. In the early 1990s, scholars began filling in this picture, including James Ralph's (1993) look at Dr. King's disastrous 1966 move into Chicago, and the sociologist William Van DeBurg's (1992) survey of Black Power as a cultural phenomenon, which lacks historical grounding but suggests how the new black consciousness was lived and understood. Also important was William Sales's (1994) study of Malcolm X's last year, and the ideological perspective and new strategy envisioned for the Organization of Afro-American Unity, prefiguring Black Power.

The 1990s were most notable, however, for a flood of memoirs, essay collections, Hollywood films, and other evocations of Malcolm X and the Black Panther Party (BPP) as embodiments of the aspiration to self-determination. Some of these are worth noting, because they "stand in" for scholarship as yet unwritten, including memoirs by BPP leaders Elaine Brown (1992) and David Hilliard (1993) and the Detroit activist Grace Lee Boggs (1998), a muckraking biography of Huey P. Newton (Pearson, 1994), many works reflecting on the contemporary significance of Malcolm X (Wood, 1992; Strickland, 1994; Dyson, 1995), and a remembrance of his travels in Africa, Europe, and the Caribbean by Jan Carew (1994) – one notes the urgent need for a comprehensive political biography of this seminal leader. The decade's end brought a wave of scholarship, enlarging our understanding of Black Power's origins and impact: a voluminous anthology on the BPP edited by Charles Jones (1998), in which Nikhil Singh's essay is a model of situating Black Power globally, and meeting the challenge of the Panthers' strategy of the spectacular gesture; Timothy Tyson's (1999) masterful biography of Robert F. Williams, demonstrating that armed self-defense against racist state and paramilitary forces had a long history predating the Panthers, and illuminating Williams's prophetic role; Suzanne Smith's (1999) engaging study of Detroit as the site of a new black entrepreneurial culture, via Motown Records, that interacted with many of the Detroit-based organizations, theorists, and cultural activities that birthed the Black Power movement; Komozi Woodard's (1999) sensitive investigation of Amiri Baraka's multifaceted "cultural nationalist" organizing project in Newark; Yohuru Williams's (2000) examination of black politics in New Haven from the mid-1950s through the arrival of the BPP; Rod Bush's (1999) broader-based study of black nationalism and leftism across the twentieth century. But we are still at the beginning.

Scholarship on the other social movements is much less developed. Women's liberation, for instance, and feminism's resurfacing as an organized political presence have been examined by only a handful of historians. Scholarship has emphasized recovering points of origin for "second-wave" feminism, including a respectful analysis of the "old" feminism, a residual, patrician radicalism embodied in the National Women's Party (Rupp and Taylor, 1990), Cynthia Harrison's (1988) study of women's issues in mainstream politics through 1968, and an influential collection (Meyerowitz, 1994), examining women's lives and politics during the 1950s, demonstrating that many women's groups never acquiesced in the *faux* Victorianism of the High Cold War. Most recently, Daniel Horowitz's (1998) biography of Betty Friedan, revealing her roots in the Popular Front left, and Kate Weigand's (2001) examination of communist women's "red feminism" post-1945 have demonstrated another source for what became women's liberation. Continuing this investigation, Susan Hartmann (1998) argues that consciously feminist women embedded in the network of mainstream liberal organizations and trade unions pursued policy agendas to bolster women's civil rights and access. Collectively, these recent books force a reexamination of the century's middle, well before "the Sixties," suggesting that liberal feminism's seemingly spontaneous emergence between 1961 and 1966 was a culmination rather than a sudden new beginning. Moving forward to women's liberation in the late 1960s and 1970s, memoirs are appearing from important activists (Smith, 1998; Brownmiller, 1999; Jay, 1999; Hollibaugh, 2000), and Ruth Rosen (2000) has published a wide-ranging cultural history of the women's movement from the 1950s onwards, with only modest attention to its political evolution. Rosalyn Baxandall's and Linda Gordon's (2000) scintillating collection of leaflets, articles, and ephemera is complemented by a "memoir project" (DuPlessis and Snitow, 1998) featuring many key leaders of women's liberation, and Miriam Schneir's authoritative documents collection (1994). Still, other than useful syntheses by Myra Marx Ferree and Beth Hess (1994) and Flora Davis (1999) we have no comprehensive organizational history, examining all parts of the country, and all the feminist roots and branches – radical, liberal, cultural, lesbian, and socialist.

The scholarship on gay and lesbian politics is more limited but follows a similar trajectory. During the 1970s, as the movement flourished, it produced numerous topical books, such as Donn Teal's (1971) early activist outline of activism, and Jonathan Katz's (1976) groundbreaking documentary work. Since then, two foundational studies by John D'Emilio (1983) and Martin Duberman (1993) traced the quiet political emergence from the 1950s on that exploded in 1969 and after. D'Emilio brought to life two decades of moderate "homophile" politics prior to the "riot" sparked by a June 1969 police raid on New York's Stonewall bar. In a pattern familiar from other movements, he demonstrated conclusively that, despite the sensibility of "newness" felt by gay liberationists in the early 1970s, they were building upon a substantial history of formal politics (lobbying, publishing, networking) and community-building in bars and neighborhoods in certain urban centers since World War II; see also Stuart Timmons's (1990) biography of Harry Hay, founder of the Mattachine Society. Turning to Stonewall, Duberman's book of that title is a highly original exercise in capturing a single disruptive event that lit the spark of a new kind of gay politics, militant, confrontational, joyful – and consciously, polymorphously, perverse. His method is to focus on a few individuals, and through their memories, deconstruct and then rebuild the meaning of the streetfight and subsequent movement-building. Generally, however, there is little scholarship on how Gay Liberation evolved into Gay Rights (and Pride) during the 1970s. The journalists Dudley Clendinen and Adam Nagourney (1999) use extensive oral histories to chronicle this transition, extending it to Clinton's 1992 election, but their work is essentially descriptive and celebratory, though its massive detail will aid later historians. For the international context, Barry Adam's (1987) compact survey of the politics of homosexuality and homophobia since the nineteenth century in Europe and America is useful, but relies on existing scholarship. An excellent account of the briefly flaming radicalism after Stonewall is Terrence Kissack's (1995) article on New York's Gay Liberation Front. Also indispensable are the essays of the publisher, historian, and activist Jeffrey Escoffier (1998), reflecting practical experience and theoretical acuity in applying the "ethnic model" of American politics to political enclaves. The next step is to begin constructing those local histories that will situate gay movement and community-building into a larger context, beyond the trope of Stonewall. An essay by Justin Suran (2001), excavating the relation of Gay Liberation to the larger antiwar movement, is a pathbreaking example of the work to be done.

The limited historiography on gay politics is relatively impressive, however, when one turns to other movements with considerable political impact. Only in the 1990s did scholarship develop on the Native American movement, and events once famous – the occupation of Alcatraz island in 1969, the 1973 siege at Wounded Knee. Troy Johnson (1996) has examined the Alcatraz occupation in detail, as the movement's defining moment, and Joane Nagel (1996) has placed the cultural politics of "Red Power" into a larger frame of Indian renascence. Paul Chaat Smith's and Robert Allen Warrior's (1996) narrative of the movement's meteoric rise and fall effectively captures the *mentalité* of activists and their Nixon administration antagonists, and critically analyzes the charismatic, quixotic American Indian Movement (AIM). The New York-based Puerto Rican movement of the Young Lords Party and the Puerto Rican Socialist Party is still undocumented, except through contemporary accounts (Abramson, 1971; Lopez, 1973) and a recent collection of essays, recollections, and interviews (Torres and Velazquez, 1998). A single book by William Wei (1993) examines Asian American radicalism, but considerably more wide-ranging is a collection of documents, evaluations, memoirs, and oral histories of this multi-ethnic tendency (Louie and Omatsu, 2001). Besides Eric Cummins's (1994) history of organizing at San Quentin, encompassing Caryl Chessman, Eldridge Cleaver, and George Jackson, the nationwide prisoners' movement is unrecorded. The Chicano movement is something of an exception. Numerous social scientists have assessed the fight to reclaim New Mexican land grants, the Raza Unida Party in Texas, and the Chicano student movement in California, tracing the move into mainstream Democratic Party electoralism since the 1970s (F. Garcia, 1974; Gomez-Quinones, 1990; I. Garcia, 1997; Navarro, 2000). Among historians, Mario Garcia's (1989) work on Mexican American organizing since the 1930s, and Carlos Munoz's (1989) politically acute study of *Chicanismo* at its radical peak, are notable.

The largest problem in the New Left's historiography, however, is the degree to which we lack a thorough historiography of the anti-war movement. Though the largest movement of the time, the most far-reaching into towns, cities, and schools in all parts of the country and into nearly all sectors of the population (church members, business people, alumni and professional associations, the State Department, trade unions, the armed services themselves), it remains mysterious, seemingly amorphous and uncoordinated. Both its effect upon the conduct of the war and its composition and political stance (student-based? Old or New Left? liberal or radical or neither?) are still debated. This cloudiness and uncertainty stand in sharp contrast to the highly advanced historiography of the other overarching movement of the New Left, for civil rights and black empowerment. Why?

The most obvious reason is that the civil rights movement can be approached through the histories of distinct national organizations, each with its own ideological positioning and grassroots base, while the anti-war movement lacked similar stable national formations to provide vertical integration at the time and historical coherence after the fact. Indeed, the multiple histories of SDS can be seen as an effort to find a way out of this impasse. Telling the story of anti-war activism via SDS is unsuccessful, however, because though it was a pole of anti-imperialist radicalization in 1965–9, it had consciously abdicated its role as an "anti-anti-communist" ecumenical movement center after leading the Easter 1965 march in Washington, DC. Further, SDS had completely disappeared by the time of the student New Left's apogee – the nation-wide campus strike after the invasion of Cambodia in April 1970, involving 2 million or more students and closing hundreds of colleges and universities as young people were randomly shot down at Jackson State in Mississippi and Kent State in Ohio.

A diffuse, decentered, multilayered movement that coordinated its major initiatives through a series of ad hoc, overlapping, rival national coalitions presents the historian with a daunting challenge – it was everywhere and nowhere, and trying to assert unequivocally "this is the anti-war movement" is akin to holding sand. Only the encyclopedic account by the eminent peace historian Charles DeBenedetti (1990) provides national coverage, because it alone posits that understanding the movement which took off like a rocket after 1965 requires a solid grounding in the immediately preceding period of intensive anti-nuclear activism, starting in 1955 and leading up to the Test Ban Treaty of 1963. The other attempts at sweeping narratives, by Tom Wells (1994) and Adam Garfinkle (1995), are marred by a looking-backward sectarianism in the former case (assigning blame to various leftists, especially the Socialist Workers Party, for the movement's purported failure), and in the latter by trying to prove something unprovable and absurd – that the movement prolonged the war.

The reason that DeBenedetti's massive account succeeds as narrative record but falls short as analysis lies in the larger myopia of "peace history": that the various constituencies that oppose unjust wars, militarism, and exploitive, imperialistic foreign policies can be adequately summed up as "peace activists." The core reality of the anti-war movement was that it became the space where all the scattered remnants, hunkered-down ideological currents, underground traditions, and new outgrowths of American radicalism regrouped: independent socialists of all sorts; pacifists; Catholic Workers; Trotskyists; anarchists; religious radicals; black, Asian, and Latino revolutionary nationalists; communists and many no longer in "the Party" but still of it; Yippies; SDS'ers and other "revolutionary youth"; left-liberals marginalized by the Democratic Party's move right after 1945. Any such movement had a lowest-common-denominator quality regarding common campaigns, and sprouted initiatives in all directions, ideologically and otherwise. But until historians are willing to approach the anti-war struggle from this angle, and with genuine neutrality toward the perspectives and contributions of every one of these political tendencies, we will lack a satisfactory narrative.

The absence of a larger perspective on the movement's composition explains why two nonscholarly, first-person accounts, plus one local case study, prove invaluable to deciphering the anti-war movement: Norman Mailer's (1968) famous reportage from the October 1967 march on the Pentagon; a partisan history by Socialist Workers Party leader Fred Halstead (1978), a key player in the national anti-war coalitions; David Farber's (1988) brilliant, multivocal account of the protests at the 1968 Democratic National Convention in Chicago.

Halstead's book was for many years the only movement history, until the journalists Gerald Sullivan and Nancy Zaroulis (1984) produced a fine, ideologically neutral survey in the 1980s. It is unapologetically a work of sectarian advocacy steeped in Trotskyist perspectives, but cogently lays out the arguments, personalities, and inner workings of the movement's highest level. Of course, that sphere of intra-coalition maneuvering and strategizing for national demonstrations often meant little locally, where the bulk of activism was self-generated by independent activists observing from a distance the movement's putative national leadership (one of the most useful, if tendentious, investigations of local activism is Kenneth Heineman's [1993] comparison of four different state university campus towns). Farber's is a bold attempt to show how three parallel actors assembled and then converged violently on the streets outside the Convention: the main body of the anti-war movement, the "Mobe" led by the pacifist Dave Dellinger; the publicity-seeking, counterculturalist agitators who called themselves "Yippies," led by Abbie Hoffman and Jerry Rubin; on the other side of the national divide, the Chicago political establishment and the police themselves, who ultimately swept the streets clean of those they perceived as enemies of all civilized order. As for Mailer, allowing for his dated hypermasculinist voice, it is still the best personal account of how the war radicalized people – even those as famous and comfortable as the celebrity author – as well as a superb moment-by-moment description of a decisive mass mobilization by a movement that defined itself through its ability to put large numbers on the streets and bodies on the line. What all three of these books share, in radically different ways, is a sense of the larger, intensely charged context – the war itself as it lurched forward from one catastrophe to another, the weight of the forces backing it, how it tore apart the larger society.

Thankfully, many smaller parts of this sprawling history have been studied, notably the disarmament movement of the 1955–65 period. Lawrence Wittner (1993, 1998), the preeminent historian of anti-nuclear activism, has authored a two-volume international history of that movement since Hiroshima. Milton Katz (1986) has traced the organizational history of the Committee for a Sane Nuclear Policy (or SANE), the major new peace formation of the late 1950s, notable for its anti-communist caution; much more needs to be written about the network of established peace organizations, including SANE, the American Friends Service Committee, Fellowship of Reconciliation, Women's International League for Peace and Freedom, and the War Resisters League, since they provided much of the left's infrastructure and political ballast throughout the Cold War. In this context, Jo Ann Ooiman Robinson's (1981) subtle and sympathetic biography of A. J. Muste, the sophisticated pacifist leader who rebuilt the peace movement after 1955, is crucial. Also important is Amy Swerdlow's (1993) portrait of Women Strike for Peace, which invoked a "maternalist" ethic to blunt McCarthyite attitudes while mobilizing women outside of the left.

For the Vietnam years, basic organizational histories are available for a few branches of the movement, including Mitchell Hall's (1990) study of Clergy and Laity Concerned About Vietnam, Andrew Hunt's (1999) account of Vietnam Veterans Against the War, and Philip Foner's (1989) survey of those parts of the labor movement that supported the anti-war struggle. Richard Moser (1996) has looked at the phenomenon of GI and veteran resistance in the larger cultural context of American history, suggesting the ways in which Vietnam reanimated a popular understanding of radical citizenship with lasting impact. Charles Meconis (1979) produced an early sketch of the Catholic left that generated unflinching direct action against the war's bureaucratic machinery through raiding draft boards, destroying records, and inviting trial, though Daniel Berrigan's (1968) impassioned writings and Garry Wills's (1971) contemporary account of the sea change in Catholicism remain useful. Still, so much more needs to be done – investigations of some of the largest national phenomena, such as the development of organized anti-war groups and caucuses in the mainstream religious denominations, and among business and professional people; even more important, comprehensive local histories, beginning with major cities like New York, San Francisco, Chicago and then moving into the heartland, where President Nixon's "silent majority" resided. Eventually, scholars should follow up on Heineman's pioneering work, by examining university communities in selected regions or states. Most difficult but necessary will be studying the war's impact on, and dissent within, small towns and rural areas, including the South and the Great Plains.

This survey of movement historiographies is incomplete because in some cases the scholarship does not exist. The community-organizing tradition associated with Saul Alinsky and the Industrial Areas Foundation predates the 1960s, and was an important current linking labor liberalism with parts of the New Left, including both the United Farm Workers and SDS's moderate wing. It surged from the 1970s on, through powerful national organizations based in door-to-door canvassing like Citizen Action (in which former SDS'ers Heather and Paul Booth and Steve Max played central roles). A related variant of citizen activism rejecting a clear-cut left-wing ideological stance, the "consumer politics" associated with Ralph Nader's organizational empire, is another product of New Left populism. Other than Sanford Horwitt's (1989) uncritical biography of Alinsky, there are no histories of this significant trend. Similarly, while environmentalism is routinely examined by social scientists as exemplary of interest-group activity, no historian has investigated its relationship to the New Left; the sole exception is Barbara Epstein's (1991) theoretically sophisticated account of how a "direct action" movement linking radical environmentalism, peace, spirituality, and third world solidarity prospered in the decade after 1975.

Finally, we are only at the beginning of international histories of the New Left. Though clearly a global trend, was it essentially a response to rising postwar affluence and a concomitant democratization of consumption in the advanced capitalist countries, as Arthur Marwick (1998) argues in his intriguing, scattershot look at "cultural revolution" in the United States, England, Italy, and France? Or a generalized rejection of the West's political order, as some authors suggest in a recent collection about 1968 edited by American and German scholars (Fink et al., 1998)? Clearly, 1968 looms large in theorizing a global New Left, as books by authors like Ronald Fraser (1988), Paul Berman (1996) and George Katsiaficas (1987) testify. The subtitle of Fraser's collective oral history, "a student generation in revolt," indicates their common thesis, for which there is ample evidence. Berman links the "generation of 1968" to the liberal revolution in Eastern Europe in 1989, the development of identity politics via Gay Liberation, and varieties of neoliberal ideology, such as the French New Philosophes and Francis Fukuyama's thesis of an "end to history," which he argues share a common moral economy. Katsiaficas's is the most ambitious, asserting a transnational confrontation with statist power, East and West, that parallels the pan-European revolutions of 1848, and initiated a new epoch in world history. The problem with this visionary argument is that Katsiaficas argues that a single, shared purpose links protest in Eastern Europe against the Soviet sphere of influence with upsurges in Western Europe and the United States, and with the third world tide of armed liberation movements stretching from Vietnam to southern Africa to the hills and barrios of Latin America. Such a claim is simply untenable: most third world guerrilla movements were led by Leninist parties, attempting to smash the existing state or imperial order in the classic fashion prescribed by Marx in "The Eighteenth Brumaire," and actively supported by the Soviet Union. That most of the Western New Left supported them, and rallied behind the banner led by Ho Chi Minh and Fidel Castro, is an evident fact, and Katsiaficas's book does bring to the fore the largest confrontation of the 1960s, between the "Free World" led by the United States, and the revolutionary-nationalist arc of Africa, Asia, and Latin America. Whether this constituted a transnational New Left is still an open question.

The Contours of Postwar Radicalism: Outline of a New Democratic Order

This essay rests upon the premise that there was a fluid, complex, self-conscious left in the United States during the Cold War era, and that the name it took circa 1960 and kept until late in the decade, as a "new left" to distinguish itself from the working-class left of 1877–1948, remains valid. Though one can move its starting point back as far as the social tumult occasioned by World War II, I see this phase in American radicalism as spanning the two decades from the Montgomery bus boycott in 1955 through the Watergate crisis and the end of the Vietnam War in 1973–5. And as indicated earlier, opening up the timeframe to include all of the radical social movements of the period, rather than positing civil rights protests as the New Left's precondition and second-wave feminism and gay liberation as its outgrowth, guarantees that this left's history cannot be summed up through one group or movement (see Gosse, 2003a).

But does grouping the totality of radical movements through these two decades under a common name merely constitute a catch-all for a series of only tangentially related struggles? Did these movements have any common politics, ultimately? Equally important, how did they relate to one another – what unity was established at different points to substantiate the claim of "a movement of movements"? Those questions bedeviled political strategists at the time, and need to be addressed here.

Reflecting my conviction that the practical mechanics of politics require as much analysis as the study of evolving ideological perspectives, even when that organizing is at its most utopian and participatory, let us begin with the question of whether there really was a functioning "Movement," a coherent New Left greater than its disparate parts. Some scholars see the cascading series of coalitions, collectives, caucuses, cooperatives, and communes spilling over each other from the later 1950s through the early 1970s as disconnected, even canceling each other out, evidence of an entropic diffusion that some praise as a prefigurative anarchism and others damn as "single-issue" tunnel vision. Against this view, I have argued that it is not adequate to define the New Left as chaotic and lacking any structure. Rather, it is properly understood as a "polycentric" left encompassing a series of overlapping, contingent social movements, each with its own centers of power, that related to each other through a series of strategic arrangements (Gosse, 1993). I further argue that in each of its two major phases, there was a locus of protest, a "moral economy" that generated a rising tide of visible radicalism and defined the politics of a particular convergence. Each of these radical convergences included significant elements of the much-disparaged "old left" of communists, Trotskyists, other socialists, and, very importantly, pacifists and religious radicals. Though difficult for many veterans both "old" and "new" to acknowledge, or many schooled in recent historiography to perceive, one cannot make sense of the New Left without recognizing that it incorporated most of the Old Left into its free-floating practice (though hardly all – the abstention by the Socialist Party's trade union-based apparatus spawned New Right neoconservatism in the early 1970s, a very unintended consequence).

In 1955–65, it is indisputable that the civil rights movement in Dixie provided a moral, political, discursive, and physical center for the new postwar radicalism. The most cursory examination of left publications during these years reveals an overriding awareness that the "Negro Revolution" was the locus of change. In a literal sense, the American left had to "go South," into that other country and semicolonial reality, to rediscover itself in struggle and find a new basis of unity. Simply reciting a litany of well-known events and tableaux, including the Kennedy-backed funding of groups from the NAACP to SNCC to do grassroots voter registration, the fight between Republicans and Democrats for the black vote from 1956 to 1964, the internal dynamics of the August 1963 March on Washington, and the famous challenge of the Mississippi Freedom Democratic Party at the 1964 Democratic Convention, indicates that this particular "movement" was the terrain of struggle, of negotiation, cooperation, co-optation, and final confrontation, between the nascent radical coalition and the institutions of Cold War liberalism.

After 1965, the focus rapidly shifted away from the South, and away from the black leadership of the civil rights movement. This shift is much debated in the literature on "the Sixties," but in truth the reasons are both overdetermined and obvious. Certainly, the black freedom movement faced a crisis because of its signal victories in 1964–5, while its internal unity was collapsing from the bottom up as grassroots organizers demanded more than liberals could or would deliver. More important, however, is that in the United States, as elsewhere, bloody, drawn-out foreign wars trump all else. Inevitably, the single unchallenged point of unity among all of the left's constituencies became opposition to the war in Vietnam. Again, virtually any source from those years indicates that radical organizers, from Black Panthers to the Catholic left to gay liberationists, began their analysis of the ills afflicting America with "the war." Crucially, the war and one's position on it was the clear marker dividing, and then ultimately reconciling, liberals and radicals, as the peeling away to an anti-war stance of successive layers of Democratic Party constituencies and politicians registered the anti-war movement's growing power.

But demonstrating that the different wings of the new, decentered left cooperated around one and then another overriding cause does not demonstrate any common ideology, a "New Left politics" transcending the particular. Asserting the lack of a shared worldview is the linchpin of the insistence that only SDS deserves the name "New Left" because it alone proposed a comprehensive, genuinely new ideological stance, versus a plethora of "single-issue" groups. This assertion is often made, but will not stand scrutiny. The various organizations and constituencies of the multigenerational, multiracial New Left were politically and ideologically united by exclusion from, and eventually a fierce anger directed at, the narrow world of Cold War liberalism, and their insistence on reasserting the radical "perfectionist" strain in American democratic thought, as James Gilbert argues in an important collection defending the radicalism of the New Left, "without apology" (Sayres et al., 1984). In that sense, the New Left represented a break not just from Cold War America and the New Deal Order, but from the frame of American politics established by Reconstruction's defeat and the grinding down of black citizenship rights coinciding with a new imperialism and a dynamic industrial order based in a new white immigrant working class.

The politics of the broad New Left asserted here stemmed from an organic, often highly personalized rejection of one, two, and then many of the bargains, seductions, and "deals" of that way of life, starting with the contradiction between a democracy supposedly based in universal suffrage and citizenship, versus a caste-like racial hierarchy. The refusal to tolerate white supremacy at home or abroad, the openness to alternative humanistic forms of socialism, the invocation of the "beloved community" – all of these strains run from King's SCLC to SNCC and SDS, and then on to the vast decentralized "Resistance" to the draft that sprang up in 1966. The most complete and wrenching statement of this New Left politics is King's famous speech at Riverside Church in 1967. Indeed, for anyone embracing the inclusive definition of the New Left, King was its preeminent articulator and popular leader, if not at all the one-man Movement founder of liberal iconography. And it is his new, radically democratic, prophetic stance that does supersede the Old Left's orthodox socialist teleology, suborning its constituencies and requiring it to operate on a new terrain.

Interestingly, the scholars who put SDS at the center will concede that a common vision, derived from the black freedom movement, animated the New Left in the early 1960s, so as to argue for the dissolution of that unity later. In a sense, the civil rights movement is put on a pedestal as it is separated from "the left" itself. Again, however, this minimizes the common radicalization of all the movements as the Indochina war escalated, especially after 1968, when the Nixon administration consciously polarized US society and implemented a domestic version of counter-insurgency. The radical sections of the left, multiracial but usually youthful, adopted a joint identity as "anti-imperialist," as any reading of literature by the Young Lords Party, the Black Panthers, the various post-SDS factions moving toward Maoism, AIM and the numberless unaffiliated local groups involved in Black Power or anti-war activities, will show. The insistence that the now truly "radical" left after 1968 can be adequately summed up via the small anarcho-populist sect called Weatherman is one of the most unfortunate claims of Sale, Miller, Gitlin, and others following their lead (its sad history can be traced in Jacobs, 1997). The newly Leninist "anti-imperialist" or "new communist" left that surged from 1969 on found numerous expressions much larger and longer-lasting than the Weather Underground and needs reasoned scholarship that dispenses with old polemics about a "death culture." A collective oral documentary of one of the anti-imperialist left's earliest projects, the Venceremos Brigades that sent several thousand people to cut sugar cane in Cuba in 1969–71, is an invaluable window into the discourse of the time (Levinson and Brightman, 1971). I have examined briefly the Chile and Puerto Rico solidarity movements, which flourished in the mid-1970s and drew support from every branch of the New Left (Gosse, 1996). Max Elbaum (2002), a perspicacious veteran, has produced the first historical examination of the "new communist" movement which drew in thousands of young organizers. The more moderate main body of the New Left, stretching across the sectoral boundaries, came to a similar conclusion, that the central problem in American politics was a pervasive urge to empire, no matter what the price in blood, treasure, and morality. By 1970, powerful US senators like J. William Fulbright were openly denouncing "militarism" in the company of avowed New Leftists, and the attraction of the McGovern campaign for radicals was the Democratic candidate's commitment to unilaterally withdraw from Vietnam and cut the defense budget by 30 percent – positions for which Nixon savaged him, but which articulated an agenda at the outer limits of radical discourse as late as 1968.

In retrospect, the New Left's legacy was embodied by the radicalized liberalism manifested in McGovern's campaign and the temporary conquest of the Democratic Party, and that institution's subsequent restructuring to accommodate once radical constituencies, rather than the revolutionary hopes of anti-imperialists as the United States retreated from Indochina in 1970–5. The new understandings about race, gender, and sexuality negotiated throughout civil society (family, church, school, workplace, union, campus) over the next decades represent the New Left's partial success in revolutionizing America, even while the New Right focused single-mindedly on accreting power in municipal, state, and federal governments, and within the Republican Party. Elsewhere I argue that this tentatively named "New Democratic Order" explains the grinding political stalemate over the past generation, and the fierceness of conservative mobilization against what right-wing activists insist on calling "the left" while many radicals deny there is any left in America (Gosse, 2003b).

Where Do We Go From Here?

Several major directions are indicated by this review of New Left historiography. First, in every respect, we urgently need local studies, of city, town, state, and countryside. Second, we should look closely at how the once new radicalism inflected and influenced institutions, communities, and constituencies, or what Latin Americans call "sectors." Third, as our understanding of "the Movement" extends backwards and forwards, every instance of this decentered radicalism should be evaluated in relation to the whole of American politics. Finally, there is the problem of anti-intellectualism – the unfortunate idea that scholarship on the New Left can be done without a thorough grounding in the international history of the left.

Case studies constitute an endless process for historians – every community or locality, rendered historically, can be compared against other communities. This process has just begun for the New Left – a few public universities, some prominent states and cities during civil rights campaigns. So, for example, examinations of gay liberation outside its coastal redoubts, women's liberation in the suburbs and the South, anti-war activism in religious colleges and high schools, Black Power in white-majority cities, and so on, are all necessary: a fine example of this kind of book is Marc Stein's (2000) study of gay and lesbian community-building and activism in Philadelphia from the end of World War II through the early 1970s. Equally important will be studies assessing the New Left in all its forms, across time and constituencies, in a single locale. There were few places where individual movements were so strong and self-contained that they did not cross-pollinate, subdivide, and collaborate – at least around the Vietnam War and civil liberties issues. Such histories would demonstrate the reality of how many movements did (or did not) make up "the Movement."

For some reason, US historians seem loath to study societal groups ("sectors") outside of the major categories of workers, women, and people of color, though this is a very practical way of looking at, or fomenting, political change. Regarding the New

Left, one can easily envision studies of students, intellectuals, the various professional groups (doctors, architects, public employees, teachers and so on), artists, and more. In particular, this methodology would enable investigations of a neglected but exceptionally significant aspect of "Sixties" radicalization – the churches, both mainline Protestant and Catholic. A little-cited but excellent example of this approach is James T. Fisher's (1989) exploration of the "Catholic counterculture" from the 1930s to the 1960s, including Dorothy Day, Thomas Merton, and Jack Kerouac. Peter Levy (1994) has initiated the study of the relationship of the New Left to organized labor at the national level, but studies of specific cities are needed to penetrate the defensive silences created by McCarthyism and locate the pockets of "old" leftists (for instance, in the United Packinghouse Workers), who played crucial roles in underwriting the New Left. The widespread movement of younger activists into the labor movement in the 1970s, effecting a "revolution from below" in some instances, is an inviting topic for research.

A larger perspective on cultural-political shifts within major social groups and institutions would help historians avoid the voluntarist fallacy – the premise that a movement's victory or defeat can be attributed primarily to its own agency, degree of perspicacity, and ideological clarity. This may be a truism, yet it is common in the historiography surveyed in this essay. Therefore, we need to turn away from hermetic accounts of organizations and campaigns, and focus on integrating radicalism during the Cold War era into the larger structure of US politics. That framework had two main axes: this nation's political, economic, military, and cultural supremacy on the world stage after 1945, and the peculiar left–right character of the rickety "New Deal Order," and an essentially unreconstructed Democratic Party. The historiography of the black freedom movement has largely met this challenge; for other movements much remains to be done. Only on this basis, paying careful attention to the post-1960s decades, can we have reasoned arguments about the New Left's real impact.

To conclude, regarding anti-intellectualism, it should no longer be acceptable to write about "new" versus "old" lefts in the United States without fully appreciating the global scope, sophisticated ideologies, and revolutionary commitments of the socialist, anarchist, and communist movements, their forebears in the revolutionary democratic traditions of 1776, 1789, and 1848, and the twentieth-century anti-colonial and anti-imperialist revolutions in Africa, Asia, and Latin America. In sum, we must demand that historians of US radicalism be as internationalist and historically minded as their subjects.

REFERENCES

Abramson, Michael: *Palante, Young Lords Party* (New York: McGraw Hill, 1971).

Adam, Barry D.: *The Rise of the Gay and Lesbian Movement* (Boston: Twayne, 1987).

Anderson, Terry H.: *The Movement and the Sixties* (New York: Oxford University Press, 1996).

Baraka, Amiri: *The Autobiography of LeRoi Jones* (Chicago: Lawrence Hill Books, 1997).

Baxandall, Rosalyn and Gordon, Linda, eds.: *Dear Sisters: Dispatches from the Women's Liberation Movement* (New York: Basic Books, 2000).

Berman, Paul: *A Tale of Two Utopias: The Political Journey of the Generation of 1968* (New York: Norton, 1996).

Berrigan, Daniel: *Night Flight to Hanoi: War Diary with 11 Poems* (New York: Harper and Row, 1968).

Boggs, Grace Lee: *Living for Change: An Autobiography* (Minneapolis: University of Minnesota Press, 1998).

Branch, Taylor: *Parting the Waters: America in the King Years, 1954–63* (New York: Simon and Schuster, 1988).

Branch, Taylor: *Pillar of Fire: America in the King Years, 1963–65* (New York: Simon and Schuster, 1998).

Breines, Wini: "Whose New Left?" *Journal of American History*, 75/2 (1988): 528–45.

Breines, Wini: *Community and Organization in the New Left, 1962–1968: The Great Refusal* (New Brunswick, NJ: Rutgers University Press, 1989).

Brown, Elaine: *A Taste of Power: A Black Woman's Story* (New York: Pantheon, 1992).

Brownmiller, Susan: *In Our Time: Memoir of a Revolution* (New York: Dial Press, 1999).

Buhle, Paul: *History and the New Left: Madison, Wisconsin, 1950–1970* (Philadelphia: Temple University Press, 1990).

Bush, Rod: *We Are Not What We Seem: Black Nationalism and Class Struggle in the American Century* (New York: New York University Press, 1999).

Carew, Jan: *Ghosts in Our Blood: With Malcolm X in Africa, England and the Caribbean* (Chicago: Lawrence Hill, 1994).

Carson, Clayborne: *In Struggle: SNCC and the Black Awakening of the 1960s* (Cambridge, Mass.: Harvard University Press, 1981).

Chafe, William H.: *Civilities and Civil Rights: Greensboro, North Carolina, and the Black Struggle for Freedom* (New York: Oxford University Press, 1980).

Chafe, William H.: *The Unfinished Journey: America Since World War II*, 4th ed. (New York: Oxford University Press, 1999).

Clendinen, Dudley and Nagourney, Adam: *Out for Good: The Struggle to Build a Gay Rights Movement in America* (New York: Simon and Schuster, 1999).

Collier-Thomas, Bettye and Franklin, V.P.: *Sisters in the Struggle: African American Women in the Civil Rights-Black Power Movement* (New York: New York University Press, 2001).

Crawford, Vicki L., Rouse, Jacqueline Anne, and Woods, Barbara: *Women in the Civil Rights Movement: Trailblazers and Torchbearers, 1941–1965* (Bloomington: Indiana University Press, 1993).

Cruse, Harold: *The Crisis of the Negro Intellectual: A Historical Analysis of the Failure of Black Leadership* (New York: William Morrow, 1967).

Cruse, Harold: *Rebellion or Revolution?* (New York: William Morrow, 1968).

Cummins, Eric: *The Rise and Fall of California's Radical Prison Movement* (Stanford, Calif.: Stanford University Press, 1994).

Curry, Constance et al.: *Deep in Our Hearts: Nine White Women in the Freedom Movement* (Athens: University of Georgia Press, 2000).

D'Emilio, John: *Sexual Politics, Sexual Communities: The Making of a Homosexual Minority in the United States, 1940–1970* (Chicago: University of Chicago Press, 1983).

Davis, Flora: *Moving the Mountain: The Women's Movement in America Since 1960* (Urbana: University of Illinois Press, 1999).

DeBenedetti, Charles, with Charles Chatfield: *An American Ordeal: The Antiwar Movement of the Vietnam Era* (Syracuse, NY: Syracuse University Press, 1990).

Dittmer, John: *Local People: The Struggle for Civil Rights in Mississippi* (Urbana: University of Illinois Press, 1994).

Duberman, Martin: *Stonewall* (New York: Dutton, 1993).

DuPlessis, Rachel Blau and Snitow, Ann: *The Feminist Memoir Project: Voices from Women's Liberation* (New York: Three Rivers Press, 1998).

Dyson, Michael Eric: *Making Malcolm: The Myth and Meaning of Malcolm X* (New York: Oxford University Press, 1995).

Echols, Alice: *Daring to Be Bad: Radical Feminism in America, 1967–1975* (Minneapolis: University of Minnesota Press, 1989).

Edsall, Thomas Byrne and Edsall, Mary: *Chain Reaction: The Impact of Race, Rights and Taxes on American Politics* (New York: W. W. Norton, 1991).

Elbaum, Max: *Revolution in the Air: 1960s Radicalism and the 1970s "New Communist Movement"* (New York: Verso, 2002).

Epstein, Barbara: *Political Protest and Cultural Revolution: Nonviolent Direct Action in the 1970s and 1980s* (Berkeley: University of California Press, 1991).

Escoffier, Jeffrey: *American Homo: Community and Perversity* (Berkeley: University of California Press, 1998).

Essien-Udom, Essien: *Black Nationalism: A Search for Identity in America* (Chicago: University of Chicago Press, 1962).

Evans, Sara: *Personal Politics: The Origins of Women's Liberation in the Civil Rights Movement and the New Left* (New York: Alfred A. Knopf, 1979).

Fairclough, Adam: *To Redeem the Soul of America: The Southern Christian Leadership Conference and Martin Luther King, Jr.* (Athens: University of Georgia Press, 1987).

Fairclough, Adam: *Race and Democracy: The Civil Rights Struggle in Louisiana, 1915–1972* (Athens: University of Georgia Press, 1995).

Farber, David R.: *Chicago '68* (Chicago: University of Chicago Press, 1988).

Farber, David R.: *The Age of Great Dreams: America in the 1960s* (New York: Hill and Wang, 1994).

Ferree, Myra Marx and Hess, Beth B.: *Controversy and Coalition: The New Feminist Movement Across Three Decades of Change* (New York: Twayne, 1994).

Fink, Carole, Gassert, Phillipp, and Junker, Detlef: *1968: The World Transformed* (Cambridge: Cambridge University Press, 1998).

Fisher, James Terence: *The Catholic Counterculture in America, 1933–1962* (Chapel Hill: University of North Carolina Press, 1989).

Fleming, Cynthia Griggs: *Soon We Will Not Cry: The Liberation of Ruby Doris Smith Robinson* (Lanham, Md.: Rowman and Littlefield, 1998).

Foner, Philip S.: *U.S. Labor and the Vietnam War* (New York: International Publishers, 1989).

Forman, James: *The Making of Black Revolutionaries* (New York: Macmillan, 1972).

Fraser, Ronald et al.: *1968: A Student Generation in Revolt* (New York: Pantheon, 1988).

Freeman, Jo: *The Politics of Women's Liberation: A Case Study of an Emerging Social Movement and Its Relation to the Policy Process* (New York: McKay, 1975).

Garcia, F. Chris: *La Causa Politica: A Chicano Politics Reader* (Notre Dame, Ind.: University of Notre Dame Press, 1974).

Garcia, Ignacio M.: *Chicanismo: The Forging of a Militant Ethos Among Mexican Americans* (Tucson: University of Arizona Press, 1997).

Garcia, Mario T.: *Mexican Americans: Leadership, Ideology and Identity, 1930–1960* (New Haven, Conn.: Yale University Press, 1989).

Garfinkle, Adam: *Telltale Hearts: The Origins and Impact of the Vietnam Antiwar Movement* (New York: St. Martin's, 1995).

Garrow, David J.: *Bearing the Cross: Martin Luther King, Jr., and the Southern Christian Leadership Conference* (New York: Random House, 1986).

Garrow, David J.: *The FBI and Martin Luther King, Jr.: From "Solo" to Memphis* (New Haven, Conn.: Yale University Press, 2001).

Georgakas, Dan and Surkin, Marvin: *Detroit: I Do Mind Dying, A Study in Urban Revolution* (New York: St. Martin's, 1975).

Geschwender, James: *Class, Race, and Worker Insurgency: The League of Revolutionary Black Workers* (Cambridge: Cambridge University Press, 1977).

Gilbert, James: "New Left: Old America," in Sohnya Sayres, Anders Stephanson, Stanley Aronowitz, and Frederick Jameson, *The Sixties, Without Apology* (Minneapolis: University of Minnesota Press, 1984).

Gitlin, Todd: *The Whole World is Watching: Mass Media in the Making and Unmaking of the New Left* (Berkeley: University of California Press, 1980).

Gitlin, Todd: *The Sixties: Years of Hope, Days of Rage* (New York: Bantam Books, 1987).

Gitlin, Todd: *The Twilight of Common Dreams: Why America is Wracked by Culture Wars* (New York: Metropolitan Books, 1995).

Gomez-Quinones, Juan: *Chicano Politics: Reality and Promise, 1940–1990* (Albuquerque: University of New Mexico Press, 1990).

Gosse, Van: *Where the Boys Are: Cuba, Cold War America and the Making of a New Left* (London: Verso, 1993).

Gosse, Van: "'El Salvador is Spanish for Vietnam': The Politics of Solidarity and the New Immigrant Left, 1955–1993," in Paul Buhle and Dan Georgakas (eds.), *The Immigrant Left* (Albany: State University of New York Press, 1996).

Gosse, Van: *The American New Left: A Brief History with Documents* (Boston: Bedford/ St. Martin's, 2003a).

Gosse, Van: "Post-Modern America: A New Democratic Order in a Second Gilded Age," in Van Gosse and Richard Moser, *A Fortunate Fall: Politics and Culture Since the 1960s* (Philadelphia: Temple University Press, 2003b).

Grant, Joanne: *Ella Baker: Freedom Bound* (New York: Wiley, 1998).

Hall, Mitchell K.: *Because of Their Faith: CALCAV and Religious Opposition to the Vietnam War* (New York: Columbia University Press, 1990).

Halstead, Fred: *Out Now! A Participant's Account of the American Movement Against the Vietnam War* (New York: Pathfinder, 1978).

Harrison, Cynthia: *On Account of Sex: The Politics of Women's Issues, 1945–1968* (Berkeley: University of California Press, 1988).

Hartmann, Susan M.: *The Other Feminists: Activists in the Liberal Establishment* (New Haven, Conn.: Yale University Press, 1998).

Hayden, Tom: *Reunion: A Memoir* (New York: Random House, 1988).

Heineman, Kenneth J.: *Campus Wars: The Peace Movement at American State Universities in the Vietnam Era* (New York: New York University Press, 1993).

Hilliard, David and Cole, Lewis: *This Side of Glory: The Autobiography of David Hilliard and the Story of the Black Panther Party* (Boston: Little, Brown, 1993).

Hollibaugh, Amber: *My Dangerous Desires: A Queer Girl Dreaming Her Way Home* (Durham, NC: Duke University Press, 2000).

Honey, Michael: *Southern Labor and Black Civil Rights: Organizing Memphis Workers* (Urbana: University of Illinois Press, 1993).

Horowitz, Daniel: *Betty Friedan and the Making of "The Feminine Mystique": The American Left, the Cold War, and Modern Feminism* (Amherst: University of Massachusetts Press, 1998).

Horwitt, Sanford D.: *Let Them Call Me Rebel: Saul Alinsky, His Life and Legacy* (New York: Alfred A. Knopf, 1989).

Hunt, Andrew E.: *The Turning: A History of Vietnam Veterans Against the War* (New York: New York University Press, 1999).

Isserman, Maurice: *If I Had a Hammer: The Death of the Old Left and the Birth of the New Left* (New York: Basic Books, 1987).

Isserman, Maurice and Kazin, Michael: *America Divided: The Civil War of the 1960s* (New York: Oxford University Press, 2000).

Jacobs, Paul and Landau, Saul: *The New Radicals: A Report with Documents* (New York: Random House, 1966).

Jacobs, Ron: *The Way the Wind Blew: A History of the Weather Underground* (London: Verso, 1997).

Jay, Karla: *Tales of the Lavender Menace: A Memoir of Liberation* (New York: Basic Books, 1999).

Johnson, Troy R.: *The Occupation of Alcatraz Island: Indian Self-Determination and the Rise of Indian Activism* (Urbana: University of Illinois Press, 1996).

Jones, Charles E.: *The Black Panther Party Reconsidered* (Baltimore: Black Classic Press, 1998).

Katsiaficas, George: *The Imagination of the New Left: A Global Analysis of 1968* (Boston: South End Press, 1987).

Katz, Jonathan: *Gay American History: Lesbians and Gay Men in the U.S.A.* (New York: Harper and Row, 1976).

Katz, Milton S.: *Ban the Bomb: A History of SANE, the Committee for a Sane Nuclear Policy* (New York: Praeger, 1986).

Kissack, Terrence: "Freaking Fag Revolutionaries: New York's Gay Liberation Front, 1969–1971," *Radical History Review*, 62 (1995): 104–35.

Klibaner, Irwin: *Conscience of a Troubled South: The Southern Conference Educational Fund, 1946–1966* (Brooklyn: Carlson, 1989).

Kofsky, Frank: *Black Nationalism and the Revolution in Music* (New York: Pathfinder, 1970).

Lawson, Steven: *In Pursuit of Power: Southern Blacks and Electoral Politics, 1965–1982* (New York: Columbia University Press, 1985).

Lawson, Steven: "Freedom Then, Freedom Now: The Historiography of the Civil Rights Movement," *American Historical Review*, 96 (1991): 456–71.

Lawson, Steven: *Running for Freedom: Civil Rights and Black Politics in America Since 1941* (New York: McGraw Hill, 1997).

Lawson, Steven: *Black Ballots: Voting Rights in the South, 1944–1969* (Lanham, Md.: Lexington, 1999).

Lee, Chana Kai: *For Freedom's Sake: The Life of Fannie Lou Hamer* (Urbana: University of Illinois Press, 1999).

Levinson, Sandra and Brightman, Carol: *Venceremos Brigade: Young Americans Sharing the Life and Work of Revolutionary Cuba* (New York: Simon and Schuster, 1971).

Levy, Peter B.: *The New Left and Labor in the 1960s* (Urbana: University of Illinois Press, 1994).

Lipsitz, George: *A Life in the Struggle: Ivory Perry and the Culture of Opposition* (Philadelphia: Temple University Press, 1995).

Long, Priscilla: *The New Left: A Collection of Essays* (Boston: Porter Sargent, 1969).

Lopez, Alfredo: *The Puerto Rican Papers: Notes on the Re-Emergence of a Nation* (Indianapolis: Bobbs Merrill, 1973).

Louie, Steve and Omatsu, Glenn: *Asian Americans: The Movement and the Moment* (Los Angeles: UCLA Asian American Studies Center Press, 2001).

McAdam, Doug: *Political Process and the Development of Black Insurgency, 1930–1970* (Chicago: University of Chicago Press, 1999).

Mailer, Norman: *The Armies of the Night: History as a Novel, The Novel as History* (New York: New American Library, 1968).

Marable, Manning: *Black American Politics: From the Washington Marches to Jesse Jackson* (London: Verso, 1985).

Marable, Manning: *Race, Reform and Rebellion: The Second Reconstruction in Black America, 1945–1990* (Jackson: University of Mississippi Press, 1991).

Marwick, Arthur: *The Sixties: Cultural Revolution in Britain, France, Italy, and the United States, c.1958–c.1974* (New York: Oxford University Press, 1998).

Meconis, Charles: *With Clumsy Grace: The American Catholic Left, 1961–1975* (New York: Seabury Press, 1979).

Meier, August and Rudwick, Elliott: *CORE: A Study of the Civil Rights Movement, 1942–1968* (Urbana: University of Illinois Press, 1975).

Meyerowitz, Joanne, ed.: *Not June Cleaver: Women and Gender in Postwar America, 1945–1960* (Philadelphia: Temple University Press, 1994).

Miller, James: *"Democracy is in the Streets": From Port Huron to the Siege of Chicago* (New York: Simon and Schuster, 1987).

Mills, Kay: *This Little Light of Mine: The Life of Fannie Lou Hamer* (New York: Plume, 1993).

Morgan, Edward P: *The 60s Experience: Hard Lessons About Modern America* (Philadelphia: Temple University Press, 1991).

Morris, Aldon D.: *The Origins of the Civil Rights Movement: Black Communities Organizing for Change* (New York: Free Press, 1984).

Moser, Richard: *The New Winter Soldiers: GI and Veteran Dissent During the Vietnam Era* (New Brunswick, NJ: Rutgers University Press, 1996).

Munoz, Jr., Carlos: *Youth, Identity, Power: The Chicano Movement* (London: Verso, 1989).

Nagel, Joane: *American Indian Ethnic Renewal: Red Power and the Resurgence of Identity and Culture* (New York: Oxford University Press, 1996).

Navarro, Armando: *La Raza Unida Party: A Chicano Challenge to the U.S. Two-Party Dictatorship* (Philadelphia: Temple University Press, 2000).

Newfield, Jack: *A Prophetic Minority* (New York: New American Library, 1966).

O'Brien, James Putnam: "The Development of a New Left in the United States, 1960–1965" (Ph.D. diss., University of Wisconsin, 1971).

Oglesby, Carl: *The New Left Reader* (New York: Grove, 1969).

Olson, Lynne: *Freedom's Daughters: The Unsung Heroines of the Civil Rights Movement from 1830 to 1970* (New York: Scribner, 2001).

Payne, Charles M.: *I've Got the Light of Freedom: The Organizing Tradition and the Mississippi Freedom Struggle* (Berkeley: University of California Press, 1995).

Pearson, Hugh: *The Shadow of the Panther: Huey Newton and the Price of Black Power in America* (Reading, Mass.: Addison Wesley, 1994).

Ralph, Jr., James R.: *Northern Protest: Martin Luther King, Jr., Chicago, and the Civil Rights Movement* (Cambridge, Mass.: Harvard University Press, 1993).

Robinson, Jo Ann Ooiman: *Abraham Went Out: A Biography of A. J. Muste* (Philadelphia: Temple University Press, 1981).

Rorabaugh, W. J.: *Berkeley at War: The 1960s* (New York: Oxford University Press, 1989).

Rosen, Ruth: *The World Split Open: How the Modern Women's Movement Changed America* (New York: Viking, 2000).

Rossinow, Douglas: *The Politics of Authenticity: Liberalism, Christianity and the New Left in America* (New York: Columbia University Press, 1998).

Rupp, Leila J. and Taylor, Verta: *Survival in the Doldrums: The American Women's Rights Movement, 1945 to the 1960s* (Columbus: Ohio State University Press, 1990).

Sale, Kirkpatrick: *SDS* (New York: Random House, 1973).

Sales, Jr., William W.: *From Civil Rights to Black Liberation: Malcolm X and the Organization of Afro-American Unity* (Boston: South End Press, 1994).

Sayres, Sohnya, Stephanson, Anders, Aronowitz, Stanley, and Jameson, Frederick: *The Sixties, Without Apology* (Minneapolis: University of Minnesota Press, 1984).

Schneir, Miriam: *Feminism In Our Time: The Essential Writings, World War II to the Present* (New York: Vintage, 1994).

Schultz, Debra L: *Going South: Jewish Women in the Civil Rights Movement* (New York: New York University Press, 2001).

Sitkoff, Harvard: *The Struggle for Black Equality, 1954–1992* (New York: Hill and Wang, 1993).

Sleeper, Jim: *The Closest of Strangers: Liberalism and the Politics of Race in New York* (New York: W. W. Norton, 1990).

Smith, Allen: "Present at the Creation and Other Myths: The *Port Huron Statement* and the Origins of the New Left," *Peace and Change*, 25/3 (2000): 339–62.

Smith, Barbara: *The Truth That Never Hurts: Writings on Race, Gender, and Freedom* (New Brunswick, NJ: Rutgers University Press, 1998).

Smith, Paul Chaat and Warrior, Robert Allen: *Like a Hurricane: The Indian Movement from Alcatraz to Wounded Knee* (New York: New Press, 1996).

Smith, Suzanne E.: *Dancing in the Street: Motown and the Cultural Politics of Detroit* (Cambridge, Mass.: Harvard University Press, 1999).

Steigerwald, David: *The Sixties and the End of Modern America* (New York: St. Martin's, 1995).

Stein, Marc: *City of Sisterly and Brotherly Loves: Lesbian and Gay Philadelphia, 1945–1972* (Chicago: University of Chicago Press, 2000).

Strickland, William: *Malcolm X: Make It Plain* (New York: Penguin, 1994).

Sullivan, Gerald and Zaroulis, Nancy: *Who Spoke Up? American Protest Against the War in Vietnam, 1963–1975* (Garden City, NY: Doubleday, 1984).

Sullivan, Patricia: *Days of Hope: Race and Democracy in the New Deal Era* (Chapel Hill: University of North Carolina Press, 1996).

Suran, Justin David: "Coming Out Against the War: Antimilitarism and the Politicization of Homosexuality in the Era of Vietnam," *American Quarterly*, 55/3 (2001): 452–88.

Swerdlow, Amy: *Women Strike for Peace: Traditional Motherhood and Radical Politics in the 1960s* (Chicago: University of Chicago Press, 1993).

Teal, Donn: *The Gay Militants: How Gay Liberation Began in America, 1969–1971* (New York: Stein and Day, 1971).

Teodori, Massimo: *The New Left: A Documentary History* (Indianapolis: Bobbs Merrill, 1969).

Timmons, Stuart: *The Trouble with Harry Hay: Founder of the Modern Gay Movement* (Boston: Alyson, 1990).

Tomasky, Michael: *Left for Dead: The Life, Death, and Possible Resurrection of Progressive Politics in America* (New York: Free Press, 1996).

Torres, Andres and Velazquez, Jose E.: *The Puerto Rican Movement: Voices from the Diaspora* (Philadelphia: Temple University Press, 1998).

Tyson, Timothy B.: *Radio Free Dixie: Robert F. Williams and the Roots of Black Power* (Chapel Hill: University of North Carolina Press, 1999).

Van DeBurg, William L.: *New Day in Babylon: The Black Power Movement and American Culture, 1965–1975* (Chicago: University of Chicago Press, 1992).

Wei, William: *The Asian American Movement* (Philadelphia: Temple University Press, 1993).

Weigand, Kate: *Red Feminism: American Communists and the Making of Women's Liberation* (Baltimore: Johns Hopkins University Press, 2001).

Weisbrot, Robert: *Freedom Bound: A History of America's Civil Rights Movement* (New York: W. W. Norton, 1990).

Weiss, Nancy J.: *Whitney M. Young, Jr. and the Struggle for Civil Rights* (Princeton, NJ: Princeton University Press, 1989).

Wells, Tom: *The War Within: America's Battle Over Vietnam* (New York: Henry Holt, 1994).

Williams, Yohuru: *Black Politics, White Power: Civil Rights, Black Power, and the Black Panthers in New Haven* (St. James, NY: Brandywine, 2000).

Wills, Garry: *Bare Ruined Choirs: Doubt, Prophecy, and Radical Religion* (New York: Dell, 1971).

Wittner, Lawrence: *The Struggle Against the Bomb: One World Or None – A History of the World Nuclear Disarmament Movement Through 1953* (Stanford, Calif.: Stanford University Press, 1993).

Wittner, Lawrence: *The Struggle Against the Bomb: Resisting the Bomb – A History of the World Nuclear Disarmament Movement, 1954–1970* (Stanford, Calif.: Stanford University Press, 1998).

Wood, Joe: *Malcolm X: In Our Own Image* (New York: St. Martin's, 1992).

Woodard, Komozi: *A Nation Within a Nation: Amiri Baraka (LeRoi Jones) and Black Power Politics* (Chapel Hill: University of North Carolina Press, 1999).

CHAPTER SIXTEEN

The Triumph of Conservatives in a Liberal Age

DAVID L. CHAPPELL

Conservatism has almost as many definitions as it has opponents. In deferential response to those opponents, Samuel Huntington (1957) modestly defined conservatism as a "positional ideology," meaning it was not an ideology at all but an ad hoc, pragmatic stance against dangerous excesses. Huntington's was a definition and a defense of conservatism fit for an age when the ruling liberals celebrated their own "end of ideology," a development that they equated with maturity, sobriety, responsibility, and the like. Albert Hirschman (1991) has much more fun boiling two hundred years of conservative thought down to three dazzlingly clear reactions: Perversity! (liberal proposal X will be counterproductive); Futility! (it will not work at all); and Jeopardy! (if it did work, it would destroy the values and institutions liberals depend on). Stephen Holmes (1993) applies a hotter flame, reducing conservatives and other "non-Marxist antiliberals" to uninformed, unconstructive naysayers. Without grounding in monarchy and an established church, Holmes believes, conservative impulses are either incoherent or crypto-fascist. Jerry Muller (1997), with greater patience, makes a useful historical case that the phrase "historical utilitarianism" fits most conservatism most of the time better than other definitions. Like most thoughtful students, however, Muller emphasizes that conservatism lives only because it changes; it retains conservative *bona fides* and self-respect by changing more carefully than liberalism and radicalism. So its definition changes and will keep changing.

So far, these definitions have to do with how conservatives work and what they reject. Does conservatism have positive content? All the definitions that ring true for late twentieth-century America have in common some fundamental value akin to "ordered liberty" or "balanced authoritarianism," as John Judis (1988) calls it. Either way, conservatives do not merely attack the left and center. Like liberals, conservatives defend liberty, at least their own. Unlike liberals, conservatives resist social experiments with untested ideals, which they fear will deplete the supply of liberty. Anxious to avoid liberty shortages, conservatives also dread gluts. They tend to see programs to expand liberty as latitudinarian and licentious rather than realistic and responsible. Conservatives think that "order" – whether its source be the bourgeois family or religious tradition or the state's police power or "the discipline of the market" – needs as much attention as liberty.

The greatest distinction between liberal and conservative has to do with equality. From the French and Industrial Revolutions through the end of the Cold War, conservatives have seen earthly equality as the most pernicious untested ideal. Most of them grant, however, that certain popular steps toward equality, such as public housing, Social Security, equal civil and voting rights, are not worth attacking and may even be worth defending. The word "conservative" represents something more specific in American political culture in the last half-century, namely, reluctance to accept the surviving achievements of the New Deal, and then opposition to the Great Society, especially the anti-poverty programs, and concomitant judicial innovations, especially the loosening of restraints on criminal and sexual activity, and the post-1965 "rights revolution." "Ordered liberty," or any other shorthand for conservatives' program, must take into account a threefold division that nearly all writing on postwar American conservatism identifies: moral (often religious) traditionalism, libertarianism, and anti-communism, with the last acting as a glue to hold the first two together until 1989.

These three elements – traditionalism, libertarianism, anti-communism – are logically irreconcilable. But that is perhaps a mark of conservatism's strength rather than a puzzle to be solved. After all, without self-contradiction, none of the following could have had such powerful appeal: the Christian Trinity, "Liberty, Equality, Fraternity," the Marxist alliance of utilitarianism and Romantic utopianism, or the feminist cohabitation of equality with difference. Ideologies ease the pressure of conflicting desires by borrowing heavily from the future.

Apart from intrinsic incompatibility, libertarianism and anti-communism also borrowed heavily from liberalism, as critics of the right often point out. Yet understanding conservatives requires understanding that they made sense to themselves. They told themselves that they were conservative, which was to say, not liberal, which was to say, for all but eight years from 1932 to 2000, not in power. As liberals could not avoid the arrogance of power, so conservatives could not avoid the irresponsibility of powerlessness. Conservatives tended to see those in power as liberals, including Presidents Roosevelt, Truman, Eisenhower, Kennedy, Nixon, Carter, and Clinton, all of whom were, arguably, conservative. Conservatives saw anything that went wrong in America – even overseas – as an indictment of liberal policies. They ultimately attracted masses of dissatisfied voters because they were able to pretend more convincingly than the left that they had a realistic alternative to the status quo. Conservatives managed to define the status quo as liberal, taking great advantage of whatever contradictions and compromises power imposed upon liberals.

Liberalism was already greatly weakened by 1945. Two of the most thoughtful books on the ideological content of the New Deal (Hawley, 1966; Brinkley, 1995), for example, argue that liberals' once popular crusade to demonize and restrain big business had run out of confidence and enthusiasm by the 1937 "recession." When war brought recovery, voters no longer craved reform. Surviving liberals reined in their ambitions, confining themselves to esoteric plans for economic growth and incremental expansions of individual rights. In 1948, liberals bent on retaining power in the Cold War turned ruthlessly against less realistic liberals – those who took too long to become disillusioned with Stalin's murderous manipulation of the Popular Front and Grand Alliance. Successfully refocusing liberalism against communism, liberals like Arthur Schlesinger, Jr. (1949) and Richard Hofstadter (1948, 1963) devoted brilliant careers to demonstrating that liberals had finally become responsible. But what turned out to be decisive is that they would be held responsible.

Weakened as they were, postwar liberals made an attractive target. Their blindness and bluster made them more attractive still. When conservatives of the 1980s–1990s looked back on the 1940s, many remembered a line from Lionel Trilling's *The Liberal Imagination* (1949) as a provocation. One of the great liberal minds of the 1940s, Trilling wrote in his famous preface, "Liberalism is not only the dominant but even the sole intellectual tradition." It was just a "plain fact" that "there are no conservative or reactionary ideas in general circulation." Conservatives only had "irritable mental gestures" that sought "to resemble ideas." It may not be fair to Trilling that later conservatives took this as such an insult. Trilling was trying to warn his fellow liberals that they lacked emotional appeal, hence were defenseless against conservatives, who, Trilling believed, were more insightful and realistic about the emotional wellsprings of political action. But it galled conservatives to be told that they had no ideas, and they were told this all the time. Trilling understood and respected conservatism's cultural sophistication. But other liberals never imagined the battle against the right would be intellectually demanding. Perhaps they were too busy fighting off their enemies to the left.

The political right nonetheless got most of the credit – and most of the blame – for fighting communism. Even Lee Edwards (1999), in an otherwise thoughtful chronicle of the resurgence of the right, indulges in tacky partisanship when claiming right-wing credit for the defeat of communism – credit that is irreconcilable with right-wing blame of liberals for everything else that happened. Conservatives may have been more sensitive and fanatical about communism before 1947 or so, but from then until Vietnam most liberals with viable public careers had been Trumanized on the issue. During the postwar years, the main institutional vehicle of conservatism was the Taft wing of the GOP, in a "conservative coalition" with southern Democrats. Robert Taft, a brilliant and effective politician, surprised many conservatives by supporting public housing legislation, which probably would not have passed without his support. The real estate lobby branded him a traitor and "socialist" (Patterson, 1972). The conservative coalition was most effective when passing the Taft-Hartley Act of 1947. The act halted the political progress of unions, which directly threatened southern Democrats and business-oriented Republicans. The coalition was also successful, until 1964–5, in blocking any effective reenfranchisement legislation, which directly threatened southern Democratic members of Congress. Logrolling and business opposition to federal power pretty well explain Republican complicity. Some Republicans may also have feared that Republican efforts to win black voters back to the Party of Lincoln were futile after Harry Truman and Hubert Humphrey's desegregation initiatives in 1948.

McCarthyism is hard to sort out: it seemed at first to threaten the liberal coalition severely. There is too much excellent work on this strange person and his strangely personalized "ism," much of it with excellent bibliography (e.g., Oshinsky, 1983; Hixson, 1992; Shrecker, 1998). Some writers (beginning with Carey McWilliams, *Witch Hunt*, 1950) suggest that Harry Truman – whom liberals generally disliked – brought the Red Scare down on his party with his loyalty program, though Truman saw it as an effort to ward off intrusive, politically motivated investigations. Partisan opportunism clearly played a role in the machinations of Nixon, who captured the headlines with his indignation over the Alger Hiss trial in 1950, and in the machinations of McCarthy, who joined the anti-communist crusade rather late. McCarthy's wild accusations were encouraged by the Taft wing of his party. Few Republicans challenged McCarthy, not even Eisenhower, who was disgusted by the Wisconsin Senator and had the position and popularity to condemn him with impunity.

But the general climate of anti-communism makes it difficult to distinguish conservative from liberal within it. Liberals who, along with all Americans and their allies, had benefited greatly from the Soviet alliance, felt genuinely betrayed by Stalinist impositions in Eastern Europe after the war. Trotskyites, socialists, and social democrats eagerly joined liberals and conservatives in what Franklin Roosevelt had once dismissed as "red-baiting": they joined in partly because the Kremlin's influence became an unmistakable and irreversible threat to freedom, indeed to socialism, outside the USSR, and partly because their own hopes for influence over various international socialist movements, not to mention American liberalism, had evaporated with the Popular Front.

Who benefited most from the Red Scare, liberals or conservatives, Republicans or Democrats? Democrats regained control of Congress in 1954; a liberal Republican remained in the White House for the rest of the decade. Taft died in 1953; McCarthy was silenced a year later. The political right languished in the rather ineffectual hands of Senators John Bricker, William Jenner, and William Knowland, all defeated or withdrawn from politics in 1958. If Nixon represented the right, he was defanged by his vice-presidency under Eisenhower. At any rate, as many conservatives hated Nixon as liberals did. Liberals who embraced the Americans for Democratic Action and Harry Truman, on the other hand, proved more tenacious and more popular, especially in the unions, than those who embraced the Progressive Citizens of America and Henry Wallace. The surviving union leaders became a great source of Democratic votes and funds, defining themselves as anti-communist liberals. Anti-communism rallied working-class Americans – and not just Catholics and those with Eastern European roots – around Truman and "defense" spending, which in turn provided generous employment. Military Keynesianism provided the only form of social welfare spending that elected leaders could sustain. Liberals like Schlesinger were confident that big business was on their side along with big labor. Anti-communism was not only the glue that held disparate right-leaning strands together, but a protective shell that hardened around liberalism.

Of greater long-term import than McCarthyism itself was the energy liberals devoted to understanding – or rather, to dismissing – McCarthyism. Daniel Bell's collection, *The New American Right* (1955), has turned out to be even more of a provocation to conservatives than Trilling's preface. It made a point similar to Trilling's: McCarthy's supporters and related right-wingers were not rational. Lacking the discipline of poverty as well as the self-confidence and mental clarity of inherited affluence, Bell's "new" right-wingers were acting on resentment about their perceived social "status," rather than a true understanding of their "interests."

Perhaps nostalgic for the New Deal, when poverty taught simple-minded majorities to vote liberal, Bell and his colleagues resented the affluence that drove ordinary people, ungratefully, to abandon liberalism. What Bell could not grasp, or could not respect, was that the widespread shame of poverty during the New Deal was hard to translate into long-term gratitude. Mass support for well-off leaders who insist that people cannot help themselves is intrinsically hard to muster. Like businessmen, ordinary folk who rose from poverty often resented the government aid they once needed, and like businessmen they hated to be reminded of it. Yet Bell and his colleagues could only see such resentment as a pathetic denial of reality. Thus Bell listed the anti-liberal order of battle:

> a thin stratum of soured patricians like Archibald Roosevelt, the last surviving son of Teddy Roosevelt, whose emotional stake lay in a vanishing image of a muscular America defying a decadent Europe; the "new rich" – the automobile dealers, real estate manipulators, oil wildcatters – who needed the psychological assurance that they, like their forebears, had earned their own wealth, rather than accumulated it through government aid, and who feared that "taxes" would rob them of that wealth; the rising middle-class strata of the ethnic groups, the Irish and the Germans, who sought to prove their Americanism, the Germans particularly because of the implied taint of disloyalty during World War II; and finally, unique in American cultural history, a small group of intellectuals, many of them cankered ex-Communists, who, pivoting on McCarthy, opened up an attack on liberalism in general. (1955, pp. 14–15 [1962, pp. 48–9])

The anger and condescension of Bell and his co-authors are evident in their portrayal of their enemies. That the anger was often justified is beside the point: these liberal opinionmakers, feeling besieged and threatened, failed to see the moral appeal their opponents had. The Bellites saw the justice in any attack on communists; none in any attack on the liberal establishment.

Yet it was precisely their lack of humility that made liberal opinion, with its nostalgia for the Depression, so galling. In the Bell volume, and in Hofstadter's later essays, "anti-intellectualism" was interchangeable with anti-liberalism: you had to be uneducated, backward, provincial, xenophobic, to oppose liberalism. The danger of such tunnel vision – the extremism of the vital center – is not simply that it made centrists incapable of co-opting and dividing their enemies. It also failed to prepare centrists to fight their enemies' ideas with ideas. Scholars who tried to test Bell's and Hofstadter's assumptions about the social origins of right-wing politics in the 1950s–1960s found that the available data did not support them. Michael Paul Rogin (1967) made this unmistakably clear, though historians proved generally immune to the lesson for another twenty-five years. The fatal error, however, was not so much Bell and others' analysis of McCarthyism, but liberals' general belief that all attacks from the right would resemble the McCarthyite one (Bell et al., 1962; Hofstadter, 1963, 1965; Lipset, 1970).

Liberal social scientists' pathologization of American conservatism justified the historical profession's disposition to ignore it – one of the most tragic blindspots the consensus liberals bequeathed to their children in the New Left. There were exceptions to the rule among historians: fine writers like Russell Kirk (1953) and Clinton Rossiter (1955) found modern American conservatism intellectually serious – and real – enough to throw full-length books about it into the teeth of the Bellite consensus. Rossiter's book was a program for the conservatism that Trilling believed liberals needed for target practice. Like Trilling, Rossiter hungered for a vigorous opposition and defined conservatism as essentially negative – a response above all to the "decisive factor" of Franklin Roosevelt. Rossiter was a lot less formulaic about this, however, than Huntington or later anti-conservatives like Hirschman and Holmes. Rossiter understood the importance of libertarianism, but, like Kirk, saw conservatism per se as depending on religion, with an organic theory of society at its core.

Kirk's history of conservative ideas, disguised as a polemic by one who embraced the conservative cause, did not deny the truth of Trilling's observation. All ideas were, to Kirk, the province of an aristocracy, of what scholars today would imprecisely (and hypocritically) call an elite. Like many aristocratic minds, Kirk had great faith in the common people, adopting Edmund Burke's admiration of their strong, prerational "prejudices" – a word that liberals had made dirty. To Kirk as to Burke, the common people were like the cattle under the English oaks, "deaf to the insects of radical innovation." (Modern conservatives and radical historians are still fighting over the noble savage legacy bequeathed to them by Montaigne and Rousseau.) It was the aristocracy's duty to articulate the people's sound conservative instincts in the form of ideas and to defend those ideas in politics. An unexplored issue in our cultural history is the extent to which the liberal-sponsored spread of higher learning after World War II brought the naturally conservative masses into a position where they demanded, and got, an increasingly articulate and literate culture. The greater participation of American masses in college and university experience may, contrary to all expectation, help explain why they have become the most religious and conservative masses in the world.

Most liberals in the 1950s were convinced that they were more educated and sophisticated than their enemies. They did not grasp that being correct about such things mattered little: what liberals needed was to cultivate their popular support. Instead, they threw their support to Adlai Stevenson, not because he was devoted to expanding the New Deal, civil rights, or the unions (he was not), but because he was an urbane and witty egghead who shared their contempt for the rubes and yahoos of the American heartland. (Republicans were trying "to replace the New Dealers with car dealers," Stevenson said [Siegel, 1984, p. 100].) Liberals' fatal assumption that conservatives were unsophisticated by nature seems to have driven them, illogically, to the inverse assumption that people who were sophisticated must be liberal. They were not preparing to fight a conservative resurgence, it seemed, but simply waiting for their opponents to die off.

Meanwhile, the right was proving its own cosmopolitanism and intellectual prowess with the influx of anti-Nazi and anti-socialist refugees from Europe, like Friedrich von Hayek, Ludwig von Mises, Eric Voegelin, Willi Schlamm, and Leo Strauss, not to mention thoughtful first-generation Americans like Peter Viereck (1949) and Frank Chodorov. It was proving its sophistication with lyrical writers like Whittaker Chambers and dazzling professors like Yale's Wilmoore Kendall; its wide-ranging knowledge of history and social thought with John Chamberlain and Robert Nisbet (1953); its philosophical depth with Russell Kirk and Richard Weaver (1949). Stewing in isolation, often desperate for an audience, such figures were impelled to work together.

The right from the mid-1950s on was every bit as learned and worldly as the left – more so, arguably, as the right was filling up with matured leftists who knew their enemy well. To be sure, the liberal center attracted matured leftists too, Reinhold Niebuhr and Dwight Macdonald among the most brilliant. But Max Eastman, James

Burnham, Frank Meyer, John Dos Passos, and others got a warmer welcome from the right (Diggins, 1975; Nash, 1976; O'Neill, 1982; Wald, 1987), and it must be said that their dark insights were more thoroughly honored and assimilated by their new right-wing allies than Niebuhr's or Macdonald's – or Trilling's – ever were by the vital centrists, who applied their pessimism only to communists.

Conservative periodicals struggled along to provide a voice on the right of the vital center. *Human Events*, founded by Henry Regnery in 1944, was often esoterically libertarian. It was anti-Nazi but campaigned against the Nuremberg trials, thinking post-Nazi Germany a bulwark against Russia. Like much of the "Old" Republican right, it clung to isolationism, which made it unpopular in the early Cold War. The *Freeman*, founded in the 1920s by the brilliant Albert Jay Nock, who loved aristocracy and hated the modern state, was revived and combined with Isaac Don Levine's anti-communist *Plain Talk* in 1950 under the editorship of John Chamberlain. Plagued with financial troubles, *Freeman* had a circulation of only 20,000 in the early 1950s. Yet it published such renowned writers and thinkers as John Dos Passos, Raymond Moley, George Sokolsky, and Virginia Senator Harry Byrd. Financial salvation from Leonard Read, a fanatical convert to libertarianism, deprived the magazine of vitality, and its best writers grew bored with it. Chamberlain and most of the rest of *Freeman*'s talent resigned in 1953. H. L. Mencken's famous old *American Mercury* (circulation: 90,000) became a bastion of literate conservatism in the early 1950s under the editorship of William Bradford Huie. But financial troubles made it dependent on an eccentric backer, too. The sponsorship of Connecticut millionaire Russell Maguire, a vicious anti-Semite, led all editors, including, after some delay, Huie, to resign. The magazine descended into disgraceful obscurity, read only by a paranoid cult and by vigilant liberals and FBI agents on the lookout for subversives. John Judis, in his indispensable biography of William Buckley (1988), observed that the decline of these magazines left an intellectual vacuum.

The forces that gathered around Buckley soon filled that vacuum. Son of a rich businessman, Buckley gained fame with *God and Man at Yale* (1951), which challenged alumni to take control of his alma mater. Buckley told alumni they held Christian and individualist principles in their hearts and should force faculty to indoctrinate students with those principles. Financed by Buckley's father and other rich sympathizers, the book became astonishingly popular. Readers who cared nothing about the future of Yale liked a good exposé of decadence and hypocrisy in institutions of privilege – an important lesson, which anti-red propagandists had learned in their attacks on the State Department and Hollywood. After dabbling in the CIA, Buckley set out to create a new institution to bring America back to the principles he believed his father and Yale alumni shared with most Americans. He founded the *National Review* in 1955, which became the greatest voice of American conservatism in the twentieth century.

Innocent of introspection and self-doubt, Buckley used his wealth, education, and debating skills as weapons against liberalism. Rare among modern intellectuals, he never seems to have questioned the basic truths he learned from his father – except the anti-Semitic ones. The younger Buckley shunned the paranoid Jew-baiting of the right-wing fringe groups on which Daniel Bell and his colleagues concentrated their fire. His editors and contributors included Jews like Willi Schlamm, Frank Meyer, Frank Chodorov, and Ralph de Toledano; *NR* drew anti-Semitic fire from such celebrated nuts as Gerald L. K. Smith (Judis, 1988, p. 30). Buckley tried to curtail bigotry on the right – not out of a patronizing desire to avoid offending minorities, but out of realism. He knew that ethnic prejudices only limited conservatism's appeal. Buckley could be as insensitive to black people as any liberal or conservative of his day. But he almost always couched his opposition to expansion of civil rights in the pragmatic and respectable defense of constitutional state rights.

Buckley also shunned the paranoid anti-communism of the John Birch Society and did his best to marginalize its influence (Judis, 1988; Edwards, 1999). He shared the Birchers' disdain for Eisenhower, but like most literate conservatives, Buckley could not countenance the Birchers' claim that Ike was an actual communist agent. It was hard enough to insist that the president was a liberal.

More than any other single force, Buckley's magazine unified the three strands of conservatism – traditionalism, libertarianism, anti-communism. Buckley was untroubled by the inconsistencies among his adherents because he only wanted to destroy their common enemy: the establishment that had rejected his father's values. Buckley was on the attack, his protégé Garry Wills recalled in a gripping memoir (1979), defining liberals as "The Enemy," and vice versa. Traditionalism (especially that of Richard Weaver, intellectual heir of the Nashville Agrarians) was useful against some liberal weak spots, libertarianism against others. With no policy to defend in practice, *NR* exposed liberalism to a confusing and easily ignored barrage. Buckley's genius, or his good luck, was to see the vast democratic appeal of his various positions, and their incompatibility with actually existing liberalism. Their incompatibility with one another did not matter until the 1980s, when conservatives finally tried to govern.

Buckley managed to appear both effete and pugilistic at the same time, giving conservatives an egghead they could call their own. He fought liberal pomposity with his own, becoming the champion of those who somehow felt left out before Buckley appeared as the token opponent of the expansive state on radio and TV talk shows. Buckley helped inspire a whole generation of student conservatives, who idealistically dreamed of taking over the party of Eisenhower and the eastern establishment. They would invigorate it with new ideals while avoiding the stigma of McCarthyism and the Birchers. With Buckley's encouragement, students David Francke and Doug Caddy, aided by former communist Marvin Liebman, formed the Young Americans for Freedom (YAF) in 1960. Soon the electoral machinery was bloated with baby boomer Republicans.

A different kind of threat the liberals should have recognized in the 1950s was the vast popularity of Billy Graham – the center of a religious revival that filled stadiums as reliably as rock and roll or football. Liberals, having defeated the fundamentalists in the 1920s, could not imagine that conservative religion could flourish in the modern world. Joel Carpenter, one of the best historians of the evangelical resurgence that began during the economic recovery of World War II, notes that scholars have been "misled repeatedly about the character, thrust, and long-term prospects of evangelical Christianity because of one overriding assumption: Modernization always produces secularization" (Carpenter, 1997, p. 234). That assumption is at the heart of liberal faith in the ultimate triumph of human reason over superstition and "prejudice." Yet anybody who bothered to look very closely could see what Martin Marty saw, "a symbiosis between unfolding modernity and developing Evangelicalism" (Carpenter, 1997, pp. 234–5; Marsden, 1980; also Ammerman, 1987). Evangelicalism and modernity grew together.

Fundamentalism – like political conservatism – is a modern philosophy, which could not have become popular before the triumph of secular authority in Western politics and culture. Fundamentalism may look to the past, but it looks to a past that was invented largely by liberals, who were bent on justifying (and exaggerating) their own triumph over superstition. It looks to an imaginary past, that is, in which the church was unified, uncritically respected, and hostile to all skepticism and critical thinking. Fundamentalists shared the mythic liberal view of the past. They were as incapable of reviving that past as liberals were of convincing ordinary Christians that it needed to be outgrown. Fundamentalists after World War II were (until their late 1970s resurgence) hopelessly schismatic, their leaders absorbed in fratricidal disputes (see Allyn Russell, 1976).

The real Christian threat to liberal hegemony in the 1950s was not fundamentalism, but the broader based, more respectable, more intellectually astute, more politically moderate, and more organized evangelicalism (Ammerman, 1987; Marsden, 1991; Carpenter, 1997). Liberals, however, could not see the difference – they only saw crowds of backward, bigoted, small-minded fanatics. David Riesman, updating his contribution to Bell's collection in 1962, wrote, "The rich and poor fundamentalists have this much in common: they fear the way the world is going, at home or abroad; they resent those more cosmopolitan people who appear to understand the world less badly and who seem less ill at ease with all the different kinds of people who mingle in our big cities or at the United Nations" (in Bell, 1962, p. 125). Yet evangelicals were growing in the cities, and in missions abroad, because, like political conservatives, they did not assume that time was on their side: they evangelized, they syncretized, they grew.

Like Buckley, Billy Graham recognized that crude prejudices only hurt his organization – not just in his African missions, but also at home. After some waffling, Graham consistently desegregated his crowds, even in the deep South, from 1954 on – the year the Supreme Court tried, less successfully, to desegregate the government-controlled schools. Graham desegregated without fanfare but with impunity: though extreme segregationists called him a communist dupe, the southern white press on the whole dared not attack such a revered and popular figure. Segregationist editors nearly always gave Graham front-page treatment, omitting to mention that his crowds and ushers were, at Graham's insistence, desegregated. Crowd photos conveniently concealed the skin color of individual worshippers. Many black preachers, including Martin Luther King, recognized Graham's value, and cooperated with him. Fundamentalists like Bob Jones, who was happy to have racist support, hated evangelicals like Graham (Martin, 1991; Chappell, forthcoming).

Graham's popularity was far greater than that of the racially exclusive white fundamentalists. This seems surprising only to those who assume that the vast masses of Christian conservatives are more devoted to racism than other Americans. Working up a publication empire as formidable as Buckley's, centered around the popular ecumenical magazine *Christianity Today*, Graham's evangelicals revitalized American religious culture with conservative alternatives to the mainline liberal *Christian Century*.

Ideological combat took place within institutional realities, of which a peculiar form of corporate capitalism seems the most important. Money, that is, shaped the battle of ideas, but a specific kind of money. America's foreign competitors were flattened by World War II and then restrained by their dependence on American largesse during much of the Cold War. American corporations grew fat on government subsidies in World War II and the Cold War. Corporate bureaucrats turned against "government," not so much out of a perverse desire to bite the hand that fed them as out of a rational recognition that the hand that fed could also restrain. Unlike individual recipients of welfare, corporate beneficiaries recognized that the hand needed to feed more often than they needed to eat. They bit selectively, gnawing the regulatory nails, but leaving the tendons of protection and the arteries of subsidy intact.

More work needs to be done on how corporate money organized the production and consumption of political opinion after World War II. Most newspapers opposed FDR, but that did not stop him from being wildly popular. Colonel McCormick's *Chicago Tribune*, and notorious right-wing editors in Texas, aggressively sought to move American opinion to the right. Millionaires like Sun Oil's J. Howard Pew funded *Christianity Today* as well as political organs, like *Human Events*, and causes, like YAF (Viguerie, 1980, p. 27), and the Goldwater movement to capture the GOP (Goldberg, 1995). (Pew had also been part of the Liberty League in the 1930s.) Precisely what did corporate money buy? Not necessarily conservatism: the Ford and Carnegie foundations were consistent targets of right-wing attack; in recent years, the Pew millions have drifted into the right's target range, and the heirs of GM and Weyerhaeuser have long been financial underwriters of left-wing opinion. But corporate funding of conservative thought and culture was and is significant. Along with Pew, Henry Regnery, the Milliken brothers (South Carolina textile magnates, who recently showed up among Ralph Nader's funders), and New York financier Jeremiah Milbank invested in a broad range of anti-liberal publications in the 1950s, hoping to legitimate more tactics and breed more tacticians. Many writers detect a split between old eastern establishment conservatism and southwestern "cowboy" money – from speculation in mining and oil – which financed a more ruthless or reckless conservatism. Yet the most important Texas oilman, H. L. Hunt, refused to fund Buckley's magazine, a refusal Buckley attributed largely to Hunt's anti-Catholicism (Judis, 1988, p. 120).

Elizabeth Fones-Wolf (1994) paints the most important part of the picture: the self-conscious promotion – the selling – of a pro-corporate ideology in the 1950s, which equated the interests of major corporations with "America" or with "the Free World," depending on whether the audience was feeling defensive or generous. Fones-Wolf emphasizes the appeal of this ideology to the labor rank and file, a different explanation from Gary Gerstle's more parochial but more influential explanation, which emphasizes traditional Catholic affinities for key elements in America's Cold War-era nationalism (Gerstle, 1989). Equally important, however, was the campaign's success in channeling the disgruntlement of small businessmen into anti-government rather than anti-corporate channels.

In various ways, money provided conservative strategists the luxury to explore every angle of attack, breed a variety of attackers, and develop resilient institutions. Unlike the emerging student left, conservatives had leaders who were well-heeled and shameless enough to teach followers the need for party discipline. Youthful idealism was not enough. Money, and the organization and self-confidence it helped to buy, were keys to the right's increasing prominence in American culture. Prominence in politics was a trickier matter. Barry Goldwater blazed the right's trail to electoral power.

Like Buckley, Goldwater was a self-conscious ideologue, extreme in his conservatism and in the intelligence and energy he applied to it. Unlike Buckley (and unlike his right-wing political predecessors, Taft, Jenner, Bricker, and Knowland), he developed a reputation as a useful partisan vote-getter and unifier. Here Goldwater resembled the conservative evangelicals who, unlike fundamentalists, remained within their denominations and helped them grow, thus being better positioned to take them over. Goldwater worked indefatigably on GOP campaigns in the late 1950s. Though known as a conservative, he did his best to cover up his disagreements with President Eisenhower, voting with the administration 66 percent of the time in 1955–6 (Goldberg, 1995). He was Republican campaign committee chairman 1955–6 and 1959–62, during which time he made over two thousand speeches and developed ties with party activists all over the country. Goldwater's *The Conscience of a Conservative* (ghostwritten by Buckley's partner Brent Bozell, and subsidized by a Birch Society board member, Clarence Manion) became a bestseller in 1960. His literary success solidified his relationship with right-wing ideologues, but also lessened his dependence on them.

In 1960, Goldwater was as hostile as liberal Republicans were to the nomination of Richard Nixon. But unlike the liberals, Goldwater campaigned with impressive vigor for Nixon: nobody could blame the GOP's defeat on the one prominent conservative ideologue in it (Rae, 1989; Brennan, 1995; Goldberg, 1995). Soon after the GOP defeat of 1960, the smart conservative money – again Pew and the Millikens were important – bet on Goldwater, beginning a "Draft Goldwater" movement. This drew on the YAF and other grassroots organizations, some of which, like the Birch Society, were filled with fanatical anti-communists. (Anti-Semites never helped Goldwater, who was half-Jewish.)

Goldwater used the fanatics, and their money (H. L. Hunt's especially), but he tried to discipline them. He sternly dissociated himself, as Buckley did, from the Birchers' Robert Welch. His 1960 convention speech urged conservative activists to "grow up" and make realistic moves to take over their party. The speech was a turning point in conservative history, more important than Reagan's more famous speech four years later. Goldwater made it clear he had no use for conservative activists if they would not capture the local offices that would give them a power base. While tempering the ideologues, Goldwater maintained enough support among the GOP regulars, through his connections in the Senate and his speaking engagements at partisan as well as ideological occasions.

Goldwater also maintained legitimacy by rejecting the outright racism that some of his southern white supporters were inclined to indulge in during campaigns. Clearly southern racists, when they were drawn to Republicans at all, were more drawn to conservative Republicans than to liberal ones: they had a common boogieman in the federal government, and a common way to insulate themselves from charges of bigotry and lawlessness by adopting the "state rights" slogan – a slogan with a serious constitutional pedigree, not at all confined to racists or the right. Goldwater strongly supported black voting rights (Goldberg, 1995), while trying to avoid alienating his supporters in the white South. That was exactly the position John F. Kennedy took until Birmingham police and firemen obliged black protesters with a widely photographed showdown that embarrassed the nation.

Nicol Rae makes clear how the ineptitude and complacency of the liberal GOP made it easy for the Goldwaterites to capture the nomination in 1964:

> The liberals had possessed a superb campaign organization, constructed by [Thomas] Dewey and Herbert Brownell, but even they had great difficulty in defeating Taft in 1952 with a national hero as their candidate. By the early 1960s, Dewey, Brownell, and the other major figures in the Eisenhower campaign organization had retired from active politics, and the machinery had atrophied. (Rae, 1989, p. 60)

Mary Brennan points out that the GOP leaders foolishly discounted Goldwater's growing popularity in 1960, ignoring the importance of grassroots organizations (Brennan, 1995). Lisa McGirr (2001) amplifies and clarifies the importance of grassroots in her recent study of southern California.

Rather than shore up their popular support, GOP liberals began betting their lives on Nelson Rockefeller's candidacy, on the "very tenuous foundation" of Rockefeller's popularity in opinion polls. That foundation crumbled after the divorced Rockefeller's second marriage to Happy Murphy in June 1963. Needing votes, the GOP poured resources into Operation Dixie – a far more effective invasion, interestingly, than that attempted under the same code-name by the Congress of Industrial Organizations (CIO) twenty years earlier. But liberal leaders failed to grasp the significance of the rising southern presence, which they had lost their ability to control in the traditional manner of federal patronage after the GOP's departure from the White House in 1961. They also failed to appreciate the changing convention rules, which amplified the power of volunteer activists (Rae, 1989).

Liberal Democrats made parallel errors. They probably never realized how much they depended on the GOP liberals to keep a leash on the right. They probably even believed their own propaganda as to how southerners in their own party – like LBJ and Sam Rayburn – were as bad as Republicans. In fact, many were to the left of Adlai Stevenson. (Like liberal Republicans, Brennan notes, Democrats "lumped all conservatives together" [Brennan, 1995, p. 50].) This is the key point in the entire history of liberal blindness. Democratic liberals, pressured by ingenious black southern preachers, had just managed their greatest post-FDR achievement by reaching across party lines and defeating the southern Democratic filibuster: they re-reconstructed the South, with the Civil Rights and Voting Rights Acts of 1964 and 1965 and the Twenty-Fourth Amendment. But that was all they could do; had liberal Democrats been less complacent about Goldwaterites, they might have helped their indispensable allies in the GOP to stave off further revolt. Instead, liberal Democrats let the GOP conservatives destroy the old GOP, without realizing that the GOP conservatives had larger prey in their sights – and enough strength to shoot effectively as soon as liberalism faltered. That did not take long.

Democratic liberal failures have to account for most of the perceived rightward drift of Nixon: he drifted in the direction the electorate was drifting, and the electorate ultimately chose him in a very close election in 1968. The liberals' greatest weakness in the 1960s was their contempt for Lyndon Johnson, their strongest leader. Though liberals always opposed and distrusted Johnson, he showed himself the truest heir of FDR by enacting more of the unfinished business of the New Deal than anyone thought possible. In one vital way, Johnson moved to the left of FDR:

he was willing and able to welcome black voters into the party in droves, and to reward them with a more severe commitment to civil rights than any president since Lincoln – and so far a more durable one. With Medicare and Medicaid, Johnson even made a dent in the pharmaceutical-medical-insurance industry's armor, something no other American politician has ever been able to do.

Turning against the war they had done so much to expand in Vietnam, liberals blamed Johnson (who was far more interested in domestic policy) essentially for continuing Kennedy's policies there. But northern liberals' hostility to the South, and their bigoted equation of bigotry with southern styles of speech and manners, hurt Johnson more than Vietnam: he might have been able to weather the controversies over that war, had radicals and centrists in his own party rallied behind him. Instead, the radicals made kamikaze attacks on the only viable trustee of the New Deal coalition, and the only politician – ever – who was able to support civil rights and retain nationwide popularity at the same time. The centrists failed to defend him. Ralph Ellison's estimate was that black Americans understood Johnson better than the liberals. LBJ would go down in history as a great president in the eyes of black Americans, Ellison said, the greatest since Lincoln, who paid an admittedly higher price.

Next, young activists began driving regular Democrats away from their exhausted party. Eugene McCarthy, the failed 1968 candidate of the anti-war movement, waited until October to endorse, half-heartedly, the Democratic nominee, Hubert Humphrey. Humphrey was a devoted liberal with the longest, most distinguished civil rights record of any member of Congress in the twentieth century, and one of the strongest pro-labor records. McCarthy and followers had failed to learn the lesson Barry Goldwater had taught Republican conservatives in 1960: that an ideological extremist is a guest and must earn his keep in a political party, which is devoted above all to its own electoral survival. Disgruntled McCarthyites nonetheless tried to seize the convention machinery. Surprisingly, they succeeded, instituting a radical form of affirmative action in delegate-selection rules, replacing old ward-heelers with young people and members of hitherto unrepresented minority groups. Whatever the symbolic justice of the new diversity, it filled the party with inexperienced people and cut out millions of loyal vote-getters. As Chicago columnist Mike Royko observed, the Democratic Party's decision to start reform this way was like a man starting a diet by shooting himself in the stomach. Historians often quote Royko now. But no liberal ever admitted what a dumb idea it was to give eighteen- to twenty-year-olds the vote, with the Twenty-Sixth Amendment of 1971.

When Nixon took over in 1969, he shrewdly began forcing liberal Democrats (especially judges) to defend his civil rights initiatives, including his aggressive enforcement of affirmative action in employment law, the revived "Philadelphia Plan" of 1969 and the Equal Employment Opportunity Act of 1972 (Graham, 1990). Nixon knew that affirmative action would force historically Democratic union members to start choosing between their own hard-won seniority rights and the rights of black workers. This would break the bond between the majority of workers and the civil rights lobby, the bond on which liberal strength in Congress depended. Nixon's bureaucrats also raised the cost to unions by forcing not just black workers on them, but "Oriental, American Indian, and Spanish Surnamed" workers. Then during the 1972 campaign, Nixon ostentatiously halted enforcement of busing orders, which had become a symbol of affluent liberal judges' contempt for white people who could not afford private schools or escape to the suburbs: the key Democratic constituencies of the ethnic urban working class and white southerners. Again and again, "limousine liberals" had to defend "minority rights" at the expense of broad popular support. As Hugh Graham observed, "Nixon's civil rights victories ironically freed him to run for re-election by taking a stand against the school integration orders and minority quota requirements that he had done so much to further" (Graham, 1990, p. 445).

Nixon's virtuosity in political opportunism helped the Republicans and the grassroots conservatives, who got tied to one another in the 1970s much as the Democrats had gotten tied to the unions in the 1930s. Indeed, the expansion of the Republican Party fed off the disillusionment of many union members, who, along with others in the lower middle and working classes, felt the Democrats, and allied union leaders, had abandoned them.

Opportunism requires opportunity, and rightward-drifting Republicans like Nixon were among the luckiest in history. Rising crime, inflation, taxes, and a costly and controversial war all hit the American voter-consumer simultaneously, on the liberal Democrats' watch (Lukas, 1985; Rieder, 1985; Edsall and Edsall, 1991). Supreme Court justices and other prominent authorities – from Dr. Spock to the Kerner Commission – seemed intent on protecting and rewarding anti-social behavior. Liberals had assumed that affluence would guarantee social order, but in many ways it appeared to have done the opposite. At any rate, affluence seemed suddenly in jeopardy, too, at least for the white voters who were still new to affluence. The rising crime and rising taxes of the 1960s formed as potent a juxtaposition as the destruction of crop surpluses and widespread hunger had formed in the Depression. High crime and taxes were further juxtaposed with a cultural rebellion – largely created by Madison Avenue, though nobody knew that at the time (Frank, 1997) – which brought millions of baby boomers into the streets, rejecting sexual restraint and manners, and the values of their parents, if not authority and order altogether. There were more young adults per capita than ever before or since. Just as important, the boomers' adolescent freedom from work, class consciousness, and other future-oriented concerns, was prolonged – by the economic boom, by the expansion of higher education, and by their parents' understandable but tragic desire to spare them the hard work and discipline they had endured before the boomers were born. All these were opportunities for Republican campaign managers, as poverty and unemployment had been for their Democratic predecessors in the realignment of 1929–32.

The right profited from liberals' insistence that they could cure social unrest without cracking down on the civil liberties of defendants or rioters, and from liberals' belief that they could have both guns (escalation in Vietnam, continuation of the arms race) and butter (expansion of the welfare state, plus health, education, and retirement subsidies for the affluent). Liberals underestimated the shrewdness, and the dumb luck, of their enemies.

Judges, recoiling from judicial excesses, helped do the liberals in: they refused to extend desegregation to the suburbs, which grew from "white flight" as the cities deindustrialized. Many cities dropped into a vicious cycle of declining tax bases, which undermined schools, street and transportation repair, police protection, and other basic services, hastening a considerable black flight of teachers and other noncriminal role models (Harrison and Bluestone, 1982; Lukas 1985; Wilson, 1987). Real estate speculators made out like bandits, driving selling prices down for panic-stricken white owners who wanted to flee "transitional neighborhoods," and buying prices up for equally panic-stricken black buyers, who found the urban homes that white people abandoned to be a hopeful step, for a while (Sleeper, 1990). Liberals got blamed, however, for their failure to squelch urban unrest, and for forced busing, inflation, and taxes. Liberals desperately clung to their conviction that the beleaguered white people who turned against busing, along with the white southerners who began to jump off the sinking Democratic ship a little earlier, were just backward racists (Lukas, 1985; Rieder, 1985; Sleeper, 1990). Historians have refined but not abandoned liberals' assumption that right-wing growth depended on racism (Berman, 1994; Carter, 1995, 1996; and see Wolters, 1996).

A new intellectual insurgency, known as neoconservatism, came to the fore in the 1970s. Disillusioned with the hasty and careless quality of much of the Great Society, some of the most thoughtful liberals – including Daniel Bell – were drawn toward a group that coalesced around the magazine *The Public Interest*: Irving Kristol, Gertrude Himmelfarb, Daniel Patrick Moynihan, Robert Nisbet, among others. A similar coalescence around Norman Podhoretz's *Commentary* broadened the movement. Very telling was the neoconservative welcome extended to some of the most gifted black intellectuals, including Glenn Loury and Bayard Rustin, whose sincere dissent from the strategies of the civil rights lobby (no longer a mass movement) added to a vigorous debate on liberalism's abandonment of the black masses, a debate whose history has yet to be written.

Many of the "neocons" claimed, as libertarians had done earlier, that they were the true liberals – that government bureaucracy and the Democratic Party had spun away from liberalism. The neocons, if they had any common values, were not libertarians: they believed the state had a strong, positive role to play in creating opportunity for the unfortunate. But they believed the liberals in power in the 1960s had gone too far to appease the young radicals in the streets, along with urban rioters and other criminals. They argued that liberalism and government had in effect become captives of anti-social forces. Kristol emphasized the need to defend capitalist institutions, on which economic growth and therefore civilization depended. He also emphasized the need to reinvigorate the spiritual and cultural values of bourgeois society. Too much of the bourgeoisie, he believed, had devoted itself too persuasively to discrediting those values – especially the young, whose cultural leadership Kristol regretted (Moynihan, 1969; Banfield, 1970; Kristol, 1978; Podhoretz, 1979; Steinfels, 1979; Ehrman, 1995). No doubt many parents did too. The youth rebellion of the 1960s has often been viewed as a mass Freudian struggle against parental authority. The rightward reaction of the 1970s makes sense as parents' itch for the switch they had set aside during the boom, with the bestselling Dr. Spock's reassurance.

Much of what Kristol defended had a liberal ring. So too, Moynihan. Bell defined himself as liberal in politics, conservative in culture, and socialist in economics (1976). Strong among neocons were the followers of Leo Strauss, who enjoyed an academic and popular revival, represented by the bestselling success of the greatest – and least populist – American conservative book since Kirk's, Allan Bloom's *Closing of the American Mind* (1987). The neocons' views on foreign affairs were as complex and as important as their views on domestic policy. Though most neocons had objected to American policy in Vietnam, they resisted what they saw as liberals' general turn away from responsibility in international affairs, particularly when it came to attacking Soviet influence and defending Israel. This influential and creative group of thinkers helped legitimate "conservatism" further, again by defining liberalism as the incoherent jumble of compromise and failure that had dominated Washington during the late 1960s and 1970s. Since many neocons were ethnic Jews and Catholics, and since many had established records in liberal journals and universities, they lent a cover of respectability to the sometimes reluctantly rightward-moving population.

The politicization of evangelical Christians was as big and important a surprise as the disappearance of the liberal wing of the Republican Party. This was in part a response to the rising street crime of the late 1960s, and the simultaneous increase (by the standards of those days) in public expression of sexual tastes, particularly of ones that were taboo. It was also a response to a perceived politicization of "secular humanism," which evangelicals made into another popular synonym for liberalism. Evangelical Christians overwhelmingly favored separation of church and state, but they saw the Supreme Court's decisions banning voluntary school prayer and Bible reading in 1962 and 1963 as extreme: the justices had sacrificed the First Amendment's protection of free exercise to an overzealous interpretation of its establishment clause (as Potter Stewart wrote in dissent).

The later reaction to the Supreme Court's compromise on abortion, in 1973, gave an opportunity to mobilize what a substantial and militant minority believed was disrespect for the sanctity of human life. Female anti-abortion activists tended to have less attractive job opportunities than their "pro-choice" sisters: they saw involuntary motherhood as a basis for their demand that society protect them against loss of dignity and freedom in the job market (Luker, 1984). Abortion gave a significant anti-liberal culture a new way to stand for generosity and compassion, and to commandeer all the cachet of "rights talk."

More surprising than the political militancy – and increasingly open Republican partisanship – of leaders like Pat Robertson and Jerry Falwell was the new solidarity of conservative Protestants with conservative Catholics and Jews. This was based on a whole range of social issues but especially abortion (Wuthnow, 1988; Hunter, 1991). Pro-lifers, as the most visible conservatives in America, were a walking refutation of the liberal equation of conservatism with bigotry, though liberals certainly scored points by outing the bigots who remained (including the anti-Semitic Robertson). Large numbers of black leaders also identified themselves as pro-life, including Jesse Jackson, before he decided to seek the Democratic presidential nomination in 1984. Jackson helped conservatives next by reminding America that anti-Semitism was far from dead on the left.

Political strategists like Richard Viguerie popularized a moralistic conservatism in the 1970s, mobilizing voters directly on behalf of conservative political candidates, including Ronald Reagan. Viguerie developed the use of direct mail for fundraising and the targeted dissemination of ideas. This was a form of technological populism similar to that of the televangelists: it allowed direct contact between a central leader, or small cabal, and millions of scattered individual supporters, who never met one another. Technopopulism gave new leaders the power to tell millions of disaffected voters (and nonvoters) that they had a voice. That was not the same as giving them a voice, but it seemed enough of an improvement to generate millions in political cash. The means to centralize and mobilize popular resentment against liberalism –

by now a synonym for the status quo – were now overwhelming. Republicans seized those means, their efforts culminating in the overwhelming popular support for Ronald Reagan in 1980 and 1984.

Reagan defeated Jimmy Carter, who had been elected not simply, as many writers assume, because the "Watergate interlude" made a rightward-turning electorate pause before plunging off the cliff with the Gipper. Democrats in 1976 did not take public revulsion with the Nixon scandals for granted – or Ford's ineptitude, or the inflation that ran away with the public's savings on Ford's watch. The Democrats finally learned the lesson of the 1960s that year, and they tried with some plausibility to jump on the rightward bandwagon: they nominated a conservative, southern, born-again Baptist, who campaigned as a homespun farmer who was completely alien to Washington, DC. Republicans, who hesitated to go too far to the right after Watergate, nominated Ford, and lost. But Carter could not shake the stigma of failure and liberalism any more than Ford could shake the stigma of Nixon's crookery. The press, having filled a certain authority-vacuum during Vietnam and Watergate, was still smelling blood through the 1970s, and somewhat indiscriminately undermined Ford and Carter. After Carter's bad luck in Iran, the press changed its tack – recognizing that it, too, needed to cultivate public support. Having effectively savaged LBJ, Nixon, Ford, and Carter, the press greeted the popular Reagan with fawning, uncritical coverage.

Many Democrats supported Reagan's tax cuts for the rich. More generally, as Democrats' union support continued to fail them in the 1980s, and the unions continued to decline in any case, Democrats could not make up their minds what to do – nominating the Humphrey-clone Walter Mondale in 1984 and the technocrat Dukakis in 1988. (Like Gary Hart and Bill Clinton, Dukakis borrowed the neocons' agenda and cachet; the press called him neoliberal, which meant, more or less, neo-conservative.) The left of the party, meanwhile, wasted its energy in moralistic hand-wringing about military expansion, which it rightly observed was strategically unnecessary. But it failed to respect how politically beneficial the military was, as the world's largest socialized housing program and one of the largest socialized medicine programs. The military kept unemployment in check, offering opportunity to thousands of capitalism's casualties. Indeed, the post-Vietnam all-volunteer military, for all its waste, came closer than any political movement in world history to fulfilling the old red slogan, Arm the Proletariat.

The Democrats' aimlessness may not have mattered, as long as the Republicans had the most popular leader since FDR carrying the ball. But by the late 1980s, following Bill Clinton's Democratic Leadership Council, Democrats were moving further and further to the right – only "diversity," environmentalism, and unlimited abortion rights remained of the "liberal" agenda – all symbolic issues that had been added after the Great Society. These issues either cost the taxpayers nothing or appealed to affluent voters who were otherwise likely to vote Republican. (Clinton's unsuccessful health proposals were radically pro-business by worldwide standards. They looked liberal only because the health industry was strong enough to demonize any encroachment on its power, and because the Clintons made the mistake of trying to appease that industry. Medical insurers did not bite the hand that tried to feed them, they amputated it.)

Republican politicians exploited the compassionate imagery of their "new abolitionism" on abortion as shrewdly as Democrats exploited their support for affirmative action and racial gerrymandering: both issues secured a key demographic base without asking much financial sacrifice from voters. Neither required much follow-through from elected officials, who shunted the most difficult decisions off onto unelected judges. Democrats and Republicans, both dependent on corporate support, converged on economic issues, with the Clinton administration adopting GOP positions on welfare reform and free trade. Republicans rightly but pathetically complained that Clinton hit the jackpot with their nickel. Clinton cut the debt that Reagan's deficits had piled up and enjoyed a boom on Wall Street, as speculators cashed in on the taxpayers' investment in new technology. Thus Clinton earned the support of the "centrist" lobbyists and campaign financiers without the ideological baggage that extreme right-wingers, like Republican House Speaker Newt Gingrich, asked their party to carry. Though Gingrich was forced to retire, the future of conservatism looked bright at the end of the twentieth century, with both major parties in the most powerful, most technologically advanced nation shunning the liberal label and doing their best to reduce government spending on behalf of the poor and unemployed.

On the other hand, there were clouds on conservatives' horizon. In the aftermath of the Reagan Revolution, there was much disappointment and disillusionment on the right, documented by thoughtful conservative partisans like R. Emmett Tyrrell (1992) and David Frum (1994), as well as by scholars (e.g., Steve Bruce, 1988; Michael Lienesch, 1993; Kenneth Heineman, 1998). Disillusionment was particularly strong among the religious right, which recognized Reagan's exploitation of it. Reagan's failure to deliver on abortion and school prayer made many realize that he had not made much effort, though many to this day continue to think of Reagan – an enigmatic popular leader like his early hero, FDR – as a personal symbol of hope. Conservatives' nostalgia for Reagan now echoes liberal Democrats' nostalgia for FDR. To some extent, the religious right retreated from politics – bruised by the "telescandals" of Jimmy Swaggart and Jim Bakker, and by Jerry Falwell's unseemly opportunism in response to the latter, as well as Pat Robertson's exposure as (among other things) an anti-Semite after all. Ralph Reed, following the pragmatic tendency long denounced by religious conservatives, revitalized the Christian Coalition as a political force during the Clinton years, but perhaps eroded its bonds with its constituency. Reed's move echoed Goldwater's move of 1960: if conservatives want to be taken seriously, they had to become more ruthless and unprincipled in seizing and retaining state power – as ruthless and unprincipled as post-FDR liberals had been.

The judicially assisted capture of the White House by George W. Bush suggests that conservatives may be following Reed's path. The younger Bush, the remarkable scion of an old eastern establishment family – the sort whom conservatives held in contempt in the 1950s – has a more genuine affinity for the religious conservatives than Reagan ever did. Though W's enemies like to call attention to his sodden past, and the possibility of his backsliding, his personal tribulations make him a familiar character in a story much loved by the born-again. His struggles, and the uncharitable abuse of those who cannot understand and forgive, may actually solidify his relationship with a constituency that believes in the reality of sin and the need to struggle, dramatically and publicly, against it. W admitted his weakness as readily as Jimmy Carter or Jesse Jackson.

The future of conservatism will probably depend on its ability to deal with its weaknesses. It is a great sign of the right's resiliency that it produces and apparently consumes such invigorating and candid works of self-criticism as Frum's and Tyrrell's – and that its young generation of writers shows vitality, resourcefulness, even humor. It is an equal and opposite sign of the left's morbidity that books like Michael Tomasky's *Left for Dead* – an earnest effort to take responsibility for the rout the left has suffered since 1968 – are greeted with such resistance by the left, and are so few and far between.

The causes of the great conservative resurgence in America are complex, involving many questions that historians have barely begun to turn loose on the evidence. Liberals' overweening self-assurance appears to be the most important single reason for their fall. That trait stands out, in part, because it is responsible for the historical ignorance of conservatism among educated Americans in the 1950s–1970s, when liberals dominated the writing and teaching of history more than they dominated politics. Louis Hartz's reading of a Lockean consensus back into American history was shared by most of the prominent historians of his generation, even those who, like Daniel Boorstin, emphasized a conservative side of the consensus. Hartz expressed a belief equivalent to liberal Manifest Destiny or liberal divine right. A ruling faction that cannot see – cannot imagine – an enemy, even in the past, is in obvious trouble, even in a society that lacks representative government.

Exceptions poked their heads above the parapet of the liberal consensus. John Higham's famous essay on the "consensus school" (1959) provided a rallying cry and a program for a generation of historians growing impatient with liberalism. At first, the rebels who got attention lined up on the left; they dug into the lives of the downtrodden and excluded, the poor and oppressed, providing these hitherto inarticulate subjects a leftish voice. In the process, they redefined left (with the help of E. P. Thompson) as a kind of traditionalism, and even, sometimes, Americanism. No right-wing historiographical school developed, but along the way, William Nelson came out with a solid account of American anti-revolutionaries (1961) and David Hackett Fischer (1965) with a solid account of the first conservative party in America. Rossiter produced an important revised edition (1966). Rogin, affiliated with a non-history department, severed the connection Hofstadter had drawn between McCarthy's supporters and the "real" late nineteenth-century Populists. Rogin led his generation of left-leaning historians in defining the right-wingers of McCarthy's grassroots as lacking historical pedigree altogether, and in redefining the true Populists (after Vann Woodward's more profound and less influential attempt) as left-leaning. Eugene Genovese (1969) brought southern conservatism, with its romantic, anti-capitalist drive, to almost blinding light, eventually connecting that conservatism with twentieth-century survivals. Linda Kerber added depth and cultural context to the Federalists Fischer had brought back to life (1970). Working closer to his own lifetime, James Patterson deserves great credit for his scholarly work on Taft (1972) and the congressional conservatives (1967) who set the stage for the anti-FDR reaction. George Nash (1976) probably did more than anybody to rescue American conservatives from the massive condescension of the professional managers of posterity. John Lukacs (1961, 1968, 1984, 1990), one of the great historical minds who worked in English in the twentieth century, elaborated (at times, single-handedly) a philosophy of history that was conservative in the historic, European sense, rather than the corporate or libertarian boosterism that wears the label in America.

Great journalists wrote a lot of the history that professional historians could or would not write: Thomas and Mary Edsall, a superb history (1991) of the connections among various elements of conservatism; John Judis, one of the most important intellectual biographies (1988) of his generation; and Godfrey Hodgson, probably the best overall history (1996) of America's turn to the right. There were others. Before the 1990s, historians tended not to assimilate all this work, but they could not ignore its growing weight and high quality.

Historians were also influenced by the cognitive dissonance injected into liberal-consensus historiography – not just by leftists who wanted (like Staughton Lynd) to find an American "radical tradition," but by less obviously present-minded historians like Caroline Robbins and Bernard Bailyn, who set in motion a reconsideration of America's ideological origins. Robbins's and Bailyn's discovery of what came to be called classical republicanism had a momentum of its own.

The Robbins/Bailyn trend culminated in J. G. A. Pocock's *Machiavelian Moment*, and the proliferation of republicanism studies in unpredictable areas, including labor history. Historians of liberalism, and of Lockean thought more specifically, responded by coming up with a more complicated, more Christian, or more virtue-oriented liberal tradition. That revised liberal tradition strained the credibility of Hartz's tradition as much as the discovery of a distinct and powerful republican tradition. Less fruitful, but equally important for a while, was the rediscovery of Scots commonsense realism and its important, often illiberal, role in American political culture in the eighteenth to nineteenth centuries.

But what really brought home the need to study conservatism was the overwhelming political reality in historians' own lifetimes: the utter rout of the left and center. When Ronald Reagan stood up in their soup, historians finally got around to finding out what conservatism might look like on a significant scale. Most important was the amazing proliferation of studies of the Klan of 1920s, a time when extremism seemed to go mainstream. Building on earlier work by Kenneth Jackson (1967), scholars like Robert Goldberg (1981) and Nancy MacLean (1994) found a complicated Klan, very different from the Klan of Reconstruction, from the Klan that "revived" after World War II, and from the radical right that Bell and Hofstadter had projected onto America. All that fine work finally begged the question whether "extreme" was really the right word for the Klan in a decade of "normalcy." Alan Brinkley followed the same impulse with great success (1982), finding that the populist-style leaders Huey Long and Charles Coughlin were more understandable and human than pathological. In 1992, Michael Kazin called for a general reassessment in the *American Historical Review*, followed two years later by a similar call in the same journal by Brinkley, and one by Leonard Moore in *Reviews in American History* (1996).

The ultimate determinant of the Bell–Hofstadter view was the McCarthy–Goldwater period, however, and there recent historians seem less sure-footed. Gary Gerstle (1989) tried to account for an ethnic Catholic, working-class cold warriorism and nonfascist corporatism in Rhode Island. Gerstle did not exactly throw off the massive condescension of posterity (to use Thompson's phrase), which in America has applied to conservatives. But he bristled defiantly under it – even if, in doing so, he sidled quaintly close to an Ortega-like fear of the rootless, anomic "mass man" who is ever drawn toward ever more frightful modern substitutes for community.

Historians of conservatism might, like most historians since the 1960s, be missing the forest for the grassroots. There are other things a full historical investigation should cover. Perhaps most important, historians have not heeded the basic principle of investigative journalism, detective fiction, and indeed all the higher forms of common sense: to follow the money. We know very little about the Milliken brothers, H. L. and Nelson Bunker Hunt, J. Howard Pew, Henry Regnery, Carleton Putnam, Richard Mellon Scaife. The left, in a more conspiratorial and political era when scholars like G. William Domhoff were prominent, paid attention to the political investments of such men and their tax-dodging foundations. Money and grassroots became blurred by the technological populism of televangelism and direct mail (were already blurred by earlier forms of populism, especially those that lean toward authoritarianism). Historians need to unblur them. More related to the connection between grassroots and what appears above the ground in politics, historians need to explore the rise of political mercenaries (see Blumenthal, 1980; Sabato, 1981), who often determine who wins and loses, and the growing role of rich lobbyists in making policy (see Philip Stern, 1987, 1992, and the vital website of the Center for Responsive Politics).

But even remaining tangled within the grassroots, historians seem to be missing issues at that level, for example, the assimilation of ethnic "minorities" – especially Catholics and Jews. Immigrants were always welcomed by the Democratic Party. As that party evolved into its "liberal" phase – in our social democrat/Progressive-New Deal-Great Society sense of the term – it helped promote the independence of neighborhoods, parishes, families, and individuals who sought assimilation and respectability (which too many historians reductively and condescendingly write off as "whiteness"). It gave them something to be conservative about. Very late in the game, northern Democrats began stealing the black bloc from the GOP, and offering "the Negro" a road to respectability, too. That vote-getting project was intertwined so much with postwar liberalism (*not* with prewar liberalism) that it is hard to disentangle the liberalism from the opportunism. But the point is that historians need to look at black conservatism – at least the so-called social conservatism that shows up in opinion polls on abortion, crime, "school choice," homosexuality; in membership in organizations like the Promise Keepers and the Nation of Islam; and in attendance at theologically and socially anti-liberal churches, which are often (especially in the Pentecostal wing) racially integrated. (Angela Dillard, 2001, has made a start by looking at black conservative intellectuals.) The missionary efforts of evangelical churches – plus the Mormons and, in recent years, American Muslims – in the decolonializing "third world" may have a lot to do with the attraction of recent immigrants from Asia, the Middle East, Africa, the Caribbean, and Latin America to the most conservative social institutions here. If these institutions are politicized, they could provide a great windfall for the shrewd Republican or Democrat willing to campaign and patronize for their vote.

The rise from poverty after the 1930s affected most Americans – not just the assimilating ethnic groups. Whether that rise was embourgeoisement of the working class or proletarianization of the middle class, or both, conservatives simply had to point out that most Americans now felt they had something to lose – something to conserve. Barbara Ehrenreich evoked the rising class consciousness of the professional-managerial class in the late 1970s – its awakening from the boom-generated illusion that it lived in a classless society (1989). American historians love to use the word class, but they lack Ehrenreich's supple way of recognizing its wily manifestations in social and political life, and do not respect its fundamental (definitional) distinctiveness from more popular classifications like gender and race.

Historians are much better than they used to be at handling the wily manifestations and fundamental distinctiveness of religion. Patrick Allitt (1993) and Lisa McGirr (2001) are good at incorporating the restructuring of American religion into their accounts, but few other historians are considering the possibility that religion – belief in the day-to-day presence in our world of a transcendent, personal, and all-powerful Other – may, with some independence of economic interest or ethnic identity, determine political and social action. Historians need to look into that possibility more.

Much scholarship remains infected with the pathologizing tendency of Bell and Hofstadter's early work, in other words, with liberal hubris. The very focus on grassroots – i.e., on extreme – conservatism denies conservatism the central place that historians like Rossiter and Kirk tried reasonably to give it. Lisa McGirr's grassroots history is exceptional, in that it defines the conservative masses as middle class, and not particularly racist, or violent, paranoid, stingy, (to use that most evasive term) antimodern: in other words, as average, mainstream Americans. She goes so far in depathologizing the right that one comes away from her book wondering how there could be any liberals. The key question she raises but does not answer is, what sometimes makes the rest of America vote the way Orange County always votes?

Grassrooting is a complex move by historians, who tend to lionize and apotheosize whatever they deem marginal: are they condescendingly looking down or patronizingly groping their way toward respect – or toward realism? Is conservatism now as American as Hartz thought liberalism was? In other words, has conservatism – still defined as a negative reaction to the status quo – become a catch-all term for all the various brands of cranky opposition to authority (Protestantism, Republicanism) that helped to motivate, if they did not determine, the transatlantic migrations that defined America – and that animated great social and political movements from the frontier and back-country revivals, to the Boston Tea Party, to the Jeffersonian and Jacksonian "revolutions," the occasional slave rebellion, the greenback labor and Agrarian movements, to some forms of Progressivism and tenant farmer agitation, and finally to the Dionysian cultural ecstasies of the Jazz and Rock and Roll eras? In the most liberal nation in the world – a nation without inherited social distinctions or an established church – is rebellion, and thus historical change, always going to draw on something like conservatism?

REFERENCES

Allitt, Patrick: *Catholic Intellectuals and Conservative Politics in America* (Ithaca, NY: Cornell University Press, 1993).

Ammerman, Nancy: *Bible Believers: Fundamentalists in the Modern World* (New Brunswick, NJ: Rutgers University Press, 1987).

Banfield, Edward: *The Unheavenly City* (Boston: Little, Brown, 1970).

Bell, Daniel, ed.: *The New American Right* (New York: Criterion, 1955); rev. ed., *The Radical Right* (Garden City, NY: Doubleday, 1962).

Bell, Daniel: *The Cultural Contradictions of Capitalism* (New York: Basic Books, 1976).

Berman, William: *America's Right Turn: From Nixon to Clinton* (Baltimore: Johns Hopkins University Press, 1994; 2nd ed., 1998).

Bloom, Allan: *The Closing of the American Mind* (New York: Simon and Schuster, 1987).

Blumenthal, Sidney: *The Permanent Campaign: Inside the World of Elite Political Operatives* (Boston: Beacon Press, 1980).

Brennan, Mary: *Turning Right in the 1960s: The Conservative Capture of the GOP* (Chapel Hill: University of North Carolina Press, 1995).

Brinkley, Alan: *Voices of Protest: Huey Long, Father Coughlin, and the Great Depression* (New York: Alfred A. Knopf, 1982).

Brinkley, Alan: "The Problem of American Conservatism," *American Historical Review* 99 (1994).

Brinkley, Alan: *The End of Reform: New Deal Liberalism in Recession and War* (New York: Alfred A. Knopf, 1995).

Bruce, Steve: *The Rise and Fall of the Christian Right: Conservative Protestant Politics in America* (New York: Oxford University Press, 1988).

Carpenter, Joel: *Revive Us Again: The Reawakening of American Fundamentalism* (New York: Oxford University Press, 1997).

Carter, Dan: *Politics of Rage: George Wallace, the Origins of the New Conservatism, and the Transformation of American Politics* (New York: Simon and Schuster, 1995).

Carter, Dan: *From George Wallace to Newt Gingrich* (Baton Rouge: Louisiana State University Press, 1996).

Chappell, David: *A Stone of Hope: Prophetic Religion, Liberalism, and the Death of Jim Crow* (Chapel Hill: University of North Carolina Press, forthcoming, 2003).

Diggins, John: *Up from Communism: Conservative Odysseys in American Intellectual History* (New York: Harper, 1975).

Dillard, Angela: *Guess Who's Coming to Dinner Now? Multicultural Conservatism in America* (New York: New York University Press, 2001).

Edsall, Thomas and Edsall, Mary: *Chain Reaction: The Impact of Race, Rights, and Taxes on Politics* (New York: W. W. Norton, 1991).

Edwards, Lee: *The Conservative Revolution: The Movement that Remade America* (New York: Free Press, 1999).

Ehrenreich, Barbara: *Fear of Falling: The Inner Life of the Middle Class* (New York: Pantheon, 1989).

Ehrman, John: *Rise of Neoconservatives: Intellectuals and Foreign Affairs* (New Haven, Conn.: Yale University Press, 1995).

Fischer, David Hackett: *Revolution of American Conservatism: Federalist Party in the Era of Jeffersonian Democracy* (New York: Harper, 1965).

Fones-Wolf, Elizabeth: *Selling Free Enterprise: The Business Assault on Labor and Liberalism, 1945–1960* (Urbana: University of Illinois Press, 1994) .

Frank, Thomas: *The Conquest of Cool* (Chicago: University of Chicago Press, 1997).

Frum, David: *Dead Right* (New York: Basic Books, 1994).

Genovese, Eugene D.: *The World the Slaveholders Made: Two Essays in Interpretation* (New York: Pantheon, 1969).

Gerstle, Gary: *Working Class Americanism: The Politics of Labor in a Textile City, 1914–1960* (Cambridge: Cambridge University Press, 1989).

Goldberg, Robert: *Hooded Empire: The Ku Klux Klan in Colorado, 1921–1932* (Urbana: University of Illinois Press, 1981).

Goldberg, Robert: *Barry Goldwater* (New Haven, Conn.: Yale University Press, 1995).

Graham, Hugh: *The Civil Rights Era* (New York: Oxford University Press, 1990).

Harrison, Bennett and Bluestone, Barry: *The Deindustrialization of America* (New York: Basic Books, 1982).

Hawley, Ellis: *The New Deal and the Problem of Monopoly* (Princeton, NJ: Princeton University Press, 1966).

Heineman, Kenneth: *God is a Conservative: Religion, Politics, and Morality in Contemporary America* (New York: New York University Press, 1998).

Higham, John: "The Cult of the American Consensus," *Commentary* (1959).

Hirschman, Albert: *The Rhetoric of Reaction: Perversity, Futility, Jeopardy* (Cambridge, Mass.: Belknap, 1991).

Hixson, William: *Search for the American Right Wing: An Analysis of the Social Science Record, 1955–1987* (Princeton, NJ: Princeton University Press, 1992).

Hodgson, Godfrey: *World Turned Rightside Up* (Boston: Houghton Mifflin, 1996).

Hofstadter, Richard: *American Political Tradition and the Men Who Made It* (New York: Alfred A. Knopf, 1948).

Hofstadter, Richard: *Anti-Intellectualism in American Life* (New York: Alfred A. Knopf, 1963).

Hofstadter, Richard: *The Paranoid Style in American Politics* (New York: Alfred A. Knopf, 1965).

Holmes, Stephen: *Anatomy of Antiliberalism* (Cambridge, Mass.: Harvard University Press, 1993).

Hunter, James Davison: *Culture Wars* (New York: Basic Books, 1991).

Huntington, Samuel: "Conservatism as an Ideology," *American Political Science Review*, 51 (1957).

Jackson, Kenneth T.: *The Ku Klux Klan in the City, 1915–1930* (New York: Oxford University Press, 1967).

Judis, John: *William Buckley, Jr.: Patron Saint of the Conservatives* (New York: Simon and Schuster, 1988).

Kazin, Michael: "The Grass-Roots Right," *American Historical Review*, 97 (1992).

Kerber, Linda: *Federalists in Dissent* (Ithaca, NY: Cornell University Press, 1970).

Kirk, Russell: *The Conservative Mind: From Burke to Santayana* (Chicago: Henry Regnery, 1953).

Kristol, Irving: *Two Cheers for Capitalism* (New York: Basic Books, 1978).

Lienesch, Michael: *Redeeming America: Piety and Politics in the New Christian Right* (Chapel Hill: University of North Carolina Press, 1993).

Lipset, Seymour Martin: *The Politics of Unreason: Right-Wing Extremism in America, 1790–1970* (New York: Harper, 1970).

Lukacs, John: *History of the Cold War* (Garden City, NY: Doubleday, 1961).

Lukacs, John: *Historical Consciousness: Or, The Remembered Past* (New York: Harper, 1968).

Lukacs, John: *Outgrowing Democracy: America in the 20th Century* (Garden City, NY: Doubleday, 1984).

Lukacs, John: *Confessions of an Original Sinner* (New York: Ticknor and Fields, 1990).

Lukas, J. Anthony: *Common Ground: A Turbulent Decade in the Lives of Three American Families* (New York: Alfred A. Knopf, 1985).

Luker, Kristin: *Abortion and the Politics of Motherhood* (Berkeley: University of California Press, 1984).

McGirr, Lisa: *Suburban Warriors: Origins of the New American Right* (Princeton, NJ: Princeton University Press, 2001).

MacLean, Nancy: *Behind the Mask of Chivalry: The Making of the Second Ku Klux Klan* (New York: Oxford University Press, 1994).

Marsden, George: *Fundamentalism and American Culture: The Shaping of 20th-Century Evangelicalism, 1870–1925* (New York: Oxford University Press, 1980).

Marsden, George: *Understanding Fundamentalism and Evangelicalism* (Grand Rapids, Mich.: Eerdman's, 1991).

Martin, William: *Prophet With Honor: The Billy Graham Story* (New York: William Morrow, 1991).

Moynihan, Daniel Patrick: *Maximum Feasible Misunderstanding: Community Action in the War on Poverty* (New York: Free Press, 1969).

Muller, Jerry, ed.: *Conservatism: An Anthology of Social and Political Thought – David Hume to the Present* (Princeton, NJ: Princeton University Press, 1997).

Nash, George: *The Conservative Intellectual Movement in America* (New York: Basic Books, 1976).

Navasky, Victor: *Naming Names* (New York: Viking, 1980).

Nelson, William H.: *The American Tory* (Oxford: Clarendon Press, 1961).

Nisbet, Robert: *Quest for Community: A Study in the Ethics of Order and Freedom* (New York: Oxford University Press, 1953).

O'Neill, William: *A Better World: The Great Schism: Stalinism and the American Intellectuals* (New York: Simon and Schuster, 1982).

Oshinsky, David: *A Conspiracy So Immense: The World of Joe McCarthy* (New York: Free Press, 1983).

Patterson, James: *Congressional Conservatism and the New Deal* (Lexington: University Press of Kentucky, 1967).

Patterson, James: *Mr. Republican: A Biography of Robert Taft* (Boston: Houghton Mifflin, 1972).

Podhoretz, Norman: *Breaking Ranks* (New York: Harper, 1979).

Rae, Nicol: *Decline and Fall of the Liberal Republicans from 1952 to the Present* (New York: Oxford University Press, 1989).

Rieder, Jonathan: *Canarsie: The Jews and Italians of Brooklyn against Liberalism* (Cambridge, Mass.: Harvard University Press, 1985).

Rogin, Michael Paul: *The Intellectuals and McCarthy* (Cambridge, Mass.: MIT Press, 1967).

Rossiter, Clinton: *Conservatism in America* (New York: Alfred A. Knopf, 1955; rev. ed., 1966).

Rovere, Richard: *Senator Joe McCarthy* (New York: Harcourt, 1959).

Russell, C. Allyn: *Voices of American Fundamentalism: Seven Biographical Studies* (Philadelphia: Westminster Press, 1976).

Sabato, Larry: *The Rise of Political Consultants: New Ways of Winning Elections* (New York: Basic Books, 1981).

Schlesinger, Jr., Arthur: *The Vital Center: The Politics of Freedom* (Boston: Houghton Mifflin, 1949).

Schrecker, Ellen: *Many Are the Crimes: McCarthyism in America* (Boston: Little, Brown, 1998).

Siegel, Fred: *Troubled Journey: From Pearl Harbor to Ronald Reagan* (New York: Hill and Wang, 1984).

Sleeper, Jim: *The Closest of Strangers: Liberalism and the Politics of Race in New York* (New York: W. W. Norton, 1990).

Steinfels, Peter: *The Neoconservatives: The Men Who Are Changing America's Politics* (New York: Simon and Schuster, 1979).

Stern, Philip: *The Best Congress Money Can Buy* (New York: Pantheon, 1987).

Stern, Philip: *Still the Best Congress Money Can Buy* (Washington, DC: Regnery Gateway, 1992).

Trilling, Lionel: *The Liberal Imagination* (New York: Viking, 1949).

Tyrrell, R. Emmett: *The Conservative Crack-Up* (New York: Simon and Schuster, 1992).

Viereck, Peter: *Conservatism Revisited* (New York: Scribner's, 1949).

Viguerie, Richard: *The New Right: We're Ready to Lead* (Falls Church, Va.: Viguerie, 1980).

Wald, Alan: *The New York Intellectuals* (Chapel Hill, NC: University of North Carolina Press, 1987).

Weaver, Richard: *Ideas Have Consequences* (Chicago: University of Chicago Press, 1949).

Wills, Garry: *Confessions of a Conservative* (Garden City, NY: Doubleday, 1979).

Wilson, William Julius: *The Truly Disadvantaged: The Inner City, The Underclass, and Public Policy* (Chicago: University of Chicago Press, 1987).

Wolters, Raymond: *Right Turn: William Bradford Reynolds, the Reagan Administration, and Black Civil Rights* (New Brunswick, NJ: Transaction, 1996).

Wuthnow, Robert: *The Restructuring of American Religion* (Princeton, NJ: Princeton University Press, 1988).

CHAPTER SEVENTEEN

Modern Environmentalism

IAN TYRRELL

Introduction

What's in a name? The etymology of the word "environmentalism" indicates that the modern movement developed before it had a self-conscious identity in the 1970s. "Environmentalism" had not been well recognized lexicographically until that time but the roots of environmentalism run deeper – to the struggles over parks, nuclear testing, and pesticides in the 1950s and to underlying intellectual change earlier still, as conservation-minded people faced novel threats to environmental quality, and absorbed new ideas and concepts to deal with those problems.

Definitions are slippery, too. To "preserve the diversity and wondrous beauty of our world" was an important goal, but the "environmental" movement was more than that, recognizing "that billions must steadily draw upon (the earth's) substance for survival" (Scheffer, 1991, p. 197). Environmentalism included the restoration and renovation of environment conditions of human existence. It encompassed issues of conserving resources as well as preserving wild nature, urban and agricultural pollution as well as wilderness, global as well as purely American problems, human health as well as the health of the rest of nature. What linked these themes was the science of ecology and its understanding of the interdependence of human activities and natural systems.

Environmentalism represented a potential challenge to dominant American political/economic institutions of the postwar period. It was more than a self-interested assertion of a new middle-class, consumer-oriented society and more than a movement concerned only with pristine nature. Environmentalism posed a nascent threat to the mass consumer capitalism of the post-World War II period by attacking the environmental consequences of economic growth, and resurrected, though in new ways and in new guises, the public regulatory activity that flourished in the Progressive era. Environmentalism thus became a battle over socioeconomic objectives and distributional structures within the American state, as well as a movement for better environmental amenities. However, this distributional aspect of environmentalism (found in such issues as energy policy, public lands controversies in the American West, population politics, and transnational environmental policy) has not been clearly articulated in American environmental discourse, and for this reason, perhaps,

I wish to thank Roy Rosenzweig, Tom Dunlap, and Richard Gowers for reading various drafts of this chapter and making useful suggestions and corrections.

not properly understood by historians, who have treated environmental issues in pragmatic interest group terms, and in terms of the politics and ideology of social movements – themes that were but part of the story.

Though new works are now appearing (for example, Rome, 2001), the post-World
War II period has been little studied by environmental historians. Most major
contributors to American environmental history, notably Donald Worster, William
Cronon, Alfred Crosby, Carolyn Merchant, and Richard White, have worked mainly
on earlier periods. Many were attracted to the colonial years, or have been closely
aligned with the history of the American West, rather than with urban and industrial
topics. A major exception for coverage of the period since 1945 is Samuel Hays.

How New is the New Environmentalism?

To sum up the concerns of modern American environmentalism, Hays (1987) titled
his book *Beauty, Health, and Permanence*. He described the modern movement as
encapsulating "new values, rooted in changing demography, improved standards of
health and living, and enhanced levels of human aspiration." Hays has an important
and sophisticated argument to explain the rise of modern environmentalism; as the
author of a major work on earlier Progressive-era conservation (Hays, 1959), he was
well placed to comment on modern environmentalism's distinctive features. Hays
argued that the postwar decline of an industrial base and rise of the service sector raised
the social, cultural, and economic importance of ecologically based ideals. He stressed
the culturally constructed desires of the newly affluent service sector professional and
middle classes and the private and public apparatus that constituted the "organizational" society. Formerly an adjunct to developmentalism and utilitarian conservation,
science now provided the perspective of ecology – the branch of biology that studies
relationships between living organisms and their physical environments. Moreover,
new sciences such as toxicology could show a larger number of potential carcinogens;
and scientific disputes were now being fought out in public rather than among experts.
From scientists came the news that human aspirations were on the point of outrun-
ning resources; elements of the educated elite argued that there were limits to growth
and that Americans would have to stress the quality of life. Hays's new middle-class
consumers began to demand better "goods and services" such as clean water and air,
and accessible but nevertheless relatively pristine national parks (Hays, 1987).

An important distinction divides the environmental movement from the earlier conservation movement. Environmental concerns had shifted from a "productionist"
ethic to a "consumerist" ethic. The ethic of conservation involved efficient use of
resources according to maximum sustained yield without destroying those resources.
The idea, first derived for fisheries in Europe, was applied in the United States to
forestry, game, and soils (McEvoy, 1986). In contrast, post-1945 environmentalists
looked at nature as independent of humans and as possessing intrinsic value, but nevertheless as providing benefits to humans beyond economic need. These were health,
recreation, aesthetics, and sustainability through treating nature not as a set of discrete resources, but as an interrelated system. Thus modern environmentalism sought
"beauty, health, and permanence."

Modern environmentalism reinvigorated old tensions between ideas of conservation and preservation. Wise-use concepts – the term was coined by preeminent

US forester Gifford Pinchot (1947) – and multiple use, in which resources would be conserved for maximum benefit to the economy *and* for public appreciation in the case of parks, had come to prominence in the Progressive era. In the pre-World War I struggle over whether to dam the Hetch Hetchy Valley in California, John Muir and supporters of the wilderness ethic argued unsuccessfully that the valley should be preserved, like Yosemite, for its own sake (Muir, 1912). But the dam was built and the valley flooded after 1913. This defeat conventionally marks the decline of preservationist agitation. The political power of conservation languished in the pro-business climate of the 1920s. But the New Deal saw a revival of conservation as efficiency, with the extension of concern to soil erosion as well as forestry, and the initiation of great projects of flood control and hydroelectric generation and irrigation. Not until the early 1950s did the emphasis on rational use of resources receive a significant setback from resurgent preservation sentiment, when the proposed Echo Park dam on the Colorado–Utah border became a cause célèbre because it would flood the unique scenery and fossils of the Dinosaur National Monument. Nurtured in the Wilderness Society (founded 1935) and the Sierra Club (founded 1892 but revitalized under David Brower in the 1950s), the preservationist ethic grew in strength. The Echo Park conflict established limits to the efficiency argument – only with the defeat of this project was the inviolability of the national parks and monuments established (Miles, 1995).

Origins of Modern Environmentalism

If the dam controversy marked the visible reassertion of preservation issues, modern environmentalism had deeper roots. Instead of the idea of "natural history" as a descriptive science cataloguing nature, there arose the science of ecology with its concept of an ecosystem independent of human values, and growing understanding of the importance of the dynamic and interactive aspects of nature (Dunlap, 1999). Though the word "ecology" can be traced back to 1873, the ecological view became more self-conscious from the late 1930s. A new ethic of symbiosis with land, both moral and ethical, based on notions of long-term ecological stability, was proclaimed by Aldo Leopold. Leopold's developing ideas were collected in his *A Sand County Almanac* in 1949; they were not widely accepted for twenty years (Opie, 1998, p. 397; Dunlap, 1999).

Economic changes helped the new land ethic develop in the 1930s. The Great Depression undermined confidence in market values and favored the preservation of wild country. Much of the land incorporated in Olympic National Park during that period, for example, seemed of little economic value. Wild lands were designated by the federal government, albeit with a tentative and insecure status, as "Primitive areas."

But longer-term trends were more important to the new environmental concerns of the 1950s. Economic changes, especially the industrialization of agriculture, distanced humans from nature and yet made them more aware of the risks of ignoring natural systems. Modern mechanized agriculture involved vast energy inputs, fertilizers, and pesticides; it received a boost from the need for more food products in World War II, and from the discovery during wartime of new chemicals that could control insect pests.

Modern media shaped popular perceptions of nature and the vast changes humans had wrought. Television news programs by the 1990s would spread environmental concern, but television much earlier aided Rachel Carson, author of the influential *Silent Spring* (1962). A program hosted by Eric Severeid on her challenge to the pesticide industry garnered 10 to 15 million viewers when shown on the CBS network. The program "amounted to nothing less than a special printing of *Silent Spring*" (Lear, 1997, p. 450). Knowledge about environmental issues spread through other media changes, too. Color photography for magazines such as *National Geographic* and as an American hobby boomed in the 1950s, helping to create identification with natural landscapes.

The Development of a Wilderness Ethic and Movement

The search for an environmental amenity preserved in national parks and wilderness sprang from these changed conditions. The black and white photography of Ansel Adams (1902–84) in the 1930s began to make the high Sierra of California famous (Boston, 1948). Stimulated by the threat to the Dinosaur National Monument, the Sierra Club and the Wilderness Society lobbied Congress in the 1950s to designate new areas and to solidify their wilderness status; these and other societies also fought to establish at the congressional level a Wilderness Act, achieved in 1964. This act created wilderness areas within the national forests, and under its powers a more ecocentric ethic developed.

Congress's definition designated areas substantially unaltered by humans. "A wilderness, in contrast with those areas where man and his works dominate the landscape, is hereby recognized as an area where the earth and its community of life are untrammeled by man, where man himself is a visitor who does not remain." The wilderness ethic itself, some commentators such as Baird Callicott have argued, is a product of Western consciousness, and modern ecological consciousness, especially Europe's encounter with the New World (Callicott, 1991; Cronon, 1996). To call North America a pristine wilderness to be preserved from development ignored the thousands of years of occupation and change by Amerindian peoples. One moral dilemma was whether urban middle-class people had the right to tell indigenous peoples how to use the land, and whether Americans ought to accept some human invention by traditional owners as worth emulating as an example of ecological sustainability. While not all environmentalists subscribed to this view of parks as formerly pristine landscapes, there is no denying that wilderness played a significant part in determining environmental values in the United States, and through the pioneering work of Roderick Nash and Alfred Runte the intellectual fascination with wilderness continues to influence historiographical debates over conservation (Nash, 1967; Runte, 1979).

Despite growing recognition of the importance of wilderness, a continuing battle raged over what kinds of access Americans should have to national parks. Tourism has compromised the very wilderness values that the act sought to promote when larger numbers of people hiked or canoed through wild areas. National Park administrators had to balance the impact of automobile and hotel development in such areas as Yosemite National Park against the right of Americans to see these attractive and supposedly "preserved" regions.

Wilderness was not the only contentious issue in modern environmental historiography. The rise of industrial cities before 1900 had produced much factory pollution, but the shift to the second stage of an industrial revolution with automobiles, oil production, mass assembly lines, and consumer goods at its center had both good and bad effects evident after World War II. The decline of smoke pollution with closer regulation of chimneys in factories and residences in such cities as Pittsburgh by the 1940s was welcome. David Stradling (1999) documents advances that were made in cleaning up industrial pollution through better local government control of emissions. But the rise of the automobile as a new form of transport was already at hand. The first American freeway had opened in Los Angeles in 1940, and it was to be in southern California in the 1940s and 1950s where a new form of pollution, photochemical smog, was noticed. Created from the interaction of nitrous oxides and hydrocarbons, the resulting cocktail included high concentrations of ozone. While global ozone depletion at high altitudes threatened global atmospheric health, ozone was dangerous to human health at low altitude.

Such air pollution signaled increased chemical contamination in the environment, but of more immediate public concern was the dramatic rise in the use of synthesized chemicals to control insect-born disease. DDT, the most famous of these substances, first appeared as a savior of humankind, and was used during World War II to prevent the spread of lice among refugees and to destroy mosquito populations which spread malaria. By the 1950s, however, scientists of an ecological bent became disturbed by the impact of this and similar chemicals when used by the US Department of Agriculture (USDA) and state departments, and by farmers themselves (Dunlap, 1978).

Carson, Chemicals, and Cancer

Through her writings, Rachel Carson (1907–64), a former biologist with the US Fish and Wildlife Service, made an important contribution to a widening of environmental awareness of toxic substances, and of their direct impact on humans as well as on ecosystems. Carson played an important role in alerting Americans to the dangers of pesticides, finding her niche as a communicator of scientific information on ecology to a wider public. In 1951 she wrote the bestselling *The Sea Around Us*, which made her reputation. *Silent Spring* is, however, the most famous of her works and provoked considerable opposition from the pesticide industry and its allies in the federal and state agriculture departments. *Silent Spring* was symptomatic of the central concerns of the new environmentalism because the book made a direct connection between amenity and health (Lear, 1993, 1997). Carson stressed the "direct killing of birds, mammals, fishes, and indeed practically every form of wildlife by chemical insecticides indiscriminately sprayed on the land" (Carson, 1962, p. 70). Pesticides were not selective and were used repetitively, affecting harmless wildlife that, she argued, enriched life by merely being there.

Carson's critique was on the mark. The aerial spraying of pesticides was increasing rapidly. In one case, some 27,000 acres of southern Michigan, including many suburbs of Detroit, were heavily dusted from the air in the fall of 1959 by pellets of aldrin, one of the most dangerous of the chlorinated hydrocarbons. The program was conducted by the Michigan Department of Agriculture with USDA cooperation to control the Japanese beetle. Carson argued that the beetle was not proven to be epidemic in Michigan, and that spraying was unjustified. Much wildlife was destroyed as a result of the spraying, yet little or no funding was available at the time to investigate the impact of the chemicals. Biological control was eschewed as too expensive. Instead, Carson persuasively argued, a chemical fix was adopted that fitted in with the prestige of "science" and technology. Related to this was an arrogant anti-democratic thrust in the bureaucracy, which had seen cozy relationships develop between large-scale farmers, the Department of Agriculture, and the pesticide industry. The bureaucrats seemed, Carson felt, to be keeping information from the people, and telling them that the chemicals were safe. Carson linked such episodes to the new ecological consciousness that Hays has subsequently analyzed. "The question is," stated Carson, "whether any civilization can wage relentless war on life without destroying itself, and without losing the right to be called civilized" (Carson, 1962, p. 82; Hays, 1987).

Carson raised an important set of questions that continues to define modern environmentalism. Human-generated pollution had changed from organic to synthesized contaminants that would not break down easily, but rather accumulated in the food chain, ultimately affecting humans. Human health, therefore, became a major reason for supporting environmentalism. Carson showed that Americans might be destroying themselves as well as the environment around them. Her work coincided with a rise of concern with cancer, stimulated by the fact that the incidence of cancer was itself increasing as more of the American population lived longer with improved public health measures, and as chemical contaminants grew in number. By the late 1970s, one-quarter of all living Americans would contract cancer and two-thirds of these would die from it (Hays, 1987; Proctor, 1995).

Nuclear Issues

Carson might not have been so effective if she had been unable to tap into the wider sense of community alarm concerning atomic power. The danger of nuclear war as well as the reality of nuclear testing raised public concern, as did pesticide abuse. Both pesticides and nuclear waste signified humanity's growing deleterious impact on nature. In fact, Carson herself drew the analogy with nuclear fallout, arguing for parallel contamination of the environment threatening human existence (Lear, 1997, pp. 373–5). Above-ground nuclear testing was already proving a danger. After a test in Nevada in 1953, fallout spread over the Northeast and was detected in a Troy, New York, rainstorm. In 1954, hydrogen bomb test fallout killed crewmen of a Japanese fishing boat in the Pacific; and in 1957, American Atomic Energy Commission (AEC) testing at Nevada exposed troops to radiation. Environmentalist Barry Commoner said "the AEC turned me into an ecologist" (Strong, 1996, p. 100). Commoner's work, often obscured by historians' attention to Carson, has recently been well documented by Douglas Strong (1996). In 1956, Commoner provided information on nuclear fallout to Adlai Stevenson for his presidential campaign, and initiated a petition to protest nuclear testing. In 1958, Commoner formed the St. Louis Committee for Nuclear Information, which showed strontium-90 to be present in baby teeth. The efforts of scientists and citizens such as those in Commoner's group helped produce the climate of opinion leading to the nuclear test ban treaty of 1963 in which the United States, Soviet Union, and Britain agreed to stop above-ground testing. The achievement of an international treaty (China did not sign) partially blunted the force of the campaign against testing, though nuclear issues continued in the form of grassroots campaigning against nuclear power plants.

Anti-nuclear power activities were of immediate relevance to the burgeoning environmental movement. The crusade against the Diablo Canyon reactor was not successful, but California's anti-nuclear protests were paradigmatic of a shift in values that, as Thomas Wellock argues, "allowed the environmental movement to transcend traditional wilderness" advocacy and draw on a broader, popular coalition including consumer, student, and other social protest movements (Wellock, 1998, p. 5). Anti-nuclear activists such as Commoner became concerned in the 1970s with wider issues of pollution and with the wasteful use of energy characterized by the high-consumption US economy. Americans had, Commoner reflected, broken out of "the circle of life" (Commoner, 1971; Strong, 1996).

Such individual activists could not have been effective without the mobilization of larger numbers of people in environmental organizations. Environmentalism became part of the new social movements of the 1960s and 1970s. Some of the key organizations were far from new, but new groups included Friends of the Earth, a breakaway from the Sierra Club concerned with conservation and preservation issues. Gallup polls showed concern with environmental issues rising to a majority position by the early 1970s, symbolized by the observance of Earth Day (1970). This single event is often taken to be the high point of environmental influence. Certainly, environmental causes were boosted by the social ferment of the Vietnam War period, just as feminism was; a back-to-the land ethic among hippies won much media coverage, yet equally difficult to ignore was the spectacle of warfare in Vietnam, with 10 percent of Vietnam defoliated by the American military with the herbicide Agent Orange (2-4-5D and 2-4-5T), and more by bombing (Opie, 1998, pp. 436, 490). Later in the 1970s the impact of Agent Orange on the health of soldiers became a separate issue in American politics, reinforcing the claims from a decade before about the damaging effects of chemical spraying.

In tandem with radical activism came greater federal government regulation in environmental matters. This activity revived ideas of public interest advocacy and consumer protection from the Progressive and New Deal eras, though masked in the concept of environmentalism as a form of middle-class consumerism (Morris, 1988). The Wilderness Act of 1964 and extensions to the national parks system were followed by reforms after 1965 concerned first with urban issues, and then with public health. Emerging from the language of "conservation," from about 1969 one could see these acts directed toward a self-conscious environmental perspective. Among the welter of regulatory measures passed by Congress were the Air Quality Act (1967); Clean Air Act (1970); Water Pollution Control Act (1970); Occupational Safety and Health Act (1970); the Drinking Water Act (1974), establishing federal standards for drinking water; and the Toxic Substances Control Act (1976). Meanwhile, the National Environmental Policy Act (1969) required an ecological impact assessment for any major federal action and the Environmental Protection Agency (EPA) itself was established in 1970 to merge government programs that had been spread across various federal authorities.

These changes in the law shifted environmental argument from torts to administrative control and crossed party and presidential lines through the Johnson, Nixon, Ford, and Carter administrations. Reduction of pollutants as a result of the 1970

EPA Act were dramatic by the 1980s. Emissions of lead declined 95 percent and six major airborne pollutants, including carbon monoxide, declined by one-third from 1970 to 1996 (Kraft, 2000).

The new regulation did not stop all problems; like dike plugging, new gaps in the defense against pollution emerged just as others were covered. Catalytic converters reduced hydrocarbons, but could not deal with rising nitrous oxide levels. The removal of lead from gasoline was accompanied by introduction of carcinogenic additives to provide the contribution to engine performance that lead had supplied. Moreover, some of the most notorious evidence of environmental decline came in the late 1970s and early 1980s as waste management and nuclear issues kept environmental concerns high. In 1978, grassroots environmental activists exposed Love Canal near Niagara Falls as the scene of a major dump of toxic chemicals. Dioxins and polychlorinated biphenyls (PCBs) could affect water supplies, polluting groundwater there and elsewhere. In 1979, the Three Mile Island nuclear alarm in Pennsylvania signaled a downturn in the US nuclear power industry, conveying a persuasive view to the public that nuclear power had little future because of its potential radioactivity and because of the unresolved problem of nuclear waste disposal. The environmental movement had moved beyond mere protest in the 1960s to shape debates and regulations; the late 1970s was the high point in influence, not 1970.

Reaction

Such influence was bound to produce a backlash, particularly since environmentalism now threatened major economic interests and could stymie capitalist growth itself by making industry and consumers cover the true costs of environmental degradation rather than leave them to future generations. The heavy hand of government regulation intended to protect the public interest in basic environmental resources such as air, public lands, and water was now subject to severe criticism from business.

Corporations targeted the Occupational Safety and Health Administration as a promoter of ill-advised and poorly written workplace regulations, and objected to full testing by the Food and Drug Administration of new chemicals prior to release. As Hays points out, "a full-scale assault on the EPA led by the Dow Chemical Company" had begun by 1980 on the grounds that the EPA's scientific procedures and advice were inferior to the company's (Hays, 1987, p. 192). Industry "adamantly" and successfully objected to "premarket testing" and, as a result of lobbying with government, only a limited system of "premarket notification" rather than a full testing of new chemicals was instituted under the Toxic Substances Control Act.

The business reaction was backed by a conservative political revolt over federal control of public lands and over the allegedly restrictive policies of federal land management. The so-called "Sagebrush rebellion" of southwestern state conservatives (1979–81) began in the state legislatures. A variety of interest groups attempted to convince the public that environmentalism threatened the nation's wellbeing, and that management of federal lands should be turned over to the states. The rebellion garnered support from westerners long resentful of federal intrusion, particularly in states such as Utah and Nevada, where the Interior Department was a major landholder. Issues such as President Carter's attempt to site MX missiles in those states

could couple genuine anti-nuclear and other environmental protest with the very different discontents of ranching interests determined to stop protection of wild animals
in federal grazing lands that competed for pasture with cattle and sheep (Glass, 1993).

No doubt, as Jacqueline Switzer (1997) argues, anti-environmentalists were
neither monolithic nor composed simply of corporations, though business interests
did try to fund and coordinate local opposition toward direct agitation against the
growth of the national-state regulatory system. Mining and grazing activities would
benefit from devolution to the states, where land was most likely to be sold off or
leased cheaply to special interests. For business groups, including those in timber and
grazing, it was fortunate that recreational users, snowmobile enthusiasts, hunters, and
farmers could be mobilized to portray the diversity of the backlash (Helvarg, 1994;
Rowell, 1996; Switzer, 1997).

The Sagebrush rebels were allied institutionally and ideologically with the New
Right political and economic agenda advanced by Ronald Reagan and his Interior
Secretary, James Watt; the latter envisioned, Brant Short (1989) explains, a "growth"
economy in which the marketplace dictated how resources would be allocated, and
championed a human-centered view of nature emphasizing economic needs. The
attempted rollback of federal land management and pollution standards of the 1960s
and 1970s raised most publicity, but these were not the only issues tackled. Among
environmentalist causes stalled were some related to global policies. For example, the
Reagan administration attempted in the so-called Mexico City policy of 1984 to stop
aid packages for governments whose family planning policies involved pro-choice
methods. President Clinton reversed this policy in 1993, but the US contribution to
global population control measures – vital to limiting environmental degradation –
had been compromised (Sharpless, 1996).

Environmentalists themselves regrouped in the 1980s and fought the New Right
backlash, which was conveniently symbolized by the wacky extremism of Reagan's
Interior Secretary and his EPA appointee Anne Gorsuch. Watt was a religious fundamentalist (a member of the Assembly of God Church), and accident prone in his
relations with the press. Gorsuch and Watt both lacked wide public support and left
the administration in 1983 after heavy media criticism. The political fallout led to
the reappointment of a more widely respected Republican, William Ruckelshaus, to
head the EPA (he had been the first EPA administrator during the Nixon presidency).
Ruckelshaus stemmed the decline in public confidence and sought to reestablish a
sense of the agency's independence from heavy-handed Republican political and
ideological interference. Later, George Bush (1989–93) promised to be a more
environmentally sound president, and his EPA appointee, William Reilly, initially
improved the Republican record, but the identification of the Republican Party with
an anti-environmentalist "backlash" came back with a vengeance in the early 1990s.
At first Bush softened the administration's regulation of polluters when economic
recession appeared, and then Republican control of Congress after 1994 led to
further attempts to roll back federal environmental regulation as part of the general
attack on big government in the Contract with America.

The Sagebrush rebellion had not been defeated; it had mutated into a more sophisticated and PR-conscious movement known as "Wise Use." Ron Arnold, affiliated
with the Campaign to Defend Free Enterprise and other right-wing causes, adopted
this term first used by Gifford Pinchot many years before, but now wise use included

many questionable practices based on a free-market approach to environmental allocation of resources, rather than the use of expertise, a scientific elite, and bureaucratic management, as conservationists conceived of efficiency conservation in the Progressive era.

Global Issues

Key struggles over national parks, forests, and public lands reflected their importance in American culture as well as the institutional structures of environmental policy-making established in the 1960s. Historians in turn have reflected this national debate and focused on such problems, while they have given relatively little attention to issues of global significance. Environmental problems were not purely national, especially where population pressure and the consumption of resources in advanced industrial economies were concerned. The world population had already reached 3 billion by 1960. Ecologists working with the concept of a "carrying capacity" became alarmed. To the young convert to ecology Paul Ehrlich, humans were not exempt from the natural laws that tied them to the resources available in their ecosystems. Stimulated by the work of Carson on pesticides to consider its implications for population research, and moved by a visit to resource-stretched India, Ehrlich wrote in *The Population Bomb* (1967): "No ecological event in a billion years has posed a threat to terrestrial life comparable to that of human overpopulation." "Hundreds of millions" of people were going to starve to death (quoted in Thompson, 1992, p. 16). The concern was fundamentally external and global, since US growth rates were significantly lower and declining. Ehrlich's book was followed by pessimistic works predicting that the increased number of humans would lead to shortages in basic food and other resources; the Club of Rome commissioned a study published as *The Limits to Growth* in 1973. The team of researchers used computer modeling to project trends in food production, resource use, industrial output, pollution, and population. They predicted that "there would be a catastrophic collapse of population around the year 2025" as resources became scarce (Thompson, 1992, p. 16).

This scenario, commonly though perhaps unfairly caricatured as a doomsday vision, coincided with the fallout from the energy "crisis" of 1973–4. The OPEC oil embargo resulting from the Yom Kippur War showed how the United States could not stand alone from resource shortages. Extended daylight saving, long gasoline queues, and frayed tempers lingered in the memory of those who experienced them, deepening the sense of new environmental limits. To reduce dependence on Arab oil, highway speed limits were lowered, Congress established a federal department of energy in 1977, and President Carter announced new energy policy initiatives.

But Carter's proposals bogged down in Congress with his attempt to raise US oil prices to world levels to stimulate further exploration, while also preventing oil companies from profiteering from the end of price controls on petroleum. The proposed windfall profits tax was particularly contentious with oil producers, but consumers and their representatives in Congress were equally reluctant to accept scarcity. The Energy Act of 1978 and the tax on oil passed in 1980 were not in line with the thinking of environmentalists. Though some tax revenue was put into solar and wind energy projects, the major thrust of Carter's policies was to shift US energy policy back from oil to coal (with potential for more environmentally damaging strip mining), and to encourage fuel switching through a new synthetic-fuel corporation to foster shale oil and other greenhouse gas-producing fuels.

After 1980, however, the international situation allowed the United States to shrug off the energy crises. The policies of the energy-consuming countries became better coordinated under the International Energy Agency, and Japan and France substituted nuclear fuels for oil, reducing demand for the latter; in the United States new oilfields were discovered and prospecting increased offshore. While the supply of fossil fuel energy undermined OPEC prices, the oil-exporting nations bickered among themselves. But in case they did not, US foreign and aid policies encouraged oil producer competition and lobbying against the rise of prices. With the decline of the oil crisis in the 1980s, larger cars became more common again, and ever-higher energy consumption was registered. In 1986, the Reagan administration rolled back the 1978 automobile fuel economy standards. The result was a marked increase in greenhouse gas emissions by the 1990s (Luger, 1995; Russell, 1997).

Doomsayers had not helped the environmental cause tackle energy, population, and other global issues effectively. Environmentalists could be denounced in pop works as neo-Malthusians who were constantly making false predictions. Typical was anti-environmentalist Ronald Bailey, affiliated with the conservative Cato Institute. His *Eco-Scam: The False Prophets of Ecological Apocalypse* repeated claims by others that the media were implicated in a "greenhouse conspiracy" (Bailey, 1993, p. 170). The most widely publicized blunder of the 1980s among environmentalists that could be pilloried by their opponents was Paul Ehrlich's bet with economist Julian Simon that the prices of key metal commodities in world trade would rise due to excessive use. Ehrlich lost his bet, as prices actually declined, not rose as the scarcity model would suggest, and Ehrlich mailed a check to Simon to cover the bet in 1990 (Bailey, 1993). This, along with the failure of the Club of Rome predictions, discredited sections of the environmental movement.

The real problem was not metals, but the more basic issue of energy consumption's environmental impacts. The United States was still consuming in the mid-1990s the largest proportion of the world's resources – about 23 percent of carbon-based energy for 5 percent of the world's population (Abramovitz et al., 1997). The "green revolution" in agriculture touted by Ehrlich's detractors simply displaced the problem of population versus resources to chemical impacts on food crops; though the United States itself was still a bountiful agricultural producer, its surpluses derived from the world's most energy-intensive agriculture, and the returns from increased inputs of fertilizer and fuels were diminishing by the 1990s. The need for a better balance between energy outputs and inputs via more efficient use of energy and restraining of consumption remained the major and largely unacknowledged environmental issue facing the United States (Pimentel and Pimentel, 1996).

International Comparisons

US environmental policies and movements reveal distinctive national features as well as important transnational similarities. Many of the distinctive features are linked to the patterns of the American state structure, rather than to an enduring set of national values concerning environment.

While the Greens entered the European parliament, ultimately becoming part of the German Social Democrat government coalition in 1998, the United States lacked strong Green political party institutions. Such parties faced numerous problems in the United States, especially the immense cost of congressional and presidential elections and the entrenched two-party system through first-past-the-post voting and single-member constituencies (Dominick, 1988).

American federalism is sometimes cited as another example of the nation's uniqueness, but the important point for modern environmentalism is the precise division of powers, a division that has been favorable to federal regulation in the American case. Some other countries, most notably Australia, also have federal constitutions and a complex federal/state division, yet the detail was different in each case. In the United States, control of the public lands was in federal hands, whereas in Australia, the states inherited at the time of federation from the self-governing colonies the power over "Crown" lands, the Australian equivalent. Thus environmental policy was more fragmented by federalism in Australia. In the United States, public lands were a major source of federal government power over environmental issues of mining and other aspects of land use. This power was mostly concentrated in the states west of the Mississippi, because it was there that the remaining public lands were located. By the same token, the strong presence of the federal state backed by environmental groups fueled the reaction in the rhetoric of states' rights. Longstanding western antipathies toward Washington were important sources of the anti-environmental backlash in the United States after 1980.

US isolationism in international environmental diplomacy was more telling than its federalism. Along with the United Kingdom and Poland, the United States did not sign in 1985 the Helsinki protocols limiting sulfur emissions; and it refused to agree in 1992 at the UN conference in Rio with the Biodiversity Convention. Though the latter agreement was ratified by over 150 countries, the Bush administration announced that if the United States joined, the activities of the fledgling biotechnology industry would be unduly limited. The Clinton administration reversed this position but the treaty remained unratified by the Senate (Elliott, 1998, p. 79; Vogel, 2000). Isolationist policies of this type partly reflected the separation of executive and legislative powers, and therefore the difficulties in getting international treaties ratified by Congress. But isolationism also registered the relative international freedom of the United States, as the only remaining superpower, to resist limits to its sovereignty over environmental matters (Moltke and Rahman, 1996).

But where US trade interests have been advantaged, the US government has strongly supported an international regime potentially inimical to global environmental quality. The United States' post-World War II push toward free trade, enshrined in the General Agreement on Tariffs and Trade (Uruguay round) leading to the establishment of the World Trade Organization (WTO) was potentially anti-environmental, many environmentalists argued, when the WTO encouraged a larger trade in forest products. In the case of quarantine, too, WTO rules tended to favor free trade over environment.

Roderick Nash has depicted concern with wilderness as a distinctive feature of "the American mind" (Nash, 1985; Morris, 1988; Cronon, 1996). Similarly, for English commentator Peter Coates, wilderness "still occupies a special, elevated position in the agenda of (American) environmentalists." Much of the rationale went back to the late nineteenth century when old-stock Americans feared new European immigrants, lamented the rise of the cities, and sought to reinvigorate pioneer values (Coates, 1989, p. 444). It is true that Americans' self-conception remained important in what people thought constituted the "environmental," especially the intellectual and spiritual values inherent in national parks and wilderness. Earth First!, the radical environmental group founded by Dave Foreman and accused by some of being "eco-terrorist," was a modern example of the high valuation given to nature for its own sake. A quasi-religious and Romantic attitude to wilderness consonant with the stereotype of American difference can be detected among some such deep ecologists. Yet wilderness has not been a purely American preoccupation, but one shared by Europeans in their encounters with Australasia and the Americas, as well as with Africa. On the other hand, a good many authorities agree with Thomas Dunlap (1999) that the ways in which wilderness has been perceived suggest national differences. These possible differences (and similarities) should be the subject of further research.

Class tends to be obscured in these American debates. Though good studies of class environmental issues are now becoming available, little attention has been paid to the social geography of pollution. As Andrew Hurley (1988, 1995) has shown for Gary, Indiana, "the age of ecology" since 1945 "coincided with changing forms of environmental degradation that discriminated along racial and class lines." Blacks fared badly in this hierarchy in experiencing "the worst consequences of industry's air, water and land use." As Carl Anthony (1994) reports, there has been little contact between middle-class and largely white environmentalist groups on the one hand, and the problems of the ghettoes on the other. By the 1990s the need for the environmental movement to consider social justice issues was becoming unavoidable and reflected in scholarship.

Ultimately, modern environmentalism must forge links with wider segments of the American public in a more hard-nosed era than the 1960s, which saw the movement's flowering. Environmentalism has implications for the struggle over resources on a global level, and if it does not speak to these issues, it may be sidelined and typecast as elitist and anti-growth. There is no sign yet that the American movement can regain the momentum of the 1970s, though the diverse history of environmentalism in the United States provides many ideas and institutions with which to forge a renewed identity for the early part of the new century and a new millennium.

REFERENCES

Abramovitz, Janet N. et al.: *State of the World, 1997: A Worldwatch Institute Report on Progress Toward a Sustainable Society* (New York: W. W. Norton, 1997).

Anthony, Carl: "Carl Anthony Explains Why African-Americans Should Be Environmentalists," in Carolyn Merchant (ed.), *Major Problems in American Environmental History* (Lexington, Mass.: D. C. Heath, 1994), 542–4.

Bailey, Ron: *Eco-Scam: The False Prophets of Ecological Apocalypse* (New York: St. Martin's, 1993).

Boston, Charlotte, ed.: *Yosemite and the Sierra Nevada: Photographs by Ansel Adams: Selections from the Works of John Muir* (Boston: Houghton Mifflin, 1948).

Callicott, J. Baird: "Wilderness Values Revisited: The Sustainable Development Alternative," *Environmental Professional*, 13 (1991): 236–45.

Carson, Rachel: *Silent Spring* (1962; London: Hamish Hamilton, 1963).

Coates, Peter A.: "'Support Your Right to Bear Arms (and Peccadillos)': The Higher Ground and Further Shores of American Environmentalism," *Journal of American Studies*, 23 (1989): 439–46.

Commoner, Barry: *The Closing Circle: Nature, Man, and Technology* (New York: Alfred A. Knopf, 1971).

Cronon, William: "The Trouble With Wilderness; Or, Getting Back to the Wrong Nature," *Environmental History*, 1 (1996): 7–28.

Dominick, Raymond: "The Roots of the Green Movement in the United States and West Germany," *Environmental Review*, 12 (Fall 1988): 1–30.

Dunlap, Thomas: *DDT: Scientists, Citizens, and Public Policy* (Princeton, NJ: Princeton University Press, 1978).

Dunlap, Thomas: *Nature and the English Diaspora: Environment and History in the United States, Canada, Australia, and New Zealand* (New York: Cambridge University Press, 1999).

Elliott, Lorraine: *The Global Politics of the Environment* (Basingstoke: Macmillan, 1998).

Glass, Matthew: *Citizens Against the MX: Public Languages in the Nuclear Age* (Urbana: University of Illinois Press, 1993).

Hays, Samuel P.: *Conservation and the Gospel of Efficiency: The Progressive Conservation Movement, 1890–1920* (Cambridge, Mass.: Harvard University Press, 1959).

Hays, Samuel P.: "Comment: The Trouble With Bill Cronon's Wilderness," *Environmental History*, 1 (1996): 29–32.

Hays, Samuel P., in collaboration with Barbara D. Hays: *Beauty, Health, and Permanence: Environmental Politics in the United States, 1955–1985* (New York: Cambridge University Press, 1987).

Helvarg, David: *The War Against the Greens: The "Wise Use" Movement, the New Right, and Anti-Environmental Violence* (San Francisco: Sierra Club, 1994).

Hurley, Andrew: "The Social Bases of Environmental Change in Gary, Indiana, 1945–1980," *Environmental Review*, 12 (Winter 1988): 1–19.

Hurley, Andrew: *Environmental Inequalities: Class, Race, and Industrial Pollution in Gary, Indiana, 1945–1980* (Chapel Hill: University of North Carolina Press, 1995).

Kraft, Michael E.: "U.S. Environmental Policy and Politics: From the 1960s to the 1990s," *Journal of Policy History*, 12 (2000): 17–42.

Lear, Linda: "Rachel Carson's 'Silent Spring,'" *Environmental History Review*, 17 (1993): 23–48.

Lear, Linda: *Rachel Carson: Witness for Nature* (New York: Henry Holt, 1997).

Luger, Stan: "Market Ideology and Administrative Fiat: The Rollback of Automobile Fuel Economy Standards," *Environmental History Review*, 19 (1995): 77–93.

McEvoy, Arthur F.: *The Fisherman's Problem: Ecology and Law in the California Fisheries, 1850–1980* (New York: Cambridge University Press, 1986).

Melosi, Martin J.: "Environmental Justice, Political Agenda Setting, and the Myths of History," *Journal of Policy History*, 12 (2000): 43–71.

Miles, John C.: *Guardians of the Parks: A History of the National Parks and Conservation Association* (Washington, DC: Taylor and Francis, 1995).

Moltke, Konrad von and Rahman, Atiq: "External Perspectives on Climate Change: A View from the United States and the Third World," in Tim O'Riordan and Jill Jager (eds.), *Politics of Climate Change: A European Perspective* (New York: Routledge, 1996), 330–42.

Morris, Desmond J. S.: "'Help Keep the Peccadillo Alive': American Environmental Politics," *Journal of American Studies*, 22 (1988): 447–55.

Morris, Desmond J. S.: "'Help Keep the Peccadillo Alive': American Environmental Politics: A Rejoinder," *Journal of American Studies*, 23 (1989): 446.

Muir, John: "John Muir Advocates Wilderness Preservation" (1912), in Carolyn Merchant (ed.), *Major Problems in American Environmental History* (Lexington, Mass.: D. C. Heath, 1994), 391–4.

Nash, Roderick: *Wilderness and the American Mind* (New Haven, Conn.: Yale University Press, 1967; 3rd rev. ed. 1985).

Opie, John F.: *Nature's Nation: An Environmental History of the United States* (Fort Worth, Tex.: Harcourt Brace College Publishers, 1998).

Pimentel, David and Pimentel, Marcia, eds.: *Food, Energy, and Society,* rev. ed. (Niwot: University Press of Colorado, 1996).

Pinchot, Gifford: *Breaking New Ground* (New York: Harcourt Brace, 1947).

Proctor, Robert: *Cancer Wars: How Politics Shapes What We Know and Don't Know About Cancer* (New York: Basic Books, 1995).

Rome, Adam: *The Bulldozer in the Countryside: Suburban Sprawl and the Rise of American Environmentalism* (New York: Cambridge University Press, 2001).

Rowell, Andrew: *Green Backlash: Global Subversion of the Environmental Movement* (New York: Routledge, 1996).

Runte, Alfred: *National Parks: The American Experience* (Lincoln: University of Nebraska Press, 1979).

Russell, III, Edmund P.: "Lost Among the Parts Per Billion: Ecological Protection at the United States Environmental Agency, 1970–1993," *Environmental History*, 2 (1997): 29–51.

Scheffer, Victor B.: *The Shaping of Environmentalism in America* (Seattle: University of Washington Press, 1991).

Sharpless, John: "World Population Growth, Family Planning, and American Foreign Policy," in Donald T. Critchlow (ed.), *The Politics of Abortion and Birth Control in Historical Perspective* (University Park, Pa.: Penn State University Press, 1996), 103–27.

Short, C. Brant: *Ronald Reagan and the Public Lands: America's Conservation Debate, 1979–1984* (College Station: Texas A&M University Press, 1989).

Stradling, David: *Smokestacks and Progressives: Environmentalists, Engineers, and Air Quality in America, 1881–1951* (Baltimore and London: Johns Hopkins University Press, 1999).

Strong, Douglas: "Barry Commoner and Environmentalism," in Randall Miller and Paul Cimbala (eds.), *American Reform and Reformers: A Biographical Dictionary* (Westport, Conn.: Greenwood Publishers, 1996).

Switzer, Jacqueline Vaughn: *Green Backlash: The History and Politics of Environmental Opposition in the U.S.* (Boulder, Colo.: Lynne Rienner Publishers, 1997).

Tarr, Joel: "The Search for the Ultimate Sink: Urban Air, Land and Water Pollution in Historical Perspective," in Kendall Bailes (ed.), *Environmental History* (Lanham, Md.: University Press of America, 1985), 525–8.

Thompson, Paul: *The Third Revolution: Environment, Population and a Sustainable World* (London: I. B. Tauris, 1992).

Vogel, David: "The Environment and International Trade," *Journal of Policy History*, 12 (2000): 72–100.

Wellock, Thomas R.: *Critical Masses: Opposition to Nuclear Power in California, 1958–1978* (Madison: University of Wisconsin Press, 1998).

PART III

Politics and Foreign Policy

CHAPTER EIGHTEEN

Beyond the Presidential Synthesis: Reordering Political Time

JULIAN E. ZELIZER

In 1948, the historian Thomas Cochran attacked the "presidential synthesis," the prevailing framework that had structured most narratives about the history of the United States. Cochran (1948) pleaded with colleagues to broaden their analysis beyond Washington, DC in order to examine the larger social and economic forces that shaped history, as well as developments at the local level. In most areas of history, Cochran's plea would be answered as social, cultural, and economic historians reconstructed our understanding of the past. Even political historians, who found themselves at the margins of the profession after the 1960s, developed complex interpretations of the revolutionary period and nineteenth centuries that were not centered exclusively on the presidency. But for post-World War II political history, the presidency remained dominant. The last major synthesis of postwar politics continued to place the presidency at the forefront of its story. Not only did presidential administrations mark political time, but the power of the presidency was itself a major theme.

The rise and fall of the presidency from Franklin Roosevelt to Richard Nixon was the central story of a newly formulated liberal presidential synthesis. Whereas historians had often explained politics through presidential administrations as a matter of convenience and familiarity, now the expanding role of the presidency became a central story. Organized around the four- to eight-year timeframes of presidential administrations, mainstream historical narratives centered on the rapid expansion of presidential power after the New Deal. The executive branch, in these accounts, was the engine for liberal domestic and international policy. The creation of the national security state during the Cold War accelerated this trend, as did the growth of domestic programs in the 1960s. Even the Supreme Court was said to reflect the president who appointed its justices (Burns, 1965, p. 316). Just as important, the president was able to dominate television in a fashion that was difficult for other politicians. While the presidency came under fire during Nixon's administration, and Watergate-era reforms in the mid-1970s triggered a resurgence of congressional power in areas such as war-making, historians argued that these reforms were unable to tame presidential power. It was in 1973 that historian Arthur Schlesinger, Jr. coined the phrase that would forever identify this understanding of political history, when he published his landmark book about the "Imperial Presidency."

Shortly after the liberal presidential synthesis crystallized in the 1960s, historians turned away from the study of government elites and institutions. There were few individuals who conducted archival research on the history of postwar political elites, other than those who were developing the existing framework. The recentness of the postwar period also constrained the historical vision of historians. The two generations who have written about postwar politics came of age in a culture that emphasized the presidency, both liberals who exalted Franklin Roosevelt's legacy in the 1950s and New Left scholars who were disillusioned by Lyndon Johnson and Richard Nixon. As a result, the synthesis remained in place and was incorporated into almost every textbook account of modern American history.

Just as historians turned away from political history, political scientists discovered crucial weaknesses in the presidential-centered history. In almost every subfield of political science, scholars found that the power of the presidency remained limited after World War II. In many political science analyses of policymaking, the president appeared as an official who faced enormous institutional constraints. In fact, exaggerated perceptions of executive power often bred frustration as presidents, and those who voted for them, discovered that the policymaking influence of the chief executive remained limited. In this context, Franklin Roosevelt seemed like more of an aberration than a norm. Furthermore, political scientists depicted a policymaking process that did not revolve around individual presidential administrations. This political science research made it clear that the liberal presidential synthesis – both its four- to eight-year timeframes for organizing political history and its emphasis on the expansion of presidential power – needed to be thoroughly reexamined by historians. But given the lack of interest in political elites within the historical profession, mainstream historians have never incorporated the findings of political scientists, resulting in a serious disjunction between historical research and that of political science. The liberal presidential synthesis lingered within the historical profession, more through intellectual inertia than any active defense of the argument.

This disjunction is particularly pertinent today, as historians seek to bring politics back into history. They must avoid blending social and cultural history with outdated narratives about political elites. Traditional political history, largely defined by the liberal presidential synthesis, must be reconceptualized by recognizing and incorporating the findings of political science. This essay begins by restating the basic narrative of the liberal presidential synthesis to revisit the important findings of the last generation of postwar political historians. These works, while providing a much richer understanding of each individual, have downplayed institutional questions about the evolution of the office over time. The essay then examines how political scientists since the 1960s have argued that presidential-centered history does not offer the best way to capture the second half of twentieth-century politics. To move beyond the presidential synthesis, it will be necessary to reorder what political scientist Stephen Skowronek (1993) called political time. Fortunately, an exciting body of interdisciplinary research has offered a solid foundation for historians who want to develop new strategies for writing about government elites and institutions. In the end, a revitalized approach to political history will provide a much richer understanding of the presidency itself.

The Master Narrative

The liberal presidential synthesis flourished in the 1960s, the last time that politics was central to the historical profession. The synthesis presented three views about the presidency: the president was engine of liberal policy; the presidency had grown in power over the course of the twentieth century; and the president was the prime mover in national politics since the New Deal. Characterized as "liberal historians," this generation of historians had ardently supported Franklin Roosevelt's New Deal agenda. Many of them, including Arthur Schlesinger, Jr. and William Leuchtenburg, had even advised Democratic politicians and were members of Americans for Democratic Action, an organization that promoted anti-communism and a progressive domestic agenda. While some of this generation stood farther to the left than others, they all praised Roosevelt for having ushered the nation through its two worst crises without resorting to totalitarianism or socialism. In their view, Roosevelt successfully built federal policies that were grounded in consensual liberal values of individualism and property rights. Their work relied heavily on political scientist Louis Hartz's (1955) argument that liberalism had been the consensual American value since the founding of the nation. Although he had overreached with his court-packing scheme, liberal historians boasted that Roosevelt had tamed the conservative Supreme Court while dragging along a reluctant Congress. On the international front, Roosevelt had forcefully responded to fascism over the opposition of an isolationist Congress. Franklin Roosevelt, in this worldview, embodied the best American politics had to offer (Schlesinger, 1959; Leuchtenburg, 1963). His policies and leadership affirmed that the presidency was now the central institution in contemporary American politics.

Roosevelt's administration served as the linchpin for subsequent accounts about the expansion of presidential power. The growth of presidential power and the triumph of liberalism went hand in hand. Roosevelt's presence in national life was overwhelming. In the 1930s and 1940s, the president had dominated national life in unprecedented style, winning four consecutive elections and achieving an intimate personal connection with citizens. Roosevelt, according to Richard Hofstadter (1955), freed the reform tradition from irrational myths that had influenced populism and progressivism. While his cousin Theodore had elevated the importance of the presidency at the turn of the century, liberal historians agreed it was Franklin who brought the office into its modern form. His fireside chats on radio, for instance, embodied the unprecedented contact he achieved with the electorate. Liberal historians also pointed to key organizational changes Roosevelt had implemented. Even though Congress watered down much of his reorganization proposal by the time it passed in 1939, the president increased the independence of his office with respect to the parties, Congress, Supreme Court, and the rest of the executive branch. But it was during World War II when Roosevelt's impact became undeniable. Defying congressional isolationism, Roosevelt harnessed presidential power to bring the nation into the war against fascism. By overcoming congressional resistance, historians credited Roosevelt for directing the defeat of totalitarianism and crafting a response to Stalinist communism.

Roosevelt's administration set the stage for historical analysis of presidential administrations after World War II. When liberal historians wrote about postwar political history, they presented a succession of presidents who preserved the spirit of New Deal politics (Goldman, 1956; Schlesinger, 1965; Hamby, 1973, 1985; Leuchtenburg, 1983). Although presidential administrations had traditionally been used as the framework through which to organize political time, now the expanding power of the office itself became a crucial focus of scholarly research. Until the 1970s, liberal historians found support from the political science profession (although many scholars straddled both intellectual worlds at this time). Before 1960, political scientists such as Clinton Rossiter (1956) and Edward Corwin (1957) had focused on the constitutional sources of presidential power. In his landmark book, Richard Neustadt (1960) claimed that there were limits to formal power but that skilled presidents could be successful through persuasion. In both cases, the scholarship focused on the preeminent power of the presidency within the political system.

James MacGregor Burns best expressed the spirit of this research with his book, entitled *Presidential Government: The Crucible of Leadership* (1965). Samuel Huntington asserted that "If Congress legislates, it subordinates itself to the President; if it refuses to legislate, it alienates itself from public opinion. Congress can assert its power or it can pass laws; but it cannot do both" (1965, p. 6; see also Polsby, 1964; Fisher, 1972). These scholars were convinced that the public agreed (Rossiter, 1956). Conservative scholars, through a critical analysis, acknowledged that Congress had declined in power since the New Deal. James Burnham (1959) warned that the ideology of "democratism" had shaped twentieth-century politics. Burnham explained that this ideology favored popular sovereignty, as expressed through the president, rather than intermediary institutions such as Congress and the rule of law. Twentieth-century US politics, he added, had also privileged bureaucratic over democratic power.

Importantly, the New Left, even while criticizing Schlesinger, Jr. and his colleagues, adhered to presidential-centered political history. They attacked the liberal presidential synthesis on its own terms, simply interpreting the inhabitants of that office as being less virtuous in their goals. Rather than using the office to protect average citizens, the New Left emphasized that twentieth-century presidents had maintained an unholy alliance with corporate America (Williams, 1959, 1961; Kolko, 1976, 1985; Matusow, 1985). Since conservatives did not have a major impact within the profession during these formative decades, their understanding of these issues remained underdeveloped.

Political historians, working within the liberal presidential synthesis, have stressed that foreign policy was the key arena where presidents usurped constitutional power. The first major expansion of presidential power after Roosevelt occurred between 1947 and 1949. Although Harry Truman did not achieve the prominence of his predecessor, the Cold War necessitated a further extension of presidential influence since the decentralized Congress could not deal with complicated and sensitive foreign policy issues. The process began with the creation of the National Security Council in 1947, a small group that centralized military decisionmaking power in the White House. Truman's subsequent entrance into the Korean War without formal congressional approval proved even more decisive. With the decline of isolationism in these years and the expansion of the military budget, historians suggested that little stood in the way of presidential decisions. Presidents would frequently enter foreign conflicts over the next two decades without receiving formal approval from Congress. Until Vietnam, this process was seen as positive since the presidents universally championed Cold War internationalism. Without a strong presidency, historians suggested, foreign policy would have fallen victim to an isolationist Congress. When recounting efforts to constrain presidential power, historians conveyed a tone of disapproval (Patterson, 1967; Porter, 1980).

Although Eisenhower at first seemed difficult to fit within the synthesis, given his mild demeanor and his initial criticism of the strong presidency, research soon showed this was not the case. Ideologically, Eisenhower forced his party to accept the presidential-centered New Deal state and Cold War internationalism. Just as important, Eisenhower did not reverse the organizational reforms that had strengthened the presidency. Despite his initial opposition to Roosevelt's expansion of the office, he ended up following the same path. For instance, in response to Senator Joseph McCarthy's attacks on executive branch personnel, Eisenhower brought in more officials under the protective privileges enjoyed by the president. Under his leadership, moreover, the size of the presidential staff grew dramatically.

While initial scholarship depicted Eisenhower as a weak leader, archival research revealed that this perception was incorrect (J. Barber, 1992). Political scientist Fred Greenstein (1982) and historian Robert Griffith (1982) both found that behind the scenes, Eisenhower maintained a strong hold on decisionmaking. In what he called the "hidden-hand presidency," Greenstein presented Eisenhower as an effective decisionmaker who maintained control over his cabinet. In foreign policy, historians Blanche Weisen Cook (1981) and Robert Divine (1981) claimed that Eisenhower had significantly advanced the Cold War by improving relations with the Soviet Union while simultaneously launching covert operations in smaller nations such as Iran, Vietnam, and Guatemala. Later archival research revealed that the allegedly "bumbling" Eisenhower was quite shrewd in crafting his relationship with the mass media (Allen, 1993). By 1990, the noted historian Stephen Ambrose confidently proclaimed that Dwight Eisenhower had been "one of the outstanding leaders of the Western world in this century" (1990, p. 11).

While the 1940s and 1950s witnessed the incremental growth of presidential power, the 1960s brought the second "big bang" (the first being the combined impact of the New Deal and World War II). "The imperial Presidency, born in the 1940s and 1950s to save the outer world from perdition," Schlesinger wrote, "thus began in the 1960s and 1970s to find nurture at home" (1973, p. 212). John Kennedy began by shifting the agenda to a more aggressive Cold War posture and launching new domestic initiatives on poverty, education, healthcare, civil rights, and the economy. In the same fashion that Eisenhower dominated public opinion because of his military service and affable personality, Kennedy enchanted the nation through his charisma and royalty-like stature. Although liberals and the New Left acknowledged that Kennedy accomplished little in domestic policy, he was credited with elevating the issues that dominated the rest of the decade. Moreover, historians pointed to his seminal confrontations with the Soviet Union, particularly the Cuban Missile Crisis of 1962, and his acceleration of US military participation in Vietnam.

If anyone doubted the centrality of the presidency under Kennedy, those feelings evaporated with Lyndon Johnson, whose larger-than-life persona seemed to overwhelm national life. "Johnson left huge footprints wherever he stepped," the historian Bruce Shulman has written, "overwhelming nearly everyone who crossed his path and achieving more than nearly any other American politician" (1995, p. 2). Since Republican presidential candidate Barry Goldwater had attacked the presidency as excessively strong, James Burns believed that Goldwater's decisive defeat in 1964 was a "historic validation both of the interlaced purpose of American domestic and foreign policy and the role of the Presidency in achieving that purpose." Burns concluded that "the power and paradox of the Presidency have reached a new peak in the administration of Lyndon B. Johnson. . . . More than ever the White House is a command post for economic, political, diplomatic, and military combat" (1965, pp. 277, 312–13). After winning the 1964 election, Johnson intensified the war in Vietnam through the Gulf of Tonkin Resolution, which allowed him to send more troops into the region without obtaining a congressional declaration of war. At the same time, Johnson's Great Society included important legislation such as Medicare and the Voting Rights Act. While Vietnam was disastrous to the War on Poverty, mainstream accounts stressed that Johnson was his own worst enemy. It was Johnson's brashness and decision to expand the Vietnam War that undermined his own agenda. Revealingly, student activists of the period condemned "Johnson's War," highlighting the grip that the presidency held on the public psyche. It seemed, explained Godfrey Hodgson, that liberals in the 1950s and 1960s had placed an impossible "burden on the institution on which the consensus had counted to carry out that program, and to which everyone turned to put things right when it became apparent that they were going wrong: the presidency" (1976, p. 492).

The liberal presidential synthesis culminated with Richard Nixon's downfall in 1974. Until the 1970s, liberal historians had presented the expansion of presidential power as a positive development. But Nixon revealed the dangerous side of Roosevelt's legacy. Suddenly, the cost of excessive presidential power became evident. Whereas the Imperial Presidency had facilitated unprecedented innovations in domestic policies and Cold War internationalism, Nixon revealed that the office could easily be used toward malicious ends. It was during these years that books and articles began to note the darker side of presidential power (see, for example, Reedy, 1970). Nixon began his presidency by reorganizing the executive branch so that he could circumvent the federal bureaucracy; he used informal channels to assert the type of control that eluded earlier presidents (Nathan, 1975; Patterson, 1996). As the Watergate investigations later revealed, the president carried these activities much further than anyone ever imagined. Nixon had used the FBI and IRS to investigate opponents, his staff broke into opposition headquarters, and his administration exchanged favorable policy decisions for large campaign contributions. Nixon's secret war in Cambodia and his impoundment of budgetary spending offered the strongest evidence that the office had become too powerful. The constitutional separation of power had almost vanished as the president was dominant. Schlesinger opened his landmark book with an apology of sorts: "It must be said that historians and political scientists, this writer among them, contributed to the rise of the presidential mystique" (1973, p. ix). Watergate encouraged scholars – who still privileged the president as the main storyline in political history – to look back in time at how previous presidents had abused their own power (Pyle, 1974; Theoharis, 1971, 1978). Lyndon Johnson, for example, became a favorite target of these works, with scholars depicting a ruthless and tyrannical Texan who had committed equally disgraceful abuses throughout his political career (Caro, 1982, 1990). The only difference between the two presidents, some books suggested, was that Congress caught Nixon.

President Nixon inspired Congress to reclaim its constitutional power. In response to Nixon's abuses, Congress increased its strength through the War Powers Act, oversight laws, the legislative veto, and budget reform (Sundquist, 1981; Fisher, 1998;

Mann, 2001). The War Powers Act of 1973 granted Congress improved authority to terminate war, while the Congressional Budget and Impoundment Act of 1974 limited presidential impoundments and centralized the legislative budget-making process. Although Nixon resigned before Congress could remove him from office, the House Judiciary Committee's impeachment proceedings represented the ultimate reassertion of congressional power. Furthermore, the Ethics in Government Act of 1978, which created the Office of the Independent Prosecutor to investigate potential wrongdoing by the executive branch, indicated that Congress had institutionally weakened the presidency. At the same time that Congress reasserted its power, the Warren Court completed a two-decade campaign that elevated the Supreme Court as an extremely powerful force in shaping policy. By Congress and the Supreme Court both acting more assertively, it seemed that the Imperial Presidency had been tamed. If anything, the reversal had gone too far. One scholar warned regarding the president's power to enter into foreign war after 1973: "While we cannot have rules which permit a stamp of constitutional approval on what Roosevelt felt was necessary, neither can our democracy survive by adopting rules which assume that every president is a Nixon" (Redlich, 1981, p. 294).

It soon became clear in updated versions of the liberal presidential synthesis, however, that the office remained strong despite Watergate. For instance, Schlesinger posited that congressional resurgence had been more of a blip than a transformation: "The indestructibility of the Presidency was demonstrated in the very years when political scientists were pronouncing presidential government as illusion. . . . Whatever else may be said about Ronald Reagan, he quickly showed that the reports of the death of the Presidency were greatly exaggerated" (1986, pp. 288, 293). Although presidential power did not return to the condition of the Roosevelt or Johnson years, it remained the preeminent political force. During the 1980s, Reagan demonstrated that the office could be used as a political battering ram. As a public official, Reagan's direct connection to citizens seemed to rival that of Franklin Roosevelt. Continuing along the path that started after World War II, Reagan's administration turned to covert warfare to pursue its Cold War agenda, over the explicit opposition of Congress. He also reorganized the Office of Management and Budget so that it could be used to curtail domestic programs such as environmental regulation (Hays, 1987). Furthermore, changes in the political process seemed to favor the president. The primacy of television as the medium of political communication, along with the decline of political parties, made presidents more prominent. Party reforms in the 1970s weakened the influence of parties in the candidate-selection process. Now the president carried his message directly to the people (Shafer, 1983). Jimmy Carter proved this to be true during the 1976 campaign when he traveled around the country to meet with news reporters rather than party bosses.

The liberal presidential synthesis, as outlined here, has proved to be remarkably durable. Liberals and New Left historians could at least agree on the expanding power of the presidency. Social and cultural historians, less interested in politics, drew on this synthesis since it was the most comprehensive and compelling account that was available. By organizing American political history around each successive administration and focusing on the expanding size of presidential power, our understanding of "traditional political history" has been shaped by this school of research. Shortly after the 2000 presidential election, popular historian Michael Beschloss published a piece for the *New York Times*, "The End of the Imperial Presidency," that repeated the 1960s traditional narrative of modern US history without qualification. He wrote: "The grand age of presidential power began in the 1930's with Franklin Roosevelt and started to decline in the early 1970's with Richard Nixon. Although presidential power has been slipping for some time, whoever was elected the 43rd president would have been the first leader to govern fully out of the wake of the imperial age" (2000, p. 27; see also Leuchtenburg, 2001). A glimpse at most high school or college textbooks (in an age when many textbooks pay little attention to politics) reveals the staying power of this narrative. Texts still rely on the presidential synthesis when dealing with government elites and institutions (see, for example, Blum et al., 1989; Brinkley and Fitzpatrick, 1997; Goldfield et al., 1998; Gillon and Matson, 2001). Presidents in these texts are usually depicted as free-floating individuals picking and choosing between the policies they want to promote. Individual presidents set the agenda and dictate the themes of government. Even while admitting that presidents lost many key battles, the liberal presidential synthesis has devoted little rigorous analysis to the forces that constrained the president. Just as important, they present the president's agenda at the center of these battles.

The soundness of the liberal presidential synthesis was not evaluated because political history – defined as the study of political elites and government institutions – became unpopular with the baby boom generation in the 1970s and 1980s (Leuchtenburg, 1986; Leff, 1995). This generation criticized "traditional" political history as elitist and irrelevant, claiming that the actions of political leaders did not reflect the experience of most Americans. Moreover, they claimed that true power rested in social relations. In this intellectual context, the social history revolution swept through the profession, and emphasized history from the "bottom up." When historians wrote about politics, they focused on grassroots social movements, contestations over race, ethnicity, class, and gender, and the social impact of policies. The "new political historians" of the 1970s focused on quantifying voting behavior in the nineteenth century (Kleppner, 1970; P. Baker, 1993).

As a result of the "bottom-up" focus in the mainstream historical profession, the history of postwar political elites was locked into the liberal presidential synthesis. For the next generation, "traditional" political history would be defined as presidential-centered history with an emphasis on the expanding power of the office.

Assessing Individual Presidents

Before examining what political scientists have said about presidential power, it is important to discuss the voluminous literature on individual presidencies. While these seminal historical works have greatly advanced our understanding of each individual president, and most of these books actually offer evidence that the policymaking process was more complex than the liberal presidential synthesis indicates, they have not produced a new framework for understanding the history of government elites and institutions. Each administration is treated as distinct in these books, while the presidents themselves are presented as the prime movers in elite politics. Other actors enter the story briefly only as they impact the administration being studied. Rarely are external forces given sustained analysis.

Focusing on each president, rather than on the evolution of the presidency, presidential history since the 1960s has centered on gauging whether individuals were "strong" or "weak" leaders and if they were "liberal" or "conservative." Historiographical debates, for example, have focused on whether Truman was an ineffective "closet conservative" or a true heir to Roosevelt who pushed forward New Deal liberalism (Hamby, 1973, 1989; McCullough, 1992; Ferrell, 1996). Kennedy has been a popular subject. Critics have asserted that Kennedy attempted to protect corporate interests and ward off radical changes in civil rights (Heath, 1975; Miroff, 1976; Shank, 1980; Parmet, 1983). Sympathetic accounts insist that Kennedy was truly committed to the liberal agenda and that he accomplished a great deal, even though he often found himself frustrated by conservative opponents (Schlesinger, 1965; Bernstein, 1991; Reeves, 1993). A similar view shaped the first scholarly assessment of Carter's presidency (Fink and Graham, 1998).

With Eisenhower, the focus of presidential history moved in the opposite direction. Scholars have tried to show the conservative bent of the president, particularly in his battles with Democrats over the budget, to counteract claims that he was nothing more than a Republican New Dealer (Morgan, 1990). In contrast to those who stressed comparisons with Franklin Roosevelt, Ambrose traced the conservatism of the 1980s directly back to Eisenhower, particularly with respect to defense, the budget, and anti-communism (Ambrose, 1990).

Research on Lyndon Johnson and Richard Nixon has been less concerned with their forcefulness as leaders, instead focusing exclusively on the underlying nature of their agenda. Studies about President Johnson have weighed his commitment to the Great Society against his enthusiasm or ambivalence about Vietnam (Sherrill, 1967; VanDeMark, 1991; Bernstein, 1996; Dallek, 1998). His 1968 decision to cut "butter" (Great Society) in favor of "guns" (Vietnam) haunts his legacy. Some studies, for example, suggest that he was dragged into the war by national military ideologies and interests despite strong reservations (Dallek, 1998). Others argue that from the start Johnson chose war over viable negotiation (Logevall, 1999). A few scholars have been interested in locating the origins of Johnson's commitment to the poor and African Americans (Kearns, 1976).

Most work on Richard Nixon has probed the details of Watergate (Kutler, 1990). Given that the crisis was so traumatic, scholars set out to determine the details of Nixon's wrongdoing, often to determine whether his actions were exceptional or rooted in the structure of political institutions (Schudson, 1992). But studies eventually turned to other aspects of Nixon's administration besides Watergate (Ambrose, 1987). Recent historiographical debates on Nixon have addressed his policy contributions as president. Revisionists such as historian Joan Hoff (1994) have asserted that Nixon was an innovator in domestic policy, as evidenced in the new federalism, affirmative action, welfare reform, and Social Security indexation. On the international front, Nixon has been credited with helping to improve relations with both China and the Soviet Union.

Research on individual presidencies has thus fit easily within the liberal presidential synthesis. Presidents established the agenda (even though they could not always pass desired legislation), they were the focus of political history, and political time was organized around each administration. Institutions such as Congress, the courts, interest groups, and the media have not been studied in as much depth, nor have they been integrated into the organization of scholarly narratives. Nonpresidential institutions appear as the supporting cast to the leads of a movie; otherwise, they are treated as outliers and roadblocks.

Political Science and the Presidency

Because of the "bottom-up" direction taken by historians since the 1970s, the profession has paid little attention to how political scientists have analyzed the presidency. While political scientists are not in the business of writing historical narratives, their work has collectively poked holes in popular historical accounts of government elites. At a minimum, political scientists have proved the need for substantial archival research to test existing interpretations of postwar elites. If those findings complicate our understanding of the past, there will be a need to reconceptualize the order and structure of political history. This is an enormous challenge given the familiarity of the existing framework and the fact that popular conceptions of politics revolve around presidents.

Since the 1960s, almost every subfield in political science has greatly qualified the power of the postwar presidency. The shift in emphasis arrived like a thunderbolt with Walter Dean Burnham's (1970) realignment synthesis. Burnham argued that America's political parties had been nonprogrammatic and politically timid. As a result, the nation usually experienced incremental politics. However, incremental politics could not handle major changes in the economic and social system such as a depression. The result, Burnham explained, were realigning periods that were ideologically volatile and transformative. Building on the work of V. O. Key and E. E. Schattschneider, Burnham claimed that during "critical elections" in 1800, 1828, 1860, 1896, and 1932, the governing party switched hands as a result of changed voting behavior. The new alignment favored a cluster of policies that seemed to meet the needs of the new voting majority. The arrangement usually dominated national politics for several decades, until the next realignment, with little major change taking place in between. What was most striking about the twentieth century, Burnham concluded, was the decline of partisan participation and identification which made realignments more unlikely. Historical political scientists, and a handful of Progressive-era historians, quickly incorporated this synthesis into their work (Ladd and Hadley, 1975; McCormick, 1981; Sinclair, 1982).

Political scientists who focused on policy analysis were likewise aware of the power Congress and the federal bureaucracy exerted, often independent of presidential desire. During the 1970s, Theodore Marmor (1973), Martha Derthick (1979), and James Sundquist (1968) were among those who developed multicausal accounts of policy development. Derthick argued that experts in the Social Security Administration played the key role in building Social Security between 1935 and 1972. Marmor believed that committee chairmen such as Wilbur Mills (D-AR) played an important role in the formation of Medicare, while Sundquist found that much of the Great Society was promoted by congressional Democrats in the 1950s.

Policy analysts were not alone. Within the American Political Science Association, behavioralist scholars examined congressional leadership through participant observation. They found that Congress played a seminal role in policymaking. Richard Fenno (1973), Randall Ripley (1969), and John Manley (1970) were among those interested in how institutional norms shaped the behavior of individual legislators. These books, particularly those focusing on the revenue committees, demonstrated that committee chairmen retained a tight grip on policymaking between the 1940s and 1970s. While Congress as an institution appeared fragmented, chaotic, and decentralized, the books portrayed committee chairmen as exercising enormous influence in policymaking. Arguing that the postwar Congress had initiated many key policies such as environmental protection, Gary Orfield (1975) criticized colleagues who dismissed Congress as "unresponsive." He warned that "it often turns out that the author uncritically assumes either that the President's program actually reflects national needs, or that Congress should respond to the author's own implicit or explicit beliefs about what the primary national needs are. In fact, these goals espoused by the critics may have little or no relationship to the real desires of the local or national public constituency" (1975, p. 20). In a recent book emphasizing the active role of congressional entrepreneurs, political scientist David Mayhew noted: "it is a fair question whether the 1930s, at least as an epic legislative era, should not be labeled 'the age of Wagner' [referring to Senator Robert Wagner of New York] as much as it is 'the age of Roosevelt' . . . one reading of the significance of the 1932 election might be: It produced a president who would sign Wagner's bills" (2000, pp. 212–13).

Studies about policy implementation, most notably the scholarship of Aaron Wildavsky and Jeffrey Pressman (1984), stressed how the success or failure of policies was only determined after they went into effect at the state and local levels. Political development, in this view, must place substantial emphasis on the implementation stage of policymaking. Here, presidents usually were far less important than in making broad proposals. Theodore Lowi (1969) had also lamented that Congress delegated authority to administrative agencies, which were then "captured" by powerful interest groups. It was in those organizations, Lowi argued, where true power rested.

During the 1980s, political scientists continued to decenter the presidency. Scholarship on agenda-setting, for example, revealed that no single player maintained strong control over the policy agenda (Kingdon, 1984; Polsby, 1984; Baumgartner and Jones, 1993). Instead, their work posited that a myriad of policymakers, inside and outside elected office, promoted issues over long periods of time. Kingdon wrote about the "policy primeval soup" where "many ideas float around, bumping into one another, encountering new ideas, and forming combinations and recombinations" (1984, p. 209). In this analysis, policy communities pushed for, and reconfigured, programs until "focusing events" created a window of opportunity to enact legislation. Policy communities extended well beyond the executive branch. In this model of policymaking, no single institution or policymaker exercised singular control. While vigorous presidential support could create a decisive window of opportunity, other factors had similar effects, including crises, scandals, and strong policy entrepreneurs. During the period that he called policy "incubation," Nelson Polsby explained:

> demand for innovation is built slowly, and specific plans or proposals are typically the work of people relatively far in social, temporal, and sometimes physical distance from ultimate decision-makers: experts and researchers working in universities or in quasi-academic settings, or technical staff employees of interest groups, government agencies, or congressional

committees. Innovations pass through a stage of *incubation*, where political actors – senators, congressmen, lobbyists, or other promoters – take the idea up, reshape it, adapt it to their political needs, publicize it, and put it into the ongoing culture of decision-makers. This culture endures in Washington and in national politics, maintaining an interest in various subject areas from generation to generation and assimilating new participants as they drift into town with the tides of electoral politics. (1984, p. 153)

A dynamic group of political scientists and sociologists in the 1980s developed the subfield of historical institutionalism. While historians ignored political elites, social scientists embraced political history. Led by Stephen Skowronek, Richard Bensel, Ira Katznelson, and Theda Skocpol, these scholars examined how institutions shaped politics over long stretches of time and how new policies reconfigured politics. Concurring that the presidency had significantly expanded its power over the twentieth century, their research simultaneously showed that other institutions maintained a strong hold on the policymaking process. Skowronek's (1982) pathbreaking book on the Progressive era revealed that when the administrative state was created at the turn of the century, Congress and the courts built mechanisms into new programs so that they would maintain power. The result, Skowronek said, was a jerry-built state where Congress, parties, and the courts competed with presidents over control of the policy.

In her work, Skocpol (1992, 1995) found that all political actors, including presidents, were constrained by the institutions within which they operated. Through the concept of policy feedback, Skocpol and others revealed how preexisting policies shaped politics. Focusing on policy retrenchment, rather than expansion, Paul Pierson (1994) concluded that Reagan failed to eliminate key domestic programs because they had created powerful constituencies. Budgetary scholars Eugene Steuerle (1996) and Eric Patashnik (2000) showed that precommitted policies, namely Social Security and Medicare, constituted such a large portion of the budget by the 1980s and 1990s that few politicians could produce dramatic changes in the allocation of federal budgeting. Their work built on the foundation laid by Aaron Wildavsky (1964), whose book stressed the incremental nature of federal budgeting. Through his theory of incrementalism, Wildavsky contended that there were only minor departures each year from the previous budget. Legislators, under pressure from entrenched interests who supported programs, built on the base of the preexisting budget. As a result of incremental politics, there was little dramatic change from year to year in the direction of federal spending despite the rhetoric of campaigns.

Even in the subfield of presidential studies, political scientists challenged the power of the "modern" office. Analyzing the constraints that faced the president has a long tradition in this subfield. In his classic treatise, Richard Neustadt (1960) had warned that the public's expectations of the president were far greater than the resources available to them. Even modern presidents had to overcome an array of external forces if they were to achieve their objectives. Reflecting the optimism of an earlier era, Neustadt believed that individuals could nonetheless overcome these constraints if they were skilled at the power of persuasion. By 2000, Paul Light, initially a strong proponent of the presidential-centered analysis of policymaking, admitted that: "The prevailing wisdom today is that this presidency-centered vision of policy making was an inappropriate reading of both constitutional intent and legislative reality. . . . To expect the president's agenda to remain dominant year after year is to ignore the normal ebb and flow of power built into the very fiber of the federal system" (2000, pp. 109–10; for an earlier argument along these lines, see McConnell, 1967).

Political scientists shifted their attention to the institutional environment that constrained the modern presidency (Shapiro et al., 2000). Tracing the roots of presidential *weakness* back to the New Deal, Sidney Milkis contended that after Roosevelt severed ties between the presidency and the parties, the strength of the office diminished because it lacked a stable base of popular support: "The modern executive that arose from the ashes of traditional parties was hardly imperial, as scholars and pundits frequently asserted by the end of Richard Nixon's ill-fated reign. Put simply, 'modern' presidents bask in the honors of the more powerful and prominent office that emerged from the New Deal, but find themselves navigating a treacherous and lonely path, subject to a volatile political process that makes popular and enduring achievement unlikely" (1993, p. ix; see also Milkis, 1999).

In the subfield of presidential studies, two books were decisive in changing the direction of scholarship. Building on the work of Mark Peterson (1990) and George Edwards (1989), Charles Jones argued that the system of separated power continued to hold sway after the New Deal – the president was never as strong as some scholars had suggested: "The American presidency carries a burden of lofty expectations that are simply not warranted by the political or constitutional basis of the office. . . . The natural inclination is to make the president responsible for policies and political events that no one can claim a legitimate right to control. Presidents are well advised to resist this invitation to assume a position of power as though it conveyed authority" (1994, p. 281; see also Edwards and Wood, 1996). Congress, according to Jones, played an enormous role in shaping the agenda and legislating. Based on extensive historical analysis, Jones found that most presidents defined their agenda through proposals that had gestated for many years. Presidents also were forced to contend with the economic and institutional context they inherited when they crafted their proposals. The book shattered many myths. He rebutted the assumption that high presidential approval ratings translated into legislative success. Truman, for example, had the highest number of proposals enacted in 1946 and 1947, when his popularity was extremely low; Eisenhower, who enjoyed tremendous approval ratings until 1956, experienced a lower rate of passing important legislation than any postwar president (Jones, 1994, pp. 128–9). Through these and other examples, Jones demonstrated how presidents were usually frustrated when they discovered that their power was so limited. Rather than a lament, the book celebrated the separation of power and claimed that it resulted in effective government. He added to Mayhew's (1991) findings that divided government worked effectively in terms of legislative production.

The second major publication in presidential studies during the 1990s came from Stephen Skowronek (1993). Presidents, Skowronek argued, amassed power not just through institutional strength but also through their authority. According to Skowronek, every president since George Washington had gained authority based on his relationship to the established political regime of his time. For example, Truman, Eisenhower, Kennedy, Johnson, Nixon, and Carter all had different relationships to the regime which had been created during the New Deal. Their relationship to the established political regime dictated their success or failure. Skowronek identified four types of presidential leaders: those who practiced the politics of *reconstruction* by creating new regimes and abandoning old commitments; those who practiced the politics of *articulation* by being faithful to the established regime but attempted to make its agenda more relevant to contemporary issues; those who practiced the politics of *disjunction* by remaining affiliated to the established regime while simultaneously insisting that its ideology and interests were no longer useful to the problems of the day; and those who practiced the politics of *preemption* by becoming opposition leaders in resilient regimes. Roosevelt, in this scheme, established a regime around certain policies, ideas, interests, and coalitions that lasted until the 1980s. Except for the few presidents who established a new regime, such as Thomas Jefferson or Franklin Roosevelt, Skowronek claimed that most presidents became frustrated when they discovered it was difficult to move beyond inherited agendas. "Power," Lyndon Johnson once lamented, "The only power I've got is nuclear . . . and I can't use that" (cited in Skowronek, 1993, p. 341). While each president attempted to break free from the past to some extent, few presidents amassed the authority needed to succeed. Moreover, Skowronek argued that the possibility of creating new regimes diminished during the twentieth century as preexisting commitments and thickening institutions left presidents with less room to innovate. Although some scholars still claimed that the president had exceptional influence, they targeted specific stages in the policymaking process. In particular, many continued to argue that presidents wielded unusual power in agenda-setting (McKay, 1989). After that stage of the process, most works agree that the president must share power.

Political science scholarship shows that political historians must seriously modify the presidential-centered synthesis if they are to provide an accurate account of the policymaking process. These subfields of political science have demonstrated that the president remained one player in a larger universe of political actors and that those who held the office confronted significant constraints on their behavior. Just as important, political scientists showed that the policymaking process extended far beyond the timeframe of any specific administration. Indeed, some of the most effective presidents had a strong sense of history, improving their ability to pass legislation if they understood their own place in larger policy streams that had unfolded over decades (May and Neustadt, 1986).

Reorganizing Political Time

If we are to take political scientists seriously, historians will have to reorganize political time during the postwar period and downplay the presidency as the central storyline of synthetic narratives. Skowronek defined "political time" as the "historical medium through which authority structures have recurred" (1993, p. 30). While he focused on the presidency, Skowronek's concept of political time offers a useful starting point for contemplating the chronology of politics. Reordering political time is essential. This type of dramatic reconceptualization will most likely become easier with greater historical perspective. There are several models – which I will call the revised organizational synthesis, political process, political culture, historical institutionalism, political regimes, policy history, and economic eras – that already offer methods to tackle this challenge.

One possibility originates with a group of maverick historians who continued to study politics in spite of the social history revolution. Their work, labeled the "organizational synthesis," directly challenged the presidential-centered understanding of elites. Given the popularity of social and cultural history, few organizational historians found their work published in the *Journal of American History* or the *American Historical Review*, nor was this view reflected in textbooks. Therefore, while the organizational synthesis dates back several decades, its findings have not yet been incorporated into mainstream historical narratives in the same fashion as the presidential synthesis. Building on modernization theory from the social sciences, organizational historians such as Samuel Hays (1957), Robert Wiebe (1967), Alfred Chandler (1977), and Louis Galambos (1970, 1976, 1983) argued that the major force driving change in the twentieth century was the evolution of large-scale national institutions such as the corporation, the professions, and the administrative state. When writing about the federal government, they concentrated on the expansion of the administrative state with its bureaucracies and expert staff. Proponents of the organizational synthesis downplayed the differences between presidential administrations in any single century. Instead, they stressed large-scale structural shifts that occurred when political institutions were transformed. In their view, the structural changes that distinguished nineteenth-century from twentieth-century politics were far more important than any differences between specific administrations. Their analysis did not ignore the presidency but looked at the office in a more complex light. Indeed, the executive branch was still central as the area of government most sympathetic to working with modern economic institutions. Revisionists attempted to bring home this point by highlighting similarities between Hoover and Roosevelt's economic policies. Collapsing the alleged differences between the two administrations, the organizational synthesis aimed to prove that all modern presidents shared certain concerns and relied on common solutions to problems of political economy (Hawley, 1979; W. Barber, 1985). By undermining the perception that the New Deal constituted a "big bang" in politics, this work provided some of the most stimulating scholarship of the last two decades. However, there were problems extending the organizational synthesis to the postwar period. Since the synthesis emphasized the centrality of the years between 1880 and 1920, they downplayed changes later in the century. Moreover, critics felt that the synthesis did not acknowledge historical contingency or resistence to modernization (Balogh, 1991b; Brinkley, 1984).

Nonetheless, some scholars brought the organizational synthesis into the modern era, while avoiding the air of inevitability that characterized initial scholarship. In fact, the best research has applied the framework to the second half of the century, when the nation confronted a series of crises and internal upheaval. Extending the organizational synthesis to the postwar period forced historians to develop a more complex analysis. In his work on civil rights, Hugh Graham (1990) showed how the civil rights bureaucracy played a pivotal role in the creation and implementation of affirmative action during the late 1960s, as opposed to the grassroots movement that dominated the first part of the decade. Samuel Hays (1987) discovered that both popular culture as well as scientific and legal experts were instrumental in shaping environmental policy after 1955. Brian Balogh (1991a), in a book overflowing with contingency and crisis, carefully traced how professional administrators within the state attempted to build a sizable domestic nuclear power program despite lacking external demand.

The result of this history was a policy that rested on an extremely unstable foundation. With its attention to bureaucracy, experts, and interest-group politics, the revised organizational synthesis has offered an extremely compelling narrative through which to construct American history since World War II that captures the full range of participants.

A second possibility would be to organize political time around changes in the political process. This approach is related to the organizational synthesis in that it emphasizes fundamental shifts in institutional structure. Studying the process has been a successful strategy for those who focus on earlier periods in political history. Most notably, nineteenth-century historians broke with the presidential synthesis by focusing on landmark changes in the way that politics operated. Joel Silbey (1991), for example, has argued that the decades between 1838 and 1893 were marked by continuity based on the primacy of parties (see also J. Baker, 1983; Shafer, 1993; Altschuler and Blumin, 2000; Kornbluh, 2000). Their work marked political time around the evolution of the democratic process. A related approach toward the nineteenth and early twentieth centuries has centered on the relationship between gender and politics. Led by Paula Baker (1984) and Molly Ladd Taylor (1994), these works looked at the existence of two gendered political worlds in the nineteenth century: one male-centered partisan world of electoral politics with voting and party events, and the other female political world that revolved around voluntary associations and social welfare initiatives. By the end of World War I, they argue, these worlds collapsed. In these accounts, individual presidential administrations fade into a larger historical story as attention shifts to the underlying rules that defined political participation at both the elite and mass levels.

A similar process-centered framework could be used for the postwar period. Based on initial scholarship, we already have sketches of seminal moments during which the political process changed. For example, some political scientists have suggested that after the 1970s, criminal investigation, legal prosecution, and scandal became the dominant modes of conducting political warfare as the importance of elections declined (Ginsberg and Shefter, 1990; Garment, 1991). It would be useful to understand how policymaking and public participation differed in each era, or if the differences were as great as these scholars suggest. In my recent work (Zelizer, forthcoming), I highlight changes in Congress during the 1970s when the insulated, committee-based system was replaced by a more porous, scandal-ridden, and partisan-based process. The political impact of changes in the institutional structure of the news media and journalistic ethics, moreover, is an issue that has received scant attention from historians. We will also learn about how presidential strategies were shaped by the evolving process, and how the process impacted the nation's unfolding policy agenda. Another compelling thesis has been put forth by social historians who claim that between the 1960s and 1980s, grassroots social movements played an unprecedented role in shaping the agenda (Chafe, 1998; Wittner, 1998). Although their work has taught us a great deal about the social movements themselves, we know little about the connections between activists and policy outcomes, as well as how grassroots movements turned into interest groups.

Baker's and Ladd Taylor's work on gender is rooted in the third strategy for reorganizing political time: studies on political culture. This scholarship is rooted in cultural studies and anthropology rather than political science. The focus of this research has been to examine how language, discourses, ideology, and symbols shaped all political action in a given period. Resembling studies on political process, scholars of political culture marked political time around key shifts in American's ideological perception about the underlying rules and questions of politics (Kelley, 1989; Sklar, 1995). While examining America's revolutionary period – one of the few eras where political history continued to thrive after the 1970s – landmark studies about culture offered bold analyses of the ideologies and discourses that united the colonists. These linked the founders to European traditions dating back to the Renaissance (Bailyn, 1967; Wood, 1969; Pocock, 1975; McCoy, 1980; Appleby, 1984; Kloppenberg, 1987). Daniel Rodgers's (1998) book on the Progressive era revealed that political ideas about government expansion originated from around the globe, as an international community of experts in Europe responded to the dilemmas of industrialism.

Looking at the political culture of the postwar period, an intriguing question has been how New Deal liberalism declined as a shared ideology and when a new style of conservatism replaced it. The nature of this shift, and the continuities between the eras, are ripe for archival research. There were also deep divisions within the new conservatism that need to be explored (Dionne, 1991). Equally important have been findings of how older ideologies, such as fiscal conservatism, continued to limit domestic and foreign policy (Hogan, 1998; Zelizer, 2000b). But historians are finding a richer story than the familiar ideological competition between conservatism and liberalism. One group of scholars has shown how a psychological-based political culture triumphed in the 1950s and 1960s (Herman, 1995; Scott, 1997). In this view, psychological rhetoric played a pivotal role in debates over policies ranging from Cold War strategy to race relations. An enormous amount of work remains to be completed on the political culture(s) that shaped political actors and citizens. In the end, by looking at the "larger picture," studies on political culture enable historians to integrate presidents with other elites and nonelites.

Historical institutionalism has offered the fourth compelling model, by using the concept of political regimes. These political scientists have argued that regimes defined politics over long stretches of time. Grounded in Burnham's realignment synthesis, they characterize regimes as a complex, albeit distinct, array of legislative coalitions, presidential administrations, grassroots movements, political discourses, and policy clusters. Regimes situate presidents in a much larger constellation of political actors and forces. One of the most notable byproducts of this approach has been a resurgence of scholarly investigation of congressional history. Recent research has shown that Congress played a strong role in the development of postwar policies, ranging from small business regulation, taxation, to foreign affairs (Bean, 1996; Hogan, 1998; Zelizer, 1998; Johnson, 1998–9; Friedberg, 2000). The power of the presidency in relation to the regime, as well as the constraints the president faced as a result of it, become much clearer in this scheme. Scholars have started to study when and why political regimes emerge, collapse, and are replaced by new ones. Thus far, one of the most elaborate versions of this approach has focused on the rise and fall of the New Deal regime (Gerstle and Fraser, 1989; Plotke, 1996). W. Elliot Brownlee (1996), moreover, traced the evolution of a tax regime between 1941 and 1986 that revolved around high progressive rates and extensive tax loopholes.

Building on the institutionalist approach, legal historians have been reminding historians that law has remained integral to politics throughout the twentieth century.

This is a fifth avenue toward a new chronology of postwar American history. Some legal scholars have recently argued that seminal changes in law served as the foundation for the modern state. The most important change that has been examined thus far took place in the late 1930s as the Supreme Court legitimated New Deal institutions and policies. The decision culminated shifts in legal thinking that had been taking place since the Progressive era (Horwitz, 1994; Ackerman, 1998). Focusing on labor policy, Christopher Tomlins (1985) and Karen Orren (1991) have both looked at important developments in law which reconstructed the relationship between business, government, and organized labor during the 1930s. Moreover, Lucas Powe, Jr. (2000) has traced how the Supreme Court under Chief Justice Earl Warren exerted a powerful influence on the 1960s political agenda. But these works are limited in number. Except for civil rights, postwar historians downplayed the law.

Policy history is the sixth strategy for organizing the postwar period. Policy history is a subfield that emerged in the late 1970s largely as a way to apply historical methods to practical policy debates and to reconstruct political history without focusing exclusively on elites (Zelizer, 2000a). In this subfield, it became clear that policies had a life of their own which revolved around the stages of the policymaking process: agenda-setting, legislation, and implementation. These stages usually outlasted any specific presidential administration and did not fit neatly into the standard chronology of political history. Social Security, for example, only became central to American domestic policy between 1950 and 1954, not during the New Deal or 1960s. Unlike many domestic programs, Social Security experienced its period of greatest expansion during the "conservative" decades of the 1970s and 1980s (Berkowitz, 1991). Policy offers an exciting opportunity to break free from traditional conceptions of political time. By focusing on policy, rather than the president, it forces the historian to consider a much larger number of actors and to consider alternative time-frames for their narratives. Delving into the implementation of housing policies in Detroit, for instance, social historian Thomas Sugrue (1996) deftly illustrated how policies were reconfigured around local racial struggles. Since many policies have lasted over the course of the entire postwar period, this style of political history also allows scholars to perceive the larger continuities that shaped that period. It simultaneously provides an avenue for historians to contribute to contemporary policy debates.

The policy history framework does pose challenges. Most important, it will produce a more fragmented account of the postwar period. Policy history requires research into unwieldy communities of policymakers, including policy experts, think tanks, academics, bureaucrats, and congressional committees (see, for example, Balogh, 1991a; Berkowitz, 1995). Nonetheless, the fragmentation must be seen as virtue, not a vice. As the modern state has become more complex, it makes sense that its history will be more multifaceted. In my first book (1998), I focused on the influence of a tax policy community that promoted moderate Keynesian economic policy and contributory social insurance. The community, which lasted from the 1950s through the mid-1970s, was not tied to a particular administration and its membership extended far beyond the executive branch.

Finally, economic historians have brought their own distinct approach to the table. They have shown that economic eras have been pivotal to politics. For example, the period of economic growth between the 1940s and the 1960s sustained the expansion of federal policies, as policymakers found themselves with extra revenue: citizens were automatically brought into higher tax brackets as a result of rising income. Policymakers were thus able to increase benefits without raising taxes. This expanding economy, moreover, dulled sharp class conflict over political economy (Collins, 2000). In his synthesis of the postwar period, James Patterson (1996) added that economic growth created rising expectations that were eventually shattered in the 1970s. These expectations shaped the contours of American political debate. Inflation and stagflation in the 1970s, on the other hand, fundamentally transformed the politics of the next two decades (Bernstein and Adler, 1994). Robert Collins (1996), for example, showed how developments in international monetary policy had a devastating effect on the War on Poverty in the late 1960s by forcing Johnson to take unfavorable actions toward his most favored programs. This type of periodization, based on economic conditions rather than presidential administrations, effectively captures broad continuities that span decades.

There are of course tensions between the different approaches to reorganizing political time. For example, while the regime approach has stressed institutional structure, scholars of the economy have been more concerned with the market context within which politicians and citizens operate. Scholars of political culture, moreover, often come into conflict with the political process literature, which stresses self-interest and institutional rules. But these tensions are healthy. Careful research will help us understand the complex relationship that existed between regimes and the economic context within which they operated, while students of political culture will strengthen their work by relating political culture(s) to a specific institutional and political infrastructure. Historians, who tend to relish multicausal explanations of the past, should be excited, rather than fearful, about the tensions between competing approaches.

These alternative frameworks are only a few of the ways that historians can reorder political time during the postwar period. All of them place greater emphasis on the policymaking process, institutional and economic contexts, and cultural boundaries than the liberal presidential synthesis. This fundamental shift in emphasis is a major intellectual change. In the coming years, as we begin to see the postwar period in greater historical perspective, other frameworks will emerge. We can assume that the president will not appear to be as imperial as once was thought and that there will be a fundamental reorganization of the postwar chronology. Far from abandoning the presidency, this approach will require a new generation of historical investigations that situate the office in its proper social, cultural, economic, and institutional contexts. It is likely that our historical understanding of the presidency itself will become much stronger as a result of this new presentation of time.

Toward a New Political History

As historians seek to revitalize and reconceptualize political history, they need to avoid blending social and cultural history with outdated narratives about political elites. At the center of this project will be a new understanding of the postwar presidency that integrates the research of political scientists. This does not mean that the president should be ignored, nor should the enormous power of the office be downplayed. Rather, we need to understand better how presidents grappled with the environment they inherited. As scholars examine the past through new eyes, narratives on politics will become more fragmented, textured, and multicausal as historians discover inter-related storylines as the state expanded its scope and its infrastructure. Since the postwar period remains historically unconstructed, this project promises unexpected turns and will produce exciting new conceptions of the path that links our past to the future.

REFERENCES

Ackerman, Bruce: *We The People: Transformations*, vol. 2 (Cambridge, Mass.: Belknap Press of Harvard University Press, 1998).

Allen, Craig: *Eisenhower and the Mass Media: Peace, Prosperity, and Prime-Time TV* (Chapel Hill: University of North Carolina Press, 1993).

Altschuler, Glenn C. and Blumin, Stuart M.: *Rude Republic: Americans and Their Politics in the Nineteenth Century* (Princeton, NJ: Princeton University Press, 2000).

Ambrose, Stephen E.: *The Education of a Politician* (New York: Simon and Schuster, 1987).

Ambrose, Stephen E.: *Eisenhower Soldier and President: The Renowned One-Volume Life* (New York: Touchstone, 1990).

Appleby, Joyce: *Capitalism and a New Social Order* (New York: New York University Press, 1984).

Bailyn, Bernard: *The Ideological Origins of the American Revolution* (Cambridge, Mass.: Belknap Press of Harvard University Press, 1967).

Baker, Jean: *Affairs of Party: The Political Culture of Northern Democrats in the Mid-Nineteenth Century* (Ithaca, NY: Cornell University Press, 1983).

Baker, Paula: "The Domestication of Politics: Women and American Political Society, 1780–1920," *American Historical Review*, 89 (1984): 620–47.

Baker, Paula: "A Reply to Byron E. Shafer: Social Science in Political History," *Journal of Policy History*, 5 (1993): 480–4.

Balogh, Brian: *Chain Reaction: Expert Debate and Public Participation in American Commercial Nuclear Power, 1945–1975* (Cambridge: Cambridge University Press, 1991a).

Balogh, Brian: "Reorganizing the Organizational Synthesis: Federal–Professional Relations in Modern America," *Studies in American Political Development*, 5 (1991b): 119–72.

Barber, James D.: *The Presidential Character*, 4th ed. (Upper Saddle River, NJ: Prentice Hall, 1992).

Barber, William J.: *From New Era to New Deal: Herbert Hoover, the Economists, and American Economic Policy, 1921–1933* (Cambridge: Cambridge University Press, 1985).

Baumgartner, Frank R. and Jones, Bryan D.: *Agendas and Instability in American Politics* (Chicago: University of Chicago Press, 1993).

Bean, Jonathan J.: *Beyond the Broker State: Federal Policies Toward Small Business, 1936–1961* (Chapel Hill: University of North Carolina Press, 1996).

Berkowitz, Edward D.: *America's Welfare State: From Roosevelt to Reagan* (Baltimore: Johns Hopkins University Press, 1991).

Berkowitz, Edward D.: *Mr. Social Security: The Life of Wilbur Cohen* (Lawrence: University Press of Kansas, 1995).

Bernstein, Irving: *Promises Kept: John F. Kennedy's New Frontier* (New York: Oxford University Press, 1991).

Bernstein, Irving: *Guns Or Butter: The Presidency of Lyndon Johnson* (New York: Oxford University Press, 1996).

Bernstein, Michael A. and Adler, David E., eds.: *Understanding American Economic Decline* (Cambridge: Cambridge University Press, 1994).

Beschloss, Michael: "The End of the Imperial Presidency," *New York Times* (December 18, 2000): 27.

Blum, John M., McFeely, William S., Morgan, Edmund S., Schlesinger, Jr., Arthur M., Stampp, Kenneth M., and Woodward, C. Vann: *The National Experience: A History of the United States, Part II*, 7th ed. (New York: Harcourt Brace Jovanovich, 1989).

Brinkley, Alan: "Writing the History of Contemporary America: Dilemmas and Challenges," *Daedalus*, 113 (1984): 121–41.

Brinkley, Alan and Fitzpatrick, Ellen: *America in Modern Times* (New York: McGraw Hill, 1997).

Brownlee, W. Elliot: *Federal Taxation in America: A History* (Cambridge: Cambridge University Press, 1996).

Burnham, James: *Congress and the American Tradition* (Chicago: Henry Regnery, 1959).

Burnham, Walter Dean: *Critical Elections and the Mainsprings of American Politics* (New York: W. W. Norton, 1970).

Burns, James MacGregor: *Presidential Government: The Crucible of Leadership* (Boston: Houghton Mifflin, 1965).

Caro, Robert A.: *The Years of Lyndon Johnson* (New York: Alfred A. Knopf, 1982).

Caro, Robert A.: *Means of Ascent: The Lyndon Johnson Years* (New York: Alfred A. Knopf, 1990).

Chafe, William H.: *The Unfinished Journey: America Since World War II*, 4th ed. (New York: Oxford University Press, 1998).

Chandler, Alfred D.: *The Visible Hand: The Managerial Revolution in American Business* (Cambridge, Mass.: Belknap Press of Harvard University Press, 1977).

Cochran, Thomas C.: "The 'Presidential Synthesis' in American History," *American Historical Review*, 53 (1948): 748–59.

Collins, Robert M.: "The Economic Crisis of 1968 and the Waning of the 'American Century,'" *American Historical Review*, 101 (1996): 396–422.

Collins, Robert M.: *More: The Politics of Economic Growth in Postwar America* (New York: Oxford University Press, 2000).

Cook, Blanche Weisen: *The Declassified Eisenhower: A Divided Legacy* (New York: Doubleday, 1981).

Corwin, Edward: *The President and Powers* (New York: New York University Press, 1957).

Dallek, Robert: *Flawed Giant: Lyndon Johnson and His Times, 1961–1973* (New York: Oxford University Press, 1998).

Derthick, Martha: *Policymaking for Social Security* (Washington, DC: Brookings Institution, 1979).

Dionne, Jr., E. J.: *Why Americans Hate Politics* (New York: Touchstone, 1991).

Divine, Robert A.: *Eisenhower and the Cold War* (New York: Oxford University Press, 1981).

Edwards, III, George C.: *At the Margins: Presidential Leadership of Congress* (New Haven, Conn.: Yale University Press, 1989).

Edwards, III, George C.: "Who Influences Whom? The President, Congress, and the Media," *American Political Science Review*, 93 (1996): 327–44.

Fenno, Richard F.: *Congressmen in Committees* (Boston: Little, Brown, 1973).

Ferrell, Robert H.: *Harry S. Truman: A Life* (Columbia: University of Missouri Press, 1996).

Fink, Gary M. and Graham, Hugh Davis, eds.: *The Carter Presidency: Policy Choices in the Post-New Deal Era* (Lawrence: University Press of Kansas, 1998).

Fisher, Louis: *President and Congress: Power and Policy* (New York: Free Press, 1972).

Fisher, Louis: *The Politics of Shared Power: Congress and the Executive*, 4th ed. (College Station: Texas A&M University Press, 1998).

Friedberg, Aaron L.: *In the Shadow of the Garrison State: America's Anti-Statism and Its Cold War Grand Strategy* (Princeton, NJ: Princeton University Press, 2000).

Galambos, Louis: "The Emerging Organizational Synthesis in Modern American History," *Business History Review*, 44 (1970): 279–90.

Galambos, Louis: *America At Middle Age: A New History of the United States in the Twentieth Century* (New York: McGraw Hill, 1976).

Galambos, Louis: "Technology, Political Economy, and Professionalization," *Business History Review*, 57 (1983): 471–93.

Garment, Suzanne: *Scandal: The Culture of Mistrust in American Politics* (New York: Random House, 1991).

Gerstle, Gary and Fraser, Steven, eds.: *The Rise and Fall of the New Deal Order, 1930–1980* (Princeton, NJ: Princeton University Press, 1989).

Gillon, Steve M. and Matson, Cathy D.: *The American Experiment: A History of the United States* (Boston: Houghton Mifflin, 2001).

Ginsberg, Benjamin and Shefter, Martin: *Politics By Other Means: The Declining Importance of Elections in America* (New York: Basic Books, 1990).

Goldfield, David, Abbott, Carl, Anderson, Virginia DeJohn, Argersinger, Jo Anne, Argersinger, Peter H., Barney, William, and Weir, Robert: *The American Journey: A History of the United States* (Upper Saddle River, NJ: Prentice Hall, 1998).

Goldman, Eric: *The Crucial Decade: America, 1945–1955* (New York: Alfred A. Knopf, 1956).

Graham, Hugh Davis: *The Civil Rights Era: Origins and Development of National Policy* (New York: Oxford University Press, 1990).

Greenstein, Fred I.: *The Hidden Hand Presidency: Eisenhower as Leader* (New York: Basic Books, 1982).

Griffith, Robert: "Dwight D. Eisenhower and the Corporate Commonwealth," *American Historical Review*, 87 (1982): 87–122.

Hamby, Alonzo: *Beyond the New Deal: Harry S. Truman and American Liberalism, 1945–1953* (New York: Columbia University Press, 1973).

Hamby, Alonzo: *Liberalism and Its Challengers: F.D.R. to Reagan* (New York: Oxford University Press, 1985).

Hamby, Alonzo: "The Mind and Character of Harry S. Truman," in Michael Lacey (ed.), *The Truman Presidency* (Cambridge: Cambridge University Press and Washington, DC: Woodrow Wilson Center Press, 1989).

Hartz, Louis: *The Liberal Tradition in America* (New York: Harcourt Brace and World, 1955).

Hawley, Ellis: *The Great War and a Search for a Modern Order: A History of the American People and Their Institutions, 1917–1933* (Boston: St. Martin's, 1979).

Hays, Samuel P.: *The Response to Industrialism, 1885–1914* (Chicago: University of Chicago Press, 1957).

Hays, Samuel P., in collaboration with Barbara D. Hays: *Beauty, Health, and Permanence: Environmental Politics in the United States, 1955–1985* (Cambridge: Cambridge University Press, 1987).

Heath, Jim F.: *Decade of Disillusionment: The Kennedy–Johnson Years* (Bloomington: Indiana University Press, 1975).

Herman, Ellen: *Romance of American Psychology: Political Culture in the Age of Experts* (Berkeley: University of California Press, 1995).

Hodgson, Godfrey: *America in Our Time. From World War II to Nixon: What Happened and Why* (New York: Vintage, 1976).

Hoff, Joan: *Nixon Reconsidered* (New York: Basic Books, 1994).

Hofstadter, Richard: *The Age of Reform: From Bryan to F.D.R.* (New York: Vintage, 1955).

Hogan, Michael J.: *A Cross of Iron: Harry S. Truman and the Origins of the National Security State* (Cambridge: Cambridge University Press, 1998).

Horwitz, Morton J.: *The Transformation of American Law 1870–1960: The Crisis of Legal Orthodoxy* (Cambridge, Mass.: Belknap Press of Harvard University Press, 1994).

Huntington, Samuel P.: "Congressional Responses in the Twentieth Century," in David B. Truman (ed.), *The Congress and America's Future* (New York: Prentice Hall, 1965).

Johnson, Robert David: "The Government Operations Committee and Foreign Policy During the Cold War," *Political Science Quarterly*, 113 (1998–9): 645–71.

Jones, Charles O.: *The Presidency in a Separated System* (Washington, DC: Brookings Institution, 1994).

Kearns, Doris: *Lyndon Johnson and the American Dream* (New York: Harper and Row, 1976).

Kelley, Robert: "The Interplay of American Political Culture and Public Policy: The Sacramento River as a Case Study," *Journal of Policy History*, 1 (1989): 1.

Kingdon, John W.: *Agendas, Alternatives, and Public Policies* (Glenview, Ill.: Scott, Foresman, 1984).

Kleppner, Paul: *The Cross of Culture: A Social Analysis of Midwestern Politics, 1850–1900* (New York: Free Press, 1970).

Kloppenberg, James T.: "The Virtues of Liberalism: Christianity, Republicanism, and Ethics in Early American Political Discourse," *Journal of American History*, 74 (1987): 9–33.

Kolko, Gabriel: *Main Currents in Modern American History* (New York: Harper and Row, 1976).

Kolko, Gabriel: *The Triumph of Conservatism: A Re-Interpretation of American History, 1900–1916*, reissue ed. (New York: Free Press, 1985).

Kornbluh, Mark L.: *Why America Stopped Voting: The Decline of Participatory Democracy and the Emergence of Modern American Politics* (New York: New York University Press, 2000).

Kutler, Stanley I.: *The Wars of Watergate: The Last Crisis of Richard Nixon* (New York: Alfred A. Knopf, 1990).

Ladd, Jr., Everett Carll and Hadley, Charles D.: *Transformations of the American Party System: Political Coalitions from the New Deal to the 1970s* (New York: W. W. Norton, 1975).

Ladd Taylor, Molly: *Mother-Work: Women, Child Welfare, and the State, 1890–1930* (Urbana: University of Illinois Press, 1994).

Leff, Mark H.: "Revisioning U.S. Political History," *American Historical Review*, 100 (1995): 829–53.

Leuchtenburg, William E.: *Franklin D. Roosevelt and the New Deal* (New York: Harper and Row, 1963).

Leuchtenburg, William E.: *In the Shadow of FDR: From Harry Truman to Ronald Reagan* (Ithaca, NY: Cornell University Press, 1983).

Leuchtenburg, William E.: "The Pertinence of Political History: Reflections on the Significance of the State in America," *Journal of American History*, 73 (1986): 585–600.

Leuchtenburg, William E.: "The Twentieth-Century Presidency," in Harvard Sitkoff (ed.), *Perspectives on Modern America: Making Sense of the Twentieth Century* (New York: Oxford University Press, 2001), 9–32.

Light, Paul C.: "Domestic Policy Making," *Presidential Studies Quarterly*, 30 (2000): 109–32.

Logevall, Fredrik: *Choosing War: The Lost Chance for Peace and the Escalation of War in Vietnam* (Berkeley: University of California Press, 1999).

Lowi, Theodore J.: *The End of Liberalism: Ideology, Policy, and the Crisis of Public Authority* (New York: W. W. Norton, 1969).

McConnell, Grant: *The Modern Presidency* (New York: St. Martin's, 1967).

McCormick, Richard L.: *From Realignment to Reform: Political Change in New York State, 1893–1910* (Ithaca, NY: Cornell University Press, 1981).

McCoy, Drew R.: *The Elusive Republic: Political Economy in Jeffersonian America* (Chapel Hill: University of North Carolina Press, 1980).

McCullough, David: *Truman* (New York: Simon and Schuster, 1992).

McKay, David: *Domestic Policy and Ideology: Presidents and the American State, 1964–1987* (Cambridge: Cambridge University Press, 1989).

Manley, John: *The Politics of Finance: The House Committee on Ways and Means* (Boston: Little, Brown, 1970).

Mann, Robert: *A Grand Delusion: America's Descent into Vietnam* (New York: Perseus, 2001).

Marmor, Theodore R.: *The Politics of Medicare* (Chicago: Aldine, 1973).

Matusow, Allen J.: *The Unraveling of America: A History of Liberalism in the 1960s* (New York: Harper Torchbooks, 1985).

May, Ernest R. and Neustadt, Richard E.: *Thinking in Time: The Uses of History for Decision Makers* (New York: Free Press, 1986).

Mayhew, David R.: *Divided We Govern: Party Control, Lawmaking, and Investigation, 1946–1990* (New Haven, Conn.: Yale University Press, 1991).

Mayhew, David R.: *America's Congress: Actions in the Public Sphere, James Madison through Newt Gingrich* (New Haven, Conn.: Yale University Press, 2000).

Milkis, Sidney M.: *The President and the Parties: The Transformation of the American Party System Since the New Deal* (New York: Oxford University Press, 1993).

Milkis, Sidney M.: *Political Parties and Constitutional Government: Remaking American Democracy* (Baltimore: Johns Hopkins University Press, 1999).

Miroff, Bruce: *Pragmatic Illusions: The Presidential Politics of John F. Kennedy* (New York: McKay, 1976).

Morgan, Iwan W.: *Eisenhower Versus "The Spenders": The Eisenhower Administration, the Democrats, and the Budget, 1953–1960* (New York: St. Martin's, 1990).

Nathan, Richard P.: *The Plot that Failed: Nixon and the Administrative Presidency* (New York: Wiley, 1975).

Neustadt, Richard E.: *Presidential Power: The Politics of Leadership* (New York: Wiley, 1960).

Orfield, Gary: *Congressional Power: Congress and Social Change* (New York: Harcourt Brace Jovanovich, 1975).

Orren, Karen: *Belated Feudalism: Labor, the Law, and Liberal Development in the United States* (Cambridge: Cambridge University Press, 1991).

Parmet, Herbert S.: *The Presidency of John F. Kennedy* (New York: Dial Press, 1983).

Patashnik, Eric M.: "Budgeting More, Deciding Less," *Public Interest*, 138 (2000): 65–78.

Patterson, James T.: *Congressional Conservatism and the New Deal: The Growth of the Conservative Coalition in Congress, 1933–1939* (Lexington: University of Kentucky Press, 1967).

Patterson, James T.: *Grand Expectations: The United States, 1945–1975* (New York: Oxford University Press, 1996).

Peterson, Mark: *Legislating Together: The White House and Capitol Hill from Eisenhower to Reagan* (Cambridge, Mass.: Belknap Press of Harvard University Press, 1990).

Pierson, Paul: *Dismantling the Welfare State? Reagan, Thatcher, and the Politics of Retrenchment* (Cambridge: Cambridge University Press, 1994).

Plotke, David: *Building a Democratic Political Order: Reshaping American Liberalism in the 1930s and 1940s* (Cambridge: Cambridge University Press, 1996).

Pocock, J. G. A.: *The Machiavellian Moment* (Princeton, NJ: Princeton University Press, 1975).

Polsby, Nelson W.: *Congress and the Presidency* (Englewood Cliffs, NJ: Prentice Hall, 1964).

Polsby, Nelson W.: *Political Innovation in America: The Politics of Policy Initiation* (New Haven, Conn.: Yale University Press, 1984).

Porter, David L.: *Congress and the Waning of the New Deal* (Port Washington: National University Publications, 1980).

Powe, Jr., Lucas A.: *The Warren Court and American Politics* (Cambridge, Mass.: Belknap Press of Harvard University Press, 2000).

Pyle, Christopher H.: "Military Surveillance of Civilian Politics, 1967–1970" (Ph.D. diss., Columbia University, 1974).

Redlich, Dean Norman: "Concluding Observations: The Constitutional Dimension," in Thomas M. Franck (ed.), *The Tethered Presidency: Congressional Restraints on Executive Power* (New York: New York University Press, 1981).

Reedy, George E.: *The Twilight of the Presidency* (New York: World Publishing, 1970).

Reeves, Richard: *President Kennedy: Profile of Power* (New York: Simon and Schuster, 1993).

Ripley, Randall B.: *Majority Party Leadership in Congress* (Boston: Little, Brown, 1969).

Rodgers, Daniel: *Atlantic Crossings: Social Politics in a Progressive Age* (Cambridge, Mass.: Belknap Press of Harvard University Press, 1998).

Rossiter, Clinton: *The American Presidency* (New York: Harcourt Brace, 1956).

Schlesinger, Jr., Arthur M.: *The Age of Roosevelt: The Coming of the New Deal* (Boston: Houghton Mifflin, 1959).

Schlesinger, Jr., Arthur M.: *A Thousand Days* (Boston: Houghton Mifflin, 1965).

Schlesinger, Jr., Arthur M.: *The Imperial Presidency* (Boston: Houghton Mifflin, 1973).

Schlesinger, Jr., Arthur M.: *The Cycles of American History* (Boston: Houghton Mifflin, 1986).

Schudson, Michael: *Watergate in American Memory: How We Remember, Forget, and Reconstruct the Past* (New York: Basic Books, 1992).

Scott, Daryl M.: *Contempt and Pity: Social Policy and the Image of the Damaged Black Psyche, 1880–1996* (Chapel Hill: University of North Carolina Press, 1997).

Shafer, Byron E.: *Quiet Revolution: The Struggle for the Democratic Party and the Shaping of Post-Reform Politics* (New York: Russell Sage Foundation, 1983).

Shafer, Byron E.: "Political Eras in Political History: A Review Essay," *Journal of Policy History*, 5 (1993): 461–74.

Shank, Alan: *Presidential Policy Leadership, Kennedy, and Social Welfare* (Lanham, Md.: University Press, 1980).

Shapiro, Robert Y., Kumar, Martha Joynt, and Jacobs, Lawrence R., eds.: *Presidential Power: Forging the Presidency for the Twenty-First Century* (New York: Columbia University Press, 2000).

Sherrill, Robert: *The Accidental President* (New York: Pyramid Books, 1967).

Shulman, Bruce J.: *Lyndon B. Johnson and American Liberalism: A Brief Biography With Documents* (Boston: Bedford Books, 1995).

Silbey, Joel H.: *The American Political Nation, 1838–1893* (Stanford, Calif.: Stanford University Press, 1991).

Sinclair, Barbara: *Congressional Realignment, 1925–1978* (Austin: University of Texas Press, 1982).

Sklar, Kathryn Kish: *Florence Kelley and the Nation's Work: The Rise of Women's Political Culture, 1830–1900* (New Haven, Conn.: Yale University Press, 1995).

Skocpol, Theda: *Protecting Soldiers and Mothers: The Political Origins of Social Policy in the United States* (Cambridge, Mass.: Belknap Press of Harvard University, 1992).

Skocpol, Theda: *Social Policy in the United States: Future Possibilities in Historical Perspective* (Princeton, NJ: Princeton University Press, 1995).

Skowronek, Stephen: *Building a New American State: The Expansion of National Administrative Capacities, 1877–1920* (Cambridge: Cambridge University Press, 1982).

Skowronek, Stephen: *The Politics Presidents Make: Leadership from John Adams to George Bush* (Cambridge, Mass.: Belknap Press of Harvard University Press, 1993).

Steuerle, C. Eugene: "Financing the American State at the Turn of the Century," in W. Elliot Brownlee (ed.), *Funding the Modern American State, 1941–1995: The Rise and Fall of the Era of Easy Finance, 1941–1995* (Cambridge: Cambridge University Press and Washington, DC: Woodrow Wilson Center Press, 1996), 409–44.

Sugrue, Thomas J.: *The Origins of the Urban Crisis* (Princeton, NJ: Princeton University Press, 1996).

Sundquist, James L.: *Politics and Policy: The Eisenhower, Kennedy, and Johnson Years* (Washington, DC: Brookings Institution, 1968).

Sundquist, James L.: *The Decline and Resurgence of Congress* (Washington, DC: Brookings Institution, 1981).

Theoharis, Athan: *Seeds of Repression: Harry S. Truman and the Origins of McCarthyism* (Chicago: Quadrangle Books, 1971).

Theoharis, Athan: *Spying on Americans: Political Surveillance from Hoover to the Huston Plan* (Philadelphia: Temple University Press, 1978).

Tomlins, Christopher L.: *The State and the Unions: Labor Relations, Law, and the Organized Labor Movement in America, 1880–1960* (Cambridge: Cambridge University Press, 1985).

VanDeMark, Brian: *Into the Quagmire: Lyndon Johnson and the Escalation of the Vietnam War* (New York: Oxford University Press, 1991).

Wiebe, Robert H.: *The Search for Order, 1877–1920* (New York: Hill and Wang, 1967).

Wildavsky, Aaron: *The Politics of the Budgetary Process* (Boston: Little, Brown, 1964).

Wildavsky, Aaron and Pressman, Jeffrey: *Implementation: How Great Expectations in Washington Are Dashed in Oakland: Or, Why It's Amazing that Federal Programs Work At All, This Being a Saga of the Economic Development Administration As Told By Two Sympathetic Observers Who Seek to Build Morals on a Foundation of Ruined Hopes* (Berkeley: University of California Press, 1984).

Williams, William A.: *The Tragedy of American Diplomacy* (Cleveland: World Publishers, 1959).

Williams, William A.: *The Contours of American History* (Cleveland: World Publishers, 1961).

Wittner, Lawrence S.: *The Struggle Against the Bomb: Resisting the Bomb – A History of the World Nuclear Disarmament Movement, 1954–1970* (Stanford, Calif.: Stanford University Press, 1998).

Wood, Gordon: *The Creation of the American Republic* (Chapel Hill: University of North Carolina Press, 1969).

Zelizer, Julian E.: *Taxing America: Wilbur D. Mills, Congress, and the State, 1945–1975* (Cambridge: Cambridge University Press, 1998).

Zelizer, Julian E.: "Clio's Lost Tribe: Public Policy History Since 1978," *Journal of Policy History*, 12 (2000a): 369–94.

Zelizer, Julian E.: "The Forgotten Legacy of the New Deal: Fiscal Conservatism and the Roosevelt Administration, 1933–1938," *Presidential Studies Quarterly*, 30 (2000b): 331–58.

Zelizer, Julian E.: *The Cost of Democracy* (Cambridge: Cambridge University Press, forthcoming).

CHAPTER NINETEEN

McCarthyism and the Red Scare

ELLEN SCHRECKER

The end of the Cold War, certainly the end of communism as a major international force, should have lowered the emotional level of the discussion about communism, anti-communism, and McCarthyism. Paradoxically, however, the debate has intensified, primarily because the recent release of previously secret Soviet and American records revealing widespread Soviet espionage in the United States has allowed some scholars to justify the events of the McCarthy period. These new documents show that as many as 300 Americans may have worked with the Soviet Union's intelligence agencies during the 1930s and 1940s. Because many of these people were communists, traditionalist historians like Harvey Klehr, John Earl Haynes, and Ronald Radosh claim that national security required federal authorities and private organizations to crack down on domestic communism (Haynes and Klehr, 1999; Weisberg, 1999). Other historians like Maurice Isserman and myself do not deny that American communists spied, but do not think that their activities justify (or explain) the massive violations of civil liberties that occurred during the early years of the Cold War (Isserman and Schrecker, 2000). Nor do we believe that Soviet espionage is the whole story. McCarthyism – misnamed as it is – requires a broader perspective.

That scholars should still be arguing about the justice and injustice of the McCarthy period shows how politically volatile the subject was – and is. Such passion complicates the task of the historian. Because of the pressure to conform one's inquiry to external and often somewhat politicized criteria, more intellectually rewarding lines of investigation can sometimes be overlooked. Thus, for example, with regard to espionage, the emphasis on guilt or innocence and our understandable hunger for certainty – "Did Ethel Rosenberg know what her husband was doing?" – can distract us from exploring the political culture that would allow a group of young New York City communists to spy for the Soviet Union. In addition, the continuing controversy blocks our access to sources and renders some of them unreliable. Because so much of what happened in the furtive and highly charged world of communism and anti-communism never made it into the written record, oral history is a necessary adjunct to the archives. But it is a tricky source. Moreover, many veterans of the period remain so deeply scarred by their experiences that they will not talk with historians – and they are rapidly passing from the scene.

Still, the fascination with what was, after all, the longest-lasting and most widespread episode of political repression in American history does not abate. Despite the political pitfalls of chronicling the McCarthy era, the historical literature on the subject is far-ranging and rich. And, it includes much more than the bizarre career of a single senator from Wisconsin. Identifying McCarthyism solely with McCarthy not only limits our understanding of what went on, but also treats it as an aberrant blip in American political history instead of the mainstream development that it actually was. After all, the anti-communist crusade to which Joe McCarthy gave his name had been in existence long before he appeared at a Wheeling, West Virginia, Republican women's banquet in February 1950, waving his ever-changing lists of alleged communists in the State Department. And it was to continue for several years after the Wisconsin senator self-destructed before the nation's television viewers at the Army–McCarthy hearings in the spring of 1954.

In order to understand McCarthyism – and I use that term in its broadest sense as a convenient term for the wave of anti-communist political repression that dominated American politics in the late 1940s and 1950s – we must recognize that it was a complicated movement that came in many different forms and extended far beyond the congressional investigations that were its most visible manifestations. Historians of all political persuasions have recognized McCarthyism's complexity. Michael J. Heale (1990) and Robert Goldstein (2001), for example, have found its antecedents in the anti-radicalism of the late nineteenth and early twentieth centuries, while Richard Gid Powers (1995) charts the variegated nature of American anti-communism.

McCarthyism and the Historians: The Successive Interpretations

The first scholarly attempt to explain McCarthyism took place while it was still going on and was designed, at least in part, to counter it. Some of this work, like the early Rockefeller Foundation-funded studies by Eleanor Bontecou (1953) and Vern Countryman (1951), has yet to be superseded. A similar set of monographs on "Communism in American Life" commissioned by the Ford Foundation, ostensibly to show that communism did not endanger the United States, is more mixed. While some of the books in that series, like those by Daniel Aaron and Nathan Glazer, remain useful, others were overly polemical or else have been supplanted by later scholarship. Perhaps the most ambitious of those works was Theodore Draper's two-volume study of the early Communist Party (CP). Though it needs revision to incorporate the new Russian materials, it remains the standard history of American communism during the 1920s (Draper, 1957, 1960). The main drawback of Draper's work, common to much of the early scholarship on American communism, is its narrowly institutional perspective. A former mid-level party functionary, Draper views the CP from the top down, focusing mainly on its leaders' squabbles and their relationship with the mother party in Moscow.

An equally important, though smaller, body of work produced in the 1950s sought to explain McCarthyism. Reflecting the Cold War liberalism of its authors, it treated McCarthy and his allies as an aberration in American politics. Because these authors were among the nation's leading public intellectuals, their analysis of McCarthyism had considerable influence. Despite a remarkable lack of empirical evidence, historian Richard Hofstadter and the other contributors to Daniel Bell's key collection of essays (1955) took McCarthy's attacks on the nation's ruling elites at face value. McCarthyism, they claimed, was a quasi-populist phenomenon that reflected the status anxieties of upwardly mobile ethnics and downwardly mobile WASPs.

By the late 1960s, younger scholars whose opposition to the war in Vietnam had led them to question Cold War liberalism began to argue that President Truman and the liberals whom McCarthy attacked were as culpable for the political repression as their Republican antagonists. By consciously using scare tactics to garner public support for America's anti-communist foreign policy, the Truman administration legitimized the notion that communism endangered the United States. In so doing it inadvertently facilitated the campaign of those conservatives who claimed to locate that threat in Washington rather than Moscow (Freeland, 1971; Theoharis, 1971). McCarthyism, according to these scholars, was a partisan political endeavor. In this they were in accord with Earl Latham (1966), who claimed that the red scare reflected the accumulated "stress of government" resulting from the Republican Party's unanticipated failure to capture the White House in 1948. Michael Rogin (1967) corroborated Latham's findings by demonstrating that the junior senator from Wisconsin was a regular Republican, not a populist maverick, while Robert Griffith (1970, rev. ed. 1987) traced the traditional political machinations behind the Senate's response to McCarthy.

When FBI records became available through the Freedom of Information Act in the mid-1970s, the interpretation of McCarthyism entered a new phase – this time focusing on the activities of J. Edgar Hoover and the FBI, as well as on some of the period's major espionage cases. Athan Theoharis (1981, 1991; Theoharis and Cox, 1988) was one of the first historians to uncover the FBI's secrets as well as one of the most diligent in obtaining Bureau records. As he and Hoover's other biographers have shown, the FBI director and his men conducted a carefully orchestrated campaign of propaganda, leaks, and criminal prosecutions that not only targeted individuals, but also constructed the scenarios of subversion and betrayal that justified the McCarthy-era violations of civil liberties (Powers, 1987; Gentry, 1991). Other scholars have used FBI files to examine the Bureau's activities in specific areas, like its collaboration with the House Un-American Activities Committee (HUAC) or its long-term surveillance of Martin Luther King, Jr., the academic community, and America's major authors (Garrow, 1981; O'Reilly, 1983; Diamond, 1992; Robins, 1992).

Another group of historians used the Freedom of Information Act to research the early Cold War espionage cases (R. Williams, 1987). Allen Weinstein's study of the Alger Hiss case (1978, rev. ed. 1997) relied heavily on FBI files, as did Ronald Radosh and Joyce Milton's *The Rosenberg File* (1983). Controversy attended both volumes, as supporters of Hiss and the Rosenbergs continued to insist on these people's innocence and to question the reliability of the FBI's heavily censored documents, while other scholars reserved judgment (Navasky, 1981; Schneir and Schneir, 1983).

By the late 1990s, the opening of some Soviet-era archives to Western scholars and the release of the VENONA decrypts, as the deciphered texts of intercepted wartime KGB telegrams were called, had convinced all but a few holdouts that the alleged spies were, in fact, real ones. These findings have not entirely stilled the controversy, for the Kremlin's holdings peter out in the late 1930s, while access to other documents remains limited. No other Western scholars have seen the KGB files that Allen Weinstein's publisher paid the Russians to open (Weinstein and Vassiliev, 1999). Nor, despite the discovery of some previously unsuspected Soviet agents in the atomic bomb project and elsewhere, do all historians agree with Haynes (2000) that espionage is the main story of American communism and anti-communism (Albright and Kunstel, 1997).

The debate, however, seems tired. Though the traditionalists claim that the new documents are rejuvenating the field by clearing up the old questions, other scholars, especially in cultural and literary studies, are asking new questions. They take an interdisciplinary approach to McCarthyism, treating it as a cultural phenomenon that, as Michael Rogin (1988) suggests, reveals much about "the countersubversive tradition" within the United States. Though this scholarship sometimes seems far-fetched and unburdened by evidentiary concerns, it may eventually incorporate our previous findings into a broader analysis of Cold War political culture (Garber and Walkowitz, 1995).

The American Communist Movement

Despite the common assumption that almost anybody could be investigated and charged with communism, there were few "innocent liberals" during the McCarthy years. Most of the men and women affected by the anti-communist purges of the late 1940s and 1950s had once been in or near the American Communist Party. Many were former members who had long since dropped out. Though unjustly persecuted, they were not incorrectly targeted. As a result, it is not possible to understand their experiences without first looking at the movement to which they belonged. Not only did the CP, with its secrecy, discipline, and devotion to the Soviet Union, shape much of the repression that was directed against it, but the specific activities of its members determined which sectors of American society that repression would touch. Though the most reactionary proponents of the red scare viewed anything to the left of center as a menace to the nation, the McCarthy-era purges were not consciously designed to wipe out radical dissent. Nonetheless, because communists had been so active in the main social movements of the 1930s and 1940s, the purges did, in fact, have that effect.

Historians have written quite a lot about American communism. Much of it, however, will have to be revised to take account of new materials from Moscow. Despite several biographies and volumes of documents that have emerged from the former Soviet archives, no comprehensive survey of American communism that incorporates the Russian materials has yet been written (Johanningsmeier, 1994; Klehr, Haynes, and Firsov, 1995; Ryan, 1997; Klehr, Haynes, and Anderson, 1998; Barrett, 1999). Until it is, we must rely on the old volume by Irving Howe and Lewis Coser (1957), or the more recent one by Haynes and Klehr (1992). There is a rich monographic literature, but it, too, will require updating. This will be especially the case for studies of party policy, like those of Draper for the 1920s, Klehr (1984) and Fraser Ottanelli (1991) for the 1930s, and Maurice Isserman (1982) and Joseph Starobin (1972) for the 1940s. Clearly, any historian who takes a traditional top-down approach and seeks to ascertain how independent the American Communist Party was from Moscow will have to use the Russian materials.

Many scholars, however, are not interested in the CP's leaders and their relationship with the Kremlin. Instead, they study American communism as a social movement, one that was the largest and most dynamic part of the left in the 1930s and 1940s. These historians examine the party's culture and the day-to-day activities of its members, focusing primarily on the organizations within its orbit and on those sectors of American society where communists were active.

Among the most useful studies are those that deal with the party's attempt to create an interracial working-class movement (Naison, 1983; Kelley, 1990). This aspect of American communism has not received as much attention as it deserves, mainly because the CP did not fully embrace the struggle for racial equality until the 1940s. By then, communists had become so thoroughly demonized that their civil rights activities simply disappeared from view. The party's participation in the labor movement has gotten more attention, no doubt because its work in organizing the major industrial unions in the 1930s and 1940s actually gave the CP some influence. Harvey Levenstein (1981) and Bert Cochran (1977) have studied the overall impact of communism and anti-communism on the Congress of Industrial Organizations (CIO), while other historians have looked at the CP's activities within other sectors of organized labor (Freeman, 1989; Kimmeldorf, 1988; Rosswurm, 1992; Filippelli and McCullough, 1995).

Though American communists focused much of their attention on labor and civil rights, they were also active in other types of organizations, ranging from literary magazines to insurance companies. At the peak of the CP's influence during the 1930s and 1940s, there were dozens of these "front groups," as these party-led organizations were (usually pejoratively) called. Among the ones that scholars have examined are those aimed at folk singers, women, summer camps, and the volunteers who fought in the Spanish Civil War (Lieberman, 1989; Weigand, 2001; Mishler, 1999; Carroll, 1994).

Because of the CP's clandestinity and the unavailability (and often nonexistence) of its archives, much of our information about it comes from memoirs and oral histories. Despite the inaccuracies and obvious biases of such sources, until more studies emerge from the Russian archives, this literature is invaluable for revealing what it was like to participate in such a demanding political movement. Particularly useful are those narratives in which long-term party members told their stories to professional historians (Painter, 1979; Nelson et al., 1981; Healey and Isserman, 1990). How else could we find out that a communist leader decided to live with a maritime worker she did not love because the party wanted to keep him on shore, or that another CP dignitary and his wife returned to the United States from a stint in Moscow, leaving their five-year-old son behind because he spoke only Russian and so would validate the opposition's charges of Soviet control (Dennis, 1977)?

The Machinery of Political Repression

Almost every communist memoir and oral history describes the repression the author faced during the McCarthy era. From the late 1940s on, America's internal security apparatus was ubiquitous in these people's lives. The onslaught came from all sides. A CP leader or trade union official might find himself or herself subpoenaed by one or several congressional committees, indicted for contempt or perjury, fired from his or her job, denied a passport, spied on by the FBI, and, if he or she was foreign born, threatened with deportation. Lesser lights might not get quite so lavish a treatment, but the sanctions they faced generally succeeded in silencing them, and, more importantly, in keeping others from engaging in left-wing political activities.

Because it is tempting to take a victim-centered approach, scholars who offer a general overview of the anti-communist crusade risk producing elaborate lists of horror stories. Still, several historians have made the attempt (Caute, 1978; Fried, 1990; Schrecker, 1998). Most, however, have focused on specific cases or institutions. While such an approach avoids overemphasizing victimization, it sometimes overlooks the connections between the different elements of repression. McCarthyism owed its efficacy to those connections, many of which developed within a network of professional anti-communists that ranged from Trotskyists and social-ists to FBI agents and right-wing politicians. Consciously collaborating with each other, these people crafted the mechanisms and ideology that came to dominate the anti-communist crusade.

Unlike political repression in less democratic polities where the state or semi-official goon squads were in charge, McCarthyism seemed almost casual. Most of the time it operated in accordance with a two-stage procedure. First, the politically undesirable individuals or organizations were identified; then they were punished. An official body like the FBI or HUAC usually handled that first stage of identification, while another agency or private employer applied the second-stage sanctions, nor-mally by firing the men and women fingered during the first stage. The diffusion of responsibility that this two-step procedure entailed allowed many moderates and even liberals to participate. While claiming to oppose McCarthyism (which they identified only with its first stage), they often imposed the sanctions that ensured its efficacy.

The federal government's loyalty-security program established the pattern. Inau-gurated by the Truman administration in March 1947, to preempt the more parti-san measure that the newly elected Republican Congress threatened to impose, the program required the FBI to check out all federal workers. If the Bureau turned up any "derogatory information" on someone, that person might lose his or her job. Communists were automatically disqualified from government service, but so too was anyone who associated with the party or with any of the front groups that the Attorney General was ordered to list. The FBI championed this method of ascer-taining "guilt by association" on the grounds that the party's secrecy made it impos-sible to identify its members except by tracing the pattern of their activities.

In practice, the loyalty-security program probably did rout most of the Reds out of the government, mainly by provoking them to resign rather than undergo the security checks they surely would have failed. The program also decimated the federal workers' left-led union. Because of the FBI's expansive notion of what constituted an association with communism, the program targeted enough ordinary liberals and apolitical types to alarm civil libertarians. At the same time, the Bureau's refusal to reveal its sources of information unjustly forced many federal workers from their jobs when they could not rebut the charges made against them by the FBI's unidentified informants.

From the start, critics recognized the program's flaws. As a result, some of the best studies are among the earliest, perhaps because so many outstanding scholars felt compelled to combat the purge (Bontecou, 1953; Brown, 1958). Unfortunately, however, these works do not reach past the early 1950s and most later studies consist mainly of human interest stories (Bernstein, 1989; S. Williams, 1993). Accordingly, except for a useful survey of the Eisenhower administration (Broadwater, 1992), historians have not charted the changes in the loyalty program nor shown how political tests for employment spread from the federal government to the rest of American society.

Scholars have paid more attention to the congressional investigating committees, the institutions that symbolized the anti-communist crusade. Though we now know that J. Edgar Hoover wielded much more influence over that crusade than either HUAC or McCarthy, the committees were crucial in publicizing the alleged dangers of communism as well as in fingering its alleged adherents. HUAC was the most notorious and longest-lived, but the Senate Internal Security Subcommittee and McCarthy's own Senate Permanent Subcommittee on Investigations were also active. These committees specialized in grilling suspected communists about their political activities and associates. Witnesses who did not want to name names could either go to prison for contempt or invoke the Fifth Amendment's privilege against self-incrimination. The latter option was the only legal protection uncooperative witnesses had, but it did not protect them from losing their jobs. With a few exceptions, like Kenneth O'Reilly's (1983) study of HUAC and the FBI, most of the scholarship relies on published transcripts and, thus, focuses on the plight of witnesses. Now, however, as the committees' records become increasingly available, historians may be able to take a more institutional perspective (Taylor, 1955; Donner, 1961; Goodman, 1968; O'Reilly, 1983).

Joe McCarthy, of course, cannot be ignored. When he blustered onto the scene early in 1950, he tapped into the preexisting network of conservative activists eager to offer him advice and information. His allegations were nothing new; for years, right-wingers had been claiming that the New Deal harbored Reds. Still, McCarthy was more flamboyant and more skilled at manipulating the media. He was also lucky; the outbreak of the Korean War in the summer of 1950 increased the salience of his unfounded charges that State Department communists had betrayed China to Mao Zedong. But the recklessness that gained McCarthy his notoriety proved his downfall. Unable to realize that the rules had changed once the Republicans came into power, McCarthy ran foul of the Eisenhower administration. He ended up having to defend himself against allegations that he had pressured the military into giving favorable treatment to one of his aides. When the Army–McCarthy hearings petered out in the summer of 1954, McCarthy's career did too. The Senate censured him soon after; and his own alcoholism killed him three years later. Despite Arthur Herman's recent effort to resuscitate his reputation, every other historian endorses the original assessment by journalist Richard Rovere that McCarthy was a blowhard and a demagogue (Rovere, 1959; Bayley, 1981; Reeves, 1982; Oshinsky, 1983; Herman, 1999).

While most of the people who refused to cooperate with McCarthy and the other congressional investigators lost their jobs, a few went to prison. So, too, did several hundred communist leaders, union officials, and other political undesirables who were prosecuted on charges that ran from espionage and perjury to "teaching and advocating" communist doctrines. During the McCarthy period, the criminal justice system, though ostensibly separate from the investigating committees, actually performed identical functions. Like congressional hearings, political trials publicized the dangers of communism and penalized its adherents. Ironically, despite the notoriety of the major Cold War trials, with the exception of a strangely ignored 1961 treatise by Otto Kirchheimer, most scholars treat those prosecutions as individual cases rather than as part of a broader program for identifying and punishing communists.

As J. Edgar Hoover well knew, a courtroom was a bully pulpit. He and his men had long viewed the CP as a criminal conspiracy they were eager to unmask. Not only would prosecuting communists eliminate the danger they allegedly posed, but it would also educate the American people about that danger (Lamphere and Schachtman, 1983). Because of the FBI's dirty tricks, we often overlook the Bureau's ordinary – and completely legal – responsibility for providing evidence to federal prosecutors, a responsibility that gave the FBI considerable influence over who to bring to trial and on what grounds. Much to Hoover's dismay, however, the Department of Justice did not always seek the indictments the Bureau recommended; its attorneys understandably shrank from prosecutions they could not sustain. That the government might be violating the First Amendment rights of the men and women it indicted never seemed to be at issue. After all, at the height of the red scare, even Supreme Court justices believed that communists were so uniquely dangerous they did not deserve the same constitutional protections as other defendants.

We know quite a lot about these Cold War prosecutions, especially about the big espionage cases that got so much attention (Weinstein, 1978, 1997; Radosh and Milton, 1983; May, 1994). Almost as well known are the major sedition trials of the CP's top leaders that provided the legal basis for treating communists as members of a criminal conspiracy (Belknap, 1977; Steinberg, 1984). Communists and alleged communists were also hauled into court for what Kirchheimer calls "offense artifacts," charges that, like perjury and contempt of Congress, punished individuals for otherwise legal behavior that an anti-communist investigation had criminalized. By the late 1950s, many of these cases began to be reversed on appeal. Nonetheless, simply having to undergo such a protracted legal proceeding was a punishment in and of itself (Kutler, 1982).

Central to these prosecutions and congressional hearings was the testimony of former communists. While some were clearly speaking under duress, others had made a career of it. Besides describing the party's intrigues and identifying its members at dozens of criminal trials, congressional hearings, and deportation proceedings, some of these professional witnesses were able to parlay their experiences into bestsellers, movies, and TV shows (Chambers, 1952; Tanenhaus, 1997; Leab, 2000). Because so few Americans knew anything at all about communism, these people's sometimes lurid stories had enormous influence in shaping popular perceptions. Though we know that some of these ex-communists perjured themselves, the testimony of others has been corroborated by the VENONA decrypts and Moscow archives.

McCarthyism began in Washington, DC, but state and local governments soon followed suit. Besides establishing their own loyalty-security programs, several states and cities set up anti-communist investigating committees, while others passed laws imposing loyalty oaths on teachers and public employees or requiring the registration of individual communists. These measures were often the products of the efforts of an ambitious politician or right-wing pressure group and reflected local rather than national politics (Gellhorn, 1952; Carleton, 1985; Heale, 1998; Jenkins, 1999). Future scholars might do well, however, to look more carefully at how the local and the national purges intersected.

The inaction of so many of the institutions and individuals that could have mitigated the political repression of the Cold War contributed to its spread. While contemporary observers described the chilling effect of the purges, in retrospect the more salient factor was not fear, but an implicit and often explicit endorsement of the anti-communist crusade on the part of many liberals who might otherwise have opposed it. Internal divisions over communism, for example, kept the American Civil Liberties Union from seriously resisting McCarthyism or defending its victims. Though we will never know if a stronger stand by the nation's liberals would have reduced the damage, their passivity is an important part of the story (McAuliffe, 1978; Gillon, 1987; Walker, 1990).

The Impact of McCarthyism

Just as McCarthyism came in many forms, so too its impact was equally diverse. Dozens of memoirs and oral histories chronicle the suffering of its victims and the toll that it took on their personal lives and careers (Schultz and Schultz, 1989; Fariello, 1995). Recently, a new genre has emerged. Beginning with the sons of the Rosenbergs, the victims' children are also telling their stories. To what extent these people were scarred by their parents' suffering is unclear, but the fact that they center their narratives around it attests to McCarthyism's lasting cultural power (Meeropol and Meeropol, 1986; Belfrage, 1994; Kaplan and Shapiro, 1998).

Its institutional damage is harder to assess. Because the CP dominated the left in the years before the Cold War, domestic radicalism suffered a near-crippling setback. Those areas of American life like the labor movement where the party had been most active took the biggest hits. Left-wing labor leaders faced congressional investigations, perjury prosecutions, and deportation proceedings. In addition, their unions came directly under attack. Taking advantage of the anti-communist provisions of the 1947 Taft-Hartley Act, hostile businessmen, politicians, and rival unions managed to force these unions and their communist officials from all positions of influence within organized labor. Historians are still debating the extent to which the marginalization of the left-led unions weakened the labor movement by depriving it of its most militant and progressive elements (Korstad and Lichtenstein, 1988; Freeman, 2000).

Because communism had appealed to artists, intellectuals, and other middle-class professionals, McCarthyism drew its most prominent victims from those fields. The blacklist in the entertainment industry has attracted the most attention. Memoirs, biographies, and monographs on the Hollywood Ten and their colleagues proliferate (Ceplair and Englund, 1979; Navasky, 1980; McGilligan and Buhle, 1997). But there is a growing literature about the impact of McCarthyism on college teachers and other professionals (Schrecker, 1986; Walkowitz, 1999).

Sometimes a particular area was affected because it intersected with sensitive Cold War issues. Thus, even before the extent of atomic espionage had been revealed, scientists came under intense scrutiny. Their work was crucial to America's defense and their politics could be unconventional. The 1954 withdrawal of his security clearance from J. Robert Oppenheimer, the nation's most famous physicist, symbolized the vulnerability of the scientific establishment at the height of the McCarthy period (Wang, 1999). A similar purge hit the nation's China specialists. Here, the most well-known victim was Johns Hopkins University Professor Owen Lattimore, singled out as the nation's number one spy by Joe McCarthy. A later investigation by Senator Pat McCarran's Internal Security Subcommittee not only destroyed Lattimore's career, but also purged most of the State Department's experienced China hands (Kahn, 1975; Newman, 1992; Klehr and Radosh, 1996).

Given its still-controversial nature, it is hard to figure out how McCarthyism affected American culture and politics. Was it a major influence or a mere blip? Many historians believe that there may have been a brief moment of opportunity before the Cold War set in during the late 1940s when the American polity might have been more open to a kind of liberal internationalism and to a wider range of social democratic reforms. The anti-communist crusade (and, of course, the Cold War) destroyed that promise (Lichtenstein, 1989; Lipsitz, 1994; Schrecker, 1998). Other historians doubt that such a moment ever existed. They cite the congenital weakness of the American left, the growing prosperity of most workers, and the racial tensions that riddled the working class as evidence that it may never have been possible to implement a social democratic agenda in this country (Edsforth, 1991; Sugrue, 1996). In foreign affairs, the fear of a replay of Joe McCarthy's attacks on the State Department probably helped pull American policymakers into the Vietnam quagmire. But when we try to look more closely at McCarthyism's impact, we find a legacy of silence. It is hard to measure all the films that were not produced, the books that were not written, the movements that were not organized, the courses that were not taught, and the ideas that were not expressed. If nothing else, the anti-communist crusade narrowed the political spectrum and made it impossible to criticize much of what was going on in the United States during the early years of the Cold War.

REFERENCES

Aaron, Daniel: *Writers on the Left* (New York: Harcourt Brace and World, 1961).

Albright, Joseph and Kunstel, Marcia: *Bombshell: The Secret Story of America's Unknown Atomic Spy Conspiracy* (New York: Times Books, 1997).

Barrett, James R.: *William Z. Foster and the Tragedy of American Radicalism* (Urbana: University of Illinois Press, 1999).

Bayley, Edwin R.: *Joe McCarthy and the Press* (Madison: University of Wisconsin Press, 1981).

Belfrage, Sally: *Un-American Activities: A Memoir of the Fifties* (New York: HarperCollins, 1994).

Belknap, Michael R.: *Cold War Political Justice: The Smith Act, the Communist Party, and American Civil Liberties* (Westport, Conn.: Greenwood Press, 1977).

Bell, Daniel, ed.: *The New American Right* (New York: Criterion, 1955).

Bernstein, Carl: *Loyalties: A Son's Memoir* (New York: Simon and Schuster, 1989).

Bontecou, Eleanor: *The Federal Loyalty-Security Program* (Ithaca, NY: Cornell University Press, 1953).

Broadwater, Jeff: *Eisenhower and the Anti-Communist Crusade* (Chapel Hill: University of North Carolina Press, 1992).

Brown, Jr., Ralph S.: *Loyalty and Security: Employment Tests in the United States* (New Haven, Conn.: Yale University Press, 1958).

Carleton, Don E.: *Red Scare! Right-Wing Hysteria, Fifties Fanaticism, and Their Legacy in Texas* (Austin: Texas Monthly Press, 1985).

Carroll, Peter N.: *The Odyssey of the Abraham Lincoln Brigade: Americans in the Spanish Civil War* (Stanford, Calif.: Stanford University Press, 1994).

Caute, David: *The Great Fear: The Anti-Communist Purge Under Truman and Eisenhower* (New York: Simon and Schuster, 1978).

Ceplair, Larry and Englund, Steven: *The Inquisition in Hollywood: Politics in the Film Community, 1930–1960* (Garden City, NY: Anchor Press/Doubleday, 1979).

Chambers, Whittaker: *Witness* (New York: Random House, 1952).

Cochran, Bert: *Labor and Communism* (Princeton, NJ: Princeton University Press, 1977).

Countryman, Vern: *Un-American Activities in the State of Washington: Canwell Committee* (Ithaca, NY: Cornell University Press, 1951).

Dennis, Peggy: *The Autobiography of an American Communist* (Westport, Conn., and Berkeley: Lawrence Hill and Creative Arts Book Company, 1977).

Diamond, Sigmund: *Compromised Campus: The Collaboration of Universities With the Intelligence Community, 1945–1955* (New York: Oxford University Press, 1992).

Donner, Frank: *The Un-Americans* (New York: Ballantine, 1961).

Draper, Theodore: *The Roots of American Communism* (New York: Viking, 1957).

Draper, Theodore: *American Communism and Soviet Russia* (New York: Viking, 1960).

Edsforth, Ronald: "Affluence, Anti-Communism, and the Transformation of Industrial Unionism Among Automobile Workers, 1933–1973," in Ronald Edsforth and Larry Bennett (eds.), *Popular Culture and Political Change in Modern America* (Albany: State University of New York Press, 1991).

Fariello, Griffin: *Red Scare: Memories of the American Inquisition* (New York: W. W. Norton, 1995).

Filippelli, Ronald L. and McCullough, Mark: *Cold War in the Working Class: The Rise and Decline of the United Electrical Workers* (Albany: State University of New York Press, 1995).

Freeland, Richard: *The Truman Doctrine and the Origins of McCarthyism* (New York: Alfred A. Knopf, 1971).

Freeman, Joshua B.: *In Transit: The Transport Workers Union in New York City, 1933–1960* (New York: Oxford University Press, 1989).

Freeman, Joshua B.: *Working-Class New York: Life and Labor Since World War II* (New York: New Press, 2000).

Fried, Richard M.: *Nightmare in Red: The McCarthy Era in Perspective* (New York: Oxford University Press, 1990).

Garber, Marjorie and Walkowitz, Rebecca, eds.: *Secret Agents: The Rosenberg Case and the McCarthy Era* (New York: Routledge, 1995).

Garrow, David J.: *The FBI and Martin Luther King, Jr.* (New York: W. W. Norton, 1981).

Gellhorn, Walter: *The States and Subversion* (Ithaca, NY: Cornell University Press, 1952).

Gentry, Curt: *J. Edgar Hoover: The Man and the Secrets* (New York: W. W. Norton, 1991).

Gillon, Steven M.: *Politics and Vision: The ADA and American Liberalism, 1947–1985* (New York: Oxford University Press, 1987).

Glazer, Nathan: *The Social Basis of American Communism* (New York: Harcourt Brace and World, 1961).

Goldstein, Robert: *Political Repression in Modern America: From 1879 to 1976* (Urbana: University of Illinois Press, 2001).

Goodman, Walter: *The Committee* (New York: Farrar, Straus, and Giroux, 1968).

Griffith, Robert: *The Politics of Fear: Joseph R. McCarthy and the Senate* (Lexington: University Press of Kentucky, 1970; 2nd ed., Amherst: University of Massachusetts Press, 1987).

Haynes, John Earl: "The Cold War Debate Continues," *Journal of Cold War Studies*, 2/1 (Winter 2000): 76–115.

Haynes, John Earl and Klehr, Harvey: *The American Communist Movement: Storming Heaven Itself* (New York: Twayne, 1992).

Haynes, John Earl and Klehr, Harvey: *Venona: Soviet Espionage in America in the Stalin Era* (New Haven, Conn.: Yale University Press, 1999).

Heale, Michael J.: *American Anticommunism: Combating the Enemy Within, 1830–1970* (Baltimore: Johns Hopkins University Press, 1990).

Heale, Michael J.: *McCarthy's Americans: Red Scare Politics in State and Nation, 1935–1965* (London: Macmillan, 1998).

Healey, Dorothy and Isserman, Maurice: *Dorothy Healey Remembers: A Life in the American Communist Party* (New York: Oxford University Press, 1990).

Herman, Arthur: *Joseph McCarthy: Reexamining the Life of America's Most Hated Senator* (New York: Free Press, 1999).

Howe, Irving and Coser, Louis: *The American Communist Party* (Boston: Beacon Press, 1957).

Isserman, Maurice: *Which Side Were You On? The American Communist Party During the Second World War* (Middletown, Conn.: Wesleyan University Press, 1982).

Isserman, Maurice and Schrecker, Ellen: "The Right's Cold War Revisionism," *Nation* (July 24/31, 2000): 22–4.

Jenkins, Philip: *The Cold War at Home: The Red Scare in Pennsylvania, 1945–1960* (Chapel Hill: University of North Carolina Press, 1999).

Johanningsmeier, Edward P.: *Forging American Communism: The Life of William Z. Foster* (Princeton, NJ: Princeton University Press, 1994).

Kahn, Jr., E. J.: *The China Hands: America's Foreign Service Officers and What Befell Them* (New York: Viking, 1975).

Kaplan, Judy and Shapiro, Linn: *Red Diapers: Growing Up in the Communist Left* (Urbana: University of Illinois Press, 1998).

Kelley, Robin D. G.: *Hammer and Hoe: Alabama Communists During the Great Depression* (Chapel Hill: University of North Carolina Press, 1990).

Kimmeldorf, Howard: *Reds or Rackets? The Making of Radical and Conservative Unions on the Waterfront* (Berkeley and Los Angeles: University of California Press, 1988).

Kirchheimer, Otto: *Political Justice: The Use of Legal Procedure for Political Ends* (Princeton, NJ: Princeton University Press, 1961).

Klehr, Harvey: *The Heyday of American Communism* (New York: Basic Books, 1984).

Klehr, Harvey, Haynes, John Earl, and Anderson, Kyrill M.: *The Soviet World of American Communism* (New Haven, Conn.: Yale University Press, 1998).

Klehr, Harvey, Haynes, John Earl, and Firsov, Fridrikh Igorevich: *The Secret World of American Communism* (New Haven, Conn.: Yale University Press, 1995).

Klehr, Harvey and Radosh, Ronald: *The Amerasia Spy Case: Prelude to McCarthyism* (Chapel Hill: University of North Carolina Press, 1996).

Korstad, Robert and Lichtenstein, Nelson: "Opportunities Found and Lost: Labor Radicals, and the Early Civil Rights Movement," *Journal of American History*, 75 (1988): 786–811.

Kutler, Stanley I.: *The American Inquisition: Justice and Injustice in the Cold War* (New York: Hill and Wang, 1982).

Lamphere, Robert J. and Schachtman, Tom: *The FBI–KGB War: A Special Agent's Story* (New York: Random House, 1983).

Latham, Earl: *The Communist Controversy in Washington* (Cambridge, Mass.: Harvard University Press, 1966).

Leab, Daniel J.: *I Was a Communist for the F.B.I.: The Unhappy Life and Times of Matt Cvetic* (State College: Pennsylvania State University Press, 2000).

Levenstein, Harvey A.: *Communism, Anticommunism, and the CIO* (Westport, Conn.: Greenwood Press, 1981).

Lichtenstein, Nelson: "From Corporatism to Collective Bargaining: Organized Labor and the Eclipse of Social Democracy in the Postwar Era," in Steve Fraser and Gary Gerstle (eds.), *The Rise and Fall of the New Deal Order, 1930–1980* (Princeton, NJ: Princeton University Press, 1989).

Lieberman, Robbie: *"My Song Is My Weapon": People's Songs, American Communism and the Politics of Culture, 1930–1950* (Urbana: University of Illinois Press, 1989).

Lipsitz, George: *Rainbow at Midnight: Labor and Culture in the 1940s* (Urbana: University of Illinois Press, 1994).

McAuliffe, Mary Sperling: *Crisis on the Left: Cold War Politics and American Liberals* (Amherst: University of Massachusetts Press, 1978).

McGilligan, Patrick and Buhle, Paul: *Tender Comrades: A Backstory of the Hollywood Blacklist* (New York: St. Martin's, 1997).

May, Gary: *Un-American Activities: The Trials of William Remington* (New York: Oxford University Press, 1994).

Meeropol, Robert and Meeropol, Michael: *We Are Your Sons: The Legacy of Ethel and Julius Rosenberg* (Urbana: University of Illinois Press, 1986).

Mishler, Paul C.: *Raising Reds: The Young Pioneers, Radical Summer Camps, and Communist Political Culture in the United States* (New York: Columbia University Press, 1999).

Naison, Mark: *Communists in Harlem During the Depression* (Urbana: University of Illinois Press, 1983).

Navasky, Victor: *Naming Names* (New York: Viking, 1980).

Navasky, Victor: "The Transformation of Historical Ambiguity into Cold War Verity," in Athan Theoharis (ed.), *Beyond the Hiss Case: The FBI, Congress, and the Cold War* (Philadelphia: Temple University Press, 1981).

Nelson, Steve, Barrett, James, and Ruck, Rob: *Steve Nelson: American Radical* (Pittsburgh: University of Pittsburgh Press, 1981).

Newman, Robert P.: *Owen Lattimore and the "Loss" of China* (Berkeley: University of California Press, 1992).

O'Reilly, Kenneth: *Hoover and the Un-Americans: The FBI, HUAC, and the Red Menace* (Philadelphia: Temple University Press, 1983).

Oshinsky, David: *A Conspiracy So Immense: The World of Joe McCarthy* (New York: Free Press, 1983).

Ottanelli, Fraser M.: *The Communist Party of the United States: From the Depression to World War II* (New Brunswick, NJ: Rutgers University Press, 1991).

Painter, Nell Irvin: *The Narrative of Hosea Hudson: His Life as a Negro Communist in the South* (Cambridge, Mass.: Harvard University Press, 1979).

Powers, Richard Gid: *Secrecy and Power: The Life of J. Edgar Hoover* (New York: Free Press, 1987).

Powers, Richard Gid: *Not Without Honor: The History of American Anticommunism* (New York: Free Press, 1995).

Radosh, Ronald and Milton, Joyce: *The Rosenberg File* (New York: Holt, Rinehart, and Winston, 1983).

Reeves, Thomas: *The Life and Times of Joe McCarthy* (New York: Stein and Day, 1982).

Robins, Natalie: *Alien Ink: The FBI's War on Freedom of Expression* (New York: William Morrow, 1992).

Rogin, Michael Paul: *The Intellectuals and McCarthy: The Radical Specter* (Cambridge, Mass.: MIT Press, 1967).

Rogin, Michael Paul: *Ronald Reagan: The Movie and Other Episodes in Political Demonology* (Berkeley: University of California Press, 1988).

Rosswurm, Steve, ed.: *The CIO's Left-Led Unions* (New Brunswick, NJ: Rutgers University Press, 1992).

Rovere, Richard H.: *Senator Joe McCarthy* (New York: Harcourt Brace Jovanovich, 1959).

Ryan, James G.: *Earl Browder: The Public Life of an American Communist* (Tuscaloosa: University of Alabama Press, 1997).

Schneir, Walter and Schneir, Miriam: *Invitation to an Inquest* (New York: Pantheon, 1983).

Schrecker, Ellen: *No Ivory Tower: McCarthyism and the Universities* (New York: Oxford University Press, 1986).

Schrecker, Ellen: *Many Are the Crimes: McCarthyism in America* (Boston: Little, Brown, 1998).

Schultz, Bud and Schultz, Ruth: *It Did Happen Here: Recollections of Political Repression in America* (Berkeley: University of California Press, 1989).

Starobin, Joseph: *American Communism in Crisis, 1943–1957* (Cambridge, Mass.: Harvard University Press, 1972).

Steinberg, Peter: *The Great "Red Menace": United States Prosecution of American Communists, 1947–1952* (Westport, Conn.: Greenwood Press, 1984).

Sugrue, Thomas J.: *The Origins of the Urban Crisis: Race and Inequality in Postwar Detroit* (Princeton, NJ: Princeton University Press, 1996).

Tanenhaus, Sam: *Whittaker Chambers: A Biography* (New York: Random House, 1997).

Taylor, Telford: *Grand Inquisition: The Story of Congressional Investigations* (New York: Simon and Schuster, 1955).

Theoharis, Athan: *Seeds of Repression: Harry S. Truman and the Origin of McCarthyism* (Chicago: Quadrangle, 1971).

Theoharis, Athan, ed.: *Beyond the Hiss Case: The FBI, Congress, and the Cold War* (Philadelphia: Temple University Press, 1981).

Theoharis, Athan, ed.: *From the Secret Files of J. Edgar Hoover* (Chicago: Ivan R. Dee, 1991).

Theoharis, Athan and Cox, John Stuart: *The Boss: J. Edgar Hoover and the Great American Inquisition* (Philadelphia: Temple University Press, 1988).

Walker, Samuel: *In Defense of American Liberties: A History of the ACLU* (New York: Oxford University Press, 1990).

Walkowitz, Daniel J.: *Working With Class: Social Workers and the Politics of Middle-Class Identity* (Chapel Hill: University of North Carolina Press, 1999).

Wang, Jessica: *American Science in an Age of Anxiety: Scientists, Anticommunism, and the Cold War* (Chapel Hill: University of North Carolina Press, 1999).

Weigand, Kate: *Red Feminism: American Communism and the Making of Women's Liberation* (Baltimore: Johns Hopkins University Press, 2001).

Weinstein, Allen: *Perjury: The Hiss–Chambers Case* (New York: Alfred A. Knopf, 1978; 2nd. ed., 1997).

Weinstein, Allen and Vassiliev, Alexander: *The Haunted Wood: Soviet Espionage in America – The Stalin Era* (New York: Random House, 1999).

Weisberg, Jacob: "Cold War Without End," *New York Times Sunday Magazine* (November 28, 1999).

Williams, Robert Chadwell: *Klaus Fuchs, Atom Spy* (Cambridge, Mass.: Harvard University Press, 1987).

Williams, Selma R.: *Red-Listed: Haunted by the Washington Witch Hunt* (Reading, Mass.: Addison Wesley, 1993).

FURTHER READING

For a more complete survey, see the bibliographical essay in Ellen Schrecker, *The Age of McCarthyism: A Brief History With Documents* (Boston: Bedford Books, 2002).

CHAPTER TWENTY

The Politics of "The Least Dangerous Branch": The Court, the Constitution, and Constitutional Politics Since 1945

MARY L. DUDZIAK

The courts, wrote Alexander Hamilton, are "the least dangerous branch" of government, "having neither FORCE, nor WILL, but only judgment." In this idealized depiction, judges stand beyond politics. They discern true principles of law and of justice, and apply them in the cases they confront. Their isolation from politics helps confer upon courts a sense of the legitimacy of their judgments. And that legitimacy is a source of the courts' power. This vision of the judiciary may have continued on in American high school civics books by the mid-twentieth century; however, the courts themselves would not have the luxury of blind faith on the part of the American public in their judgments.

American courts have never been far from the political fray, but in the twentieth century, as highly charged cases found their way before the US Supreme Court, constitutional questions – including the proper role of the courts themselves – more frequently occupied American politics. From the scope of federal regulatory power, to the legality of racial segregation, to the "right to life," crucial political issues came before the United States Supreme Court, and the Court, in turn, became a political issue.

As the courts took up many of the most important political and social questions, it is not surprising that scholarship on the courts and on constitutional history was highly charged. All scholarship has consequences, but the consequences of legal scholarship are particularly visible and immediate. Scholarship on the intentions of the framers of the equal protection clause, or on the history of the legal status of abortion, would find its way into briefs before the US Supreme Court, and then would be cited by justices in support of a Court ruling. The line between scholarship and advocacy, always tenuous, is more questionable than ever here. It is not just that some legal scholars who write about the history and theory of the Constitution also write briefs advocating that the "correct" vision of history dictates a particular outcome in a case. Professional historians have served as consultants in cases, briefs by historians have increasingly been filed in high-profile cases, and as if to complete the circle, some judges have themselves written constitutional history, advocating a vision of history that also certainly informs their approach to deciding cases. And at no time were the role of the courts and the nature of constitutional history more heatedly debated than at the end of the twentieth century, when the Supreme Court decided perhaps its most political case of all, ending the 2000 presidential election and handing the presidency to George W. Bush.

Scholarship on the courts often focuses on particular iconic moments, like the 2000 election, and sometimes focuses on Chief Justices who become iconic figures. Prior to the 2000 election case, there were three events that would most affect post-1945 thinking about the courts: first, the 1937 "switch in time that saved nine," when the Supreme Court appeared to abruptly shift course to uphold New Deal programs and state labor regulation; second, the 1954 decision in *Brown v. Board of Education* invalidating racial segregation in public schools; and third, the 1973 ruling protecting abortion rights, *Roe v. Wade*. The Supreme Court Chief Justice whose tenure on the Court has evoked most scholarly commentary is Chief Justice Earl Warren, who served from 1953 to 1969.

The "Switch in Time" and Constitutional Theory

American legal history in the late 1930s is a subject of great debate. For many years the standard account, as developed especially by New Deal scholars like William E. Leuchtenburg, has held that the Supreme Court dramatically altered course in 1937. During the preceding years, called the "*Lochner* era" after a 1905 case in which the Court struck down a state law regulating hours and working conditions of bakers, the Court had played a judicially activist but politically conservative role. Many of President Franklin Delano Roosevelt's New Deal programs had been struck down because they had gone beyond what the Court thought were appropriate limits on Congress's power. The Court also had carefully scrutinized state labor regulations, invalidating those that interfered with the rights of workers and employers to freely bargain over labor conditions. In early 1937, FDR proposed a plan to pack the Court. In the midst of the political controversy over the Court's role, the Supreme Court itself appeared suddenly to change course. It seemed to many that the Court was responding to political pressure, although later archival research would show that the crucial "switch in time" vote occurred before Roosevelt's court-packing plan was announced (Leonard, 1971; Leuchtenburg, 1996).

Through the rest of the twentieth century, the *Lochner* era would continue to haunt constitutional history. Seen as a period of judicial excess, the lesson of the *Lochner* era would appear to be that judges should be deferential to the political branches, that less judicial involvement in scrutinizing federal and state statutes would keep the Court more properly confined to its legitimate role. Judges and scholars advocating a strong role for the courts, for example in protecting individual rights, faced the challenge of distinguishing new forms of judicial activism from the judicial missteps of the *Lochner* era.

How the Court's actions in the 1930s were understood would come to have a profound impact on scholars' views about the basic nature of constitutional analysis in later years. Bruce Ackerman argued that FDR's landslide victory in the 1936 presidential election was a ratification of a new constitutional vision embodied in FDR's New Deal. The Court fell in line with this new constitutional vision when it changed course in 1937. Although the formal process of constitutional amendment had not been used, the Constitution had nevertheless been transformed during this "constitutional moment," Ackerman argued. The consequences were significant. For Ackerman, later judges were bound to interpret the scope of government regulatory power in light of the constitutional transformation of the 1930s. The result was that a stronger role for Congress in regulating labor and other areas of American life was legitimate. Ackerman provided a theory that justified the path the Court had, in fact, taken from 1937 to the 1990s (Ackerman, 1991, 1998).

Political scientists and legal historians challenged Ackerman's theory, and put into question the long-accepted historical narrative about the Court during the New Deal. Barry Cushman argued that there was no clean break in 1937 and that the Court's decisions in the late 1930s were based on case-law that had been developing in earlier years. The 1937 cases were best seen as an outgrowth of earlier developments in legal doctrine. If, as Cushman argued, there was no dramatic turnabout in 1937, then there could have been no "constitutional moment" and no public ratification of a constitutional transformation. If the Constitution had not been transformed, then legitimate questions could be raised about whether congressional enactments throughout the rest of the century had transgressed constitutional limits on Congress's power (Cushman, 1998).

The ensuing scholarly debate ultimately turned on what were thought of as "internalist" and "externalist" views of legal history. Externalists, including Laura Kalman, viewed legal history as being driven by forces outside of the law itself. In the New Deal period, an important external influence was American politics, popular criticism of the Court, and support for FDR's efforts to pull the nation out of depression. Internalists like Cushman and G. Edward White argued that external accounts had given short shrift to the role of legal analysis. Judges were constrained by case-law, they argued, and legal doctrine itself played a critical role in the way American legal history unfolded (Symposium, *Yale Law Journal*, 1999; White, 2000).

Much of the debate about the 1930s has operated within the frame of the New Deal period. A full "external" account of the courts, however, would require more. As David Bixby (1981) has shown, the Court and American political culture in the 1930s came to confront the specter of totalitarianism in other parts of the world. Many Americans, Bixby argues, believed that the judiciary served as a brake on the excesses of democracy, and that the courts were a necessary constraint on majoritarian politics. And indeed, once the Court changed course in 1937 and adopted a posture of deference toward economic legislation, the Court also crafted a new approach to individual rights. The Court would more closely scrutinize legislation that harmed minorities, since some groups, especially racial and religious minorities, were not fairly treated in a majoritarian system of government (Cover, 1982). Richard Primus (1999) also shows how anti-totalitarianism infused US rights discourse during this period. There were limits to the Court's new solicitude for minority rights, however, as illustrated most dramatically when the Court upheld aspects of the program to remove persons of Japanese heritage from their homes on the West Coast, and send them to internment camps. Peter Irons shows that the evidence the Court relied on was tainted by race-based assumptions, yet ironically in the internment cases the Court reaffirmed its commitment to strict scrutiny of race-based government action (Irons, 1993).

By 1945, the Court was well on its way toward charting a new approach to the practice of judicial review. Whether the product of an abrupt shift or of incremental change, a new jurisprudence had been framed in a time of crisis. The directions this new jurisprudence would take in later years was affected by the new constitutional challenges of the Cold War years.

The Cold War Constitution

Constitutional historians have long debated whether the Constitution serves as a meaningful restraint on government during times of crisis, or whether constitutional limits are malleable. While some suggest that it is unfortunate but inevitable that the Court will close ranks and support the executive branch during wartime, Chief Justice William Rehnquist has gone further, arguing in *All the Laws But One: Civil Liberties in Wartime* (1998) that the Court *should* be more deferential to the executive during such times. Yet if the Court simply falls in line behind the executive during times of crisis, of what value is a Constitution? The role of the Court and the Constitution during crisis times is most often discussed in the context of World Wars I and II, but is also at issue during early Cold War years. While cases on loyalty oaths and anti-subversive prosecutions went to the heart of the domestic Cold War, the Cold War context affected other cases as well. If communists might infiltrate American society through unseen "fifth column" activity, surely all aspects of American life were at risk and had broader implications for national security (Shrecker, 1998).

Dennis v. United States, decided by the Court in 1951, dealt directly with the government efforts to prosecute members of the Communist Party. The eleven defendants in the case were charged with violating the Smith Act, which had made it unlawful to advocate or teach the overthrow of the government by force or violence, or to organize or help to organize a group of persons so teaching and advocating, or conspiring to do so. As Michael Belknap (1977) has shown, the evidence against the defendants revealed no overt actions to target government officials or disrupt government actions. Instead, the defendants had read writings by communists, including the *Communist Manifesto*. They had hoped for the day when workers would rise up and topple American capitalism, but they had taken no steps to bomb factories or to sabotage government operations. The Court believed that these hopes were enough. It is a government's prerogative to defend itself, Chief Justice Fred Vinson argued, even against a small band of revolutionaries who had no chance of success. This low point in First Amendment jurisprudence provoked a strong dissent from Justice William O. Douglas. Under the First Amendment, speech should counter speech in the marketplace of ideas, he argued. Even revolutionaries should be able to speak openly unless their words truly pose an imminent "clear and present danger."

Constitutional limits had more force in one of the most important cases of the early Cold War years, *Youngstown Sheet and Tube v. Sawyer* (1952), also known as the Steel Seizure Case. The classic work on this episode remains Maeva Marcus's *Truman and the Steel Seizure Case: The Limits of Presidential Power* (1977). The United Steelworkers of America had called a strike against a number of steel companies that threatened to shut down the steel mills. For President Harry S. Truman, the implications of the threatened strike were global, for it threatened American military readiness during the Korean War. So the president issued an executive order directing the federal government to seize the steel mills and keep them operating. The steel companies went to court, arguing that Truman had exceeded his powers as president by seizing private property. The Supreme Court agreed. Authority to act may have seemed necessary, but as Justice Douglas put it, necessity did not expand the president's power under the Constitution. Unbridled executive authority might not have been abused by Harry Truman, but the Court was reluctant to establish a precedent that could be abused in the future. "It is absurd to see a dictator in a representative product of the Mississippi Valley. The accretion of dangerous power does not come in a day," Douglas wrote. "It does come, however slowly, from the generative force of unchecked disregard of the restrictions that fence in even the most disinterested assertion of authority."

At the same time that the Court was cracking down on communism, it was expanding rights in another area: racial equality. The Court's desegregation cases are a crucial focal point of two important scholarly debates: first, about the nature of judicial review, and second, about the effectiveness of courts as an agent of social change.

The story of the desegregation cases is often framed as the "road to *Brown*," since these cases laid the doctrinal groundwork for the Supreme Court's landmark desegregation decision. The literature on this history is vast. Richard Kluger's *Simple Justice* (1976) remains the classic narrative of the events leading to *Brown*, while James T. Patterson's recent account (2001) carries the story through the post-*Brown* years. At first glance, the Supreme Court cases seem to tidily chip away at the doctrine of "separate but equal," but Mark Tushnet's careful (1987) study of the National Association for the Advancement of Colored People's (NAACP's) legal strategy shows that there was nothing inevitable about this story. In 1938, in *Missouri ex rel. Gaines v. Canada*, the Supreme Court did not question the constitutionality of racial segregation per se, but invalidated Missouri's practice of sending black students out of state to go to law school since legal education was not offered to them in the state. It was the first time that the Court had looked seriously at the equality side of the separate-but-equal formula.

In *Shelly v. Kramer* (1946), the Court ruled racially restrictive covenants could not be enforced. These covenants typically forbade landowners from selling to persons of color, and they were used to foster residential segregation. In *Shelly*, the Court held that when private individuals invoked the support of state courts to enforce such agreements, that was "state action" in violation of the Fourteenth Amendment. Then in 1950, in *Sweatt v. Painter* and *McLaurin v. Oklahoma*, the Court found that legal education and graduate education could not be equal under the conditions of segregation. *Sweatt* and *McLaurin* significantly undermined Jim Crow in higher education. It was not clear at the time, however, whether the Court would extend these rulings to primary and secondary education, and whether the Court would find that government-sponsored segregation in all respects violated the Constitution.

Scholarly discussion of these cases often isolates them from their Cold War context. Yet as detailed in Mary L. Dudziak's *Cold War Civil Rights: Race and the Image of American Democracy* (2000), connections with the Cold War permeate primary documents related to these cases and to other civil rights developments. The US Justice Department argued in each case leading up to and including *Brown* that racial segregation embarrassed the United States internationally at a time when it was argued that American democracy was a model for the world. From this perspective, the segregation cases can inform the broader story of the Court's Cold War jurisprudence.

The Warren Court and the Countermajoritarian Difficulty

When the Supreme Court took up *Brown v. Board of Education*, the Warren Court era had begun. The Court under Chief Justice Earl Warren's leadership has captured the imagination of scholars and has played a critical role in scholarly debates about judicial review and the effectiveness of courts as a vehicle for social change. Yet some Warren Court historians acknowledge the awkwardness of periodizing Court history by the tenure of a Chief Justice, even one of Warren's reputation. Lucas A. Powe, Jr., in *The Warren Court and American Politics* (2000), for example, divides these years into three periods, with only the 1962–8 years seen as "History's Warren Court." While the Court had undermined the legal status of Jim Crow in the years before Warren's appointment, most scholars believe that Warren played a critical role, if not in the outcome of *Brown* itself, then certainly in the unanimity of the Court's verdict and in the nature of the ruling itself, which Warren authored (Hutchinson, 1979; Tushnet with Lezin, 1991).

Brown has been celebrated as one of the Supreme Court's greatest moments, but the *Brown* opinion itself has been the target of much scholarly criticism. The Court's ruling in *Brown* was, in many ways, a simple moral judgment: racial segregation in public schools was wrong. The difficulty for Chief Justice Warren in writing the opinion was the question of why it was the Court's job to make that moral judgment and to enforce it on local school systems. In a footnote of the opinion, Warren relied on social science evidence to support the finding that racial segregation was harmful to children. The evidence was useful not only because, at the time, it seemed powerful, but because reliance on modern scientific evidence also provided a means of arguing that the Court had learned something new about conditions of segregation, and that new knowledge required a different interpretation of the Fourteenth Amendment's guarantee of equality, one that justified a departure from past rulings.

Many constitutional scholars have criticized the Court's reliance on social science evidence, especially when some of the findings in *Brown*'s social science footnote 11 were criticized by social scientists themselves. If the Court had relied on dubious social science, then it could be argued that the very foundation for *Brown* was shaky (Powe, 2000). But if the legal and social science analysis in *Brown* was lacking, the opinion may still have been politically astute. By resting the decision on a new understanding of the facts, by arguing that modern science had only now shown us that segregation was harmful, the opinion was certainly less inflammatory than a ruling addressing the legacy of American racism would have been. Justice Warren did not point a finger of blame at southern whites, the individuals who would ultimately be charged with implementing the ruling. He also wrote *Brown* simply and plainly, so that all could read it, and many did as the opinion was reprinted in full in the nation's newspapers. *Brown* was also broadcast to the world on the Voice of America, and used effectively in State Department efforts to placate foreign critics of American race discrimination.

What was missing from *Brown*? It is not just that *Brown* sidestepped the question of the "intent of the framers" of the equal protection clause, something the Court itself had asked southern states to file briefs on. Throughout the entire *Brown* opinion, no reference was made to racism or to the legacy of Jim Crow. It was an opinion sanitized of context. It would not be until 1967 in a case invalidating

Virginia's ban on interracial marriage, a case appropriately titled *Loving v. Virginia*, that the Court finally directly addressed what all the civil rights cases in the 1940s, 1950s, and 1960s had been about. In *Loving*, the Court said that the purpose of the Virginia law had been to maintain white supremacy, thus setting the case in the context of the painful history of American racism. It was that context, and the recognition of continuing racial subordination, that was the reason the separate schools in *Brown* violated the Fourteenth Amendment. By failing to address this context in 1954, Warren undermined the legal basis for the Court's important opinion.

While *Brown* served as a helpful reassurance that American democracy was on the side of racial equality, the case did not end up requiring the integration of southern school districts during the 1950s. In 1955 in *Brown v. Board of Education II*, the Court denied the plaintiffs in the desegregation cases a timely remedy, calling instead for "all deliberate speed" in the enforcement of *Brown*. As many legal scholars and social scientists have shown, it would not be until the middle of the 1960s, when Congress and the president also got behind strong civil rights enforcement, that the Court would reenter the fray and begin defining just what desegregation should look like (Hochschild, 1983; Rosenberg, 1991; Patterson, 2001).

A crisis over the role of the courts developed in the aftermath of *Brown*. Southern politicians stood in the schoolhouse door, claiming that their states' rights had been violated and wrapping their resistance in the cloak of the Constitution. Southern members of Congress submitted a manifesto arguing that the Supreme Court had subverted the Constitution.

Criticism of *Brown* was not restricted to southern politicians and segregationist mobs. Throughout the academy, the *Brown* decision was heavily criticized as lacking a basis in law, precedent, or history, criticisms that would plague the Warren Court in other areas as well. Some scholars supported the outcome in *Brown*, but were uncomfortable with the way the Court got there. In an influential 1959 article, "Toward Neutral Principles of Constitutional Law," Herbert Weschler suggested that *Brown* was more politics than law because it was not based on neutral, generalizable principles. Instead, Weschler argued, an alternative basis for *Brown* was freedom of association.

While such scholars as Charles Black (1960) responded to Weschler by defending *Brown* as appropriately applying principles of equality to victims of discrimination, other scholars expanded the critique of *Brown* to an attack on judicial activism in general. In 1962, Yale law professor Alexander Bickel, a former law clerk and protégé of Supreme Court Justice Felix Frankfurter, published a book that would become the bible of advocates of judicial restraint: *The Least Dangerous Branch: The Supreme Court at the Bar of Politics*. Bickel's title was borrowed from Alexander Hamilton, who had written in the *Federalist Papers* that the judiciary was the least dangerous of the branches of government. This branch, Bickel wrote, had become "the most extraordinarily powerful court of law the world has ever known." Yet the courts played a problematic role in our political system. A democracy is based on majority rule, yet each time a court strikes down a statute, it acts counter to the will of the majority. Because of this "countermajoritarian difficulty," Bickel argued that the courts should not play an activist role in striking down unwise popular enactments. He shared Frankfurter's fondness for what he called the "passive virtues" – the exercise of court power in a restrained way so as to conserve the court's authority (Bickel,

1962, p. 201). Bickel's analysis of the countermajoritarian difficulty set the terms of debate over the role of the courts for the remainder of the twentieth century. Conservative scholars found in Bickel a justification for narrow theories of judicial power and constitutional interpretation. Liberals such as John Hart Ely took Bickel as their starting point and crafted a theory of judicial activism limited to contexts where the majoritarian political process was likely to fail (Ely, 1980).

There was yet more fodder for Warren Court critics in a series of cases on the constitutionality of state voting districts. The Court had avoided the issue of apportionment in the past. Justice Felix Frankfurter argued in 1946 that it would be impossible for the Court to get involved in apportionment cases and still maintain its independence from the other branches. To cross this line would be to enter the "political thicket," an area strictly forbidden to the judiciary (Powe, 2000). The Court nevertheless took up this question in *Baker v. Carr* (1962). In Tennessee, many residents had moved from rural to urban areas, but voting districts had not changed in sixty-one years. As a result, congressional districts were more populous in the cities. This diluted the strength of the votes of city dwellers and magnified political power in the less populous, and often more conservative, rural areas. Unequal voting power seemed unjust, but was it the Court's job to redress this problem?

In *Baker*, the Court addressed the issue of the Court's role in political controversies. Justice William Brennan's majority opinion found that unfairness in state voting schemes was not a "political question" outside the bounds of judicial power. In later cases the Court established a constitutional standard of "one man, one vote": each person's vote must have equal weight. These cases resulted in an uproar of accusations that the Court had overstepped its bounds, had departed from the meaning and purpose of the Constitution, and had taken over a legislative function. However, this time the furor arose principally from scholars and politicians. The general public appeared to accept, and even welcome, the results of the cases (Cox, 1968; Bickel, 1986).

Scholarly reactions to *Baker* often set themselves within the terms of the countermajoritarian debate, a sign of Bickel's influence. For example, Robert Bork argued that the reapportionment cases were a perfect example of the Court's disregard for the Constitution, because the "one man, one vote" principle was "forced upon people who have chosen democratically to arrange their state governments in part upon a different principle" (Bork, 1990, pp. 84–5). In contrast, John Hart Ely believed that "unblocking stoppages in the democratic process is what judicial review ought preeminently to be about, and denial of the vote seems the quintessential stoppage" (Ely, 1980, p. 117; Horwitz, 1998).

Another critical area of social change was criminal justice. Beginning in 1961, the Court under Earl Warren transformed the rights of those accused of crimes. In *Mapp v. Ohio* (1961), the Court held that illegally obtained evidence could not be used in prosecutions in state courts. This extended the federal exclusionary rule to the states, and began the criminal procedure revolution of the 1960s. *Gideon v. Wainwright* came in 1963, holding that the Sixth Amendment guaranteed a right to counsel, and required states to provide indigent criminal defendants with a lawyer. According to Powe, this case was Warren's only popular criminal procedure decision. *Miranda v. Arizona* in 1966 was one of the Warren Court's most controversial decisions. The Court held that the Fifth Amendment right against self-incrimination required police officers to notify a defendant of his or her rights before an interrogation in police custody. The "Miranda warning," as it came to be called, informed defendants of their right to be silent and their right to an attorney. Although the *Miranda* case was heavily criticized, Miranda warnings became a standard aspect of police procedures. They became well known through popular television programs featuring fictional police stories, so that even children would incorporate Miranda warnings into their play. The criminal law revolution then came to a halt after *Miranda*, as the Court allowed police to "stop and frisk" suspects without showing probable cause in 1968 in *Terry v. Ohio* (Horwitz, 1998; Powe, 2000). Some scholars would view these cases as another aspect of judicial usurpation and "government by judiciary" (Berger, 1977). For a later generation of scholars, however, the criminal justice cases were an important element of the Warren Court's efforts to achieve racial justice (Klarman, 2000).

Reactions to these and other judicial innovations put the Supreme Court at the center of American politics in the 1960s. In the spring of 1964, Alabama Governor George Wallace, who had already lambasted the Court for its civil rights rulings, broadened his critique. According to Wallace, the Court was responsible for a rise in "crime in the streets," for the "Supreme Court is fixing it so you can't do anything about people who set cities on fire." Moving beyond sectional concerns, Wallace helped to nationalize court bashing. The 1964 Republican presidential nominee, Barry Goldwater, picked up this theme, criticizing the Court for having abandoned the principle of judicial restraint (Carter, 1995, p. 313).

Women's Rights and "Privacy" Rights

The focus on iconic figures and cases, while helping to give focus to the writing of constitutional history, can leave important issues outside of the master narrative. In legal studies, the move to "canonize" a set of texts has particular power. The legal canon becomes the limited set of cases chosen for placement in law school casebooks. The canon becomes the legal doctrine learned by new generations of legal scholars, and relied on by courts as precedent for the future. Sanford Levinson (2000) has argued that the canon should be expanded, particularly to take account of foundational constitutional issues that arose in the context of American imperial expansion at the beginning of the twentieth century. The existence of a legal canon nevertheless continues to structure the study of American constitutional law in a way that renders marginal some important topics, such as the rights of women.

The Constitution was amended to protect women's right to vote in 1920. While Reva Siegel (1999) has argued that the suffrage amendment should be understood as having more transformative power for women's rights, the Supreme Court relegated the suffrage amendment to the periphery of constitutional analysis. While the Fifteenth Amendment, barring discrimination on the basis of race in voting, became part of the constitutional underpinnings for a broader vision of equality for persons of color, the woman suffrage amendment remained the equivalent of constitutional marginalia. Faced with a case involving sex discrimination against female bartenders in 1948, for example, Justice Felix Frankfurter wrote for the Court that "beguiling" as the issue in the case may be, "it need not detain us long." Against a lone dissent, the Court upheld sex distinctions as obviously legitimate.

Before the Court would develop a gender equality jurisprudence, the Court took important steps to protect reproductive rights. In the landmark case *Griswold v. Connecticut* (1965), the Court held that a state ban on the use of contraceptives that applied even to married couples violated the Constitution. Such laws intruded on intimate relationships and so violated a constitutional right to privacy. Since privacy rights are not mentioned in the text of the Constitution, the Court struggled to find a rationale for this outcome. Justice Douglas's majority opinion found that there were "penumbras, formed by emanations" from those rights specified in the Bill of Rights that created "zones of privacy" protected by the Constitution. Put together, these constitutional essences made it clear that the Constitution would not tolerate state intrusions into marital privacy.

The Court's struggle to find an acceptable theory in *Griswold* was tied in part to the Court's own history. The most likely home for a right to privacy was in the substantive right to be treated lawfully by government, which was implicit in the right to "due process of law," guaranteed by both the Fifth and the Fourteenth Amendments. But "substantive due process" had been a basis for judicial activism during the early twentieth-century *Lochner* era. The *Lochner* case, a symbol of wrong-headed judicial activism that had undermined progressive reform efforts, continued to have a hold on the Court's jurisprudence. In order to distinguish its own creation of rights from that of the *Lochner* Court, the justices struggled to find another, though ultimately unsatisfactory, constitutional mooring. Only Justice John Marshall Harlan embraced substantive due process, in an opinion that took on the legacy of *Lochner* and distinguished the right to privacy from *Lochner*'s form of judicial activism. And ultimately it would be Harlan's approach that a majority would adopt in later years (Garrow, 1994).

In the meantime, however, although the right in *Griswold* seemed of obvious importance, the Court's awkward analysis made the right to privacy an easy target for scholarly critics. Sylvia Law (1984) has argued that the context of *Griswold* – before the Court developed its sex discrimination jurisprudence – helps us to see a missing element of *Griswold* and later reproductive rights cases: a discussion of the importance of reproductive freedom to women's equality. Instead, the rights in the reproductive freedom cases are rights to *privacy* in one's intimate relationships and in one's relationship with medical professionals. As Ruth Bader Ginsburg (1985) argued before her appointment to the Supreme Court, a more robust understanding of women's constitutional equality would have provided an alternative legal basis for women's reproductive rights.

"Government by Judiciary" or a "Hollow Hope"?

The landmark cases of *Griswold*, *Miranda*, *Brown*, *Baker v. Carr*, and others during the Warren years have led scholars to look upon this period in the Court's history as characterized by judicial activism in the service of individual rights. For some scholars, this record epitomizes the Court at its best (Fiss, 1991). For critics, it is an example of judicial overreaching. Among the Warren Court's contemporaries, Raoul Berger argued that Court decisions striking down state and federal statutes resulted in "government by judiciary" (Berger, 1977). For Archibald Cox the Warren Court's involvement was crucial because the other branches of government were not acting on reapportionment, criminal procedure reforms, and racial inequality. Either the Court had to do something, or nothing would be done at all (Cox, 1968).

Notwithstanding all the clamor about the Court entering the arena of politics, did the Warren Court really accomplish social change? Scholars identified with the critical legal studies movement have long argued that the law is indeterminate, and as a result legal precedent is never a firm foundation. Rulings always involve choices that are at base political. Alan Freeman and others brought these insights to bear on the Court's developing equality jurisprudence, arguing that these rulings held out a promise of reform while masking continuing inequalities (Freeman, 1978).

In *The Hollow Hope* (1991), political scientist Gerald Rosenberg crystallized this line of analysis. He argued that the courts are not a source of meaningful social change, and when litigants rely on courts, their energies are deflected from the political process, where real change can occur. According to Rosenberg, the Supreme Court is not "dynamic" and by itself cannot produce significant social change. To the contrary, the Court is "constrained" because: (1) as an institution, it is limited as to the scope of issues it can address (limited to the Constitution, for example); (2) it lacks sufficient independence from the other branches of government; and (3) it lacks the power to develop appropriate policies and implement decisions. Thus, the Court can only facilitate change when other specific social and/or political factors work to reinforce Court rulings and provide incentives for compliance. The result is a "fly-paper Court" that lures in movements for social reform, causing them to pour resources into an institution that, without actually serving their needs, provides only an illusion of change. Turning to *Brown*, Rosenberg notes that meaningful school desegregation did not occur until after the passage of the Civil Rights Act of 1964, which gave the executive branch enforcement authority in the area of school desegregation (Rosenberg, 1991). Taking a somewhat different emphasis, Michael Klarman argued that it was not *Brown* that achieved social change on civil rights. Instead, *Brown* led to massive resistance, and it was the national reaction against massive resistance that led to significant social change such as the Civil Rights Act (Klarman, 1994).

Some legal scholars and social scientists suggest that legal culture and the power of law are more complex than Rosenberg allows. Michael McCann, for example, criticizes Rosenberg's "top-down, unmediated view of judicial power," which results in a "narrow understanding of causality and impact." According to McCann, it is "surely correct . . . that landmark decisions by themselves rarely change either citizens' behavior or personal values in a dramatic and uniform fashion." Rosenberg's approach, however, "tends to discount the reciprocal, interactive, relational terms of law's constitutive power." For McCann, litigation can have an impact on social movements, for example, by generating support from middle-class contributors who would be unwilling to support more "disruptive" forms of grassroots activity. In this way, "legal tactics can produce as well as consume financial resources." McCann emphasizes that "legal norms and institutions neither guarantee justice nor are they simply obstacles and diversions to the pursuit of a more just society." Both of these characterizations are overly simplistic. In his view, "given the overwhelming systemic inequalities and scarcities in basic resources that oppress subordinate groups, even limited, contingent, uncertain resources such as our legal traditions offer should be appreciated" (McCann, 1994, pp. 290–4, 309; see also Schultz, 1998).

For other scholars, the answer has been to turn away from the courts but not from the Constitution itself. Richard Parker argues for a "populist" non-court-centered constitutional politics, and Mark Tushnet proposes that people should "take the Constitution away from the courts," looking to the political branches to give meaning to individual rights (Parker, 1994; Tushnet, 2000).

"The Counter-Revolution that Wasn't?"

Whether or not scholars believe that Warren-era decisions led to effective social change, rulings in the areas of reproductive rights, apportionment, racial equality, criminal justice, and other areas became a focus of electoral politics in the 1968 presidential election. Richard Nixon attacked the Court in his campaign. Borrowing George Wallace's argument that the federal courts were responsible for increased "crime in the streets," Nixon's 1968 campaign focused on "law and order." He attacked the Supreme Court and its liberal rulings protecting the rights of defendants as standing in the way of government crime-fighting efforts. As an antidote to the liberal bench, Nixon promised to appoint strict constructionists who would interpret and not make law (T. White, 1969; Carter, 1995). Nixon's first Supreme Court appointee was Warren Burger, who replaced the retiring Earl Warren. Burger's ideology fit well with Nixon's agenda. He had publicly attacked the Warren Court and the expansion of individual rights. According to David O'Brien, "Burger came to the Court with the agenda of reversing the 'liberal jurisprudence' of the Warren Court and restoring 'law and order'" (O'Brien, 2000, p. 69).

Since judicial politics was on the national agenda when Burger was appointed to the Court, and since the change in the Chief Justice was so stark – from liberal activist to conservative strict-constructionist – it was widely expected that under Chief Justice Burger the Court would take a sharp turn to the right. That was, after all, what Richard Nixon had had in mind. However, the "Burger Court" continued many of the doctrinal strands begun under Warren's tenure. In the protection of individual rights, the Court took some dramatic steps forward that went beyond even what the Court had accomplished during the Warren years, most notably in the area of abortion rights, in *Roe v. Wade* (1973). During the 1970s the Court also developed for the first time a gender equality jurisprudence. Yet so widely was a conservative turn expected that a book on the Court during Burger's tenure was subtitled "The Counter-Revolution that Wasn't" (Blasi, 1983).

Scholars writing about race and the Burger Court tend to compare it with the Warren years. The trend of desegregation begun in the Warren years continued into the cases and decisions of the Burger era, but with notable setbacks. *Swann v. Charlotte-Mecklenburg County School District* (1971), for example, upheld cross-town busing as an appropriate remedy for school segregation, and *Keyes v. School District No. 1* made it clear that the principles in the desegregation cases would be applied in northern and western schools that had not been subject to segregation statutes but were nevertheless racially segregated (Schwartz, 1986; Douglas, 1995). Perhaps a more important decision was *Washington v. Davis*, in which the Court ruled that in order to gain relief from a discriminatory policy, plaintiffs must prove that it was motivated by a "discriminatory purpose." According to Derrick Bell, since discriminatory motive is often impossible to prove, *Davis* "raised beyond reach the barriers to relief in a range of cases in housing, criminal justices, and education" (Bell, 1998, p. 62). In an influential article, Charles Lawrence argued that the intent requirement was inconsistent with the basic psychology of race in America. In a culture in which racial ordering had played a dominant role, actions that resulted in discrimination would often be the product of unconscious racial motivation. Yet unconscious racism was now beyond the reach of the Constitution (Lawrence, 1987).

One of the most contentious issues on the Court during this period was the issue of affirmative action. A divided Court barred racial quotas, yet left room for some consideration of race in university admissions in *Regents of the University of California v. Bakke* (1978). As the Court's affirmative action case-law developed, a rich debate among legal scholars explored the questions of whether the Fourteenth Amendment envisioned a "colorblind" society in which any consideration of race was suspect, or whether the basic purpose of the Fourteenth Amendment was to overcome the enforced subordination created by a system of slavery. Under an anti-subordination model, affirmative steps taken to overcome racial hierarchy would be in keeping with the basic purpose of equal protection. The discussion would go beyond constitutional history and abstract legal reasoning, as scholars associated with the critical race theory movement enriched the discussion of race and the law by relentlessly confronting legal subjectivity, bringing the concrete experience of race-based oppression to legal analysis. Patricia Williams and others challenged the notion that race neutrality should be the remedy for race bias. Williams argued that affirmative action was not a constitutional harm but "an act of social as well as professional responsibility" (Williams, 1991, p. 50).

The Court would ultimately come together on affirmative action. As staunch conservatives joined the Court, the center shifted, creating a majority firmly on the side of colorblindness in *Adarand Constructors v. Pena* (1995). As Justice Antonin Scalia put it in his concurrence, "To pursue the concept of racial entitlement – even for the most admirable and benign of purposes – is to reinforce and preserve for future mischief the way of thinking that produced race slavery, race privilege and race hatred. In the eyes of government, we are just one race here. It is American" (Brest et al., 2000, p. 949).

In *Roe v. Wade*, the Court drew upon the right to privacy developed in *Griswold*, and struck down a Texas statute that made abortion a crime. With access to abortion blocked, many desperate women had sought what were called "back-alley abortions" from unregulated providers who operated in secret, while others attempted self-abortion, often with disastrous results. For this reason, the bloody coathanger became a symbol of the abortion rights movement. For some religious groups, however, human life began at conception, and so an abortion resulted in the intentional taking of a human life. The meaning of abortion seemed to turn on the moral status of the fetus and the unanswerable question of when human life begins (Luker, 1984; Garrow, 1994). In *Roe v. Wade* the Court held that the constitutional right to privacy protected the right to terminate a pregnancy, but also allowed states to regulate abortion. Since the Court deemed the question of the beginnings of human life unanswerable, and since important rights were at stake for pregnant women, Justice Harry Blackmun's majority opinion balanced these interests. The further a pregnancy had developed, the stronger the interests of the state, and the more likely they were to outweigh a woman's right to choose to have an abortion, so that in the third trimester, when the fetus would reach the point that it could survive outside the woman's womb, the state could prohibit abortion unless it was necessary to save a woman's life or safeguard her health.

Roe v. Wade set off a firestorm of criticism, and galvanized the "right to life" movement. Massive marches to the Supreme Court were organized on January 22, the anniversary of the day the decision was handed down. The combination of a high-profile case in a controversial area and a well-organized national right to life movement ensured that the Court would be at the center of political controversy for some time to come. Among scholars of the Court, the reaction to *Roe* initially mirrored reactions to *Brown*, with much criticism of the Court's constitutional analysis, although this time there was less consensus that the outcome was correct.

At the same time that the Court was expanding women's reproductive rights under a privacy rationale, the Court expanded women's right in another area: the right to equality. For most of the Court's history, gender equality was not given serious thought. As Linda Kerber (1999) has detailed, in 1961 the Court relied on gender stereotyping and the idea that women's role was principally in the home when it upheld Florida rules that resulted in nearly all-male juries. It would not be until 1971 that the Court would strike down a statute for the first time on the grounds that it violated women's constitutional right to equality. The Court's about-face on sex discrimination happened in the context of a revived feminist movement and a renewed attempt to gain ratification of an Equal Rights Amendment (ERA) to the Constitution (Ginsburg, 1983; Seymour, 1998). In an argument reminiscent of Rosenberg, some scholars have suggested that when the Court decided its 1970s sex discrimination cases, it derailed political efforts to amend the Constitution (Mansbridge, 1986). Although the ERA was not ratified, by the end of the twentieth century the first two women justices on the US Supreme Court, Sandra Day O'Connor and Ruth Bader Ginsburg, ensured that the Court would continue to take sex discrimination claims seriously.

There were limits to the Court's new privacy jurisprudence. Access to reproductive freedom had often been heavily affected by class standing, as women with resources were able to get around restrictions, while women needing publicly funded reproductive services were not. With abortion rights, the Court would codify that difference in a series of cases that refused to find any unconstitutional burden on the right to women's freedom of choice posed by state and federal medical programs for the poor that banned use of government funds for abortion services. It was a woman's poverty, the Court reasoned, not the government's funding scheme, that made access to abortion difficult for poor women. Poverty was seen as a natural phenomenon that preceded the state and for which the government was not responsible. The result was that women had a right to choose, as long as they could pay for it (Dudziak, 1991).

The Court also declined to extend the right to privacy to gays and lesbians. In *Bowers v. Hardwick* (1986), the Court held that a Virginia anti-sodomy law was not unconstitutional, at least in the context of a prosecution of a gay man for homosexual sex, even though the consensual sex occurred in his own home. William Eskridge has argued that cases like *Bowers* both reinforced the "apartheid of the closet" but also helped galvanize the gay rights movement (Eskridge, 1999).

Judicial Politics at the End of the Century

President Ronald Reagan was particularly effective at using court appointments to further a political agenda. He instituted an anti-abortion "litmus test" for judicial appointees. Seeing the courts as a means to achieve a conservative social agenda over time, the Reagan administration sought steadfast conservatives who were also young, and therefore likely to have a long-lasting impact on the courts. President George H. W. Bush followed a similar strategy. By the end of the century, seven out of nine justices of the Supreme Court had been appointed by Republican presidents, so that the new conservative Chief Justice, William H. Rehnquist, had more allies in his efforts to roll back Warren Court-era reforms. The Reagan and Bush court appointments also had a profound effect on the lower federal courts as, by 1992, approximately 70 percent of lower court judges were Reagan and Bush appointees (Schwartz, 1988; Savage, 1992; O'Brien, 2000).

There was a limit to what could be accomplished by such an aggressively political strategy, however, as demonstrated by the defeat of Supreme Court nominee Robert Bork. Nominated in July 1987 to fill the vacancy created by the resignation of Justice Lewis F. Powell, Bork was immediately opposed by a broad coalition of civil rights groups appalled by his conservative views. In testimony before the Senate Judiciary Committee, Bork advocated judicial restraint and a theory of constitutional interpretation based on the constitutional text and the intentions of the framers. Bork believed that *Roe v. Wade* was not authorized by the framers' intentions and also that the right to privacy in the use of birth control articulated in *Griswold v. Connecticut* was something the framers had not contemplated, and therefore something the Constitution did not protect. Bork's widely televised testimony provoked a strong, negative public reaction. Some commentators likened the Bork hearings to a national teach-in on the Constitution, with a final public referendum in favor of a constitutional right to privacy. Bork was ultimately defeated by the widest margin of votes in the Senate in the history of the confirmation process (Schwartz, 1998).

Following Bork, the next nomination to generate especially widespread controversy was Bush's nomination of Clarence Thomas in 1991 to fill a vacancy created by the retirement of Justice Thurgood Marshall. The selection of Thomas, a conservative black Court of Appeals judge who formerly served as chair of the Equal Employment Opportunity Commission, in part reflected a sense that it was important for a black person to fill the seat of the only black justice ever to serve on the Supreme Court. President Bush also rightly calculated that it would be more difficult for liberals to mount an effective challenge to a black appointee. Ultimately it would not be his conservative ideology that would be the greatest hurdle to the Thomas nomination. Rather, it was a charge of sexual harassment by Anita Hill, a former Thomas subordinate at the Equal Employment Opportunity Commission. Senate hearings were held to air the Hill allegations. Even though many praised Hill for raising the nation's consciousness about sexual harassment, Thomas was ultimately confirmed. By the end of his first Supreme Court term, his harshly conservative opinions led the *New York Times* to call him "The Youngest, Cruelest Justice" (Savage, 1992).

By 1992, a staunchly conservative Court majority was thought to be ready to overturn *Roe v. Wade*. The threat to *Roe* helped galvanize supporters of abortion rights, including members of Congress and presidential candidates. In *Planned Parenthood of Southeastern Pennsylvania v. Casey* (1992), however, a new coalition of justices – Sandra Day O'Connor, Anthony Kennedy, and David Souter – voted with Court moderates to uphold most aspects of a Pennsylvania statute restricting access to abortion, but not to overturn flatly *Roe v. Wade*. While *Casey* vastly expanded the ability of states to regulate abortion and to encourage women not to have the procedure, *Roe* remained on the books as a precedent, albeit a substantially weakened one; as a result, *Casey* diffused abortion as a political issue among progressives (Garrow, 1994).

Because most commentators viewed *Casey* as an affirmation rather than an evisceration of *Roe*, the case seemed to fit a pattern, reinforcing the belief that a conservative counterrevolution on the Court had once again failed to materialize. In the last decade of the twentieth century, however, the Court appeared to move in a new direction. Increasingly vocal opponents of affirmative action saw the Court as protecting their vision of individual rights, and opponents to government regulation argued that the Court was protecting liberty. Since 1937 the Court had been deferential to the political branches in the area of economic legislation, but with *United States v. Lopez* in 1995, the Court began to develop a new federalism jurisprudence. In the name of states' rights, the Court struck down congressional attempts to regulate firearms near schools, to criminalize violence against women, to protect persons with disabilities from discrimination by state governments, and other areas. The most marked change was the Court's refusal to defer to choices made by Congress. Ironically, countermajoritarianism, once a conservative critique of a liberal court, had come to characterize a conservative judiciary. Legal scholars began the 1990s debating whether a conservative revolution had or had not happened. By the end of the century it was clear that the Court had carved out for itself an activist role – both to restrict the reach of congressional power and to protect a new vision of individual rights, the rights of supposed victims of state and federal affirmative action programs (Symposium, *Stanford Law Review*, 2001).

Critics of the Court continued to divide along political and ideological lines. One act would bring many Court critics together, however, at least for a moment. In the close 2000 election, Florida's disputed votes would determine the winner. The Court intervened. Notwithstanding an earlier judgment that the Court risked its legitimacy any time it entered the political arena, the Court first issued an order blocking a recount of disputed ballots, and then blocked the Florida State Supreme Court's efforts to bring the election to a resolution with a recount by ruling that the state court's efforts violated the US Constitution. Because the five members of the Court majority seemed to disregard their own views of federalism and equal protection in reaching this result, the Court's creative constitutional analysis was quickly criticized, momentarily bringing legal scholars together across ideological lines. In the aftermath, some asked whether it had not finally become clear that politics was necessarily at the center of judicial action. The Court was seen as having damaged its legitimacy by raising the veil and exposing itself as a partisan actor (Gillman, 2001).

Yet just as it appeared that a wide range of legal scholars had joined the critical legal studies camp, the process of "renormalization" set in, according to Mark Tushnet (2001). Just as statisticians normalize data so that outliers do not disrupt the results, so too, he argued, were legal scholars finding ways of explaining *Bush v. Gore* that did not disrupt their fundamental need to believe in the rule of law. In the showering of legal scholarship that followed the decision, Alan Dershowitz (2001) argued that the Court had committed a criminal act, while Judge Richard Posner (2001) argued that the Supreme Court had stepped in to protect the nation from an impending constitutional crisis. In a careful analysis, Howard Gillman (2001) argued that the Supreme Court had indeed acted in a partisan manner in the election case, but that the many other state and federal judges involved in the complex litigation had not been partisan. As a result the overall picture was more salient to the hope of judicial impartiality. Still the glaring reality that the Supreme Court had cast the vote that counted the most in the election case ensured that the century ended with a new, if troublesome, icon.

The five members of the *Bush v. Gore* majority did not seem to garner the same level of public opprobrium that the New Deal-era Court had. Yet they may have made a mark on the image of the Court at least as clear as that of their predecessors during the "switch in time." As *Bush v. Gore* settles uncomfortably into the legal canon, its lessons are sure to be constructed by scholars to inform new visions of the Court in generations to come.

REFERENCES

Ackerman, Bruce: *We the People: Foundations*, vol. 1 (Cambridge, Mass.: Harvard University Press, 1991).

Ackerman, Bruce: *We the People: Transformations*, vol. 2 (Cambridge, Mass.: Harvard University Press, 1998).

Belknap, Michael: *Cold War Political Justice: The Smith Act, the Communist Party, and American Civil Liberties* (Westport, Conn.: Greenwood Press, 1977).

Bell, Derrick: "The Burger Court's Place on the Bell Curve of Racial Jurisprudence," in Herman Schwartz (ed.), *The Burger Court: Counter-Revolution or Confirmation?* (New York: Oxford University Press, 1998).

Berger, Raoul: *Government by Judiciary: The Transformation of the Fourteenth Amendment* (Cambridge, Mass.: Harvard University Press, 1977).

Bickel, Alexander: *The Least Dangerous Branch: The Supreme Court at the Bar of Politics* (New Haven, Conn.: Yale University Press, 1962; 2nd ed., 1986).

Bixby, David: "The Roosevelt Court, Democratic Ideology, and Minority Rights: Another Look at *United States v. Classic*," *Yale Law Journal*, 90 (1981): 741–815.

Black, Charles: "The Lawfulness of the Segregation Decisions," *Yale Law Journal*, 69 (1960): 421–30.

Blasi, Vincent, ed.: *The Burger Court: The Counter-Revolution that Wasn't* (New Haven, Conn.: Yale University Press, 1983).

Bork, Robert H.: *The Tempting of America: The Political Seduction of the Law* (New York: Free Press, 1990).

Brest, Paul, Levinson, Sanford, Balkin, Jack, and Amar, Akhil: *Processes of Constitutional Decisionmaking: Cases and Materials*, 4th ed. (New York: Aspen Publishers, 2000).

Carter, Dan T.: *The Politics of Rage: George Wallace, the Origins of the New Conservatism, and the Transformation of American Politics* (New York: Simon and Schuster, 1995).

Cover, Robert: "The Origins of Judicial Activism in the Protection of Minorities," *Yale Law Journal*, 91 (1982): 1287–1316.

Cox, Archibald: *The Warren Court: Constitutional Decision as an Instrument of Reform* (Cambridge, Mass.: Harvard University Press, 1968).

Cushman, Barry: *Rethinking the New Deal Court: The Structure of a Constitutional Revolution* (New York: Oxford University Press, 1998).

Dershowitz, Alan M.: *Supreme Injustice: How the High Court Hijacked Election 2000* (New York: Oxford University Press, 2001).

Douglas, Davison M.: *Reading, Writing, and Race: The Desegregation of the Charlotte Schools* (Chapel Hill: University of North Carolina Press, 1995).

Dudziak, Mary L.: "Just Say No: Birth Control in the Connecticut Supreme Court Before *Griswold v. Connecticut*," in P. S. Finkelman and S. Gottlieb (eds.), *Toward a Usable Past: Liberty Under State Constitutions* (Athens: Georgia University Press, 1991), 915–39.

Dudziak, Mary L.: *Cold War Civil Rights: Race and the Image of American Democracy* (Princeton, NJ: Princeton University Press, 2000).

Ely, John Hart: *Democracy and Distrust: A Theory of Judicial Review* (Cambridge, Mass.: Harvard University Press, 1980).

Eskridge, William: *Gaylaw: Challenging the Apartheid of the Closet* (Cambridge, Mass.: Harvard University Press, 1999).

Fiss, Owen: "A Life Twice Lived," *Yale Law Journal*, 100 (1991): 1117.

Freeman, Alan: "Legitimizing Racial Discrimination Through Antidiscrimination Law: A Critical Review of Supreme Court Doctrine," *Minnesota Law Review*, 62 (1978): 1049–1119.

Garrow, David: *Liberty and Sexuality: The Right to Privacy and the Making of Roe v. Wade* (New York: Macmillan, 1994).

Gillman, Howard: *The Votes that Counted: How the Court Decided the 2000 Presidential Election* (Chicago: University of Chicago Press, 2001).

Ginsburg, Ruth Bader: "The Burger Court's Grapplings with Sex Discrimination," in Vincent Blasi (ed.), *The Burger Court: The Counter-Revolution that Wasn't* (New Haven, Conn.: Yale University Press, 1983).

Ginsburg, Ruth Bader: "Some Thoughts On Autonomy and Equality in Relation to *Roe v. Wade*," *North Carolina Law Review*, 63 (1985): 375–86.

Gottlieb, Stephen E.: *Morality Imposed: The Rehnquist Court and Liberty in America* (New York: New York University Press, 2000).

Hochschild, Jennifer L.: *The New American Dilemma: Liberal Democracy and School Desegregation* (New Haven, Conn.: Yale University Press, 1983).

Horwitz, Morton: *The Warren Court and the Pursuit of Justice* (New York: Hill and Wang, 1998).

Hutchinson, Dennis: "Unanimity and Desegregation: Decisionmaking in the Supreme Court, 1948–1958," *Georgetown Law Journal*, 68 (1979): 1–87.

Irons, Peter H.: *Justice at War: The Story of the Japanese American Internment Cases*, 2nd ed. (New York: Oxford University Press, 1993).

Kerber, Linda: *No Constitutional Right to Be Ladies: Women and the Obligations of Citizenship* (New York: Hill and Wang, 1999).

Klarman, Michael J.: "How *Brown* Changed Race Relations: The Backlash Thesis," *Journal of American History*, 81 (1994): 81–118.

Klarman, Michael J.: "The Racial Origins of Modern Criminal Procedure," *Michigan Law Review*, 99 (October 2000): 48–97.

Kluger, Richard: *Simple Justice: The History of Brown v. Board of Education and Black America's Struggle for Equality* (New York: Random House, 1976).

Law, Sylvia A.: "Rethinking Sex and the Constitution," *University of Pennsylvania Law Review*, 132 (1984): 955–1040.

Lawrence, III, Charles R.: "The Id, the Ego, and Equal Protection: Reckoning with Unconscious Racism," *Stanford Law Review*, 39 (1987): 317–88.

Leonard, Charles A.: *A Search for a Judicial Philosophy: Mr. Justice Roberts and the Constitutional Revolution of 1937* (New York: Kennikat Press, 1971).

Leuchtenburg, William E.: *The Supreme Court Reborn: The Constitutional Revolution in the Age of Roosevelt* (New York: Oxford University Press, 1996).

Levinson, Sanford: "Why the Canon Should Be Expanded to Include the Insular Cases and the Saga of American Expansionism," *Constitutional Commentary*, 17 (2000): 241–66.

Luker, Kristin: *Abortion and the Politics of Motherhood* (Berkeley: University of California Press, 1984).

McCann, Michael: *Rights at Work: Pay Equity Reform and the Politics of Legal Mobilization* (Chicago: University of Chicago Press, 1994).

Mansbridge, Jane J.: *Why We Lost the ERA* (Chicago: University of Chicago Press, 1986).

Marcus, Maeva: *Truman and the Steel Seizure Case: The Limits of Presidential Power* (New York: Columbia University Press, 1977).

O'Brien, David M.: *Storm Center: The Supreme Court in American Politics*, 3rd ed. (New York: W. W. Norton, 2000).

Parker, Richard D.: *"Here, The People Rule": A Constitutional Populist Manifesto* (Cambridge, Mass.: Harvard University Press, 1994).

Patterson, James: *Brown v. Board of Education: A Civil Rights Milestone and Its Troubled Legacy* (New York: Oxford University Press, 2001).

Posner, Richard: *Breaking the Deadlock: The 2000 Election, the Constitution, and the Courts* (Princeton, NJ: Princeton University Press, 2001).

Powe, Jr., Lucas A.: *The Warren Court and American Politics* (Cambridge, Mass.: Belknap Press, 2000).

Primus, Richard: *The American Language of Rights* (New York: Cambridge University Press, 1999).

Rehnquist, William: *All the Laws But One: Civil Liberties in Wartime* (New York: Alfred A. Knopf, 1998).

Rosenberg, Gerald: *The Hollow Hope: Can Courts Bring About Social Change?* (Chicago: University of Chicago Press, 1991).

Savage, David G.: *Turning Right: The Making of the Rehnquist Supreme Court* (New York: John Wiley, 1992).

Schrecker, Ellen: *Many Are the Crimes: McCarthyism in America* (New York: Little, Brown, 1998).

Schultz, David A., ed.: *Leveraging the Law: Using Courts to Achieve Social Change* (New York: Peter Lang, 1998).

Schwartz, Bernard: *Swann's Way: The School Busing Case and the Supreme Court* (New York: Oxford University Press, 1986).

Schwartz, Herman: *The Burger Years: Rights and Wrongs in the Supreme Court, 1969–1986* (New York: Viking, 1987).

Schwartz, Herman: *Packing the Courts: The Conservative Campaign to Rewrite the Constitution* (New York: Charles Scribner's Sons, 1988).

Schwartz, Herman, ed.: *The Burger Court: Counter-Revolution or Confirmation?* (New York: Oxford University Press, 1998).

Seymour, Stephanie K.: "Women as Constitutional Equals: The Burger Court's Overdue Evolution," in Herman Schwartz (ed.), *The Burger Court: Counter-Revolution or Confirmation?* (New York: Oxford University Press, 1998).

Siegel, Reva B.: "Collective Memory and the Nineteenth Amendment: Reasoning About 'the Woman Question' in the Discourse of Sex Discrimination," in Austin Sarat and Thomas R. Kearns (eds.), *History, Memory and the Law* (Ann Arbor: University of Michigan Press, 1999), 131–82.

Symposium, "Moments of Change: Transformation in American Constitutionalism," *Yale Law Journal*, 108 (June 1999): 1917–2349.

Symposium, "Shifting the Balance of Power? The Supreme Court, Federalism, and State Sovereign Immunity," *Stanford Law Review* (May 2001).

Tushnet, Mark V.: *The NAACP's Legal Strategy Against Segregated Education, 1925–1950* (Chapel Hill: University of North Carolina Press, 1987).

Tushnet, Mark V.: *Taking the Constitution Away from the Courts* (Princeton, NJ: Princeton University Press, 2000).

Tushnet, Mark V.: "Renormalizing *Bush v. Gore*: An Anticipatory Intellectual History," *Georgetown University Law Review* (forthcoming, 2001).

Tushnet, Mark V., with Katya Lezin: "What Really Happened in *Brown v. Board of Education*," *Columbia Law Review*, 91 (1991): 1867–1930.

Weschler, Herbert: "Toward Neutral Principles of Constitutional Law," *Harvard Law Review*, 73 (1959): 1–35.

White, G. Edward: *The Constitution and the New Deal* (Cambridge, Mass.: Harvard University Press, 2000).

White, Theodore H.: *The Making of the President, 1968* (New York: Atheneum, 1969).

Williams, Patricia J.: *The Alchemy of Race and Rights* (Cambridge, Mass.: Harvard University Press, 1991).

FURTHER READING

Abraham, Henry J.: *Justices, Presidents, and Senators: A History of the U.S. Supreme Court Appointments from Washington to Clinton*, rev. ed. (Lanham, Md.: Rowman and Littlefield, 1999).

Ariens, Michael: "A Thrice-Told Tale, or Felix the Cat," *Harvard Law Review*, 107 (1994): 620–76 (on Felix Frankfurter).

Balkin, J. M. and Levinson, Sanford, eds.: *Legal Canons* (New York: New York University Press, 2000).

Bell, Derrick, ed.: *Shades of Brown: New Perspectives on School Desegregation* (New York: Teachers' College Press, 1980).

Cain, Patricia: *Rainbow Rights: The Role of Lawyers and Courts in the Lesbian and Gay Civil Rights Movement* (Boulder, Colo.: Westview Press, 2000).

Crenshaw, Kimberle, Gotanda, Neil, Peller, Gary, and Thomas, Kendall, eds.: *Critical Race Theory: The Key Writings that Formed the Movement* (New York: New Press, 1996).

Currie, David P.: *The Constitution in the Supreme Court: The Second Century, 1888–1986* (Chicago: University of Chicago Press, 1990).

Delgado, Richard and Stefanic, Jean, eds.: *Critical Race Theory: The Cutting Edge*, 2nd ed. (Philadelphia: Temple University Press, 2000).

Feldman, Stephen M.: *American Legal Thought from Premodernism to Postmodernism: An Intellectual Voyage* (New York: Oxford University Press, 2000).

Friedman, Barry: "The History of the Countermajoritarian Difficulty, Part Four: Law's Politics," *University of Pennsylvania Law Review*, 148 (2000): 971–1064.

Friedman, Lawrence M. and Scheiber, Harry N., eds.: *American Law and the Constitutional Order: Historical Perspectives*, rev. ed. (Cambridge, Mass.: Harvard University Press, 1988).

Gillman, Howard and Clayton, Cornell, eds.: *The Supreme Court in American Politics: New Institutionalist Interpretations* (Lawrence: University Press of Kansas, 1999).

Higginbotham, A. Leon: *Shades of Freedom: Racial Politics and Presumptions of the American Legal Process* (New York: Oxford University Press, 1996).

Kahn, Ronald: *The Supreme Court and Constitutional Theory, 1953–1993* (Lawrence: University Press of Kansas, 1994).

Kairys, David: *With Liberty and Justice for Some: A Critique of the Conservative Supreme Court* (New York: New Press, 1993).

Kammen, Michael: *A Machine that Would Go of Itself: The Constitution in American Culture* (New York: Alfred A. Knopf, 1986).

Kelly, Winifred A., Harbison, Alfred H., and Belz, Herman: *The American Constitution: Its Origins and Development*, 7th ed., vol. 2 (New York: W. W. Norton, 1991).

Kull, Andrew: *The Color-Blind Constitution* (Cambridge, Mass.: Harvard University Press, 1992).

Lazarus, Edward: *Closed Chambers: The Rise, Fall, and Future of the Modern Supreme Court*, rev. ed. (New York: Penguin, 1999).

McCloskey, Robert G. and Levinson, Sanford: *The American Supreme Court*, 3rd ed. (Chicago: University of Chicago Press, 2000).

Mason, Alpheus T.: *Harlan Fiske Stone: Pillar of the Law* (New York: Viking, 1956).

Minda, Gary: *Postmodern Legal Movements: Law and Jurisprudence at Century's End* (New York: New York University Press, 1996).

Sarat, Austin, ed.: *Race, Law, and Culture: Reflections on Brown v. Board of Education* (New York: Oxford University Press, 1997).

Scheingold, Stuart A.: *The Politics of Rights: Lawyers, Public Policy and Political Change* (New Haven, Conn.: Yale University Press, 1974).

Siegel, Reva B.: "Reasoning From the Body: A Historical Perspective on Abortion Regulation and Questions of Equal Protection," *Stanford Law Review*, 44 (1992): 261–381.

Tribe, Laurence H.: *American Constitutional Law*, 3rd ed. (New York: Foundation Press, 2000).

Tushnet, Mark V., ed.: *The Warren Court in Historical and Political Perspective* (Charlottesville: University Press of Virginia, 1993).

Urofsky, Melvin I.: *Division and Discord: The Supreme Court Under Stone and Vinson, 1941–1953* (Columbia: University of South Carolina Press, 1997).

Whitman, Mark, ed.: *Removing a Badge of Slavery: The Record of Brown v. Board of Education* (Princeton, NJ: Markus Wiener, 1993).

Williams, Wendy W.: "Sex Discrimination: Closing the Law's Gender Gap," in Herman Schwartz (ed.), *The Burger Years: Rights and Wrongs in the Supreme Court, 1969–1986* (New York: Viking Penguin, 1987).

Woodward, Bob and Armstrong, Scott: *The Brethren: Inside the Supreme Court* (New York: Simon and Schuster, 1979).

CHAPTER TWENTY-ONE

The Cold War in Europe

CAROLYN EISENBERG

Though now forgotten, the Cold War was an unpleasant surprise. When World War II ended in 1945, there was a widespread expectation in the United States and elsewhere that there would be a long period of peace. The successful wartime alliance between the United States, Britain, and the Soviet Union had seemed to show that, despite large differences in social systems, under skillful leadership nations could cooperate for shared goals.

The crucial arena was Europe, where the three Allied armies had converged in the heart of Germany. With the Red Army occupying much of Eastern Europe and the combined American and British forces in the West, the prospects for peace depended on the ability of the three powers to compromise their differences in this theater.

What was known of the Yalta agreements seemed a positive augury. In addition to a Declaration on Liberated Europe with its promise of self-determination for all nations, there was agreement on unified control for postwar Germany. American, British, French, and Soviet troops would each be given their own zone of occupation, with the understanding that common policies would be set by a quadripartite Allied Control Council.

The arrangements for Berlin exemplified the high expectations. The German capital had been conquered by the Red Army at an estimated cost of 100,000 casualties and lay entirely inside the Soviet zone. Nevertheless, it had been agreed that each of the four powers would occupy a sector of the city and through a quadripartite Kommandatura make collective decisions. In July 1945, a most promising development was the regrouping of Allied armies, as the Soviets withdrew from the western sectors of Berlin and the Americans and British pulled out of Saxony and Thuringia in the eastern zone. By early summer, the machinery had been put in place for a new era of European harmony.

Yet four years later, the early hopes had been completely shattered. By 1949, Europe was clearly divided into Eastern and Western blocs, Germany had split into two separate and hostile states and, in the aftermath of a ten-month blockade, the line across Berlin marked the fracture of the continent. Rival military alliances were being assembled and shortly thereafter nuclear weapons became the instrument of choice for defending each side.

In this evolution lies the origin of the Cold War. During the ensuing decades, the contest was expanded into a global competition and the nuclear arms race became a

menace unto itself. As crises proliferated, it became increasingly difficult to determine which of these conflicts was fundamental. However, among historians there has
been broad agreement that the source of the US–Soviet conflict was in Europe, and
a growing recognition that the core issue was the future of Germany.

I

As the wartime alliance fell apart, American policymakers articulated a clear
explanation of the reasons. In their account, it was the Soviet refusal to respect the
self-determination of nations and their unbridled expansionism that had created the
need for a policy of "containment." Though desiring peace, the Western countries
had no choice but to strengthen themselves economically, politically, and militarily
in order to prevent a communist juggernaut from sweeping across Europe.

This point of view was subsequently elaborated in works of history, some of which
were written by individuals who had themselves participated in American decisionmaking. In books by Herbert Feis (1957), Louis Halle (1967), Joseph Jones (1955),
and others, US policymakers were portrayed as willing to cooperate with Stalin and
prepared to effect reasonable compromises toward that goal. These writers stressed
Soviet misdeeds in Eastern Europe, especially its crimes in Poland. In 1944 Stalin
had cynically denied assistance to the Polish Underground, which had risen up against
the Nazi occupiers. By facilitating the slaughter of people who might be too
independent, refusing to work with the official Polish government-in-exile, and
eventually imposing the communist-based Lublin regime, he displayed a clear
determination to control the country's destiny.

For the first generation of Cold War historians, Poland set the pattern. Wherever
the Red Army went, across Eastern Europe and even into eastern Germany, an
"Iron Curtain" fell. Stalin insisted that the political, social, and economic structures
of other nations conform to the Soviet model. Any notion of democratic rights was
immediately snuffed out.

Nor did this exhaust Stalin's acts of aggression. Not content with new holdings
in Eastern Europe, he was also moving to control northern Iran and to force
concessions from the Turks in the Dardanelles. Most frightening, however, was his
apparent threat to Western Europe. Lacking troops on the ground, he appeared to
be cleverly using the West European communist parties to take advantage of the
economic dislocations produced by the war. As of 1947, US policymakers were faced
with the possibility that in Italy, France, and Greece, and perhaps other places, the
communists might come to power either through free elections or revolutionary
upheaval.

Fearing that the Soviets might soon control all of Europe, the Truman administration acted defensively to forestall this. In March 1947 the president enunciated
the Truman Doctrine, warning Congress that "it must be the policy of the United
States to support free peoples who are resisting subjugation by armed minorities
or by outside pressures." Under this rubric, Washington provided substantial military and economic assistance to the government of Greece to quash a left-wing
rebellion.

Two months later, Secretary of State George Marshall gave a historic speech at
Harvard in which he proclaimed America's willingness to underwrite a large-scale

economic recovery program for Europe. As presented by orthodox historians, the Marshall Plan represented a high point of American diplomacy. Under friendly US pressure, West European officials were brought together to craft a realistic, integrated plan for revival, finally abandoning the nationalistic economic policies that had proved so ruinous in the past. In one bold stroke, the American government ameliorated the misery of millions, placed the economies of Western Europe on a healthy foundation, and protected US security by thwarting the communists.

Integral to the Marshall Plan were the western zones of Germany. This area had always played a vital role in the economic life of Europe – as a source of coal, steel, and chemicals for other industrial nations, and as a market for their goods. One of the great merits of the European Recovery Plan (ERP) was that it provided a framework for western Germany to be rebuilt without the associated dangers of military revival. Yet western Germany could not participate in the program as three separate zones. By the spring of 1948, there was an agreement to fuse them into a new West German state.

Unfortunately, the creation of ERP and the inclusion of western Germany enraged Stalin. As described by orthodox historians, the Soviet leader was faced with the imminent demise of his expansionist plans. In a daring attempt to halt this trend, he instructed the West European communist parties to engage in illegal acts of sabotage, provoked a coup in the still democratic government of Czechoslovakia, and in June 1948, launched a blockade of Berlin.

In the traditional account, the Berlin blockade emerged as the central drama of the early Cold War. Having sealed off eastern Germany, the Soviet government was attempting to wrest control of the city by preventing the flow of food and other supplies into the western sectors. As a response, the United States and Britain initiated an extraordinary airlift in which their planes flew over the Soviet Zone, bringing necessary goods to the beleaguered Berliners. This dangerous confrontation in the former German capital exemplified the ruthlessness and rapacity of the Soviets, as well as the courage and magnanimity of their western opponents.

After ten months Stalin was compelled to acknowledge defeat, and by May of 1949 he had lifted the blockade. Yet the trauma of his aggression had left the United States and its West European allies convinced that military strength was a necessary accompaniment to economic revival. It was therefore no coincidence that the termination of the blockade occurred simultaneously with the creation of the North Atlantic Treaty Organization (NATO). Under its provisions, the United States and eleven European signatories agreed that "an attack against one or more of them . . . shall be considered an attack against all," and that there would be mutual consultation and assistance in such a contingency.

The creation of NATO and the establishment of a West German government were rapidly succeeded by the formation of a Soviet-led Warsaw Pact and a new communist-dominated East German state. With these developments, the basic structure of Cold War Europe was set, with no significant changes for many decades. To orthodox writers, the dynamics of the Cold War were simple. In flagrant disregard of the principle of self-determination, Stalin had attempted to control Europe. Unable to dislodge the Russians from the east, the United States and its allies had taken the necessary economic and military steps to "contain" them.

II

This perspective on the Cold War remained the conventional wisdom until the late 1960s. Its persistence was partially due to the intellectual climate created by McCarthyism. The atmosphere of conformity that pervaded politics, journalism, the entertainment industry, and the academy was nowhere more stifling than on the subject of Cold War culpability. The content of the history books both promoted and reflected the black and white interpretation of the conflict that was being articulated in these other sectors.

It was not until the Vietnam War disrupted the national consensus about America's role in the world that the historiography of the early Cold War became more diverse and controversial. There had been some early mavericks. In two thoughtful but neglected volumes, historian D. F. Fleming (1961) had challenged the traditional accounts of many specific Cold War episodes, demonstrating that the United States as well as the Soviets had contributed to post-1945 tensions.

At the University of Wisconsin, William Appleman Williams was training a new generation of American historians to see the Cold War as "only the most recent phase of a more general conflict between the established system of western capitalism and its internal and external opponents" (Williams, 1962, p. 10). For Williams, expansionism had been a central feature of American foreign policy throughout the twentieth century, more rooted in its *domestic* political economy and ideology than in external danger.

Within a few short years, these isolated contributions were assimilated into a rapidly growing "revisionist literature" that found its way into the academic mainstream. Reflecting the controversial perceptions of the Vietnam era, revisionist writers emphasized the cautiousness of Soviet foreign policy, the indigenous roots of foreign left-wing movements, and the American habit of imposing its ideological predilections on other nations (Alperovitz, 1965; LaFeber, 1968; Gardner, 1970; Paterson, 1973).

As applied to the European theater, revisionists questioned whether Stalin had ever seriously threatened Western Europe, and many pointed out that even in Eastern Europe, the Soviets were slow to bolshevize the countries they initially occupied. Meanwhile US officials had used their nuclear advantage and economic strength to create a bloc of like-minded states, while denying the Russians the right to do the same.

Yet while revisionists held in common a critical stance toward American policy, they did not always agree on how to explain it. At one end of the spectrum were those who focused on economic concerns, claiming that US efforts to shape the political economy of Europe reflected a perceived domestic need for foreign markets and outlets for investment. On the other end were those who believed that US officials were motivated by an exaggerated, albeit genuine, fear of Soviet aggression. For the latter, as for more orthodox analysts, it was "national security" concerns that underpinned American decisionmaking.

Among those historians who emphasized the economic imperatives of US policy, the two-volume work of Gabriel and Joyce Kolko (1972) provided the most single-minded and comprehensive account. In their treatment of Europe, they focused on the devastation that had resulted from depression and war, and highlighted the associated collapse of traditional elites. As a consequence, the defeat of the Axis set the stage for bitter internal struggles within all the nations of Europe, struggles in which left-wing movements held an advantaged position.

The Kolkos demonstrated that while communist parties played a prominent role, they were by no means the most radical element. Quite frequently, it was the social democratic and sometimes the agrarian parties that were pressing for more drastic change. Also noteworthy were the many grassroots formations – the anti-fascist committees, works councils, and new labor unions – that had sprung up spontaneously to challenge the existing order.

These developments were deeply troubling to the Americans, who had exited the war determined to reform international capitalism by sweeping away the nationalist barriers to the free flow of capital, labor, and goods. As described by the Kolkos, it quickly became the unanticipated but urgent task of America's European policy to check the advance of the left.

Meanwhile, the Soviet role was an essentially conservative one. Having suffered 20 million casualties fighting the Nazis and with much of their agriculture and industry demolished, the Russians were preoccupied with issues of rehabilitation and security. In Eastern Europe they sought a buffer zone that could insulate them from future attack, but they hoped to achieve this by installing friendly coalition governments, in which the communists would carefully limit assaults on private property. The Kolkos provided a detailed narrative showing that, contrary to the American image of an "iron curtain," during the early postwar years there were hybrid political regimes in most Eastern countries.

In Western Europe, where communist parties were popular and initially seemed poised to take over in several countries, Moscow discipline held them back. The French communist leader Maurice Thorez and Italian party chief Palmiro Togliatti were specifically instructed to surrender arms garnered in the Resistance struggles and to participate in parliamentary elections. In Greece, a civil war was raging against the British-supported monarchy, but although communists were participating actively in the People's Liberation Army (ELAS), Stalin refused it any assistance.

Given this timid record, the Kolkos rejected the notion that the Cold War was fundamentally a conflict between the United States and the Soviet Union. They contended that "no one can understand Soviet–American relations save as one of a number of vital aspects of the larger advancement and application of American power in the post-war world, a greater undertaking that time and again was never caused by Russian policy and very often in no way involved Moscow" (Kolko and Kolko, 1972, p. 31).

The signal contribution of the Kolkos was to transform the study of the European Cold War from a geopolitical chess game to a rich social history. In their rendering, the continent was something more than an empty chessboard upon which American and Soviet actors made their moves. Rather, it was a collection of individual nations, torn apart by deep divisions over what their future should be. How these were resolved had direct consequences for the quality of life of millions of people.

Following the insights of William Appleman Williams, the Kolkos had introduced a degree of economic determinism that the Wisconsin professor had skirted. This made their analysis of US foreign policy at once clearer, but also more problematic. For if US policy was driven by the need to prevent economic radicalism in Europe, and if Stalin was prepared to consign Western Europe to the Americans and to limit social experiments in the East, it was difficult to understand why an accommodation could not be reached. In theory, intelligent policymakers on both sides should have been able to harmonize the Soviet need for security and reconstruction with the American need for stability.

For those revisionists who took more seriously US policymakers' concerns about "national security," one possible explanation for American behavior was misperception. Perhaps there was a self-fulfilling prophecy at play in which American leaders held misplaced fears about Soviet intentions in Western Europe, and made provocative decisions that generated a more aggressive counterresponse?

A seminal work, which espoused this point of view, was Daniel Yergin's *Shattered Peace* (1977). In a lucid narrative of the early Cold War, Yergin traced the evolving ideas of American leaders. He showed that at the end of World War II, Roosevelt's advisers were divided into two camps. One group, which included FDR himself, believed that Stalin had abandoned a Marxist revolutionary mission and was mainly preoccupied with protection from attack. Therefore, by acting in a friendly and sympathetic fashion, the United States could reduce distrust and pave the way for a collaborative relationship.

According to Yergin, these softliners were opposed by a more hawkish group based in the State Department. The latter stressed the revolutionary, totalitarian character of Soviet society and maintained that the imperatives of despotism required unlimited expansion. American concessions to Stalin were viewed as potentially catastrophic since they would be perceived as signs of weakness. Any hope of controlling Russian behavior depended on Western military and economic strength.

In the immediate postwar period, the two American factions competed for the allegiance of President Harry Truman and Secretary of State Byrnes. By late 1946, the hardliners had prevailed and put the United States on a confrontational course. This was a great misfortune because, "In the international arena, Stalin's policies were not those of a single-minded world revolutionist. The truth is that the Soviet Union's policy was often clumsy and brutal, sometimes confused, but usually cautious and pragmatic" (Yergin, 1977, p. 12). However, by acting in this fashion, the United States created needless polarization.

Yergin illustrated the self-defeating dynamic by taking a critical look at US policy in occupied Germany. The Soviet goals there were to extract large-scale reparations and to insure that Germany would not be resurrected as a major world power. However, the Americans incorrectly read Soviet reparations demands as threatening to the economic stability of Germany and Western Europe, and misconstrued the Soviet desire for security as an interest in dominating the country. As a consequence, US officials moved toward the partition of the country – incorporating the three western zones into the Marshall Plan, and by the spring of 1948 creating the machinery to establish a new West German state.

Yergin shows how these American-inspired decisions stimulated a negative reaction from the Soviets. Stalin introduced the Cominform, which tied together the European communist parties behind a more militant politics. West European parties, which had originally been encouraged by the Soviets to participate in parliamentary arrangements, were spurred on to acts of sabotage. Meanwhile, the East European parties cast aside their nationalistic practices and embraced the Soviet top-down model of socialization.

Gravest of all was the Soviet decision to blockade Berlin. The purpose of that intervention was to reopen the possibility of reunifying Germany. However, for the United States and its West European allies, the closing of the access routes into the former German capital was viewed as an aggressive act, betokening Soviet designs on the city. By launching an airlift, the Western powers were able to supply the inhabitants without resort to war. Yet the net effect of the crisis was to freeze the division of Europe and accelerate the trend toward militarization of the two blocs.

As a description of the evolving American approach to the USSR, Yergin's book was especially illuminating. However, he did not adequately answer his own central question: "why . . . an interpretive structure that posited unlimited Soviet ambitions became so generally adopted if, at least arguably, Stalin was pursuing a conservative, limited, even traditional foreign policy?" (Yergin, 1977, p. 138). He did identify several major factors: the ideological preconceptions of the State Department, the crudeness of Russian diplomacy, the dyspeptic personalities of some key US officials, the desire of the individual armed services to enhance their own bureaucracies, and the hostile Soviet response to American provocations.

Yet even when these considerations are aggregated, it is difficult to see why over a period of years such highly educated and astute policymakers failed to notice Soviet restraint or to explore the possibility that the security of the United States might be better served by sensible compromises with the Russians than by a nuclear competition, which entailed a risk of catastrophic war. In this respect, the weakness in Yergin's argument resembled the flaw in the Kolkos' case and of revisionism in general. Having painstakingly described Soviet weakness, caution, and conservatism as manifested through a series of European crises, it was hard to understand why American leaders did not push harder for European unity as the optimal way to satisfy both economic and national security objectives. This was not a question faced by more orthodox writers, for whom Soviet expansionism was an overriding threat.

III

During the late 1980s and early 1990s two challenging new books, *America's Half-Century* (1989) by Thomas McCormick and *A Preponderance of Power* (1992) by Melvyn Leffler, cast fresh light on the question of how a conservative Soviet Union had become transformed into a revolutionary menace. Significantly, both works were conceived during the Reagan era, when the Cold War was again heating up and the gravity of US–Soviet conflict seemed undeniable.

A former student of William Appleman Williams, McCormick approached the study of American foreign policy from an economic perspective. However, in a significant departure he drew upon the "world systems" theory of sociologist Immanuel Wallerstein, placing at the center of his analysis the concept of "hegemony," i.e., the ability of a single capitalist nation to exercise "such predominant influence in economic power, military might, and political-ideological leadership, that no other power, or combination of powers can prevail against it" (McCormick, 1989, p. 5).

McCormick argued that by achieving hegemony, the capitalist nation-state was able to resolve the tension between the "internationalist imperatives" of capitalism and the "nationalist biases" of the state. For five centuries, the "key to accumulating capital . . . and maximizing profits" was long-distance trade (McCormick, 1989,

p. 2). While the nation-state sometimes cooperated, there were also many occasions when it interfered with the free flow of capital, goods, and labor in order to preserve the prosperity of the population as a whole or the physical safety of the society. The virtue of being a hegemonic power was that the state could promote unobstructed commerce while simultaneously maintaining prosperity and security for its people.

At the end of World War II, the United States emerged as the new hegemon with an overriding mission to create an integrated capitalist world economy. This generated conflict not only with left-wing movements, but with weaker capitalist states that feared the impact of unrestrained market forces. Against this backdrop, the Cold War – defined as a US–Soviet clash – appeared as a significant but by no means decisive phenomenon.

Like most revisionists, McCormick did not regard the Soviet Union as an inherently revolutionary society. The Marxist trappings notwithstanding, he maintained that Stalinist Russia represented a type of state capitalism in which an autocratic government had assumed responsibility for capital accumulation and industrial development. At the end of World War II, the United States wished to draw the USSR into the world system and the Soviet leadership was inclined to join. In his view, what ultimately ruined the bargain was America's acquisition of a nuclear monopoly, which made US officials "giddy" with power and less willing to accommodate legitimate Soviet interests.

If there was a "*causa belli* of the Cold War," McCormick contends that the breakdown of the Allied Control Council in occupied Germany was surely it (McCormick, 1989, p. 67). As late as Potsdam, the Americans and Soviets were still discussing arrangements under which Russia would achieve significant reparations through a restriction of Germany's industrial capacity. For US officials this posed a potential problem because they viewed the economic revival of Germany as essential for the recovery of Europe. But many were actively seeking a middle ground, until the successful use of the atomic bomb removed their incentive to compromise.

Flouting Soviet wishes, the US Military Government suspended all reparations deliveries in mid-1946 and joined with Britain in creating a bizonal economic structure that would be independent of the Allied Control Council. Effectively banished from western Germany and faced with an American government that seemed determined to maintain its nuclear advantage, the Soviets abandoned any effort to join the American-led world economy.

From 1947 onward the USSR stood outside this system, an ever-present magnet for the many discontented countries and political movements. Through propaganda, economic aid, and the accumulation of military might, the Soviets "ultimately proved the greatest obstacle to American hegemony and its blue-print for a new world order" (McCormick, 1989, p. 53). Herein lay the foundations of the Cold War, which had emerged despite the Russians' indifference to Marxist imperatives.

Having explained the rift, McCormick also noted a certain falsity in the American posture. In striving to "contain" the Soviet challenge, US policymakers were not so distressed as they claimed since they readily apprehended the uses of the Soviet threat, as both a justification for profitable military spending and a means of disciplining recalcitrant allies.

Although McCormick's notion of hegemony specifically encompasses the idea of a national (state) interest that is not simply coterminous with that of the capitalists, he cannot bring himself to embrace the notion of "national security" as it has been conventionally articulated. The Soviets may be a real enemy in the sense that they perennially obstruct the workings of the world economy, but he ignores their threat to the physical safety of Western Europe and the United States. That omission makes it difficult to understand the centrality of NATO in American foreign policy or the unrelenting pursuit of nuclear superiority.

By contrast to McCormick, Melvyn Leffler's formidable book, *A Preponderance of Power: National Security, the Truman Administration and the Cold War* (1992) put military considerations at the center of his analysis. Winner of the Bancroft, Ferrell, and Hoover prizes, the study was remarkable in its thoughtful synthesis of the existing literature and in the use of archival materials. During almost two decades of intensive research, the author steeped himself in the writings of US policymakers and formed a sharp impression of their thinking. As suggested by his book title, he believed them to be preoccupied with issues of power and national security.

From the harsh experiences of the twentieth century, American leaders had concluded that when a hostile state or combination of states was able to achieve control over the resources, skilled labor, industrial infrastructure, and military bases of Eurasia, US interests were seriously imperiled. It was certainly true that for Washington, "a viable international economy was the surest way to defend the health of core industrial nations and to protect friendly governments" (Leffler, 1992, p. 10). However, in Leffler's account the economic project appears as the handmaiden of geopolitics. By promoting an integrated capitalist system, the Americans were attempting to insure a "favorable correlation of power."

As World War II drew to a close, it was clear that the USSR was the only nation in a position to eventually gain control of the Eurasian land mass. But it was by no means certain that it would make this attempt, particularly in view of the immense damage wrought by the German army invaders. Despite the many indications of Stalin's caution and efforts at cooperation, Leffler repeatedly points out that US officials were quick to reach the most pessimistic conclusions and to apply a double standard to his actions.

By contrast to Yergin, he does not emphasize their misperceptions. Indeed, his most important and arresting argument is that US policymakers were never focused on Russian purposes. The critical factor for them was the social turmoil and economic stagnation on the Eurasian continent, which nurtured the growth of diverse left-wing movements that everywhere included powerful communist parties. The Americans feared that the Russians would "capitalize on developments they did not cause but could redound to their long-term advantage" (Leffler, 1992, p. 6). From this standpoint it made no difference whether Moscow was really encouraging the left to seize power. Nor did it improve matters if the left enjoyed popular support and won elections. Once in office, radicals "would pursue policies that directly or indirectly served the purposes of the Soviet government" (Leffler, 1992, p. 7).

Determined to maintain "a preponderance of power," American leaders did what they could to shore up Western Europe by pouring in economic aid, forcing out leftists from government coalitions, and, most provocative of all, promoting the partition of Germany so that the western zones could be incorporated into the Marshall Plan. This was "high-risk" diplomacy which was bound to stimulate a harsh Soviet reaction, thereby confirming policymakers' negative expectations.

Leffler differed sharply from revisionists in his conviction that, however costly and dangerous, the US decisions to stop accommodating the Russians, to divide Germany, and to create an exclusive Western European bloc were "prudent." Regardless of Soviet intentions, "the threats emanating from the postwar socioeconomic dislocation and power vacuums were too great to allow for a policy of reassurance" (Leffler, 1992, p. 516).

The potential coalescence of European radical movements with the power of the Soviet state was surely a great danger. Yet like US policymakers themselves, Leffler took for granted what needed to be explained: namely, *why* radical groupings would accept Russian control and *why* the security-minded Soviets should incite foreign insurgency given their initial reluctance? Those choices cannot be understood without reference to US behavior, which from the beginning was geared to the creation of an integrated capitalist system in postwar Europe, not as the handmaiden to security but as its matrix.

By using their power on the continent to preserve private ownership, to constrain the activities of working-class organizations, and to limit government interference with the market, the Americans provoked not only indigenous leftists but also the USSR, which, at least for Germany, desired far-reaching structural change.

While Leffler had tentatively endorsed American policy choices in Europe, he was quite critical of the offshoots – the "huge" (and to him superfluous) US buildup of nuclear weapons and the expanded commitments in the third world. Moreover, his retelling of the postwar history left little doubt that in its quest for security the United States had been seeking economic, political, and military ascendancy in Europe. This was far different than the interpretation of the orthodox historians, for whom Soviet aggression had always been the main factor.

It was also quite different from the American public's understanding of the Cold War. Indeed, beginning in the late 1960s, there was a widening gulf between the work of academic historians and the larger society. One striking expression of this was the success of David McCullough's Pulitzer prize-winning biography of Harry Truman (1992), which painted a heroic picture of the plain-spoken man from Missouri, who rose unexpectedly to the pinnacle of world power and saved Western Europe from the Soviet hordes. By contrast, in his 1999 presidential address to the Society for Historians of American Foreign Relations (SHAFR), Arnold Offner summarized two decades of scholarship with the observation that "Truman's parochialism . . . caused him to disregard contrary views, to engage in simplistic analogizing, and to show little ability to comprehend the basis for other nation's policies . . . his foreign policy leadership intensified Soviet–American conflict, hastened the division of Europe, and brought tragic intervention in Asian civil wars" (Offner, 1999, p. 129).

Revisionism had by no means swept the field of diplomatic history. And there was certainly never a consensus that it was the United States that had brought about the Cold War, or that it was internally generated economic causes that had triggered it. Indeed, as long as Soviet records were closed to scholars, many fundamental questions about the dynamic interaction of the two powers could not be satisfactorily answered. Nevertheless, several of the themes that appeared in Leffler's complex account had achieved wide acceptance: most crucially, the notion that it was the United States that possessed the "preponderance of power" in the postwar era and that Soviet expansion was less than imagined.

IV

Among historians the most prominent dissenter from this view was John Lewis Gaddis, a prolific writer of books and essays, who had long faulted revisionists for minimizing the Soviet role. He was therefore quick to draw upon the rich documentary materials that began tumbling out of the Russian and East European archives in the wake of the Soviet collapse. As the consultant to CNN's *The Cold War* history series, and the author of a major book, *We Now Know* (1997), Gaddis helped to popularize an emerging post-revisionist perspective (Kuniholm, 1980; Harbutt, 1986; Lundestad, 1986).

In a series of tightly argued essays, Gaddis probes the question of alternatives. Could the Cold War have been avoided? And if not, could it have been waged in some other fashion? His conclusion is negative on both counts. He considers the decisive actor to be Joseph Stalin, one of the most ambitious and paranoid figures in the twentieth century, whose insatiable need for security put his country on a path of "revolution and war" (Gaddis, 1997, p. 25). Given the "vacuum of power" in Europe and the divergence in American and Soviet ideology, some measure of conflict was unavoidable. But it was Stalin's unbridled need for control and his contempt for the interests of others that created an unbridgeable gap. Gaddis acknowledges that Soviet behavior in Eastern Europe was variable, that in Poland there was an early suppression of domestic dissent, whereas in Hungary the vestiges of political pluralism lingered until 1948, when the communists finally took charge. However, in his judgment this was simply a matter of tactics, of Stalin cannily biding his time until he could discern what the traffic would bear.

In a nod toward contemporary scholarship, Gaddis concedes that the Cold War was a reciprocal process, that the United States did seek "preponderant power," and that it pursued a definite agenda of political democracy and capitalist integration. But the American preference was to be inclusive, to find a formula for Soviet participation in a new international order. When that effort failed, the United States constructed its own "empire" in Western Europe. This was a distinctive "invited empire" in which West European nations voluntarily accepted the leadership and occasional interventions of the United States out of a well-grounded fear of Soviet aggression.

The decisive clash took place in occupied Germany. Prior to the publication of *We Now Know*, historians of diverse persuasions had emphasized the centrality of the German question, and many suggested that it was the United States that had spearheaded the drive for partition over Soviet objections (Backer, 1978; Smith, 1980; Eisenberg, 1996). Gaddis shares their perception that "Stalin never wanted a separate German state," but contends that his real goal was "a reunified Germany within Moscow's field of influence" (Gaddis, 1997, p. 127).

Stalin's fatal mistake was to delay unification until the eastern zone could be a magnet for the West. As with citizens elsewhere in the Soviet imperium, those in East Germany came to loathe their Russian occupiers and with even greater reason. Upon entering the country in 1945, the undisciplined members of the Red Army may have raped as many as 2 million German women. And during the ensuing two years, the Soviet military ravaged the country's industrial structure, shipped off tens of thousands of people to prison and forced labor, all the while imposing their unpopular political and economic ideas on the general population.

By contrast, the Americans in Germany "with a breezy audacity that seems remarkable . . . fell back upon domestic instincts and set about transplanting democracy into the part of Germany they controlled" (Gaddis, 1997, pp. 44–5). In conjunction with the prospect of Marshall Plan aid, this created an upsurge of enthusiasm for the American way. US officials never had a formal plan to create a separate West German state. It was the British who initiated the move and pressure from the Germans that propelled it forward. As for the latter, the choice was clear: they could "follow the Stalinist path toward national unity," or they "could seek alignment with the United States and its allies, knowing that the effect might be to postpone unification for years to come"(Gaddis, 1997, p. 120). The division of Germany was a profound disappointment to the Soviet leader, but his own behavior had brought it about.

Because *We Now Know* seemed to be based on the new Soviet sources, the book gained special credibility. Yet as Gaddis forthrightly acknowledges in his introduction, he primarily utilized the records translated and printed by the Cold War International History Project and the monographs of other scholars who had done archival work. Indeed, his essays on the division of Europe are particularly thin on direct documentation and reliant on historians, who disagree with one another and who do not necessarily share Gaddis's conclusions (Staritz, 1992; Naimark, 1995; Zubok and Pleshakov, 1996).

The new scholarship certainly provides ample evidence of the cruelty, arrogance, and cynicism of Soviet foreign policy, points that orthodox and post-revisionist writers have stressed. But it also gives support to claims that Stalin expected the alliance with the United States to continue, that he did not have clear plans for Eastern Europe, and that he was open to compromise on the future of Germany.

With regard to the latter, Gaddis sidesteps the many manifestations of Soviet conservatism, among them Stalin's bridling of the German communists, his quashing of the radical anti-fascist committees, his constraints on trade union activity, and his insistence on the need for a "bourgeois-democratic" stage of German development. Stalin and his confederates may well have entertained long-term hopes that a unified Germany might some day fall into their sphere of influence, but their actual decision-making was shaped by the need to conciliate the West.

As for the alleged decision to delay reunification, the historian Norman Naimark, who has looked most closely at Soviet behavior in the eastern zone, renders a more complex judgment. In his portrayal, during the early years of the occupation, Moscow was animated by competing goals: a need for substantial reparations from all zones of Germany, a desire to tighten control in the east, and a wish for a unified, neutral state that would remain demilitarized. As late as January–February 1947, the Soviets were still looking for a deal with the West and were priming their East German minions to prepare for free elections (Naimark, 1995, pp. 298–302).

It is not just the eastern sources that pose a challenge to Gaddis and to post-revisionist analysis. There are, for example, the thousands of pages of American postwar planning papers that reveal an intention to maintain far-flung military bases and to reshape the political and economic institutions of other nations. Although Gaddis sidesteps the point, it is also worth recognizing that for US policymakers their neighboring region was not after all in Europe, but in Central and Latin America, where there is no paucity of data about US intervention and high-handedness.

But even within the European context, the suggestion that the United States con-structed "a new kind of empire – a democratic empire" is a form of special pleading. It is a fair point that US interventions in the politics of West European countries were welcomed by many inhabitants and that, by contrast to the Soviets, they were not accompanied by violence. However, American military aid to the repressive Greek government, the bribery of the Italian parties, and the infiltration and disruption of the West European labor movement must surely count as undemocratic acts.

With regard to the German question, for almost two decades historians have "known" from the papers of Military Governor Dwight Eisenhower and his Deputy Lucius Clay that they found the early Soviet behavior in occupied Germany to be constructive. Upon his visit to the United States in November 1945, Clay told State Department officials that he "took sharp issue with the point of view that it was the USSR that was failing to carry out the Berlin Protocol" and stressed that the "entire record of the Control Council showed that the USSR was willing to cooperate . . . in operating Germany as a single political and economic unit" (Smith, 1974, p. 113).

One year later, Clay was still suggesting to Secretary of State James Byrnes that if the United States responded to Soviet reparations needs, this might result in German unification and "the right to contest for its philosophy . . . to the borders of Poland and Czechoslavakia" (Smith, 1974, p. 284). Especially meaningful to Clay and his associates in Military Government were the October 1946 elections in the Soviet zone and Berlin, in which the Soviet-backed Socialist Unity Party had done poorly. Gaddis alludes to these elections as a sign of Stalin's absurd beliefs about German political attitudes. But for the American officials at the scene, the significance of these races was that in the interest of Allied unity, the Soviets were still permitting them.

This consideration caused the leaders of US Military Government to press hard for an agreement at the 1947 Council of Foreign Ministers meeting in Moscow. To their intense frustration, they were thwarted by Washington officials, who had already determined that the western zones of Germany must be integrated into an economic recovery program for Western Europe. Gaddis reverses the sequence, affirming that the new Secretary of State George Marshall was so disheartened by his experience in Moscow that he returned to the United States with a new idea for a recovery plan. But as State Department records make clear, the work on this was already underway.

Over the succeeding months, the United States and its western allies maintained the fiction of continuing negotiations. But for US and British policymakers the issue was settled: Germany would be partitioned. Their tactical problem was how to conceal their responsibility for that choice. From the November 1947 London Conference of Foreign Ministers, US Ambassador Walter Bedell Smith cabled Eisenhower: "The difficulty under which we labor is that in spite of our announced position, we really do not want nor intend to accept German unification in any terms that the Russians might agree to, even though they seem to meet most of our requirements" (Eisenberg, 1996, p. 318).

Having decided to create a separate West German state, the Americans and British anticipated certain costs, including increased repression in Eastern Europe, a crackdown on the noncommunist political parties in East Germany, and Soviet pressure on Berlin. That expectation was the major stimulus for early moves toward a western military alliance.

Gaddis conveys the impression that a divided Germany was the spontaneous creation of eager Europeans, including the West Germans. However, outside of Britain there was great reluctance to take this step, especially in France. It was only the promise of Marshall Plan aid and the implied threat of its suspension that achieved the consent of the Western nations. Among West Germans, their desire for greater self-government and financial assistance did not reflect a preference for partition. Fearful of their opinion, the Americans and British ruled out a referendum on the issue and ignored the many cautionary pleas of the minister-presidents from the western zones.

Aware of this dissension, Stalin launched the Berlin blockade hoping to derail the plans for a West German government. This was his most serious mistake, which led to the famed airlift and a consolidation of West European opinion behind the American agenda. Yet it is significant that neither the American nor the West European publics were ever apprised of the strong Soviet interest in reunifying the country.

None of this shows that the Americans "caused" the Cold War or that they were less humane than the Russians. But what it does suggest is that in their zeal to control events in Western Europe, American policymakers prematurely abandoned eastern Germany and perhaps even Eastern Europe to Stalin.

V

With the settlement of the Berlin blockade, the line across Europe was clearly drawn. In short order, NATO was founded and a new West German government was born. The Soviets responded by establishing the German Democratic Republic (DDR) in the east and intensifying their political subjugation of Eastern Europe.

With the onset of the Korean War, American policymakers were increasingly disposed toward German rearmament. As a prelude to that step, the United States, Britain, and France signed contractual agreements with the Bonn government, granting it sovereignty although holding certain powers in reserve. This opened the door for West Germany's acceptance into NATO in 1955, prompting the Soviets to grant sovereignty to the DDR and to incorporate it into the newly formed Warsaw Pact. As both sides built up their armies and enlarged their nuclear arsenals, there was a growing probability that any military effort to breach the East–West line would lead to a global conflagration.

Over the course of the decade, the Soviets made various efforts to alter the German situation. In 1952 Stalin sent a note proposing reunification and offering free elections, with the proviso that the occupying armies would be withdrawn and that Germany would be prohibited from participating in any military alliance. This proposal was briefly taken up by his successors, Georgi Malenkov and Lavrenti Beria. However, policymakers in both Washington and Bonn doubted the sincerity of these offers and for their own part, they did not wish to jeopardize West Germany's tie to the West.

In 1958 Soviet Premier Nikita Khrushchev pugnaciously challenged the arrangements for Berlin, pointing out that the existence of the two Germanies removed the legal basis for Western occupation rights. Unlike his predecessors, Khrushchev seemed reconciled to the division of Germany, and was demanding Western recognition of the Ulbricht government and a changed status for West Berlin. With thousands of East Germans escaping every month, Khrushchev announced his intention to sign a separate peace treaty, giving the DDR control of the Berlin access routes.

President Eisenhower was unable to resolve the matter and left the festering crisis to his successor. Fearful of appearing weak and pressured by West German Chancellor Konrad Adenauer, Kennedy fanned his own "war scare," stepping up draft calls, mobilizing the reserves, and speeding up plans for civil defense. Khrushchev's shocking response was to erect a wall across Berlin, thereby halting the exodus of East Germans and sealing the division of the city. With this decisive act, the second Berlin crisis began to wind down, although not until 1963 did Khrushchev apprise the East German Party Congress that a separate peace treaty was no longer a priority.

In understanding the events of this period, historians are generally agreed that they flowed from the more fundamental policy decisions of the early postwar years. Yet the interpretive debates have remained. Was the European stalemate the product of an aggressive Soviet Union held in check by the military might of an American-led NATO? Or were there real opportunities for reconciliation, which US policymakers forfeited through some combination of misperception, bureaucratic inertia, and economic interest?

With the collapse of the Soviet bloc, American triumphalism has steered the debate in a self-congratulatory direction. In taking the story of the European Cold War from its origins in 1945 through the achievement of the nuclear test ban in 1963, the most widely acclaimed new book is Marc Trachtenberg's *A Constructed Peace*, which seeks to explain "how peace came to the world of the great powers" (Trachtenberg, 1999a, p. viii).

According to this account, the outlines of the peace were already evident at Potsdam where Stalin and Truman tacitly agreed to a de facto division of Germany. The Soviets would manage their own zone of occupation and the three Western powers would control the rest. Had this arrangement been followed, Germany and the rest of Europe would have been divided but in an amicable way. What spoiled the deal, argues Trachtenberg, were the Stalinist forays into Iran and Turkey, which aroused fear in Washington that he was bent on world conquest. Reneging on Potsdam, in 1946 the Americans made claims on eastern Germany, demanding a common reparations program and the "first use" of German exports to pay for necessary imports.

Having aggravated the Soviets with no tangible result, the Americans and British chose to rebuild the western zones as part of an integrated West European system. At first glance, the emergence of the two Germanies in 1949 might appear similar to the original bargain. However, Trachtenberg's point is that this was an embittered and unstable division, in which each side feared the other's encroachments and began amassing military power.

Although the United States briefly enjoyed a nuclear monopoly, its effectiveness was dubious. Should the Soviets launch an attack, their troops would quickly overrun Western Europe, necessitating American nuclear strikes on friendly territory. The antidote was to build up NATO forces and to include West German troops so that a non-nuclear defense would become plausible.

This animated deep Soviet fears of their old enemy, so intense that they derived reassurance from the continued presence of the United States military in Western

Europe. Trachtenberg suggests that so long as the Americans dominated NATO and maintained control of nuclear weapons, the Kremlin leadership felt confident that the East–West line would be respected.

In 1955 this fragile equilibrium was jeopardized by the efforts of Eisenhower and Dulles "to get out of Europe" and to make the allies responsible for their own defense (Trachtenberg, 1999a, p. 145). For Western Europe to become a kind of Third Force, it needed independent access to nuclear weapons, something that was acceptable to Eisenhower. But that raised the possibility of a West German hand on the nuclear trigger, whether as part of a centralized decisionmaking structure or an independent national force.

Trachtenberg suggests that it was Eisenhower's tilt toward military disengagement that stimulated Khrushchev's Berlin ultimatum. To the Russians, "a non-nuclear Federal republic, dependent on the western powers for protection, was no problem" (Trachtenberg, 1999a, p. 246). However, "a nuclearized Germany able to play an independent role in international politics, was another matter entirely." To prevent that outcome, Berlin was the only lever that Khrushchev possessed.

What averted international disaster was not the erection of the Berlin Wall, as is commonly thought, but a broader set of understandings that were forged during the Kennedy years. In contrast to Eisenhower, Kennedy recognized the need for the United States to remain in Europe and he was unequivocally opposed to West Germany's acquisition of nuclear weapons. Although not negotiated directly, there was an implicit trade: Khrushchev would stop challenging Western rights in Berlin, while Kennedy would guarantee the non-nuclear status of the Bonn government. Thus the true conclusion of the second Berlin crisis was the Nuclear Test Ban Treaty in 1963, which effectively prevented the West Germans from developing their own arsenal.

So emerged the "constructed peace" which, according to Trachtenberg, lasted until the dissolution of the Soviet bloc. In the interim, the security interests of the United States, the Soviet Union, and West Germany were all well protected. From 1963 on, the Cold War became a different kind of conflict – "more subdued, more modulated, more artificial, and, above all less terrifying" (Trachtenberg, 1999a, pp. 398–401). The years of incremental decisions had brought stability to Europe, yielding "a system in which free nations could live in peace."

Marc Trachtenberg's book is a profoundly complacent work, as its title suggests. Though it concedes that the world passed through some frightening moments en route to equilibrium, the eventual outcome was benign. So benign, in fact, that its major elements have survived the ending of the Cold War and exist today: the presence of American troops in Europe, a non-nuclear Germany, and a reunified country still held in check by membership in NATO.

Trachtenberg has elsewhere prodded historians to put their "political beliefs aside and frame questions in such a way that the answers turned on what the evidence showed" (Trachtenberg, 1999b, p. 9). Toward that end, he has supplemented the footnotes from *A Constructed Peace* with a personal website, containing more elaborate documentation for his views. Yet despite the many citations, what is striking about this book is its disregard of the existing literature and the bending of unwelcome evidence.

Thus Trachtenberg's claim that at Potsdam, the Americans and Soviets had a tacit understanding to divide Germany rests almost entirely on James Byrnes's demand for zonal reparations. And while there is some basis for claiming that the Secretary of State personally preferred partition, this is not what the Potsdam Protocol stipulated, it was not what Truman instructed, and it was not the initial policy of US Military Government. Even more far-fetched and undocumented is the notion that Stalin was satisfied with a scheme that excluded Soviet influence in Western Germany.

The records of US Military Government clearly demonstrate that until early 1947, it was attempting to achieve central German agencies and common policies. The failure of that effort stemmed directly from differences between the occupying powers over such matters as reparations and foreign trade, control of the Ruhr, German political rights, de-Nazification, labor policy, and, most crucially, the organization and reconstruction of German industry. Trachtenberg's own ideology, with its exclusive focus on military power and national security, prevents him from appreciating the deep economic worries of American officials – their distress over the continuing stagnation in the western zones and their fear that this would undermine a capitalist restoration in Western Europe.

Nor does the author grasp the affront to the Soviets inherent in the western decision to divide Germany. While Stalin was obviously reluctant to surrender the eastern zone, he was even more fearful of a partitioned nation in which the most industrially rich and populated area would go to the West. Trachtenberg dismisses almost out of hand subsequent Russian efforts to bring about a neutral, demilitarized state. And he underrates the larger consequences of a split in Europe that was so disadvantageous to the Soviet side.

Here the Eurocentric focus is a particular problem, because it obscures the extent to which Soviet setbacks in Europe had profound global results. Among other things, these losses fueled a powerful desire to right the imbalance elsewhere, most immediately in Asia where a successful Chinese Revolution created the possibility for large-scale gains.

As a general proposition, the fact that there were no new wars in Europe does not demonstrate a stable peace. Like John Gaddis, Trachtenberg has a sanguine attitude toward the accumulation of nuclear weapons, believing that since they were not used, they did not pose a serious danger. Since the nuclear competition continues, one wonders if their assessment would change should there be some future nuclear conflagration. It is noteworthy, in any case, that the American-driven arms race relied in the final analysis on the caution and good sense of the Soviet leadership. This was perhaps a reasonable calculation, but not an especially safe or "prudent" way to organize international relations.

Trachtenberg's enthusiasm for the 1963 settlement is based on his conviction that, for the Russians, the prevention of West German nuclear weapons was the decisive factor. Yet there is a paucity of evidence on this point, not even a formal agreement with the United States that might symbolize their satisfaction. Equally plausible is the hypothesis that by 1963 both sides had learned from the Cuban Missile Crisis how quickly world conflagration could come.

The obvious moral was to avoid heating up events near each other's borders, while moving the competition to locations in which direct confrontation could be more easily averted. Was this a positive development? As judged against the prospect of nuclear annihilation, the answer is surely yes. But should that be the only standard for evaluating international behavior? Here again Trachtenberg's ideology, so closely reflective of US policymakers', creates its own blinders.

Absent from *A Constructed Peace* are any values apart from that of great power stability. That superpower conflict would migrate to other places, causing millions of deaths in countries like Korea and Vietnam, that the self-determination of people around the world might be hostage to US–Soviet rivalry, that the rights of individuals even in Europe itself would be suspended for decades, none of this features in the narration.

Trachtenberg grants that certain subjects "are more or less ignored" (1999a, p. ix), including such events as the East German uprising of 1953 and the Hungarian revolt of 1956. But his book is not intended to be "an encyclopedia," instead he is trying to "get at the heart of the story." Yet in passing judgment on the European settlement, it is remarkable that four decades of repression in the East carry so little weight.

The most orthodox historians would say that it should, that this is precisely the reason why United States policy was not only pragmatic but just. Yet this returns full circle to the central historiographic issue of the Cold War: was there a positive alternative to the militarized division of Europe?

There is no disputing Stalin's malevolence, but there is reason to ponder whether postwar Europe would have been so cruelly and lastingly split had American policymakers been more open to compromise, particularly in Germany. The choices they made were not irrational, nor did they flow from exclusively economic imperatives. US officials did worry about "national security" and most saw cooperation with the Soviets as a way to achieve it. However, once they concluded that the allied project in Germany imperiled free-market economies in Western Europe, their prescription for safety was overwhelming military power and continental schism.

REFERENCES

Alperovitz, Gar: *Atomic Diplomacy: Hiroshima and Potsdam* (New York: Vintage Books, 1965).

Backer, John H.: *The Decision to Divide Germany: American Foreign Policy in Transition* (Durham, NC: Duke University Press, 1978).

Backer, John H.: *Winds of History: The German Years of Lucius Dubignon Clay* (New York: Van Nostrand Rinehold, 1983).

Cumings, Bruce: "'Revising Postrevisionism' or, the Poverty of Theory in Diplomatic History," *Diplomatic History*, 17 (Fall 1993): 539–69.

Eisenberg, Carolyn Woods: *Drawing the Line: The American Decision to Divide Germany, 1944–49* (New York: Cambridge University Press, 1996).

Feis, Herbert: *Churchill, Roosevelt and Stalin: The War They Waged and the Peace They Sought* (Princeton, NJ: Princeton University Press, 1957).

Feis, Herbert: *From Trust to Terror: The Onset of the Cold War, 1945–1950* (New York: W. W. Norton, 1970).

Fleming, D. F.: *The Cold War and Its Origins 1917–60*, 2 vols. (Garden City, NY: Doubleday, 1961).

Gaddis, John Lewis: *Strategies of Containment* (New York: Oxford University Press, 1982).

Gaddis, John Lewis: *The Long Peace: Inquiries Into the History of the Cold War* (New York: Oxford University Press, 1987).

Gaddis, John Lewis: *We Now Know: Rethinking Cold War History* (Oxford: Clarendon Press, 1997).

Gardner, Lloyd: *Architects of Illusion: Men and Ideas in American Foreign Policy, 1941–49* (Chicago: Quadrangle, 1970).

Gimbel, John: *The Origins of the Marshall Plan* (Stanford, Calif.: Stanford University Press, 1976).

Halle, Louis J.: *The Cold War as History* (New York: Harper and Row, 1967).

Harbutt, Fraser: *The Iron Curtain: Churchill, America and the Origins of the Cold War* (New York: Oxford University Press, 1986).

Jones, Joseph Marion: *The Fifteen Weeks* (New York: Harcourt Brace, 1955).

Kolko, Gabriel: *Politics of War: The World and United States Foreign Policy, 1943–45* (New York: Random House, 1968).

Kolko, Gabriel and Kolko, Joyce: *The Limits of Power: The World and United States Foreign Policy, 1945–1954* (New York: Harper and Row, 1972).

Kuklick, Bruce: *American Policy and the Division of Germany: The Clash With Russia Over Reparations* (Ithaca, NY: Cornell University Press, 1972).

Kuniholm, Bruce Robellet: *The Origins of the Cold War in the Near East: Great Power Diplomacy in Iran, Turkey and Greece* (Princeton, NJ: Princeton University Press, 1980).

LaFeber, Walter: *America, Russia and the Cold War* (New York: John Wiley, 1968).

Leffler, Melvyn: *A Preponderance of Power: National Security, the Truman Administration and the Cold War* (Palo Alto, Calif.: Stanford University Press, 1992).

Leffler, Melvyn: "Inside Enemy Archives: The Cold War Reopened," *Foreign Affairs*, 75 (July/August 1996): 120–35.

Leffler, Melvyn: "Review Essay – The Cold War: What Do 'We Now Know'?" *American Historical Review*, 104 (April 1999): 501–24.

Loth, Wilfred: "Stalin Plans for Post-War Germany," in Francesca Gori and Silvio Pons (eds.), *The Soviet Union and Eastern Europe During World War II* (New York: St. Martin's, 1996), 23–36.

Lukacs, John: *A New History of the Cold War* (New York: Anchor, 1966).

Lundestad, Geir: "Empire By Invitation? The United States and Western Europe, 1945–52," *Journal of Peace Research*, 23 (September 1986): 263–77.

McCormick, Thomas J.: *America's Half-Century: United States Foreign Policy in the Cold War* (Baltimore: Johns Hopkins University Press, 1989).

McCullough, David: *Truman* (New York: Simon and Schuster, 1992).

Mastny, Vojtech: *The Cold War and Soviet Insecurity: The Stalin Years* (New York: Columbia University Press, 1997).

Naimark, Norman M.: *The Russians in Germany: A History of the Soviet Zone of Occupation, 1945–49* (Cambridge, Mass.: Harvard University Press, 1995).

Offner, Arnold: "Another Such Victory," *Diplomatic History*, 23 (Spring 1999): 127–55.

Paterson, Thomas G.: *Soviet–American Confrontation* (Baltimore: Johns Hopkins University Press, 1973).

Smith, Jean Edward, ed.: *The Papers of General Lucius Clay*, vols. 1 and 2 (Bloomington: University of Indiana Press, 1974).

Smith, Jean Edward: *Lucius D. Clay: An American Life* (New York: Henry Holt, 1980).

Staritz, Dietrich: "The SED, Stalin and the German Question," *German History*, 10 (October 1992): 274–89.

Steininger, Rolf: *The German Question: The Stalin Note of 1952 and the Problem of Reunification* (New York: Columbia University Press, 1990).

Symposium, "Soviet Archives: Recent Revelations of Cold War Historiography," *Diplomatic History*, 21 (Spring 1997): 217–307.

Trachtenberg, Marc: *A Constructed Peace: The Making of the European Settlement, 1945–63* (Princeton, NJ: Princeton University Press, 1999a).

Trachtenberg, Marc: "The Past Under Siege: A Historian Ponders the State of his Profession

– and What to Do About It," in Elizabeth Fox Genovese and Elisabeth Lasch Quinn (eds.), *Reconstructing History* (New York: Routledge, 1999b), 9–11.

Williams, William Appleman: *The Tragedy of American Diplomacy* (New York: Delta Books, 1962).

Yergin, Daniel: *Shattered Peace: The Origins of the Cold War and the National Security State* (Boston: Houghton Mifflin, 1977).

Zubok, Vladislav and Pleshakov, Constantine: *Inside the Kremlin's Cold War: From Stalin to Khrushchev* (Cambridge, Mass.: Harvard University Press, 1996).

Chapter Twenty-Two

Off the Beach: The United States, Latin America, and the Cold War

Greg Grandin

Poets may see the world in a grain of sand, says William Blake, but only diplomatic historians could reduce the Latin American Cold War to a Cuban beach. The Cold War radically transformed Latin America, yet historians of US policy toward the region inevitably focus on the period's most rousing events. These episodes more often than not have to do with Cuba – the 1959 Revolution, the Bay of Pigs, the Missile Crisis, and plots to murder Fidel Castro. Yet just as Fidel eventually made it off the beach and into the mountains, the time has come for US historians to assess the Latin American Cold War from a higher vantage point, one less preoccupied with what motivated United States policymakers and more concerned with identifying what was being fought over in Latin America itself. As some of the best social history done on the region in the last fifteen years makes clear, the Cold War in Latin America had less to do with geopolitical superpower conflict than it did with bitterly fought battles over citizenship rights, national inclusion, and economic justice.

The Latin American Cold War began not in 1959, with the triumph of the Cuban Revolution, nor in 1954, with the United States' first Cold War Latin American intervention, but in the years following World War II, when movements pushing for political and economic change swept the continent. In country after country, the emerging international fight against communism provided elites with new strategies, technologies, and ideologies to effectively and often brutally beat back these movements. At the risk of homogenizing diverse experiences, one could say that in nearly every Latin American nation the conflict that emerged in the immediate period after World War II between the promise of reform and efforts taken to contain that promise profoundly influenced the particular shape of Cold War politics in each country. To make the point even more crudely, in many countries the promise of a postwar social democratic nation was countered by the creation of a Cold War counterinsurgent terror state.

The use of social history to study the Cold War has received the recent imprimatur of John Lewis Gaddis, perhaps the most influential diplomatic historian working today. In his acclaimed *We Now Know: Rethinking Cold War History*, Gaddis argues that historians have failed to understand that the Cold War was a war of ideas. The promise of liberal democracy, he says, had great resonance among women and men in Western Europe and Japan. Because New Left critics have refused to acknowledge this fact, he adds, they have not taken seriously the United States' "strong base of popular support, confirmed repeatedly [by] free elections" that kept allies of the

United States in power (1998, p. 285). The Soviet Union, he goes on, "never won such acceptance" and therefore used bloody repression to maintain its empire. Any adequate history of the Cold War, concludes Gaddis, must also be a social history. It must take ideas seriously, examining the beliefs and actions not only of political elites but ordinary people as well (1998, p. 285).

It is a valuable insight, but unfortunately one that Gaddis neglects to apply to the victims of United States foreign policy. Following a review of the literature on US–Latin American relations, this essay turns to a discussion of the importance of the immediate post-World War II period in setting the contours of the Latin American Cold War. It then revisits the US-supported 1954 overthrow of Guatemalan President Jacobo Arbenz, who, notwithstanding the free election and strong base of popular support that brought him to power, earned the enmity of the United States for his nationalism, agrarian reform program, and close ties to the Communist Party. To focus on this event is not to argue simply that the United States fired the first shot in the Latin American Cold War. Nor is it to imply some kind of moral equivalency between the actions of the United States and those of the USSR. The point, rather, is to use the event to help define a domestic history of the Cold War in Latin America, to show what was at stake and what were some of the consequences of a broader continent-wide social conflict.

I

Starting in the mid-1960s, a young, radicalized, and frustrated generation of Latin American intellectuals – spurred by the 1959 Cuban Revolution and a succession of right-wing military coups – began to work out a broad, new historical perspective on Latin American history; they argued not only against the mainstream theories of development of Walt Rostow and Bert Hoselitz, but also against the failed reform strategies and goals of orthodox Latin American communist parties. While theoretical distinctions and points of contention were many, *dependentistas* such as Fernando Henrique Cardoso and Enzo Faletto sought to demonstrate that Latin America's seemingly chronic underdevelopment and intractable militarism were not remnants of an archaic colonial past, but consequences of a vibrant international political and economic order maintained to the benefit of the developed countries of Europe and the United States. And while their political passions varied, many of these theorists shared a belief that development could not come through collaboration with "nationalist" bourgeoisie or with participation in a world system, as many Latin American "Old Left" reformers had hoped, but rather by breaking with that system and establishing autonomous forms of national development (see also Furtado, 1970; Dos Santos, 1978).

At the same time, the New Left in the United States was producing its own cohort of dissenting intellectuals. Against liberals such as Samuel Flagg Bemis and realists such as George Kennan, who argued that US nineteenth-century expansion and early twentieth-century gunboat diplomacy were merely "adolescent" or "idealistic" transgressions, historians influenced by William Appleman Williams began to detect a structural pattern. Building on earlier, radical economic critics such as Charles Beard and Scott Nearing, New Left scholars argued that US turn-of-the-century adventures in the Caribbean and the Pacific represented, as Walter LaFeber put it, "not a break in history, but a natural culmination" of an expanding industrial capitalism that had taken off after the Civil War and demanded new markets, new resources, and new outlets for domestic conflicts (1963, p. vii).

David Green's *The Containment of Latin America: A History of the Myths and Realities of the Good Neighbor Policy* (1971) was one of the first fully developed New Left critiques of early US foreign policy toward Latin America in the Cold War. Green argued that Truman's promotion of regional organizations and military alliances like the 1947 Rio Pact, which bound Latin American nations in a mutual defense treaty, and the 1948 creation of the Organization of American States (OAS) was designed to counter the growing importance of international bodies and treaties such as the United Nations. Cold War anti-communism, Green wrote, allowed US foreign policymakers to use these regional alliances to establish hegemony and suppress economic nationalism, in effect creating a "closed hemisphere" in an increasingly open and interdependent world (p. 291). Following Green came similar studies that critically examined the means by which the United States maintained regional political and economic power (Francis, 1977; Frank, 1979; Grow, 1981).

By fusing dependency theory with New Left interpretations of US foreign policy, these historians crafted a powerful interpretive lens through which many scholars continue, implicitly or explicitly, to understand US–Latin American Cold War relations. Noam Chomsky and Richard Barnet, for example, have argued that the mutually reinforcing desires to maintain hemispheric stability, preserve access to resources and markets, protect investments abroad, and ward off foreign threats, be they economic or political, remain the motor forces of US actions abroad (see also Morley, 1987; O'Brien, 1999). When after World War II Latin American economic nationalism threatened one or more of these interests, the United States mobilized the rhetoric of anti-communism and the techniques of diplomatic pressure, covert action, counterinsurgency, or, when all else failed, direct military intervention. While Latin Americans from Simón Bolívar to José Martí have long been suspicious of the economic and political ambitions of the United States, dependency theory and the New Left came together most forcefully in LaFeber's important *Inevitable Revolutions: The United States in Central America* (1984). Written as Ronald Reagan was transforming Nicaragua, Guatemala, and El Salvador into one of the Cold War's final killing fields, LaFeber's study highlights the contradiction created by a US foreign economic policy that generates chronic poverty and revolt and a diplomatic policy that enforces, at whatever price, political stability (see also Baily, 1976; Haines, 1989).

By any measure, the cost of hemispheric enforcement was high. Today, no one can seriously deny the atrocities the United States either committed or condoned in order to wage the Cold War in Latin America. From John Gerassi's *The Great Fear* (1963) to Martha Huggins's *Political Policing: The United States and Latin America* (1998), the literature on topics ranging from US invasions and the orchestration of coups to obstacles placed in the way of social reform and political and technical support provided to repressive military regimes is vast and damning (Americas Watch, 1985; Blasier, 1985; Black, 1986; Schoultz, 1987; LeoGrande, 1998; Cullather, 1999). The slow and limited, but nevertheless illuminating, declassification of information from US foreign service agencies – documenting, for instance, US support of Augusto Pinochet's murderous 1973 coup and regime in Chile – suggests that we still have much to learn about US actions in Latin America (Kornbluh, forthcoming).

What is debated is the motivation for such actions. The end of the Cold War brought about a general retreat from New Left diplomatic history. While many investigations into the United States' Cold War Latin American policy still engage its critical perspectives (Benjamin, 1990; Paterson, 1994), few if any studies produced in the last decade have continued in the tradition of Green or LaFeber. A new post-Cold War cohort of diplomatic historians has produced many finely researched but less conceptually ambitious works on specific Latin American Cold War episodes and policies (Rabe, 1988, 1999a; Weis, 1993). This new generation seems intellectually paralyzed by the persistent dissonance between the democratic values that the United States purported to defend and the consequences of its foreign policy. (This conflict ran through the work of Williams himself, who, as Marilyn Young points out, "always seemed to feel that the United States could, if only it just would, abandon its imperialist career and go into another more modest business"; in Copelman and Smith, 1991, p. 69.)

Take, for example, Stephen Rabe, whose *The Most Dangerous Area in the World: John F. Kennedy Confronts Communist Revolution in Latin America* (1999a) is quite critical of the New Frontier's obsessive anti-communism. It was on Kennedy's watch that the United States, building on hemispheric military relations established during World War II, helped lay the material and ideological foundations for subsequent Latin American terror states. In the wake of the Cuban Revolution, the United States stepped up the export of counterinsurgency training, material, and doctrines. In country after country, the United States helped establish intelligence systems that were not only capable of spying on civil society – the seedbed of subversion in the fevered counterinsurgent imagination – but of capturing and interrogating, often to deadly effect, individuals deemed dangerous. It was during Kennedy's administration that US military aid to Latin America skyrocketed, with military officers receiving training in US military schools in sociology, psychology, economics, and management, as well as other, less enlightened skills (see Carlos Osorio's 1997 analysis of the manuals the United States used to train Latin American military officials); thus bolstered, these officers began to expand on their already well-established tendency to intervene in civilian politics. Yet after two hundred fairly unfavorable pages, Rabe's last paragraph laments that "Kennedy brought high ideals and noble purposes to his Latin American policy. Ironically, however, his unwavering determination to wage Cold War . . . led him and his administration ultimately to compromise and even mutilate those grand goals for the Western Hemisphere" (Rabe, 1999a, p. 199). As subsequent Latin American truth commissions document in bloody detail, however, the consequences of US counterinsurgency aid and training mutilated a good deal more than Kennedy's ideals.

If only it could be definitively proven that the Dulles brothers had been motivated by political rather than economic considerations, then, it seems, the ghost of William Appleman Williams could finally be put to rest. Consider the strategic use that diplomatic historians have made of Piero Gleijeses's *Shattered Hope: The Guatemalan Revolution and the United States, 1944–1954* (1991). Gleijeses revisits the 1954 overthrow of democratically elected Guatemalan President Jacobo Arbenz – arguably the most well-known covert operation in CIA history. Prior to Gleijeses's minutely researched, detailed study, previous accounts, such as Stephen Schlesinger and Stephen Kinzer's *Bitter Fruit* (1982), stressed the influence on Eisenhower's decision to intervene of the United Fruit Company, which lost land under Arbenz's agrarian reform. Openly sympathetic to the economic and political goals of Arbenz and his advisers and admiring of their intelligence, vision, and integrity, Gleijeses documents Arbenz's close relationship with the Guatemalan Communist Party. In doing so, he downplays economic motivations and places the actions of the Eisenhower regime within the cultural and political milieu of the Cold War.

Some historians have seized on Gleijeses's book like Christians on the Turin Shroud: they see what they want to see. Both John Lewis Gaddis and Gaddis Smith cite it as if it were the final nail in Williams's coffin, while Paul Dosal, an historian of the United Fruit Company, uses *Shattered Hope* to mitigate US culpability in ending Guatemala's democratic revolution. "Arbenz apologists," Dosal writes, "have long felt compelled to deny Arbenz's communist inclinations to maintain the case against the CIA" (2000, p. 634). "None of this justified the American intervention," Dosal concedes, "but assessing responsibility for the collapse of the Arbenz regime hangs in the balance" (p. 635). Likewise, in his review of *Shattered Hope*, Robert Pastor writes that Eisenhower truly desired democracy in Latin America but "mistakes" led "well-intentioned men to produce a tragedy" (1993, p. 125). In response, Gleijeses, who knows well the distinction between the motivations of individuals and the larger social consequences of their actions, writes:

> I disagree that the men [who overthrew Arbenz] were well-intentioned. Their intentions were as old as international relations: they believed they were acting in the U.S. national interest. . . . My own study . . . showed that the Eisenhower administration acted with supreme indifference toward the fate of the Guatemalan people. This cannot be described as being well-intentioned. It is, rather, wanton criminal negligence. . . . [Guatemala] still has the most regressive fiscal system and the most unequal land-ownership pattern in Latin America. Its army, victorious on the battlefield, has evolved into an all-powerful mafia, stretching its tentacles into drug-trafficking, kidnapping, and smuggling. . . . Guatemala is still paying for the American 'success.' (1999, pp. xxviii–xxix, xxxii)

As Gleijeses makes clear in *Shattered Hope*, to argue that it was the activities of the Guatemalan Communist Party rather than the land reform that moved the United States to intervene ignores the evident fact that there would have been no land reform, nor a significant expansion of political democracy for that matter, if it were not for Guatemalan communists. It seems as if the specter of William Appleman Williams is not so easily exorcised.

II

Neither New Left scholarship, with its focus on larger historical frames, nor diplomatic history, with its myopic obsession with the motives of US policymakers, has provided a satisfying account of the Latin American Cold War. For their part, recent social historians, hoping to fill in dependency theory's abstractions with grassroots studies of local relations and values, have paid only cursory attention to politics and diplomacy. They have refrained from fully developing the term "Cold War," instead using it as shorthand to describe either direct US (or Cuban) intervention in Latin American politics or the collateral damage from superpower conflict. Rather than forcing the rich diversity of Latin American politics into a Cold War template, however, Leslie Bethell and Ian Roxborough (1992a, 1992b, 1994) use that diversity to provide a framework helpful in understanding the indigenous origins of the Latin American Cold War.

Bethell and Roxborough argue that following World War II, Latin America experienced a continent-wide democratic spring. In 1944, only four Latin American countries – Uruguay, Chile, Costa Rica, and Colombia – could nominally call themselves democracies. By 1946, only five countries still could not. After World War II, dictators toppled throughout Latin America, the franchise was extended, unions were legalized, and governments, to varying degrees, enacted social welfare programs. Everywhere, it seemed, liberal, nationalist, socialist, and communist reform parties took power or gained influence in coalition governments. With the exceptions of Paraguay, El Salvador, Honduras, Nicaragua, and the Dominican Republic, all Latin American countries moved toward political liberalization. "No single country moved in the opposite direction" (Bethell and Roxborough, 1992a, p. 5).

Politicians, nationalists, and reformers in all Latin American countries sought to achieve industrialization through economic planning, state regulation of capital, and other initiatives that favored the domestic manufacturing sector. As Bethell and Roxborough write, "at the end of the Second World War, and to a large extent because of the Second World War, not only was there in Latin America a forward march by democracy, the Left, and labor, but there was also a shift in the nature of political discourse and ideology" (1992b, p. 327). Democracy came to mean a "commitment to popular, more particularly working-class participation in politics, and social and economic improvements for the poorer sections of the population. Democracy increasingly became identified with development and welfare. This was a vision of the Latin American Left, both Communist and non-Communist" (1992b, pp. 327–8).

A number of factors seeded this postwar continental democratic spring. The experience of the war itself and wartime propaganda promoting democratic values and freedoms strengthened a "strong liberal tradition in Latin American political ideas and culture" reaching back at least to independence from Spain in the early nineteenth century (1994, p. 295). Wartime exigencies, as well as encouragement from the United States, led Latin American military and economic elites to acquiesce to popular demands for greater democratization. Fidel Castro's evocation of Thomas Paine and the US Declaration of Independence in his 1953 "History Will Absolve Me" speech captures the inspiration the progressive currents of US history continued to hold for Latin American intellectuals and politicians well into the Cold War. The widely reported anecdote that a fourteen-year-old Castro sent Franklin Delano Roosevelt a letter to congratulate him on his 1940 electoral victory (he also asked FDR for a dollar!) likewise highlights the importance the New Deal state held as a model to would-be Latin American reformers.

To varying degrees in different countries, urbanization, industrialization, and population growth created both an expanded middle class and an urban working class that joined with students, intellectuals, and, in some cases, a mobilized peasantry to demand economic and political reform. Following the war, invigorated labor unions in Mexico, Brazil, Peru, Guatemala, Colombia, Argentina, and Chile led strike waves of unparalleled militancy. In a number of countries populist reform parties, many of them organized in the 1920s, came to power by tapping into this increased mobilization. Legitimized by anti-fascist patriotism and largely neglected by Moscow, many Latin American communist parties hoped to continue a wartime strategy of alliance with other "progressive" sectors of society in nationalist, popular movements in order to break the "feudal" power of an atavistic landed class that, it was believed, stood in the way of economic and political reforms (Bethell and Roxborough, 1992a, 1992b).

What made this postwar opening particularly threatening to local elites was that it had been brought into being or immediately seized on by sectors of the population historically marginalized from political participation. Latin American labor historians, writing in the 1960s and 1970s, tended to judge this reform period as a failure, highlighting the demobilization of popular movements brought about by their incorporation into populist or social welfare projects (Berguist, 1986). Viewing working-class aspirations through the lens of dependency theory, these historians downplayed the importance that claims to citizenship and national inclusion had for peasant and working-class movements; for these scholars, the state was the enemy and appeals to nationalism and citizenship rights were all but unintelligible to the great mass of the disfranchised and the marginalized. Even historians who had initially emphasized the importance of popular mobilization and political culture in the forging of national identity and state formation turned sour, as did John Womack, whose 1969 book on Emiliano Zapata's peasant army continues to inspire new generations of historians. By the late 1980s, Womack was describing the Mexican Revolution as little more than a "bourgeois civil war" that resulted in the creation of a decidedly unpopular, leviathan state (1991, p. 128).

Over the last decade, however, historians of Latin America have begun to offer fine-grained, on-the-ground studies of social movements, successfully incorporating analyses of gender, race, and ethnic relations and ideologies into their interpretations. Much of this work parallels efforts by historians of the United States to recover the radical potential of the 1930s and 1940s without reducing that potential to a specific party, project, ideology, or identity. New work by historians such as John French on Brazilian working-class populism (1992), Daniel James on Peronism (1988), Jeffrey Gould (1990) on peasant mobilization in Nicaragua, Karin Rosemblatt (2000) on gender in the Chilean Popular Front, and Thomas Klubock (1998) on copper miners in Chile are forcing a reconsideration of oppositional models of state formation that present the state as inherently predatory. Klubock writes that far from defanging the Chilean working class, the expansion of state-directed labor relations and social welfare system in the 1940s helped create a "radical nationalism and ideology of citizenship" that offered workers not only a language to define their interests but a lever to press for them (1998, p. 289). This new work has been complemented by recent histories (Mallon, 1995; Grandin, 2000) of nineteenth-century popular politics which argue that the state and claims to citizenship held "emancipatory potential," to borrow the words of David Nugent in his study of Peruvian peasants (1997, p. 8). Peter Guardino, for instance, in his work on nineteenth-century Mexican peasants concludes that "popular liberalism" posed a "haunting challenge" in demanding that the "ideals of post-Enlightenment liberal nation-states" be taken seriously (1996, p. 220). In many countries, these popular claims to liberal ideals, national inclusion, and state action, often grouped under the bloodless rubric "economic nationalism" by critics and apologists of US foreign policy, reached their apex in the 1930s and 1940s, only to come under violent, relentless assault during the Cold War years.

In nearly every Latin American country, when the threat of the postwar opening became clear, economic and military elites moved to contain it. By the early 1950s, by 1948 in most nations, the democratic opening had been shut down. In Peru and Venezuela military coups overthrew democracies. In countries that maintained the trappings of democratic governance there was a sharp veer to the right. Reform parties lost their dynamism and communist parties almost everywhere were repressed and outlawed. Governments intervened against work stoppages and passed legislation restricting the right to strike. Militants were purged from unions, while labor confederations either fractured or were placed under government control.

Bethell and Roxborough list a number of causes to explain this reaction, reminding us that the "strength of the authoritarian as well as the liberal tradition in Latin American political culture should never be forgotten" (1994, p. 305). The ongoing power of the dominant classes, particularly the landed class, led to a rollback of social reform and attacks on organized labor. The emerging Cold War reinforced domestic anti-communism, which already had deep roots in the military, the middle class, and the Catholic Church throughout Latin American society, and provided elite reaction with "ideological justification" (1994, p. 306).

While the United States largely neglected Latin America in the early years of the Cold War, Bethell and Roxborough insist that it would be a "mistake to underestimate its importance" (1994, p. 306). World War II had marked the culmination of a century-long process of US hemispheric ascendance. A realistic assessment of Soviet aims and strength led the State Department to ignore Latin America, sending little economic or military assistance to the region in the late 1940s. The United States was concerned with internal threats, however, and began to monitor communist activities immediately following the war, first through the FBI and embassy officials, then through the Central Intelligence Agency (CIA), which was founded in 1947. US embassies applied a range of economic and political pressure on local governments to restrict communist activities, particularly in Chile, Brazil, Cuba, Guatemala, and Bolivia, and the American Federation of Labor worked with Latin American labor leaders to purge unions of militants. Foreign policy analysts, when they paid attention, viewed the rightward shift with approval. Indigenous popular fronts that "might have been acceptable in 1944 and 1945 or even 1946," write Bethell and Roxborough, "[were] no longer so in 1947 or 1948" (1994, p. 310).

The two authors end their survey with a discussion of the "perception the ruling groups had of the new international economic order, and its consequences, short- and long-term, for Latin American economic development" (1994, p. 312). Capital starved and diplomatically slighted by the United States in terms of economic aid, Latin American elites had to look to private capital to fund industrialization. "If U.S. capital were to be attracted the right climate had to be created: political stability . . . a commitment to liberal, capitalist development and to an 'ideology of production,' nationalism curbed, the left marginalized, the working class firmly under control, unions not necessarily weaker but bureaucratized" (1994, p. 312). Thus the authors argue a number of competing national and international agendas were fused in the crucible of Cold War anti-communism: "The attack on labor and the left, especially the Communist left, was, in this sense, clearly overdetermined" (1994, p. 312). It was the condition of the region's "participation in the unprecedented expansion of the international economy, in which the United States played the dominant role" (1994, p. 314).

In different countries, a single event came to symbolize the defeat of the postwar democracy. In Cuba, Fulgencio Batista's 1952 coup evoked an earlier year, 1933, of frustrated reform. The 1948 murder of Jorge Gaitán likewise marked for many Colombians the beginning of their descent into civil war. In Chile, Gabriel González Videla's 1947 violent turn against striking coal miners and his erstwhile communist allies severed a popular front alliance that had elected three presidents since 1938. From his exile in Mexico, poet Pablo Neruda, a Communist Party senator forced to flee Chile following González Videla's crackdown, surveyed the continent-wide ruins of failed reform in his epic 1950 poem, *Canto General*: "How will it end . . . this bleak year? . . . This bleak year of rage and rancor, you ask, you ask me how will it end?"

It ended badly. The Cold War unfolded in its own way in each country, yet in many Latin American nations political strategies were radicalized and political visions polarized. The dynamic established in the immediate postwar period between the hope of reform and measures taken to contain that hope would repeatedly resurface, in ever-intensifying cycles, as the Cold War played itself out. Despite the setbacks suffered in the late 1940s, reformers and nationalists worked with some success to reestablish democracies. By 1961, there were once again only a handful of Latin American governments that were not, at least nominally, democratic. And once again, many of these new governments attempted to enact social and political reforms. In many nations, this reform was impelled by the imperatives of anti-communism and was backed up by the Kennedy administration's launch of the Alliance for Progress, which promised to donate as much as $10 billion in exchange for significant land and tax reforms that would hopefully create a prosperous, stable middle class. In 1962, political scientist Victor Alba viewed the period with such hope that he gushed that Latin American militarism would soon wither away.

But of course it did not. The promised financial aid never materialized. And at the same time that the United States was promoting economic and political modernization, it was also invigorating Latin American militaries and police forces in an effort to counter real and perceived insurgent threats. Starting in Argentina in 1962, these militaries toppled democratically elected administrations, often with the tacit approval if not direct assistance of the United States. Once again the wheel had turned. By 1976 there were only three Latin American nations that could be considered democratic. While historians and social scientists have engaged in chicken-and-egg debates about which came first, the fact is that both the guerrilla insurgencies and the military regimes that dominated Latin American politics in the 1960s and 1970s were less a reaction to each other and more the outcome of the postwar dynamic set in motion between the hope of reform and the beefed-up propensity for repression.

That many of the most famous Latin American Cold War actors received their political education in the years following World War II highlights the importance of the period to subsequent hemispheric politics. Salvador Allende and Augusto Pinochet stood on opposing sides as Chile's postwar popular front crumbled under the weight of state repression. Fidel Castro was in Bogotá in 1948 when Gaitán was murdered and witnessed the widespread riots and protests that followed. And in Guatemala, a young and socially conscious Ernesto Guevera sought asylum in the Argentine embassy following the 1954 US-backed coup. While he awaited safe conduct to Mexico (where he would meet Castro), he started a lifelong friendship with a young activist named Ricardo Ramírez, who went on to lead the Guerrilla Army of the Poor, Guatemala's most formidable armed movement in the 1970s and 1980s. Both men would cite the experience of the 1954 coup as central to their subsequent rejection of reform politics and embrace of armed revolution.

III

In important ways, Guatemala, rather than Cuba, set the pace of much of Latin American Cold War politics. In October 1944, Guatemala experienced a revolution that was among the most ambitious of any in post-World War II Latin America. That revolution came to an abrupt end in 1954, when Guatemala suffered the first US Cold War direct intervention in Latin American politics, an intervention that not only toppled Arbenz, but definitively ended the hemisphere's postwar democratic opening. Emboldened by this easy success, the United States would employ the same tactics seven years later in its disastrous Bay of Pigs operation, which was launched from Guatemala. For the next four decades, US advisers in Guatemala rehearsed coun- terinsurgency tactics that would later be used throughout Latin America (Streeter 2000). If Vietnam came to symbolize the failure of US counterinsurgent policy, Guatemala was considered a success. (A recent UN truth commission, which found the Guatemalan military responsible for 200,000 murders and charged the state with genocide, documents US involvement in political repression; see Comisión para el Esclarecimiento Histórico, 1999.)

What made Guatemala's 1944 Revolution unique was its duration. While all other Latin American postwar democracies were short-lived, the commitment of the Guatemalan state to reform intensified over its ten-year course. By ending forced labor, legalizing unions, establishing labor rights, extending the franchise to women, Mayans, and the propertyless, and enacting an unprecedented program of agrarian reform, the October Revolution not only threatened the political and economic power of Guatemala's landed elite but undercut the culture, privilege, and racism that justified that power (Porras, 1992; Handy, 1994; Grandin, 2000). According to Piero Gleijeses, Guatemala was never more free or democratic than it was between 1944 and 1954.

There were many reasons for the failure of Guatemala's social democracy. Endemic divisions among nationalists and reformers failed to provide a united front against the alliance forged between a landed class bent on regaining power and by the US Department of State intent on restoring the status quo ante. And although the goals of the earlier Mexican Revolution and Guatemalan Revolution were similar, in Mexico, decades of rural violence forced elites to hold to their promises of reform. That the more radical elements of the Mexican Revolution – land reform and nation- alization of oil production – occurred prior to the Cold War speaks to the impor- tance of anti-communism in containing political and economic reform. In Guatemala, as popular agitation and demands increased in the years following 1944, government opponents effectively used the rhetoric of anti-communism to tap middle-class and military anxiety about peasant and Indian rebellion.

The US Department of State and the CIA took advantage of this internal insta-bility and anxiety to promote, plan, and execute the overthrow of Arbenz in 1954. The most thorough description of this operation comes from Nick Cullather, who was hired by the CIA to write an internal history of its Guatemalan operation. Declas-sified and published as *Secret History: The CIA's Classified Account of Its Operations in Guatemala, 1952–1954,* Cullather's study offers a truly extraordinary account of the scope, ambition, and hubris of the operation. From Langley to Madison Avenue, the CIA mobilized every facet of US power to oust Arbenz. Agents planned an operation in Guatemala that would be "applied on a grander scale, over a longer period, and for higher stakes than ever before" (1999, p. 39). The CIA used the OAS to isolate Guatemala diplomatically; it worked with US businesses to create an eco-nomic crisis there; it cultivated dissidents within the military, oligarchy, Catholic Church, and student organizations; and it funded and equipped an exile invasion force based in Honduras. The State Department threatened to withhold much-needed trade con-cessions and credit from other Latin American countries unless they acceded to US plans for Guatemala. Information released subsequent to Cullather's research has revealed that in the event its operation failed, the CIA intended to assassinate fifty-eight key Guatemalan government officials (US Central Intelligence Agency, 1954).

The CIA also "placed tremendous faith in the new science of advertising," Cullather writes. "Touted as the answer to underconsumption, economic recession, and social ills, advertising, many thought, could be used to cure Communism as well" (1999, p. 40). Radio shows claiming to be broadcast from "deep in the jungle" by rebel forces were in fact taped in Miami and beamed into Guatemala from a neighboring country. Agents planned an "Orson Welles type 'panic broadcast'" to coincide with the invasion from Honduras. Operatives mined pop sociologies such as Robert Maurer's *The Big Con* (1940) for disinformation tactics. The CIA used rumors and posters, planted stories (both in the Guatemalan and international press), and engineered death threats and sabotage to create dissension and confusion within the Arbenz government.

Limited by its exclusive reliance on CIA documents, *Secret History* contributes little to the debate discussed above as to whether President Eisenhower acted pri-marily to defend the economic interests of the United Fruit Company, which had lost land under Arbenz's agrarian reform, or to stem the growing importance of the Guatemalan Communist Party (PGT) in the Guatemalan government. Organized in 1949 by politicians and intellectuals from the left wings of reform parties, the PGT was largely independent from Moscow; its belated formation freed it from some of the historical baggage that weighed down other Latin American communist parties. The party combined the promise of Roosevelt's Four Freedoms with a comprehen-sive Marxist critique of Guatemala's ills. The PGT was legalized in 1950 and quickly went on to have a great deal of influence on Arbenz, who found in the PGT the most coherent vision for how to "modernize" Guatemala.

Whatever the case, Cullather, as does Gleijeses, makes it clear that the debate is moot: the politics and culture of anti-communism cannot be divorced in any mean-ingful way from the political economy of the Cold War. He writes that the CIA's objectives were not just the removal of Arbenz and his advisers but a "radical, revolutionary change in Guatemalan politics. They sought the reversal of the Revolution of 1944, the termination of land reform, and the replacement of Arbenz with a liberal, authoritarian leader. Afterwards, they foresaw a prolonged period of dictatorial rule during which the regime would depend on United States aid and arms" (1999, p. 60).

After 1954, reform strategies divided. A new generation of revolutionaries dismissed the PGT's attempt to usher in progressive capitalism as misguided in light of US intervention and irrelevant in the wake of the Cuban Revolution. By the early 1960s, these new leftists came together in a socialist insurgency that would continue to operate for more than three decades. But the PGT, banned and persecuted, was still influential. While the PGT allied with the rebels, it did so grudgingly, viewing armed resistance more as a pressure tactic than a way of taking state power (in most cases, Latin American Cuban-inspired insurgencies and communist parties were at odds with each other). Many of its leaders, together with other reformers and nationalists, continued to believe that the 1944 Revolution could be remade.

Responding to the Cuban Revolution in 1959 and the growing opposition to the Guatemalan government, US policymakers actively pushed for the creation of a national and Central American-wide intelligence apparatus. Following another military coup in 1962, the United States upgraded Guatemala's military intelligence system with new weapons, vehicles, and telecommunication equipment. This revamped intelligence apparatus was put to a lethal test with the arrival in November 1965 of US security adviser John P. Longan. Summoned to Guatemala to help stem a rise in kidnappings and urban political unrest, Longan trained an elite squad, commanded by Guatemala's notoriously brutal future defense minister, to gather intelligence and conduct rapid raids on the homes and meeting places of suspected subversives.

The unit carried out its most ambitious operation in March 1966 when, during a three-day period, it kidnapped, tortured, and executed close to thirty people.[1] This operation took place on the eve of the election of a civilian president who repeatedly evoked the legacy of the 1944 Revolution. Many in the PGT and its allied guerrilla organization thought the imminent election of the new civilian government provided the possibility to reenter the political arena, and they encouraged their rank and file to cast their vote in his favor. Opposing these plans stood the Guatemalan military and the CIA, which, declassified documents reveal, were nervous about a possible negotiated end to the insurgency and a return of the PGT to legal status and influence (US Central Intelligence Agency, 1966). Whatever the motivation for the executions or the complicity of US agents, the operation had a profound impact on Guatemalan politics, shutting down the possibility of peaceful reform. In a sense, the 1966 killings – the first systemic wave of counterinsurgent disappearances in Latin America – offered in one act a repeat performance of Guatemala's democratic decade: reformers and revolutionaries hoping to recreate the alliances that had led to nationalist and social democratic reform (among those killed were a number of politicians and activists from the Arbenz period) now confronted a new set of international relations that ensured that those coalitions could never again be replicated. Following this collective "disappearance," repression aimed at the PGT and noncommunist reformers destroyed any conceit that 1944 could be recreated. In the 1970s, the PGT passed into irrelevance, overshadowed by a growing Cuban-inspired insurgency intent on overthrowing, not reforming, the state. Guatemala's October Revolution ended in 1966, not 1954.

IV

Nick Cullather's account, if not the very notion of a CIA historian, would seem a curious contradiction in terms, for documents declassified over the past ten years suggest that political repression functions best when it is accompanied by historical amnesia. Consider this 1986 State Department history of political disappearances in Guatemala:

> Guatemala is a violent society. The conscious acceptance and use of violence as an instrument of politics contributes to the extraordinary levels of murder, kidnapping and disappearances.
>
> First used systematically by the security forces against the Communist Party and members of the moderate left beginning in 1966, the practices of kidnappings became institutionalized over time. . . .
>
> Guatemala's high violence levels cannot be accounted for by economic or political variables. Equally poor nations in Africa, Asia, and Latin America have lower violence levels. The explanation for Guatemala's high level of violence probably is rooted in cultural and sociological factors unique to Guatemala. Guatemala is distinguished from other Central American nations by the duality of its culture where a wealthy ladino [non-Indian] minority lives side by side with an impoverished Indian majority largely marginalized from national political and economic life. . . . The use of violence to settle disputes of almost any nature is accepted in Guatemala's indigenous culture.
>
> The plantation system which historically generated Guatemala's exports and wealth has relied on Indian labor to function. . . .
>
> Fear of revolution stems from the Arbenz period when the first political efforts to involve peasants and Indians in national life began in earnest. . . . Following Arbenz' ouster in 1954, saving the country from communism and personal self interest thus blended to form a psychology conducive to supporting physical repression of workers and peasants in the name of anti-communism. (US Department of State, 1986)

In this document and in many like it, the imaginative projection of violent propensities upon Guatemalans abetted official amnesia about US collusion in repression – an amnesia that, to borrow from the document itself, became institutionalized over time. Denial became deniability. While acknowledging the importance of the years 1954 (the overthrow of Arbenz) and 1966 (the collective disappearance described earlier), the analysis conveniently omits any actions taken by the United States at these two junctures. By expunging the United States from the narrative, a fairly perceptive critique of how anti-communism had been used to protect the economic and political privileges of an entrenched elite turned into a dubious armchair anthropology of "cultural and sociological factors unique to Guatemala" – an anthropology that holds Indians accountable for counterinsurgent disappearances. Brutality is a thing of the past in which Guatemala is trapped. Guatemala's failure to modernize, to move beyond its native particularity toward a tolerant American pluralism, thus explains, or rather explains away, a system of violence that the United States was instrumental in creating.

Precisely the same rhetorical strategies are at play in an 1986 interview given by John Longan, the official who trained Guatemalans in the tactics that led to Latin America's first counterinsurgent disappearances. Joining the US foreign service in 1957 and the newly created Office of Public Safety (OPS) in 1962, Longan trained foreign security forces of Guatemala, Venezuela, the Dominican Republic, and Thailand in counterinsurgent and counterterrorist techniques. In recounting his life's work, Longan displayed a law-and-order, countersubversive sensibility (similar to what Ellen Schrecker describes as fueling the rise of domestic anti-communism [1998, pp. 50–1]), honed by his earlier career with the Oklahoma police department and the Texas Border Patrol. Transplanted in foreign soil, Longan's reactive anti-communism melded with the Black Legend of Spanish barbarism: "Guatemala," Longan remarked, "is a society that's conducive, I guess, to reacting with violence. . . . Under the Arbenz – that was the communist regime – . . . they cut off the hands of thieves, so it's, it was traditional, I guess, from the time of the Spanish conquest for some of these countries to react like that to criminals and violence – or over-react, I'd say" (Institute of Inter-American Affairs Collection [IIAC], 1986, p. 21). In his only reference to the 1966 killings, Longan blamed the murders on "[Guatemala's] underlying vein of violence – I'm not sure I can explain it – it's inbred in them, and they hate pretty deeply" (IIAC, 1986, p. 20).

Like many foreign service agents, Longan conducted his activities within a bureaucratic division of labor that compartmentalized the benevolence of US intentions, hiving it off from the often horrific consequences of US actions. While Longan believed that there was "no question about the U.S. policy always being on the side of human rights," he stressed that the United States had little influence on the governments it was training: "you didn't control the country that you were trying to upgrade their – capabilities" (IIAC, 1986, pp. 12–13). As to his role, he was just a "technician [whose] job was to try to implement the policies of our government at that particular time on those particular things. If it was to upgrade this or upgrade that, I didn't ask why. If you had a corrupt government or something like that, as long as they were our crooks – there wasn't anything I could do about it" (IIAC, 1986, p. 22).

V

This chronic official refusal to reckon seriously with the consequences of US policy in Latin America has its parallels in the work of many of the most respected and influential diplomatic historians. Consider John Lewis Gaddis's analysis of the United States' 1954 Guatemalan intervention: "Arbenz's attraction to Moscow resembled that of a moth for a distant star," he writes. "Like many Latin American intellectuals," Arbenz "found in the sweeping totality of Marxist theory a substitute for *caudillismo* and Catholicism. He read extensively on the Soviet Union and learned a few simple things. . . . The Guatemalan president, in short, was Don Quixote, with Moscow the alluring and incorruptible Dulcinea" (Gaddis, 1998, p. 178). After painting Arbenz as a picaresque character out of a Cervantes novel (suggesting a projection of neoconservative contrition over an earlier left revolutionary romanticism onto Arbenz himself), Gaddis goes on to argue that "the CIA's intervention was a massive overreaction to a minor irritant. It did little to alter the course of events inside Guatemala, where Arbenz's regime had made so many enemies among the landowners and the military that it probably would not have lasted in any event" (Gaddis, 1998, p. 178).

Gaddis's dismissal of the 1944 Revolution as a "minor irritant" effectively understates its power and importance. The revolution's promise, its vision of economic rights and claims to citizenship, sprang from longstanding moral visions and material conflicts over what a just society should look like – visions and conflicts that were energized by an expanding political and economic horizon that followed Allied victory in World War II. The revolution's unleashed hopes and frustrated reforms created a social democratic vista that inspired successive generations of reformers, revolutionaries, and nationalists and defined the contours of the next four decades of war. Gaddis's dismissal of the importance of the US intervention – the claim that Arbenz would have been eventually overthrown by internal opposition – is equally myopic; his counterfactual proposition denies the transformation of domestic politics that the 1954 coup represented, both in Guatemala and throughout Latin America: the revolution's violent overthrow established a new set of internationalized political relations that ensured that the conditions that brought about the 1944 Revolution would never be replicated. In the context of the Cold War, all political actions – in defense or defiance of the status quo – divided according to Cold War priorities. While Cold War repression called upon older practices of social violence, a new set of international political alliances transformed its intensity, efficiency, and effect.

John Gaddis's reassessment of the historical and moral legacy of the Cold War depends in turn upon his containment of the larger significance of the CIA's 1954 Guatemalan intervention, and other similar events – to keep the focus "on the beach," so to speak, away from the messy political and social consequences (intended or otherwise) of a half-century of lethal counterinsurgent aid.

For Gaddis to include such consequences in his analysis would undercut the triumphalist cast of his conclusions. For decades, he observes, "we wrote Cold War history pretty much in the way we used to look at the moon: we could see only one side of it" (Gaddis, 1996). The opening of archives in the former Soviet Union and Eastern Europe has given us the first view of the "dark side." From this new information, Gaddis has come to believe that Caspar Weinberger, Reagan's Secretary of Defense, was right when he argued in 1984 in his famous Oxford debate with British historian E. P. Thompson that the Cold War "really was . . . about individual freedom and the ability to pass it along to our kids" (Gaddis, 1996). Weinberger's boast, it need only be added, was made at the beginning of the Contra War in Nicaragua.

It would behoove historians who work on the foreign relations of the United States to impose a moratorium on this kind of moralizing until the US archive is fully opened. Since the end of the Cold War, the United States has declassified a significant amount of information, but not nearly enough to provide a thorough understanding of what it did to win the conflict. While the State Department has been more forthcoming with material, albeit often heavily censored, the CIA continues to defy efforts to release information pertaining to covert actions. Did US agents directly participate in Latin America's first collective counterinsurgent disappearance? We still do not know, and probably will not know anytime soon. As the CIA's current director, George Tenet, put it during his Senate confirmation hearings: "I would turn our gaze from the past. . . . It is dangerous, frankly, to keep looking over our shoulders" (Cullather, 1999, p. xv).

A recent volume of declassified materials dealing with Latin America covering the years 1961 to 1963, for example, contains few documents on CIA activity in the Dominican Republic and no information at all on CIA actions in British Guyana, where in 1962 the Agency worked to stop Cheddi Jagan from becoming prime minister, or in Brazil, where a large-scale, covert operation eventually led to the overthrow of president João Goulart in 1964. Nor does the volume contain information on CIA activity in Argentina leading up to the 1962 military coup against Arturo Frondizi. Frondizi had relatively good relations with the United States yet complained to President Kennedy of CIA involvement with the Argentine military. Stephen Rabe writes that without "full access to CIA documents, it cannot be ascertained whether the administration played the dangerous game of inciting Argentine military officers to enter the political arena" (1999b, p. 544).

Notwithstanding these enforced silences, new information reveals that the United States played an indispensable role in the functioning of Operation Condor, an intelligence consortium made up of the security forces of Chile, Argentina, Brazil, Uruguay, Paraguay, Ecuador, and Bolivia responsible for the death, torture, and disappearance of thousands. Condor, like many other Cold War counterinsurgent operations, gave states unprecedented repressive capability, which, as we have seen, deeply polarized Latin American politics. General Augusto Pinochet, for instance, used Condor to kill or terrorize centrist political opponents in order to avert the formation of a broad-based democratic alliance that could effectively challenge his rule. The United States has stonewalled requests for information on Condor's operations that would help criminal investigations taking place in Spain, France, Argentina, and Chile. The Clinton administration, for instance, ignored a French judge's petition to question former Secretary of State Henry Kissinger in the investigation of five French citizens believed to have been disappeared by Pinochet. Declassified documents reveal that Kissinger not only knew about Condor, he covertly encouraged and perhaps abetted Pinochet's murderous behavior (Kornbluh, 1999). With no assistance forthcoming from the United States, the judge, upon learning Kissinger had traveled to Paris, issued a summons requesting his testimony (*Le Monde*, 2001a, 2001b). Shielded by bodyguards, Kissinger refused the summons and left town. As of this writing, the United States has failed to respond to petitions from France, Argentina, and Chile to question Kissinger.

Returning to Gaddis's lunar metaphor, historians know that all claims – historical or moral – are relative to the information available. When it comes to what "we now know" of the United States' Cold War role in Latin America, there has been less of an illumination than a revolution. It is we, now, who live on the dark side of the moon.

NOTE

1   The most detailed description of these executions, from which the account below is based, is from the United Nations-administered Guatemalan truth commission, the Comisión para el Esclarecimiento Histórico, vol. 6, pp. 89–98.

REFERENCES

Alba, Victor: "The Stages of Militarism in Latin America," in John Johnson (ed.), *The Role of the Military in Underdeveloped Countries* (Princeton, NJ: Princeton University Press, 1962).

Americas Watch: *With Friends Like These: The Americas Watch Report on Human Rights and U.S. Policy in Latin America* (New York: Pantheon, 1985).

Baily, Samuel: *The United States and the Development of South America, 1945–1975* (New York: New Viewpoints, 1976).

Barnet, Richard J.: *Intervention and Revolution: America's Confrontation with Insurgent Movements Around the World* (New York: New American Library, 1968).

Beard, Charles A.: *The Open Door at Home: A Trial Philosophy of National Interest* (New York: Macmillan, 1934).

Bemis, Samuel Flagg: *A Diplomatic History of the United States*, 5th ed. (New York: Holt, Rinehart, and Winston, 1965).

Benjamin, Jules R.: *The United States and the Origins of the Cuban Revolution: An Empire of Liberty in an Age of National Liberation* (Princeton, NJ: Princeton University Press, 1990).

Berguist, Charles: *Labor in Latin America: Comparative Essays on Chile, Argentina, Venezuela, and Colombia* (Stanford, Calif.: Stanford University Press, 1986).

Bethell, Leslie and Roxborough, Ian: "Introduction: The Postwar Conjuncture in Latin America: Democracy, Labor, and the Left," in Leslie Bethell and Ian Roxborough (eds.), *Latin America Between the Second World War and the Cold War, 1944–1948* (Cambridge: Cambridge University Press, 1992a).

Bethell, Leslie and Roxborough, Ian: "Conclusion: The Postwar Conjuncture in Latin America and Its Consequences," in Leslie Bethell and Ian Roxborough (eds.), *Latin America Between the Second World War and the Cold War, 1944–1948* (Cambridge: Cambridge University Press, 1992b).

Bethell, Leslie and Roxborough, Ian: "The Impact of the Cold War on Latin America," in Melvyn Leffler and David Painter (eds.), *Origins of the Cold War: An International History* (New York: Routledge, 1994).

Black, Jan Knippers: *Sentinels of Empire: The United States and Latin American Militarism* (New York: Greenwood Press, 1986).

Blasier, Cole: *The Hovering Giant: U.S. Responses to Revolutionary Change in Latin America, 1910–1985* (Philadelphia: University of Pittsburgh Press, 1985).

Cardoso, Fernando Henrique and Faletto, Enzo: *Dependencia y desarrollo en América Latina: Ensayo de interpretación sociológica* (Mexico City: Siglo Veintiuno Editores, 1969).

Chomsky, Noam: *Turning the Tide: U.S. Intervention in Central America and the Struggle for Peace* (Boston: South End Press, 1985).

Comisión para el Esclarecimiento Histórico: *Guatemala: Memoria del silencio*, 12 vols. (Guatemala City: Oficina de Servicios para Proyectos de las Naciones Unidas, 1999).

Copelman, Dina M. and Smith, Barbara Clark: "Excerpts from a Conference to Honor William Appleman Williams," *Radical History Review*, 50 (1991): 39–70.

Cullather, Nick: *Secret History: The CIA's Classified Account of Its Operations in Guatemala, 1952–1954* (Stanford, Calif.: Stanford University Press, 1999).

Dos Santos, Theotonio: *Imperialismo y dependencia* (Mexico City: Ediciones Era, 1978).

Dosal, Paul: "Review of Stephen Schlesinger and Stephen Kinzer's *Bitter Fruit: The Story of an American Coup in Guatemala*, and Nick Cullather's *The CIA's Classified Account of Its Operations in Guatemala, 1952–1954*," *Hispanic American Historical Review*, 80/3 (2000): 633–7.

Francis, Michael J.: *The Limits of Hegemony: United States Relations with Argentina and Chile During World War II* (Notre Dame, Ind.: University of Notre Dame Press, 1977).

Frank, Gary: *Struggle for Hegemony in South America: Argentina, Brazil and the United States During the Second World War* (Coral Gables, Fla.: Center for Advanced International Studies, University of Miami, 1979).

French, John: *The Brazilian Workers' ABC: Class Conflict and Alliances in Modern São Paulo* (Chapel Hill: University of North Carolina Press, 1992).

Furtado, Celso: *Economic Development of Latin America: Historical Background and Contemporary Problems*, trans. Suzette Macedo (Cambridge: Cambridge University Press, 1970).

Gaddis, John Lewis: "On Moral Equivalency and Cold War History," *Ethics and International Affairs*, 10 (1996).

Gaddis, John Lewis: *We Now Know: Rethinking Cold War History* (Oxford: Oxford University Press, 1998).

Gerassi, John: *The Great Fear: The Reconquest of Latin America* (New York: Macmillan, 1963).

Gleijeses, Piero: *Shattered Hope: The Guatemalan Revolution and the United States, 1944–1954* (Princeton, NJ: Princeton University Press, 1991).

Gleijeses, Piero: "Afterword: The Culture of Fear," in Nick Cullather, *Secret History: The CIA's Classified Account of Its Operations in Guatemala, 1952–1954* (Stanford, Calif.: Stanford University Press, 1999).

Gosse, Van: *Where the Boys Are: Cuba, Cold War America and the Making of a New Left* (New York: Verso, 1993).

Gould, Jeffrey: *To Lead as Equals: Rural Protest and Political Consciousness in Chinandega, Nicaragua, 1912–1979* (Chapel Hill: University of North Carolina Press, 1990).

Grandin, Greg: *The Blood of Guatemala: A History of Race and Nation* (Durham, NC: Duke University Press, 2000).

Green, David: *The Containment of Latin America: A History of the Myths and Realities of the Good Neighbor Policy* (Chicago: Quadrangle, 1971).

Grow, Michael: *The Good Neighbor Policy and Authoritarianism in Paraguay: United States Economic Expansion and Great-Power Rivalry in Latin America during WWII* (Lawrence: Regents Press of Kansas, 1981).

Guardino, Peter: *Peasants, Politics, and the Formation of Mexico's National State: Guerrero, 1800–1857* (Stanford, Calif.: Stanford University Press, 1996).

Haines, Gerald K.: *The Americanization of Brazil: A Study of U.S. Cold War Diplomacy in the Third World, 1945–1954* (Wilmington, Del.: Scholarly Resources Books, 1989).

Handy, Jim: *Revolution in the Countryside: Community, Land, and Reform in Guatemala* (Chapel Hill: University of North Carolina Press, 1994).

Hoselitez, Bert F.: *Sociological Factors in Economic Development* (Glencoe, Ill.: Free Press, 1960).

Huggins, Martha K.: *Political Policing: The United States and Latin America* (Durham, NC: Duke University Press, 1998).

Institute of Inter-American Affairs Collection (IIAC): "John P. Longan Memoir" (V. I. University of Illinois, Springfield, 1986).

James, Daniel: *Resistance and Integration: Peronism and the Argentine Working Class, 1946–1976* (Cambridge: Cambridge University Press, 1988).

Kennan, George F.: *American Diplomacy, 1900–1950* (New York: Mentor, 1951).

Kimball, Warren: "Letter to Madeleine K. Albright" (March 6, 1998). Federation of American Scientists, Washington, DC. http://www.fas.org/sgp/advisory/state/hac97.htm/, 1998.

Klubock, Thomas Miller: *Contested Communities: Class, Gender, and Politics in Chile's El Teniente Copper Mine, 1904–1951* (Durham, NC: Duke University Press, 1998).

Kornbluh, Peter: "Kissinger and Pinochet," *Nation* (March 29, 1999).

Kornbluh, Peter, ed.: *The Pinochet File: A Declassified Dossier of Atrocity and Accountability* (New York: New Press, forthcoming).

LaFeber, Walter: *The New Empire: An Interpretation of American Expansion, 1860–1898* (Ithaca, NY: Cornell University Press, 1963).

LaFeber, Walter: *Inevitable Revolutions: The United States in Central America* (New York: W. W. Norton, 1984).

Le Monde: "Affaire Pinochet: un juge français veut entendre Henry Kissinger" (June 22, 2001a).

Le Monde: "Henry Kissinger rattrapé au Ritz, à Paris, par les fantômes du Plan Condor" (May 29, 2001b).

LeoGrande, William: *In Our Own Backyard: The U.S. in Central America* (Chapel Hill: University of North Carolina Press, 1998).

Mallon, Florencia: *Peasant and Nation: The Making of Postcolonial Mexico and Peru* (Berkeley: University of California Press, 1995).

Morley, Morris H.: *Imperial State and Revolution: The United States and Cuba, 1959–1985* (Cambridge: Cambridge University Press, 1987).

Nearing, Scott: *The American Empire* (New York: Rand School of Social Science, 1921).

Nugent, David: *Modernity at the Edge of Empire: State, Individual, and Nation in the Northern Peruvian Andes, 1885–1935* (Stanford, Calif.: Stanford University Press, 1997).

O'Brien, Thomas F.: *The Century of U.S. Capitalism in Latin America* (Albuquerque: University of New Mexico Press, 1999).

Osorio Avaria, Carlos: "¿Buenas vecinos? La doctrina de seguridad nacional en América Latina," *Anuario de Ciencias Sociales*, 2/2 (1997).

Pastor, Robert A.: "A Discordant Consensus on Democracy," *Diplomatic History*, 17/1 (1993): 117–28.

Paterson, Thomas G.: *Contesting Castro: The United States and the Triumph of the Cuban Revolution* (New York: Oxford University Press, 1994).

Porras Castejón, Gustavo: "Análisis estructural y recomposición clasista de la sociedad guatemalteca de 1954–1980," in Centro de Estudios Integrados de Desarrollo Comunal (ed.), *Seminario estado, clases sociales y cuestión etnico-nacional* (Mexico City: Editorial Praxis, 1992).

Quijano, Aníbal: "Imperialism and International Relations in Latin America," in Julio Cotler and Richard Fagan (eds.), *Latin America and the Changing Political Realities* (Stanford, Calif.: Stanford University Press, 1974).

Rabe, Stephen G.: *Eisenhower and Latin America: The Foreign Policy of Anticommunism* (Chapel Hill: University of North Carolina Press, 1988).

Rabe, Stephen G.: *The Most Dangerous Area in the World: John F. Kennedy Confronts Communist Revolution in Latin America* (Chapel Hill: University of North Carolina Press, 1999a).

Rabe, Stephen G.: "John F. Kennedy and Latin America: The 'Thorough, Accurate, and Reliable Record' (Almost)," *Diplomatic History*, 23/3 (1999b): 539–52.

Rosemblatt, Karin: *Gendered Compromises: Political Cultures and the State in Chile, 1920–1950* (Chapel Hill: University of North Carolina Press, 2000).

Rostow, Walt W.: *The Stages of Economic Development: A Non-Communist Manifesto* (Cambridge: Cambridge University Press, 1960).

Schlesinger, Stephen C. and Kinzer, Stephen: *Bitter Fruit: The Untold Story of the American Coup in Guatemala* (New York: Doubleday, 1982).

Schoultz, Lars: *National Security and United States Policy Toward Latin America* (Princeton, NJ: Princeton University Press, 1987).

Schrecker, Ellen: *Many Are the Crimes: McCarthyism in America* (Boston: Little, Brown, 1998).

Smith, Gaddis: *The Last Years of the Monroe Doctrine, 1945–1993* (New York: Hill and Wang, 1994).

Streeter, Stephen M.: *Managing the Counterrevolution: The United States and Guatemala, 1954–1961* (Athens: Ohio University Center for International Studies, 2000).

US Central Intelligence Agency: "Guatemalan Communist Personnel to be Disposed of During Military Operations" (National Security Archive, Washington, DC, 1954).

US Central Intelligence Agency: "Guatemala on the Eve of the Elections" (National Security Archive, Washington, DC, 1966).

US Department of State: "Incoming Telegram from Guatemala City to Secretary of State, October 16th, 1962," Reference Embassy Telegram 206 (National Security Archive, Washington, DC, 1962).

US Department of State: "Guatemala's Disappeared, 1977–1986" (National Security Archive, Washington, DC, 1986).

US Department of State: *Foreign Relations of the United States, 1961–1963, American Republics*, vol. 12 (Washington: Government Printing Office, 1996).

Weis, W. Michael: *Cold Warriors and Coups d'État: Brazilian–American Relations, 1945–1964* (Albuquerque: University of New Mexico Press, 1993).

Womack, John: "The Mexican Revolution, 1910–1920," in Leslie Bethell (ed.), *Mexico Since Independence* (Cambridge: Cambridge University Press, 1991).

CHAPTER TWENTY-THREE

The United States and East Asia in the Postwar Era

JAMES I. MATRAY

World War II was a watershed in American involvement in East Asia. Before Pearl Harbor, businessmen, missionaries, and independent diplomats favored passive and reactive US policies. But after 1945, the United States asserted its military power and political influence in East Asia in pursuit of regional hegemony. No longer satisfied with offering a model for emulation, postwar US policymakers believed that they had a special talent for restructuring the lives of liberated colonial people. To be sure, the reality of the Cold War in Europe was a powerful force behind the conviction of US leaders that an assertive policy was essential to prevent the Soviet Union from persuading people in Asia to embrace communism. But the United States already had made plain its intention to impose an American vision of social, economic, and political affairs on East Asia during the war at the Cairo Conference in 1943 and the Yalta Conference in 1945. The American quest to remake East Asia in its own image would become the unifying theme of postwar affairs across the Pacific, creating a predictable pattern of US frustration and failure.

Historian Paul Schroeder (1958) has argued that China was at the heart of the Japanese–American dispute that led to war in 1941, and it was also at the center of US foreign policy calculations toward postwar Asia. President Franklin D. Roosevelt had expected that China would be one of the four major powers acting to preserve peace and stability in the postwar world. But the contest between the Guomindang or Nationalist Party of Jiang Jieshi and the Communist Party under Mao Zedong resumed after Japan surrendered. Mao prevailed, establishing the People's Republic of China (PRC) in October 1949. Anti-communist conservatives in the United States, especially Republicans, charged that President Harry S. Truman had "lost China" because he had allowed communist sympathizers in the State Department to subvert Jiang's government. Historians initially focused their research on this question, quickly concluding that the United States, short of military intervention, could not have prevented the triumph of communism in China. In August 1949, the State Department issued the "China White Paper" to disarm its critics, blaming Jiang for his own demise. Although Herbert Feis (1953) and Foster Rhea Dulles (1972) supported this view, Tang Tsou (1963) and Ernest R. May (1975) blamed the US failure in China on misguided idealism.

Early writings about US China policy mostly recounted the interactions between governments and their leaders. "Traditionalist" historians in the decade after World

War II – notably Thomas A. Bailey, Armin Rappaport, and Richard W. Leopold – wrote top-down history that focused on elites and consistently portrayed the United States as a nation seeking idealistic and altruistic objectives in world affairs. The Cold War reinforced their conviction in the fundamental goodness of US foreign policy. During the 1950s, however, a new school of writers known as the "realists" challenged traditionalist assumptions. Hans Morgenthau, Robert E. Osgood, and Norman A. Graebner argued that US pursuit of idealistic goals abroad had ignored the vital necessity of advancing and protecting fundamental national interests. While viewing American motives as admirable, realists described US policies as invariably unwise and often disastrous. The debate between idealism and realism would dominate the field of US diplomatic history until the Vietnam War shattered this framework.

Trade had been a central motive behind initial American expansion into the Pacific, yet surprisingly historians did not stress the economic motives behind postwar US policy in Asia until the 1960s. Fred Harvey Harrington (1944) set the stage for moving analysis in this direction with his study of US relations with Korea at the end of the nineteenth century. And William Appleman Williams, who followed Harrington at the University of Wisconsin, created a new interpretive school with his *Tragedy of American Diplomacy* (1959) that relied on economic determinism to explain a US foreign policy obsessed with opening new commercial and financial markets overseas. His students, especially Walter LaFeber, Thomas McCormick, and Lloyd C. Gardner, published prolific studies that portrayed the United States as an aggressive power seeking to impose its will on a reluctant world for economic gain. US intervention in Vietnam during the 1960s seemed to support this interpretation, causing many young historians to join the "Wisconsin School." These New Left revisionists wrote passionately about malevolent US policies in East Asia, but at times without the benefit of access to still-classified government documents.

Traditionalists, realists, and revisionists would fight their most heated historiographical battle over the origins of the Cold War, with their attention focused primarily on Europe. But Joyce and Gabriel Kolko (1972), Richard J. Barnet (1968), and Walter LaFeber (1967) advanced a revisionist critique of postwar US policy in East Asia. During the 1970s, the availability of an increasing number of US government documents resulted in studies that seemed to belong to a new so-called post-revisionist synthesis school. John Lewis Gaddis (1982) led this school, but applied its perspective mainly to US policy in Europe rather than Asia. Many scholars – including Akira Iriye (1974), Nagai Yonosuke and Iriye (1977), John Chay (1977), and Dorothy Borg and Waldo Heinrichs (1980) – rejected the Cold War framework for understanding postwar US–East Asian relations. Among the issues that post-revisionist writers addressed was not whether the United States "lost" China, but if it could have found the new China. Warren I. Cohen (1980), William Stueck (1981), and Nancy B. Tucker (1983) argued that the United States missed an opportunity to reach an accord with the PRC after 1949. Chinese oral and written accounts later led Chen Jian (1994), Shu Guang Zhang (1995), and Michael Sheng (1997) to conclude that Mao's revolutionary ideology ruled out accepting US offers of reconciliation, if in fact extended.

Vietnam moved China from center stage in writings on US–East Asian relations. As the war ended in 1975, younger scholars predictably began to investigate the assertive postwar involvement of the United States elsewhere in Asia as a way to explain the disastrous American experience in Vietnam. For most of these writers, anti-communism, containment, and the Cold War were the motivating forces behind US policy in Asia. Truman initiated the pattern for global American intervention when he relied on alarmist rhetoric in his Truman Doctrine speech of March 1947 to build public support for a policy to contain the perceived Soviet threat to Western Europe. Russell H. Fifield (1973), Gary R. Hess (1987), and Marc S. Gallicchio (1988) portrayed US containment in Asia as an incremental policy to defend its interests. But by 1949, Truman had deserted Roosevelt's policy of accelerating the liberation of colonial peoples and was actively opposing Asia's revolutionary nationalist movements. Andrew J. Rotter (1987) and Lloyd C. Gardner (1988) point to this shift as evidence of a purposeful neocolonialist policy aimed at achieving regional economic hegemony. Washington, for example, strongly supported Britain's efforts beginning in 1946 to reassert colonial rule over Malaya where it faced military opposition from the Malay Communist Party.

Containment dictated Truman's policy in the Dutch East Indies as well. The popular nationalist leader Sukarno had proclaimed an independent Republic of Indonesia in August 1945, but the Dutch were determined to reassert colonial sovereignty over the sprawling archipelago that they had ruled with an iron fist before World War II. At first, the Truman administration was neutral, but Robert J. McMahon (1981) has shown how a need for European partners in the Cold War caused US leaders not to contest the legal right of the Netherlands to resume its position as "territorial sovereign." Thereafter, US Marshall Plan aid facilitated indirectly two unsuccessful "police actions" to suppress the Indonesian independence movement. Washington's policy shifted only after Sukarno suppressed a communist rebellion within its ranks in 1948. In the end, the Truman administration's threat to withhold economic and military aid to the Netherlands unless it clearly and irrevocably committed itself to terminating colonial rule brought independence for Indonesia in December 1949. Similar pressure persuaded Britain to grant independence to Burma in 1948, although US officials were unsure about the new leader, U Nu, and concerned about his anti-communist credentials.

Cold War concerns also dominated US policy in the Philippines. In 1946, the United States fulfilled its 1934 promise to grant independence to the island nation. In return for economic assistance, the new Philippine Republic's foreign policy followed the American anti-communist line. The US government maintained its strategic interests in the Philippines through a series of military agreements that allowed continued use of the Philippines as a military base for projecting its power in postcolonial Asia. Stephen R. Shalom (1981) sees US dominance extending to economic relations and neocolonial exploitation, but Nick Cullather (1994) and H. W. Brands (1992) maintain that Philippine leaders manipulated the United States to achieve their own agenda. Still, US efforts led to the election of Ramon Magsaysay as president, who worked with Central Intelligence Agency (CIA) operative Edward G. Lansdale to crush the communist Hukbalahap insurgency.

Postwar American fears of communist expansion in Asia also shaped US policy toward Japan. Richard B. Finn (1992) supports Edwin O. Reischauer's (1950) and Justin Williams's (1979) view that the United States was a benevolent occupier with the admiration, support, and trust of the Japanese people. William Borden (1984), however, maintains that Washington restructured Japan to serve its economic interests, while John W. Dower (1999) presents US policy as ambiguous, arrogant, bungling, and culturally insensitive. Retaining Emperor Hirohito and working through existing parliamentary institutions and the bureaucracy, occupation officials, in the initial phase, tried to demilitarize and democratize Japan to prevent a revival of the militaristic imperialism that had led to war. In 1947, the new Japanese Constitution renounced war as an instrument of national policy and accepted parliamentary democracy. Steps to democratize Japan's economy made landholders out of tenant farmers, broke up large economic combines (*zaibatsu*), and encouraged trade unionism.

Howard B. Schonberger (1989) and Michael Schaller (1985) also see the Cold War, rather than altruism, as dictating US occupation policy in Japan. The "reverse course" in 1947 and 1948 ended reform and enacted measures to build Japan into a bulwark against communist expansion in Asia. Japanese conservatives exploited this reverse course to justify purging leftists from government and revoking those reforms they disliked. During the Korean War, the United States and Japan created their security partnership with the Japanese Peace Treaty and the US–Japan Security Treaty of 1951. US occupation formally ended in 1952, leaving a divided legacy, Aaron Forsberg (2000) has observed, of democratic reform and an alliance with Japan's conservative establishment that would be an enduring source of inspiration and friction for future Japanese–American relations.

Simultaneous US military occupation of Korea from 1945 to 1948 led to a far less favorable outcome, mainly because in August 1945, with the defeat of Japan at hand, Truman hastily persuaded the Soviets to accept division of the Korean peninsula into two zones of military occupation. As the Cold War deepened, the temporary division at the 38th parallel became permanent in 1948, separating two hostile regimes. While Carl Berger (1957), Soon Sung Cho (1967), and Charles M. Dobbs (1981) praise the United States for saving half the nation from communism, they criticize it for not building a stronger South Korea and inviting an attack from the North. But James I. Matray (1985), John Merrill (1989), and Ronald L. McGlothen (1993) show how, in fact, Washington implemented a policy of qualified containment in Korea. US leaders knew that South Korea's survival was in jeopardy when Moscow and Beijing signed the Sino-Soviet Pact in February 1950, establishing a bilateral defense commitment and initiating a modest Soviet aid program to China. Equating Korea with Vietnam, however, Bruce Cumings (1981) and Peter Lowe (1986) assert that Washington had blocked revolutionary change in Korea, resulting in the imposition of a repressive dictatorship on the South.

On June 25, 1950, when North Korea's attack on South Korea ignited the Korean War, Truman sent ground forces a week later after self-defense failed because he saw communist control over Korea as a threat to Japan, Taiwan, and the Philippines. Robert Leckie (1962), T. R. Fehrenbach (1963), Glenn D. Paige (1968), and Joseph Goulden (1982) agree with the Truman administration that the Soviet Union ordered North Korea to attack. During the 1980s, however, a consensus emerged that, as Burton I. Kaufman (1986), Callum A. McDonald (1986), and Bruce Cumings (1990) contend, Washington had intervened in a civil war. War, in fact, had been underway in Korea for two years, as violent border clashes occurred at the 38th parallel, with the South Koreans usually acting as the instigators. Soviet documents released during the 1990s reveal that Joseph Stalin consistently refused before April 1950 to approve North Korean leader Kim Il Sung's plans for invasion. But following Mao's victory in China, pressure grew on Stalin to support the same outcome in Korea, which Kim said would be swift because of guerrilla operations and a popular uprising in the South. Most historians agree that US action in Korea was necessary to preserve US credibility, but Truman, acting on what Ernest R. May (1973) has called the "Lessons of the Past" and rejecting appeasement, erroneously portrayed intervention as a collective security operation under the United Nations.

Sergei Goncharov, John W. Lewis, and Xue Litai (1993), James I. Matray and Kim Chull Baum (1993), and William Stueck (1995) argue convincingly that Korea can best be seen as an "international civil war" fought in a restricted geographic space. Robert E. Osgood (1958), Trumbull Higgins (1960), and David Rees (1964) applaud this limited conflict, but Rosemary Foot (1985) shows how unrestrained was the US application of its military power, including near use of atomic weapons. UN troops retreated to the Pusan Perimeter, but then General Douglas MacArthur's Inchon landing led to liberation of South Korea. Cold War and domestic political considerations motivated Truman's decision to order an offensive across the 38th parallel, which ensured China's intervention. Chinese forces were unable to evict UN troops from Korea and, by the fall of 1951, trench warfare characterized the ground fighting mostly just north of the 38th parallel, while US warplanes pummeled North Korea. Truce negotiations began in July 1951 and peace was near in April 1952, when a stalemate over repatriating prisoners of war prolonged the war for another fifteen months. In the spring of 1953, the Eisenhower administration considered attacking China with atomic bombs in coordination with an offensive in Korea. Robert A. Divine (1981) argues that Beijing agreed to a truce because of US nuclear threats, but Rosemary Foot (1995) sees communist domestic political and economic problems as producing the armistice agreement in July 1953.

The Korean War had great global repercussions, including, for example, the remilitarization of the United States, the emergence of a unified North Atlantic Treaty Organization (NATO), the rearmament of West Germany, and the destruction of hopes of reconciliation between the PRC and the United States. Two days after the war began, Truman deployed the Seventh Fleet in the Taiwan Strait to protect Jiang's regime that had fled to Taiwan in 1949. After China intervened in Korea, Truman fully implemented his containment strategy, signing with Taiwan a Mutual Security Treaty in 1954. When the PRC began bombing offshore islands under Nationalist control during 1954, President Dwight D. Eisenhower persuaded Congress to pass the "Formosa Resolution" granting him emergency power to take independent action to protect Taiwan. His commitment to Taiwan almost ignited nuclear war. For Stephen E. Ambrose (1984), Eisenhower's handling of the two Taiwan Strait crises demonstrated skillful diplomacy, which kept the final decision in his hands. Robert D. Accinelli (1996), however, judges it unduly risky, given the negligible strategic value of the offshore islands.

Fred I. Greenstein (1982) and Melanie Billings-Yun (1988) – known along with Divine and Ambrose as Eisenhower revisionists – praise Eisenhower for practicing a "hidden-hand" foreign policy that protected US interests while averting war. But Gordon Chang (1990), David L. Anderson (1991), and Zhai Qiang (1994) see his commitment to containment in Asia as having lasting adverse effects. Eisenhower continued Truman's policy of support for France against Ho Chi Minh's Vietminh, but during the spring 1954 crisis at Dien Bien Phu, he withheld direct military assistance to stop communist forces from seizing that French stronghold. He could not prevent the division of Vietnam at the Geneva Conference that July, but then acted to block reunification through internationally supervised elections in 1956. By then, the United States had replaced France in Vietnam, moving to build an anticommunist state in the South. To deter further communist advances in the region, the United States was responsible for the creation in 1954 of the Southeast Asia Treaty Organization (SEATO), which placed Laos, Cambodia, and South Vietnam under its defense umbrella. SEATO included as members Australia, New Zealand, Pakistan, the Philippines, and Thailand, along with France, Britain, and the United States. But Indonesia, India, and Burma refused to join, preferring neutrality in the Cold War.

Eisenhower believed that SEATO would deter communist aggression in East Asia. Indeed, the insurgency in Malaya diminished greatly after 1954 and in 1960 the "Malay Emergency" ended. Meanwhile, the United States was sponsoring economic and military assistance programs to attract and strengthen former colonies in Asia as regional allies. Bernard B. Fall (1969), Timothy N. Castle (1993), and Roger Warner (1995) see the Laotian crisis of the late 1950s as showing how the containment policy prevented US leaders either from understanding or effectively handling revolutionary nationalism in Southeast Asia. As part of French Indochina, Laos, along with Cambodia and Vietnam, had been economically exploited and politically oppressed. After Laos gained independence in 1954 under the Geneva Accords, American influence quickly eclipsed that of France. US threats to withhold aid initially prevented the communist Pathet Lao from joining a coalition government, while the CIA promoted schemes to boost rightist political groups. Just prior to leaving office, Eisenhower told President-Elect John F. Kennedy that Laos was the nation's most critical problem. As president, Kennedy, in a show of strength that Norman B. Hannah (1987) later would insist should have been sustained, ordered preliminary military moves, but then sought compromise. The 1962 accord neutralized Laos, but only increased the determination of Kennedy to keep other Asian nations out of communist hands.

Richard J. Walton (1972), Gabriel Kolko (1985), Marilyn B. Young (1991), and Lloyd C. Gardner (1995) point to US involvement in Vietnam as evidence of an American imperialism seeking dominance in Asia. More dispassionate are George C. Herring (1986), Robert D. Schulzinger (1997), and David E. Kaiser (1999), who have attributed intervention to an illusion of American omnipotence that combined with the containment policy to draw the United States into an unwinnable war against Vietnamese nationalism – the subject of another essay in this volume. But Harry Summers (1982), Timothy J. Lomperis (1984), and Philip B. Davidson (1988), part of a right revisionist school, all claim that a US military victory was possible if the war had been waged directly against North Vietnam rather than on guerrillas in the South.

Richard M. Nixon became president in 1969 and significantly altered the thrust of US policy across East Asia. Most important, his "Vietnamization" policy withdrew US forces and strengthened the South Vietnamese army to assume combat responsibilities. Nixon explained the regional significance of this new policy on Guam after visiting troops in Vietnam, stating that Asians directly facing communist aggression had to defend themselves, but that the United States would provide necessary military and financial support. The "Nixon Doctrine" was a major revision in the containment policy in Asia, as by 1972, although war raged in most of Indochina, US participation was generally limited to aerial bombing and provision of weapons and assorted supplies to indigenous forces. This was enough, according to Bruce Palmer (1985), to persuade North Vietnam to accept the Paris Peace Accords after the intensive "Christmas Bombing" of Hanoi late in 1972. Gareth Porter (1975) and Anthony Short (1989) argue that the United States could have negotiated a better agreement years earlier, while Frank Snepp (1977) asserts that Nixon merely wanted to gain a "decent interval" after US departure before the certain fall of his client in South Vietnam. Once there were no more Americans on the ground, Congress reduced military aid to pro-US regimes in South Vietnam, Cambodia, and Laos.

Nixon's Vietnam policy devastated Cambodia and Laos. During the 1960s, Cambodia's Norodom Sihanouk tried to avoid involvement in the war without angering either the Americans or the North Vietnamese, who were using Cambodian border territory to launch attacks. When Nixon became president in January 1969, he ordered the secret bombing of Cambodia, eventually dropping more tons of bombs there than in Japan during all of World War II. The bombing radicalized the peasants and fostered support for the communist Khmer Rouge. Dissatisfaction with Sihanouk led to the March 1970 coup that brought to power Lon Nol, who received immediate US backing and acquiesced to Nixon's decision late in April to invade Cambodia from South Vietnam. Although US troops quickly withdrew, the war intensified. Thereafter, the Cambodian government teetered on the edge of extinction until the communists triumphed in April 1975 and the Khmer Rouge embarked on a fanatical ideological crusade that led to the extermination of more than 3 million Cambodians. William Shawcross (1979) and Arnold Isaacs (1983) blame Nixon and National Security Adviser Henry Kissinger for this genocide, while Wilfred P. Deac (1997) attributes it to internal forces.

Laos experienced a similar, though not as horrific, fate. US bombing of the Ho Chi Minh Trail within Laos intensified after President Lyndon B. Johnson halted bombing of North Vietnam in 1968. Thereafter, the struggle for political power saw the communist Pathet Lao getting the upper hand during the dry season and the government with US support regaining territory in the rainy season. A secret US air war in Laos ended early in 1973, allowing the Pathet Lao and North Vietnamese to continue their hostilities at will. The 1975 collapse of South Vietnam and Cambodia hastened the fall of the Royal Lao government, as there was no serious effort at resistance when the communists took power in December. The new communist regime was politically repressive and diplomatically isolated. In 1995, US relations with Laos started to improve, as Washington ended its ban on assisting this exceedingly poor country.

The United States justified its actions in postwar Indochina as necessary for the defense of Japan. Robert Blum (1982) contends that the ultimate aim was to create a "Great Crescent" of economic development in Asia, with Japan as its industrial engine. But many Japanese opposed US containment policies, aiming harsh criticism against the US–Japan Security Treaty that not only gave US base rights in Japan, but denied a voice to the Japanese in the deployment of US troops from them to other countries in Asia. Despite extensive protests, the treaty became the bedrock of US–Japanese relations for decades thereafter. After 1960, the central element in the

American–Japanese relationship increasingly became bilateral trade that brought benefits to both countries, but also provoked bitter rivalry. The initial postwar expansion of US–Japan trade was inseparable from the Cold War, as US spending on the Korean War in particular created a market for Japanese manufactures, while the US-imposed embargo of the PRC ended Japan's traditional reliance on trade with China. Japanese manufacturers exported an increasing volume of consumer goods to the United States, as Japan's economy surged forward during the "miracle" years. Expanding Japanese exports to the United States prompted pressure for protection on textiles in the 1950s, steel in the 1960s, and automobiles in the 1980s. The two countries frequently resorted to "voluntary exports restraints" or "voluntary import expansion" to resolve trade conflicts.

American relations with Japan began to experience a painful transition during the Nixon years. In 1969, the president agreed to return Okinawa, where US occupation had become a contentious issue in Japanese politics. Then, in the summer of 1971, the United States made three moves known as the "Nixon shocks" in Japan. The first was the announcement that the president would visit China. Since US occupation, Japan had supported the US policy of isolating the PRC, recognizing instead the government on Taiwan. Prime Minister Sato Eisaku learned about the dramatic change in policy just three minutes before Nixon went public with the news. For Walter LaFeber (1997), this illustrates basic flaws in a contradictory partnership, while Matray (2000) counters that Japan should not have been surprised, since Washington and Beijing had been exchanging signals for two years. The substantive result of the Nixon visit was the Shanghai Communiqué, in which both nations declared that they would not seek to dominate Asia, and would oppose efforts of a third nation to gain regional superiority, an obvious reference to the Soviet Union. As for Taiwan, the United States recognized that it was part of China, while the PRC implied a commitment to peaceful unification alone. Nixon's visits symbolized the new military and economic balance of power in Asia emerging with US withdrawal from Vietnam.

A second "Nixon shock" was the American abandonment of the gold standard in August 1971, which made American goods cheaper and Japanese products more expensive. The third shock came in September when the American trade representative warned his Japanese counterpart that the United States intended to impose import quotas on textile goods, unless Japan adopted voluntary restraints. Nixon's actions showed how economic competition with Japan, along with Vietnam, had ended American confidence about its dominance in Asia. Japan's trade surplus continued to grow into the 1980s, making trade a divisive political issue. Bilateral agreement to revaluate the yen in 1985 had little effect. Not surprisingly, the Japanese resented criticism for selling quality goods that Americans wanted to buy. Ishihara Shintaro (1989) complains that Japan was being blamed unfairly for US economic shortcomings. Clyde Prestowitz (1988) charges that Japan traded according to a different set of rules and calls for retaliation. Trade friction peaked just as the Cold War ended. But the American–Japanese partnership endured, despite profound changes in world affairs. Roger Buckley (1992), Timothy P. Maga (1997), and Michael Schaller (1997) have described how the two nations despite their struggles have managed to maintain cooperation, especially on security issues.

Meanwhile, the United States struggled to redefine its political role in Southeast Asia. Gerald R. Ford, who replaced Nixon as president in August 1974, was unable to persuade Congress to provide the military assistance he requested for South Vietnam. According to Nguyen Tien Hung and Jerrold Schechter (1986) and P. Edward Haley (1982), he did so in a cynical and deceitful effort to shift blame to Congress for the communist victory in Vietnam. In fact, Nixon himself (1985), Norman Podhoretz (1982), and Jeffrey P. Kimball (1998) believe that Congress was responsible for losing the peace and forcing Ford to watch helplessly in April 1975 while North Vietnam seized the South. Ford privately feared a resurgence of isolationist sentiment domestically and the development of international contempt for the United States. In May, he therefore reacted strongly, and critics argue needlessly, to Cambodia's seizure of the *Mayaguez*, even though the Khmer Rouge already had released the US freighter. R. B. Smith (1986) later implied that the US exercise of power in East Asia had thrown communist parties in the region on the defensive as early as 1965, pointing to events in Indonesia as proof. There, Sukarno's determined pursuit of a nonaligned foreign policy clashed with Washington's desire to convert Indonesia to the anti-communist cause. His rabid support for incorporation of the disputed territory of West Irian into the Indonesian state also generated tensions, as the United States endorsed its Dutch ally's desire to retain the territory.

Jakarta's warm relations with both Moscow and Beijing, as well as the growing power and influence of the Indonesian Communist Party (PKI), led the United States in late 1957 to make a bold attempt to undermine if not actually topple Sukarno. The CIA supported regional rebellions against the central government that Sukarno's military crushed decisively. Thereafter, the Eisenhower administration tried to cultivate the Indonesian military as a counterweight to the PKI. Kennedy went further, mounting a major effort to win over Sukarno that culminated in his successful role in mediation of the West Irian dispute. Nevertheless, the PKI by 1963 was the largest nonruling communist party in the world, and Sukarno increasingly relied upon it for support. Relations deteriorated further under Johnson, as Sukarno told the United States to "Go to hell with your aid!" Washington feared that another Southeast Asian country soon might join the communist camp. But a failed coup in 1965 then gave the United States an unexpected diplomatic windfall. General Suharto moved quickly to restore order and repress the left. After establishing himself as the country's new strongman, he replaced Sukarno in 1966 as president. Southeast Asia's largest and richest nation had almost overnight transformed itself into a reliable US regional partner. George McT. and Audrey R. Kahin (1995) and Paul F. Gardner (1997) have argued that neither Vietnam nor the CIA had anything to do with Suharto's victory.

Robert J. McMahon (1999) has discussed how Suharto's victory signaled less about the future of US relations in East Asia than did the formation in August 1967 of the Association of Southeast Asian Nations (ASEAN), its five original members being Indonesia, Malaysia, Philippines, Singapore, and Thailand. The organization sought to achieve mutual economic development through regional cooperation that would promote both social progress and political democracy. ASEAN also adopted, however, a cardinal principle of noninterference in the domestic affairs of its members, which made it difficult for the organization to deal with human rights issues. Thailand and the Philippines would propose after the Vietnam War that ASEAN broaden its ability to involve itself in cases in which internal policies affected other nations in the region, such as the genocide in Cambodia and the stream of refugees into Thailand. This coincided with President Jimmy Carter's human rights campaign in 1977, but also exposed its fundamental policy weaknesses in a region that contained some notoriously repressive, authoritarian regimes. The Philippines, Indonesia, and Thailand were major violators of human rights. In each case, Carter, more concerned about economic and security issues, refused to apply sanctions or significantly reduce aid to those governments. Eventually, he even reembraced containment, joining with ASEAN to condemn Vietnam's occupation of Cambodia in 1978.

Carter's efforts to move US policy in East Asia away from containment and toward human rights by then had focused attention on South Korea, which during the 1950s had been faithfully supportive of US priorities in defense and economic relations. In 1961, a military junta had seized power under Pak Chong-hui. Carter spoke about the need to reconsider the US security commitment to Pak's regime because of its "repugnant" repression of internal critics, as well as stating his desire to remove US troops from South Korea. Typically, he backed away from both threats, but US policy then faced a new crisis with Pak's assassination in October 1979. President Ronald Reagan had little difficulty in dealing with South Korea, inviting Chun Du-hwan, Pak's authoritarian successor, as his first foreign visitor in 1981. For Reagan, it was far more important that under Pak and Chun, South Korea had achieved dramatic industrial growth and had become a world economic power. The gap between economic prosperity and political backwardness spurred rising public discontent, leading to the end of the military rule in 1987. By 1992, South Korea's embrace of democracy led to the election of its first civilian leader since 1960 and the world's eleventh largest economy.

As in Korea, Reagan viewed other East Asian issues and problems largely through the prism of a reenergized containment strategy that was central to his foreign policy. He successfully pressed the Japanese to assume greater responsibility for their own defense, strengthening security ties with Japan and persuading Prime Minister Nakasone Yasuhiro to inaugurate a modest defense buildup. But Reagan showed little concern as Japan's multinational companies invested heavily in US bonds, property, and businesses. Reagan pursued a strategic partnership with Beijing, seeing a cooperative China as an indispensable strategic asset. Revival of the Soviet–American Cold War under Carter already had resulted in the formal recognition of the PRC in January 1979 and absence of criticism when China initiated a brief border conflict with Vietnam. But Deng Xiaoping's common commitment to check Soviet expansion delighted Reagan, contributing to the signing of several agreements governing trade, nuclear cooperation, and technical, scientific, and cultural exchanges. Two-way trade between the United States and the PRC rose. Reagan liberalized US technology transfer policy to the PRC and the United States became a major arms supplier to its former adversary.

Reagan's support for ASEAN increasingly became the pivot around which US policy toward Southeast Asia revolved, as trade between these countries and the United States grew during the 1980s. He also sought close political and security bonds with ASEAN members, operating on the premise that human rights pressures just served as irritants to East Asia's more friendly, stable, and anti-communist regimes. Vice-President George Bush went so far as to toast Philippine dictator Ferdinand Marcos during his 1981 visit for his "adherence to democratic processes." Marcos was his own worst enemy, taking actions so repressive and destabilizing that even the forgiving Reagan ultimately had to renounce him. After the blatant fraud in the presidential election of February 1986, Reagan recognized the opposition government on the same day Marcos fled to exile in Hawaii. But Reagan offered unqualified support to the equally repressive, venal, and authoritarian Suharto regime in Indonesia. He also courted Thailand. After providing a base for US military operations in Vietnam, Bangkok had repositioned itself as a leading player in Southeast Asian political and economic life. Thailand's engagement with the world economy made it one of the "tiger" economies of the early 1990s.

Containment no longer was the driving force behind US East Asia policy after the Cold War ended during 1989. Thereafter, Presidents Bush and Bill Clinton sought expanded economic relations and greater political stability in the region, with promoting human rights an ancillary concern. Reflecting this pattern was Washington's movement toward normalization of relations with the Socialist Republic of Vietnam. Carter had abandoned his efforts in this direction because of disagreements over the issues of US reparations to Vietnam and Vietnamese cooperation in finding US servicemen missing in action (MIA). Reagan sought to isolate and punish Vietnam, although he did make deals on searching for MIAs and orderly emigration of Vietnamese. As the Soviet Union collapsed, Vietnam withdrew its forces from Cambodia in 1989, persuading Bush to permit sale of humanitarian supplies to Vietnam and allow US companies to negotiate contracts for business ventures there. The Clinton administration ended all economic sanctions and announced plans to open mutual liaison offices in 1994. Full diplomatic relations came in 1995, paving the way for Vietnam to join ASEAN that July. Communist Laos gained admission in July 1997, along with Myanmar (the new official name for Burma), despite its brutal repression of political dissenters.

Pursuit of economic interests dominated US policy toward East Asia in the first half of the 1990s, as economies along the Pacific Rim boomed. But in 1997 a financial crisis dramatically altered relationships in the region. Asian nations had borrowed large amounts of then cheap capital to finance risky business ventures that went sour when export growth began to stall in the middle of the decade. Various Asian nations had no choice but to devalue their currencies, creating a financial catastrophe. After its currency collapsed, Thailand sought a $17 billion loan package from the International Monetary Fund (IMF). Indonesia also turned to the IMF, but the economic downturn ignited a mass uprising that forced Suharto from power in 1998. Financial distress spread to Japan, where the banking industry teetered on the brink of collapse. Washington used the crisis to press Tokyo to boost domestic demand and lower tariffs, thereby reducing the US trade deficit. South Korea was hard hit because the government had encouraged banks to make cheap loans to big businesses, resulting in an inefficient allocation of resources. Massive layoffs and a $57 billion IMF loan request contributed to the election of former dissident Kim Dae-jung as president.

Declining per capita income, growing unemployment, and rising prices seemingly put a damper on the previously lauded Asian economic miracle. This only encouraged a preference for cooperation rather than confrontation in relations between the United States and East Asia in the 1990s. There were meetings of the new Asia-Pacific Economic Cooperation (APEC) forum. In 1993, the United Nations sponsored elections in Cambodia that saw over 90 percent of the eligible population vote in defiance of Khmer Rouge threats of violence. Reviving Cold War fears that year, however, was the evidence that North Korea was near completion of a program to develop nuclear weapons. Negotiation of an Agreed Framework in 1994 temporarily defused the crisis, as South Korea, Japan, and the United States pledged funding to construct power plants in North Korea that did not produce weapons-grade nuclear waste. When the financial crisis caused Tokyo and Seoul to delay action on the deal, an impatient Pyongyang launched a missile over Japanese territory in 1998. Tensions relaxed thereafter because South Korean President Kim Dae-jung implemented a "Sunshine Policy" of engagement, with the strong support of the Clinton administration, that led to his personal meeting in Pyongyang in June 2000 with North Korean leader Kim Jong Il.

Harry Harding (1992), Rosemary Foot (1995), and Robert S. Ross (1995) applaud US China policy after 1972 because it successfully integrated the PRC into the world system, while advancing the interests of the United States in East Asia. But the fall of the Soviet Union in 1991 removed a key element in maintaining this fragile relationship, causing the United States to have trouble in the 1990s developing mature and stable relations with China. While still sensitive about threats to Taiwan, Washington was mainly at odds with Beijing over its suppression of political freedom in China. In June 1989, the human rights issue exploded when the Chinese army killed hundreds of pro-democracy demonstrators gathered in Tiananmen Square. Bush condemned the massacre, but opposed a boycott or ending the PRC's most-favored-nation trading status, insisting that engagement with Beijing kept the way open for capitalist development and greater personal freedom. Despite criticizing Bush for not punishing China as a presidential candidate, Clinton followed a "constructive engagement" policy that differed little from that of his predecessor.

Taiwan remained the main source of friction in relations between the United States and China. During the 1980s, US–Taiwan relations achieved greater equality because of the transformation of Taiwan from a one-party, authoritarian dictatorship to a fledgling democracy and from a developing country to a modern, highly industrialized nation. Congressional pressure to end its isolation caused the Clinton administration to allow US officials to attend high-level bilateral meetings on Taiwan, but it refused to support its bid for representation at the United Nations. Relations between the United States and the PRC were strained severely in June 1995 when President Li Denghui of Taiwan visited the United States. In March 1996, Clinton sent naval forces to the Taiwan Strait after the PRC staged military exercises in the area. Another source of friction was Hong Kong, which Britain returned to China's rule in July 1997, where critics charged Beijing with violating its pledge not to interfere internally with the former colony.

Since the mid-1970s, the United States has tried to reverse the steady decline of its power and influence in East Asia and reassert itself, without appearing to seek hegemony. Writings on events during these years either have been tentative scholarly studies or journalistic commentaries without foundation in primary sources. But US diplomatic historians will address these events as the documents become available, and their conclusions are certain to be enlightening because, as Warren I. Cohen noted in 1985, writing on East Asia is on the "cutting edge of the historical profession." In this view, he challenges Charles S. Maier's (1980) claim that diplomatic historians had stopped dealing with important issues and were writing books that were a mere compilation of what "one clerk wrote to another." Yet the 1980s and 1990s saw an outburst of analytical innovation in the field of US foreign relations that resulted in imaginative new interpretive frameworks ranging from world systems theory to corporatism. Regarding East Asia, there was renewed interest in probing the role of culture, a factor that Frances FitzGerald (1972) had addressed earlier in Vietnam. Recently, writers have revived this analytical approach, in particular William O. Walker (1991) on the opium trade, Inoue Kyoko (1991) on Japan's Constitution, T. Christopher Jespersen (1996) on the American vision of China, and Mark P. Bradley (2000) on American images of Vietnam. US policymakers would be wise to read recent and forthcoming studies on US–East Asia relations as a reminder of the limits on American power to reorder the world.

REFERENCES

Accinelli, Robert D.: *Crisis and Commitment: United States Policy Toward Taiwan, 1950–1955* (Chapel Hill: University of North Carolina Press, 1996).

Ambrose, Stephen E.: *Eisenhower: The President* (New York: Simon and Schuster, 1984).

Anderson, David L.: *Trapped by Success: The Eisenhower Administration and Vietnam, 1953–1961* (New York: Columbia University Press, 1991).

Barnet, Richard J.: *Intervention and Revolution: The United States in the Third World* (Cleveland: World, 1968).

Berger, Carl: *The Korean Knot: A Military-Political History* (Philadelphia: University of Pennsylvania Press, 1957).

Billings-Yun, Melanie: *Decision Against War: Eisenhower and Dien Bien Phu, 1954* (New York: Columbia University Press, 1988).

Blum, Robert M.: *Drawing the Line: The Origin of the American Containment Policy in East Asia* (New York: W. W. Norton, 1982).

Borden, William: *The Pacific Alliance: United States Foreign Economic Policy and Japanese Trade Recovery, 1947–1955* (Madison: University of Wisconsin Press, 1984).

Borg, Dorothy and Heinrichs, Waldo, eds.: *Uncertain Years: Chinese–American Relations, 1947–1950* (New York: Columbia University Press, 1980).

Bradley, Mark P.: *Imaging Vietnam and America: The Making of Postwar Vietnam, 1919–1950* (Chapel Hill: University of North Carolina Press, 2000).

Brands, H. William: *Bound to Empire: The United States and the Philippines* (New York: Oxford University Press, 1992).

Buckley, Roger: *U.S.–Japanese Alliance Diplomacy, 1945–1990* (Cambridge, Mass.: Harvard University Press, 1992).

Castle, Timothy N.: *At War in the Shadow of Vietnam: U.S. Military Aid to the Royal Lao Government, 1955–1975* (New York: Columbia University Press, 1993).

Chang, Gordon: *Friends and Enemies: The United States, China, and the Soviet Union, 1948–1972* (Stanford, Calif.: Stanford University Press, 1990).

Chay, John, ed.: *The Problems and Prospects of American–East Asian Relations* (Boulder, Colo.: Westview Press, 1977).

Chen Jian: *China'a Road to the Korean War: The Making of the Sino-American Confrontation* (New York: Columbia University Press, 1994).

Cho, Soon Sung: *Korea in World Politics, 1940–1950: An Evaluation of American Responsibility* (Berkeley: University of California Press, 1967).

Cohen, Warren I.: *America's Response to China: An Interpretive History of Sino-American Relations* (New York: John Wiley, 1980).

Cohen, Warren I.: "The History of American–East Asian Relations: Cutting Edge of the Historical Profession," *Diplomatic History*, 9 (1985): 101–12.

Cullather, Nick: *Illusions of Influence: The Political Economy of United States–Philippines Relations, 1942–1960* (Stanford, Calif.: Stanford University Press, 1994).

Cumings, Bruce: *The Origins of the Korean War*, 2 vols. Vol. 1: *Liberation and the Emergence of Separate Regimes, 1945–1947* (Princeton, NJ: Princeton University Press, 1981).

Cumings, Bruce: *The Origins of the Korean War*, 2 vols. Vol. 2: *The Roaring of the Cataract, 1947–1950* (Princeton, NJ: Princeton University Press, 1990).

Davidson, Philip B.: *Vietnam at War: The History, 1946–1975* (New York: Oxford University Press, 1988).

Deac, Wilfred P.: *Road to the Killing Fields: The Cambodian War of 1970–75* (College Station: Texas A&M University Press, 1997).

Divine, Robert A.: *Eisenhower and the Cold War* (New York: Oxford University Press, 1981).

Dobbs, Charles M.: *The Unwanted Symbol: American Foreign Policy, the Cold War, and Korea, 1945–1950* (Kent, OH: Kent State University Press, 1981).

Dower, John W.: *Embracing Defeat: Japan in the Wake of World War II* (New York: W. W. Norton, 1999).

Dulles, Foster Rhea: *American Policy Toward Communist China, 1949–1969* (New York: Crowell, 1972).

Fall, Bernard B.: *Anatomy of a Crisis: The Laotian Crisis of 1960–1961* (Garden City, NY: Doubleday, 1969).

Fehrenbach, T. R.: *This Kind of War: A Study in Unpreparedness* (New York: Macmillan, 1963).

Feis, Herbert: *The China Tangle: The American Effort in China from Pearl Harbor to the Marshall Plan* (Princeton, NJ: Princeton University Press, 1953).

Fifield, Russell H.: *Americans in Southeast Asia: The Roots of Commitment* (New York: Crowell, 1973).

Finn, Richard B.: *Winners in Peace: MacArthur, Yoshida, and Postwar Japan* (Berkeley: University of California Press, 1992).

FitzGerald, Frances: *Fire in the Lake: The Vietnamese and the Americans in Vietnam* (New York: Vintage Books, 1972).

Foot, Rosemary: *The Wrong War: American Policy and the Dimensions of the Korean Conflict, 1950–1953* (Ithaca, NY: Cornell University Press, 1985).

Foot, Rosemary: *Substitute for Victory: The Politics of Peacemaking at the Korean Armistice Talks* (Ithaca, NY: Cornell University Press, 1990).

Foot, Rosemary: *The Practice of Power: U.S. Relations with China Since 1949* (New York: Oxford University Press, 1995).

Forsberg, Aaron: *America and the Japanese Miracle: The Cold War Context of Japan's Postwar Economic Revival, 1950–1960* (Chapel Hill: University of North Carolina Press, 2000).

Gaddis, John Lewis: *Strategies of Containment: A Critical Appraisal of Postwar American Security Policy* (New York: Oxford University Press, 1982).

Gallicchio, Marc S.: *The Cold War Begins in Asia: American East Asian Policy and the Fall of the Japanese Empire* (New York: Columbia University Press, 1988).

Gardner, Lloyd C.: *Approaching Vietnam: From World War II through Dienbienphu* (New York: W. W. Norton, 1988).

Gardner, Lloyd C.: *Pay Any Price: Lyndon Johnson and the Wars for Vietnam* (Chicago: Ivan Dee, 1995).

Gardner, Paul F.: *Shared Hopes, Separate Fears: Fifty Years of U.S.–Indonesian Relations* (Boulder, Colo.: Westview Press, 1997).

Goncharov, Sergei N., Lewis, John W., and Xue Litai: *Uncertain Partners: Stalin, Mao, and the Korean War* (Stanford, Calif.: Stanford University Press, 1993).

Goulden, Joseph C.: *Korea: The Untold Story of the War* (New York: McGraw Hill, 1982).

Greenstein, Fred I.: *The Hidden-Hand Presidency: Eisenhower as Leader* (New York: Basic Books, 1982).

Haley, P. Edward: *Congress and the Fall of South Vietnam and Cambodia* (Rutherford, NJ: Fairleigh Dickinson Press, 1982).

Hannah, Norman B.: *The Key to Failure: Laos and the Vietnam War* (Lanham, Md.: Madison Books, 1987).

Harding, Harry: *A Fragile Relationship: The United States and China Since 1972* (Washington, DC: Brookings Institute, 1992).

Harrington, Fred Harvey: *God, Mammon, and the Japanese: Dr. Horace N. Allen and Korean-American Relations, 1884–1905* (Madison: University of Wisconsin Press, 1944).

Herring, George C.: *America's Longest War: The United States and Vietnam, 1950–1975* (New York: Alfred A. Knopf, 1986).

Hess, Gary R.: *The United States' Emergence as a Southeast Asian Power, 1940–1950* (New York: Columbia University Press, 1987).

Higgins, Trumbull: *Korea and the Fall of MacArthur: A Precis on Limited War* (New York: Oxford University Press, 1960).

Inoue Kyoko: *MacArthur's Japanese Constitution: A Linguistic and Cultural Study of Its Making* (Chicago: University of Chicago Press, 1991).

Iriye, Akira: *The Cold War in Asia: A Historical Introduction* (Englewood Cliffs, NJ: Prentice Hall, 1974).

Isaacs, Arnold: *Without Honor: Defeat in Vietnam and Cambodia* (Baltimore: Johns Hopkins University Press, 1983).

Ishihara Shintaro: *The Japan That Can Say No: Why Japan Will Be First Among Equals*, trans. Frank Baldwin (New York: Simon and Schuster, 1989).

Jespersen, T. Christopher: *American Images of China, 1931–1949* (Stanford, Calif.: Stanford University Press, 1996).

Kahin, George McT. and Kahin, Audrey R.: *Subversion as Foreign Policy: The Secret Eisenhower and Dulles Debacle in Indonesia* (New York: New Press, 1995).

Kaiser, David E.: *An American Tragedy: Kennedy, Johnson, and the Origins of the Vietnam War* (Cambridge, Mass.: Harvard University Press, 1999).

Kaufman, Burton I.: *The Korean War: Challenges in Crises, Credibility, and Command* (New York: Alfred A. Knopf, 1986).

Kimball, Jeffrey P.: *Nixon's Vietnam War* (Lawrence: University Press of Kansas, 1998).

Kolko, Gabriel: *Anatomy of a War: Vietnam, the United States, and the Modern Historical Experience* (New York: Pantheon, 1985).

Kolko, Joyce and Kolko, Gabriel: *The Limits of Power: The World and United States Foreign Policy, 1945–1954* (New York: Harper and Row, 1972).

LaFeber, Walter: *America, Russia, and the Cold War, 1945–1966* (New York: John Wiley, 1967).

LaFeber, Walter: *The Clash: A History of U.S.–Japan Relations* (New York: W. W. Norton, 1997).

Leckie, Robert: *Conflict: A History of the Korean War* (New York: Putnam, 1962).

Lomperis, Timothy J.: *The War Everyone Lost – And Won: America's Intervention in Viet Nam's Twin Struggles* (Baton Rouge: Louisiana State University Press, 1984).

Lowe, Peter: *Origins of the Korean War* (New York: Longman, 1986).

McDonald, Callum A.: *Korea: The War Before Vietnam* (New York: Free Press, 1986).

McGlothen, Ronald L.: *Controlling the Waves: Dean Acheson and U.S. Foreign Policy in Asia* (New York: Columbia University Press, 1993).

McMahon, Robert J.: *Colonialism and Cold War: The United States and the Struggle for Indonesian Independence, 1945–49* (Ithaca, NY: Cornell University Press, 1981).

McMahon, Robert J.: *Limits of Power: The United States and Southeast Asia Since World War II* (New York: Columbia University Press, 1999).

Maga, Timothy P.: *Hands Across the Sea? U.S.–Japan Relations, 1961–1981* (Athens: Ohio University Press, 1997).

Maier, Charles S.: "Marking Time: The Historiography of International Relations," in Michael Kammen (ed.), *The Past Before Us: Contemporary Historical Writing in the United States* (Ithaca, NY: Cornell University Press, 1980), 265–82.

Matray, James I.: *The Reluctant Crusade: American Foreign Policy in Korea, 1941–1950* (Honolulu: University of Hawaii Press, 1985).

Matray, James I. and Kim Chull Baum, eds.: *Korea and the Cold War: Division, Destruction, and Disarmament* (Claremont, Calif.: Regina, 1993).

Matray, James I.: *Japan's Emergence as a Global Power* (Westport, Conn.: Greenwood Press, 2000).

May, Ernest R.: *"Lessons" of the Past: The Use and Misuse of History in American Foreign Policy* (New York: Oxford University Press, 1973).

May, Ernest R.: *The Truman Administration and China, 1945–1949* (Philadelphia: Lippincott, 1975).

Merrill, John: *Korea: The Peninsular Origins of the War* (Newark: University of Delaware Press, 1989).

Nagai Yonosuke and Iriye, Akira, eds.: *The Cold War in Asia: A Historical Introduction* (New York: Columbia University Press, 1977).

Nguyen Tien Hung and Schechter, Jerrold: *The Palace File* (New York: Harper and Row, 1986).

Nixon, Richard M.: *No More Vietnams* (New York: Arbor House, 1985).

Osgood, Robert E.: *Limited War: The Challenge to American Strategy* (Chicago: University of Chicago Press, 1958).

Paige, Glenn D.: *The Korean Decision: June 24–30, 1950* (New York: Free Press, 1968).

Palmer, Jr., Bruce: *The 25-Year War: America's Military Role in Vietnam* (Lexington: University of Kentucky Press, 1985).

Podhoretz, Norman: *Why We Were in Vietnam* (New York: Simon and Schuster, 1982).

Porter, Gareth: *A Peace Denied: The United States, Vietnam and the Paris Agreement* (Bloomington: Indiana University Press, 1975).

Prestowitz, Clyde V.: *Trading Places: How We Allowed Japan to Take the Lead* (New York: Basic Books, 1988).

Rees, David: *Korea: The Limited War* (New York: St. Martin's, 1964).

Reischauer, Edwin O.: *The United States and Japan* (New York: Macmillan, 1950).

Ross, Robert S.: *Negotiating Cooperation: The United States and China, 1969–1989* (Stanford, Calif.: Stanford University Press, 1995).

Rotter, Andrew J.: *The Path to Vietnam: Origins of the American Commitment to Southeast Asia* (Ithaca, NY: Cornell University Press, 1987).

Schaller, Michael: *The American Occupation of Japan: The Origins of the Cold War in Asia* (New York: Oxford University Press, 1985).

Schaller, Michael: *Altered States: The United States and Japan Since Occupation* (New York: Oxford University Press, 1997).

Schonberger, Howard B.: *Aftermath of War: Americans and the Remaking of Japan, 1945–1952* (Kent, OH: Kent State University Press, 1989).

Schroeder, Paul W.: *The Axis Alliance and Japanese–American Relations, 1941* (Ithaca, NY: Cornell University Press, 1958).

Schulzinger, Robert D.: *A Time for War: The United States and Vietnam, 1941–1975* (New York: Oxford University Press, 1997).

Shalom, Stephen R.: *The United States and the Philippines: A Study in Neocolonialism* (Philadelphia: Institute for the Study of Human Issues, 1981).

Shawcross, William: *Sideshow: Kissinger, Nixon and the Destruction of Cambodia* (New York: Simon and Schuster, 1979).

Sheng, Michael: *Battling Western Imperialism: Mao, Stalin, and the United States* (Princeton, NJ: Princeton University Press, 1997).

Short, Anthony: *The Origins of the Vietnam War* (New York: Longman, 1989).

Smith, R. B.: *An International History of the Vietnam War*, 2 vols. (New York: St. Martin's, 1986).

Snepp, Frank: *Decent Interval: An Insider's Account of Saigon's Indecent End* (New York: Random House, 1977).

Stueck, William W.: *The Road to Confrontation: American Policy Towards China and Korea, 1947–1950* (Chapel Hill: University of North Carolina Press, 1981).

Stueck, William W.: *The Korean War: An International History* (Princeton, NJ: Princeton University Press, 1995).

Summers, Jr., Harry G.: *On Strategy: A Critical Analysis of the Vietnam War* (Novato, Calif.: Presidio Press, 1982).

Tsou, Tang: *America's Failure in China, 1941–1950*, 2 vols. (Chicago: University of Chicago Press, 1963).

Tucker, Nancy B.: *Patterns in the Dust: Chinese–American Relations and the Recognition Controversy, 1949–1950* (New York: Columbia University Press, 1983).

Walker, William O.: *Opium and Foreign Policy: The Anglo-American Search for Order in Asia, 1912–1954* (Chapel Hill: University of North Carolina Press, 1991).

Walton, Richard J.: *Cold War and Counterrevolution: The Foreign Policy of John F. Kennedy* (New York: Penguin, 1972).

Warner, Roger: *Back Fire: Secret War in Laos and Its Link to the War in Vietnam* (New York: Simon and Schuster, 1995).

Williams, Sr., Justin: *Japan's Political Revolution Under MacArthur: A Participant's Account* (Athens: University of Georgia Press, 1979).

Williams, William Appleman: *The Tragedy of American Diplomacy* (Cleveland: World, 1959).

Young, Marilyn B.: *The Vietnam Wars, 1945–1990* (New York: Harper Collins, 1991).

Zhai Qiang: *The Dragon, the Lion, and the Eagle: Chinese–British–American Relations, 1949–1958* (Kent, OH: Kent State University Press, 1994).

Zhang, Shu Guang: *Mao's Military Romanticism: China and the Korean War, 1950–53* (Lawrence: University Press of Kansas, 1995).

FURTHER READING

Allison, John M.: *Ambassador of the Prairie or Allison in Wonderland* (Boston: Houghton Mifflin, 1973).

Antolik, Michael: *ASEAN and the Diplomacy of Accommodation* (Armonk, NY: M. E. Sharpe, 1990).

Berman, Larry: *Planning a Tragedy: The Americanization of the War in Vietnam* (New York: W. W. Norton, 1982).

Berman, Larry: *Lyndon Johnson's War: The Road to Stalemate in Vietnam* (New York: W. W. Norton, 1989).

Braestrup, Peter: *Big Story: How the American Press and Television Reported and Interpreted the Crisis of Tet 1968 in Vietnam and Washington* (New Haven, Conn.: Yale University Press, 1977).

Buhite, Russell D.: *Soviet–American Relations in Asia, 1945–1954* (Norman: University of Oklahoma Press, 1981).

Cumings, Bruce, ed.: *Child of Conflict: The Korean–American Relationship, 1945–1953* (Seattle: University of Washington Press, 1983).

Fifield, Russell H.: *Diplomacy of Southeast Asia: 1945–1958* (New York: Harper, 1958).

Fineman, Daniel: *A Special Relationship: The United States and Military Government in Thailand, 1947–1958* (Honolulu: University of Hawaii Press, 1997).

Gelb, Leslie H. and Betts, Richard K.: *The Irony of Vietnam: The System Worked* (Washington, DC: Brookings Institute, 1979).

Goodman, Allan E.: *Lost Peace: America's Search for a Negotiated Settlement of the Vietnam War* (Stanford, Calif.: Hoover Institution Press, 1978).

Hilsman, Roger: *To Move a Nation: The Politics of Foreign Policy in the Administration of John F. Kennedy* (Garden City, NY: Doubleday, 1967).

Iriye, Akira: "Contemporary History as History: American Expansion into the Pacific Since 1941," *Pacific Historical Review*, 53 (1984): 191–212.

Jespersen, T. Christopher: "The Politics and Culture of Nonrecognition: The Carter Administration and Vietnam," *Journal of American–East Asian Relations*, 4 (1995): 397–412.

Kahin, George McT.: *Intervention: How America Became Involved in Vietnam* (New York: Alfred A. Knopf, 1986).

Karnow, Stanley: *Vietnam: A History* (New York: Penguin, 1983).

Karnow, Stanley: *In Our Image: America's Empire in the Philippines* (New York: Random House, 1989).

LaFeber, Walter: *The New Empire: An Interpretation of American Expansion, 1960–1898* (Ithaca, NY: Cornell University Press, 1963).

Liefer, Michael: *ASEAN and the Security of South-East Asia* (London: Routledge, 1989).

Logevall, Fredrik: *Choosing War: The Lost Chance for Peace and the Escalation of War in Vietnam* (Berkeley: University of California Press, 1999).

McMahon, Robert J.: "United States Relations with Asia in the Twentieth Century: Retrospect and Prospect," in Gerald K. Haines and J. Samuel Walker (eds.), *American Foreign Relations: A Historiographical Survey* (Westport, Conn.: Greenwood Press, 1981), 237–70.

McMahon, Robert J.: "The Cold War in Asia: Toward a New Synthesis?" *Diplomatic History*, 12 (1988): 307–27.

McMaster, H. R.: *Dereliction of Duty: Lyndon Johnson, Robert McNamara, the Joint Chiefs of Staff, and the Lies that Led to Vietnam* (New York: Harper Collins, 1997).

McNamara, Robert S.: *In Retrospect: The Tragedy and Lessons of Vietnam* (New York: Vintage Books, 1995).

May, Ernest R. and Thomson, James C., eds.: *American–East Asian Relations: A Survey* (Cambridge, Mass.: Harvard University Press, 1972).

Oberdorfer, Don: *The Two Koreas: A Contemporary History* (New York: Basic Books, 1997).

Palmer, Ronald D. and Reckford, Thomas J.: *Building ASEAN: Twenty Years of Southeast Asian Cooperation* (New York: Praeger, 1987).

Ross, Robert S., ed.: *East Asia in Transition: Toward a New Regional Order* (Armonk, NY: M. E. Sharpe, 1995).

Sheehan, Neil: *A Bright Shining Lie: John Paul Vann and America in Vietnam* (New York: Random House, 1988).

Smith, Gaddis: *Morality, Reason, and Power: American Diplomacy in the Carter Years* (New York: Hill and Wang, 1986).

Thomson, James C., Stanley, Peter W., and Perry, John Curtis, eds.: *Sentimental Imperialists: The American Experience in East Asia* (New York: Harper and Row, 1981).

VanDeMark, Brian: *Into the Quagmire: Lyndon Johnson and the Escalation of the Vietnam War* (New York: Oxford University Press, 1991).

Westmoreland, William C.: *A Soldier Reports* (Garden City, NY: Doubleday, 1972).

Whiting, Allen S.: *China Crosses the Yalu: The Decision to Enter the Korean War* (Stanford, Calif.: Stanford University Press, 1960).

CHAPTER TWENTY-FOUR

Washington Quagmire: US Presidents and the Vietnam Wars – A Pattern of Intervention

DAVID HUNT

Scholarship on presidential decisionmaking in the era of the Vietnam Wars conveys a somber message. Unable to conceive of an independent Vietnam, Roosevelt endorsed the return of French colonialism. Beginning in 1946, the Truman administration covertly armed France against the Viet Minh, then expanded and went public with its assistance in 1950. Eisenhower subverted the Geneva Accords and conjured up South Vietnam. Kennedy dispatched helicopter crews and Green Berets and rained down Agent Orange on the Vietnamese. Johnson sent troops and planes in 1965 and to the end of his administration sought military victory. Demonstrating a similar obduracy, Nixon turned up the firepower all over Indochina. Every US president plunged in deeper when he could have pulled back, and the result was thirty years of war in Vietnam.

Presidential initiatives again and again steered the country in the same direction with an inevitability that commands our attention and eludes our understanding. Perhaps ideological factors explain why historians only occasionally evoke the economic, the imperial, character of US foreign policy. But an impression persists that, at least in its early manifestation, "revisionism" fell short of explaining events in Vietnam. The specter of international communism has aged even less gracefully and, indeed, is largely absent from the literature. A variant, that a Cold War mentality, however inadequate as a guide to Soviet or Chinese behavior, influenced policymakers, can be affirmed with confidence. But references to "anticommunist paranoia" in the White House (Olson and Roberts, 1996, p. 25) do no more than open the inquiry.

In this essay, I dwell on works that lead toward new or significant revision of old interpretations. Recent publications demonstrate how race and gender constructions promoted intervention. They explore policymaking dynamics that impeded strategic thinking and blocked out dissenting views. They underscore the limits of US power and the stubbornness of chief executives who refused to admit defeat. They raise hopes that higher levels of understanding of the Vietnam War are within our grasp.

The Prism of Racialized Hierarchies

Deciding where to begin may appear a simple matter. But it is not. Accounts of US intervention in Vietnam often start in 1950 or 1954. But George Kahin (1986) establishes that US leaders welcomed the French return to Indochina in the spring of 1945 and were quick to support France's campaign against the Viet Minh.

The Cold War did not prompt these moves. In 1945, the Americans were worried about the Red Army presence in Eastern Europe, but they did not feel a similar concern over Soviet intrusion in Southeast Asia, and with good reason. No scholarly treatment suggests that the USSR was meddling in or even paying attention to Vietnam in the last days of World War II. "The Soviet Union took virtually no interest in the Viet Minh's problems," Gary Hess declares. "It did not extend diplomatic recognition to the DRV [Democratic Republic of Vietnam] and continued to regard France as the legitimate ruler of Indochina" (Hess, 1990, p. 37).

Great power rivalries loomed larger in 1950, when Harry Truman publicly embraced the anti-Viet Minh cause. Some argue that this escalation was a response to Soviet success in exploding an atomic device, the victory of communism in China, and the North Korean invasion of South Korea. But American policymakers were not simply reacting to threats from the enemy camp. Because their bipolar construction of the world was not wholeheartedly embraced by US allies, they felt all the more compelled, in the words of Lloyd Gardner, to insist on "Cold War unities" (Gardner, 1988, p. 90). Even the French seemed less committed than the Americans to achieving victory in Indochina, a curiosity noted, but not explored, in a number of accounts. Washington's fear of international communism is itself a phenomenon, requiring explanation.

In pursuing the analysis, some scholars have stressed economic considerations. Yet in that respect as well, a 1945 starting point is awkward. Michael Schaller (1982) and Andrew Rotter (1987) analyze US efforts to safeguard Japanese interests in Southeast Asia, but only in the 1947–50 period, after the United States decided to rebuild Japan. The case for economic motives at an earlier date remains to be established.

Some treatments suggest that the Americans were obliged to follow their allies in Paris. "Not wanting to raise French ire over Indochina, Truman acquiesced" (Olson and Roberts, 1996, p. 25); US leaders were "fearful of antagonizing France" (Herring, 1994, p. 13); they showed themselves anxious to "placate" the French (Moss, 1998, p. 29). Yet no one seriously argues that De Gaulle was strong enough to dictate to the United States.

Perhaps at a later date Washington adopted a conciliatory approach in hopes of securing French backing for German integration into the European defense system. But such considerations hardly applied in 1945, when the United States and the USSR were still fighting against Nazi Germany. In the following years, if "Europe" explains US policy in Asia, then one would expect the White House to have discouraged a war that "retarded France's economic recovery" (Herring, 1996, p. 15). It makes more sense to assume that the United States had its own reasons for blocking Vietnamese independence and that the French role in Indochina was desired by the Americans.

The Vietnam/Korea parallel clarifies the US agenda. In both countries at the end of World War II, an "August Revolution" brought leftist regimes to power. In Vietnam, the Americans lined up with French colonialism; in Korea, they counted on Koreans who had collaborated with the Japanese and on Japanese instruments of control, most notably the National Police. The US occupation force in Korea declared war on the indigenous left, while the State Department trailed behind this anticipation of the Cold War. By contrast, Americans stationed in Vietnam looked askance at the returning French and remained open to dialogue with the Democratic Republic of Vietnam (DRV) after pro-French Foreign Service officers had abandoned the "trusteeship" option in Washington. But within weeks, disjunctures between the home front and its agents in the field disappeared, and the entire US team opted for counterrevolution in both Korea and Vietnam (on Korea, see Cumings, 1989).

Franklin Roosevelt's role in these developments remains in dispute. Stein Tonnesson argues that Roosevelt wanted an end to French Indochina and hoped that trusteeship would succor Vietnamese people newly liberated from colonialism (see the review of the literature in Tonnesson, 1991, pp. 13–19). But, in *Approaching Vietnam* (1988), Lloyd Gardner maintains that the president envisioned "a liberal empire" in Asia. Intended to obstruct both French colonialism and Vietnamese independence, trusteeship, with a Guomindang-governed China joining the United States in providing oversight, was a chimera. Not surprisingly, "in a sudden gust at Roosevelt's death, the pieces all flew apart." There is a link, Gardner adds, in a blunt passage, between FDR's "dream" and John Foster Dulles's plan for a strong US presence in postcolonial Vietnam (Gardner, 1988, pp. 52–3).

Elaborating on the imperial theme, Mark Bradley dwells on longstanding anti-Asian biases that influenced Roosevelt and other policymakers. For them, the Vietnamese were a weak, unintelligent, deceitful people. Some State Department personnel supported and some opposed trusteeship, but all saw Vietnam through the same "prism of racialized hierarchies" (Bradley, 2000, p. 77). When Roosevelt expressed hope that American tutelage would allow Vietnam to achieve self-government, he was anticipating that independence would be granted twenty, thirty, or even fifty years after the end of World War II. While criticizing French colonialism, US leaders scorned the Vietnamese people.

Bradley does not spare Archimedes Patti, who later claimed to have perceived the mettle of the Viet Minh, but whose cables at the time took no distance from racial stereotypes. Patti and other OSS personnel were well disposed toward Ho Chi Minh because he seemed an anomaly, an intelligent and honest native who would serve "as a vehicle to transfer American values and aims onto the Vietnamese movement for independence" (Bradley, 2000, p. 139). In light of this paternalism, one might doubt that there was a lost opportunity for rapprochement between an independent Vietnam and the United States.

Bradley suggests that Orientalism rather than anti-communism shaped Washington choices. In the last days of World War II, the Americans were more worried that Chiang Kai-shek might try to extend Chinese influence into Indochina than about Soviet imperialism. The communist threat did not enter into their deliberations until September 1946, and then only after prompting from the French, who knew what chord to strike in order to mobilize American support for their cause. US leaders bought into this conception not because of anything Moscow was thought to be doing, but based on a longstanding assumption that the Vietnamese were incapable of self-government. If France and the United States were pushed out of the country, they reasoned, Vietnam would gravitate by default into the Soviet orbit.

Mounting Cold War tensions in 1949–50 do not make American choices easier to understand. At that time, US anxiety about communism was not felt elsewhere with the same urgency, not even by the most vulnerable "dominos." Save for Thailand, the governments of South and Southeast Asia declined to recognize the State of Vietnam, set up by the French in 1949, and several maintained communications with the DRV, in spite of the US insistence that Hanoi was an outpost of the Kremlin and Communist China.

Scholars have labored to make sense of the 1945–6 period. But progress was made when George Kahin demonstrated that Roosevelt belongs in the story and Lloyd Gardner proposed a way of interpreting FDR's approach. Amplifying on these overtures, Mark Bradley's meditation on trusteeship establishes that "the prism of racialized hierarchies" ranks among causes of the Vietnam Wars.

Limits of Eisenhower Revisionism

Unimpressed by "Eisenhower revisionism," Vietnam War historians do not see Dwight Eisenhower as a statesman who exercised power in a restrained, responsible fashion (see references and development of the argument in Anderson, 1991). They indicate that the president wanted Paris to concede Vietnamese independence, follow Washington directives, and allow US advisers a free hand within the Saigon government. When the French refused these terms, Eisenhower decided against a rescue operation at Dien Bien Phu, while looking for other ways to thwart the Viet Minh. The result was perhaps the most drastic escalation in the 1945–75 period, involving sabotage of the Geneva Accords and consolidation of a separate state below the 17th parallel.

The motives for these commitments remain unclear. Some historians mention Eisenhower's April 1954 "tin and tungsten" press conference, in which he dwelt on strategic raw materials in Southeast Asia, but without developing the point into a larger interpretation of American policy. Standing on their own, references to international communism also fail to resolve the problem, given that Washington's fear of Soviet and Chinese expansion was not shared by US allies, including Winston Churchill, who made explicit his rejection of the domino theory. At the Geneva Conference, the USSR placed a priority on détente with the United States, and Chou En-lai worked with the French and the British and tacitly with the Americans to dash Viet Minh hopes for a united, independent Vietnam. In short, Eisenhower and Dulles adopted an adversarial posture toward Vietnamese communism, not in response to an objective necessity, but because of the peculiar construction they placed on the Cold War.

"McCarthyism" helped to produce this outcome, but not in the way one might expect. In his biography of Tom Dooley (1997), James Fisher argues that elements within the CIA and European-born social democrats such as Joseph Buttinger encouraged the administration to create South Vietnam. Edward Lansdale and others aimed to keep the Vietnamese in the Free World while also foiling McCarthy and his allies and carving out more political space for liberal anti-communism. In a titanic miscalculation, they saw Ngo Dinh Diem as a "democratic socialist," a progressive ally who would bolster the US position in Asia and provide an alternative to dictators sponsored by reactionary forces in the United States.

The youthful, vaguely countercultural Tom Dooley, with his breezy Catholicism, was an effective front man for the CIA. His *Deliver Us From Evil* (1956), an account of Vietnamese Catholics fleeing from a satanic communism, is a Cold War classic. At the same time, he was able to charm newspaper people and the public in a way that the dour McCarthy and his ilk were not. But then, in an astonishing turn, the gay, sexually active Dooley was driven out of the military by homophobic security agents. Friends in the intelligence community helped him land on his feet as a "jungle doctor" and CIA asset in Laos. While Lansdale pulled the strings and the United States intruded into Laotian affairs, Dooley's celebrity grew in ways that carried beyond the Cold War script.

Fisher's biography of Dooley is among the first works on the Vietnam War to comment simultaneously on policymaking and on American society. There were links between decisions at the top and social trends, he argues. Vietnam choices in the era of Eisenhower and Dulles constituted a moment in the history of liberalism, Catholicism, and gay subcultures in the United States.

Similarly interested in the interplay between politics and sexuality in the McCarthy era, Robert Dean (2001) argues that anti-communist purges were reinforced by a ferocious patrolling of gender boundaries. Showing that government employees were cashiered for sexual as well as for political offenses, Dean argues that "perverts" were even more persecuted than "reds." As domestic spying overran private life and character assassination came to dominate political quarrels, the struggle for control over sexual secrets ran parallel to and merged with the struggle for control over US foreign policy.

Taking for granted its access to high office and drawing inspiration from the likes of Teddy Roosevelt and Henry Stimson, patrician elements within the foreign policy establishment were caught in a web of surveillance and repression. Whereas earlier accounts linked partisan quarrels to class and regional hatreds, Dean goes further to demonstrate how culturally based definitions of manhood also came into play. Forming an "imperial brotherhood," the patricians were imbued with a masculinity inculcated in the prep schools and Ivy League universities they had attended and reinforced by service in war and the national security state. McCarthyite allegations that they were incompetent and effete challenged their public careers and their male identities.

Political figures who lived through McCarthyism responded by placing an even greater emphasis on "toughness" in public life. The result was a loss of analytic flexibility, a hardening of imperial arrogance, a tendency toward symbolic as opposed to substantive deployments of power. "Credibility" was not just an ideological quirk. For elite survivors of the sexual inquisition, it became an obsession.

Our understanding of Vietnam decisionmaking in the McCarthy period has been changed by recent scholarship. Of course the presidents and their advisers paid attention to the Soviet threat and to "tin and tungsten." But at a moment when political discourse was manifestly overdetermined, it makes sense, indeed it seems imperative, to explore the social and cultural forces that energized and limited their actions. Disputed and reconfigured gender identities added impetus to US intervention in Vietnam.

Experiment in Counterinsurgency

Kennedy nostalgia still glimmers around the edges of recent scholarship. Passing over "flexible response" and counterinsurgency, not to speak of John Kennedy's infatuation with the Green Berets, David Kaiser makes much of the president's "personal grace," which "enabled him to maintain his emotional equilibrium" and also "helped the vast majority of his fellow citizens to maintain theirs as well" (Kaiser, 1999, p. 266). Equally inattentive to what the administration was actually doing in Vietnam, A. J. Langguth (2000) asserts that, in the weeks before his death, JFK envisioned a fundamental change in US policy (for references to what might be called the "Oliver Stone" view of the assassinated president, see Buzzanco, 1996, p. 82).

Fredrik Logevall's interpretation is more complicated, but he, too, regards Kennedy as a thoughtful leader who took his distance from Cold War orthodoxies. Responsibility for escalation, Logevall argues, rests on the shoulders of Lyndon Johnson, Robert McNamara, Dean Rusk, and McGeorge Bundy. Or perhaps LBJ alone was to blame. If Kennedy had lived, his advisers might have been more inclined "to ask the really fundamental questions about the war," to achieve a rapprochement with the USSR, and even to address the "difficult frictions between rich and poor nations" (Logevall, 1999, pp. 399, 412).

These wistful passages appear out of place in an otherwise rigorously argued text. Kennedy "would not have seen the war as a test of his manliness to the same degree as did Johnson," asserts Logevall, "for though himself imbued with a good dose of *machismo*, he was less prone to extending it to the nation, to the complex world of foreign policy" (p. 399). But this nonanalytic formulation seems sentimental in light of Robert Dean's work. As Dean (1998) shows, Kennedy's class-based and historically determined conception of masculinity disposed him to personalize foreign policy issues and to see Cold War competition precisely as a test of manhood.

In any case, Logevall rejects the suggestion that Kennedy aimed to reduce the US commitment in Vietnam and dismisses his much-touted recall of 1,000 US personnel as a "token" gesture (Logevall, 1999, pp. 69–70). Other historians agree. "There is not a shred of evidence," George Herring declares, that Kennedy planned to reverse course. Herring paints a portrait in vacillation, far different from the bold and decisive image of JFK cultivated by his admirers. The president refused "to face the hard questions" (Herring, 1996, pp. 104, 119). William Turley ("improvisational, incremental, tentative, and temporizing") seconds the view that Kennedy lacked the imagination and courage to break from the Cold War (Turley, 1986, p. 41).

A number of texts highlight Kennedy's sponsorship of counterinsurgency, including the use of defoliants. If the United States "could not locate the enemy because of the jungle, then eliminate the jungle," write James Olson and Randy Roberts (1996, p. 110). Marilyn Young states that Kennedy wanted to turn Vietnam into a "laboratory for counterinsurgency techniques" and estimates that 100,000,000 pounds of herbicides were eventually dropped (Young, 1991, p. 82). Guenter Lewy cites polls taken in Vietnam indicating that "eighty-eight percent of the villagers interviewed blamed the US/GVN for the destruction of their crops and 74 percent expressed outright hatred" (Lewy, 1978, p. 260).

Many studies indicate that Kennedy insiders reacted to Cold War events, such as the "wars of national liberation" speech delivered by Nikita Khrushchev in January 1961, in an idiosyncratic fashion. The Soviet leader launched "a passionate appeal for peaceful co-existence," affirms Young, with "generalized support for wars of national liberation in the colonial world" expressed only in passing. Kennedy seized on the aside because it better fit his preconceptions (Young, 1991, p. 76).

In the same spirit, Robert Buzzanco cites JFK's "strident" anti-communism and agrees with the notion that he was "a consummate cold warrior." When military leaders expressed doubts about Vietnam, the president brushed them aside. His "critical ruminations," which Logevall takes as expressions of Kennedy's contemplative bent, were "little more than devil's advocacy" (Buzzanco, 1996, pp. 81, 111). The argument is different, but the balance sheet is just as negative in H. R. McMaster's book (1997), which portrays Kennedy and McNamara as dilettantes, unfit to lead the country into war.

The "Oliver Stone thesis" lingers in popular culture and along the margins of academic inquiry. But the scholarly view of JFK is less indulgent. Some portray him as reckless, others as temporizing, and a few insist that he was both. But there is a general consensus that Kennedy was a primary architect of the Vietnam debacle.

The Biggest Hawk of Them All

After his death, a certain sympathy made its way into accounts of Lyndon Johnson's war policies. LBJ was seen as "a bound Prometheus" (Karnow, 1997, p. 574), a reformer who was frantic as Vietnam "strangled his beloved Great Society" (Moss, 1998, p. 159). Several studies affirm that he showed restraint in the face of enemy provocations until the National Liberation Front (NLF) attack on Pleiku in February 1965 forced his hand. Carrying the argument further, George Kahin (1986) states that the president resisted escalation and was induced to act only under pressure from truculent advisers.

In rebuttal, Fredrik Logevall declares that Johnson plotted for a wider war in 1964 and had committed himself to intervene by December of that year. Examining the domestic political situation and the mood in London, Paris, Moscow, Beijing, and Hanoi, he suggests that, outside of the small circle of policymakers, no one wanted a confrontation in Vietnam. Even in the countries of Southeast Asia, where one might expect to find support for the American stand, there was "skepticism and fear" as the administration's bellicose intent became apparent (Logevall, 1999, p. 181).

Historians may disagree in specifying the moment when the Johnson administration decided to escalate. But, Logevall avers, since peaceful alternatives were never explored or even considered, it was inevitable from as early as March 1964. "The biggest hawk of them all" (p. 335), LBJ was responsible for this outcome. Logevall's demonstration that Johnson, and Kennedy, too, "chose war" sets a standard that future scholars will have to take into account.

Equally telling is the author's portrait of politicians who privately opposed war, but publicly rallied to Johnson's defense. The administration's 1965 "White Paper" labored to prove that the Vietnam crisis was caused by external aggression. But Senator Mike Mansfield, an off-the-record critic of the president's rationale for action, went out of his way to state that the document indicated "why this nation has been compelled to take the steps it has in recent weeks." European allies of the United States, and especially the British, who kept their reservations about the American course to themselves, were also culpable in fashioning a "permissive context" for US intervention (pp. 358–9, 400–4).

At a deeper level, Logevall asks readers to think in a different way about the policymaking process. What looks like give-and-take among leaders earnestly seeking answers is better understood as self-serving manipulation of the transcript. The counterfeit character of this posturing is nowhere more apparent than in the "devil's advocacy" of George Ball, whose arguments nobody listened to and whose memos were never read, as Ball himself well understood. Logevall thinks that he "hoped one day to be Johnson's secretary of state" and was not prepared to go beyond discreet criticisms of Johnson's approach (p. 249).

This line of thought is elaborated in McMaster's riveting work. Vietnam decisionmaking was a charade, he argues, where recommendations were drawn up before officials were dispatched on fact-finding trips to determine what to do and where decisions were made in advance of the meetings convened to discuss them. The real quagmire was in Washington, a place where everyone lied to everyone else, where choices taken by the commander in chief were based on domestic political considerations, and where military men who knew that US strategy would not work were bought off with increased budget outlays for the services they represented.

McMaster comes close to saying that US leaders did not care about or even pay much attention to what was happening in Vietnam. He agrees with Logevall that before the 1964 presidential election, LBJ put campaign needs first. But whereas Logevall argues that policymakers were awaiting the moment, styled "D day" (Logevall, 1999, p. 194), when they would be free to escalate, McMaster insists that Johnson remained preoccupied by home front politics after November 1964. "Blinded by his desire to pass the Great Society legislative program, the president had found Vietnam a nuisance that he hoped would go away" (McMaster, 1997, p. 298).

Turning logic upside-down, LBJ and his cohorts convinced themselves that a bloody stalemate was preferable to a timely, if embarrassing, retreat. Robert McNamara thought "that a loss at the current [January 1965] level of commitment would be worse than failure after the commitment of hundreds of thousands of American soldiers, airmen, and Marines." Anticipating the consequences of escalation, McGeorge Bundy "admitted that 'U.S. casualties would be higher – and more visible to American feelings,' but dismissed that expense as 'cheap' relative to the costs of withdrawal" (pp. 207, 219). Through a magical alchemy, futile killing would make its perpetrators appear more "credible."

Although *Dereliction of Duty* never spells out what a winning strategy might have looked like, some passages hint that a plan for victory could have been implemented if generals and politicians had been interested in formulating one. But the author makes clear, and Buzzanco agrees, that internecine rivalries within the Pentagon got in the way of strategic thinking. When he thought the honor of the Air Force had been slighted, Curtis LeMay challenged Army Chief of Staff Harold Johnson to an aerial duel ("I'll shoot you down and scatter your peashooter all over the goddam ground"). Wallace Greene tried to promote realistic discussion, but was then diverted by promises that the Marines would be allowed to send more troops to Vietnam and even by planning sessions to improve "press coverage of Marine Corps actions" (pp. 114, 317, 304).

Logevall and McMaster reject older explanations for US intervention. They do not believe that the socialist bloc played a significant role in Vietnam, or even that such considerations weighed heavily in the minds of policymakers. "The Vietnam War was not forced on the United States by a tidal wave of Cold War ideology,"

McMaster asserts (1997, p. 323), and the USSR and the People's Republic of China (PRC) are only bit players in the narrative he constructs. Logevall states that the Americans "do not appear to have worried much about increased Soviet penetration" in the third world. As for the Chinese, "it is startling how seldom analyses of China's posture and aims appear" in government documents. Also discounted are economic factors. McMaster shows no interest in the topic, and Logevall states that, "In the high-level policy deliberations of 1964–1965 concerns for the fate of world capitalism appear to have been *entirely* absent, while the main worry about the American economy was that it would be harmed by a larger war" (Logevall, 1999, pp. 382, 291, 386 [author's emphasis]).

This approach comes at a cost insofar as it leaves readers without an explanation for the president's actions. Having ruled out "deep structural forces," a perplexed Logevall notes that "the Americanization of the war becomes difficult to understand." By default, he blames "Johnson's profound personal insecurity and his egomania" (pp. xxii, 298). McMaster's disdain is even more bitingly expressed, but he, too, does not say why a pack of impostors happened to be in power when the country plunged into war. The two books do not find the origins of the fiasco they so tellingly chronicle.

After being denounced by the anti-war movement, Lyndon Johnson gained a brief reprieve in the 1980s, when historians appeared willing to give him the benefit of the doubt. But recent works condemn LBJ's conduct and policies. Talking peace while plotting war, he corrupted the 1964 election (with less success, he was to try the same tactic in 1968). Buzzanco, Logevall, and McMaster read him in different ways, but all agree on his deviousness and irresponsibility and all fix him with a major share of the blame for the catastrophe that followed on escalation.

Refusal of a Decent Interval

President Johnson's speech of March 31, 1968, in which he announced a partial bombing halt and a willingness to negotiate with the North Vietnamese, as well as his decision not to seek reelection, opened the most surreal phase in the Vietnam War. "Peace" replaced "victory" in presidential discourse, and US troops started to come home. But blood continued to flow in Indochina.

George Herring offers the most emphatic reading of Johnson's last months in office. According to Herring, the March 31 speech "did not represent a change of policy, but a shift of tactics to salvage a policy that had come under bitter attack." Indeed, key elements of Nixon's strategy originated under Johnson. In the fall of 1967, "Vietnamization" before the letter was broached, and the president launched a political offensive on behalf of "peace with honor," aimed at "the silent center" (compare to Nixon's "silent majority"). Meanwhile, extralegal attacks on enemies, including the CIA's "Operation CHAOS" (a program for domestic surveillance), anticipated Nixon's deployment of the "plumbers" (Herring, 1996, pp. 227, 198–201; for more, see Herring's detailed treatment in *LBJ and Vietnam*, 1994).

The uncertainty surrounding Johnson's last days in office carries over into discussions of the Nixon administration. Stanley Karnow asserts that Nixon "ruled out victory" but "refused to contemplate defeat," while Kissinger hoped for an agreement giving "the Saigon government a 'reasonable' chance to survive – a 'decent interval,' as he later said privately" (Karnow, 1997, p. 604). Gary Hess thinks the president was determined to "end the war" and also that he was "no more prepared than his predecessors to accept defeat" (Hess, 1990, p. 115). George Moss's assessment is similarly puzzling. Nixon "did not delay ending the war," he affirms, "because he was trying to win it, as some radical and liberal antiwar critics have charged." A page later, he adds, "although Nixon never tried to win the war, he fought ferociously for years not to lose it, or at least to appear not to lose it" (Moss, 1998, pp. 337–8).

Jeffrey Kimball's ambitious study tries to dispel the confusion. Within days after being sworn in, Nixon and Kissinger began the secret bombing of Cambodia. Confident that they could out-negotiate and outgun the enemy, the two men opened secret diplomatic channels to the USSR and the DRV and put forward Vietnamization as an antidote to the withdrawal of US combat forces. In July 1969, the administration warned Hanoi that measures "of great consequence and force" would ensue if concessions at the bargaining table were not forthcoming and contemplated various escalations (Operation "Duck Hook"), including the use of "a nuclear device" (Kimball, 1998, pp. 153, 163). In February 1970, "protective reaction strikes" began against North Vietnam, and B-52s hammered the Plain of Jars in Laos. In April, US and ARVN troops invaded Cambodia, and in February 1971 the Saigon army crossed into Laos with US air support. The following year brought intensified assaults on the North, culminating in the Christmas Bombing.

Nixon's tactics were unlikely to succeed. The DRV would not be bluffed by Vietnamization or by the administration's feints at the bargaining table. Nor were Hanoi leaders going to yield to "Duck Hook" or other threats. To compound the problem, the president knew that "it would be very hard to hold the country together while pursuing a military solution" (cited in Kimball, 1998, p. 172), an insight whose prescience was confirmed in the wake of the Cambodia invasion.

Trying to seize the initiative, Nixon and Kissinger broke new ground with their overture to the People's Republic of China. But, like earlier great-power maneuvers, this gambit betrayed an unwillingness to credit Vietnamese desires and capabilities and therefore could not transform the balance of forces. Still more original was the "madman theory," the notion that the president's reputation for instability, backed by spasms of violence, would unnerve the enemy. The "theory" was itself a symptom of folly.

These moves testify to the self-delusion of their authors. Nixon, who compared himself favorably to Lincoln, Churchill, and De Gaulle, and the equally vainglorious Kissinger persuaded themselves that they could surmount obstacles that had defeated their predecessors. They were not alone. In the spring of 1968, when President Johnson sent Averill Harriman to the Paris peace talks, Harriman still "wanted to believe that somehow a negotiated settlement could produce a viable, independent South Vietnam" (Isaacson and Thomas, 1986, p. 712). The prototypical "dove," Harriman was at that moment trying to persuade other leaders that Vietnam had been a mistake and that the United States should find a way out of the war. Yet even he could not bring himself to envision an outcome short of victory.

There was no "decent interval" policy. At times, high-level officials seemed to be saying that the United States should withdraw and leave the GVN to its fate, even if that course eventuated in a communist victory. But no president was ever willing to implement such a strategy. In an intriguing passage, Kimball affirms that by the end of 1970 Nixon and Kissinger began to envision a face-saving retreat. But the author is quick to add, "they had not, however, abandoned the hope that Thieu could survive into the indefinite future." A year later, Nixon is portrayed as "eager to withdraw, but loathe to lose." He was still "banking on triangular diplomacy and the hole card of airpower to retrieve victory from the jaws of defeat" (Kimball, 1998, pp. 240, 285). If Nixon had served out his term, surely he would again have launched B-52 strikes in 1975 in defense of the South Vietnamese Government. When Gerald Ford did not respond in force to prevent the disappearance of the Saigon regime, an era came to a close.

"Right" and "Left" Explanations on the Margins

The history of US intervention demonstrates that every president from Roosevelt to Nixon contributed to a consistent policy orientation. Archimedes Patti and John Foster Dulles and Curtis LeMay and George Ball and Averill Harriman and Henry Kissinger were all part of the team. Ad hominem explanations do not, cannot, account for this uniformity. So it seems worthwhile to take another look at systemic interpretations and to ask why they have ceased to enjoy much currency.

Vietnam War scholars have tabled Cold War orthodoxy. In his defense of US intervention, Guenter Lewy (1978) occasionally mutters about international communism, but for the most part his book argues that the war was decided within South Vietnam. Other conservative treatments (Podhoretz, 1983; Joes, 2001) take a similar approach, showing minimal interest in the external aspect, while asserting that Vietnamese communism on its own posed a challenge, more moral than strategic, that the United States could and should have met.

R. B. Smith is more insistent on the "international" aspect. "Sino-Soviet talks in September and October [1960] *appear* to have succeeded in narrowing the differences between the two principal Parties," he suggests. Of course, this was the moment when the gravity of the quarrel within the socialist bloc was becoming apparent. But "it is important not to underestimate the degree of genuine unity that emerged, which was none the less real for being shortlived." A putative consensus was spelled out at the Moscow Conference of Communist Parties in December, and Khrushchev's speech of the following month "*seemed* to accept" the desirability of "national liberation" wars. Smith goes on to state, "The Vietnamese struggle *might* even become a logical focus for international solidarity within the 'socialist camp,' despite continuing Sino-Soviet differences on other issues." "Given all this," he hazards, "it was difficult for the Americans to regard" the NLF "as anything more or less than a specific application of the international Communist line contained in the Moscow Statement"(Smith, 1983, vol. 1, pp. 224–5, emphases added).

Smith's analysis often relies on conjecture of this sort, a tentative address that may explain why it is not more frequently cited in other works on the war. But at least he presents an ambitious and scholarly treatment, worth consulting. By contrast, John Lewis Gaddis comments on Vietnam only in passing. After claiming that Chinese support was "maybe even the critical reason" for Viet Minh victory over the French, he concedes that "paradoxically" the USSR and the PRC worked at the Geneva Conference to prevent Vietnamese communism from extending its "triumph south of the

17th parallel" (Gaddis, 1997, p. 186). Readers of William Duiker's measured and richly researched biography of Ho Chi Minh (2000) are likely to wince when Gaddis assigns Ho to a rogues gallery of "all the little Stalins and Maos," "brutal romantics" who "promised liberation for their peoples but delivered repression" (Gaddis, 1993, p. 11).

Name-calling figures even more prominently in Michael Lind's recent book. Lind echoes Gaddis in declaring that Ho was "a minor clone of the major communist tyrants," then, for good measure, compares him to Franco and Mussolini as well (Lind, 1999, p. 42). Who knows what the next generation of research will bring. But for the time being, when it comes to understanding the Vietnam War, the "Foreign Other" is in limbo.

Echoes of the anti-imperialist critique of the 1960s are more frequently, but not much more frequently, heard in the literature. A review of the Indonesian case illustrates the point. There, in 1965, half a million leftists were killed by death squads linked to the armed forces. Lyndon Johnson later argued that this defeat of the Indonesian Communist Party (PKI) "would probably never have occurred" if not for his Vietnam escalation. The American "policy of helping those who wished to remain free and who were willing to help themselves" emboldened "the brave men who put their lives on the line" in Indonesia (Johnson, 1971, p. 357).

Perhaps the PKI would have been crushed even if the United States had not escalated. It is also true that Johnson's comment is self-serving, not to say brutal ("we regretted the bloodshed involved," he notes in an aside). Still, LBJ provides a plausible explanation for what "credibility" was all about and raises the prospect that Indonesia 1965 has something to do with the Vietnam War. Could one of the lessons of Vietnam have been that no amount of "bloodshed" was too great for the United States when it came to backing allies "willing to help themselves"?

Persuaded that LBJ's hypothesis warrants attention, R. B. Smith is one of the few scholars to examine it in detail. The United States aimed "to defeat any attempt by the Communist powers to draw individual countries away from existing political and economic relations with the West," he affirms. "In that context the most important country in the region was not South Vietnam but Indonesia." Declining to acknowledge that mass murder was the instrument ("a military campaign to restore full control – that is to suppress the PKI" is as far as he is willing to go), Smith notes that the liquidation of the Indonesian left was seen as "a welcome change" by the Americans, one which "held out the possibility of a return to regional stability in South-East Asia, allowing the adoption of measures conducive to the kind of economic development" that they desired. Positing a domino theory in reverse, he links the elimination of the PKI to Washington's "grand design," which was to mobilize "the whole of South-East Asia (except for North Vietnam) into an anti-Communist, anti-Chinese alliance" (Smith, 1985, vol. 2, p. 14; 1991, vol. 3, pp. 208, 210).

Gabriel Kolko agrees with Smith that the United States placed a high strategic and economic value on Indonesia and thought that its future would be influenced by what happened in Vietnam. But Kolko goes further, in order to emphasize US complicity with the massacre. Cable traffic between the US Embassy and Secretary of State Dean Rusk makes clear that the Americans were "generally sympathetic with and admiring of what [the] army [is] doing." When killing with knives and other primitive implements yielded a disappointing murder rate, the United States promised to send communications equipment and small arms, "dubbed 'medicines' to prevent embarrassing revelations" (Kolko, 1988, p. 181).

Kolko's *Anatomy of a War* (1994) might have been expected to pursue the point. But while it is a great book indeed on the Saigon milieu and an important book on the Vietnamese Revolution, its treatment of the US aspect is modest in scope. Not pausing overlong over markets and raw materials, Kolko shows more interest in "inherited geopolitical frustrations and conventional class wisdom" (p. 195), which precluded strategic thinking about the Vietnam battlefield and about economic costs and benefits as well.

A sense of how Vietnam fit into a larger perception of interests is implicit in *Confronting the Third World* (1988), which appeared three years after the first edition of *Anatomy* and was perhaps intended by Kolko as a companion volume to it. But the connections are not spelled out in the later work, leaving readers to imagine what a continent-wide interpretation of the Vietnam War might look like. In the chapter on Indonesia 1965, cited above, Vietnam is mentioned only in passing, and there is no testing of President Johnson's hypothesis on the link between the two.

When Michael Schaller (1982) and Andrew Rotter (1987) established that concern for Japanese recovery influenced Washington's thinking about Southeast Asia in the late 1940s, and when Paul Joseph (1981) and Gabriel Kolko (1994) demonstrated that economic pressures turned large segments of the capitalist class against the war in 1968, these affirmations worked their way into the treatments put forward by other scholars. But there is no study of economic considerations prompting Kennedy in 1961 or Johnson in 1965. As for Nixon, Jeffrey Kimball notes that in 1970 "even loyal Republican corporate executives were expressing a longing for peace" (Kimball, 1998, p. 176). But he does not say anything about the impact of such sentiments on the president. The anti-imperialist interpretation of US intervention remains stillborn.

Conclusion

In *The Perfect War* (1986), James William Gibson developed another kind of critical thinking about US intervention. While Robert Buzzanco and H. R. McMaster examine conflicts between military and civilian leaders, Gibson probes for the logic underlying perceptions of war-making that were common to the Pentagon and the White House. According to his analysis, the American way of fighting in Vietnam, which Gibson calls "technowar," was rooted in a corporate and political culture going back to World War II.

"Technowar" remains a strikingly ambitious formulation, with more explanatory power than, say, "dereliction of duty." But *The Perfect War* has made little impact on the Vietnam field. It could be that the same fate awaits studies by Mark Bradley and Robert Dean, which also offer a social interpretation of policymaking and bring back into discussion racism and imperialism and other conceptions once deployed by the left of the anti-war movement. Or perhaps, after recent calls for new departures (Appy, 2000; Rotter, 2000), there will be a more receptive audience for such approaches.

I hope these breakthroughs will be followed up in future work. Some might call this a "cultural turn," a usage I resist because it implies a gap between the "cultural" and the "material," when the point is to see how these spheres are indissoluble and constitutive elements, shaping the behavior of policymakers. Worries about Indonesian communism and worries about toughness came into their minds from the same historical experience, and "credibility" is misconstrued if either the global ("dominos") or the affective ("machismo") is left out. Our picture of Vietnam War decisionmaking will remain unfinished if the presidents are not positioned within society, which imposes on all who seek to make history its own conceptions of interest and power.

REFERENCES

Anderson, David: *Trapped by Success: The Eisenhower Administration and Vietnam, 1953–1961* (New York: Columbia University Press, 1991).

Appy, Christian, ed.: *Cold War Constructions: The Political Culture of United States Imperialism, 1945–1966* (Amherst: University of Massachusetts Press, 2000).

Bradley, Mark: *Imagining Vietnam and America: The Making of Postcolonial Vietnam, 1919–1950* (Chapel Hill: University of North Carolina Press, 2000).

Buzzanco, Robert: *Masters of War: Military Dissent and Politics in the Vietnam Era* (New York: Cambridge University Press, 1996).

Cumings, Bruce: *Origins of the Korean War: Liberation and the Emergence of Separate Regimes, 1945–1947* (1981; Princeton, NJ: Princeton University Press, 1989).

Dean, Robert: "Masculinity as Ideology: John F. Kennedy and the Domestic Politics of Foreign Policy," *Diplomatic History*, 22 (1998): 29–62.

Dean, Robert: *Imperial Brotherhood: Gender and the Making of Cold War Foreign Policy* (Amherst: University of Massachusetts Press, 2001).

Duiker, William: *Ho Chi Minh* (New York: Hyperion, 2000).

Fisher, James T.: *Dr. America: The Lives of Thomas A. Dooley, 1927–1961* (Amherst: University of Massachusetts Press, 1997).

Gaddis, John Lewis: "The Tragedy of Cold War History," *Diplomatic History*, 17 (1993): 1–16.

Gaddis, John Lewis: *We Now Know: Rethinking Cold War History* (1997; New York: Clarendon Press, 1998).

Gardner, Lloyd: *Approaching Vietnam: From World War II through Dienbienphu* (New York: W. W. Norton, 1988).

Gibson, James William: *The Perfect War: The War We Couldn't Lose and How We Did* (1986; New York: Vintage, 1988).

Herring, George: *LBJ and Vietnam: A Different Kind of War* (Austin: University of Texas Press, 1994).

Herring, George: *America's Longest War: The United States and Vietnam, 1950–1975* (1979; New York: McGraw Hill, 1996).

Hess, Gary: *Vietnam and the United States: Origins and Legacy of War* (Boston: Twayne, 1990).

Isaacson, Walter and Thomas, Evan: *The Wise Men: Six Friends and the World They Made* (1986; New York: Touchstone, 1988).

Joes, Anthony James: *The War for South Viet Nam, 1954–1975* (1989; Westport, Conn.: Praeger, 2001).

Johnson, Lyndon Baines: *The Vantage Point: Perspectives of the Presidency, 1963–1969* (New York: Holt, Rinehart, and Winston, 1971).

Joseph, Paul: *Cracks in the Empire: State Politics in the Vietnam War* (Boston: South End Press, 1981).

Kahin, George: *Intervention: How America Became Involved in Vietnam* (New York: Anchor, 1986).

Kaiser, David E.: *An American Tragedy: Kennedy, Johnson, and the Origins of the Vietnam War* (Cambridge, Mass.: Harvard University Press, 1999).

Karnow, Stanley: *Vietnam: A History* (1983; New York: Penguin, 1997).

Kimball, Jeffrey: *Nixon's Vietnam War* (Lawrence: University Press of Kansas, 1998).

Kolko, Gabriel: *Confronting the Third World: United States Foreign Policy, 1945–1980* (New York: Pantheon, 1988).

Kolko, Gabriel: *Anatomy of a War: Vietnam, the United States, and the Modern Historical Experience* (1985; New York: New Press, 1994).

Langguth, A. J.: *Our Vietnam: The War 1954–1975* (New York: Simon and Schuster, 2000).

Lewy, Guenter: *America in Vietnam* (New York: Oxford University Press, 1978).

Lind, Michael: *Vietnam, The Necessary War: A Reinterpretation of America's Most Disastrous Military Conflict* (New York: Free Press, 1999).

Logevall, Fredrik: *Choosing War: The Lost Chance for Peace and the Escalation of War in Vietnam* (Berkeley: University of California Press, 1999).

McMaster, H. R.: *Dereliction of Duty: Lyndon Johnson, Robert McNamara, the Joint Chiefs of Staff, and the Lies that Led to Vietnam* (New York: HarperCollins, 1997).

Moss, George: *Vietnam: An American Ordeal* (1990; Upper Saddle River, NJ: Prentice Hall, 1998).

Olson, James and Roberts, Randy: *Where the Domino Fell: America and Vietnam, 1945–1995* (1991; New York: St. Martin's, 1996).

Podhoretz, Norman: *Why We Were In Vietnam* (1982; New York: Simon and Schuster, 1983).

Rotter, Andrew: *The Path to Vietnam: Origins of the American Commitment to Southeast Asia* (Ithaca, NY: Cornell University Press, 1987).

Rotter, Andrew: "Saidism Without Said: Orientalism and U.S. Diplomatic History," *American Historical Review*, 105 (2000): 1205–17.

Schaller, Michael: "Securing the Great Crescent: Occupied Japan and the Origins of Containment in Southeast Asia," *Journal of American History*, 69 (September 1982): 392–413.

Smith, R. B.: *An International History of the Vietnam War*, 3 vols. Vol. 1: *Revolution Versus Containment, 1955–1961*; vol. 2: *The Struggle for Southeast Asia, 1961–1965*; vol. 3: *The Making of a Limited War, 1965–66* (New York: St. Martin's, 1983, 1985, 1991).

Tonnesson, Stein: *The Vietnamese Revolution of 1945: Roosevelt, Ho Chi Minh and De Gaulle in a World at War* (London: Sage Publications, 1991).

Turley, William: *The Second Indochina War: A Short Political and Military History, 1954–1975* (New York: Mentor, 1986).

Young, Marilyn: *The Vietnam Wars, 1945–1990* (New York: HarperCollins, 1991).

CHAPTER TWENTY-FIVE

The End of the Cold War

DAVID S. PAINTER AND THOMAS S. BLANTON

The sudden and surprising end of the Cold War in the late 1980s closed an epoch in modern history. As a superpower confrontation, ideological contest, arms race, and competition for geopolitical influence, the Cold War dominated international relations for forty-five years (1945–90). It shaped the foreign policies of the United States and the Soviet Union and deeply affected their societies and their political, economic, and military institutions. By justifying the projection of US power and influence all over the world, the Cold War facilitated the assertion of global leadership by the United States. By providing Soviet leaders with an external enemy to justify their repressive internal regime and external empire, it helped perpetuate the grip of the Communist Party on power. In both countries, the Cold War compelled ongoing mobilization for war, locking the Soviet Union even tighter into the bifurcated command economy that led to its downfall, while pushing the United States toward a stronger central state and hybrid economic management that produced progress by reducing social inequalities and creating a "social bargain" within reformed capitalism.

In addition to its impact on the superpowers, the Cold War caused and sustained the division of Europe, and within Europe, Germany. It also facilitated the reconstruction and reintegration of Germany, Italy, and Japan into the international system following their defeat in World War II. The impact of the Cold War was especially great in the third world, where it overlapped and interacted with longer-term trends like decolonization and sweeping social and economic changes. The Cold War led to the division of Vietnam and Korea and to costly wars in both nations, and it exacerbated conflicts throughout the third world. During crises, the Cold War's nuclear arsenals threatened the end of human civilization. In short, the Cold War was at the center of world politics in the second half of the twentieth century.

Debates about the end of the Cold War are inextricably bound up with assumptions about the nature of the Cold War. As Richard Ned Lebow (2000, p. 208) has noted, "the debate about the end of the Cold War is at its core a controversy about the validity of the principles that shaped Western understanding of the Soviet Union and its foreign policy." Defenders of US policies blame the Cold War on an expansionist and ideologically motivated Soviet Union and argue that victory in the Cold War vindicates US policies during the conflict. In contrast, more critical scholars argue that US policies and actions played an important role in starting and sustaining the Cold War and that less confrontational US policies could have led to the end of the Cold War sooner and at a lower cost.

The end of the Cold War was largely the result of long-term processes, most of which were internal to the Soviet Union. Although we will not neglect long-term processes or Soviet internal policies, our focus will be on the impact of US policies and actions, especially in the 1980s. Following an overview of the key events of the Cold War in the 1980s, we evaluate major interpretations of the end of the Cold War. Next, we discuss some of the sources on this topic that have become available in the last decade and point to new directions for research.

Conventional wisdom in the United States conflates the breakup of the Soviet Union, the collapse of communism, and the end of the Cold War, but these processes, while closely related, were not the same. In long-term perspective, the breakup of the Soviet Union can be seen as the long-delayed result of a process of disintegration of multinational empires that was one of the key legacies of World War I. While that war destroyed other empires, the Russian Empire continued "under new management" as the Soviet Union. Initially unaffected by the end of European colonial empires set in motion by World War II, that process also caught up with the last of the great multinational and colonial empires. In the end, nationalism and democratization proved incompatible with empire, dooming the Soviet Union. Jacques Lévesque (1997) argues that the transformation of Soviet communism was the result of the gradual social democratization of the Soviet elite, a process that had already occurred in other countries. Similarly, Jack Snyder (1987–8) and David Lane (1996) point to shifts in Soviet society resulting from the economic transformation of the Soviet Union that led to changes in the composition and interests of the country's dominant groups.

As for the more immediate factors that led to the "end of the Communist revolution," to use Robert Daniels's (1993) phrase, Jerry Hough (1997) and other Soviet specialists point to the disastrous and unintended consequences of the economic policies initiated by Mikhail Gorbachev. In addition, David Kotz and Fred Weir (1997), drawing on the work of Russian scholars, focus on the defection of a significant portion of the Soviet elite whose continued privileges were threatened by Gorbachev's reforms, and argue that Boris Yeltsin and his supporters forced the breakup of the Soviet Union in order to consolidate their hold on power in Russia.

The Cold War in the 1980s

As the 1980s began, the end of the Cold War seemed nowhere in sight. Following a brief period of relaxed tensions and better relations (détente) in the mid-1970s, that decade ended with a "new Cold War" and the Soviet invasion of Afghanistan in December 1979. In Washington, President Jimmy Carter was about to lose his job to Ronald Reagan not only because of high inflation and soaring interest rates, but also because of Soviet-supported revolutions in the third world, the hostage crisis in Iran, and changes in the strategic balance that had ended US strategic superiority.

Warning that the Soviet Union had surpassed the United States in military strength, Reagan intensified the military buildup begun during the last years of the Carter administration, and between 1981 and 1989 added more than $2.1 trillion to the US defense budget (see Arkin, 1989). The Reagan administration also expanded covert action and sharply increased military assistance to pro-United States governments and groups, including anti-communist insurgents in Afghanistan,

Angola, and Nicaragua. The Reagan administration revived the B-1 bomber, continued development of the B-2 (Stealth) bomber, expanded the navy from 450 to 600 ships, and accelerated deployment of the MX mobile missile and the Trident submarine missile system – both highly accurate delivery systems capable of carrying multiple warheads.

One deployment in particular symbolized the new antagonism, and the old misunderstandings. In the fall of 1983, after almost four years of the highest-level alliance negotiations, front-page headlines, and a rising tide of anti-nuclear protest in Western Europe, the United States began placing Pershing II intermediate-range missiles and Tomahawk cruise missiles in Western Europe. In NATO eyes, this upgraded intermediate-range missile capacity was a necessary response and deterrent to the Soviet deployment, beginning in the late 1970s, of hundreds of SS-20 intermediate-range missiles, with highly accurate multiple warheads aimed at Western Europe. In Soviet eyes, the SS-20s were merely a normal modernization of forces, much as NATO had junked its Jupiter and Thor missiles in the 1960s for Pershing I's – a modernization that actually stabilized deterrence by being more mobile, less vulnerable to preemption, and carrying less total megatonnage. But to NATO, the SS-20s challenged its basic war-fighting strategy, which called for tactical nuclear superiority in Europe to counterbalance assumed Soviet and Warsaw Pact conventional superiority.

The Soviets apparently never considered the political impact on NATO of their deployment. For its part, the Reagan administration had proposed negotiating positions on intermediate-range missiles that sounded serious ("the zero option"), but in reality only offered to trade a NATO bird in the bush (plans for future Pershing deployment) for the Soviet birds on the ground. In response to the deployment of the Pershing II and Tomahawk missiles, the Soviets broke off both the Intermediate Nuclear Forces (INF) talks and Strategic Arms Reduction Talks (START).

In part, the vehemence of the Soviet response was due to Reagan's announcement, in March 1983, of the Strategic Defense Initiative (SDI), a technologically ambitious and extremely expensive plan to develop a nationwide ballistic-missile defense system that would deploy weapons in outer space to destroy enemy warheads in flight. As former Soviet Foreign Minister Alexander Bessermertnykh pointed out in a 1993 oral history conference (Wohlforth, 1996, p. 48), SDI violated the whole structure of US–Soviet arms control that had as its cornerstone the Anti-Ballistic Missile (ABM) Treaty of 1972 by threatening mutual deterrence, which was based on each side's ability to retaliate against a nuclear attack. Bessermertnykh also noted Soviet fears that SDI had the potential to provide the United States with the capacity and confidence to launch a preemptive nuclear strike.

Reagan, as Frances Fitzgerald (2000) notes, saw SDI in fundamentally moral terms, as a way to prevent nuclear war through defensive means. He seemed not to know or to care whether such a system would likely set off a new arms race, and genuinely wanted to share anti-missile technology with the world. Hardliners in the Reagan administration like Secretary of Defense Caspar Weinberger embraced SDI from different and multiple motives: to increase defense spending even more; to take the initiative in developing space weapons; and to undercut the existing arms-control framework with the Soviets, whom they believed could not be trusted. In contrast, Secretary of State George Shultz and other top officials saw SDI primarily as a bargaining chip to help bring the Soviets to the table and force them to moderate their behavior. Congress liked the idea of spending several billion dollars on missile defense every year even if there was little to show for it but jobs and votes. SDI's Hollywood-originated nickname, "Star Wars," summed up American public opinion, which was skeptical of the technical possibilities but generally supportive of the idea of defending against an attack rather than initiating one.

Judged on its own terms, without the hindsight provided by the end of the Cold War, Reagan's foreign policy during his first term might well be assessed, on balance, as a failure, as in the first edition of Raymond Garthoff's *Détente and Confrontation* (1985). Reagan administration policies and rhetoric exacerbated tensions within the Western alliance and contributed to the strength of a powerful and at times explicitly anti-US peace movement in Western Europe. Reagan's policies in the third world, especially Central America, also evoked widespread protest, never gaining majority support even in the United States. In late 1986, the revelation that administration officials had been covertly violating a congressional ban on aid to the anti-communist insurgents in Nicaragua (known as *contras*), while simultaneously shipping arms to Iran to gain the freedom of Americans held hostage in Lebanon, led to a serious constitutional crisis, the resignation of several of Reagan's top aides, and a dramatic decline in public and congressional support for administration policies in Central America. Finally, the mushrooming budget deficits that resulted from increased military spending combined with tax cuts swelled the national debt and led to an inflow of foreign capital that drove up the value of the dollar and contributed to a skyrocketing trade deficit.

During his second term, however, Reagan found a partner, in the person of Mikhail Gorbachev, who could actually produce the movie Reagan had always wanted to make about US–Soviet relations. Soviet-related documentation from Reagan's first term has begun to be declassified, and it reveals that Reagan secretly sent a handwritten (but staff-drafted) letter to Soviet leader Yuri Andropov only four months after the "evil empire" speech – one in a series of secret Reagan approaches to the three Soviet general secretaries during his first term – suggesting talks and offering "private and candid" communications at the highest level. However, as Reagan later commented, Soviet leaders kept dying on him. Before Gorbachev took office in March 1985, the Soviet Union had gone through three general secretaries in the four years Reagan was in the White House. The deaths in quick succession of Leonid Brezhnev (November 1982), Yuri Andropov (February 1984), and Konstantin Chernenko (March 1985) added even more uncertainty to a Soviet system characterized by secrecy, stagnation, and government by committee.

As Archie Brown (1996) and others point out, Gorbachev took charge of a Soviet Union beset by declining economic performance, a widening technology gap, a demoralized set of elites and Party cadres, an increasingly restive population, and a confrontational relationship with the United States and its allies. To meet these challenges, Gorbachev ordered more investment in the machine-building industries, expecting the kinds of major productivity and output gains the Soviet Union had realized from a similar strategy in the 1950s. He sought to keep his military happy with increased spending on weapons procurement and a free hand, with a one-year deadline, in Afghanistan. When these policies failed to produce immediate improvements, Gorbachev moved to a more radical reform agenda: encouraging open debate on government policies (*glasnost*), economic restructuring (*perestroika*), and improved relations with the West (new thinking). These policies were linked. Brown (1996), Robert English (2000), and other Soviet specialists have pointed out that Gorbachev hoped that political reform would break bureaucratic opposition to his economic reforms. Similarly, he hoped that a less competitive relationship with the West would permit a drastic reduction in military spending and allow the Soviet Union to devote greater attention and resources to internal renewal.

Gorbachev focused first on arms control. In April 1985, he suspended the countermeasures the Soviets had taken in response to the NATO INF deployments and halted further deployment of SS-20 intermediate-range missiles. In August, he announced a unilateral moratorium on nuclear testing, and offered to extend it indefinitely if the United States would also stop testing. He also agreed to on-site inspection of Soviet test facilities. Gorbachev met with Reagan in Geneva in November 1985. The two leaders established a personal relationship, and Gorbachev gained Reagan's assent to a joint statement that nuclear war could never be won and must never be fought. In October 1986 at the Reykjavik summit, Gorbachev offered to remove all SS-20s from Europe and limit the number deployed in Asia to 100, and also proposed a plan to cut US and Soviet nuclear forces in half. As detailed accounts by Fitzgerald (2000), Jack Matlock (1995), and Anatoly Chernyaev (2000) make clear, Gorbachev and Reagan almost reached agreement on eliminating "offensive" nuclear weapons entirely, but Reagan's refusal to limit SDI to laboratory research, and Gorbachev's refusal to believe Reagan was sincere about sharing SDI, prevented any agreement.

Following Reykjavik, Gorbachev dropped his previous insistence that agreement on SDI was a prerequisite for progress on all arms control matters and accepted the earlier US "zero option" offer that all US and Soviet intermediate-range forces in Europe and Asia be scrapped. In addition, Gorbachev proposed eliminating shorter-range intermediate forces. These proposals became the basis for the Intermediate Nuclear Forces (INF) Treaty signed in Washington in December 1987, the first arms reduction (as opposed to arms control) agreement of the Cold War.

Turning his attention to conventional forces, Gorbachev, in a December 1988 address before the United Nations, announced a 12 percent unilateral reduction in Soviet conventional forces, including a 20 percent reduction in forces west of the Urals. A large part of these cuts would come from Soviet forces in Eastern Europe, significantly reducing the Warsaw Pact's offensive capabilities. These cutbacks, as well as the proposals on nuclear weapons, grew out of a drastic revision of Soviet military strategy that replaced the previous objective of not losing a war with the West with the objective of preventing such a war. As Michael MccGwire (1991) and Gerard Snel (1998) make clear, the new strategy, in contrast to previous ones, did not require maintaining a strategic sphere of influence in Eastern Europe. As Matthew Evangelista (1999) notes, Gorbachev's speech also ruled out use of force as an instrument of policy and pledged to respect freedom of choice for Eastern Europe.

At the same time that he was moving to wind down the arms race, Gorbachev was also taking steps to end the Cold War in the third world. In February 1988, Gorbachev announced his intention to pull all Soviet troops out of Afghanistan. Negotiations under the auspices of the United Nations led to a series of agreements in the spring of 1988 that called for the withdrawal of Soviet forces by February 15, 1989. Reversing an earlier commitment to stop aiding the Afghan resistance once

Soviet forces left Afghanistan, the Reagan administration announced that the United States would continue to provide aid to the resistance as long as the Soviet Union provided aid to the Afghan government. Soviet forces left on schedule in February 1989, but the war continued for three more years.

Withdrawing forces from Afghanistan not only reassured the West but also helped repair relations with the People's Republic of China (PRC). Gorbachev also pressured Vietnam to remove its forces from Cambodia, where they had been since 1978. By the fall of 1989, Vietnamese forces had left Cambodia, and in October 1990, the various Cambodian forces reached a peace agreement under UN auspices. The Soviets also phased out their military assistance to Vietnam and withdrew their forces from bases in Vietnam.

In Africa, Soviet and US negotiators helped mediate a settlement linking withdrawal of foreign forces from Angola with Namibian independence. The December 1988 agreements provided for the withdrawal of all foreign forces from Angola by mid-1991, and South African acceptance of a UN-sponsored plan for Namibian independence, which occurred in March 1990. South African forces had already left Angola by the time the agreement was signed, and all Cuban troops left by June 1991. As in Afghanistan, fighting continued as the United States continued to send arms to anti-communist insurgents and the Soviet Union continued to aid the Angolan government. In 1990, the Soviets cut back their assistance and withdrew their advisers from Ethiopia, and the Cubans withdrew their combat forces and advisers. After the Ethiopian government fell to regional rebel forces in May 1991, the Soviets evacuated their base in the Dahlak Islands.

Although aided by the changes in Soviet policies, the end of the Cold War in Central America, as William Leogrande (2000) and others have shown, was primarily the result of a regional peace process led by Costa Rican president Oscar Arias Sánchez, which called for ceasefires in each of the war-torn nations of the region, free elections, and the end of all aid to irregular forces or insurrectionary movements. Helped by millions of dollars in US aid, opposition forces in Nicaragua won free elections in February 1990, which were followed by a peaceful transfer of power. Although fighting dragged on until the early 1990s in both El Salvador and Guatemala, the end of the Cold War helped facilitate ceasefires and elections in both nations.

By early 1989, Cold War tensions had lessened markedly. The arms race was abating and the Cold War in the third world was winding down. Eastern Europe remained under communist control, however. Still skeptical about Soviet intentions and determined to put its own mark on US foreign policy, the incoming Bush administration put relations with the Soviet Union on hold for almost six months as it conducted a detailed strategic review of US foreign policy. President George Bush and his advisers also decided to test Soviet sincerity by focusing on the future of Eastern Europe (see Wohlforth, forthcoming).

Eastern Europe's communist regimes lacked legitimacy and depended on Soviet support to stay in power. As Gorbachev and his supporters struggled to restructure the Soviet economy and open up the Soviet political system they recognized that using coercion to maintain control of Eastern Europe could undermine their efforts at reform. Moreover, as Andrew Bennett (1999, forthcoming) argues, Gorbachev, his Foreign Minister Eduard Shevardnadze, and most of their advisers regarded earlier

Soviet uses of force in Eastern Europe as major mistakes. Economic factors also played a role. As Randall Stone (1996) demonstrates, subsidies to Eastern Europe were a chronic drain on Soviet resources.

Beginning with elections in Poland in June 1989, the region's communist regimes collapsed over the next six months. With the exception of Romania, the revolutions of 1989 came about peacefully. Gorbachev not only rejected the use of force to stave off the collapse of communist control, but, as Lévesque (1997) shows, at critical junctures in Poland and East Germany, he actively promoted political liberalization.

Germany had been at the center of the Cold War from its outset (see chapter 21), and the division of Germany and especially Berlin had served as potent symbols of the East–West divide. The Berlin Wall came down on November 9, 1989, and on November 28, West German Chancellor Helmut Kohl announced a ten-point plan for the rapid reunification of Germany. Elections in the German Democratic Republic (GDR) in March 1990 revealed overwhelming support for its absorption into an expanded Federal Republic. After extensive negotiations, Gorbachev, in September 1990, agreed to German reunification and membership of a unified Germany in NATO.

According to Lévesque (1997), Gorbachev had hoped to preserve the Warsaw Pact as the institutional basis for a negotiated new European security order in which the Soviet Union would play a major role. The collapse of communism in much of Eastern Europe and German reunification within NATO meant, James Davis and William Wohlforth (forthcoming) point out, that the post-Cold War order in Europe would be on US terms and would exclude the Soviet Union. In October 1990, NATO and the Warsaw Pact signed a treaty drastically reducing the size and armament of their conventional forces in Europe, with the Soviet Union accepting deeper cuts in its forces than those required of NATO and the United States. By the time the United States ratified the treaty in November 1991, the Warsaw Pact had ceased to exist, having disbanded in July 1991.

The reunification of Germany marked the end of the Cold War. Even before that occurred, the Soviet nonresponse to the end of communist rule in Eastern Europe had convinced President Bush and his advisers that the Soviet Union was no longer an adversary. Indeed, as Thomas Blanton (1998) has argued, by December 1989, the United States was willing to support Soviet intervention in Romania to prevent Romanian dictator Nicolae Ceausescu from crushing reform forces. The momentous changes set in motion by Gorbachev thus ended the Cold War well before the Soviet Union collapsed and disintegrated in December 1991.

Interpretations

In the United States, the prevailing popular interpretation of the end of the Cold War is the so-called "Reagan victory school," which argues that the Soviets shifted to less confrontational policies in the late 1980s because the US military buildup and political offensive in the early 1980s raised the costs of confrontation and forced the Soviets into a corner from which there was no escape save for surrender. This interpretation (popularized by Schweizer, 1994, 2000; Winik, 1996) begins with a highly critical view of US policies during the 1970s, claiming that the Soviets took advantage of détente and American weakness to take the lead in the arms race and to make gains in the third world. Victory school advocates claim that Reagan administration strategists, recognizing that the Soviet Union, and especially the Soviet economy, was in deep trouble, developed and implemented a series of actions designed to burden and undermine the Soviet system.

According to this view, US covert action programs in Poland, Afghanistan, Angola, and Nicaragua cost the Soviets billions of dollars a year and forced the Soviets to accept regional settlements on US terms. Similarly, victory school advocates argue that the US military buildup was a purposeful strategy designed to put unbearable strains on an economically and technologically inferior foe. They place special emphasis on SDI, claiming that it convinced the Soviets they could not hope to keep up with the United States in the next phase of military-technological competition. They also claim that US export control programs designed to limit Soviet access to Western technology and US efforts to drive down oil prices and hamper Soviet gas exports retarded Soviet economic growth and cost the Soviet Union billions of dollars. Richard Pipes (1995) even claims that the Reagan administration's "tough" policies were a key factor in Gorbachev's selection as Soviet leader in 1985.

Promoted primarily by former Reagan administration officials and conservative journalists, the Reagan victory school, with few exceptions (Gaddis, 1989; Pateman, 1999), has found little support among scholars. Craig Nation (1992), Brown (1996), and Garthoff (1994b) argue that the Reagan victory school greatly exaggerates Soviet strength and aggressiveness at the beginning of the 1980s. Rather than a strong and aggressive "evil empire" on the march, they see a Soviet Union ruled by a sclerotic group of gerontocrats presiding over a stagnant economy falling ever further behind the West, a hollow military bogged down in an unwinnable war in Afghanistan, a dramatic geopolitical imbalance featuring former comrades in China and Egypt as new US allies, and a workers' revolt in Poland personifying the international proletariat's rejection of communism. In addition, CIA figures (Firth and Noren, 1998) show that Soviet defense spending throughout Carter's four years and the first four of Reagan stayed relatively flat.

Studies of détente by Garthoff (1994a), Mike Bowker and Phil Williams (1988), and Odd Arne Westad (1997) agree that US concerns about Soviet strategic forces were overblown and ignored continuing US advantages, and that the Soviet conventional buildup of the early 1970s was, in part, a response to the modernization of NATO forces in the 1960s. They also argue that the third world revolutions of the 1970s were rooted in indigenous developments and regional rivalries rather than being the products of Soviet expansionism.

Research in Soviet records by Westad (1997) and Bennett (1999), for example, reveals that the 1979 invasion of Afghanistan was largely motivated by defensive concerns, including Soviet paranoia that the CIA would somehow recruit the erstwhile communist head of state in Kabul. Similarly, studies by Westad (1996–7), Piero Gleijeses (1996–7), and Bennett (1999) of Angola, and numerous studies of the situation in Central America in the 1980s (for example, LeoGrande, 2000), reveal a much more complex story of Soviet involvement than that held by victory school advocates. Finally, documents unearthed by Vojtech Mastny (1998) and others ("New Evidence on the Polish Crisis," 1998) suggest that the 1980–1 noninvasion of Poland was deeply influenced by Soviet acceptance of their own weakness and inability to police Stalin's empire in Eastern Europe, thus presaging 1989.

Second, most of the major national security initiatives now identified with Reagan actually began during the last year of Carter's presidency: a major military buildup, large increases in defense spending, changes in US nuclear targeting guidance, mass procurement of precision-guided munitions, and covert support for the Afghan muja-hedin were all underway before Reagan came to office in January 1981. Carter never produced as ringing a phrase as Reagan's "evil empire," but some of Reagan's actions, such as lifting the grain embargo on the Soviet Union, were actually less harsh than Carter's in 1980 (boycotting the Olympics in addition to the grain embargo).

Recent scholarship also disputes the claim that the changes in Soviet policy were due to US pressure. English (2000) has shown that the new generation of Soviet leaders that emerged in the 1980s had already concluded that the policies of their predecessors were counterproductive and that continued conflict threatened their goal of overcoming the disastrous legacy of Stalinism, reforming their economy, democratizing their politics, and revitalizing their society. English (1997) and Brown (forthcoming) also argue that claims that Gorbachev's selection was influenced by Reagan's policies have no basis in the evidence that has thus far come to light. Rather than causing the changes in Soviet foreign policy that led to the end of the Cold War, Brown, English, and numerous other scholars (for example, Garthoff, 1994b; Cordovez and Harrison, 1995; Mendelson, 1998; Evangelista, 1999; Zubok, 2000) argue that US policies and actions delayed, and almost derailed, them by providing opponents of reform with arguments against better relations with the West and relax-ation of internal controls. Bennett (1999, pp. 248–9) argues that Gorbachev suc-ceeded in changing Soviet policies in spite of US aggressiveness by viewing US actions as, in part, "a reaction to Soviet policies rather than merely an indicator of the inher-ently aggressive nature of capitalism."

It is difficult to assess the efficacy of covert aid to Solidarity with any degree of certainty. Those who see US actions as crucial should reflect, however, on the fact that the Soviets and their local allies in Poland and throughout Eastern Europe had for forty years been unable to extinguish opposition to Soviet dominance. It is also difficult to assess, with any degree of accuracy, the impact of US economic sanctions on the Soviet Union. While it is clear that the Soviet Union suffered a huge drop in export earnings due to the collapse of oil prices in 1986, this came after Gorbachev took office. Moreover, while US pressures and inducements no doubt played a role in Saudi decisions to increase production, the Saudis had sufficient reasons of their own to prefer lower prices. In addition, reduced demand for oil due to high prices, conservation, and use of alternative energy sources, and expanded production outside the Middle East, were more important factors in the price collapse than any con-certed campaign by the Reagan administration to drive prices down (see Painter, 1991).

Numerous studies of the Cold War in the third world demonstrate not only that Reagan victory school adherents fundamentally misunderstand the sources and nature of these conflicts, but also that their version of how and why the conflicts ended is seriously flawed. As Richard Herrmann (forthcoming), Diego Cordovez and Selig Harrison (1995), Sarah Mendelson (1998), and Bennett (1999) make clear, the Soviets were already moving toward withdrawing their forces from Afghanistan before the Reagan administration stepped up military aid to the mujahedin, and US actions probably delayed a settlement and prolonged the fighting. US aid to anti-communist forces in Angola and Nicaragua also prolonged the fighting and suffering, and in both cases the eventual settlements were more the result of regional forces than of US actions. As Herrmann (forthcoming) points out, the Soviet-allied Afghan government did not fall to insurgent forces until April 1992 after Russian President Boris Yeltsin, who had displaced Gorbachev and extinguished the Soviet Union in late December 1991, cut off aid. Likewise, the Soviet-allied government in Angola won free elections in October 1992 and is still in power. In Nicaragua, a government of national reconciliation, rather than the *contras*, replaced the Sandinistas, who remained the largest and best-organized party in the country.

Although the Soviets deeply opposed SDI, at least initially, Garthoff (1994b) and Evangelista (1999) argue that its main impact on Soviet policy was to delay progress in arms control. The Soviets continued research on space-based and other high-tech weapons, but they neither tried to develop their own SDI-type weapons nor devoted significant efforts to developing countermeasures against SDI, in part because the United States never developed a workable system. In any event, the Soviets could have countered SDI by building more missiles, a response that would have cost far less than the requisite US countervailing defensive measures. This was economically feasible because Soviet spending on offensive nuclear forces made up less than 10 percent of overall Soviet military spending, as Fitzgerald (2000, pp. 474–5) notes.

Finally, critics of the Reagan victory school point out that there is little contemporary evidence that US policymakers believed in the early 1980s that the Soviet Union was on the verge of collapse. Indeed, at the time these same polemicists saw Soviet power on the rise, not in decline, and warned that the Soviet Union was about to win the Cold War. As Robert McMahon (1995) has noted, even if these claims were true, such a strategy was reckless since it could have resulted in desperate Soviet responses rather than a peaceful end to the Cold War. Indeed, by the fall of 1983 Soviet leaders seem genuinely to have believed that the United States was preparing a preemptive nuclear attack, a perception heavily influenced by memories of Hitler's 1941 surprise attack on the USSR (see Benjamin Fischer, 1997). Had the Soviets taken measures to counter the expected US attack, it could have initiated a disastrous chain reaction that would have made August 1914 look like a minor mishap.

While the Reagan victory school has been largely discredited, at least among scholars, the view that "containment worked" and led to US victory in the Cold War is widely held. Advocates of this view, such as Shultz (1993), Matlock (1995), and John Gaddis (1997), explain the end of the Cold War by claiming that US policies and actions, in particular the related policies of containment and nuclear deterrence, finally convinced Soviet leaders that their goal of world domination was unobtainable and that trying to achieve it was not only dangerous but also incompatible with the economic health of the Soviet Union. In this interpretation, the policies of containment and deterrence prevented war, held the line against the expansion of Soviet power and influence, raised the costs of competing with the West, and eventually convinced Soviet leaders that communism was not the wave of the future but rather a dead end.

The Soviet Union devoted a much larger share of a much smaller economy to defense spending, thus siphoning off resources needed for economic modernization, and many advocates of the "containment worked" school focus on economic factors. As Stephen Brooks and Wohlforth (2000–1) and Geir Lundestad (2000), among others, show, Soviet defense and "imperial" expenditures were quite high (analysts

now put Soviet defense spending at 15–20 percent of GNP) and imposed a significant burden on the Soviet economy. By the 1980s the Soviet economy was in serious
trouble. Most scholars also agree that a key motivation behind Gorbachev's foreign
policy initiatives was a desire to reduce these expenditures.

There is less agreement over the impact of US policy and actions, however. The
militarized command economy of the Soviet Union with its emphasis on the rapid
buildup of heavy industry took shape in the 1930s, and the roots of Russian economic backwardness reach even further into the past. While agreeing that the global
balance of power was important, Lévesque (forthcoming) also argues that any analysis that sees the changes in Soviet foreign policy under Gorbachev as merely a
response to changes in the distribution of power "is far off the mark."

In the end, assumptions about Soviet foreign policy are at the heart of debates
about the end of the Cold War. If the Soviets were intent on world revolution and
global domination, the main interpretive question is why did they abandon this goal?
If, however, they were not trying to take over the world, what were they trying to
do and why, and what caused the changes in Soviet policies that led to the end of
the Cold War? Answering these questions requires a sophisticated understanding of
Soviet intentions, something notably lacking in most of the studies that argue US
policies won the Cold War.

Before turning to this question, it is important to remember that US policies also
changed. Beth Fischer (1997) has even described the dramatic foreign policy differences between Reagan's first and second terms as "The Reagan Reversal." Fischer,
Shultz (1993), Matlock (1995), and Don Oberdorfer (1998) claim that the changes
in US policies occurred in 1983, before Gorbachev became leader of the Soviet
Union. Fitzgerald (2000) and Michael Cox (1990) attribute Reagan's shift to domestic politics and the fallout from the Iran–Contra affair. In contrast to the Reagan
victory school's emphasis on the hardline policies of Reagan's first term, critics like
Brown (1996, forthcoming) and Garthoff (1994b, forthcoming) praise the Reagan
of 1985–8 for "his willingness to enter into serious negotiations and treat the Soviet
leader more as a partner than an enemy" (Brown, forthcoming).

Although the end of the Cold War has brought an outpouring of memoirs by participants and the opening of a vast amount of formerly unavailable archival records
on Soviet foreign policy, it is still difficult to discern Soviet motives with certainty.
Gaddis (1997) and like-minded scholars have seized on recently released Soviet and
other communist records to argue that the foreign policy of the Soviet Union and
other communist regimes was ideologically motivated and aggressively insecure. (For
a discussion of Gaddis's work, see chapter 21.) Wohlforth (1997) and others have
argued that available documents are too limited and ambiguous to draw such sweeping conclusions. As a result, the sources of Soviet conduct, to echo the title of George
Kennan's famous essay, remain a contested issue.

While scholars like Gaddis still see Stalin and his successors as incorrigible ideologues and expansionists, others question the long-assumed links between the Soviet
Union's repressive internal regime and Soviet foreign policy. Michael MccGwire
(1991), Nation (1992), and David Holloway (1994), for example, highlight such
factors as Russian history and geography, bureaucratic differences within the Soviet
decisionmaking elite, and the security requirements arising from the Soviet Union's
unique geopolitical position. Geoffrey Roberts (1999), Vladislav Zubok and

Constantine Pleshakov (1996), Bennett (1999), and Mark Kramer (1999) have taken closer and more nuanced looks at Soviet ideology and operational beliefs and the precise nature of their impact on Soviet foreign policy.

While there is no consensus alternative view, many scholars have stressed what international relations scholars call the security dilemma, which argues that actions taken by one nation for its security can easily be construed by its adversary as threatening and lead to countermeasures which further reduce security for both sides. Drawing on this insight, MccGwire (1991) and Richard Ned Lebow and Janice Gross Stein (1994) argue that the US policies of containment and deterrence were part of the problem rather than the solution because they increased Soviet insecurity and led to Soviet counteractions. Although the security dilemma affected the United States as well as the Soviet Union, it had especially stark implications for the Soviets. Most of the measures the Soviets adopted to improve their security provoked countermeasures by the more powerful United States and its allies that preserved or increased Western supremacy and thus diminished Soviet security. Seen in this light, the Cold War ended when Soviet leaders consciously took steps to redefine their security requirements and objectives in ways that would allow them to escape the constraints of the security dilemma.

Focusing solely or primarily on Soviet policies and actions distorts the history of the Cold War and its end. As Melvyn Leffler (2000) has noted, the Cold War was a product of interaction. His pioneering work (1984, 1992) stresses the importance of a global conception of US national security interests that emerged during World War II and dominated US policy throughout the Cold War. US leaders sought to prevent any power or coalition of powers from dominating Europe and/or Asia, to maintain US strategic supremacy, to fashion an international economic environment open to US trade and investment, and to maintain the integration of the third world in the world economy in an era of decolonization and national liberation. By the end of the Cold War, the United States had added maintaining access to the oil resources of the Persian Gulf to its list of vital interests.

This expansive definition of US interests clashed with Soviet security concerns and resulted in the Soviets taking counteractions to protect their security. This pattern of action and counteraction was a key dynamic of the Cold War. For example, US efforts to reconstruct and reform the world economy and to maintain a favorable balance of power in Europe and Asia involved the rebuilding of Germany and Japan, prospects the Soviets viewed with great concern. The Soviets responded by tightening their control of Eastern Europe. Similarly, a key element in US containment policy, the strategy of extended deterrence, was predicated on overall US strategic superiority. According to this view, the function of US strategic forces was not only to deter a Soviet attack on the United States, but also to deter possible Soviet advances elsewhere in the world. US strategists believed that strategic superiority was needed to compensate for assumed Soviet conventional superiority in Europe and to discourage Soviet "adventurism" in the third world. Soviet strategists believed that strategic parity was necessary to discourage an attack on the Soviet Union, and the Soviets tried to match each US advance.

The recognition that US policies and actions contributed to Cold War tensions leads to very different explanations for the origins, persistence, and end of the Cold War. Evangelista (1999) and others argue that the Western policies that contributed the most to the end of the Cold War were those such as Ostpolitik, détente, and the actions of Western peace activists that reduced Soviet anxieties. Similarly, Daniel Deudney and G. John Ikenberry (1991) argue that the "benign" nature of US power, especially compared to Imperial and Nazi Germany, and possession of nuclear weapons gave Soviet leaders the confidence that their basic security needs would be respected even as their power declined. In addition, Zubok (2000) and Snyder (1987–8) point to the passing of the generation of Soviet leaders that had most directly experienced the horrors of World War II, and consequently were almost obsessively concerned with conventional definitions of security. Finally, Leffler (2000) argues that Western successes in reforming capitalism, ending colonialism, combating racism, and avoiding another depression and further fratricidal wars were more important factors in "winning" the Cold War than policies that built up Western military power in order to contain Soviet power and influence.

Sources

The end of the Cold War is replete with ironies, not the least of which is that historians now have available, at least on the Soviet side, more primary sources on the end than on the beginning or the middle of the Cold War. In fact, on some topics, there are more high-level Soviet than US documents available. Ordinarily, scholars have to wait twenty or thirty years before the archives open, at which point most of the witnesses who could provide context, interpretation, affirmation, or refutation of the documents have passed from the scene. But the epochal transformations that centered around the year 1989 brought new, more open political systems to Eastern Europe and the former Soviet Union, not to mention the disappearance of an entire country, East Germany. Enterprising journalists, scholars, former political prisoners, and former officials themselves rushed to open the files, excavate the archives, debate the meanings, and shrink the elapsed time between journalism and history.

This cornucopia of primary sources has reached the public record under a variety of auspices. Much is still missing, and what has been released has often been influenced by political calculations. The greatest bonanzas have come precisely in those countries whose transitions (or "refolutions," in the incisive phrase of Timothy Garton Ash) led the way to the collapse of communism in 1989 – Poland, Hungary, the Czech Republic, and the former East Germany. The Central European University is bringing out in English a series of four volumes compiling the most important of the new primary sources from communist files on the end of the Cold War (one on the superpowers, and one each on Poland, Hungary, and Czechoslovakia). Similarly, the Cold War International History Project at the Woodrow Wilson International Center for Scholars in Washington, DC, regularly publishes selections from these new sources. But even combined, these collections barely skim the surface.

If there is a single language for aspiring graduate students to learn that would open the greatest variety of primary sources on the end of the Cold War, it would be German. The most open archive in the world today of recent, high-level political and national security documents, ironically enough, is that of the former East German Communist Party (the Socialist Unity Party, known by its German initials, SED). In the interregnum between the fall of the Berlin Wall in November 1989 and the reunification of Germany in October 1990, the younger generation of reform communists curried public favor by opening the SED files through 1989 for researchers, thus distancing themselves from and discrediting their elders. Also during this time, East German protesters stormed various headquarters buildings of the secret police, the Stasi, to halt the shredding and destruction of files, and won the East German parliament's approval for an independent authority to hold these files and make them public.

After reunification, when Chancellor Helmut Kohl's government attempted to close the SED and Stasi files under the West German thirty-year rule, the Bundestag's deputies from the East forced Kohl to retreat – not, however, before he succeeded in sequestering the East German Foreign Ministry files. Kohl apparently did not apply the thirty-year rule to his own activities, since in 1998 his Interior Ministry's Bundesarchiv produced a massive 1,667-page documentary volume on the reunification process in 1989 and 1990 (Kusters and Hoffmann, 1998), with Kohl as the protagonist in dozens of verbatim memoranda of conversations with every world leader from Gorbachev and Bush to Lee Yuan Kew of Singapore.

The East German military files are also open at the archives in Freiburg, and include a complete run of the Warsaw Pact meeting minutes for the defense ministers and the political coordinating committee from 1955 through 1991. Despite the extraordinary detail captured by the East German note takers, the careful researcher will note a German-centricity to these materials that requires balancing by comparing them with the records of other Pact member countries. An international consortium of scholars has established the Parallel History Project on NATO and the Warsaw Pact, which has published a number of revelations including a detailed set of Bulgarian documents on the end of the Cold War (see the PHP website: http://www.isn.ethz.ch/php).

While German openness is largely a function of the disappearance of the GDR, the plethora of primary sources now available in Poland, Hungary, and the Czech Republic testifies to the pioneering work of former dissidents turned scholars. In Warsaw, various intellectuals affiliated with Solidarity established a new institute of the Polish Academy of Sciences, the Institute of Political Studies (ISP), to study the recent past and the present. In addition, an independent authority, the National Institute of Remembrance, was established to hold, analyze, and release the secret police files. The ISP has reconstituted from the personal recollections of former nomenklatura the files that were destroyed by the Communist Party as it gave up power, including a large collection of Politburo records. In addition ISP scholars and former Interior Ministry officials have compiled and published the complete transcripts of the Roundtable negotiations and the secret meetings at Magdalenka that set up the 1989 elections; and the "Karta" archives have opened the complete records of the Solidarity movement from 1980 through 1989.

In Budapest, veterans of the 1956 Hungarian revolution organized the 1956 Institute in the late 1980s to open that censored history and by so doing ease the transition out of communism. Scholars associated with the Institute and Hungary's National Archives have published an extraordinary array of primary sources on the end of the Cold War. For example, they have obtained, annotated, and published the complete series of minutes from the Hungarian Socialist Workers Party central committee during 1989, and the complete transcripts of the Hungarian Roundtable talks between the Party and the opposition during 1989. In addition, they have obtained the declassification of the Party Politburo minutes for the entire communist period.

In Prague, Charter 77 activists came back in 1989 to run the Czech Academy of Sciences' Institute for Contemporary History and to move back to Prague the extensive samizdat collections maintained outside the country since at least the Soviet invasion in 1968. These scholars have published seven volumes of sources on 1989, and have compiled the complete archive of the opposition groups Civic Forum (Czech) and People Against Violence (Slovak), including the audio recordings of their closed sessions during the tumultuous days of the Velvet Revolution in November 1989. An edited collection of English-language transcripts of these recordings is currently in preparation by President Havel's long-time translator, Paul Wilson. Also available to scholars are the complete stenographic minutes of the Czechoslovak Communist Party central committee meetings.

Primary source availability is much more spotty in Moscow. The "golden age" of archival openness in the former Soviet Union in 1992–3 was short-lived. The most egregious withdrawal from the public record consists of the telegram and cable traffic of the Soviet Foreign Ministry, now completely closed for the dubious reason that releasing the texts would allow the codes to be broken (this has not actually been an issue since the adoption of one-time code pads in the late 1930s). Also, the Kremlin archive of Politburo decisionmaking from Lenin through Gorbachev remains under the Russian President's direct control and closed to all but a few favored and government-sponsored researchers. Some remnants of the golden age may be found in the Chadwyck-Healey/Hoover Institution microfilm series, especially in "Fond 89," the court record of the trial of the Soviet Communist Party before the Constitutional Court in 1992. This particular collection has become a grab-bag of selective releases since 1992 on topics like the Soviet invasion of Czechoslovakia in 1968 or noninvasion of Poland in 1980–1.

One of the few archival bright spots in Moscow is the Gorbachev Foundation, whose archivist and senior staff have successfully opened their copies of much of the most important primary source material on the Gorbachev period. For example, Anatoly Chernyaev, Gorbachev's top foreign policy aide from February 1986 through 1991, has generously opened to researchers his notes of Politburo sessions and all of Gorbachev's meetings with foreign heads of state. The Foundation also plans to publish a complete set of the Politburo minutes of Gorbachev's tenure, and has already published minutes of Gorbachev's negotiations with the United States, including the lengthy minutes of the historic Reykjavik summit with Ronald Reagan in 1986.

The primary sources available in English are also enormous. Freedom of Information Act (FOIA) requests by the National Security Archive have produced declassification of thousands of pages of the US Embassy cables reporting on the revolutions of 1989 as well as the briefing books prepared for Secretary of State George Shultz for each of his meetings with top Soviet officials. The interest of Reagan acolytes and former officials in proving that Reagan's policies "won" the Cold War has combined with FOIA requests from openness advocates to obtain declassification of tens of thousands of pages on US–Soviet relations now available in the Ronald Reagan Presidential Library. Vociferous criticism by prominent officials like Senator Daniel Patrick Moynihan of the Central Intelligence Agency (CIA) for missing the coming collapse of communism has resulted in the unprecedented release by the CIA of 95,000 pages of its intelligence analysis on the Soviet Union. These documents undercut the critics by providing a more nuanced and balanced portrait of the CIA's successes and failures at the end of the Cold War.

This plethora of primary documentation also allows scholars to use with much greater confidence the outpourings of memoirs from former officials, veterans, and eyewitnesses to the events. Ordinarily, of course, such memoirs must be taken with grains if not entire shakers of salt, given the self-serving rationalizations endemic to the genre. Moreover, memoirs, like oral history, are subject to "contamination," whereby a participant's memories of decisions and events have been altered by subsequent events and experiences, and even by reading secondary accounts. Placed alongside the actual transcripts of the meetings described or the actual texts of the documents alluded to, the memoirs no longer have to be relied on for evidentiary value, but rather may be mined more appropriately for the perceptions, atmospherics, and context that only eyewitnesses and participants can provide.

Almost every leader, foreign minister, and top national security aide involved in the end of the Cold War has felt the need to unburden themselves of what they did and saw at the highest levels; so much so, in fact, that some of the best books now available on the period (for example, Fitzgerald, 2000) have constructed their narratives almost exclusively from comparing and contrasting the various memoir volumes. For a relatively complete list of the most useful memoirs, see the bibliography appended to this essay. In addition, Michael Ellman and Vladimir Kontorovich (1997) list over seventy Russian memoirs. The best memoir from the Soviet side is Anatoly Chernyaev's *My Six Years With Gorbachev*, which presents an unvarnished and often critical portrait of Gorbachev's actions, and of the author's own. On the US side, the best memoir remains Jack F. Matlock's *Autopsy On an Empire*, which ranges far beyond the subtitle, *The American Ambassador's Account of the Collapse of the Soviet Union*, to cover the entire period of Reagan and Bush policymaking at the end of the Cold War.

In addition to the primary sources and the voluminous memoir literature, several oral history projects have added new data to the available sources. Princeton University has hosted two major conferences around the tenures of alumni George Shultz and James Baker as Secretaries of State (Wohlforth, 1996, forthcoming); the Russian Academy of Sciences' Institute of Universal History sponsored two separate interview projects, one focused on Gorbachev aides and the other focused on Gorbachev critics and the hardliners who led the August 1991 attempted putsch. In the realm of critical oral history, in which the veterans debate with each other, with scholars, and with the documents, Brown University's Watson Institute hosted a major gathering in 1998 including key arms control negotiators from both sides of the end of the Cold War; Ohio State University's Mershon Institute hosted an additional conference with hardliners in Moscow in 1999; and the National Security Archive in 1998 brought together key US and Soviet officials at the Musgrove conference center in Georgia, and followed up in 1999 with conferences in Warsaw, Budapest, and Prague co-organized with the Institute for Political Studies, the 1956 Institute, and the Institute for Contemporary History, respectively.

Even in the midst of this cornucopia of sources, much is still missing. Each of the communist regimes in Eastern Europe, and no doubt in Moscow as well, managed to cull, edit, and destroy some of its documentary record before abandoning power – the most prominent examples being General Jaruzelski's destruction of the Politburo record in Poland and the East German spy chief Markus Wolf's destruction of the GDR's foreign intelligence files. In Romania and Bulgaria, where the transition was protracted (in Romania, the post-communists held power until 1996), scholars are convinced that the surviving files have long since been weeded.

Probably the most important missing material is still classified within the CIA, the KGB, and each side's intelligence apparatus. It is still a mystery, for example, what the KGB was actually up to in each of the Eastern European countries during their revolutions, particularly in the case of the violent collapse of the Ceausescu dictatorship in Romania. Likewise, the CIA's covert operators have been eager to claim credit for the success of Solidarity in Poland (see Schweizer, 1994), but have denied any release of documentation on their role either in Poland or elsewhere in Eastern Europe. Finally, neither side has released its signals intercepts of the other's communications during the end of the Cold War.

Scholars may take some consolation in the fact that, while there will doubtless be future volumes that focus on the role of intelligence in the end of the Cold War, these sources are not likely to revise substantially the history currently being written on the basis of the primary source flood described above. This reality stands in contrast to that of World War II, where we now know that Enigma and Ultra and the other code-breaking successes of the Allies played major roles in the decisions at the highest levels. For the end of the Cold War, however, we know from the transcripts of meetings at the highest levels, summits, politburos, and roundtables, how little the raw intelligence seems to have come up for discussion (although it may well have informed the top leaders' decisions and ideas more than we can tell now), and how little the surveillance capabilities of the communist states seem to have availed them in their final throes. Indeed, in the case of East Germany, it may well have been exactly the overload of surveillance information, a kind of arteriosclerosis, that helped prevent timely intervention by the Stasi to prevent the Party's collapse.

The ratio of sources to historians working on them is probably higher for the end of the Cold War than for any other period since World War II. Despite this richness, different philosophical and methodological approaches, as well as different political beliefs and commitments, will continue to produce differing explanations for the end of the Cold War. Nevertheless, as Wohlforth and Brooks (forthcoming) point out, "in the final analysis no theory or analytical framework can substitute for careful empirical research; and no argument about the meaning of the end of the Cold War for policy and theory that is unsupported by such research will stand the test of time."

REFERENCES

Arkin, William: "The Buildup That Wasn't," *Bulletin of the Atomic Scientists* (January/February 1989): 6–10.

Bennett, Andrew: *Condemned to Repetition: The Rise, Fall, and Reprise of Soviet-Russian Military Interventionism, 1976–1996* (Cambridge, Mass.: MIT Press, 1999).

Bennett, Andrew: "Trust Busting Out All Over: The Soviet Side of German Unification," in William C. Wohlforth (ed.), *Cold War Endgame: Oral History, Analysis, Debates* (University Park, Pa.: Pennsylvania State University Press, forthcoming).

Blanton, Thomas S.: "When Did the Cold War End?" *Cold War International History Project Bulletin*, 10 (March 1998): 184–91.

Bowker, Mike and Williams, Phil: *Superpower Détente: A Reappraisal* (London: Sage Publications, 1988).

Brooks, Stephen G. and Wohlforth, William C.: "Power, Globalization, and the End of the Cold War: Reevaluating a Landmark Case for Ideas," *International Security*, 25 (Winter 2000–1): 5–33.

Brown, Archie: *The Gorbachev Factor* (Oxford: Oxford University Press, 1996).

Brown, Archie: "Gorbachev and the End of the Cold War," in Richard K. Herrmann and Richard Ned Lebow (eds.), *Learning from the Cold War* (forthcoming).

Chernyaev, Anatoly S.: *My Six Years with Gorbachev*, trans. and ed. Robert D. English and Elizabeth Tucker (University Park, Pa.: Pennsylvania State University Press, 2000).

Cordovez, Diego and Harrison, Selig: *Out of Afghanistan: The Inside Story of the Soviet Withdrawal* (New York: Oxford University Press, 1995).

Cox, Michael: "Whatever Happened to the 'Second' Cold War? Soviet–American Relations: 1980–1988," *Review of International Studies*, 16 (1990): 155–72.

Daniels, Robert V.: *The End of the Communist Revolution* (London: Routledge, 1993).

Davis, James A. and Wohlforth, William C.: "German Unification," in Richard K. Herrmann and Richard Ned Lebow (eds.), *Learning from the Cold War* (forthcoming).

Deudney, Daniel and Ikenberry, G. John: "Soviet Reform and the End of the Cold War: Explaining Large-Scale Historical Change," *Review of International Studies*, 17 (July 1991): 225–50.

Ellman, Michael and Kontorovich, Vladimir: "The Collapse of the Soviet System and the Memoir Literature," *Europe–Asia Studies*, 49 (March 1997): 259–79.

English, Robert D.: "Sources, Methods, and Competing Perspectives on the End of the Cold War," *Diplomatic History*, 21 (Spring 1997): 283–94.

English, Robert D.: *Russia and the Idea of the West: Gorbachev, Intellectuals, and the End of the Cold War* (New York: Columbia University Press, 2000).

English, Robert D.: "The Road(s) Not Taken: Causality and Contingency in Analysis of the Cold War's End," in William C. Wohlforth (ed.), *Cold War Endgame: Oral History, Analysis, Debates* (University Park, Pa.: Pennsylvania State University Press, forthcoming).

Evangelista, Matthew: *Unarmed Forces: The Transnational Movement to End the Cold War* (Ithaca, NY: Cornell University Press, 1999).

Firth, Noel and Noren, James H.: *Soviet Defense Spending: A History of CIA Estimates, 1950–1990* (College Station: Texas A&M University Press, 1998).

Fischer, Benjamin B.: "A Cold War Conundrum: The 1983 Soviet War Scare" (Center for the Study of Intelligence Monograph, Washington, DC: Central Intelligence Agency, 1997).

Fischer, Beth A.: *The Reagan Reversal: Foreign Policy and the End of the Cold War* (Columbia: University of Missouri Press, 1997).

Fitzgerald, Frances: *Way Out There in the Blue: Reagan, Star Wars, and the End of the Cold War* (New York: Simon and Schuster, 2000).

Gaddis, John Lewis: "Hanging Tough Paid Off," *Bulletin of the Atomic Scientists*, 45 (January–February 1989): 11–14.

Gaddis, John Lewis: *We Now Know: Rethinking Cold War History* (New York: Oxford University Press, 1997).

Garthoff, Raymond L.: *Détente and Confrontation: American–Soviet Relations from Nixon to Reagan* (Washington, DC: Brookings Institution, 1985; rev. ed., 1994a).

Garthoff, Raymond L.: *The Great Transition: American–Soviet Relations and the End of the Cold War* (Washington, DC: Brookings Institution, 1994b).

Garthoff, Raymond L.: "Process and Outcome," in Richard K. Herrmann and Richard Ned Lebow (eds.), *Learning from the Cold War* (forthcoming).

Gleijeses, Piero: "Havana's Policy in Africa, 1959–1976: New Evidence from the Cuban Archives," *Cold War International History Project Bulletin*, 8–9 (Winter 1996–7): 5–18.

Herrmann, Richard K.: "Regional Conflicts as Turning Points: The Soviet and American Withdrawal from Afghanistan, Angola, and Nicaragua," in Richard K. Herrmann and Richard Ned Lebow (eds.), *Learning from the Cold War* (forthcoming).

Herrmann, Richard K. and Lebow, Richard Ned, eds.: *Learning from the Cold War* (forthcoming).

Holloway, David: *Stalin and the Bomb: The Soviet Union and Atomic Energy, 1939–56* (New Haven, Conn.: Yale University Press, 1994).

Hough, Jerry F.: *Democratization and Revolution in the USSR, 1985–1991* (Washington, DC: Brookings Institution, 1997).

Kotz, David and Weir, Fred: *Revolution from Above: The Demise of the Soviet System* (London: Routledge, 1997).

Kramer, Mark: "Ideology and the Cold War," *Review of International Studies*, 25 (October 1999): 539–76.

Kusters, Hans Jürgen and Hoffmann, Daniel, eds.: *Deutsche Einheit: Sonderedition aus den Akten des Bundeskanzleramtes 1989–90* (Munich: R. Oldenbourg, 1998).

Lane, David: *The Rise and Fall of State Socialism: Industrial Society and the Socialist State* (Cambridge: Polity Press, 1996).

Lebow, Richard Ned: "Social Science, History, and the Cold War: Pushing the Conceptual Envelope," in Odd Arne Westad (ed.), *Reviewing the Cold War: Approaches, Interpretations, Theory* (London: Frank Cass, 2000), 103–25.

Lebow, Richard Ned and Stein, Janice Gross: *We All Lost the Cold War* (Princeton, NJ: Princeton University Press, 1994).

Leffler, Melvyn P.: "The American Conception of National Security and the Origins of the Cold War," *American Historical Review*, 89 (April 1984): 346–81.

Leffler, Melvyn P.: *A Preponderance of Power: National Security, the Truman Administration, and the Cold War* (Stanford, Calif.: Stanford University Press, 1992).

Leffler, Melvyn P.: "Bringing it Together: The Parts and the Whole," in Odd Arne Westad (ed.), *Reviewing the Cold War: Approaches, Interpretations, Theory* (London: Frank Cass, 2000), 43–63.

LeoGrande, William M.: *Our Own Backyard: The United States in Central America, 1977–1992* (Chapel Hill: University of North Carolina Press, 2000).

Lévesque, Jacques: *The Enigma of 1989: The USSR and the Liberation of Eastern Europe* (Berkeley and Los Angeles: University of California Press, 1997).

Lévesque, Jacques: "The Emancipation of Eastern Europe," in Richard K. Herrmann and Richard Ned Lebow (eds.), *Learning from the Cold War* (forthcoming).

Lundestad, Geir: " 'Imperial Overstretch,' Mikhail Gorbachev, and the End of the Cold War," *Cold War History*, 1 (August 2000): 1–20.

MacEachin, Douglas J.: "CIA Assessments of the Soviet Union: The Record Versus the Charges" (Center for the Study of Intelligence Monograph, Washington, DC: Central Intelligence Agency, 1996).

MccGwire, Michael: *Perestroika and Soviet National Security* (Washington, DC: Brookings Institution, 1991).

McMahon, Robert J.: "Making Sense of American Foreign Policy in the Reagan Years," *Diplomatic History*, 19 (Spring 1995): 367–84.

Mastny, Vojtech: "The Soviet Non-Invasion of Poland in 1980–81 and the End of the Cold War" (Cold War International History Project Working Paper 23, Washington, DC: Woodrow Wilson Center, 1998).

Matlock, Jr., Jack F.: *Autopsy On an Empire: The American Ambassador's Account of the Collapse of the Soviet Union* (New York: Random House, 1995).

Mendelson, Sarah: *Changing Course: Ideas, Politics, and the Soviet Withdrawal from Afghanistan* (Princeton, NJ: Princeton University Press, 1998).

Nation, R. Craig: *Black Earth, Red Star: A History of Soviet Security Policy, 1917–1991* (Ithaca, NY: Cornell University Press, 1992).

"New Evidence on the Polish Crisis 1980–1981," *Cold War International History Project Bulletin*, 11 (Winter 1998): 1–133.

Oberdorfer, Don: *From the Cold War to the New Era: The United States and the Soviet Union, 1983–1991* (Baltimore: Johns Hopkins University Press, 1998).

Painter, David S.: "International Oil and National Security," *Daedalus*, 120 (Fall 1991): 183–206.

Pateman, Robert G.: "Reagan, Gorbachev, and the Emergence of 'New Political Thinking,'" *Review of International Studies*, 25 (October 1999): 577–601.

Pipes, Richard: "Misinterpreting the Cold War: The Hard-Liners Had It Right," *Foreign Affairs*, 74 (January–February 1995): 154–60.

Roberts, Geoffrey: *The Soviet Union in World Politics: Coexistence, Revolution and Cold War, 1945–1991* (London: Routledge, 1999).

Schweizer, Peter: *Victory: The Reagan Administration's Secret Strategy that Hastened the Collapse of the Soviet Union* (New York: Atlantic Monthly Press, 1994).

Schweizer, Peter, ed.: *The Fall of the Berlin Wall: Reassessing the Causes and Consequences of the End of the Cold War* (Stanford, Calif.: Hoover Institution Press, 2000).

Shultz, George P.: *Turmoil and Triumph: My Years as Secretary of State* (New York: Scribner's, 1993).

Snel, Gerard: "'A (More) Defensive Strategy': The Reconceptualization of Soviet Conventional Strategy in the 1980s," *Europe–Asia Studies*, 50 (March 1998): 205–39.

Snyder, Jack: "The Gorbachev Revolution: The Waning of Soviet Expansionism?" *International Security*, 12 (Winter 1987–8): 93–131.

Stone, Randall: *Satellites and Commissars: Strategy and Conflict in the Politics of Soviet-Bloc Trade* (Princeton, NJ: Princeton University Press, 1996).

Westad, Odd Arne: "Moscow and the Angolan Crisis, 1974–1976: A New Pattern of Intervention," *Cold War International History Project Bulletin*, 8–9 (Winter 1996–7): 21–32.

Westad, Odd Arne, ed.: *The Fall of Détente: Soviet–American Relations During the Carter Years* (Oslo: Scandinavian University Press, 1997).

Winik, Jay: *On the Brink: The Dramatic Behind the Scenes Saga of the Reagan Era and the Men and Women Who Won the Cold War* (New York: Simon and Schuster, 1996).

Wohlforth, William C., ed.: *Witnesses to the End of the Cold War* (Baltimore: Johns Hopkins University Press, 1996).

Wohlforth, William C.: "New Evidence on Moscow's Cold War: Ambiguity in Search of Theory," *Diplomatic History*, 21 (Spring 1997): 229–42.

Wohlforth, William C.: *Cold War Endgame: Oral History, Analysis, Debates* (University Park, Pa: Pennsylvania State University Press, forthcoming).

Wohlforth, William C. and Brooks, Stephen G.: "Economic Constraints and the End of the Cold War," in William C. Wohlforth (ed.), *Cold War Endgame: Oral History, Analysis, Debates* (University Park, Pa: Pennsylvania State University Press, forthcoming).

Zubok, Vladislav: "Why Did the Cold War End in 1989? Explanations of 'The Turn,'" in Odd Arne Westad (ed.), *Reviewing the Cold War: Approaches, Interpretations, Theory* (London: Frank Cass, 2000), 343–67.

Zubok, Vladislav and Pleshakov, Constantine: *Inside the Kremlin's Cold War: From Stalin to Khrushchev* (Cambridge, Mass.: Harvard University Press, 1996).

FURTHER READING

Video

British Broadcasting Company: *The Romanian Revolution*. Broadcast December 16, 1995.
Brook Lapping Productions: *The Reagan Agenda – Star Wars*.
CNN and Jeremy Isaacs Productions: *Cold War*. Episodes 22 ("Star Wars, 1980–1988"), 23 ("The Wall Comes Down, 1989"), and 24 ("Conclusions, 1989–1991").

On-line

Blanton, Thomas S., ed.: *The Revolutions of 1989: New Documents from Soviet/East Europe Archives Reveal Why There Was No Crackdown During the Collapse of Communism in Eastern Europe* (National Security Archive Electronic Briefing Book No. 22, Washington, DC: National Security Archive, 1999). www.gwu.edu/~nsarchiv/NSAEBB/NSAEBB22/index.html.
CNN.com/COLD WAR.
Cold War International History Project, Woodrow Wilson International Center for Scholars: www.cwihp.si.edu.
Digital National Security Archive: www.chadwyck.com/dnsa.
Domber, Gregory, ed.: *Solidarity's Coming Victory: Big or Too Big: Poland's Revolution as Seen from the U.S. Embassy* (National Security Archive Electronic Briefing Book No. 42). www.gwu.edu/~nsarchiv/NSAEBB/NSAEBB42/index.html.
Mastny, Vojtech, ed.: Did NATO Win the Cold War? (National Security Archive Electronic Briefing Book No. 14). www.gwu.edu/~nsarchiv/NSAEBB/NSAEBB14/index.html.

Documentary Collections

Fischer, Benjamin B., ed.: *At Cold War's End: U.S. Intelligence on the Soviet Union and Eastern Europe, 1989–1991* (Washington, DC: Central Intelligence Agency, 1999).
Haines, Gerald K. and Leggett, Robert E., eds.: *CIA's Analysis of the Soviet Union, 1947–91* (Washington, DC: Central Intelligence Agency, 2001).
Kornbluh, Peter and Byrne, Malcolm, eds.: *The Iran–Contra Scandal: The Declassified History* (New York: New Press, 1993).
Simpson, Christopher, ed.: *Presidential Directives: National Security During the Reagan–Bush Years: The Declassified History of U.S. Political and Military Policy, 1981–1991* (Boulder, Colo.: Westview Press, 1994).

Memoirs (US)

Baker, III, James A.: *The Politics of Diplomacy: Revolution, War, and Peace, 1989–1992* (New York: G. P. Putnam's Sons, 1995).
Bush, George and Scowcroft, Brent: *A World Transformed* (New York: Alfred A. Knopf, 1999).
Crocker, Chester A.: *High Noon in Southern Africa: Making Peace in a Rough Neighborhood* (New York: W. W. Norton, 1993).
Gates, Robert M.: *From the Shadows: The Ultimate Insider's Story of Five Presidents and How They Won the Cold War* (New York: Simon and Schuster, 1997).
Haig, Jr., Alexander M.: *Caveat: Realism, Reagan, and Foreign Policy* (New York: Macmillan, 1984).
MacFarlane, Robert C., with Zofia Smardz: *Special Trust* (New York: Cadell and Davies, 1994).
Meese, III, Edwin: *With Reagan: The Inside Story* (Washington, DC: Regnery Gateway, 1992).

Reagan, Ronald: *An American Life* (New York: Simon and Schuster, 1990).
Weinberger, Caspar W.: *Fighting for Peace: Seven Critical Years in the Pentagon* (New York: Warner Books, 1990).

Memoirs (Soviet)

Dobrynin, Anatoly: *In Confidence: Moscow's Ambassador to America's Six Cold War Presidents* (New York: Times Books, 1995).
Gorbachev, Mikhail: *Memoirs* (New York: Doubleday, 1995).
Ligachev, Yegor: *Inside Gorbachev's Kremlin: The Memoirs of Yegor Ligachev* (Boulder, Colo.: Westview Press, 1996).
Palazchenko, Pavel: *My Years With Gorbachev and Shevardnadze: The Memoir of a Soviet Interpreter* (University Park, Pa.: Pennsylvania State University Press, 1997).
Shevardnadze, Eduard: *The Future Belongs to Freedom* (New York: Free Press, 1991).

Secondary Sources

Beschloss, Michael and Talbott, Strobe: *At the Highest Levels: The Inside Story of the End of the Cold War* (Boston: Little, Brown, 1993).
Hogan, Michael J., ed.: *The End of the Cold War: Its Meaning and Implications* (New York: Cambridge University Press, 1992).
Lebow, Richard Ned and Risse-Kappen, Thomas, eds.: *International Relations Theory and the End of the Cold War* (New York: Columbia University Press, 1995).
Painter, David S.: *The Cold War: An International History* (London: Routledge, 1999).
Westad, Odd Arne, ed.: *Reviewing the Cold War: Approaches, Interpretations, Theory* (London: Frank Cass, 2000).

CHAPTER TWENTY-SIX

From the "Atomic Age" to the "Anti-Nuclear Age": Nuclear Energy in Politics, Diplomacy, and Culture

J. SAMUEL WALKER

Within a short time after the United States bombed the Japanese cities of Hiroshima and Nagasaki with nuclear weapons in August 1945, many observers labeled the coming era as the "atomic age." They also expressed deep ambivalence about the potential consequences – military, diplomatic, political, economic, and cultural – that might accompany the scientific achievement of nuclear fission. Their gratitude that the bombs had brought a prompt end to the war in the Pacific was tempered by obvious uneasiness. "With the controlled splitting of the atom, humanity, already profoundly perplexed and disunited, was brought inescapably into a new age in which all things were split – and far from controlled," declared *Time* magazine in its first coverage of the bomb ("The Bomb," 1945, p. 19).

The dawn of the atomic age offered both an unprecedented threat and, perhaps, abundant promise. The threat was that the same weapons that forced the Japanese surrender could be used against the United States in future wars or could even destroy the world. The promise was that nuclear energy could be employed for peaceful applications that would improve the quality of life throughout the world, including power plants, treatments for cancer, and more fancifully, airplanes, trains, and automobiles. *Newsweek* told its readers that atomic energy could produce "a civilization which would make the comic-strip prophecies of Buck Rogers look obsolete" ("For the Future," 1945, p. 59). The atomic age began with a rush of mixed emotions and disquieting uncertainty. "The whole revelation of the fission of the atom has come with such a sudden thunderclap," commented the *New York Times* three days after Hiroshima, "that one is left bewildered and at a loss to know which of its many implications . . . may prove to be substantial and real, and which chimerical" ("Atomic Power," 1945, p. 20).

Although the term "atomic age" has commonly served since 1945 as a catch-all phrase to refer to the postwar world, its explanatory power is limited. The term itself was used as early as 1921 in *Science* magazine, but it remains an imprecise and inchoate concept. In some cases, it appears as a synonym for the "Cold War," and the influence of atomic weapons on the course of the decades-long confrontation between the United States and the Soviet Union was, by any standard, enormous.

Nevertheless, much of what happened during the Cold War – Soviet–American tensions, the division of Europe, rivalry in the developing world, arms competition, the space race, and intense fear of communism in the United States – could have and probably would have occurred if the atomic bomb had never been invented. Nuclear weapons made every international crisis a potentially terrifying event, but the "atomic age" remained a subset of the Cold War era. In this essay, "atomic age" refers to the ways in which the fears and the hopes about atomic energy that became prominent immediately after World War II played out in the ensuing decades. In keeping with the limited utility of the term, scholars have not provided an overall interpretive framework for the "atomic age." They have generally written about discrete topics relating to nuclear weapons and nuclear power, and used those topics to shed light on themes that were not strictly nuclear, such as the Cold War, détente, energy policies, the performances of different presidential administrations, and social and cultural developments.

The subject that has received the most attention and debate is President Harry S. Truman's decision to use atomic bombs against Japan. Immediately after the war, the American people overwhelmingly approved Truman's action, despite their misgivings about the long-term dangers that the bomb imposed. Strong popular support reflected the conviction that the atomic bombs had been essential to compel the Japanese surrender and end the war. A few critics questioned the need for and the morality of dropping the atomic bombs, but the influence of their arguments, at least initially, was slight. In later years, however, the question of whether the atomic bomb was needed to bring about a Japanese surrender at the earliest possible moment generated sharp debate among scholars.

The traditional interpretation, advanced by such scholars as Herbert Feis (1961), Robert H. Ferrell (1994), Robert James Maddox (1995), and Robert P. Newman (1995), was that the bomb was required to end the war promptly and prevent an invasion of Japan that would have caused hundreds of thousands of American casualties. It drew heavily on the explanations for the use of the bomb that Truman and his chief advisers offered. Writers who took this position asserted or implied that Truman faced a categorical choice between the bomb and an invasion that was forced on him by the refusal of the Japanese to surrender. In their view, the United States dropped the bomb primarily for military purposes – to shorten the war and save huge numbers of American lives.

The traditional interpretation was sharply disputed by scholars known as revisionists, including Gar Alperovitz (1965), Robert Jay Lifton and Greg Mitchell (1995), Ronald Takaki (1995), and Kai Bird and Lawrence Lifschultz (1998). The revisionist argument that Alperovitz offered in his controversial 1965 book gained credibility during the late 1960s and early 1970s as a part of increasing scholarly criticism of Truman's foreign policies. Revisionists contended that the bomb was not necessary for victory because the Japanese were so weak by the summer of 1945 that they were ready to quit the war on the sole condition that their emperor be retained. Revisionists further insisted that American policymakers were well aware of Japan's intentions. In their judgment, the United States used atomic weapons more for political than for military reasons, especially to intimidate the Soviet Union in the emerging Cold War.

The revisionist view made a considerable impact on scholarly accounts of Truman's decision, though few accepted it in unadulterated form. By the mid-1970s scholars had reached a general but hardly unanimous consensus that combined features of both the traditional and revisionist interpretations. It held that Truman used the bomb primarily for military reasons and secondarily for political ones. Scholars further concurred that Truman and his closest advisers were well aware of alternatives to the bomb that might have ended the war within a relatively short time, though their agreement did not extend to the more important question of whether the options would have been preferable to dropping the bomb.

After decades of research and debate, specialists on the subject had moved far beyond the traditional view that Truman's options for ending the war were either the bomb or an enormously costly invasion of Japan. They showed that the situation that faced Truman was vastly more complex. Their research and conclusions, however, were not widely known to the general public, which remained wedded to the traditional interpretation. The chasm between the mythological dogma that the public embraced and the findings of scholars who studied the documentary sources led to a bitter controversy when the Smithsonian Institution's National Air and Space Museum made plans in the early 1990s to present a major exhibit on the bomb and the end of World War II. Museum curators designed an exhibit that was intended both to commemorate the valor and sacrifices of American war veterans on the fiftieth anniversary of the end of the war and to reflect recent scholarly investigations on the use of the atomic bomb. By raising questions about the traditional interpretation of why the United States dropped the bomb, the original script for the exhibit set off a firestorm of protest. Critics claimed that the Smithsonian had adopted a revisionist perspective, which in their analyses usually meant any departure from the traditional position. Historians who defended the script pointed out that a large volume of historical evidence did not support a view that Truman faced a categorical choice between the bomb and an invasion. But their arguments made no discernible impact on those who objected to the script, and the Smithsonian, in an effort to still the controversy, sharply scaled back the exhibit.

Within a short time after the planned Enola Gay exhibit commanded national headlines, several scholars, including Barton J. Bernstein (1995), J. Samuel Walker (1997), Richard B. Frank (1999), and Herbert Bix (2000), published new studies that, without endorsing the discredited elements of the traditional view, pointed out serious flaws in the revisionist interpretation. They demonstrated major weaknesses in the most cherished revisionist contention – that Truman and his advisers knew that alternatives to the bomb, especially guaranteeing the status of the emperor, would end the war promptly on a basis satisfactory to the United States. They showed beyond reasonable doubt that the Japanese government had not decided to surrender and did not do so until after Hiroshima. The new studies also suggested, with varying but still high levels of certainty, that the available alternatives to the bomb would not have ended the war as quickly. The newer scholarship reaffirmed the broad consensus that had originally emerged in the 1970s, which held that neither the traditional nor the revisionist interpretation of Truman's decision to use the bomb was sound in its pure form.

Nevertheless, heated debate over specific issues continued. The issue that generated the most controversy between 1995 and 2000 was estimated American casualties for an invasion of Japan that military experts calculated in the summer of 1945. During the 1980s, newly opened documentary sources indicated that top military analysts had not predicted American casualties in the hundreds of thousands if a landing proved to be necessary. Supporters of the traditional view insisted that Truman received projections in the hundreds of thousands before he authorized dropping the bomb, while revisionists cited the smaller numbers as evidence that the bomb was unnecessary. Moderates who stood between the extremes pointed out that the tens of thousands of American deaths that military experts estimated before Hiroshima were very large numbers that in Truman's mind provided ample reason to use the bomb, even if the projections were far lower than he claimed after the war.

Much of the debate over the use of atomic bombs against Japan centered on counterfactual arguments, that is, judgments that were not based on hard evidence but on speculation about what might have happened. They included, for example: how long the war would have continued if the bomb had not been dropped; how many casualties American forces would have suffered if an invasion had occurred or even if the war had gone on for a few more weeks without an invasion; whether Japan would have responded favorably to an American offer to guarantee the status of the emperor before Hiroshima or whether such an offer would have prolonged the war; and whether any of the other alternatives to the use of the bomb would have ended the war as quickly in a way that was acceptable to the United States. Those questions go to the heart of the historiographical conflicts over Truman's decision, and although much important new evidence about the end of the war has opened over the past two decades, it cannot settle in a definitive way the debate over counterfactuals. The rich abundance of documentary sources on the use of the bomb shows that both the traditional and the revisionist interpretations are oversimplified, incomplete, and inadequate. But there still is ample room for disagreement among scholars, and the battle over the events that led to Hiroshima seems destined to carry on.

The nuclear arms race that followed quickly in the wake of Hiroshima and Nagasaki was a major component of the immense volume of literature on the origins of the Cold War. The scholarly debate over the Cold War that erupted in the 1960s focused on the question of whether the United States or the Soviet Union was primarily responsible for provoking it. In contrast to the traditional view that the US buildup of nuclear arms was necessary to contain Soviet expansion, critics suggested that the American monopoly of the bomb made it more aggressive, dogmatic, and imperious than it would otherwise have been. In that way the bomb was a major contributor, if not the leading cause, of the Cold War. The culmination of the emerging nuclear arms race was Truman's approval of a crash program to develop a hydrogen bomb in early 1950. The hydrogen bomb promised an explosive yield a thousand times greater than the comparatively primitive weapons that the United States employed against Japan. Success in designing and building a hydrogen bomb, which were not sure things, opened a new and more ominous phase of the growing nuclear competition between the world's superpowers.

The judgments that scholars made about Truman's nuclear weapons programs ranged, on the one hand, from resigned acceptance that he was forced to ensure American superiority to, on the other hand, condemnation that he deserved the bulk of the blame for the arms race. For most of the Cold War era, those positions were based on the information available from American sources. The collapse of the Soviet

Union made it possible for scholars to examine important Soviet documentary collections that previously had been tightly closed. The availability of Soviet sources, though far from comprehensive, placed the early Cold War and the beginning of the arms race in a new light. As David Holloway made clear, once the United States demonstrated the power of the atomic bomb, Stalin was determined to have his own. Stalin qualified as the first revisionist on why Truman used the bomb. Although nearly all scholars now agree that Truman dropped the bomb primarily to end the Pacific war as quickly as possible, Stalin immediately concluded that it was aimed at him. He regarded the bomb as a serious threat to the long-term position of the Soviet Union by distorting the balance of power. "Hiroshima has shaken the whole world," he reportedly remarked. "The balance has been destroyed" (Holloway, 1994, p. 132).

Given Stalin's reaction to the bomb, it appears that the arms race, at least in some form, was inevitable. The Soviets immediately launched a massive effort to build an atomic bomb, supported not only by their own cadre of able scientists but also by information that they had received from spies on the Manhattan Project. Their commitment to matching the atomic achievement of the United States made it improbable that they would have agreed to any meaningful limitations on developing nuclear weapons. There certainly was no chance that they would go along with the proposals that the United States offered. The Soviets tested their first atomic bomb in August 1949 and immediately accelerated their work on a hydrogen bomb.

Within a short time after the end of World War II, the principal feature of the atomic age was an increasingly perilous and terrifying nuclear arms race. When Dwight D. Eisenhower became president in January 1953, both the United States and the Soviet Union were well on their way to staggering increases in the size and power of their nuclear arsenals. Eisenhower's nuclear programs have received a great deal of attention, much of it framed within a context of his performance in the White House. In the early 1980s, several scholars, notably Robert A. Divine (1981), Fred I. Greenstein (1982), and Stephen E. Ambrose (1984), advanced the view that, contrary to earlier perceptions, Eisenhower was a strong, active, and capable leader who was fully in charge of the diplomatic policies of his administration. The so-called "Eisenhower revisionists" (who should not be confused with atomic bomb or Cold War revisionists) hailed the president for recognizing the dangers of the arms race and taking meaningful steps to curtail it.

Most scholars accepted the argument that Eisenhower was a forceful and skillful leader but many took issue with revisionist claims about his approach to nuclear arms. They pointed out that despite his abhorrence of the prospect of nuclear war, the size of the US nuclear arsenal increased astronomically under his administration. As David Alan Rosenberg (1983) demonstrated, for example, Eisenhower presided over the "origins of overkill" even as he sought ways to limit the arms buildup. Further, critics of the revisionist position, such as H. W. Brands (1989), Peter J. Roman (1995), and Jeremi Suri (1997), argued that whatever Eisenhower's intentions, he failed to slow the arms race, adopt a clear position on US nuclear strategy, or substantially improve relations with the Soviet Union.

During Eisenhower's presidency, another alarming aspect of the atomic age rose to prominence – radioactive fallout from atmospheric nuclear bomb testing. Initial reactions to the bombings of Hiroshima and Nagasaki focused on the force of the blasts rather than the effects of radiation. Knowledge of and concern about radiation gradually increased after the war, and, as a result of the atmospheric testing of atomic and hydrogen bombs, the public health risks of radioactive fallout became the source of a major scientific and political controversy. The magnitude of the risks of population exposure to low levels of radiation generated sustained and deepening public anxiety because bomb tests by the United States, the Soviet Union, and Great Britain produced radioactive fallout that spread to populated areas far from the sites of the explosions.

The US Atomic Energy Commission (AEC), which was responsible for conducting the American tests, insisted that the levels of radiation in fallout were too low to threaten public health significantly and that the risks of testing were less dangerous than losing ground to the Soviets in the arms race. Critics of the AEC contended that it underestimated the chances that fallout would cause increased rates of cancer, birth defects, and other afflictions. By moving radiation effects from scientific journals to a featured subject in the popular news media, the fallout debate greatly expanded public awareness of and concern about the hazards of low-level exposure. It also seriously damaged the credibility of the AEC because the agency's responsibilities for testing nuclear weapons made its evaluations of fallout risks highly suspect. The fallout controversy sharply elevated public fears of radiation and doubts about weapons testing, and in that way had an important impact on the atomic age. It has received some attention from scholars, including Robert A. Divine (1978), George T. Mazuzan and J. Samuel Walker (1984), Richard G. Hewlett and Jack M. Holl (1989), and Allan M. Winkler (1993), but perhaps less than it deserves.

When John F. Kennedy replaced Eisenhower as president, the nuclear arms race had taken on new and more dangerous dimensions because of the availability of ballistic missiles that could deliver warheads within a matter of minutes after launching. During the presidential campaign of 1960, Kennedy criticized the Eisenhower administration for creating a "missile gap" by allowing the Soviets to move ahead of the United States in missile development. There was indeed a missile gap, but contrary to Kennedy's assertions, it heavily favored the United States. After taking office, Kennedy still authorized the construction of new nuclear delivery systems – missiles, submarines, and bombers – that fueled the arms race, though he approved fewer than his military advisers sought. Both the United States and the Soviet Union strove to improve and enlarge their nuclear capabilities. In the summer of 1961, Soviet premier Nikita Khrushchev decided to stop observing a voluntary moratorium on atmospheric nuclear weapons testing. Kennedy reluctantly followed suit. The result was a series of tests that heightened already growing international tensions and renewed concern about the effects of fallout.

In a diplomatic climate of mutual fear and suspicion, the gravest crisis of the Cold War era erupted when Khrushchev decided to place nuclear missiles in Cuba. The Cuban Missile Crisis, which came closer to causing a nuclear war between the United States and the Soviet Union than any other event, has been the focus of enormous interest. Scholars offered a variety of evaluations of how it came about and how it was handled by the Kennedy administration. The first accounts of the missile crisis were laudatory, if not hagiographical, treatments of Kennedy's performance. Arthur M. Schlesinger, Jr. (1965, p. 841), for example, maintained that the president's response to Khrushchev's reckless venture was "so brilliantly controlled, so matchlessly calibrated, that [it] dazzled the world." By the early 1970s, however, critics of Kennedy's foreign policies, including Richard J. Walton (1972), Louise FitzSimons (1972), and Henry Fairlie (1973), had offered a considerably less favorable view of his actions. They suggested that at best he overreacted to the Soviet challenge, and at worst, caused the crisis by his efforts to oust Fidel Castro from power in Cuba. Those allegations received support later in the 1970s from revelations that the Kennedy administration, perhaps with the president's knowledge, had conspired to assassinate Castro.

The opening of new evidence from both US and Soviet sources, including oral histories and conferences in which former high-level officials of both nations recounted their experiences, provided a much more thorough and balanced view of the Cuban affair. Several studies that drew on the new sources, such as books by Raymond L. Garthoff (1989), Michael R. Beschloss (1991), Mark J. White (1997), and Aleksandr Fursenko and Timothy Naftali (1997), did not confirm the portrait of Kennedy as either a peerless hero or a malevolent villain. Scholars generally concluded that once the crisis began, both Kennedy and Khrushchev acted responsibly and prudently to avoid a nuclear war. Operating under tremendous pressure and bewildering uncertainty, they elected to seek a negotiated settlement to the crisis rather than opting for a military confrontation. Recent scholarship has demonstrated that despite the efforts of the two leaders, the situation could have spun out of control. One major revelation, for example, was that unbeknownst to American officials, the Soviets had placed several tactical nuclear warheads in Cuba (in addition to the strategic missile sites that the United States discovered). An American attack on Cuba, which was one option favored by Kennedy's more militant advisers, could have triggered a nuclear response that escalated into nuclear war.

The missile crisis continues to provide fertile ground for debate among scholars on a number of vital questions. They center on matters that include the motivations that led Khrushchev to send missiles to Cuba, the importance of Castro in initiating and sustaining the crisis, the influence of various considerations (especially domestic politics) that Kennedy and his advisers weighed in reaching decisions, and the role of diplomatic issues such as tensions over Berlin and the presence of American missiles in Turkey. Whatever conclusions scholars may reach on those issues, there is little question that the missile crisis convinced Kennedy and Khrushchev that they must try to reduce Cold War hostilities. In the wake of the Cuban face-off, both sought to ease ill-will. One significant result was the first nuclear arms control agreement, the Limited Test Ban Treaty of 1963. It prohibited nuclear weapons testing in the atmosphere and underwater by signatory nations. Although it did not terminate nuclear testing underground by signatories or in the atmosphere by nonsignatory nations, most Americans regarded it as a useful step that greatly diminished the problem of radioactive fallout from weapons tests.

In the aftermath of the Cuban Missile Crisis and the Limited Test Ban Treaty, nuclear arms issues lost much of their visibility and at least some of their urgency. The arms race continued, but in the next two decades, other problems generated much more controversy, including the civil rights movement, the energy crisis, the Watergate scandal, and on the foreign policy front, the Vietnam War. Questions relating to nuclear weapons development and proliferation and their impact on relations with the Soviet Union were hardly ignored, but they did not command the paramount importance with which they were treated during the Truman, Eisen-hower, and Kennedy administrations. Presidents Lyndon B. Johnson, Richard M. Nixon, Gerald R. Ford, and Jimmy Carter sought ways to curb the arms race and to ease Cold War tensions. Their efforts paid off with major achievements such as the Nuclear Non-Proliferation Treaty (1968), the Strategic Arms Limitation Talks (SALT) agreement (1972), and at least for a time, progress toward détente with the Soviets.

The arms control agreements of the 1970s, including the first SALT treaty and a second one that was aborted, generated considerable debate. Opponents of the agree-ments insisted that the Soviet Union could not be trusted to observe the limitations, and furthermore, that SALT-I and SALT-II were giveaways that favored the Soviets. Supporters contended that they would prevent the Soviets from racing ahead of the United States in their nuclear capabilities. The debate over arms control was critical to the fate of US–Soviet détente. Those issues have been well covered and well ana-lyzed by many scholars of the period, but no major historiographical disputes have emerged – probably a reflection of the diminished importance attached to issues of nuclear arms development and control.

Although the objective of arms control won wide popular support, the provisions of the SALT agreements were so complex and so arcane that only knowledgeable experts could discern their meaning and potential impact. The accounts of John Newhouse (1973) on SALT-I and Strobe Talbott (1979) on SALT-II, for example, demonstrated how mind-numbing arms control issues had become. This made them susceptible to oversimplified analyses that opponents of the treaties marshaled to claim that the agreements delivered one-sided advantages that would enable the Soviet Union to achieve nuclear superiority. By the late 1970s, critics of the Carter administration's foreign policies, including former high-level government officials, had organized a well-publicized campaign that asserted that the United States had fallen behind the Soviets and made itself vulnerable to nuclear blackmail. They claimed that the very survival of the United States was threatened by a massive Soviet military expansion that would enable the Soviet Union to fight and win a nuclear war. This view gained new prominence in 1980 when presidential candidate Ronald Reagan charged that Carter had weakened American defenses and called for a rapid military buildup to counter the Soviet offensive.

Immediately after assuming office in 1981, Reagan secured enormous increases in the defense budget, which was already growing at the end of Carter's presidency. He used the funds to, among other things, augment and modernize US nuclear forces with new strategic bombers, missile-launching submarines, and ballistic missiles. Administration officials insisted that those measures were essential to protect against the Soviets' potential for successfully waging nuclear war. One prominent feature of Reagan's program was his proposal in 1983 to build a defense system that could intercept ballistic missiles launched against the United States. This was called the "Strategic Defense Initiative" (SDI), but was more commonly referred to as "Star Wars."

Reagan's national security policies redefined the political landscape, and in so doing, created a great deal of controversy in the popular and scholarly literature. The major source of debate was whether Reagan's arms buildup and his missile defense proposal caused the demise of the Soviet Union and won the Cold War. Reagan sup-porters asserted that the president's programs were instrumental in bankrupting the

Soviets and making clear to them that they could not defeat the United States. Others took issue by arguing that the Soviet Union was teetering on the brink of collapse in any event, and that it was mostly Soviet premier Mikhail Gorbachev's actions rather than Reagan's that ended the Cold War. Much of the literature is partisan, and little is based on still-closed primary sources. The book that is likely to serve as the focal point for debate is Frances Fitzgerald's *Way Out There in the Blue* (2000). She sharply criticized Reagan and his advisers, notably Secretary of Defense Caspar Weinberger, for pursuing costly military technologies, especially "Star Wars," rather than less glamorous but more substantial and more feasible arms control agreements. She not only denied that SDI played any significant role in the dissolution of the Soviet Union, but also maintained that Reagan's commitment to it prevented fruitful negotiations on arms limitation.

The end of the Cold War occurred long after the end of the "atomic age," which had largely disappeared by the mid-1960s, at least in the ways that had been predicted shortly after Hiroshima. By that time, the prominence and frequent dominance of atomic energy issues in diplomacy, politics, and culture had declined, without being entirely replaced, by other concerns. In the immediate aftermath of World War II, popular attitudes toward the atom had shown keen ambivalence – anxiety about the threat of nuclear weapons mixed with hopes, many of them inflated, about the promise of peaceful uses of atomic energy. In a lecture he gave in 1963, David E. Lilienthal, who had served as the first chairman of the AEC from 1946 until 1950, addressed the question of "whatever happened to the peaceful atom?" He argued that although progress had been made in developing nuclear power and other civilian technologies, the "glamour, the excitement of the boundless possibilities of power from the peaceful atom is gone." "The peaceful atom," he added, "has not ushered in a 'new world' but has rather become a part, a minor part, of the old one" (Lilienthal, 1963, pp. 709, 714).

The ambivalence about nuclear energy that had emerged in the wake of World War II gradually gave way to growing opposition. As anxieties about the atom prevailed over hopes for its peaceful applications, the atomic age was supplanted by what might be termed the "anti-nuclear age." Although anti-nuclear attitudes were far from universal, after the mid-1960s, the dominant political and cultural trends increasingly emphasized the dangers and risks of nuclear energy over its potential benefits. The crucial event in transforming popular views of nuclear energy was the fallout controversy of the late 1950s and early 1960s. The debate alerted the American people to the possible risks of exposure to low levels of radiation and raised their concern about radiation hazards from any source. Although it was clear that acute doses of radiation could cause serious injury or death, the scientific evidence about the effects of low-level radiation was inconclusive.

Greater public knowledge about fallout was accompanied by heightened fear of radiation from nuclear power and other sources. The nuclear power industry did not exist until after Congress enacted a law in 1954 that eased restrictions on access to information about atomic energy and that made commercial applications of nuclear technology possible for the first time. The law assigned the AEC responsibility for both promoting the development and regulating the safety of nuclear power. In the late 1960s, nuclear power underwent a sudden and unexpected boom as utilities ordered nuclear units in record numbers. As the number of nuclear plants on order rapidly expanded, the size of individual facilities also dramatically increased. The arrival of commercial nuclear power placed unprecedented demands on the AEC by raising new safety problems.

The growth of the nuclear power industry coincided with the emergence of the environmental movement in the United States. Nuclear power soon became a prime target of environmentalists. In the early 1960s, protests against the construction of some nuclear plants, based largely on public fear of radiation, helped lead to their cancellation. In the late 1960s and early 1970s, several critics of nuclear power made headlines by charging that the AEC's regulations for protecting against radiation hazards were too lax. They suggested that even routine emissions of low levels of radiation from nuclear plants could cause thousands of cancer deaths annually. The AEC and most radiation experts denied those allegations, but their arguments were not convincing to those who had doubts about the impact of the nuclear boom. E. F. Schumacher, an economist and technology critic, for example, described radiation in 1973 as "the most serious agent of pollution of the environment and the greatest threat to man's survival on earth" (Schumacher, 1989, p. 143).

In addition to radiation emissions, environmentalists raised questions about other aspects of nuclear power, including thermal pollution of waterways from the discharge of waste heat, the disposal of radioactive wastes, and the safety of plants. Nuclear power safety became a front-page issue in the early 1970s when the AEC held hearings on the performance of emergency core cooling systems, which were designed to dump huge quantities of water into the reactor core in the event of a serious accident. The reservations cited by opponents of nuclear power produced a highly visible and bitter controversy during the 1970s. Those who objected to the technology asserted that it was unsafe and unnecessary. Supporters of nuclear power countered that it was essential for meeting the nation's energy needs and that its risks were small. They insisted that the chances of an accident that threatened public health were remote.

The anti-nuclear position won new recruits when the most serious nuclear plant accident in the United States occurred at the Three Mile Island station near Harrisburg, Pennsylvania, on March 28, 1979. Following a series of mechanical failures, compounded by human errors, the accident uncovered the reactor's core and melted about half of it. Uncertainty about the causes of the problem and confusion about how to deal with it among utility and government officials fed public fears that the plant would release large and dangerous amounts of radiation to the environment. By the time that the plant was finally brought under control, the credibility of nuclear critics who had argued that no facility as complex as a nuclear plant could be made foolproof was greatly enhanced. The *Washington Post* captured this feeling in a headline that read: "The Day Few Believed Possible Arrives in the Atomic Age" (1979). Although the accident destroyed the plant, only small amounts of radiation, far below the permissible limits allowed by federal regulations, escaped into the environment. Several studies of the population in areas surrounding the plant over a twenty-year period conducted by the Pennsylvania Department of Health and by other researchers showed no increase in the incidence of cancer from radiation, though those results were contested by some critics.

Surprisingly, given the enormous controversy over the technology, there has been little historiographical debate over the subject of nuclear power. Indeed, historians have not accorded it a great deal of attention. Most scholars who examined the subject took a position that leaned, sometimes sharply, toward the arguments of nuclear opponents. Although their tone, focus, and quality varied greatly, books by Gerard H. Clarfield and William M. Wiecek (1984), Peter Stoler (1985), John L. Campbell (1988), Catherine Caufield (1989), James M. Jasper (1990), Howard Ball (1993), Robert J. Duffy (1997), and Steven Mark Cohn (1997) were critical of the AEC's regulatory performance. They depicted it as an ineffective regulator that was more attentive to the health of the nuclear industry than the health of the public. Those authors accepted at least some of the major allegations that nuclear activists made about the AEC's safety programs, including: (1) the AEC's dual responsibilities for promoting and regulating nuclear power made it a weak regulator that was disinclined to place tough requirements on the nuclear industry; (2) the AEC was so committed to the expansion of nuclear power that it disregarded, downplayed, or postponed vital reactor safety issues; (3) the AEC's licensing process was unresponsive to public concerns and rigged to advance industry objectives; (4) the AEC's radiation protection regulations failed to protect the public adequately and threatened to allow radiation exposures that could increase the incidence of cancer by alarming proportions; and (5) the AEC was largely indifferent to the environmental costs of nuclear power.

Few scholars questioned the negative treatment of the AEC that those books presented. The most comprehensive studies of the AEC's regulatory programs took issue, however, with some important aspects of the prevailing view. A book by George T. Mazuzan and J. Samuel Walker (1984), and two others by Walker (1992, 2000), agreed that the AEC's regulatory performance was hardly flawless and that the agency's promotional priorities compromised its regulatory responsibilities. But they also pointed out that the AEC imposed many stringent safety requirements and argued that it did not operate in meek and heedless complicity with the interests of the nuclear industry. They suggested that the AEC was a more independent and conscientious regulator than its critics claimed.

Although most works on nuclear power focused on the AEC, and, to a lesser extent, on the nuclear industry, some books evaluated the dynamics of the nuclear debate by examining the growth of opposition to nuclear power. Brian Balogh (1991) showed that experts who became concerned about the safety of nuclear technology initially expressed their reservations within the bureaucratic channels of the AEC, which held a virtual monopoly on technical expertise in the early years of nuclear development. Gradually, other federal agencies, state and local governments, and outside organizations acquired their own expertise and were able to challenge the regulatory policies and decisions of the AEC. This process laid the foundations for the broad-based public debate over nuclear power that emerged by the early 1970s. Thomas R. Wellock (1998) took another approach by examining the development of grassroots challenges to nuclear power in California. He showed how local activists, motivated by reasons ranging from aesthetic sensibilities to the preservation of rural values, won their battles against the construction of nuclear plants. Citizen protests, he concluded, were instrumental in causing the decline of the nuclear industry in California and across the nation. Christian Joppke placed the rise of anti-nuclear protests in the United States and Germany in the context of differing political cultures. He found that although the movement in Germany was more radical than that in the United States, in both nations it showed a "tendency . . . to demonize nuclear power as an imminent threat" (Joppke, 1993, p. 10).

The "anti-nuclear age" gathered momentum in response to growing doubts about nuclear power. It reached new heights in the 1980s in response to Reagan's arms buildup and his anti-Soviet rhetoric and policies. A plethora of books, articles, films, television shows, and other presentations that reached a vast audience graphically described the horrors of nuclear war. In 1982, over 700,000 demonstrators participated in an anti-nuclear rally in New York City. The same year, Jonathan Schell's widely circulated and influential book, *The Fate of the Earth*, took issue with the idea that a nuclear war could be won and vividly reminded readers that the existence of nuclear weapons could destroy the world. Nuclear arms, he wrote, held "this entire terrestrial creation hostage to nuclear destruction, threatening to hurl it back to the inanimate darkness from which it came" (Schell, 1982, p. 181). In 1983, the ABC television network ran a special, "The Day After," watched by an estimated 100 million viewers, that dramatized the ghastly aftermath of a nuclear attack. At about the same time, scientists, religious leaders, politicians, and other citizens spearheaded a movement for a nuclear freeze that aimed to halt the arms race at existing levels of deployment. Despite strong opposition by the Reagan administration, it gained impressive support from a broad cross-section of American society. There was no ambivalence in the intensity of concern that critics expressed in a variety of forums about nuclear energy; their abhorrence of nuclear war often extended to all things nuclear.

The events of the "atomic age" and the "anti-nuclear age" made a great impact on American culture, and in turn, nuclear developments after World War II were significantly influenced by cultural trends. Some of the most original work done by scholars examined the cultural aspects of the history of nuclear energy. Margot A. Henriksen went so far as to claim that the atomic bomb played the "defining role" in American society between 1945 and the early 1980s. In her view, the government suppressed cultural dissent and public doubts about nuclear weapons during the 1950s, but a cultural rebirth during the 1960s forced America to come to grips with "previously disguised Cold War reality," which she described as "immoral, insane, deadly – and ridiculous" (Henriksen, 1997, pp. 187, 318). Although other scholarly work did not substantiate Henriksen's thesis about the centrality of the bomb in practically every aspect of postwar American culture, much of it presented a decidedly negative view of the atomic age. Paul Boyer, in a pioneering study of the cultural impact of the bomb, argued that by 1950, the public fears that immediately followed Hiroshima had been replaced by a resigned acceptance that he called the "complacency of despair" (Boyer, 1985, p. 351). He attributed this deadened cultural mood to the efforts of government officials and other opinion leaders to emphasize the future benefits of the peaceful atom, the feasibility of civil defense, and the need for supremacy in the arms race. Elaine Tyler May (1988) suggested that concern about atomic war during the 1950s played a significant role in reasserting traditional domestic responsibilities and gender roles for American women. Her findings received support from Laura McEnaney, who argued that the civil defense programs of the Truman and Eisenhower administrations not only "amplified the cacophony of voices preaching domesticity," but also contributed heavily to the militarization of everyday life in the United States (McEnaney, 2000, p. 113). Like McEnaney, Guy Oakes traced the efforts of the US government to alert its citizens to the dangers of nuclear war without immobilizing them with fear. He concluded that the government failed to inform the public fully and frankly about the horrors of nuclear war, and as a result, "the principles of liberalism were sacrificed to the exigencies of national security" (Oakes, 1994, p. 167).

Some treatments of American postwar culture took a position that, while hardly celebratory, assessed with greater balance the efforts of those of different persuasions who sought to address the problems of the atomic age. Allan M. Winkler traced popular responses to the postwar era in books, articles, songs, poems, films, television shows, and other cultural artifacts to demonstrate that fear was an "undeniable part of our nuclear age." He suggested that the bomb was, "like a heart condition," something that people had to live with. Without fully endorsing their arguments, he commended anti-nuclear activists for forcing governments to adopt "a more reasonable approach to nuclear issues" (Winkler, 1993, pp. 5, 212). In a study of public attitudes toward nuclear energy, Spencer R. Weart (1988) found that the roots of nuclear fear went back to cultural images that predated the scientific achievement of nuclear fission by decades. In his discussions of the postwar era, he faulted government officials, on the one hand, and anti-nuclear activists, on the other hand, for trying to manipulate public opinion with images that supported their own positions. The result, he concluded, was to inhibit well-informed discussions.

Most of the scholarly literature of the 1980s and 1990s reflected American society's prevailing attitudes by supporting an anti-nuclear position. A few scholars, however, without understating the horrors of nuclear war or underestimating the risks of nuclear power, have provided more favorable perspectives on some key issues. Their judgments, perhaps, will provide the basis for future historiographical debates. McGeorge Bundy, who served as national security adviser to Presidents Kennedy and Johnson and later turned to scholarly pursuits, concluded that from World War II into the 1980s, the United States, the Soviet Union, and other nuclear powers had been well aware of the limited value of the bomb as a military and diplomatic weapon, keenly alert to its dangers, and firmly committed to avoiding a nuclear war. "On balance," he wrote, "the major lessons of this history are more encouraging than not." Bundy faulted American leaders (including Kennedy and Johnson) for some of their decisions on nuclear matters, but he maintained that all postwar presidents, including Reagan, understood that a nuclear war should never be fought and could never be won (Bundy, 1988, p. 584).

John Lewis Gaddis supported Bundy's evaluation of the role of nuclear weapons in international affairs by suggesting that they had contributed in significant ways to world stability and peace in the postwar era. Although it was apparent that nuclear arms had not eliminated war, he argued, the demonstration of their power at Hiroshima and Nagasaki had helped to prevent a great-power conflict on the scale of World War II. Gaddis submitted that the invention of the bomb was such a revolutionary development that it changed international behavior in dramatic ways. "The fact that no great power has gone to war with another great power since 1945 is," he wrote, "a remarkable record, unparalleled in modern history" (Gaddis, 1992, p. 110). Gaddis's conclusion that the existence of nuclear weapons, despite the risks they presented, served a worthwhile purpose was self-consciously counterfactual, and like counterfactuals on other nuclear issues, triggered strong objections from those who disagreed.

Just as Bundy and Gaddis proposed some positive features to the history of nuclear weapons in the postwar period, there are reasons to view the history of nuclear power more favorably than it has been treated by most scholars. For example, those who wrote on the subject almost invariably quoted a 1954 speech in which AEC chairman Lewis L. Strauss declared that in the future nuclear power could provide electricity "too cheap to meter." Scholars generally cited this statement to demonstrate the unrealistic hopes of the AEC and other nuclear proponents. But they usually failed to note that Strauss did not articulate a common view among government or industry officials, who had no illusions that nuclear power would be inexpensive. Indeed, the heavy capital costs of nuclear power were a major impediment to its development. The basis of Strauss's flight of fancy is unclear, but it did not represent a widely held opinion or provide the rationale for AEC programs.

In a similar manner, historians frequently asserted that in preparing regulations for the protection of the public from radiation hazards, the AEC and scientific experts assumed the existence of a threshold level, below which exposure was harmless. They argued that by adopting a threshold theory, the AEC greatly underestimated the risks of low-level radiation. But the AEC and the scientific experts who made recommendations on radiation standards did not accept the threshold concept and stated explicitly that no quantity of radiation was certifiably safe. They attempted to provide an ample margin of safety by using very conservative standards; AEC regulations for emissions from nuclear plants, for example, assumed that a person stood at the boundary of a facility 24 hours a day, 365 days a year. The effects of low-level radiation are still hotly disputed by professionals in the field of radiation protection. Scholars have too often oversimplified a complex and controversial issue that is a major component in the history of nuclear energy.

Those examples raise questions about some of the shibboleths that have become conventional wisdom in the anti-nuclear consensus. They indicate that the history of nuclear power, like the political and cultural history of other nuclear subjects, still requires an abundance of careful scholarly work. They also suggest that scholars should apply the same methods of judgment and analysis to all participants in the debate over nuclear issues. Researchers should continue to view the promises and performances of government officials and business leaders with healthy skepticism, but they should hold nuclear critics to the same standards. If we are to understand the history of the atomic age (and the anti-nuclear age), scholars must provide accounts that fully recognize complexities, ambiguities, and uncertainties while avoiding the emotional and partisan approaches of the popular debate. This has occurred on vital topics such as the atomic bombings of Japan and the Cuban Missile Crisis, and we can hope that balanced, accurate, and sober scholarship will likewise enrich the study of other nuclear issues.

REFERENCES

Alperovitz, Gar: *Atomic Diplomacy: Hiroshima and Potsdam* (New York: Simon and Schuster, 1965).
Ambrose, Stephen E.: *Eisenhower: The President* (New York: Simon and Schuster, 1984).
"Atomic Power," *New York Times* (August 9, 1945): 20.

Ball, Howard: *Cancer Factories: America's Tragic Quest for Uranium Self-Sufficiency* (Westport, Conn.: Greenwood Press, 1993).

Balogh, Brian: *Chain Reaction: Expert Debate and Public Participation in American Commercial Nuclear Power, 1945–1975* (New York: Cambridge University Press, 1991).

Bernstein, Barton J.: "Understanding the Atomic Bomb and the Japanese Surrender: Missed Opportunities, Little-Known Near Disasters, and Modern Memory," *Diplomatic History*, 19 (1995): 227–73.

Beschloss, Michael R.: *The Crisis Years: Kennedy and Khrushchev, 1960–1963* (New York: HarperCollins, 1991).

Bird, Kai and Lifschultz, Lawrence, eds.: *Hiroshima's Shadow* (Stony Creek, Conn.: Pamphleteers Press, 1998).

Bix, Herbert: *Hirohito and the Making of Modern Japan* (New York: HarperCollins, 2000).

Boyer, Paul: *By the Bomb's Early Light: American Thought and Culture at the Dawn of the Atomic Age* (New York: Pantheon, 1985).

Brands, H. W.: "The Age of Vulnerability: Eisenhower and the National Security State," *American Historical Review*, 94 (1989): 963–89.

Bundy, McGeorge: *Danger and Survival: Choices About the Bomb in the First Fifty Years* (New York: Random House, 1988).

Campbell, John L.: *Collapse of an Industry: Nuclear Power and the Contradictions of U.S. Policy* (Ithaca, NY: Cornell University Press, 1988).

Caufield, Catherine: *Multiple Exposures: Chronicles of the Radiation Age* (New York: Harper and Row, 1989).

Clarfield, Gerard H. and Wiecek, William M.: *Nuclear America: Military and Civilian Nuclear Power in the United States, 1940–1980* (New York: Harper and Row, 1984).

Cohn, Steven Mark: *Too Cheap to Meter: An Economic and Philosophical Analysis of the Nuclear Dream* (Albany: State University of New York Press, 1997).

Divine, Robert A.: *Blowing On the Wind: The Nuclear Test Ban Debate, 1954–1960* (New York: Oxford University Press, 1978).

Divine, Robert A.: *Eisenhower and the Cold War* (New York: Oxford University Press, 1981).

Duffy, Robert J.: *Nuclear Politics in America: A History and Theory of Government Regulation* (Lawrence: University Press of Kansas, 1997).

Fairlie, Henry: *The Kennedy Promise: The Politics of Expectation* (Garden City, NY: Doubleday, 1973).

Feis, Herbert: *Japan Subdued: The Atomic Bomb and the End of the War in the Pacific* (Princeton, NJ: Princeton University Press, 1961).

Ferrell, Robert H.: *Harry S. Truman: A Life* (Columbia: University of Missouri Press, 1994).

Fitzgerald, Frances: *Way Out There in the Blue: Reagan, Star Wars, and the End of the Cold War* (New York: Simon and Schuster, 2000).

FitzSimons, Louise: *The Kennedy Doctrine* (New York: Random House, 1972).

"For the Future," *Newsweek* (August 20, 1945): 59–60.

Frank, Richard B.: *Downfall: The End of the Imperial Japanese Empire* (New York: Random House, 1999).

Fursenko, Aleksandr and Naftali, Timothy: *"One Hell of a Gamble": Khrushchev, Castro, and Kennedy, 1958–1964* (New York: W. W. Norton, 1997).

Gaddis, John Lewis: *The United States and the End of the Cold War: Implications, Reconsiderations, Provocations* (New York: Oxford University Press, 1992).

Garthoff, Raymond L.: *Reflections on the Cuban Missile Crisis*, rev. ed. (Washington, DC: Brookings Institution, 1989).

Greenstein, Fred I.: *The Hidden-Hand Presidency: Eisenhower as Leader* (New York: Basic Books, 1982).

Henriksen, Margot A.: *Dr. Strangelove's America: Society and Culture in the Atomic Age* (Berkeley and Los Angeles: University of California Press, 1997).

Hewlett, Richard G. and Holl, Jack M.: *Atoms for Peace and War: Eisenhower and the Atomic Energy Commission* (Berkeley and Los Angeles: University of California Press, 1989).

Holloway, David: *Stalin and the Bomb: The Soviet Union and Atomic Energy, 1939–1956* (New Haven, Conn.: Yale University Press, 1994).

Jasper, James M.: *Nuclear Politics: Energy and the State in the United States, Sweden, and France* (Princeton, NJ: Princeton University Press, 1990).

Joppke, Christian: *Mobilizing Against Nuclear Energy: A Comparison of Germany and the United States* (Berkeley and Los Angeles: University of California Press, 1993).

Lifton, Robert Jay and Mitchell, Greg: *Hiroshima in America: Fifty Years of Denial* (New York: Grosset/Putnam, 1995).

Lilienthal, David E.: "Whatever Happened to the Peaceful Atom?" (Printed in Joint Committee on Atomic Energy, *Hearings on Development, Growth, and State of the Atomic Energy Industry*, 88th Congress, 1st Session, 1963, pp. 705–14).

McEnaney, Laura: *Civil Defense Begins at Home: Militarization Meets Everyday Life in the Fifties* (Princeton, NJ: Princeton University Press, 2000).

Maddox, Robert James: *Weapons for Victory: The Hiroshima Decision Fifty Years Later* (Columbia: University of Missouri Press, 1995).

May, Elaine Tyler: *Homeward Bound: American Families in the Cold War Era* (New York: Basic Books, 1988).

Mazuzan, George T. and Walker, J. Samuel: *Controlling the Atom: The Beginnings of Nuclear Regulation, 1946–1962* (Berkeley and Los Angeles: University of California Press, 1984).

Newhouse, John: *Cold Dawn: The Story of SALT* (New York: Holt, Rinehart, and Winston, 1973).

Newman, Robert P.: *Truman and the Hiroshima Cult* (East Lansing: Michigan State University Press, 1995).

Oakes, Guy: *The Imaginary War: Civil Defense and American Cold War Culture* (New York: Oxford University Press, 1994).

Roman, Peter J.: *Eisenhower and the Missile Gap* (Ithaca, NY: Cornell University Press, 1995).

Rosenberg, David A.: "The Origins of Overkill: Nuclear Weapons and American Strategy, 1945–1960," *International Security*, 7 (Spring 1983): 3–71.

Schell, Jonathan: *The Fate of the Earth* (New York: Alfred A. Knopf, 1982).

Schlesinger, Jr., Arthur M.: *A Thousand Days: John F. Kennedy in the White House* (Boston: Houghton Mifflin, 1965).

Schumacher, E. F.: *Small Is Beautiful: Economics As If People Mattered* (1973; New York: HarperCollins, 1989).

Stoler, Peter: *Decline and Fail: The Ailing Nuclear Power Industry* (New York: Dodd, Mead, 1985).

Suri, Jeremi: "America's Search for a Technological Solution to the Arms Race: The Surprise Attack Conference of 1958 and a Challenge for the 'Eisenhower Revisionists,'" *Diplomatic History*, 21 (1997): 417–51.

Takaki, Ronald: *Hiroshima: Why America Dropped the Bomb* (New York: Little, Brown, 1995).

Talbott, Strobe: *Endgame: The Inside Story of SALT II* (New York: Harper and Row, 1979).

"The Bomb," *Time* (August 20, 1945): 19.

"The Day Few Believed Possible Arrives in the Atomic Age," *Washington Post* (March 31, 1979): 1.

Walker, J. Samuel: *Containing the Atom: Nuclear Regulation in a Changing Environment, 1963–1971* (Berkeley and Los Angeles: University of California Press, 1992).

Walker, J. Samuel: *Prompt and Utter Destruction: Truman and the Use of Atomic Bombs Against Japan* (Chapel Hill: University of North Carolina Press, 1997).

Walker, J. Samuel: *Permissible Dose: A History of Radiation Protection in the Twentieth Century* (Berkeley and Los Angeles: University of California Press, 2000).

Walton, Richard J.: *Cold War and Counterrevolution: The Foreign Policy of John F. Kennedy* (New York: Viking, 1972).

Weart, Spencer R.: *Nuclear Fear: A History of Images* (Cambridge, Mass.: Harvard University Press, 1988).

Wellock, Thomas Raymond: *Critical Masses: Opposition to Nuclear Power in California, 1958–1978* (Madison: University of Wisconsin Press, 1998).

White, Mark J.: *Missiles in Cuba: Kennedy, Khrushchev, Castro and the 1962 Crisis* (Chicago: Ivan R. Dee, 1997).

Winkler, Allan M.: *Life Under a Cloud: American Anxiety About the Atom* (New York: Oxford University Press, 1993).

FURTHER READING

Alperovitz, Gar: *The Decision to Use the Atomic Bomb and the Architecture of an American Myth* (New York: Alfred A. Knopf, 1995).

Aron, Joan: *Licensed to Kill? The Nuclear Regulatory Commission and the Shoreham Power Plant* (Pittsburgh: University of Pittsburgh Press, 1997).

Ball, Howard: *Justice Downwind: America's Atomic Testing Program in the 1950s* (New York: Oxford University Press, 1986).

Bedford, Henry F.: *Seabrook Station: Citizen Politics and Nuclear Power* (Amherst: University of Massachusetts Press, 1990).

Bernstein, Barton J: "Roosevelt, Truman, and the Atomic Bomb, 1941–1945: A Reinterpretation," *Political Science Quarterly*, 90 (Spring 1975): 23–69.

Divine, Robert A.: "Alive and Well: The Continuing Cuban Missile Crisis Controversy," *Diplomatic History*, 18 (Fall 1994): 551–60.

Hacker, Barton C.: *Elements of Controversy: The Atomic Energy Commission and Radiation Safety in Nuclear Weapons Testing, 1947–1974* (Berkeley and Los Angeles: University of California Press, 1994).

Herken, Gregg: *The Winning Weapon: The Atomic Bomb in the Cold War, 1945–1950* (New York: Alfred A. Knopf, 1980).

Hogan, Michael J., ed.: *America in the World: The Historiography of American Foreign Relations Since 1941* (New York: Cambridge University Press, 1995).

Immerman, Richard H.: "Confessions of an Eisenhower Revisionist: An Agonizing Reappraisal," *Diplomatic History*, 14 (1990): 319–42.

Johnson, John W.: *Insuring Against Disaster: The Nuclear Industry on Trial* (Macon, Ga.: Mercer University Press, 1986).

Morone, Joseph G. and Woodhouse, Edward J.: *The Demise of Nuclear Energy? Lessons for Democratic Control of Technology* (New Haven, Conn.: Yale University Press, 1989).

Nash, Philip: *The Other Missiles of October: Eisenhower, Kennedy, and the Jupiters, 1957–1963* (Chapel Hill: University of North Carolina Press, 1997).

Rhodes, Richard: *Dark Sun: The Making of the Hydrogen Bomb* (New York: Simon and Schuster, 1995).

Sherwin, Martin J.: *A World Destroyed: The Atomic Bomb and the Grand Alliance* (New York: Alfred A. Knopf, 1975).

Weisgall, Jonathan M.: *Operation Crossroads: The Atomic Tests at Bikini Atoll* (Annapolis: Naval Institute Press, 1994).

Wittner, Lawrence S.: *One World or None: A History of the World Nuclear Disarmament Movement through 1963* (Stanford, Calif.: Stanford University Press, 1993).

Wittner, Lawrence S.: *Resisting the Bomb: A History of the World Disarmament Movement, 1954–1970* (Stanford, Calif.: Stanford University Press, 1997).

PART IV

Essential Reading

CHAPTER TWENTY-SEVEN

J. Anthony Lukas, *Common Ground: A Turbulent Decade in the Lives of Three American Families* (1985)

ALAN BRINKLEY

Almost every morning in the fall of 1975 and the spring of 1976, I woke up to sounds of fury and hatred. I was a graduate student at Harvard, living in a quiet neighborhood in Cambridge. But my clock radio was tuned to a left-leaning Boston public radio station, and it spent most mornings playing recordings of the ugly confrontations that were accompanying the first months of "forced busing" in the city's public schools. Day after day, I lay in bed listening to Irish parents from South Boston and Charlestown railing against Judge W. Arthur Garrity, who had ordered the busing; against the *Boston Globe*, which they considered biased against them; against Ted Kennedy, who they felt had betrayed them; and against the frightened and bewildered African American students who had been suddenly thrust into the heart of hostile neighborhoods. One morning in April, the reporters interviewed Ted Landsmark, a Yale-educated, African American lawyer who ran a trade association for black contractors in Boston. No one living in Boston in those years can ever forget the extraordinary, Pulitzer prize-winning photograph of Landsmark (who up to that point had had no connection at all to the busing crisis) being beaten by white demonstrators in City Hall Plaza with the staff of the American flag they were carrying. Nothing seemed better to epitomize the stark and mindless racism that many liberals, myself among them, assumed drove the anti-busing demonstrators.

Less often, but not infrequently, the station aired interviews with the black participants in this drama, and they were angry too – at the hostility and racism their children were confronting, certainly, but also, many of them, at the unwanted controversy into which Garrity's decision had plunged them. Their children were no more eager to attend school in South Boston or Charlestown than the South Boston kids were eager to attend school in Roxbury. Why did they have to suffer because of a policy formulated in the chambers of federal judges?

To me, and I assume to most other listeners, these jarring and discordant voices made the harrowing drama unfolding before us in our city seem not less, but more bewildering. Nothing seemed adequately to explain the depths of the anger, the hatred, and the bitterness that people on both sides of this question were expressing. Boston seemed caught up in a kind of spiraling irrationality from which, for a time, there appeared to be no exit.

About ten years later, in 1985, in the midst of the stiff, self-congratulatory aura of the Reagan years, J. Anthony Lukas – a former *New York Times* reporter turned free-lance writer – published a book about the busing crisis: *Common Ground*. I had been hearing about this book for years, and had even seen Lukas talk about it at a seminar I arranged at MIT, where I taught for a while. But there was no particular reason to expect anything out of the ordinary in this reconstruction, one among many, of the busing controversy. Most of what one heard about *Common Ground* before it was published were vaguely ungenerous comments about how long it was taking Lukas to finish it. And yet today, if I were to draw up a shortlist of books crucial to under-standing American life in the last third of the twentieth century, *Common Ground* would be at or near the top of it.

Common Ground is the story of three Boston families, each of which became caught up in the tragedy of the city's busing crisis. Collectively, they provide a window into the experiences and, more importantly, the perceptions of three different communities.

Colin and Joan Diver represented well-meaning white liberals. Colin was a pro-fessor of law at Boston University (and later became the dean of the University of Pennsylvania Law School), and Joan was a bright, energetic foundation officer. Not long before the busing crisis began, they had moved into a town house in Boston's South End, a once prosperous neighborhood just on the other side of the Massa-chusetts Turnpike from the more fashionable Back Bay. In the 1950s and 1960s, the South End was a poor, minority-dominated community. By the time the Divers moved in, middle-class white families were beginning to rediscover the neighbor-hood and its large, attractive, still inexpensive houses. Even so, it was still too early in 1975 to think of the South End as truly "gentrifying," and so the Divers were – as they themselves believed – urban pioneers, painstakingly restoring their house at the same time that they hoped their presence would help restore the neighborhood. Their son was enrolled in a public elementary school that had become an innovative experiment in unstructured education. The Divers were among the small group of committed parents who had fought to improve the school and who continued to fight to preserve it.

Rachel Twymon was a single African American woman raising her four children alone in a housing project built on the edge of the same neighborhood – the South End – in which the Divers lived. The project was near the border of Boston's largest black community, Roxbury, and so this part of the South End was not a likely can-didate for gentrification. Like many poor single mothers, Rachel drifted back and forth between work and welfare. In 1968, she was running a clothing store in Roxbury (which was damaged in the riots following the assassination of Martin Luther King, Jr. and went out of business a little over six months later). By 1975, she was living on welfare, struggling with the recurrent effects of lupus, deeply involved in the affairs of her church, and increasingly concerned about her children, who were – she believed – being shortchanged by the city's public schools. She feared, not without reason, that they would fall victim to early pregnancies, drugs, crime, and violence.

Alice McGoff was a widow with seven children living in a housing project in Charlestown, which was – like South Boston – one of the epicenters of the busing crisis. She survived precariously on her late husband's small pension and her own low-paying job in the Charlestown Navy Yard. Charlestown was a close-knit, largely Irish Catholic neighborhood presided over by its high school. All of Alice's children had either attended it or expected to do so. In the early 1960s, she had watched the civil rights movement from afar, and she had sympathized with Martin Luther King, Jr. and the demonstrators who had braved fire hoses, police dogs, and worse in the South. But she had soured on the movement once it moved North and once its leaders, white and black, began to promote the idea of affirmative action. Her family had it hard too, she believed, but they asked for no special favors. Increasingly she came to believe that Democratic political leaders – among them many Irish Catholic politicians in Massachusetts – had come to care more about African Americans than they did about working-class whites.

By following the lives of these three families through the searing events that affected them all, Lukas revealed layers of both experience and sentiment that neither daily journalistic accounts nor later historical reconstructions could provide. Well before the postmodern critique of the linear narrative and the omniscient narrator became popular, Lukas created a tapestry of multiple perspectives and managed to do so without privileging, or even judging, any of them. There are no heroes in this story, but no real villains either – only ordinary people struggling, and often failing, to make sense of a series of profound changes in their lives and in the life of the nation.

But while Lukas did not take sides in this story, he did provide a muted but powerful interpretation of the events he described. And in doing so, he suggested a more promising basis for understanding many of the social conflicts of the last forty years than many of those created by academic scholars. The Boston busing crisis, he gently insisted, was not only, perhaps not even primarily, about race. It was also, fundamentally, about class. The men, women, and children caught up in this conflict were divided by race, certainly. But they were also divided by their economic circumstances, and that division – at least as much as the racial one – helped determine the character of this conflict. Busing in Boston – as in many other American cities in the aftermath of the Supreme Court's 1970 *Swann* decision banning the transport of children across municipal lines to achieve racial balance – was an experiment in compelling working-class white children and working-class black children to change places with one another in attending similarly inferior schools. Affluent families, white and black, managed to escape the ordeal – by moving to prosperous suburbs whose schools were exempt from busing, sending their children to private schools, or (like the Divers) using their skills and influence to reverse a court-ordered movement of their son from their local, progressive school to a far less favored public school blocks away.

Thirty years ago, class was the principal analytical category of scholars working in the "new history," attempting to uncover the experiences of ordinary men and women and of forgotten groups in the American past. Gradually, and appropriately, historians began to add other new categories to their arsenal: race, ethnicity, gender, culture, and identity. Eventually, these new categories moved to the fore of historical interpretation and class faded into the background. The most influential work of history in the 1960s and 1970s was probably E. P. Thompson's epic *The Making of the English Working Class* (1963). It would be hard to point to a similarly influential book in the 1980s or 1990s, but virtually all of the candidates would be works that give scant attention to class and a great deal of attention to other categories.

This downgrading of class analysis in the scholarly world has been matched by an effective public effort to banish class from public discourse. Many groups on the left see class as a far less important category than race, culture, or identity. Many people on the right consider class an incendiary concept and pounce on discussions of power and wealth as "class warfare." In a time in which the values of the "free market" have revived as a central principle of public life, talk of inequality and privilege has become tinny and unconvincing.

But despite the longstanding and often successful effort by many Americans to deny the importance, even the existence, of class, and despite the increasing neglect of the concept by historians, it remains one of the most powerful dividing lines in American society and one of the most important determinants of the worldview and behavior of everyone in it. No one can deny the power of race or ethnicity or gender or identity as forces in modern life, but there is no reason that acknowledging them should require us to minimize the importance of class – which is intimately bound up in the workings of all other categories. "The more I delved into Boston's crisis," Lukas wrote in the introduction to his next, and last, book, *Big Trouble*, the story of a labor controversy in the American West, "the more I found the conundrum of race and class inextricably intertwined." Even today, more than fifteen years after the publication of *Common Ground*, Lukas's invitation to take seriously that crucial relationship remains a powerful challenge to American society and American scholarship.

REFERENCE

Lukas, J. Anthony: *Common Ground: A Turbulent Decade in the Lives of Three American Families* (New York: Alfred A. Knopf, 1985).

CHAPTER TWENTY-EIGHT

Charles Payne, *I've Got the Light of Freedom* (1995)

LINDA GORDON

Even in the rich field of scholarship on the civil rights movement, Charles Payne's *I've Got the Light of Freedom* shines – a superb study of the severest test for that movement, Mississippi. It also does something that other studies fail to do: it advances the historical scholarship on social movements in general by applying a powerfully analytic inquiry to a local, grassroots struggle. The result is a spellbinding narrative whose protagonists are not Martin Luther King, Jr. or other national figures, but local activists. This ambitious study seeks to explain the sources and processes of bottom-up, grassroots organizing. It combines sophisticated scholarship with a gripping story, told with spiritual and moral as well as emotional power.

Payne's book stands virtually alone in the field because historians have been underdeveloped in analyzing and theorizing social movements and social movement leadership. *Light of Freedom* lights a path for historians to follow. Payne is not by disciplinary training an historian but a sociologist. Yet he writes in a manner more characteristic of historians, allowing his theoretical assumptions and axes of analysis to spring, seemingly "naturally," from within a narrative. Its generalizations and arguments are embedded in, and flow from, nuanced, detailed understandings of the particular place, time, and actors. As a result the book does not intimidate a general audience as so many other scholarly studies do. It is, moreover, a wonderful book to teach because it offers the students a sophisticated analysis along with the challenge of discovering that analysis within a narrative.

Payne's book is a close examination of the civil rights movement in Mississippi, particularly the work of the Student Nonviolent Coordinating Committee (SNCC, pronounced "snick"). The story is based on decades of interviews and research and, like many such microcosmic works, reaches far beyond Mississippi and back several decades in order to explain how this movement came about. That this militant movement arose takes some heavy-duty explaining, because African Americans in Mississippi faced an apartheid, terrorist state and suffered devastating reprisals for challenges to the system. Sociological theorists have taken up this explanatory challenge with hypotheses that delineate the structural factors that condition social movements and their shape. These conditions include, for example, political opportunities, that is, contradictions and weak points within dominant political structures; and the resources, including "human resources," that advocates can mobilize.

Payne, by contrast, focuses on human agency and culture. He does not disregard the structural conditions that allowed the civil rights movement to happen, such as the decline of demand for plantation labor, but considers less-often-studied sources. Using what were once called "free-will" rather than determinist assumptions, Payne is interested in different questions. He wants to know why people step into risky activism, and structural theories will never explain this because, no matter how ample the political opportunity, some will lead, some will act, some will remain inactive. One of Payne's most important themes is that good leaders (and good followers too) devote care, thought, practice, and skill to constructing their political projects; that they have often imbibed a culture of social responsibility; that they have often been apprenticed, mentored by older leaders; that their leadership rests on a great deal of knowledge and expertise.

Payne writes, "I once heard a journalist who had covered the movement remark that two decades after its height the civil rights movement had inspired no great works of art – no great novels or films, no great plays. He rather missed the point. The movement was its own work of art" (p. 256). A social movement is not just an emanation of beauty, or of justice, or of rage, but a product of art, even artifice – that is, of craft, skill, strategy, hard work, and discipline. Social movement leaders are often master artists (note that we have no feminine or ungendered word for mastery in that sense). In the political arts, a social movement may also be as close as human beings will ever get to full democracy, which would have to mean not just a liberal democracy – choosing between alternatives defined by others, but a republican democracy – participating in shaping alternatives.

Charles Payne begins his study by distinguishing between mobilizing and organizing. In his usage, mobilizing is what Martin Luther King, Jr. and other great orators, often ministers, did in social movements: they used words, music, charisma, passion, and courage to motivate; projected their own self-confidence to inspire others to think that justice was possible. Mobilization, in Payne's sense, was vital to grassroots social movements because it allowed those normally excluded from or indifferent to politics to demonstrate their political power, and it allowed individuals to gain strength from feeling part of a larger community of the just. Mobilization not only exerted power on leaders, but also served to inspire, encourage, and rededicate those who need social change. Not only through demonstrating and rallying but also through creating drama, stimulating media coverage, and threatening disruption, mobilizations forced concessions from the powerful. These mobilizations have worked even when they were not victorious. The 1965 Selma, Alabama, demonstration where protestors were brutally beaten on the Pettus bridge was arguably as influential as the 1963 march on Washington. In Selma the mobilizers of the march turned the fact that they were driven back by force – defeated, in other words – into a moral, spiritual, and media victory.

Payne uses organizing to mean, not building organizations, but transforming popular consciousness so as to make individuals active, not passive, members of a democratic order. Organizing in Payne's definition thus involves not just different tactics but actually a different vision of what freedom and democracy can mean. He shows how the best civil rights organizers aimed to self-destruct as leaders – that is, to make people need them less, to build leadership in others. Organizing works through developmental politics, in which the immediate objective, the demands, may matter less than bringing people to see themselves as having the right and the capacity to have a say in the community or polity. Ella Baker said, "SNCC demonstrated the possibility of taking uninitiated people and working with them to the point that they began to understand where their interest really was and the relationship to their own capacity to do something about it." This is not just empowerment, as the concept is used in pop psychology. It is intellectual and political because it requires understanding one's place in the social world and being able to evaluate realistically how to exert influence. On the other hand, it does have a significant psychological dimension: master organizers like Ella Baker also understood and practiced an insight that in the late twentieth century was more often associated with psychotherapy – that people have to discover the most profound things for themselves.

In organizing, as opposed to mobilizing, personal transformation became a part of political empowerment. Charles Payne examines this process closely, and evaluates it as a process rather than measuring it by the achievement of specific goals. He does not trivialize the movement's goals, but suggests that self-transformation was a condition of achieving them. His analysis implies that organizing worked primarily through face-to-face contact. When social movements are risky, or challenge hegemonic presumptions, the printed word or even a public lecture was unlikely to bring a new person to a meeting or a picket line populated by strangers – only personal connections would do so.

In this analysis Payne disrupts a conventional public/private distinction, in which social movements are categorized on the public side. In perhaps the greatest historical tradition of examining social movements, that of Marxism, the private has usually been associated with quietism, conservatism, cowardice. Payne's refusal to accept this public/private distinction is an intellectual move consonant with the new women's history, and his emphasis on Ella Baker along with Robert Moses as consummate leaders reinforces that association. He shows that civil rights activists were often continuing family traditions, building on kinship and personal friendships, judging people's character as well as their ideas and words.

Previous work on SNCC has emphasized its defiance of and break from the conservatism of an older generation of southern black leaders. Payne, by contrast, emphasizes generational continuity. He shows how the SNCC youngsters who moved into Mississippi began by searching out old activists and succeeded by depending on them. He shows how the most effective young activists found ways to include and value the contributions of even the most timid and conventional rather than deride them for their lack of militance.

Yet this focus on human agency does not morph into an idealist or starry-eyed sensibility. On the contrary, within the analyses of strategies and tactics, Payne focuses persistently on the balance of power. This is illustrated by his forthright and subtle discussion of violence. The movement gained substantially from its commitment to nonviolence, but too many observers and scholars of the movement took that to be an absolutist, religious commitment, and for many it was not. Payne shows us the black men who sat up on their porches at night with a shotgun or a rifle to watch for marauding white racists who believed they could shoot blacks with impunity. One said, "I wasn't breaking with nonviolence, I was just defending myself." This defensive posture was of course multilayered: it was simultaneously an insistence on upholding a "manly" obligation to protect women and children, a declaration of willingness to sacrifice one's own life, and a tactical determination to raise the cost to the terrorists of intimidating blacks. Its message was, you can shoot me but which of you will die first? Payne interprets white violence equally subtly. The fact that racist vigilantes in the 1960s turned to attacks at night was a sign, he points out, of their increasing timidity, of the "lessening return from racist violence" (p. 40).

In his class analysis Payne reunifies structure and agency with his characteristic complexity. Civil rights in Mississippi was not primarily a middle-class black movement, he shows, but it did gain disproportionate contributions from those who were not entirely economically dependent on whites. Yet he avoids determinism. He refuses, for example, to attribute the disproportionately great contributions of women activists to their alleged insulation from economic reprisals, but examines how they strategically politicized their personal and church experience and connections.

In his introduction to the book, Payne insists that courage was the least of the organizers' gifts. A puzzling comment at first, since we know how extraordinary was the courage of those who faced beatings, water hoses, dogs, and sheer terror. Payne's comment is the essence of the book's contribution, however: its insistence that social movements are not mere emanations of desperation, faith, or blind passion, but one of the great human creative, intellectual, and political achievements. They deserve much more serious analysis by historians than they have received, and for anyone wanting to do this, *I've Got the Light of Freedom* is a good place to begin.

REFERENCE

Payne, Charles M.: *I've Got the Light of Freedom: The Organizing Tradition and the Mississippi Freedom Struggle* (Berkeley: University of California Press, 1995).

CHAPTER TWENTY-NINE

Samuel Lubell, *The Future of American Politics* (1952, 1956, 1965)

NELSON LICHTENSTEIN

At the center of twentieth-century US politics stand the great reforms of the New Deal era and the fate of the social forces that sustained them. The two are closely linked but not identical, which is why historians and social scientists continue to debate how, why, and when the electoral coalition that proved so potent during the presidency of Franklin Roosevelt lost its majoritarian character. Was the New Deal merely a set of specific economic reforms that appealed to an electorate desperate for security and relief during the Great Depression? Or was it a more profound transformation in government and society that cast a shadow well into the postwar era?

These were some of the issues Samuel Lubell tried to answer when he published *The Future of American Politics* in 1952. In those early postwar years, the electoral future of the New Deal impulse was very much in play. Although his polling and journalistic investigations are now more than half a century old, Lubell's broadly conceived social analysis remains remarkably insightful, more prescient and powerful than many books written in more recent decades. The New Deal fused a demographic revolt with key economic and social reforms, argues Lubell. Thus the party of FDR remained for more than a generation the political "sun" around which all other parties, fractions, and tendencies were forced to revolve. But this electoral coalition was hardly monolithic, and it was under attack from without, while inside the encampment hidden fissures and incipient revolts threatened to undermine its majoritarian power.

Samuel Lubell was a journalist, a member of that left-liberal, largely Jewish cohort that at mid-century included I. F. Stone, Theodore White, A. H. Raskin, Daniel Bell, and Benjamin Stolberg. He was born in Poland in 1911, came to New York as an infant, and graduated from City College and Columbia's School of Journalism in the early 1930s. He worked for various newspapers, but made his unique mark as a polling and electoral analyst in a series of investigative essays for the *Saturday Evening Post*. Lubell's first book, *The Future of American Politics*, had its origins in the essays he wrote for the *Post* on how and why Harry Truman won in 1948. Instead of writing about the "principal politicians strutting across the stage in Washington," he "deliberately swung the spotlight out into the country." Lubell was therefore a shoe-leather pollster: he used the electoral returns to identify key wards and precincts, and then he went out and interviewed scores, even hundreds, of voters to get at the history and texture of their lives.

He thought voting returns were "like radioactive isotopes": as key districts shifted their vote, he sought to trace how various class strata, ethnic groups, regions, and occupations recast their loyalties, allegiances, and mentalities. Thus Lubell saw voting behavior as linked not only to current events, or even to a particular ethnicity or class, but to an historical set of circumstances that formed, froze, and sometimes broke political allegiances. He therefore returned again and again to those key precincts where a shift in the vote reflected not just the momentary appeal of one candidate or policy, but the reconfiguration of an entire ethnogenerational set of loyalties.

Lubell calls the New Deal political realignment the "Roosevelt Revolution." This is a phrase that certainly went out of fashion in the 1950s when Dwight Eisenhower was president, and it stayed out during the 1960s and 1970s when New Left historians and journalists devalued so much of what the New Deal wrought. But it has once again come into play and into parlance, for as Lubell makes clear, the power and popularity of the New Deal's social democratic initiatives were amplified by a demographic coming of age that put his own immigrant generation at the center of American politics. By the early 1950s these working-class ethnics were moving on to an "urban frontier," out of the tenements and into the new suburbs and the middle-class apartment blocks. Their lives had been transformed by the New Deal, the new unions, and the war-era prosperity over which Roosevelt presided. In 1952 Jews, Italians, and Poles still gave upwards of 90 percent of their vote to the Democrats.

But the counterrevolution was knocking at the door. Lubell understood that the greatest threat to the postwar New Deal came from the right, or from those internal fissures from which the opponents of a nationalizing, interventionist, laborite state could easily profit. His analysis therefore stands counterpoised to that of some of the giants of American historiography. Unlike many liberal intellectuals, he was not worried about the emergence of a leviathan state, or the insertion of an ideological strain into partisan politics. In *The Future of American Politics* Lubell sees the Rooseveltian New Deal in far more ideological terms than did Richard Hofstadter (1948, 1955), whose influential essays painted the New Dealers as a pragmatic, experimental, even a cavalier cohort, who broke with the moralism that had so constipated the American reform tradition. Nor does Lubell's work share much in common with the outlook of Arthur Schlesinger, Jr., who also celebrated the creative opportunism of FDR. In *The Vital Center* (1949) Schlesinger still saw a sinister threat to American social progress coming from those who took their politics a bit too seriously, namely, the communists and the dough-faced liberals they had seduced. In contrast, Lubell knew that the impact of the New Deal was profoundly ideological; there was no such thing as a pragmatic calculus or a pluralist equilibrium in American politics. Partisan politics had moral, ideological content, whatever the episodic program of those politicians who briefly strut across center stage. And this is why he spent so much time investigating the way voters rationalized a shift in their electoral loyalties even as they clung for generations to the core of their ethnoclass identity.

Lubell is remarkably prescient in identifying those tensions that would weaken or fracture the Roosevelt coalition. These are fourfold: the conservative transformation of the labor movement; the persistence of a resentful, isolationist strain within

sections of the Democratic polity; inflation, which the upwardly mobile often linked to what they saw as overweening New Deal statecraft; and most explosively, the racial tensions that were generating a white southern revolt and a growing fission among the urban frontiersmen and women who had earlier been stalwart troops in the Roosevelt line of march.

I first read Lubell's chapter on labor, "The Dynamo Slows Down," almost thirty years ago: then, now, and in 1952 it hit the target. Lubell sees labor as increasingly conservative, both in terms of its internal bureaucratization, and as a bloc that seeks to preserve the industrial status quo generated by the New Deal. But the very existence of the new industrial unions nevertheless gave to US politics a polarizing character which often divided the working class itself. This explains part of the reason that Robert Taft won such a stunning reelection victory in Ohio, where in 1950 Lubell found that many working-class voters repudiated the Congress of Industrial Organizations (CIO) as the embodiment of a dangerous, unresponsive "big labor." Fears of inflation were an equally divisive threat to labor–liberal hegemony, "the breaking point of the Roosevelt coalition," wrote Lubell. In the 1940s and 1950s inflationary worries, especially within the nonunion middle class, trumped every other issue in the opinion polls: communism, corruption, race, the Cold War. But few historians know what to do with this ever-present question. Most have come to think of it as something like the weather: always there, sometimes unpleasant, but a near-laughable subject when considered in terms of party politics. However, Lubell understood that the inflationary pressures that arose after World War II had a real political bite, and they worked insidiously against the integrity of the New Deal coalition. Inflation undercut working-class purchasing power and peeled away those layers of the Roosevelt majority most concerned with union power and welfare/warfare state spending.

Regional political currents were also threatening to fracture the Roosevelt coalition. For Lubell, isolationism and internationalism had little to do with the actual content of foreign policy. They reflected instead longstanding attitudes and postures *vis-à-vis* those who ruled, and who did not, inside the nation's boundaries. In particular, twentieth-century isolationism stood for the longstanding resentment held by many in the old Northern European immigrant groups, by the Irish, Germans, and Scandinavians, who had resisted or resented US participation in World Wars I and II. In its heyday, midwestern political progressivism had linked together the economic radicalism of many of these immigrant farmers and townspeople with the anti-war sentiment of the La Follette progressives. In 1918 Congressman Charles Lindbergh, the flyer's father, had been Minnesota's leading opponent of the war. But after 1938 these currents diverged, with the economic radicals turning into Farmer-Labor Democrats, while the isolationists moved to the Republican right where they became part of the voting bloc that cheered on Joseph McCarthy, Douglas MacArthur, and Robert Taft. In truth, Lubell's analysis devalues the McCarthyite political project. He fails to see how and why Cold War elites deployed anti-communism against the legacy of the New Deal and its left-liberal supporters. But Lubell nevertheless explains a good deal about the mass base enjoyed by the embittered anti-communists of that era, and without recourse to the crude anti-populist, anti-democratic discourse put forward by Richard Hofstadter (1963), Seymour Martin Lipset (1960), and Daniel Bell (1955) just a few years later.

And finally there are the racial tensions at work undermining the New Deal coalition. These came in two parts, one southern, the other on the urban frontier. After the Dixiecrat rebellion of 1948, it was clear that the white South was ready to bolt the Democrats. In a brilliant chapter detailing the infamous defeat of New Dealer Frank Graham in the 1950 North Carolina primary, Lubell identifies a racial counterrevolution that was energized, not ameliorated, by the urbanization and industrialization that was sweeping the South. Lubell was writing before the *Brown* decision and before the rise of massive resistance, but he nevertheless broke from the Whiggish liberalism that was so characteristic of the Roosevelt reformers, who thought southern economic progress would automatically lead to a moderation of racial attitudes and policies. Instead, Lubell demonstrates that the specter of black enfranchisement, either through the unions or through federal pressure, had begun to generate the kind of white solidarity of a sort not seen since the demise of Populism. In Charlotte, North Carolina, then a model of New South progressivism, Lubell found that Graham made his worst showing in Myers Park, heretofore the city's most progressive, upper-crust district. A GOP-southern realignment of party politics was in the making.

Lubell is somewhat more optimistic about racial politics along the northern, urban frontier. The New Deal itself gave rise to the modern civil rights impulse, when the newly empowered unions attempted to organize the South; and when black unionists and civil rights leaders realized that they too could make effective demands upon an intrusive, ambitious welfare/warfare state. Lubell thinks the passage of state-level fair employment practice laws, union success in recruiting African Americans, and the integration of many urban schools held out the prospect of black political assimilation. But Lubell sheds his rose-colored glasses when the lay of the social terrain forces him to recognize that huge numbers of working-class Democrats resisted black entry into their political and economic world. The fate of the Roosevelt coalition will therefore hinge upon the outcome "of this battle for racial and religious tolerance among its own elements." And the prospects for victory were hardly assured. In a passage that foreshadows the latter-day scholarship of Jonathan Reider (1985), John McGreevy (1996), and Thomas Sugrue (1996), Lubell finds that "the frustrations of the urban frontier fall most heavily on the older residential areas, along the line where expanding Negro settlement pushes in on those unable to rise higher on the social ladder. Along this racial 'middle border,' where the rainfall of social status is so uncertain, the emotions stirred up by the civil rights issue assume their most violent form."

This postwar stalemate thus explains why President Truman won in 1948 and why he proved so ineffectual a president, certainly in terms of the Rooseveltian yardstick by which Lubell measures Democratic politicians and their policies. Truman got himself reelected, not because of his celebrated whistlestop campaign, but because the third and fourth party defections of 1948, the Dixiecrat and Henry Wallace Democratic splitoffs, actually helped reforge the old Roosevelt coalition. The absence of these splinter elements made many wayward elements once again comfortable with Truman and the Democrats. These included the overwhelming bulk of the labor movement, the isolationists who had once followed Father Charles Coughlin out of the party, conservative midwestern farmers who were nevertheless dependent on federal crop subsidies, and all but the most radical African Americans and Jews. But

Truman's electoral success assured that the president would continue as a domestic policy failure, for as Lubell makes clear, his very presence at the top of the Democratic ticket was the product of, and dependent upon, the political stalemate that had frozen US politics in the years after 1938. Given the hagiographic treatment that has so infected our more recent studies of the Missouri politician (McCullough, 1992; Ferrell, 1994; Hamby, 1995), it is positively refreshing to read Lubell's succinct analysis. Truman was a border-state politician who made a career of straddling the issues. He was "resolutely indecisive," writes Lubell, "happiest when able to make a dramatic show of activity, secure in the knowledge that nothing much was going to happen." Thus "the secret of Truman's political vitality was that he shrewdly planted himself on the furiously dead center of stalemate to which irreconcilables must repair if they are to make a bargain . . . deadlock was the essence of the man. Stalemate was his Midas touch."

Samuel Lubell continued as an active journalist for a quarter-century after the appearance of *The Future of American Politics*. He wrote six more books, including *The Revolt of the Moderates* (1956) and *White and Black: Test of a Nation* (1965), but none enjoyed the influence of his initial book-length probe into the heart of mid-century social politics. Lubell died in 1987, by which time *The Future of American Politics* was out of print. For all students of the New Deal legacy it bears rereading.

REFERENCES

Bell, Daniel, ed.: *The New American Right* (New York: Criterion, 1955); rev. ed., *The Radical Right* (Garden City, NY: Doubleday, 1962).

Ferrell, Robert H.: *Harry S. Truman: A Life* (Columbia: University of Missouri Press, 1994).

Hamby, Alonzo: *Man of the People: A Life of Harry S. Truman* (New York: Oxford University Press, 1995).

Hofstadter, Richard: *The American Political Tradition* (New York: Alfred A. Knopf, 1948).

Hofstadter, Richard: *The Age of Reform: From Bryan to FDR* (New York: Alfred A. Knopf, 1955).

Hofstadter, Richard: *Anti-Intellectualism in American Life* (New York: Alfred A. Knopf, 1963).

Lipset, Seymour Martin: *Political Man: The Social Bases of Politics* (Garden City, NY: Doubleday, 1960).

Lubell, Samuel: *The Future of American Politics* (New York: Doubleday, 1952, 1956, 1965).

McCullough, David G.: *Truman* (New York: Simon and Schuster, 1992).

McGreevy, John T.: *Parish Boundaries: The Catholic Encounter With Race in the Twentieth Century Urban North* (Chicago: University of Chicago Press, 1996).

Reider, Jonathan: *Canarsie: The Jews and Italians of Brooklyn Against Liberalism* (Cambridge, Mass.: Harvard University Press, 1985).

Schlesinger, Jr., Arthur: *The Vital Center: The Politics of Freedom* (Boston: Houghton Mifflin, 1949).

Sugrue, Thomas J.: *The Origins of the Urban Crisis: Race and Inequality in Postwar Detroit* (Princeton, NJ: Princeton University Press, 1996).

CHAPTER THIRTY

Stephanie Coontz, *The Way We Never Were* (1992)

ELAINE TYLER MAY

When it first appeared in 1992, Stephanie Coontz's myth-shattering book, *The Way We Never Were: American Families and the Nostalgia Trap*, gained wide attention, both inside and outside the academy. It arrived just in time for the 1992 presidential campaign, when "family values" rhetoric filled the airwaves. The book offered an important antidote to Reagan-era celebrations of the "traditional" American family, which harked back to a mythic golden age that presumably reached its apex in the 1950s. Decades of scholarship in family history had shown conclusively that there never was a "traditional" family that resembled the idealized vision of the self-sufficient domestic unit with the breadwinner father, full-time homemaker-wife-and-mother, and children – all fulfilling normative expectations of gender and age behavior. But until Coontz's sweeping and politically charged synthesis, the insights of family historians did not permeate other areas of scholarship; nor did they fully enter the public policy debates that swirled around "family values." Stephanie Coontz effectively brought the lenses of race, class, and gender to focus on the political uses and abuses of family history, providing a thorough critique of the myth of the self-sufficient American home. Today, nearly a decade after it first appeared, these insights are as important and timely as ever.

In her preface, Coontz writes that she began the book as a history of the family in the twentieth century, but that she quickly realized that to tell that story, she would need to confront the widespread myths that prevail in our society about the past. She found that the model of the family that held the most power in the national imagination was grounded in a glossy vision of the 1950s, in which affluent white middle-class families lived in tidy single-family suburban homes behind trimmed lawns and white picket fences. Dad went to work in the city, while Mom took care of the house and the kids. Presumably, these families adhered to proper gender and sexual codes, and provided the basis not only for social order but also for the American way of life, the essence of democracy, the foundation of the Free World during the Cold War. Coontz points out that very few families actually lived according to this model, and those who were able to do so were supported by a vast array of government programs that subsidized this way of life, from the GI Bill of Rights that gave federal low-interest loans to veterans to tax laws that rewarded homeownership. Government funds poured into suburban developments and highways, while red-lining policies and racial exclusions prevented people of color from participating in the "good life" that defined the essence of what it meant to be an American.

The Way We Never Were argues that families in the United States have never fit the myths that surround the "traditional" family in the popular culture, political rhetoric, and common assumptions. Most important, Coontz demonstrates that families have always relied upon various forms of support – from the government, the community, and wider kinship and fictive-kin networks – in order to survive. In popular memory today, the 1950s still represents the last gasp of the "traditional" self-sufficient nuclear family. Some people applaud this ideal and struggle to restore it; others claim that it thwarted women's opportunities, put too much pressure on male breadwinners, and stifled children's independence. But either way, the myth of the "traditional" family rests on the notion of self-sufficiency, which has influenced political debates, public policies, and cultural wars. Coontz demonstrates that the post-World War II suburban ideal, propped up by massive government funding and restrictive public policies, was neither "traditional" nor "typical," yet it quickly grew into mythic proportions, further marginalizing "nontraditional" families, such as single-parent families or gay and lesbian households.

Coontz's powerful synthesis illuminates the deep assumptions about class, race, and gender that have shaped debates about the family. Because the model of the mythical family is white and middle class, families that do not conform to the model are often denigrated as morally lacking. Such assumptions allow policymakers and privileged citizens to blame the nation's most vulnerable families – those most exploited by capitalism, and most disadvantaged by racism – for their own marginality. Political rhetoric about "family values" implies that anyone whose family life does not conform to the mythic ideal causes harm to themselves, their children, and the society at large. Coontz makes it clear that the society bears some responsibility for the wellbeing of its families. She neither laments the "decline" of the family nor celebrates the diversity of family forms. Rather, she acknowledges that many American families are struggling for a variety of reasons, and she calls upon citizens and policymakers to move beyond the myths and address the structural and economic factors that cause domestic hardship.

The book is a model of academic writing for a wide public audience, written with the intention of shaping current debates about the family and influencing public policy. Considering that this is a historical investigation loaded with data, the book achieved considerable attention in the public press, with reviews in major newspapers and magazines. Coontz traveled and spoke widely on the lecture circuit. She continued to engage in spirited public debates around policy issues affecting American families, with op-ed pieces, revisions of the book to keep it current, and a follow-up analysis of contemporary families, *The Way We Really Are*. Coontz has become an activist public intellectual since the initial publication of *The Way We Never Were*, putting to rest any arcane academic claims that if a book is "popular" or "relevant," it is not serious scholarship.

The book remains important today because the political impulse toward privatization has accelerated. Democrats as well as Republicans have called for smaller government and the "end of welfare as we know it." Few would argue that the welfare system worked perfectly – the work of Linda Gordon and other scholars of welfare has shown its flawed logic from the beginning. Yet underlying the debates around welfare reform and a host of other public policies is the assumption that healthy families are and always have been self-sufficient. In the current political climate, that assumption reinforces the conservative argument that most Americans are better off when the government steps back and lets individuals take care of themselves and their families through private effort, with the help of unfettered capitalism. As the new century unfolds, George W. Bush, heir to Reagan-era politics, tacitly accepts the widening gap between the rich and poor by calling upon the nation's wealthy to take care of the poor, through faith-based initiatives and private charity, in the classic *noblesse oblige* tradition of aristocratic societies. This *laissez-faire* approach does nothing to alleviate the structural causes of poverty, and ignores the fact that much of the wealth of today's affluent elite rests on the benefits reaped by white suburban families in the 1950s, when property ownership and capital accumulation was facilitated by generous government subsidies. Filled with evidence of the government's historical role in helping as well as hindering family wellbeing, Coontz's book is as relevant to public policy debates today as it was when it first appeared.

In addition to its essential political message, *The Way We Never Were* remains important for scholars as well as students. Coontz brought the insights of feminist scholarship, labor history, and studies of race to reshape the history of the family. Her book provides a model for scholars on how to integrate analyses of public and private life, demonstrating that it is virtually impossible to understand one side without the other. The book is particularly useful as a classroom text. Although the analysis is complex and sophisticated, the book is written in a clear and accessible prose that encourages students to think in new ways about the world around them, especially their most immediate and familiar environment.

The book also provides an excellent introduction for students to the field of family history. The field has produced scholarship that illuminates the history of the family itself – its many different forms and structures, the various roles of family members, the functions it serves – as well as the political, cultural, social, and economic purposes American families have been expected to fulfill in American society. It is by now well understood by scholars that there never was a single family form, and that factors such as religion, race, ethnicity, nationality, socioeconomic status, occupation, sexual orientation, and a host of other factors and characteristics affect what families look like and how they function, both for their members and within the larger society. Coontz synthesizes these findings into a book with a powerful political argument, allowing students to critique and debate her thesis as well as their own assumptions.

The Way We Never Were also raises a number of questions that call for further study. The task for scholars is to take up where Coontz left off. She does an outstanding job of demolishing the myth of the traditional family, but she does not explain how and why that myth emerged and why it continues to hold such power. Why is it that the family continues to be the source of so many illusions, the center of so many controversies, the flashpoint in the culture wars? What is it about American society and history that places such heavy ideological weight on the family as the foundation of American citizenship and identity? For these future investigations, Coontz's book provides an essential foundation upon which to build.

REFERENCE

Coontz, Stephanie: *The Way We Never Were: American Families and the Nostalgia Trap* (New York: Basic Books, 1992).

CHAPTER THIRTY-ONE

Alphonso Pinkney, *The Myth of Black Progress* (1984)

ROBERT E. WEEMS, JR.

As a result of the mid-twentieth-century civil rights movement, overt de jure racial discrimination has disappeared in this country. Once widely used signs designating separate "colored" and "white" restrooms and water fountains are now found in museum exhibits. Nevertheless, more than a generation after the passage of the Civil Rights Act of 1964 and the Voting Rights Act of 1965, a disproportionate number of African Americans remain unemployed, undereducated, or incarcerated. One of the pioneering works that sought to address this disturbing discrepancy in American life was Alphonso Pinkney's *The Myth of Black Progress* (1984).

Written during the Reagan presidency, Pinkney's book reflected the dismay and anger that many African Americans felt toward the fortieth president of the United States. Because of the enormous cost associated with the US military's dramatic buildup during the 1980s, domestic programs, especially those associated with African Americans, were given extremely low priority. This "dismissal" of African American interests appeared linked to the fact that the vast majority of blacks had not supported the successful Reagan presidential campaign of 1980. Moreover, President Reagan surrounded himself with such neoconservative black advisers and appointees as Thomas Sowell and Clarence Thomas, who themselves rejected giving special consideration to African Americans. Consequently, African Americans, from entrepreneurs to welfare recipients, saw government support of their activities diminish. Even before Ronald Reagan took office, an increasing amount of scholarly research during the 1970s suggested that government programs aimed at ameliorating the plight of African Americans were no longer necessary. In an important section of his book entitled "Social Scientists and the Myth of Black Progress," Pinkney criticized the tendency of such scholars to both exaggerate the extent of black progress, and to blame any lingering instances of African American social and economic deprivation on the moral and intellectual deficiencies of blacks themselves.

Two of the works cited by Pinkney that reflected this disturbing trend were Robert Fogel and Stanley Engerman's two-volume book, *Time on the Cross* (1974), and William Julius Wilson's monograph, *The Declining Significance of Race* (1978). Fogel and Engerman, two economists who used computer-generated data to analyze the institution of slavery, concluded that American slavery was not as horrific as most had been led to believe. Wilson, an African American sociologist, stated that class rather than race was now the primary factor in determining people's life chances in America.

From Pinkney's perspective, *Time on the Cross* was dangerous in that it suggested that affirmative action programs (which were instituted to redress past racial discrimination and oppression) were unnecessary since alleged historic racial discrimination and oppression (exemplified by slavery) were not as bad as people thought. Similarly, *The Declining Significance of Race* incorrectly implied that historic discrimination based upon race had quickly vanished in the aftermath of the civil rights movement. It bears noting that, while Pinkney characterized Wilson as a black conservative scholar, Wilson's later works, most notably *The Truly Disadvantaged: The Inner City, the Underclass, and Public Policy* (1987) and *When Work Disappears: The Work of the New Urban Poor* (1996), clearly convey his liberal/social democrat inclinations. It appears plausible that Pinkney's (and others') criticism of *The Declining Significance of Race* helped prompt Wilson's later clarification of his ideological predilections.

For his part Pinkney, rather than solely react to the work of conservative scholars, sought to analyze the status of African Americans in the post-civil rights movement United States. To do this, his analysis stressed the dichotomy between "equality in principle" and "equality in practice." Although African Americans after the passage of 1960s civil rights legislation achieved equality in principle, they by no means had achieved equality in practice. As one of the many statistics contained in *The Myth of Black Progress* revealed, in 1970, African American families earned 63 percent of the median income of white families; by 1980, this figure had dropped to 58 percent. According to Pinkney, this and other disparities between black and white economic and educational achievement could be attributed to ongoing American individual and institutional racism.

One of the ways to measure a book's importance is whether its basic thesis is substantiated by subsequent scholarship. Among the later works that echoed Alphonso Pinkney's book were Fred R. Harris and Roger Wilkins's co-edited volume, *Quiet Riots: Race and Poverty in the United States* (1988), and Andrew Hacker's *Two Nations: Black and White, Separate, Hostile, Unequal* (1992). Harris and Wilkins's *Quiet Riots*, compiled to survey race relations in the United States twenty years after the Kerner Commission Report of 1968, confirmed Pinkney's thesis of "the myth of black progress." While some African Americans had indeed improved their socioeconomic position between 1968 and 1988, a significant number of blacks had not materially benefited from affirmative action and other 1960s civil rights legislation. Similarly, Hacker's *Two Nations* reaffirmed the persistence of white individual and institutional racism (which limited the extent of African American socioeconomic mobility). Yet, while Harris, Wilkins, and Hacker employed Pinkney's paradigm, neither *Quiet Riots* nor *Two Nations* makes any reference to *The Myth of Black Progress*.

Despite its significance, the relegation of Alphonso Pinkney's book to (undeserved) obscurity may be attributed to the fact that some of his published works, before and after *The Myth of Black Progress*, contained unmistakable elements of black nationalist and radical sentiment. For instance, after citing black militant H. Rap Brown's famous quote, "Violence is as American as cherry pie," Pinkney's *The American Way of Violence* (1972) proposed a clear historical linkage between the massacre of Native Americans, the brutal enslavement of Africans, the dropping of atomic bombs on Hiroshima and Nagasaki, atrocities perpetrated against Vietnamese peasants during the war in Vietnam, and the extermination of the Black Panther

Party. Similarly, his *Lest We Forget: White Hate Crimes: Howard Beach and Other Racial Atrocities* (1994) documented more contemporary instances of racial violence against African Americans.

Although Ronald Reagan has been out of the White House for several years, the conservative reverberations of the 1980s remain alive and well in the United States. In this climate, Alphonso Pinkney and other black nationalist and radical scholars, while not silenced, have been marginalized. Although "political" considerations have contributed to the marginalization of *The Myth of Black Progress*, the book can be justifiably criticized for occasionally crossing the line that separates scholarly discourse from polemics. Pinkney, clearly, is an impassioned critic of the Reagan administration and the conservative academic genre that helped form the ideological basis of the so-called "Reagan Revolution." Yet, even this perceived weakness can be instructive for students. Although the Reagan presidency, in many circles, is portrayed as an extremely positive period in recent American history, there is an alternative view-point. Alphonso Pinkney eloquently articulates this contrarian position regarding the Reagan years. More important, until the majority of African Americans (and not just a relative few) are provided the opportunity to fully realize their potential in the United States, the title of Pinkney's book will remain a reasonable assessment of their condition.

REFERENCES

Fogel, Robert William and Engerman, Stanley L.: *Time on the Cross: The Economics of American Negro Slavery* (Boston: Little, Brown, 1974).

Hacker, Andrew: *Two Nations: Black and White, Separate, Hostile, Unequal* (New York: Scribner's, 1992).

Harris, Fred R. and Wilkins, Roger, eds.: *Quiet Riots: Race and Poverty in the United States* (New York: Pantheon, 1988).

Pinkney, Alphonso: *The American Way of Violence* (New York: Random House, 1972).

Pinkney, Alphonso: *The Myth of Black Progress* (New York: Cambridge University Press, 1984).

Pinkney, Alphonso: *Lest We Forget: White Hate Crimes: Howard Beach and Other Racial Atrocities* (Chicago: Third World Press, 1994).

Wilson, William Julius: *The Declining Significance of Race: Blacks and Changing American Institutions* (Chicago: University of Chicago Press, 1978).

Wilson, William Julius: *The Truly Disadvantaged: The Inner City, the Underclass, and Public Policy* (Chicago: University of Chicago Press, 1987).

Wilson, William Julius: *When Work Disappears: The Work of the New Urban Poor* (New York: Alfred A. Knopf, 1996).

CHAPTER THIRTY-TWO

Garry Wills, *Nixon Agonistes: The Crisis of the Self-Made Man* (1970)

ROBERT WESTBROOK

Richard Nixon is the most pathological of postwar American presidents, though the competition is fierce. Journalist John Osborne recalled that "reporters who followed and observed Nixon as closely as I tried to did so in part because, way down and in some instances not so far down in their consciousness, there was a feeling that he might go bats in front of them at any time" (Osborne, 1975, p. 5). No president has better exemplified what Richard Hofstadter termed the paranoid style in American politics, perhaps because no president edged so close to clinical paranoia. Nixon's pathology no doubt helps explain the exceptional attention he has drawn, not only from biographers and historians, but from novelists, playwrights, poets, filmmakers, and even one major composer (John Adams). Nixon haunts postwar culture as he haunts postwar politics.

But lurking in these multimedia portraits of psychosis in power is the suspicion that – strange as he was – Nixon embodied deep-seated and widespread American dreams and nightmares. As Gore Vidal put it, "As individuals presidents are accidental; but as types, they are inevitable and represent, God help us, us. We are Nixon; he is us" (Vidal, 1970, p. 58).

No one has better captured the us that was Nixon than Garry Wills in *Nixon Agonistes*. Published in 1970 – well before Watergate – *Nixon Agonistes* propelled Wills to prominence in American intellectual life (Wills, [1970] 1979). There he has remained over the course of an extraordinary career that has witnessed exceptional books on subjects ranging from St. Augustine to Shakespeare to John Wayne, from the American founding to the Gettysburg Address to contemporary Catholicism. Not least of Wills's books are fine studies centering on two other postwar presidents, John Kennedy (*The Kennedy Imprisonment*) and Ronald Reagan (*Reagan's America*). Yet neither can compare to *Nixon Agonistes*, arguably the most revelatory book on a postwar president. That it is out of print says less about the book than about a political culture understandably wary of owning up to Wills's Nixon. Better the pathetic lush of Oliver Stone's *Nixon*, on whom we may invest the distancing contempt of pity, than a Nixon who mirrors the republic.

Wills's Nixon is, to be sure, plenty strange. The book opens on the eve of the 1968 Republican primary in Wisconsin, and features an account of Wills's telling interview with Nixon on a plane bound for Chicago, in which the candidate chose to sit shrouded in darkness as if seeking respite from the face-time of public life in which his face was a liability. Having himself offered a cruel anatomy of Nixon's visage ("when he smiles, the space under his nose rolls up [and in] like the old sunshades hung on front porches"), Wills remarks sympathetically that Nixon "must be aware that people vote for him despite his appearance; he speaks, always across a barrier. To carry that barrier about with one, to *be* that barrier, must introduce a painful complexity into one's approach toward fickle things like television and reporters and New Hampshire voters" (pp. 25, 29). Nixon was at war with himself as well as his enemies. The latest and newest "Nixon" whom he willed into being for the campaign moved with "unintended syncopation," unable to shake older Nixons "jerking still at one part of his frame or face" (pp. 22–3).

Yet for Wills, Nixon's strangeness was the consequence not of that which divided him from his fellow Americans, but of the manner in which he caricatured a deep-seated national creed. This creed, Wills argues, is *liberalism*. Liberalism, as Wills sees it, is "the philosophy of the marketplace, and America is distinguished by a 'market' mode of thought in all its public (and even private) life, a mode that is Nixon through and through" (p. ix). At the heart of liberalism lay an "emulative ethic" that held that "proving oneself in the free arena of competition is the test of manhood, truth, and political wisdom" (p. 531). This was the ethic of the individualist, of the "striver." This was the *agon* of the self-made man. Nixon – "so totally this sweaty moral self-doubting self-made bustling brooding type" – was its Samson (p. 531). Nixon's "pure expression" of the emulative ethic of the market "made him an eccentric at the center of our national experience, the *individual* as a *social measure*, our aberrant norm" (p. vii).

Nixon Agonistes is a full-throated attack on this aberrant norm, "a lover's quarrel with my country," Wills calls it (p. x). Because Wills was no less a reporter than a political theorist, his assault on liberalism was launched as much by the particulars of reportage as by the abstractions of theoretical debate. Trained at Yale as a classicist in the early 1960s while making ends meet as a freelance writer, Wills was denied tenure at Johns Hopkins in 1966 for refusing to abandon journalism. Turning then to full-time reporting, he had by the late 1960s found a place among the stable of "new journalists" working for editor Harold Hayes at *Esquire*. *Nixon Agonistes* grew out of assignments for this and other popular magazines. Hence throughout the book Wills moves "from observed particulars to argued generalities," seeking to keep the argument "based cumulatively upon observed detail, on small things widely known and discussed, analyzed and shared, things summonable still to the mind's inquest" (p. x).

As a reporter, Wills offers incisive accounts of the 1968 campaign and party conventions (including a gripping first-hand report on the oft-ignored "other riot" in the black neighborhoods of Miami during the GOP gathering, as well as the oft-described police assault on demonstrators later in Chicago). A carefully crafted portrait of Nixon's life and thought makes the case that he personified the liberal market ethos. But Wills also provides acid-etched sketches of other major political figures of the 1960s, including Spiro Agnew ("a guided missile, swung into place, aimed, activated, launched with the minute calculation that marks Nixon" [p. 257]); Daniel Berrigan ("he wears a clerical suit with a black turtleneck pullover, like an ecclesiastical U-boat commander" [p. 51]); Barry Goldwater ("he had an inferiority simplex – the plain knowledge, never shirked, that he is a lightweight" [p. 235]); Richard

Goodwin ("a Left-Wing Roy Cohn" [p. 474]); George McGovern ("pinching oratory through his stone smile" [p. 365]); Daniel Moynihan ("he obviously thinks an urbanist should be urbane – the bow tie and startled eyebrow arcs bend toward others at cocktail parties as the florid raconteur nudges his points home" [p. 474]); Nelson Rockefeller ("black comedy Falstaff, not only disastrous in himself, but the cause of disaster in others" [p. 183]); and George Wallace ("he has a dingy attractive air of a B-movie idol, the kind who plays a handsome garage attendant" [p. 56]). Not the least of the virtues of *Nixon Agonistes* is its provocative panorama of the political culture of the 1960s. Precisely by decentering Nixon, Wills better explains him.

Wills mobilizes his particulars in service of a blistering attack on four idealized markets that he argues underpin liberalism: the moral market, the economic market, the marketplace of ideas, and the political market. Each imagines a self-regulating mechanism that produces happy results, be it the triumph of the striving puritan, the success of the competitive entrepreneur, the adoption of the best idea, or the election of the superior candidate for office (or, internationally, a concert of self-determining nations). For all their differences, each of these markets inscribes the emulative ethic: "All our liberal values track back to a mystique of the earner" (p. 529).

Putting his Jesuit education to good use, Wills demonstrates in exquisite detail that none of these markets works as promised. The moral market celebrates an impossible self-sufficiency. The economic market supposes an unlikely efficiency. The marketplace of ideas invests in an impossible neutrality. The political market favors mediocrity at home and a corrosive combination of nationalism and imperialism abroad. The market mode of thought, Wills concludes, is less logical than mythological.

Wills realizes that the liberalism he speaks of is – as a whole – the "classical liberalism" of the nineteenth century and he struggles with its fracturing in the twentieth century. Those who adhere most closely to its tenets in the United States we call "libertarian conservatives." American "liberals" are commonly thought to be those who have their doubts about the virtues of unregulated economic markets. Even Nixon, whom Wills argues was trying to reassemble the classical liberal creed, cannot be said to have been a friend of academic freedom, and his was the one peacetime administration to institute wage and price controls on the economic market. Wills would have been on more solid ground simply to insist that market modes of thought and the emulative ethic had – in one form or another – penetrated the political thought of liberals and conservatives alike in twentieth-century America.

It was difficult, that is, for Wills to find anyone who believed in all four idealized markets, but it was easy enough to find at all points on the political spectrum those who believed in one or another of them. And liberals and conservatives alike were wedded to the emulative ethic, even when they disagreed about its implications for public policy. This shared worldview Wills brings home brilliantly in a meditation on the peculiarity of the metaphors of the "race" and the "starting line" which have ruled American thinking about distributive justice:

> The Left has stressed *equality* of opportunity. The Right has stressed opportunity to *achieve*. Yet each side allows for considerable adjustment. The Left, as it addresses the

voter, stresses that welfare is meant to "put a man on his feet," so he can be a productive competitor; and its strongest argument for governmental intervention is that welfare should not be considered a "dole," an act of charity, but a basic right – the right, that is, to an equal place at the starting line. And the Right does not deny the need to help some men get started; it just argues points of fact (i.e., does this or that welfare scheme destroy initiative instead of creating it?). Such a debate is not only inevitable but endless, once one accepts the metaphor of the starting line. Does a man begin the race at birth? Or when he enters school? When he enters the work force? When he attempts to open a business of his own? Or is the starting line at each of these points? And if so, then why not at all the intermediate points as well? And how does one correlate this man's starting line (or lines) with the staggered, endlessly multiplied starting lines of every other individual? How do we manage the endless *stopping* of the race involved in *starting* it so often? One second after the gun has sounded, new athletes pop up all over the field, the field itself changes shape, and we must call everybody in, to line them up once more. We never get to surmise where, in this science-fiction world of continual starting and racing, the finish line might be. Or, rather, the staggered, infinite finishing lines for each runner. The metaphor is a mess. (p. 274)

Here, in his inquisition against the emulative ethic of competitive individualism, Wills is devastating to "liberals" and "conservatives" alike. By the end of the book, Arthur Schlesinger, Jr. (his favorite "liberal" whipping boy) is no less bloodied than Nixon.

Wills's own political theory is all too implicit in his book, revealed only in an occasional vague reference to "the great lack in our political theory – its blindness to the facts of community life" (p. 543). Wills was – and is – a quirky Catholic conservative of the Burkean – or, better, Augustinian – sort. He began his career in the late 1950s as a key contributor to William F. Buckley's *National Review*. By 1970, he had been banished by his right-wing comrades for apostasy, above all on the matter of anti-communist absolutism – the chapter attacking the justification, or lack thereof, for the war in Vietnam is one of the highlights of *Nixon Agonistes*. But although the *National Review* signaled its horror with Wills in a 1973 cover featuring his head on the body of Huey P. Newton, Wills has remained true to the conservatism he had sketched in an early essay on "The Convenient State" (1964). Wills uses "convenience" in an older sense of "coming together," and he argues that the point of the state and of politics is not justice but social peace. He came to admire disruptive "prophets," like Martin Luther King, who called their fellow citizens to greater justice, but he nonetheless believes that those politicians are best who negotiate imperfect compromises that serve stability and comity. As Wills sees it, the greatest rewards of human experience are to be found not in the solitary striving of one sort of market or another, but in the interdependent social bonds (sometimes hierarchical) of civil society – in families, neighborhoods, churches, unions, and voluntary associations. *Nixon Agonistes* was perhaps the first of the important "communitarian" attacks on liberal individualism, which in the work of intellectuals such as Benjamin Barber, Jean Bethke Elshstain, Christopher Lasch, Alasdair MacIntyre, Michael Sandel, and Michael Walzer form such a prominent part of American political thought (if not American politics) of the last thirty years. And it remains one of the best.

Wills took comfort in the signs he thought he saw all around him in the late 1960s that the market myths had run their course. Discontented African Americans and young people appeared to reject them, while the members of the "silent majority" gave vent to a resentment at this discontent that, Wills contended, only thinly veiled their own disappointment that things did not work out as the myths had promised. Nixon, himself seething with "a continued sense of grievance," was the candidate of their faded values and resentment (p. vii). He was the "last liberal" (p. 534). Nixon's ascent to the presidency was thus proof of the bankruptcy of the emulative ethic – surely the markets were awry if *this* was the leader they threw up. "Nixon's victory was the nation's concession of defeat, an admission that we have no politics left but the old individualism, a web of myths that have lost their magic" (p. 536).

Here Wills was wrong, as he later admitted. Myths, as he well knew, might readily survive rational scrutiny, even scrutiny as intense as that he provided. There proved life aplenty in market modes of thought. The rapid eclipse of the American left, which began shortly after *Nixon Agonistes* was published, witnessed a shift of American political discourse back toward the "classical liberalism" he thought was on its last legs. Like Nixon himself, the ethos he embodied was rehabilitated in the two decades after Watergate. Market logic now reigns supreme under the sign of "globalization," and a Democratic president has triangulated his way to a welfare reform act that forces impoverished single mothers to lace up their track shoes and join the emulative race from which they had once been exempt. One is more likely to find Americans today who embrace all of Wills's four markets than one would have in 1970. Ironically, *Nixon Agonistes* is a book all the more worth reading because Nixon was not the last liberal.

REFERENCES

Osborne, John: *The Last Nixon Watch* (Washington: New Republic, 1975).
Vidal, Gore: "Richard Nixon: Not *The Best Man's* Best Man," in *At Home: Essays, 1982–1988* (New York: Vintage, 1970).
Wills, Garry: "The Convenient State," in Frank S. Meyer (ed.), *What Is Conservatism?* (New York: Holt, Rinehart, and Winston, 1964).
Wills, Garry: *Nixon Agonistes: The Crisis of the Self-Made Man* (New York: Houghton Mifflin, 1970; rev. ed., New York: Mentor, 1979).

CHAPTER THIRTY-THREE

Victor Navasky, *Naming Names* (1980)

JON WIENER

Victor Navasky describes *Naming Names*, a book about the Hollywood blacklist, as a "moral detective story." Navasky is not a historian; at the time the book was published, 1980, he had just been named editor of *Nation* magazine. Unlike historians of McCarthyism or the House Un-American Activities Committee (HUAC) or the Hollywood blacklist, Navasky puts moral issues, arguments about right and wrong, at the center of his work. He focuses on the witnesses who cooperated with HUAC, and asks why – why they provided the committee with the names of communists or fellow travelers in the film industry. He begins by noting the longstanding tradition in American culture that views informing as wrong. The vocabulary says it all: "rat," "stoolie," "fink," "squealer," "Judas" – characters and themes often dramatized in the movies made by the people who were subpoenaed.

The moral questions are important also because of the consequences of the decision to cooperate: those who were named would be blacklisted, their careers ended, unless they also agreed to name names. The lines were especially sharp in this case because no crime was at issue – the committee was not seeking evidence of espionage or sabotage or treason. And the committee already had the names of all the communists in Hollywood, which it obtained when the FBI infiltrated the Communist Party (CPUSA).

Those who named names were some of the most important people in Hollywood: Sterling Hayden, Lee J. Cobb, Budd Schulberg, and at the top of the list, Elia Kazan. In the heart of the book, Navasky goes back to those who named names, almost thirty years after the fact, and asks each why he did it. All of his respondents are smart, articulate, political people, and most have been thinking about the question for decades. After recording their answers, Navasky engages in a kind of moral argument about whether their reasons were good reasons, whether what they did was right.

The intensity of the arguments Navasky has with his subjects gives the book its special power. Navasky identifies three reasons for cooperating with the committee. The first is a "lesser evil" argument – HUAC was bad, but the communists were worse. The Party did not believe in freedom. It defended Stalin, who had killed millions. In the United States, communists lied, manipulated, and bullied people. Why protect them? Why sacrifice one's own career to protect a totalitarian group? Some of the friendly witnesses go farther and argue that they had a moral obligation to help expose the evil of communism. "Defending the Communist Party was something worse than naming names," Edward Dmytryk says. "I did not want to remain a martyr to something that I absolutely believed was immoral and wrong" (p. 238). Dmytryk spoke of "remaining a martyr" because he had originally refused to testify and went to jail with the Hollywood Ten, but changed his mind after the Korean War broke out.

Navasky criticizes the "lesser evil" position. He agrees that of course Stalin was a greater evil than HUAC, but argues that cooperating with HUAC was the wrong way to fight Stalinism. HUAC was attacking freedom and undermining democratic rights. Those who wanted to criticize Stalin and the CPUSA should have done so outside of HUAC, in their writing or speaking. It is significant for Navasky that none of the friendly witnesses took a stand until they faced a subpoena from HUAC.

The second argument for cooperating with the committee is "I didn't hurt anybody." These people agree on the wrongness of HUAC's quest, and avoided being blacklisted by providing names – but, they insist, they named only people who had been named already. Some claim they named only those people who had already been named ten times. Their testimony was not harmful, they argue, and thus it was not wrong.

Navasky criticizes this argument on the grounds that naming any names contributed to HUAC's legitimacy and gave credence to the committee's methods as well as its claims. Naming names made it harder for subsequent witnesses to resist. He adds that in fact each time a person was named they were "hurt" – each time their name appeared in the news they faced additional pressures and risked ostracism. And friendly witnesses had no control over how the committee and the media would publicize the names they provided. Navasky also goes to the trouble of examining the testimony of each of the people who make this argument. He finds that they sometimes made mistakes: Lee J. Cobb said he had only given the names of people who had already been named, but in fact he was the first person to publicly name Lloyd Bridges.

The third reason friendly witnesses give Navasky is "I had no choice – I had higher obligations." In this case the informer agrees that providing names was a bad thing, that it was wrong, that it hurt people, but they argue it was the only thing they could have done. Their responsibilities to support wives and children required that they do what was necessary to keep their jobs rather than sacrifice the present and future of their families for an abstract political idea. Lee J. Cobb, for example, resisted the committee for two years. During that time he was denied work and ran out of money and his wife was institutionalized as an alcoholic. Finally he named twenty people and concluded his testimony with the required statement: "I want to thank you for the privilege of setting the record straight" (p. 270). Almost thirty years later he tells Navasky, "I didn't act out of principle. I wallowed in unprincipledness. . . . If I had not been in need, I'd never have cooperated" (p. 272).

Navasky's critique of "I had no choice" consists of a single devastating fact: two-thirds of everyone who was subpoenaed refused to name names. They too had wives and children and family obligations. They too were subjected to terrible pressures. It was hard to stand up for a principle, to refuse to betray your friends; nevertheless, most of the people HUAC targeted were able to resist – even if it meant leaving Hollywood and finding a different job.

In teaching the book over the last decade, I've found that this last issue divides students along ethnic lines. The white students for the most part find Navasky's critique convincing and powerful. But students from immigrant families, especially the Chinese, Taiwanese, and Koreans, tend to support the argument for family obligations. For them, family obligations are real and powerful and compelling, and political values and ideals are clearly secondary. Indeed, they are often puzzled by what seems to them a kind of empty rhetorical posturing by their white classmates: if the government – the American government – requires that you name names, and it is clear that your family will pay the price if you refuse, of course you should cooperate.

Latino students and especially black students in my classes have been divided on this point. They often appreciate the power of family obligations more acutely than the typical native-born whites, but at the University of California in the 1990s, black and Latino students were intensely politicized by the Republican campaign to end affirmative action. These students tended to be part of a more left-wing political culture than the Asian Americans, and to understand the logic of taking a stand against an unjust governmental policy or practice.

And of course Latino and black students have a different view of the US government than their Asian American classmates. For the Asian immigrants, the United States is a land of freedom and democracy compared to their countries of origin – flawed and imperfect, of course, but still greatly appreciated. In contrast, the Latinos and especially the blacks often can articulate the many forms of discrimination and injustice their people have suffered at the hands of the US majority and its government.

Naming Names considers one additional response to Navasky's question of why: the response of Elia Kazan, probably the most powerful person in Hollywood to be subpoenaed. If he had refused to cooperate, the blacklist might have been broken. But he named names in 1952 – and then took out a full page ad in the *New York Times* declaring his position. When, almost thirty years later, Navasky asks him why, he refuses to answer. Indeed, he had refused to give interviews about his naming names to anyone else either. He says he feels no obligation to justify his actions, to explain himself to posterity.

In the book Navasky then searches Kazan's work for a statement about naming names, and finds one in Kazan's film *On the Waterfront*: he reads it as an allegory of HUAC, in which the protagonist, played by Marlon Brando, has to overcome the cultural aversion to "ratting on your friends" and tell the truth about union corruption on the docks to the Waterfront Crime Commission – a stand-in for HUAC. Here the government's cause is good; the claims made by its opponents only serve to justify wrongdoing and exploitation.

Navasky makes the most of "Elia Kazan and the Case for Silence," as he titles that chapter, in the first edition of the book. (He calls Kazan's refusal to talk "taking a retrospective Fifth" [p. 221].) But in 1988 Kazan published his autobiography, in which he broke his decades of silence on the topic. It turned out he did want to explain himself to posterity – but he did not have anything particularly original to say. He defended his cooperation by reiterating that communism was evil. In the second edition of *Naming Names*, Navasky's new introduction takes note of Kazan ending his silence, but in fact the book worked better when Navasky's key witness refused to talk.

The reviews of the book provide a brief intellectual history of America in the age of Reagan. At the time the book was published – 1980 – the principal criticism came from Cold War liberals like Arthur Schlesinger, Jr., who complained that it made heroes out of communists. "His general tone," Schlesinger wrote in the *New Leader*, "is that, while Stalinism was not so good, anti-Stalinism was really unforgivable" (Schlesinger, 1980, p. 9). The *New Republic* assigned the book to William Phillips, editor of *Partisan Review*, who criticized *Naming Names* for failing to distinguish liberal anti-communists like himself from the reactionaries on HUAC. "It was the liberal anti-communists and not the Communists who stood for a humane and open society," he wrote (Phillips, 1981, p. 32). *New Republic* publisher Martin Peretz also criticized the book in his column in the magazine, calling it a "whining and partisan narrative" and declaring Navasky wrong to view unfriendly witnesses as "virtuous heroes" and the cooperative ones as "unmitigated villains" (Peretz, 1981, p. 38).

The scholarly reviews were less ideologically engaged. The reviewer for the *Journal of American History* criticized the book for "unbelievable" flaws in taping interviews, and for a "lack [of] overall coherence" (Culbert, 1981, p. 185). The *American Political Science Review* concluded that the book "should spur our generation to become ever more vigilant in protecting its civil liberties" (Weinstock, 1981, p. 1054), and Randy Robertson declared in *Reviews in American History* that the book was "profound" (Robertson, 1983, p. 448). The reviewer for *American Historical Review* declared that, "because of the subject, this volume cannot be considered a pleasant one"; nevertheless, the author was praised for being "both dispassionate and compassionate" (Plesur, 1981, p. 953).

Indeed, most reviewers praised Navasky for his fairness in treating people with whom he disagreed. (See also the reviews by Aaron, 1980; Fremont-Smith, 1980; Gordon, 1984; and Sennett, 1980.) That fairness indeed is the key to the success of this "moral detective story" – along with the sense of urgency underlying the entire project. The book is not simply a condemnation of the friendly witnesses. It makes a strong case for the subjects of the book, it takes their arguments seriously – and then dissects and exposes their various alibis and excuses, and sorts out their motives and opportunities. The questions Navasky poses continue to have relevance after the end of the Cold War. Liberated from concerns about a communist threat, readers today can consider the ways "patriotism" has required betraying friends and colleagues – as well as democratic ideals – in our not-so-distant past.

REFERENCES

Aaron, Daniel: "Informing on the Informers," *New York Review of Books* (December 4, 1980): 6–8.
Culbert, David: Review of *Naming Names*, *Journal of American History*, 68 (1981): 184–6.
Fremont-Smith, Eliot: "Ritual in Shame," *Village Voice* (November 5–11, 1980): 43–5.
Gordon, Max: Review of *Naming Names*, *Labor History*, 25 (1984): 133–5.
Kazan, Elia: *Elia Kazan: A Life* (New York: Alfred A. Knopf, 1988).
Navasky, Victor S.: *Naming Names* (1980; rev. ed., New York: Penguin, 1991).

Peretz, Martin: "Unfriendly," *New Republic* (January 3 and 10, 1981): 38.

Phillips, William: "Radical Chic," *New Republic* (April 18, 1981): 30–2.

Plesur, Milton: Review of *Naming Names, American Historical Review*, 86 (1981): 952–3.

Robertson, Randy: "Requiem for the Body Snatchers," *Reviews in American History*, 11 (1983): 447–53.

Schlesinger, Jr., Arthur: "Liberals, Stalinists and HUAC," *New Leader* (December 15, 1980): 6–8.

Sennett, Richard: "Informing," *New York Times Book Review* (October 19, 1980): 1–4.

Weinstock, Carolyn: "Review of *Naming Names*," *American Political Science Review*, 75 (1981): 1052–4.

CHAPTER THIRTY-FOUR

Edward Said, *Orientalism* (1978)

MELANI MCALISTER

After the violence of September 11, 2001, Americans became painfully conscious of the presence of Islam as a powerful source of identity for peoples in the Middle East and elsewhere. That strong and transnational religious identification, coupled with the deep anti-Americanism engendered by decades of the arrogant imposition of US world power, signaled the obsolescence of Cold War dichotomies between communism and capitalism, and even liberal dichotomies between first and third worlds, as ways of understanding geopolitical relations. The attacks on the World Trade Center and the Pentagon, and the war in Afghanistan that followed, make it all the more pressing that, as historians, we rethink our understanding of the US relationship to the Middle East in the period since 1945.

One essential tool in that reassessment is Edward Said's 1978 study, *Orientalism*, a paradigmatic work for examining the role of culture in colonial and postcolonial relationships between the "West" and the "East." This is a particularly appropriate moment to consider the enormous value of Said's work as well as its limits. The concept of Orientalism makes certain kinds of power relationships visible, but it can also constrain our ability to comprehend fully the political and cultural encounters between the United States and the Middle East in the past half-century.

Orientalism argues that since the eighteenth century, European, and later, American, scholars and artists helped to produce a very particular understanding of the "Orient" (what is now known as the Middle East was generally understood as part of the Orient in the eighteenth and nineteenth centuries). In Said's formulation, "Orientalism" was a certain type of lens, a way of understanding the history and culture of the Middle East that consistently marked it as mysterious, decadent, irrational, and backward. "Orientalist" had once been the term that scholars of ancient Middle Eastern languages and cultures had used to define themselves; in Said's hands, the label provided an elegant shorthand for his contention that both the cognitive mapping of spaces (East v. West) and the stereotyping of peoples were intimately connected with economics, politics, and state power.

Orientalism was primarily a study of French and British intellectual and cultural life, but it would eventually have a deep and abiding influence on the study of US history, largely because of the role it played in arguing for the political significance of culture. In Said's classic formulation, Orientalism is a large and multifaceted discourse, an "imaginative geography," that became central to European self-representation in the eighteenth and nineteenth centuries and to US world understandings in the twentieth century. Orientalism operates on a binary logic: Orient v. Occident, Europeans v. Others, Us v. Them. These binaries parallel and draw heavily upon the logic of gender construction: the Orient is "feminized," thus posited as mysterious, overly sexual and tied to the body, irrational, and inclined toward despotism; by contrast, the European is "masculinized" and represented as civilized, restrained, rational, and capable of democratic self-rule.

Said's analysis of Orientalism is, at one level, the analysis of a certain set of stereotypes; the fact that Orientalist representations distorted the experiences and the capabilities of real human beings is part of what makes them so morally repugnant. But Said's argument goes well beyond looking at the limits of such stereotypes by defining the productive nature of Orientalist representations for Europeans. Orientalism mattered because it had an extraordinary identity-forging power for both its authors and their audiences. Orientalism provided one primary grid through which Europeans in the eighteenth and nineteenth centuries made sense of their imperial project. The moral logic of imperialism involved what Etienne Balibar has described as an "imperialist superiority complex," through which the project of imperialist expansion was able to transform itself, in the minds of its practitioners, "from a mere enterprise of conquest into an enterprise of universal domination, the founding of a 'civilization'" (Balibar, 1991, p. 62). For Said, Orientalist scholarship, art, and travel narratives were an integral part of the structures of European imperial power; they did not simply legitimate a political relationship after the fact. Instead, by offering Europeans the certainty that they already knew what there was to know of the East, representations became practices: they laid the foundation for imperial rule.

In the quarter-century since its publication, Said's study has served as the inspiration for a broad variety of academic and political analyses of colonial and postcolonial power. *Orientalism* was immediately and profoundly influential in both Middle East studies and East Asian studies, where it provided the groundwork for an extensive self-examination within each field. In British and European literary studies, and in European cultural history, Said's focus on the power of culture inspired detailed analyses of the imperial imagination, as it played a role in the work of writers ranging from E. M. Forster to Gustave Flaubert (Lowe, 1991; Suleri, 1993; Behdad, 1994); in art, including studies of American landscape painters' images of the Holy Land and photographs of Middle Eastern women (Davis, 1996; Graham-Brown, 1988); and in popular culture, from boys' adventure stories to popular occultism (Green, 1979; Brantlinger, 1988). And not only the Orient was at issue: the colonial imagination, it was argued, reached as far as colonialism itself, and during the 1980s and 1990s, scholars produced extraordinary work on primitivism, "Africanist" discourse, and the cultural meanings of India and Latin America, among others (Miller, 1985; Torgovnick, 1990; Pratt, 1992; McClintock, 1995).

Building on Said's intervention, scholars in recent years have also challenged and revised important aspects of his argument. Two major critiques were to prove particularly important for Americanists. The first challenge was that Said had not adequately accounted for the complexities and open-endedness of Orientalist discourse; it was never as unified and internally coherent as he had posited. Thus scholars would need to analyze Orientalism in terms of its many occasions and multiple uses. This critique recognized that there were many writers and intellectuals who had an investment in representing the "Orient," and they often did so in ways that drew on the tropes that Said had outlined: they were exoticizing, and inclined to represent "Orientals" as irrational and decadent. But like all cultural texts, these representations were also chaotic and open to a variety of potential meanings. As Lisa Lowe has argued, Orientalism consisted of "an uneven matrix of orientalist situations across different cultures and historical sites" (Lowe, 1991, p. 12). Both the Orient *and* the Occident, as produced by Orientalism, were marked by instability, changing meanings, internal contradictions, and slippages. To suggest, as Said does, that the practices of Orientalism were so totalizing as to frame almost every utterance by Europeans is also, at least implicitly, to elide the possibility of transformations, challenges, or alternatives (Behdad, 1994). It thus becomes very difficult to account for change over time.

This is precisely the criticism that has often been leveled against the philosopher and historian Michel Foucault, to whom Said is indebted. Discourses are not simply self-authorizing, and they are never unaffected by the behaviors and practices that contest them. The postcolonial critic Homi Bhabha has suggested that colonial discourse is always "ambivalent," that European imperialists were generally torn by a dual tendency: toward distancing and denigration of the colonized, on the one hand, and toward exoticization and sexual desire, on the other (Bhabha, 1994). When audiences went to a World's Fair exhibit that promised a faithful reproduction of the buildings and inhabitants of a Cairo street, they were *invited* to see the colorful poverty and fascinating-but-disgusting habits of the "other" (Mitchell, 1988). What they *did* see in the multiple and chaotic displays was almost certainly less uniform and less coherent than the official narrative: they might feel superior, but tourists might also and simultaneously feel a longing that veered into a critique of their own culture. Because of this tension – a tension that exists in the fact that all representations carry the possibility of multiple interpretations, and indeed often invite that diversity – imperialist or colonialist representations can never have the totalizing effect they seem to seek.

A second and related critique observes that Orientalism changes depending on who is mobilizing it. Said posits Orientalism as a masculinist enterprise, one that tends to imagine the Orient as feminine (and thus linked to irrationality, sexuality, and lack of capacity for democracy). And in many respects, this argument parallels the work done by political theorists and women's historians in analyzing the ways in which industrializing nations in the eighteenth and nineteenth centuries began to separate out certain spaces designated as "private" – those signified by home and hearth – and to gender those spaces as "feminine." Women's association with the private world was supposed to provide a space of tranquility for men, an escape from their stresses in the industrializing, competitive, market-driven "public." But this private world also functioned to assure women's unequal access to citizenship, voting, and public life (Cott, 1977; Fraser, 1989). Similarly, Said and others have suggested that the representations of "Orientals" as feminized (sensual, domestic, nonrational) and the West as masculinized (rational, intellectual, and public) served to legitimate the exclusion of colonized peoples from democratic rights. In this model, citizenship and nationality were necessarily represented as white and male.

Yet many women in Europe and the United States have been active participants in Orientalism, and in ways that complicated its assumptions. Lowe's reading of European women writers, for example, describes the ways in which, at some periods,

European women's rights discourse simultaneously drew upon and subverted Orientalist logic. Anne McClintock offers a similar analysis, in a rather different context, of the resourceful, unexpected, and sometimes dangerous ways that European women mobilized (and were framed by) the imperial discourse on Africa, particularly its obsessive conflation of "whiteness" and "cleanliness."

But perhaps the most important issue for Americanists has simply been that *Orientalism* did not adequately account for the particular modes of US power, especially post-World War II. Only the final section of *Orientalism* deals with US engagements with the Middle East, and it is the least nuanced and interesting of the book. Focused primarily on policymakers' statements or the work of area studies scholars, this criticism is essentially an ideological critique of US foreign policy, but it fails to account for the complexities of that policy. After World War II, the official rhetoric of US policymakers, along with journalistic accounts of international relations and loosely connected popular culture images, worked to establish the United States as different from the old colonial powers. They did so in part by fracturing the East–West binary on which traditional Orientalism had depended, separating the United States from the rest of the "West"; the United States would take up its superpower status in explicit opposition to older models of colonialism. In addition, certain subcultural groups, such as black Muslims or Christian fundamentalists, began to make their own claims on the Middle East, and their writings often contested some of the presumptions of official US policies. This diversity of voices does not mean that American culture or US policy developed a fully accurate and nuanced view of the region, but rather that the style of representation changed noticeably, from a general East–West binary to a model of "benevolent" American hegemony supplanting colonial rule. But if US appropriations and representations of the Middle East did *not* follow a simple Orientalist paradigm, that was because the project of separating the United States from European imperialism, or distinguishing the Middle East from the rest of the Orient, functioned strategically: in the post-Orientalist logic of the last fifty years, one alternative to European power/knowledge over the Orient was American power in the modern Middle East (McAlister, 2001).

If Said's discussion of the United States fails to live up to the rich analysis of intersecting grids of culture, intellectual life, and state policy that distinguishes the first part of the book, US scholarship in recent years has taken up the challenge of more clearly delineating the specific character of Americans' understandings of their postwar global role. It was Said's model for thinking about culture and power, and the fruitful challenges and additions to that model, that established *Orientalism*'s influence on the work of American historians. Since the 1980s, US historians have built on Said's work to explore the superpower role of the United States not only in terms of diplomatic or Cold War history, but also in relationship to American culture.

The scholarly conversation that *Orientalism* launched was undoubtedly part of the impetus behind the 1993 groundbreaking anthology edited by literary scholars Amy Kaplan and Donald Pease, *The Cultures of United States Imperialism*. In her introduction, Kaplan defined three major absences in the scholarship of the 1970s and 1980s: "the absence of culture from the history of U.S. imperialism; the absence of empire from the study of American culture; and the absence of the United States from the postcolonial study of imperialism" (Kaplan, 1993, p. 11). The collection's aim was to place the history of US global power at the heart of the study of US cultures, and to give culture a central place in an analysis of the production and reproduction of US power. Looking at US engagements with the Philippines, Latin America, and elsewhere, scholars paid particular attention to the remarkable impact of mass culture in the United States, with essays on Buffalo Bill's "Wild West" show, science fiction writing, a museum exhibit, and popular newspaper accounts of Pancho Villa, among others (Slotkin, Brown, Haraway, Wilson, all 1993). Like many of the heirs to *Orientalism*, these studies attended to the circumstances in which cultural texts were received: representations were assumed to be made meaningful only in specific contexts of reception.

But scholarship on the United States, in this collection and in the years to follow, would need to diverge from even the most nuanced study of European colonial power, because the specific contexts of US history demanded new analytical frameworks. First, since the United States had most often eschewed formal colonies, turning instead to economic and political influence, its "imperial" project itself was different. In fact, US power was often defined, both by policymakers and by popular audiences, in *opposition* to old-style European power: what underlay US engagement with the world was not so much imperialism as what one scholar adroitly called "anti-imperial Americanism" (Michaels, 1993). The political will to hegemony was still very much present, but the style and meaning of that hegemony were new, especially after World War II, when the United States consciously inherited and revised the role of world superpower.

Second, racial difference *within* the United States would necessarily be a factor in the ways in which diverse cultural texts imagined the rest of the world. In *Orientalism*, Said argued that Europe represented itself to itself as homogeneous, a single "us" against a "them" somewhere outside the borders. But Latinos, African Americans, Native Americans, and Asian Americans, as well as a mind-boggling variety of white ethnics, have populated the United States, and concerns about "internal" racial difference have never been far from discussions of the US role in the world. In the decades after World War II, the successes of the civil rights movement and later other liberation movements increasingly meant that even the most bland popular culture would need to account for American racial and cultural diversity. Popular movies might insist that "we" were facing a world of evil Russians and Arab terrorists, but the "we" of America would have to be understood as heterogeneous: thus the multicultural "ethnic" platoons that arose in World War II movies and made their way, with an increasingly diverse cast, into the post-Gulf War era.

Race was also an issue for people who identified part of their heritage with a region of the world where the United States was investing, be it Asia or Latin America, Africa or the Middle East. For example, African American poets and activists may have sometimes been as exoticizing as white authors when they wrote about Africa or the Middle East, but they also frequently (and often in the same work) suggested alternatives to the terms of American hegemony. When Richard Wright wrote *The Color Curtain*, his remarkable report on the 1955 Asian–African Conference at Bandung, Indonesia, he engaged in no small bit of exoticizing of the "mystical" and "irrational" peoples of the third world who were forming the nonaligned movement (Wright, 1994, pp. 218–19). But he also knew that in writing favorably about their struggle for liberation, he was arguing for the rights and liberties of African

Americans: his racial consciousness did not prohibit an "Orientalizing" gaze, but it did transform its meaning.

As scholars of US history have taken up the call to analyze culture and American power together, they have often moved well beyond the terrain defined by *Orientalism*. This is a very useful counter to the overuse of the idea of Orientalism in the 1980s and 1990s; too often, activists and writers mobilized the term Orientalism to characterize any representation of any part of the "East," from *Madame Butterfly* to television news accounts of the Viet Cong to movies about Middle Eastern terrorism. Yet not all stereotypes, even those of Asians or Arabs, are Orientalist; they might be racist, or even exoticizing, without engaging in the particular logic of Orientalism: binary, feminizing, and self-authorizing. (For example, in recent decades Arabs in film have often been represented as hypermasculine, not feminine and sensual.) When Orientalism becomes the term used to describe every Western image of every part of the eastern half of the world, the definition has become too flexible for its own good.

Yet the debt to Said's pioneering analysis remains, first and foremost in the fact that it has moved scholars so decisively beyond simple stereotype studies to instead analyze the cultural work done by representations. We do not only point out that certain images were negative, or inaccurate, or denigrating; we go on to ask why they appeared when they did, and what kind of changes in perception or self-understanding they helped to bring about. And despite the theoretical and historical limitations to the Orientalism framework, it remains a useful and evocative characterization of a certain European and American "way of seeing" (Berger, 1977). In the globalizing era, amid the confusion of transnational cultures and global flows of people, we have also seen the rise of significant new imaginative geographies, such as Benjamin Barber's "Jihad v. McWorld," or Samuel Huntington's seductively simple "clash of civilizations." People are indeed different from each other, but our desires, needs, and hopes are not organized along clear lines of geography or even by commitments to "modernity" or anti-modernity. Instead, human beings all over the world exist in modernity together, affected in diverse ways by technology, globalization, unequal distribution of resources, and the increased flow of information. Our relations with each other are as layered as the interactions of global capital and as slippery as the worldwide passages of migration. In the face of this enormously complex reality, we ignore at our peril the force of Said's fundamental argument: the tendency to divide the world into two "unequal halves," in which one part of the world is understood to be irrational, anti-democratic, and profoundly unlike "us," is the failed logic of imperial thinking.

REFERENCES

Balibar, Etienne: "Racism and Nationalism," in Etienne Balibar and Immanuel Wallerstein, *Race, Nation, and Class: Ambiguous Identities* (New York: Verso, 1991), 37–68.

Barber, Benjamin: *Jihad v. McWorld* (New York: Ballantine, 1996).

Behdad, Ali: *Belated Travelers: Orientalism in the Age of Colonial Dissolution* (Durham, NC: Duke University Press, 1994).

Berger, John: *Ways of Seeing* (New York: Penguin, 1977).

Bhabha, Homi: *The Location of Culture* (New York: Routledge, 1994).

Brantlinger, Patrick: *Rule of Darkness: British Literature and Imperialism, 1830–1914* (Ithaca, NY: Cornell University Press, 1988).

Brown, Bill: "Science Fiction, The World's Fair, and the Prosthetics of Empire, 1910–1915," in Amy Kaplan and Donald Pease (eds.), *The Cultures of United States Imperialism* (Durham, NC: Duke University Press, 1993), 129–63.

Cott, Nancy: *The Bonds of Womanhood: "Woman's Sphere" in New England* (New Haven, Conn.: Yale University Press, 1977).

Davis, John: *Landscape of Belief: Encountering the Holy Land in Nineteenth-Century American Art and Culture* (Princeton, NJ: Princeton University Press, 1996).

Fraser, Nancy: *Unruly Practices: Power, Discourse, and Gender in Contemporary Political Theory* (Minneapolis: University of Minnesota Press, 1989).

Graham-Brown, Sarah: *Images of Women: Portrayals of Women and Photography in the Middle East, 1860–1950* (New York: Columbia University Press, 1988).

Green, Martin: *Dreams of Adventure and Deeds of Empire* (New York: Basic Books, 1979).

Haraway, Donna: "Teddy Bear Patriarchy: Taxidermy in the Garden of Eden, New York City, 1908–1936," in Amy Kaplan and Donald Pease (eds.), *The Cultures of United States Imperialism* (Durham, NC: Duke University Press, 1993), 237–91.

Huntington, Samuel: *The Clash of Civilizations and the Remaking of World Order* (New York: Simon and Schuster, 1996).

Kaplan, Amy: "Left Alone With America," in Amy Kaplan and Donald Pease (eds.), *The Cultures of United States Imperialism* (Durham, NC: Duke University Press, 1993), 3–21.

Kaplan, Amy and Pease, Donald, eds.: *The Cultures of United States Imperialism* (Durham, NC: Duke University Press, 1993).

Lowe, Lisa: *Critical Terrains: French and British Orientalism* (Ithaca, NY: Cornell University Press, 1991).

McAlister, Melani: *Epic Encounters: Culture, Media, and U.S. Interests in the Middle East, 1945–2000* (Berkeley: University of California Press, 2001; updated ed., 2005).

McClintock, Anne: *Imperial Leather: Race, Gender, and Sexuality in the Colonial Contest* (New York: Routledge, 1995).

Michaels, Walter Benn: "Anti-Imperial Americanism," in Amy Kaplan and Donald Pease (eds.), *The Cultures of United States Imperialism* (Durham, NC: Duke University Press, 1993), pp. 365–91.

Miller, Christopher: *Blank Darkness: Africanist Discourse in French* (Chicago: University of Chicago Press, 1985).

Mitchell, Timothy: *Colonising Egypt* (New York: Cambridge University Press, 1988).

Pratt, Mary Louise: *Imperial Eyes: Travel Writing and Transculturalism* (New York: Routledge, 1992).

Said, Edward: *Orientalism* (New York: Vintage, 1978).

Slotkin, Richard: "Buffalo Bill's 'Wild West' and the Mythologization of the American Empire," in Amy Kaplan and Donald Pease (eds.), *The Cultures of United States Imperialism* (Durham, NC: Duke University Press, 1993), 164–84.

Suleri, Sara: *The Rhetoric of English India* (Chicago: University of Chicago Press, 1993).

Torgovnick, Marianna: *Gone Primitive: Savage Intellects, Modern Lives* (Chicago: University of Chicago Press, 1990).

Wilson, Christopher P.: "Plotting the Border: John Reed, Pancho Villa, and *Insurgent Mexico*," in Amy Kaplan and Donald Pease (eds.), *The Cultures of United States Imperialism* (Durham, NC: Duke University Press, 1993), 340–64.

Wright, Richard: *The Color Curtain: A Report on the Bandung Conference* (1956; Jackson: University of Mississippi Press, 1994).

Index

Lightning Source UK Ltd.
Milton Keynes UK

178581UK00004B/6/P